THE MAISKY DIARIES

THE
MAISKY
DIARIES

RED AMBASSADOR
TO THE COURT OF ST JAMES'S
1932–1943

EDITED BY GABRIEL GORODETSKY

Translated by Tatiana Sorokina and Oliver Ready

YALE UNIVERSITY PRESS
NEW HAVEN AND LONDON

For information about this and other Yale University Press publications, please contact:
U.S. Office: sales.press@yale.edu   www.yalebooks.com
Europe Office: sales@yaleup.co.uk   www.yalebooks.co.uk

Typeset in Minion Pro by IDSUK (DataConnection) Ltd
Printed in Great Britain by Gomer Press Ltd

Library of Congress Cataloging-in-Publication Data

Maiskii, I. M. (Ivan Mikhailovich), 1884–1975.
   The Maisky diaries : red ambassador to the Court of St James's, 1932–1943 / edited by Gabriel Gorodetsky.
      pages cm
   Includes bibliographical references and index.
   ISBN 978-0-300-18067-1 (alk. paper)
1. Maiskii, I. M. (Ivan Mikhailovich), 1884–1975. 2. World War, 1939–1945—Diplomatic history. 3. Soviet Union—Foreign relations—1917–1945. 4. Ambassadors—Great Britain—Diaries. 5. Ambassadors—Soviet Union—Diaries. 6. Soviet Union—Foreign relations—Great Britain—Sources. 7. Great Britain—Foreign relations—Soviet Union—Sources. I. Gorodetsky, Gabriel, 1945- editor. II. Title. III. Title: Red ambassador to the Court of St James's, 1932–1943.
   D754.R9M28 2015
   327.47041092—dc23
                                                                                    2015016351

A catalogue record for this book is available from the British Library.

10 9 8 7 6 5 4 3

Contents

Acknowledgements

This diary is published with the permission of the Scheffer-Voskressenski family – Ivan Maisky's heirs. I am most grateful for their cooperation and assistance in the preparation of this volume. I should also like to thank the Russian Foreign Ministry, the custodians of the Maisky diaries, for allowing me access to the original diaries, and for their help with archival sources and photographs. Particular gratitude is due to Professor Itamar Rabinovich, former president of Tel Aviv University, for his assistance in raising a generous grant towards the costs of the translation of the diary into English.

Few publishers today would enthusiastically embrace a project which involves the publication of three large volumes of a heavily annotated diary. I am grateful to John Donatich, the director of Yale University Press, and his team for their continuing unstinting support. I owe a special debt to Robert Baldock, the managing director of the London office of Yale University Press (who had commissioned my earlier book, *Grand Delusion: Stalin and the German Invasion of Russia*), for his abiding faith in me. No one could wish for a more perceptive, knowledgeable and supportive editor. It was he who convinced me, in addition to the complete three-volume edition, to produce a single compendium of excerpts from Maisky's diaries, which would be accessible to a wider audience. The result, a lavish book, beautifully produced, is a testament to his unrivalled skills.

This book is the fruit of more than ten years of extensive research. I was most fortunate to profit from a series of generous fellowships at the Institute for Advanced Study at Princeton, the Institute for Advanced Studies at Freiburg, and the Rockefeller Foundation's Bellagio Center. They provided most conducive conditions for pursuing my work, and a fertile ground for testing and sharing my ideas with leading fellow historians. The lion's share of my work, however, was done under the auspices of All Souls College, Oxford. It was Isaiah Berlin, a legendary fellow of the college, who first introduced me to Oxford in 1969 and encouraged me to write my dissertation there; the circle was miraculously closed for me when I was first offered a visiting fellowship at All Souls in 2006 and subsequently elected as a fellow. I can hardly find the proper words to describe the friendships I have forged at All Souls, and the challenging yet congenial environment I have encountered at the college – undoubtedly a guardian of scholarship in its purest form. Sir John Vickers, the warden of the college, and John

Davis, the former warden, made me feel at home and spared no effort in providing me with the utmost assistance and encouragement.

I was extremely fortunate to have Tatiana Sorokina and Oliver Ready as translators of the diary. Their combined efforts have produced a meticulous and elegant translation that is convincingly idiomatic yet faithful to Maisky's unique literary prose. I was equally fortunate in having Clive Liddiard as my copy-editor. His succinct yet wise and punctilious interventions improved the text considerably, as did his mastery of the Russian language and familiarity with Slavic and East European cultures.

Special appreciation is due to Hillel Adler, who initially helped me set up a most sophisticated database which allowed us to tame and master a voluminous body of archival sources. Dr Ruth Brown was equally helpful in organizing the glossary of the more than a thousand people mentioned in the diary. Dr James Womack produced some exquisite translations from the Russian of various letters in Maisky's private archives.

Finally, Ruth Herz, my wife, friend and companion, would be the first to admit that, rather than a burden in our life, the years spent with Maisky represented a fascinating joint journey.

1. Portrait of Maisky.

Introduction

The unique and fascinating diary of Ivan Mikhailovich Maisky, Soviet ambassador to London from 1932 to 1943, is one of the few kept by a Soviet dignitary in the 1930s and during the Second World War.[1] Stalin discouraged his entourage from putting pen to paper and would not allow notes to be taken during meetings at the Kremlin. Keeping a diary, we are reminded, was 'a risky undertaking when people scared to death were burning papers and archives. Diaries were particularly vulnerable, sought after by the police when they searched the dwellings of suspected "enemies of the people".' Indeed, Maisky's journals were eventually seized by the Ministry for State Security, together with his vast personal archive, following his arrest in February 1953 (two weeks before Stalin's death) on accusations of spying for Britain.[2] Pardoned in 1955, Maisky led a protracted – yet ultimately futile – campaign to retrieve them. His pleas were turned down by the Ministry for Foreign Affairs on the grounds that the diary 'contained various official material'. He was given only one year of limited access to it while he wrote his memoirs, but was denied access to any other archival sources. The diary remained inaccessible to researchers for decades.

Serendipity often lies at the heart of scholarly discoveries. In 1993, under the aegis of both the Israeli and the Soviet foreign ministries, I launched a research project which culminated in the joint official publication of documents on Israeli-Soviet relations. It is hard to describe my excitement when, while seeking information on Maisky's involvement in the Soviet decision to support the partition plan for Palestine in 1947,[3] the archivist at the Russian Foreign Ministry emerged from the stacks with Maisky's voluminous diary for the eventful year of 1941. No personal document of such breadth, value and size had emerged from the Soviet archives to throw fresh light on the Second World War and its origins. Flipping through the volume, I was struck by its immediacy and frankness, by Maisky's astute and penetrating insights, and by his superb prose. The diary comprises over half a million words, minutely and candidly depicting the observations, activities and conversations of the ubiquitous Soviet ambassador in London.

---

[1] The other exception was Aleksandra Kollontay, the Soviet ambassador in Stockholm, who, prompted by Maisky, kept a scrappy diary.
[2] See the chapter 'The Price of Fame'.
[3] See pp. 542–3.

Maisky typed his daily impressions in the evening, though there are also handwritten entries (remarkably missing from the Russian edition) which were often written away from the scrutinizing 'oeil de Moscou' within his office at the embassy.

Recognizing the distinctive value of the diary, Yale University Press generously agreed to publish it in its entirety, with my extensive commentary, in three volumes. I was, however, encouraged to produce this abridged version, to make it accessible to a wider audience. Making the selections for the compendium volume (25 per cent of the original diary and of my commentary) was particularly painful, as the text left out proved to be just as fascinating and compelling as that which was included. My guidelines were to retain the character and flow of the narrative. This volume is therefore stripped of the vast referential apparatus which will shortly be available to the interested reader in the full three-volume version. Abridgements are indicated by an initial space followed by ellipsis and a subsequent space. Wherever Maisky himself uses ellipsis, there is no initial space. When Maisky employs a word (or phrase) in English, that word appears in *italics*; whenever Maisky underlines a phrase for emphasis, an underscore is used here.

The process of having the diaries declassified and then published in Russia (a legal prerequisite for any publication of such documents in the West) was long and arduous. The editorial work on the Russian version was shared between the Institute of General History of the Russian Academy of Sciences, under the guidance of its director, Alexander Oganovich Chubarian, and Vitaly Yurevich Afiani, director of the Archives of the Russian Academy of Sciences, which houses Maisky's vast personal archives. I am much indebted to both for their cooperation. Their competent edition nonetheless gives the strong sense of being an official tome, and tends to uphold the traditional Russian historiography of the events leading up to the Second World War.

The commentary and annotations in the present volume bear no resemblance to those in the Russian edition. The initial temptation was to reduce any editorial intervention to the minimum and allow Maisky to tell his own tale. However, a detailed contextual commentary seemed indispensable, considering the repressive conditions under which Maisky kept his diary – forcing him to leave many blank spots in the otherwise rich and informative account – when the storm battered the gates of his own embassy. Fearful and concerned that the diary might be confiscated and denied to future generations, Maisky in fact kept at least three copies of it. The commentary is therefore by no means confined to the common practice of providing the reader with the basic auxiliary tools. It involves juxtaposing Maisky's entries with the voluminous correspondence in his private archives (which I unearthed in Moscow), as well as with the telegrams he sent to the Russian Foreign Ministry, his own apologetic memoirs written with hindsight following his arrest, and a multitude of other archival sources. Detailed references to the sources used here will be available in the extended three-volume edition of the diary. I was also privileged to gain access to Maisky's personal photo albums: some of the images (many of which feature and reflect the

2. A sample page from the diary – recording a meeting with Eden, 10 June 1941.

events described in the diary) are reproduced here. They often convey what thousands of words fail to do. I am most grateful to Dr Alexei D. Voskressenski, Maisky's great-nephew and heir, for allowing me to share with readers Maisky's incredibly personal, and at times intimate, gaze.

Maisky's diary is not the typical Soviet diary, a vehicle to 'self-perfection', which was encouraged by the regime as a means of political education and transformation. It is a personal diary, which would have been classified by the Soviet authorities as 'inherently bourgeois', revolving as it does largely around the theme of the self, rather than being a self-critical effort to become a good communist. It is a testament to the pivotal role played by personal friendships, conflicts and rivalries in early Soviet politics, transcending controversies over policy and ideology. It confirms that Soviet society and politics cannot be appropriately described without resorting to the human factor that exposes the unknown personal bonds. While Maisky's commitment to communism is manifestly proclaimed, he is fully immersed in the tradition of diary-writing among the Western 'bourgeois' intelligentsia. In fact, regardless of the obvious cultural differences, it resembles Pepys's diary in its astute observation of the British political and social scene, spiced with anecdotes and gossip. Like Churchill, Maisky surprisingly hails the role of 'great men' in history. He further acknowledges the uniqueness of events, rather than following the Marxist interpretation, which subsumes the individual into larger social patterns. Far from dismissing 'the "personal contribution" to the great general cause', Maisky openly argued in a letter to Georgy Chicherin, the commissar for foreign affairs, that one could 'scarcely deny that "personality" plays or can play a certain role in history. At times, even not a minor one.' It was 'enough to remember', he reminded Chicherin, 'what Ilyich[4] meant for our revolution'.

Maisky was obviously conscious of his own central role in shaping history. Describing a crucial meeting with Churchill in September 1941, when the fate of Moscow hung in the air, he wrote:

> I left home a quarter of an hour before the appointed time. The moon shone brightly. Fantastically shaped clouds raced from west to east. When they blotted the moon and their edges were touched with red and black, the whole picture appeared gloomy and ominous. As if the world was on the eve of its destruction. I drove along the familiar streets and thought: 'A few more minutes, and an important, perhaps decisive historical moment, fraught with the gravest consequences, will be upon us. Will I rise to the occasion? Do I possess sufficient strength, energy, cunning, agility and wit to play my role with maximum success for the USSR and for all mankind?'

The diary spans a dramatic and crucial epoch and covers a vast spectrum of topics. It was manifestly written with an eye to posterity.[5] Maisky found himself at the forefront of events, which he believed (far earlier than others) were likely to drag Europe into a world war. He dwells on the shift in Soviet foreign policy in the early thirties and on the motives for joining the League of Nations and for adherence to 'collective security'. It was Maisky who first alerted Moscow to the danger of appeasement. He fervently attempted to harmonize Soviet and British interests. His task, however, became increasingly difficult when Chamberlain arrived as prime minister in 1937, against the backdrop of the ferocious purges raging in Moscow. The voluminous entries for 1938 provide an insight into the events leading up to the Munich Conference and their devastating repercussions on collective security, as well as on the personal and political fate of

---

[4] Lenin.
[5] See his entry for 19 January 1943.

both Maisky and Maksim Litvinov, the Soviet commissar for foreign affairs. The diary for 1939 reveals the tremendous psychological pressure under which Maisky acted in his desperate attempts to hasten the conclusion of a tripartite agreement between the Soviet Union, Great Britain and France, intended to forestall a Soviet drift towards isolation. It reveals how often he found himself at odds with his own government, culminating in a stormy meeting at the Kremlin on 21 April, at which both he and Litvinov were harshly criticized and which led to the dismissal of the latter two weeks later. The diary further exposes the confusion which engulfed Soviet diplomats in the wake of the Molotov–Ribbentrop Pact and bears witness to Britain's transition from peace to war.

Just as gripping is Maisky's description, as an informed outsider, of London during the Blitz, and of his frequent intimate meetings with Churchill and Eden. The significance of his war reminiscences can hardly be overstated. While it was the practice of the foreign secretary to keep a record of his meetings with ambassadors, this did not apply to the prime ministers. Consequently, no records are to be found in the British archives of the many crucial conversations held between Maisky and Churchill before and during the Second World War. The only records preserved are therefore Maisky's detailed and immediate accounts in his diary and his more succinct telegrams to the Foreign Ministry. The diary thus becomes an indispensable source, replacing the retrospective accounts – tendentious and incomplete – which have served historians so far. It would hardly be an exaggeration to suggest that the diary rewrites some of the history that we thought we knew. The unprecedented and extraordinary relations Maisky had forged with the British leaders are well reflected in a farewell letter that the ambassador wrote to Churchill after his recall:

> Looking back now on these eleven years, I can say without hesitation that from a personal and political point of view my associations with you, extending over such a long time, have been the highlight of my Ambassadorship here ... I greatly enjoyed all our meetings and talks, irrespective of whether you were in or out of office, as I always felt that I was dealing with one of the most remarkable Englishmen of our time.

The leitmotif interwoven with Maisky's principal historical narrative is his personal struggle for physical survival during the great terror, at the end of which only he and his friend, the feminist Aleksandra Kollontay, Soviet ambassador in Stockholm, remained at their posts in Europe. Throughout his ambassadorship, Maisky had to walk a tightrope: being frank in his conversations with his British interlocutors and yet careful not to antagonize the Kremlin. The inner tensions are evident throughout the diary. Fearing that relations between the two countries were poisoned by mutual suspicion, and aware of his own precarious position, Maisky often withheld vital information from the Kremlin. A striking example was the suppression of information concerning Churchill's admission in 1943 that he could not even undertake to launch a cross-Channel attack in 1944.

The intertwined narratives are highlighted by penetrating – at times amusing – observations and anecdotes on British society, politicians, royalty, writers and artists which enliven the historical narrative. Maisky's penchant for writing prose and poetry betrayed a compulsive urge for self-expression. The result is a hybrid of literature and history. 'I had had literary inclinations since childhood', he reminisces:

> As a boy I was fond of keeping a diary and corresponding with relations and friends ... As far back as I remember, I was always composing or describing something – a forest after rain, an ambulance station, a trip to Chernoluchye, a pine wood not far from Omsk, and so on. Having grown up a little, I tried my powers in diaries, school essays and articles on current topics.

In later years, Maisky would confess to the Fabian Beatrice Webb, who also entertained literary aspirations, that 'he dislikes the profession of diplomacy; he and his wife would have been far happier in the academic or professional world; in the lecture room, library or laboratory'. Indeed, when he was incarcerated at the age of 70, he wrote a compelling novel *Close and Far Away*.

Maisky was further blessed with an extraordinary memory which, enhanced by penetrating psychological insight, powerful observation and insatiable curiosity, turned him into one of the most astute witnesses to the dramatic events and personalities of the 1930s. 'Long diplomatic practice', he explained,

> had trained my memory to act as a sort of photographic plate, which could without difficulty take up all the characteristics of the people I met. Their appearance, words, gestures and intonations were rapidly recorded on this plate, building up into sharply defined, detailed images. Often I would reach a mental conclusion about a person – positive or negative, with or without qualifications – on the spot, straight after our first acquaintance.

'You used to look down upon us from the Gallery in Parliament', recalled Harold Nicolson – author, diplomat and diarist – in a letter to Maisky, 'with benevolent interest rather like a biologist examines the habits of newts in a tank.' Having spent two years in London in exile during the First World War, followed by two years as chargé d'affaires at the embassy in the 1920s and eleven years as ambassador, his circle of acquaintances was vast. The very intimacy Maisky enjoyed with the top echelons of British politicians and officials, as well as with intellectuals and artists, gave him a perfect vantage point. Records of his conversations cover *inter alia* five British prime ministers – Lloyd George, Ramsay MacDonald, Stanley Baldwin, Neville Chamberlain and Winston Churchill – as well as King George V, Edward VIII and an impressive array of prominent figures, such as Anthony Eden, Lord Halifax, Lord Beaverbrook, Lord Simon, Nancy Astor, Samuel John Hoare, Herbert Morrison, Clement Attlee, Sidney and Beatrice Webb, Hugh Dalton, Stafford Cripps, John Maynard Keynes, John Strachey, Robert Vansittart, Joe Kennedy, Harry Hopkins, Jan Christian Smuts, Jan Masaryk, Bernard Shaw and H.G. Wells, to name just a few.

For non-experts, with limited access to the rich and fascinating documents published by the Russians on the events leading up to the war, the diary provides a rare glimpse into the inner state of the Soviet mind: its entries question many of the prevailing, often tendentious, interpretations of both Russian and Western historiography. For experts, it supplements the documents published in the *Dokumenty vneshnei politiki* by providing a colourful and candid description of Maisky's interlocutors, disclosing his own emotional, ideological and political thoughts, which are missing in the official documents. Moreover, it is stunning to discover the extent to which British politicians and officials such as Beaverbrook, Lloyd George, Eden and Vansittart spoke candidly and openly with the Soviet ambassador – at times with more sympathy for the Soviet cause than has been conceived so far. It was one thing to hear from Beatrice Webb 'that in her opinion the capitalist system had only 20–30 years left to live', but quite another to learn from Brendan Bracken, Churchill's confidant, that he was 'unsure about capitalism's future ... that the world is heading for the triumph of socialism, even if not exactly the socialism we have in the Soviet Union'. In one of their intimate fireside talks, Eden reacted to Maisky's passing remark that capitalism was 'a spent force' thus:

Yes, you are right. The capitalist system in its present form has had its day. What will replace it? I can't say exactly, but it will certainly be a different system. State socialism? Semi-socialism? Three-quarter socialism? Complete socialism? I don't know. Maybe it will be a particularly pure British form of 'Conservative socialism'.

The plethora of memoirs and diaries of Western politicians that revolve around the Second World War is striking in comparison with the dearth on the Soviet side. The only significant memoirs to have emerged from Russia were those written by the military in the 1960s. Because of the paucity of personal recollections, Maisky's series of memoirs[6] (quoting selectively from his diary) have been an indispensable source for historians in reconstructing Soviet policy. Compelling as they are, the memoirs, written with hindsight at the height of the Cold War, are highly contentious and misleading. That is why Maisky's extemporary and spontaneous diary assumes

---

[6] *Before the Storm* (London, 1943); *Journey into the Past* (London, 1962); *Who Helped Hitler?* (London, 1964); *Spanish Notebooks* (London, 1966); *Memoirs of a Soviet Ambassador: The War, 1939–43* (London, 1967).

tremendous historical significance. The memoirs present Soviet foreign policy as morally and politically righteous, glossing over issues of contention, whereas the diaries convey the immediate and far less biased impressions.

The discrepancy between the memoirs and the diary is hardly surprising. By the late forties, Maisky's star was already on the wane. At the height of the anti-Jewish frenzy following the Doctors' Plot of 1952, Maisky was arrested and charged with espionage, treason and involvement in Zionist conspiracy.[7] Although Stalin's death two weeks later, in March 1953, spared his life, his incarceration was extended by two more years for alleged association with Stalin's former henchman, L.P. Beria. Beria, who apparently wished to see Maisky installed as foreign minister in 1953, assigned him to coordinate intelligence activities in Britain at the Ministry of Home Security. In July 1953, however, Beria himself was arrested and soon afterwards executed. Maisky's alleged association with Beria and his imprisonment clearly reinforced the memory of his never forgotten past association with the Mensheviks.

As soon as Stalin died, Maisky hastened to approach Georgy Malenkov, the newly elected chairman of the Council of Ministers, from his prison cell. He proposed to atone for his past mistakes by assisting in setting up a group of young, capable Soviet historians who would 'specialize in combating the bourgeois falsification of contemporary history ... in case it was found possible to save my life'. In 1955, at the age of 72, frail and sick after two and a half years of humiliation and imprisonment, Maisky faced a long and frantic struggle to reinstate his party membership and his position at the Academy of Sciences, and above all to secure full rehabilitation. Hardly out of prison, Maisky complained to Nikita Khrushchev that he was being 'ostracized', and vowed to do 'his utmost for the benefit of the party' by 'effectively serving the Soviet State as an academic-historian'. He proposed to engage in research into the historiography of the Second World War which would 'critically evaluate the literature published in the West'. Likewise he expressed to Voroshilov, the chairman of the Presidium of the Supreme Soviet, the 'most ardent desire ... to best serve the Soviet State' in the remaining years of his life by becoming the '*in-house historian of the USSR's foreign policy* ... unmasking the most eminent bourgeois falsifiers of contemporary history, particularly of the period of the Second World War' (Maisky's emphasis). The historical value of the memoirs was further compromised by the severe censorship to which they were subjected in the first place, and when he was forced to remove criticism of Stalin from the final Russian edition of his memoirs in 1971.

The history of Maisky's long ambassadorship in London, as candidly portrayed in his diaries, is indeed breathtaking. Early in the nineteenth century, the British diplomat Stratford Canning predicted that public opinion might turn out to be 'a power more tremendous than was perhaps ever yet brought into action in the history of mankind'. His French colleague, Jules Cambon, an experienced diplomat, suggested that in getting

---

[7] On the arrest and trial, see the chapter 'The Price of Fame'.

to know a country fully, an ambassador should not confine himself to ministerial contacts, and on occasion might find that 'even the friendship of women of high social standing would be of great value to him'. But it was really Maisky who heralded a revolutionary style of diplomacy, which at the time irritated many of his interlocutors, but which has since been so much in vogue. He certainly was the first ambassador to systematically manipulate and mould public opinion, mostly through the press. A guest at the embassy recalled seeing Maisky's first secretary in the corridor 'lecturing to Cummings, the political editor of News Chronicle, that his writings on the Finnish war had been "grossly exaggerated"'. A superb 'public relations' man at a time when the concept hardly existed, Maisky did not shy away from aligning himself with opposition groups, backbenchers, newspaper editors, trade unionists, writers, artists and intellectuals. 'I have never known a representative of a foreign power', recalled John Rothenstein, the director of the Tate Gallery, 'who spoke so disarmingly, as though his listener had his entire confidence, or who took so much trouble to make the policy, or the ostensible policy, of his Government understood by the politically insignificant. And unlike most of his Soviet colleagues he seemed very ready to form private friendships.'[8]

Iverach McDonald, the young foreign correspondent of The Times, left a captivating recollection of Maisky's modus operandi:

> Most British officials were scandalised at the way Maisky would sail along, when it suited him, unhampered by normal diplomatic conventions ... He would never hesitate, by means of timely and artful disclosures, to give his hearers ammunition which they could use against Chamberlain, John Simon, and the others. His luncheon parties could be formal and orthodox, or they could be like meetings of opposition cliques ... Whenever I went to see him at his embassy in Millionaires' Row, he seemed to have all the time in the world to talk to a young man. In a flattering way he would unplug his telephone as a sign we were not to be disturbed. Or he would take me down to the end of the garden, with Kensington Gardens just over the hedge, where we could walk and talk with all the benefits of warm sunshine and complete privacy.

Maisky cultivated a significant segment of the British press with consummate skill. He read the whole British press, practically without exception, daily and weekly. He used to boast that he could place a letter in The Times whenever he chose to. His 'grasp of day-by-day changes in thought and emotion and his genial but unruffled contemplation of the whole war in all its details', remarked an American journalist, rendered him 'one of the most thoroughly competent observers' in London. What an ambassador has to aim at, Maisky told his friend Beatrice Webb, 'is intimate relations with all the live-wires in the country to which he is accredited – among all parties or circles of

---

[8] Maisky gave Molotov a fascinating description of his modus operandi; see pp. 268–70.

influential opinion, instead of shutting himself up with the other diplomatists and the inner governing circle — whether royal or otherwise'. Naturally he was first and foremost his own government's agent, but when he spoke in his quiet, often humorous way he always gave the impression of 'speaking as an individual rather than a mere record of his master's voice'.

Courting the press magnate Lord Beaverbrook certainly paid off. His *Daily Express* hailed the rise of Stalin as a defender of Soviet national interests rather than of the idea of a world revolution. In autumn 1936, Beaverbrook reminded Maisky of his newspapers' 'friendly attitude' towards Stalin and promised that 'nothing shall be done or said by any newspaper controlled by me which is likely to disturb your tenure of office'. In 1939, Beaverbrook arranged through Maisky for one of his young journalists to go to Russia. The journalist, he wrote to the ambassador, 'follows in his Master's footsteps in all his political opinions. Of course, it is commonly said that the Master follows after Maisky.' Eventually Beaverbrook became an ardent champion of a second front in 1942.

Persuasion was often rewarded by boons. 'I venture to keep my promise to you,' Maisky wrote to Beaverbrook, 'and hope you will find to your liking the sample of Russian vodka I am sending. My wife told you, I believe, something of the Russian liqueur called "Zapenkanka", and she is enclosing a sample of that which she hopes you will enjoy.' William Camrose, the editor of the conservative *Daily Telegraph*, clearly appreciated the ambassador's yearly supply of Russian caviar for Christmas:

> My dear ambassador
>   No gift could have come more appropriately or welcome than did the delightful cases of caviar which I received last night.
>   If nothing else good ever came out of Russia, caviar alone has been a great gift to civilisation!... Very many thanks for your kind thought.

At the Foreign Office they were extremely frustrated by the fact that 'no restrictions were placed on [Maisky] to prevent him doing pretty well anything he likes', and that he had and was making 'very plentiful use of free access to all Cabinet Ministers and others'. And yet Alexander Cadogan, the permanent undersecretary of state, reluctantly conceded that 'It has not yet been possible to detect any personal weakness of M. Maisky that would be gratified by a present from the Secretary of State or Prime Minister.' Official remonstrations proved just as ineffective.

His ideological predilections drove Maisky to seek particularly close contacts with the City, which he assumed controlled British politics. As soon as he landed in London, he asked his old friend H.G. Wells to organize an 'informal meeting with a "few intelligent bankers" … so that there may be an opportunity for a proper talk'. Wells complied. 'We have done nothing', he urged Brendan Bracken, 'to gratify Maisky's morbid craving to smack Bankers on their backs and call them by their Christian names.' Francis Williams, editor of the *Daily Herald*, recalls how he was caught off guard during a delicious *tête-à-tête* luncheon at the embassy by 'a very agreeable and civilized conversation' on the London theatre and literature. However, as soon as the 'English-seeming butler' had withdrawn, leaving them to coffee and brandy, Maisky spoke of his esteem for Williams' City column. Williams confesses to having felt 'a little uncomfortable' when, after discovering the extent of German dealings in the City, Maisky went on to interrogate him about the general outlook of the City and the influence it exercised on the British Government. It dawned on him, as he later admitted, 'that in the most delicate possible way the extent of my "reliability" from the Russian point of view was being probed'. In parting, Maisky expressed the hope that he could lunch with the journalist in the future, and did not shrink from making the following proposal:

> I suppose you would not contemplate sending me written reports from time to time on City institutions and affairs in the City? I would find it very interesting if you could. There must be much that you do not find it possible to print. It would be most valuable and we (the 'we' was stressed ever so slightly) would be most grateful.

This was supplemented every Christmas by a jar of caviar and a bottle of vodka with the ambassador's personal compliments. Indeed, the grey zone between being recruited and retaining professional integrity was manifestly crossed by many of the leading publicists and journalists, if not politicians, as the diary clearly reveals.

Then, as now, the legacy of preconceived ideas about Russia and its people – the most lethal feature of relations between Britain and Russia since the eighteenth century – rendered Maisky's position in London particularly precarious. He was hardly assisted by the traditional Russian xenophobic point of view, enhanced by the Soviet revolutionary tendency to demonize the Western bourgeoisie. Although Maisky was universally acclaimed as perhaps the most outstanding and informed ambassador to the Court of St James's, he was met with suspicion bordering on hostility. The long legacy of mistrust and mutual suspicion posed a formidable hurdle for the success of his mission. Moreover, the wide popularity he enjoyed among the people became a source of 'irritation and contempt' in the higher echelons, where he was often referred to as 'that little Tartar Jew'. Even friends could not refrain from alluding to his 'sub-fallstaffian figure'. 'He sits there in his ugly Victorian study,' flowed the venomous ink of Harold Nicolson in his diary, 'like a little gnome in an arm-chair, twiddling his thumbs, twinkling his eyes and giving the impression that his feet do not reach the floor.' The ambivalence was perhaps best encapsulated in General Edward Spears' observation of Maisky: 'sturdily built, obviously very strong and clever, a typical Tartar and no doubt basically cruel as are the people of his race' – oblivious to the fact that Maisky's roots (at least on his father's side) were Polish from the Russian pale of settlement. Beatrice Webb, who was particularly close to Maisky, wondered:

what the aristocratic Eden, the fascist charmer Grandi, the Nazi bounder Von Ribbentrop feel towards the stocky, ugly Jew-tartar Soviet emissary, who compares more to a shrewd business man negotiating in a world market than to a professional diplomatist manoeuvring among the governments of the world. Half the government and half the Foreign Office regard him as enemy No. 1, whilst the others glance nervously towards him as a possible ally in saving the British Empire from the militant envy of Germany and Italy.

A graphic description of such perceptions appears in Harold Nicolson's impressions of a lunch hosted by Maisky at the Soviet embassy:

> The door was opened by a gentleman in a soft collar and a stubby yellow moustache. I was ushered into a room of unexampled horror where I was greeted with effusion by Mr Maisky ... We stood in this grim ante-room while we were given corked sherry, during which time the man with a yellow moustache and a moujik's unappetizing daughter carried tableware and bananas into the room beyond.
>   We then went into luncheon, which was held in a winter-garden, more wintery than gardeny. We began with caviar, which was all to the good. We then had a little wet dead trout. We then had what in nursing-homes is called 'fruit jelly' ... During the whole meal, I felt that there was something terribly familiar about it all. It was certainly not the Russia of my memory. And then suddenly I realized it was the East. They were playing at being Europeans ... They have gone oriental.[9]

However, to others, such as the Labourite Herbert Morrison, Maisky appeared to be 'a cogent talker' who could 'argue reasonably and vividly, but with an almost Western objectivity which made discussion with him, in contrast with the case of most communists, stimulating and useful'. Likewise Rab Butler (then undersecretary for foreign affairs) recognized that Maisky was 'certainly the most pertinacious' of all foreign representatives in London. Bernard Pares, the doyen of the British historians of Russia, marvelled at Maisky who had 'never given [him] any forecast which did not prove true'. Finally, Bruce Lockhart[10] conceded that Maisky 'certainly knew his England thoroughly, indeed too thoroughly for some people. But when I said goodbye, I thought that we might wait long before we were sent as good a Russian ambassador.'

---

[9] Reading the memoirs years later, Maisky thought the 'references to me and Soviet embassy are not very profound but at times very amusing. I didn't realize being in London that he is such a "gourmand" – always writing about food which he is offered.'

[10] Sir Robert Hamilton Bruce Lockhart, acting consul-general in Moscow, 1914–17; headed special mission to Russia, 1918; imprisoned and exchanged for Litvinov; in charge of Political Warfare Executive, 1941–45.

Unlike the reserved and harsh demeanour which characterized the later 'Stalinist school of diplomacy', Maisky and his wife Agniya worked as a team and did their utmost to influence British public opinion by a display of sheer friendliness. Conservatives were just as welcome at their luncheon parties as Labourites. When Maisky arrived in London he asked Bruce Lockhart to introduce him to London society. Lockhart expressed surprise, suggesting that Maisky surely new the British socialists better than he did. 'Yes,' replied Maisky, 'but I want to meet more of the people who are running this country.' It was observed that at first Maisky's receptions were 'filled with Leftists dressed in queer clothes ... gradually the guests had progressed from red ties to stiff shirts and evening dress, until one evening H.G. Wells who had come to a large party in an ordinary day suit found himself the only person so dressed'.

Indeed Maisky lost few of his British friends even in the most difficult period, during the Soviet–German Pact and the Soviet–Finnish war. Louis Fischer, the well-informed international journalist, commented on how Maisky 'diligently and with infinite care ... cultivated numerous important individuals in British political life', while 'his attractive wife added to his popularity in high society'. Agniya was omnipresent in his life, and on the rare occasion when she indulged herself with a shopping expedition, staying longer in Paris *en route* from a League of Nations meeting in Geneva, he would seem to lose his bearings. 'My dearest Turchik,' he wrote to her on such an occasion:

> I am bored to death. It's not just that I am alone, completely alone within the four walls of this flat, but also that up to yesterday I didn't even go down to the street ... I'm reading a lot, listening to the radio and to records. Marusiya is feeding me well enough and the domestic side of things is in general 'all right' ... Can't wait to see you again soon. I kiss my dear sweet Turchik hard, and wait for her impatiently. Mikhailichi.

The image they projected was of 'strongly contrasting temperaments: she was gay, confident and an uncompromising revolutionary, he was quiet, with an occasional air of apprehension, and, though a loyal and devoted ambassador, rather liberal in his outlook'.[11] Like her husband, Agniya seems to have been lured by the comfort and the glittering facet of life in London. Herbert Morrison observed that she 'enjoyed her stay in London, for she admired the Londoners and liked their ways. I remember at a reception at the Soviet Embassy obliging her as best I could when she begged me to teach her the Lambeth Walk.[12] She always remembered it.' A woman of 'conventional charm and good manners, pretty' and 'attractively dressed', she was criticized in Parliament for 'spending 1,500 guineas on a mink coat' while the Russian armies were 'being battered

---

[11] At times her brazenness could have devastating consequences for Maisky; see p. 431.
[12] The song from the 1937 musical *Me and My Girl* lent its name to a fashionable Cockney dance describing working-class life in London.

3. The team.

by the Germans' and she was raising money for the Red Cross in the factories. In the late twenties, Narkomindel (the Soviet foreign ministry) had set up a sartorial and dressmaking establishment to produce garments for the wives, as well as for the diplomats themselves. They were, observed Beatrice Webb (who was attracted by high couture), 'carefully designed according to the fashions prevalent at the courts or capitals concerned. Which accounts for the elegance of Madame Maisky and Madame Litvinoff, much commented on in the fashion papers.' This was not the case with the ambassador, whose 'stocky figure', she observed, was often dressed 'in a holiday attire, loose light garments of the most unconventional cut and colour'. Far more ideologically militant than her husband, Agniya could at times be pugnacious and allow her emotions to run wild. At a reception at Buckingham Palace she came across one of the Russian Empress's ladies in waiting wearing a medallion with the tsarina's portrait. It was rumoured that she 'spat on the picture'.

It is most amazing to glean from Maisky's diary how much room for manoeuvre was left for ambassadors, even under Stalin's most ruthless authoritarian regime. Many of his initiatives were adopted as policy, at times even against the prevailing views held in the Kremlin – the most striking examples being his unstinting support for the negotiation of a triple alliance with the West in early 1939 and the campaign for the second front in 1941–43. To get his way, Maisky often had to attribute his own ideas to his

4. Tea in the conservatory of the embassy.

interlocutors, although the archives show that it was he who had initiated them. I have drawn the reader's attention to a handful of such instances in my commentary. A typical example would be Maisky's attempts to discourage Stalin from moving towards isolation and Nazi Germany, following the exasperating experience of the Munich agreement.

Maisky was not as successful in his attempts to halt Stalin and Litvinov from retreating from Spain. In the diary entry of 1 October 1938, he describes the advice he had given the government to adhere to collective security by citing a conversation with Lloyd George (well manipulated by him), who apparently exclaimed: 'Just don't leave Spain, whatever you do!', further urging that 'isolationism would be a bad policy for the USSR'. It was Maisky who early on warned of the impact the purges were having on British public opinion, proposing that justice should be seen to be done through public trials. Later, he went on to warn Moscow of the dire impact of the purges of the military on the prospects for concluding a triple alliance. He also engineered Eden's ground-breaking trip to Moscow and his meeting with Stalin in 1935, preferring him to Lord Simon, the then foreign secretary. As early as the end of 1937, Maisky advised Stalin how to address the appeasers: 'Let "Western Democracies" reveal their hand in the matter of the aggressors. What is the point of us pulling the chestnuts out of the fire for them? To fight *together* – by all means; to serve as cannon fodder for them – never!' Stalin indeed repeated the ambassador's ideas and words almost verbatim in his famous speech of

March 1939. During his heyday in London, after the German attack on Russia, it was Maisky who forged the alliance when paralysis struck the Kremlin, prompting Churchill's famous speech and paving the way for the visit of Harry Hopkins, Roosevelt's right-hand adviser, to Moscow in July 1941, as well as for Eden's trip that December, and Churchill's first visit to Moscow in August 1943.

* * *

The special circumstances in which Maisky wrote his diary inevitably require a reconstruction of the gaps and missing dimensions in the record. Moreover, the diary makes sense only once the context in which it was written is unfolded. This required thorough archival research of both Russian and Western archives. It was necessary further to juxtapose the entries with the private and official records of the meetings made by Maisky's interlocutors. His own official reports were also examined against the diary entries. The three volumes of the full diary and commentary will include detailed references, as well as a full list of the archival sources consulted. The prime collections were the records of the Foreign Office, the Prime Minister's Office, the Chiefs of Staff and Joint Planners, the Military Intelligence, as well as various private collections within the Foreign Office's papers at the UK's National Archives. The papers consulted in the National Archives in Washington were from the State Department and the Department of War, as well as from various other branches of government. Through painstaking efforts, I succeeded in obtaining access to a vast array of Russian archival sources – mostly in the Russian Foreign Ministry Archives, but also in the Military Archives and the Presidential Archives – as well as to Stalin's papers, which were recently placed in the State Archives. Some 80 collections of private papers were consulted, the main ones being those of Maisky, Churchill, Lord Beaverbrook, Rab Butler, Alexander Cadogan, Stafford Cripps, David Lloyd George, Lord Halifax, Harry Hopkins, John Maynard Keynes, Robert Bruce Lockhart, General George Marshall, President Roosevelt, Henry Stimson, Albert J. Sylvester, Robert Vansittart and Beatrice Webb. Those were supplemented by an exhaustive study of the wide spectrum of printed documentary material, printed diaries and secondary sources which will be fully acknowledged in the full three volumes.

Attached to the original text there were numerous relevant press clippings, occasional correspondence and copies of some of the telegrams exchanged between Churchill and Stalin during the war. As most of those sources are easily available in print, they have been largely excluded from the present collection. On a few occasions, the long reports of conversations in the diary served Maisky as the basis for his official reports, some of which have previously been published, but only in Russian compilations.

The introductory notes about individuals appear on first mention. In most cases the reference is to the position held by the individual during the period covered by the diary. To help the reader grasp the impact of the purges on the diplomatic corps, an attempt has been made to trace the fate of those at the London embassy and among the old cadre of Narkomindel who were purged during the repression.

While the guidelines of the Library of Congress remain broadly the basis for the transliteration of names, in many cases a simplified form is used: for example, 'ю' is rendered throughout as 'yu' and 'я' as 'ya', while 'ей' becomes 'ei'. To remain faithful to the conventions of the time, the endings of proper names in 'ий' are transcribed throughout as 'y' (Maisky, Trotsky, etc.). Strictly speaking, until 1946 the title of the Soviet foreign minister was 'people's commissar for foreign affairs', while that of Soviet ambassadors was *'polpred'*. I have employed mostly the Western terms, which were used indiscriminately, even by the ambassadors themselves at the time.

The Making of a Soviet Diplomat

Ivan Mikhailovich Lyakhovetsky was born on 7 January 1884 in the ancient Russian town of Kirillov, near Nizhny-Novgorod, in the comfortable environment of a nobleman's castle, where his father was a tutor to the son of the family. Maisky ('Man of May'), was a *nom de plume* he assumed in 1909 while in exile in Germany. His childhood was spent in Siberia, in Omsk, where his father, having studied medicine in St Petersburg, served as a medical officer. Maisky's father was of Jewish Polish descent, a fact that Maisky preferred to conceal. In his enchanting childhood memoirs he went a long way to stress the atheist atmosphere at home, but made the point that 'officially, of course, we were considered to be Orthodox ... as a schoolboy I was obliged to learn the catechism in class, to attend Vespers on Saturdays and Mass on Sundays, and to go to confession without fail before Easter'. Maisky, though, would find it difficult to shake off the 'Jewish image'. Both in England and in the Soviet Union, he was often perceived by others to be Jewish. The nephew of the famous Russian historian Evgeny Tarle remembers that his Aunt Manechka, who 'had a nose for Jews who'd been promoted at the time of the "proletarian revolution" confided in me that she thought Maisky wasn't really called Maisky, let alone "Ivan Mikhailovich": "Isaak Moiseevich", more likely'. One of Maisky's closest friends in Britain, the Jewish leftist publisher Victor Gollancz, remembered that Maisky used to tell 'wonderful Jewish stories, which he called Armenian, and loved listening to mine, which he called Armenian too'.

His father's 'secret love' and the 'mainspring of his soul' was his 'passion for science'. He served as a formidable role model for Maisky and as a source of inspiration for an insatiable intellectual aptitude and curiosity, professional dedication and unbridled ambition. His father's rigidity and somewhat reserved nature were cushioned by Maisky's mother, Nadezhda Ivanovna (*née* Davydova), who was a village teacher with a strong literary and artistic proclivity. In his memoirs, Maisky depicts her fondly as being 'of a choleric temperament – lively, inconsistent, quick-tempered and talkative ... She had something unique in herself, a kind of charm, which attracted people to her and easily made her the centre of attention.'

Maisky was exposed to literature from an early age. The packed bookshelves at home housed beautifully bound collected works of Shakespeare, Byron and Schiller, as well as the writing of the more radical intelligentsia, such as Nekrasov, Dobrolyubov,

Ю. Штейнбергъ.

5. Jan Lyakhovetsky (Maisky) with his young sister.

Herzen and Pisarev. Maisky was well aware of the debate raging at the time on the purpose of literature and art, and on realism and aestheticism. Though claiming in later years, for obvious reasons, to have sided with the 'utilitarians', the young Ivan uncritically devoured 'stacks of books and periodicals'. He was particularly captivated by Heine, his lifetime compass and companion, whose portrait was to hang over his desk. Barely 16 years of age, he expressed this admiration in a letter to Elizaveta, his confidant cousin:

> I have never seen a finer face than Heine's. Every day I discover more and more excellence in Heine and I am convinced that his perpetually satirical, perpetually sceptical Aristophanes of the nineteenth century is one of the greatest geniuses and judges of the human soul in general, and of the people of our times in particular. Heine is humanity. He personifies it to perfection as nobody else has done. In him is reflected all the good and bad in humanity, the wide and motley panorama of the human marketplace, all its suffering and sorrow, all its anger and indignation.

The literary atmosphere at home refined Maisky's acute powers of observation, which were enhanced by his rich imagination and his curiosity. It helped forge his complex personality, which, while romantic and artistic, was also governed by a belief in 'reason, science, knowledge, and the right of man to be master of life on earth'. The novels opened a window on Europe and awakened in Maisky a longing for travel and an interest in geography which would gradually shape his cosmopolitan outlook once in exile. That particular inquisitiveness was enriched by exposure to the bustling life of Omsk's port, where Maisky spent any free moment he had strolling about the wharves and by the steamers, 'looking at everything, listening and nosing about ... I listened to the stories of the pilots and sailors about their work and adventures and about the distant towns and places they visited.'

In reconstructing a revolutionary past, Maisky would later identify a rebellious streak in the family – a dissident member of the clergy who went off the rails and joined certain revolutionary circles in the mid-nineteenth century. Likewise he would claim that his own parents sympathized with the Populist movement, that his mother had even 'gone down to the people', and that his father had come into conflict with the authorities at the hospital in which he worked over his failure to prevent the young medical cadets from expressing revolutionary ideas in 1905. Maisky makes much of the special relationship he cultivated with his artist uncle, M.M. Chemodanov, who worked as a *zemstvo* doctor in a remote village and was mildly involved in revolutionary activities. However, at their core, Maisky's background and education were typical of the professional middle class, void of any political awareness.

Having graduated from the local gymnasium at the age of 17 with a gold medal, Maisky enrolled at St Petersburg University where he read history and philology. His literary talents were noticed around that time, when his first poem, 'I Wish to Be a Great Thunderstorm', was published in *Siberian Life* under the pseudonym 'New Man'. His university education at St Petersburg, however, came to an abrupt and premature end when he was arrested and charged with revolutionary agitation. He was put under police surveillance in Omsk, where he joined the Menshevik wing of the Russian Social Democratic Movement. In 1906 he was detained once again for taking an active part in the 1905 revolution and was sentenced to exile in Tobolsk, where he produced a manuscript inspired by the Webbs' *The History of Trade Unionism*. Maisky had stumbled upon this by sheer chance when he was a student in St Petersburg. He would later confess to Sidney and Beatrice Webb that it 'greatly contributed to my political education and to a certain extent helped me to find the path which I followed in my subsequent life'. 'Never indeed', he wrote to his cousin in 1901, 'have I read any novel with such a thrill as the Webbs' book! How feeble, miserable and nonsensical all my former literary enthusiasms seem to me!' The evolutionary Fabian stream, with its strong social-humanist bent, suited Maisky's temperament and served him as a political beam of light. Its residue was always close to the surface, even when he had to break with his Menshevik past and display loyalty to Bolshevism. Once in England, he cultivated

6. An exemplary pupil in the gymnasium (Maisky is seated fourth from left in the front row).

intimate relations with the Webbs which lasted until their death, as is well attested in both his and Beatrice Webb's diaries.

Maisky's sentence was eventually commuted to exile abroad. In his memoirs, written under the cloud of the purges in the wake of the Molotov–Ribbentrop Pact (when his stock was low in Moscow), Maisky claims that his desire to emigrate was driven by a wish to study 'socialism and the European workers' movement'. However, the attraction of exile seems to have been more profound, revealing a cosmopolitan streak and a prodigious curiosity which can be traced back to his childhood, when he used to accompany his father – who believed that 'nothing develops a child so much as travel and getting to know new places, new people, new races and customs' – on his distant missions across Siberia. When the family moved to St Petersburg for a year, we find the nine-year-old Ivan still fascinated, 'standing a long while on the granite quays of the Neva, watching the complicated manoeuvres of the Finnish boats, the loading of foreign ships, the tiny Finnish steamers darting briskly in all directions like dark blue beetles'. His exile further enhanced an enduring admiration for European (particularly German) culture, as he openly confessed in a letter to his mother: 'I am still extremely happy with being abroad. I feel that I am growing quickly and powerfully here, in mind and in spirit. And, in fact, I'm almost grateful to the circumstances which have forced me to quit Russian soil.' 'I like travel,' he confessed to Bernard Shaw years later, 'and I have travelled much over Europe and Asia ... When I see people boarding a train, a ship or a plane, I feel a sort of romantic glow.'

C. Reisener   S.T. PÉTERSBOURG.

7. The breeding of a revolutionary: Maisky as a student at St Petersburg University.

After a brief stay in Switzerland, Maisky settled in Munich, then the hub for Russian immigrants and artists, notably Kandinsky and his circle. Though associated with the Russian revolutionary movement, Maisky was as much involved in the activities of the German Social Democratic Party and the trade unions. He obtained his Master's degree in economics at Munich University, and was well on with his doctoral dissertation when the gathering clouds of war led to an unanticipated and fateful new emigration – to London. The nomadic life suited his nature:

> After Germany, it'll be very good to get acquainted with life and people in the United Kingdom, and ultimately I don't mind where I live: Munich or London. On the way to England I'll stop off for a week in Paris, to have a look at the city ... And then I'll head on from there to the British capital. I go to new countries with great interest and great expectations; we'll see whether the latter come true. Ultimately, I think the main charm in life is a constant change of impressions, and nothing aids that so much as travel, rapid movement from one place to another.

However, Maisky's first encounter with London, in November 1912, rather belied his later fascination with England. His Russian upbringing and life in the German socialist milieu did not predispose him to the kind of blind admiration for British liberalism that seized many of the romantic exiles of the nineteenth century. London, he felt, 'swallowed and suffocated' him. He did not know the language and felt lost in that 'giant stone ocean'. Indeed, those early gloomy impressions are evident in a letter to his mother:

> Of course, I find London very interesting – from the political and socio-economic points of view – and I'm not at all sorry that I'm spending the current winter here. But I wouldn't want to stop in these parts too long. Just the thought of getting stuck here permanently brings on a freezing ennui. No, I definitely don't like London! It's huge, dark, dirty, uncomfortable, with boring rows of identical little houses, permanently shrouded in fog ... You don't see the sun here for weeks, and that's terribly depressing. I now understand why spleen is called the English disease, and I also understand why Heine so disliked the country of the proud Britons. 'The ocean would have swallowed England long ago,' he once commented, 'if it weren't afraid of an upset stomach.' And he wasn't far wrong: to digest a 'nut' like England wouldn't be that easy.

The years in London and his friendship with Georgy Vasilevich Chicherin and Maksim Maksimovich Litvinov (who, for two decades, as commissars for foreign affairs, were to steer Soviet foreign policy) were, however, to have a profound impact on Maisky's later career. The three were brought together by Litvinov's future wife, Ivy, who was born in London, the product of an implausible union between a Jewish intellectual and an Indian army colonel's daughter. A nonconformist writer and rebel, she found solace from her despised employment (with an insurance firm) at the Golders Green home of her aunt and uncle, the Eders, who were left-wing thinkers. They held lively intellectual soirées, with revolutionaries, Freudians, Fabians and literary figures such as Bernard Shaw and H.G. Wells. It was at the Eders' house that Maisky, a frequent visitor, cemented his friendship with Litvinov and Chicherin.

The three lived just around the corner from each other, first in Golders Green and then Hampstead Heath, amidst a thriving colony of political exiles who found a bond with one another which transcended the schism within the Russian socialist movement. Chicherin, whose aristocratic family could trace its origins and name to an Italian courtier who had settled in Russia at the time of Tsar Ivan III, had worked in the archives of the tsarist foreign minister. He was something of a polymath, endowed with an encyclopaedic memory. A renaissance man, well versed in literature and culture, he was also a fine pianist and the author of a highly acclaimed book on Mozart's operas. He cut an eccentric and ascetic figure in London, leading a rather bohemian life. The conscience-stricken Chicherin had initially been a disciple of Tolstoy, before he joined the Russian revolutionary movement in exile, leaning towards Menshevism. This short-lived deviation did not deter Lenin from later appointing him commissar for foreign affairs. His signature would adorn the Brest-Litovsk and Rapallo agreements, the pillars of Soviet diplomacy.

Litvinov, who had an obscure Jewish background and did not entertain any intellectual pretensions, was later to be meticulous in his work in Narkomindel, fastidiously observing the rules and etiquette of diplomatic work, and almost dismissive of the ideological constraints imposed on him. Surprisingly, despite his conspicuous personal contempt for Chicherin, the two were able to work together harmoniously for almost a decade.

By the time they met in England, Litvinov, who was eight years older than Maisky, had already gained a reputation as a seasoned revolutionary. It was therefore only natural for him to become Maisky's mentor, introducing him to the country, its political institutions, its culture and a wide circle of people. What most endeared Litvinov to Maisky was his strong character, as well as his ability to grasp the essentials of a question without getting bogged down in the details, and his penchant for irony.

The outbreak of the First World War, however, brought an estrangement between the two which was to mar their future working relationship. While Litvinov adopted Lenin's position in favour of militant defeatism, Maisky sided with the Menshevik's internationalist pacifist position, which sought an end to the war. For a while, Maisky even displayed great interest in the then all-encompassing popular ideas of the 'Middle Europe' movement, propagated by F. Neumann, which tried to merge the two most powerful waves of German history – the national-bourgeois wave and the socially oriented proletarian. It further sought to synthesize the precepts of Christianity with

8. For old times' sake: Ivy and Maksim Litvinov having tea with Ivan and Agniya at the Soviet embassy, 1935.

German idealism, humanism with class solidarity, and democracy. Maisky's ingrained pragmatism and humanistic outlook, further enhanced by his English experience, came to the fore as the First World War dragged on. He was particularly obsessed with the fate of Western civilization and the European intelligentsia, who were being slaughtered in great numbers on the front line, and wanted humanism to be placed before any party considerations. 'You see,' he responded to a rebuke from Martov, the Menshevik leader:

> the longer the war drags on, the more a very serious danger appears before the belligerent nations: an enormous number of intellectuals – writers, artists, scholars, engineers, etc. – will die on the battlefields. The countries are exhausting their spiritual aristocracy, without which, whatever you say, no mental, social or political progress is possible ... Of course, any losses are difficult to bear: losses of peasants, losses of workers, etc.; but I still think that losses among the intelligentsia are, in relative terms, the hardest, because they are the most difficult to make good. The intelligentsia is a fruit that grows slowly, and it might need a whole generation before the depletion in its ranks caused by the war is even partly put right.
>
> That's why I think that a period has now begun when nations, for their own self-preservation, will have to protect intellectuals the way they protect, for instance, skilled mechanics, chemists, trained armaments workers, etc.

Although Maisky is at pains to demonstrate in his diary (and even more so in his autobiography) the kinship and warmth that characterized his relations with Litvinov – a presentation that has led historians to pair the two men – at times that relationship was troubled. Their temperaments were hardly compatible, and Litvinov was quick to rebuke Maisky, criticizing his essays on foreign affairs; on several occasions he even complained about him to Stalin. It was typical of Litvinov to keep people at arm's length, though much of this was a deep-seated disdain for cosmopolitan intellectuals. 'Litvinov had no friends,' recalled Gustav Hilger, a veteran and well-informed counsellor at the German embassy in Moscow. 'There was one member of the *kollegia* of the Foreign Commissariat with whom I had established a relationship of mutual confidence. I asked him once how he got along with Litvinov, and received the significant answer "You don't *get along* with Litvinov; you only work with him – if you have no other choice."'

Moreover, Litvinov detested those diplomats (and Maisky was certainly one of them) who sought the limelight. 'Dignity', it was said of him, 'came natural to him ... Flattery and bootlicking were entirely foreign. Nor could he bear these traits in others.' And yet the two men shared a common view of the international scene in the 1930s, and Litvinov did not shy away from supporting Maisky and even shielding him from the repressions that engulfed the ministry in 1938. Maisky was to continue to cultivate the special relationship which had been forged in exile. Congratulating Litvinov on his negotiations in Washington, which would lead in 1934 to American recognition of the Soviet Union, Maisky wrote: 'Perhaps it's because you and I are joined by a 20-year acquaintance and by the years of emigration we shared in London that I always follow your work and your speeches on the Soviet and international arena with a very special interest and an emotion of an almost personal character ... Our long acquaintance gives me the right to tell you frankly things which, in other circumstances, could only seem out of place.'

Entirely different were Maisky's relations with Aleksandra M. Kollontay, the flamboyant and militant feminist and future Soviet ambassador to Norway and then Sweden, at whose house he first met Litvinov. With her he maintained a warm personal friendship throughout his life. 'I find it interesting to be with Maisky', Kollontay noted in her diary, 'because we don't only talk business. He is a lively man with eyes, mind and feelings open to perception of life in all its manifestations and in all fields. He isn't a boring, narrow-minded person who doesn't step beyond current business and issues.'

Shortly after the February Revolution of 1917, which toppled the tsarist regime, Maisky returned to Russia and was asked by Alexander Kerensky to join the Provisional Government as the deputy minister of labour. His politics were fast veering to the right of the Menshevik Party. In the wake of the dissolution of the Constituent Assembly by the Bolsheviks, in January 1918, and the outbreak of the Civil War, Maisky failed to convince the Mensheviks to support the Samara-based committee for the re-convocation of the assembly (*Komuch*) in its struggle against the Bolsheviks. His appeal to them was in keeping with his belief – a legacy of his European social-democratic experience – that staying neutral in the Civil War was 'contrary to human nature and logic', and that the *Komuch* government, composed of refugees from the Assembly, was a 'democratic counter-revolution'. Acting on his personal convictions, Maisky defied the party, and in July 1918 crossed the front line to join the forlorn *Komuch* government as its minister for labour. He thus emerged as the champion of the sole armed socialist insurgence against Bolshevism. This was a move that would haunt him for the rest of his life and would lead to an ignominious repentance, which was dismissed by the Mensheviks as 'memoirs of a renegade'. The 'newly baptized' convert was duly expelled from Menshevik ranks and admitted to his adopted church, branded with the eternal mark of Cain.

When the White Admiral Kolchak seized control of the rebel government in 1919, persecuting the socialists, Maisky had to flee again, this time to Mongolia. His year there, spent 'crossing Genghis Khan's former homeland on horseback and camel-back ... among the deserted mountains and steppes, far from the political struggle, the heated public atmosphere, the influence of party traditions and prejudices', made him reflect on the nature of the revolution – and on his own personal future.

Maisky's earlier timid and procrastinating attempts in summer 1919 to break with the past and make it up with the Bolsheviks – undertaken at a time when their fate was still hanging in the balance – were regarded as inadequate contrition. A year later, he wrote to People's Commissar for Education A.V. Lunacharsky, whom he had befriended during his years in exile:

I now see that the Mensheviks were virtuous but talentless pupils of the past, timid imitators of long-outlived models, thinking in old clichés and formulae from books, without that precious feel for life, feel for the epoch ... The Bolsheviks, on the other hand, excelled in boldness and originality, felt no particular piety towards the behests of the past or towards dogmatic incantations. They were flexible, practical and decisive ... they spoke a new word in the field of revolutionary creativity, they created new forms of state, of economic life, and of social relations ... which others lacked the boldness to realize.

Throughout his life, and particularly during the dark days of the 'great terror', Maisky's earlier association with the Mensheviks, and above all the role he played in the Civil War (something that was meticulously glossed over in his memoirs and writings), cast a huge shadow over his career and credibility in Moscow. The constructed narrative of his conversion to Bolshevism that he sent to Lunacharsky – atonement for his failure to recognize the Bolshevik revolution as a legitimate socialist one – concealed the torment of soul-searching that the transition involved and which was never to be fully resolved.

Maisky's inner conflict was reflected in *The Peaks* (*Vershiny*), a four-act drama in verse which revealed the everlasting Romantic nature of his thinking, deeply immersed as it was in the nineteenth-century universal humanist tradition of the Russian intelligentsia and coloured by utopian visions. The distinctive codex of the intelligentsia was the formation of a Russian intellectual, independent of his class origin. The title page of *The Peaks* bore an epigraph from Maisky's favourite poet, Heinrich Heine, in German with a Russian translation: 'We want to create the kingdom of heaven here, on earth!' Its theme was 'humanity's endless movement towards the glittering peaks of knowledge and freedom, which were visible and beautiful, but which could never be reached, because the movement was endless'. The extent to which Maisky genuinely repented and fully identified with the Bolsheviks (as he manifestly claimed to do in the first volume of his memoirs, written in dire circumstances in 1939–40) is hard to ascertain. In a self-reflective mood, Maisky related with empathy to Chicherin's account of his conversion to Bolshevism which seemed to be a mirror image of how he felt:

'Although I was once a Menshevik our ways have parted. The war has taught me a lot and now all my sympathies are on the side of the Russian Jacobins.' He hesitated for a moment and then added: 'I mean the Bolsheviks.' I cannot be certain that at the time of this conversation Georgy Vasilevich was a convinced Bolshevik.

Later on, in her diary, Beatrice Webb, one of Maisky's most trusted and intimate friends, painted a succinct and precise picture of Maisky's intellectual and political character:

9. Beatrice Webb – Maisky's inspiration and most intimate friend in Britain.

> Certainly Maisky is one of the most open minded of Marxists, and is fully aware
> of the misfits in Marxian terminology – scholastic and dogmatic. But then he
> has lived abroad among infidels and philistines and his mind has been perhaps
> slightly contaminated by the foreign sophistical agnostic outlook on the closed
> universe of the Moscow Marxians.

Concerned about the 'earthly punishments' awaiting him in Moscow for his 'political sins', Maisky hoped to secure through Lunacharsky an amnesty for his past and a
guarantee of safe passage as surety 'against arrest, search, conscription, etc., on the
road'. Lunacharsky passed on the poem and the covering letter to Lenin, recommending
rehabilitation and even admittance to the Bolshevik Party. The Politburo approved,
though in guarded terms, suggesting that Maisky's expertise in economics should 'first
be used in the provinces'. He was accordingly instructed to proceed to Omsk, where he
eventually established the first Siberian State Plan (*Gosplan*). Meanwhile his repentance was published in *Pravda*.

Maisky's ambitions, however, were intellectual rather than political. They led him at
the first possible opportunity to Moscow, where he immediately established contact
with Chicherin and Litvinov – 'for old times' sake', as he later recalled, but clearly in the
hope of enhancing his credibility, which had been shattered by his association with the
Mensheviks. He grudgingly accepted a proposal to become head of the press department of the People's Commissariat for Foreign Affairs (Narkomindel), regarding the
position as merely a springboard to greater things. At the ministry he met Agniya
Aleksandrovna Skipina, a strong-willed socialist activist, who was to become his third
wife (a brief earlier marriage had produced a daughter, who went to live with her
mother in St Petersburg and with whom Maisky, who had no further children, maintained sporadic contact; he had also had a short marriage of convenience to help a
Russian stranded in London).

Hardly had he settled in his new post than Maisky quarrelled with Lev Karakhan, Chicherin's protégé, seeking his dismissal. Having failed to achieve his goal, he did succeed in steering Molotov, then the organizational secretary of the party's Central Committee, to send him to St Petersburg, where he briefly acted as the deputy editor of *Petrogradskaya Pravda*. This interlude as second fiddle ended in harsh discord with the chief editor, who, as Maisky complained to Molotov, had 'taken care to make it impossible for [him] to work at the paper'. A brief spell as editor of the social and literary journal *Zvezda* (*The Star*) came to a similar end in early 1925, following a squabble within the editorial board. On the whole, life in Leningrad did not agree with Maisky (or, more likely, with his young wife). He felt, as he explained to Molotov, like an 'outsider ... a second-class citizen'. In the relatively calm days of the New Economic Policy (NEP), Maisky could still comfortably manoeuvre his career, informing Molotov that he was 'seriously contemplating returning' to work in Narkomindel.

Maisky's first steps in his Bolshevik career revealed an inflated self-esteem, marked by a sense of intellectual superiority and a stubbornness which did not endear him to his colleagues and superiors, and often set him on a collision course with them. Although the survival instinct somewhat suppressed those traits during the oppressive 1930s, they would nonetheless keep resurfacing throughout his ambassadorship in London, particularly in his encounters with British officials.

Back in Moscow, Maisky's fraternal relations with Litvinov, who was gradually taking over from Chicherin as the strong man in Narkomindel, proved propitious. In 1925 he was appointed counsellor at the Soviet embassy in London, a position which he clearly cherished. As he wrote to his mother, he and his wife Agniya:

have taken a small house where no one else lives, we have a maid and we look after our own household ... Agniya is learning singing and English and she's starting to chatter a little in English. Our house is in one of the best London suburbs, next to the botanical garden, the air is beautiful, but it's just a shame we don't get more chance to enjoy it.

But his stay in London was again marred by poor relations with his superiors at the embassy. Maisky opted to go back to Moscow, but within a year was persuaded by Litvinov to return to the embassy. Those were turbulent years in Anglo-Soviet relations, following the 'Zinoviev letter' affair of 1924 and the 'Russian gold' contribution to the miners during the General Strike of 1926. There was a fear in Moscow of a rupture in relations, and perhaps even of renewed military intervention. Matters were further exacerbated by the premature death of Leonid Krasin, the Soviet ambassador in London. As one of the few revolutionaries fluent in English and well versed in British affairs, Maisky found his services required. It is rarely recognized that, with no ambassador in London, Maisky as counsellor actually functioned as the *de facto polpred*. 'In the old days,' he boasted in a letter to his father, 'a counsellor would have figured very high on the "table of ranks". Nowadays, the table of ranks has lost any significance for us; however I can assure you that the work of a counsellor in a place like London is highly interesting and important ... London today is the powerful centre of world politics which can only be compared to Moscow.'

His enforced departure from England, following the severance of diplomatic relations in May 1927, left Maisky, as he confided to C.P. Scott, the pro-Russian editor of the *Manchester Guardian*, with 'a feeling very much akin to personal grief'. His years in exile in London and the experience in the embassy had led him 'to understand and respect British culture, which, although so unlike Russian Culture, contains much which is both valuable and great'.

After six weeks of rest and treatment 'on doctors' orders' at the Kislovodsk sanatorium in the Caucasus, Maisky was appointed counsellor at the Soviet embassy in Tokyo, where he spent the next two years. For a while, the appointment suited him well. 'I arrived in Tokyo at the end of October,' he wrote to H.G. Wells, 'and at the present time look around with the greatest possible interest studying this most extraordinary country, which some twenty years ago gave you a good deal of inspiration to write "Modern Utopia"'. Writing to the left-wing publicist Henry Brailsford, Maisky hailed Japan as a 'unique country ... combining in some extraordinary manner Oriental Mediaeval with the most modern Americanism ... Add to this beauty of Nature, "Eigentumlichkeit" of people, of habits and customs ... No wonder that so far I had no reasons to complain that our Foreign Office has sent me to this country.'

Always resentful when placed in a subordinate position, Maisky was glad to see the Soviet ambassador transferred to Paris, as this put him (temporarily at least) in charge of the embassy. His experience in Japan helped shape his views on diplomacy, and particularly the belief that diplomats should be fully immersed in the culture and language of the country to which they were posted. As a way of introducing the Russian public to Japanese culture, he organized an extensive visit by the leading Kabuki theatre to Russia, which encountered resistance within Japanese conservative circles. Indeed, at the troupe's first performance back in Japan following its triumphant tour of Russia, hired thugs released 'live snakes under chairs all around the hall, just before it began. During the show, the snakes began hissing and crawling amidst the audience. A fearful panic broke out. Men snarled, women shrieked, children cried, the curtain had to be lowered and the performance was interrupted.'

Several months later, once again in a subordinate position far from Moscow and Europe, and on the fringes of diplomacy, Maisky was feeling depressed. Moreover, as would be manifested time and again, he was easily led by the whims of his wife, who, he confided to a friend, was 'feeling herself insignificant: primarily unemployed'. The embassy had become a hotbed of intrigue and calumny. Agniya and the wife of the trade representative were 'at daggers drawn' as to who should be the 'First Lady' at state functions. This antagonism between the two, which led to a flurry of correspondence

10. Apprenticeship at the Tokyo embassy.

between the embassy and Narkomindel, was not settled in Agniya's favour, and split the Russian colony into factions. Barely a year into his mission, Maisky complained to Chicherin that living in Japan was 'generally dull and wearisome: there is little political work (not enough for two), and any even slightly important question is dealt with in Moscow'. By now, however, Chicherin was ravaged by severe diabetes and was losing his grip on Narkomindel.

Maisky therefore turned to Litvinov with an explicit demand for a prompt transfer, motivated by the Ménière's disease which had troubled his wife since their sojourn in London and which, he claimed, had worsened in Tokyo, leaving her deaf in one ear. He further complained about the havoc that the weather in Tokyo was playing with his own health. Although it was up to the Collegium of Narkomindel to decide on his future appointment, Maisky did not fight shy of stating his own preference for spending a year or two in Moscow (though he was quick to add that he had 'no objection whatsoever to returning to the West'). Litvinov responded favourably, proposing an ambassadorial role in Kovno, which he presented as the fourth most important post after Berlin, Paris and Warsaw. He was, however, also prepared to discuss alternatives if the offer did not appeal to Maisky. It is remarkable that, at the turn of the decade, it was still possible for a Soviet diplomat to dictate his own terms of employment.

It was with great relief that Maisky received the news of the Politburo's decision to withdraw him from Tokyo in January 1929. 'Your attitude', he wrote to Litvinov in his now

familiar supercilious yet cunning way, 'inevitably invigorates my "Narkomindel patriotism" and wish to work in this environment.' On 4 April he was assigned to Narkomindel's
press department, but within a week the decision was taken to appoint him as minister
plenipotentiary to Helsinki, where he spent the next three years. His stay there culminated in the successful conclusion of the Helsinki Agreement on non-aggression in 1932.
Though a weighty post, even Helsinki was far from attractive to Maisky, who clearly
aspired to a much more prestigious and challenging position in Central or Western
Europe. 'The Russophobia and Sovietophobia here', he lamented to H.G. Wells, 'are
supreme. It is a sort of a general delirium's attack.' For the moment, however, he tried to
maintain 'a cheerful and a good fighting spirit'.

Service in London clearly continued to attract Maisky. Even after his expulsion
from England in 1927 he had remained attuned to the British political scene. He was
thoroughly briefed by Brailsford, H.G. Wells and others about the prospects of the
1929 general election, which could signal the resumption of diplomatic relations –
if not indeed his return to London. Those hopes, however, were dashed after the
elections, when Ramsay MacDonald's foreign secretary, Arthur Henderson, made the
re-establishment of relations with the Soviet Union conditional on a settlement of
tsarist debts. MacDonald, so Maisky learned from his sources in London, 'whether by
accident or design, tumbled right into the Tory trap, and repeated his old declaration
about the identity of the Soviet Government with the Komintern [sic]'. The three
months he spent in Moscow before taking up his post in Helsinki convinced Maisky
that, despite the critical domestic situation, the Soviet Government was 'at present not
at all in the mood to pay that exorbitant price'. His main focus, therefore, now became
Central Europe.

Maisky's prospects of advancement brightened when Litvinov replaced the ailing
Chicherin as commissar for foreign affairs in July 1930. Maisky was quick off the mark in
congratulating Litvinov, though in a somewhat condescending way, reminiscing about
their shared dreams and hopes while in exile in London, and the endless evenings
spent together discussing world affairs in a 'murky, sooty flat at 72 Oakley Square'. This
was only a prelude to repeated requests for a transfer from Helsinki, a 'small political
nowhereville ... and a very dull one', hardly a place where 'an active and energetic *polpred*
can remain for long'. Maisky again tried to dictate his own terms, this time by setting the
beginning of the year as the deadline for his transfer – even to the extent of apparently
being prepared to forsake his position at Narkomindel. 'My intention to seriously
commit myself to a long-term diplomatic work, of which I wrote to you a few years ago
from London, has not weakened in the intervening years but rather intensified,' he
informed Litvinov, 'so that I should be reluctant to leave Narkomindel. Of course, if any
concrete prospects for transfer do turn up, I would ask you first to consult with me.'

By now Stalin's firm grip on the commissariat was restricting Litvinov's room for
manoeuvre. Neither Maisky's personal pleading while on vacation in Moscow at the
start of 1931, nor a later appeal, again harping on Agniya's failing health (which he

claimed could only be treated in Vienna), seemed to move an increasingly disgruntled Litvinov. 'As you ought to know,' he reminded Maisky, 'this issue is not decided by me alone, but by other authorities who are least of all inclined to take account of personal considerations.' Little deterred, Maisky went on pushing forward his own plan, alas in vain: 'Are you certain that working in Vienna would condemn me to diplomatic passivity? Is it really impossible to work on Hungary and the Balkans from Vienna? Won't it be possible to make Vienna our immediate link in dealings with the League of Nations, etc.?'

In the absence of any response, Maisky confined himself to heaping praise on Litvinov, while vigilantly awaiting new opportunities: 'I have no affairs for you today, I just wanted to congratulate you even at a distance on your recent successes in Geneva … The diplomats here are also showing a heightened interest in your person-ality, and talk quite often of your Geneva successes.'

Resigned to a prolonged stay in Helsinki, Maisky was dumbfounded when the unexpected news of his appointment as plenipotentiary to London was conveyed to him by telephone on 3 September 1932. When, a month or so earlier, the Maiskys had visited Kollontay in Stockholm and candidly confided in her, the appointment to the United Kingdom was certainly not on the cards. 'After a minor post as plenipotentiary to Finland,' an amazed Kollontay commented in her diary, 'suddenly London and at such a troublesome period.' Many of his colleagues were shocked by the appointment, remembering his dubious past in the Samara Government during the Civil War. The decision was obviously made in great haste and reflected a change in the orientation of Soviet foreign policy. Litvinov had succeeded in convincing Stalin that Maisky's famili-arity with England – and particularly his ability to communicate and engage people in conversation – was vital. Stalin saw in it 'some sort of an experiment'. Within two days, Litvinov sought an *agrément* for Maisky. The feeble excuses he offered for Ambassador Sokolnikov's abrupt withdrawal were the latter's desire 'to assume work in the Soviet Union' and 'the London climate which does not suit him'. As Maisky's name did not appear on the Home Office's 'black list' of Soviet diplomats who were engaged in subversive activities during the crisis of 1927, the Foreign Office agreed that there was 'nothing in M. Maisky's record that would make him persona non grata to H.M.G.'. The more so as his record in Finland was 'not too bad'.

The appointment, perfectly tailored to Maisky's temperament and ambitions, was perceived by him as recognition of his talents and status, placing him as a lead actor at the front of the stage. 'London', he wrote to his father, 'is a world centre. The other world centre is Moscow. I have to work at the intersection of these two world systems, so it's no surprise that all my time and energy goes on dealing with the many problems that arise from the simultaneous existence of the Soviet and capitalist worlds.' To Whitehall, the appointment of Maisky signalled the Soviet Union's wish to shake off its revolutionary image in Britain by adopting a pragmatic and gradualist course towards socialism. Sokolnikov was evidently ill-suited to the position. Like Maisky, he was the

son of a Jewish doctor in the provinces. He had signed the Brest-Litovsk peace agreement with Germany in 1918 and excelled as a minister of finance during the NEP. However,
his association in 1924 with the 'new opposition' of Kamenev and Zinoviev, who were
calling for the removal of Stalin as general secretary of the party, led to his exile as
ambassador to London in 1929–32. As long as relations with Britain remained on a low
flame, Sokolnikov could be safely kept in England. However, his isolation clearly took its
toll and undermined his ability to act in the quickly changing circumstances which now
rendered relations with Britain vital to Russian national interests. His English was poor,
and even the benevolent Beatrice Webb found him 'studious and ascetic – a veritable
puritan – non smoker, did not drink his wine ... with a naive faith in communism as the
last word of science'. He spent most of his leisure time in the British Museum's reading
room. He was, she thought, 'a strange member of the diplomatic circle ... a nonentity'.

Maisky, on the other hand, was chosen by Litvinov precisely because of his engaging
personality. When Sir Esmond Ovey, the British ambassador in Moscow, met Maisky for
the first time, he found him 'affable and talkative ... a much better "mixer" than his predecessor'. Mentioning those qualities to Litvinov drew an immediate response: 'That is
why I appointed him!' In Stockholm, Kollontay attributed Maisky's appointment to the
growing fear in Moscow that deteriorating relations might again, as in 1927, lead to their
severance. The fact that she had been inundated by telegrams from Litvinov, seeking any
possible piece of information about British politics, implied that the ambassador in
London was no longer trusted.

The timing of the appointment was propitious, as Stalin's desire to remove Sokolnikov
from his post coincided with Litvinov's wish to shift his diplomatic efforts from Berlin to
London and to break through the wall of Conservative hostility. Maisky's success in
concluding a non-aggression pact with Finland and his constant lobbying surely played
their part, the more so as Litvinov was apprised of his wide range of acquaintances in
England, his command of the language and his familiarity with the country. Sokolnikov's
outspoken militancy, observed Beatrice Webb after first meeting Maisky, was replaced
by 'a more accomplished diplomat and less ardent Communist'. Indeed Maisky's
Menshevik past did not go unnoticed in the Foreign Office, and nor did the circumstances which led to his admittance 'to the Bolshevik fold' only after he had made 'a
formal recantation'. Soviet communism, as Maisky confided to Beatrice Webb, was 'in
the making'. He brushed off the 'fanatical metaphysics' (a substitute term for 'ideology')
and the repressions as an inevitable transition stage. He believed in 'the *new civilisation*'
established in the Soviet Union as a '*next* step' in human progress, but not the 'final one',
without being 'fanatical'. The human race, he told her, would 'go on marching to ever
increasing knowledge, love and beauty'. He indulged in utopian dreams about a time
when the individual would 'be absorbed in the pursuit of the interests of the whole
community. Through the advance of knowledge man would conquer this planet and
then he would proceed to conquer Venus!' Playing with the Webbs the 'dangerous game'
of what would happen 'after the disappearance of Stalin', Maisky dismissed the idea that

he would be replaced by another 'idolised' leader. An idol leader would be 'dispensed with and a completely free communist democracy established'.

On 5 September 1932, Maisky was informed by Litvinov that he had 'carried the decision on [his] appointment with the *instantsia* [Stalin], so it only needs to be passed by the Central Executive Committee, which will be done upon receiving the *agrément*'. Maisky, who had already agreed to give up his summer vacation, was encouraged to proceed to Moscow for a week of briefings before being whisked off to London. The instructions he received, Litvinov assured him, were not a reflection of his 'own personal views, but the directives of our higher authorities'. Maisky was made privy to the apprehension in the Kremlin that Weimar Germany was on its 'last legs' and that Hitler's imminent seizure of power was bound to introduce chaos on the international scene and threaten peace, which was indispensable for the domestic, economic and political transformation of the Soviet Union. Litvinov had already commented with irony that it was hardly possible to make five-year plans in international politics. The advance of Nazism therefore required a dramatic *volte-face* in relations with Great Britain, hitherto considered to be the spearhead in the crusade against the Russian Revolution. Foreign policy, unlike domestic politics, had become largely reactive, flexing according to shifting challenges.

The harsh reality dictated a shift from attempts to mobilize socialist solidarity and support for the Russian Revolution among Labour circles, to courting the Conservatives, who were, as Litvinov never tired of stressing, 'the real bosses in Britain!' Within days Maisky returned to Litvinov with a working plan that would characterize his unconventional diplomacy, particularly his recourse to the press and to personal diplomacy, aimed at 'extending as widely as possible the series of visits which diplomatic etiquette imposes on a newly appointed Ambassador, and in doing so to include not only the narrow circle of persons connected with the Foreign Office but also a number of members of the Government, prominent politicians, people of the City and representatives of the cultural world'.

Working with the Conservatives was particularly challenging, heightening the ingrained tension which characterized the work of Soviet diplomats. Maisky had already been grappling with the nature of a revolutionary diplomacy while in Helsinki. He had sought guidance from the socialist intellectual Brailsford: 'Do you know of any work describing diplomatic activities/diplomatic relations, position of revolutionary diplomats at foreign courts and governments, etc. of English, American (1776) and French (1789) revolutions? Do not you know perhaps some interesting memoirs of such revolutionary diplomats?' He was still preoccupied with the subject in 1933, trying to find out, as he confided to Beatrice Webb, 'how the revolutionary diplomats were received and how they behaved'.

The dilemma for the often ostracized Bolshevik diplomat, allured by the charm of the bourgeoisie, was how to adopt a conformist manner and way of life and to fraternize (if not identify) with the 'enemy', while keeping the revolutionary zeal and ethos

11. The alluring bourgeois environment at the embassy.

alive. This became particularly testing after the diplomatic setbacks inflicted on the Russians in 1927, a consequence of their involvement in the 1926 General Strike, which resulted in the collapse of the 'united front' tactics, deprived Soviet ambassadors of the cushion of Labour support and threw them into the Conservative lion's den.

This dichotomy haunted Maisky throughout his long diplomatic career, and he had only a modicum of success in coping with it. Considering his Menshevik and 'counter-revolutionary' past, he was particularly susceptible to accusations of betrayal, which he fervently tried to wave away. When an article in *Pravda* spelled out the problem, Maisky was quick to exonerate himself in a long letter, implying his full awareness of the issue:

> Among the people we have working abroad there is a constant internal struggle between two elements: the healthy revolutionary and proletarian element, which can give a true assessment of 'protocol', and a more sickly, opportunist element, comparatively easily subjected to the influence of the bourgeois surroundings ... The struggle between these two elements follows the rule that 'now one, now the other is driven to one side'. In particular, there is a danger that the supporters of 'protocol' might gain a certain advantage ... It would be very important if you would continue not to forget our 'abroad' and from time to time to publicize questions of the life of Soviet diplomacy outside the USSR.

That would be a strong support for those elements among our overseas workers who consider 'protocol' merely a necessary evil and who therefore try to reduce all bourgeois conventionalities to the absolutely necessary minimum. For I myself have heard more than once how in doubtful cases, where it was unclear where exactly the unavoidable minimum lay, Soviet diplomats have said 'Better too much than not enough', 'You don't spoil the gruel with butter', etc.

Similar pangs of conscience were expressed in Maisky's personal letter to Chicherin, congratulating him on ten years at the helm of Narkomindel:

You were faced with a very difficult task: to create a completely new type of foreign minister ... That task was far harder than creating, say, a new type of finance minister or a new type of agriculture minister, because by the nature of your work you have always had to tread the fine line that divides us from the bourgeois world. You had a devilishly difficult position.

It is most telling that Maisky preferred to be known in Britain, and indeed signed his letters, as Jean – the French variant of John, or the Polish Jan, as he was named by his father in his youth – rather than the archetypical Russian rendition of Ivan.

Prologue

27 October 1937[1]

The first 'five-year plan' of my ambassadorship in England has come to an end! I vividly remember 27 October 1932.

My appointment as ambassador in London came as a complete surprise to me. True, I had read in the *Manchester Guardian* in Helsingfors that Sokolnikov[2] would soon be leaving and I had often wondered who might succeed him. But, running through the candidates in my mind, I for some reason never considered myself. I felt I was as yet 'unworthy' of such a lofty and responsible post. Yes, rumours had reached me that NKID[3] considered me one of the most successful ambassadors and that I would probably be transferred soon from Finland to some other place ... but my imagination stretched no further than Prague or Warsaw.

Then suddenly, on 3 September, I received a notification from M.M. [Litvinov[4]] that I had been appointed ambassador to Britain. I could hardly believe my eyes. The telegram arrived early in the morning. I went to the bedroom, where Agniya[5] was still sleeping, woke her up and said: 'I have some important news.'

---

[1] Reflections on the fifth anniversary of his arrival in England, entered in the diary on 27 October 1937.

[2] Grigory Yakovlevich Sokolnikov (Grish Yankelevich Brilliant) was, like Maisky, the son of a Jewish doctor in the provinces. He was a signatory of the Brest-Litovsk peace agreement with Germany in 1918 and excelled as a minister of finance during the New Economic Policy, a post he lost after demanding the removal of Stalin from the position of general secretary and criticizing collectivization. He was ambassador in London, 1929–32 and deputy people's commissar for foreign affairs, 1933–34. Arrested in 1936, he was convicted of Trotskyite activities and sentenced to ten years' imprisonment, but on Beria's orders was murdered by prison inmates in 1939.

[3] Narkomindel, People's Commissariat for Foreign Affairs, intermittently appearing as Soviet Foreign Ministry. Though not officially, by the early 1930s it was referred to as such, and the *polpreds* were more often than not referred to as ambassadors.

[4] Maksim Maksimovich Litvinov (Meir Moiseevich Vallakh), member of the Russian Social Democratic Party from 1898; Soviet diplomatic representative in London, 1917–18, and in the USA, 1918; deputy people's commissar for foreign affairs, 1921–30; people's commissar for foreign affairs, 1930–39; ambassador to the USA, 1941–43; deputy people's commissar for foreign affairs, 1943–46 (frequently referred to as M.M. in the diary).

[5] Agniya Aleksandrovna Maiskaya (*née* Skipina), wife of I.M. Maisky (frequently referred to as A. or A.A. in the diary). Agniya had been married before and had had a daughter who died in childhood. When they were in England, in 1926, Maisky's daughter came to live with them, but Agniya complained that the arrangement strained their marriage, and so the daughter was sent to live with her mother in St Petersburg. Agniya remained the gatekeeper, monitoring those who were allowed access to her husband until his death.

'What? What has happened?' she asked, immediately worried. 'It's about N., isn't it?'

We were having great difficulties at the time with one of our staff, and I was expecting a decision any minute from Moscow.

'Forget N.!,' I exclaimed. 'This is a lot more serious.'

I told Agniya about my new appointment. She was no less astonished than me. There, in the bedroom, we began to discuss the new situation from every possible angle and to draft our plans for the immediate future.

I was greatly touched by the trust that M.M. and the 'high instance' [Stalin[6]] had shown in me and I expressed my feelings in a return telegram. The news of my transfer to London astounded our Helsingfors colony ... They congratulated me, shook my hand, and wished me every success and happiness. We took several photographs of the whole colony and in various groups. The colony gave us a warm send-off.

I dropped in at the Foreign Ministry a few days later and told Yrjö-Koskinen,[7] then minister of foreign affairs, that I was leaving Finland for good.

... Then the wait began for the British *agrément*. London did not hurry to reply: nearly three weeks passed before a response finally arrived from England.

M.M. wrote to say that I must be in London by the second half of October at the latest and suggested, therefore, that I immediately take a month's leave. But I was finishing my editing of the second edition of *Contemporary Mongolia* and I understood that I would have no time in England for literary activity, especially in the first six months, so I declined a holiday in order to stay in Finland to complete the work ...

I left Helsingfors on 2 October and, after a short stop in Leningrad, finally arrived in Moscow. I have vague memories of my stay in Moscow. We spent a fortnight in the capital and we were always in a hurry. I had several meetings with M.M., and familiarized myself with the materials. Before leaving, I visited V.M.[8] He gave me the following instruction: 'Develop as many contacts as possible, in all strata and circles! Be *au fait* with everything that happens in England and keep us informed.'

---

[6] Iosif Vissarionovich Stalin (Dzhugashvili), general secretary of the Central Committee of the Communist Party of the Soviet Union (CPSU) from April 1922, and member of its Politburo, 1919–53; concurrently chairman of the USSR Council of People's Commissars from May 1941. During the Great Patriotic War, served as people's commissar for defence, supreme commander-in-chief, marshal of the Soviet Union in 1943, and generalissimo of the Soviet Union in 1945.

[7] Aarno Armas Sakari Yrjö-Koskinen, foreign minister of Finland, 1931–32; ambassador to the USSR, 1932–39.

[8] Apparently Vyacheslav Mikhailovich Molotov (Skryabin), member of the Politburo, 1926–52; chairman of the USSR Council of People's Commissars, 1930–57; people's commissar for foreign affairs, 1939–49 and 1953–56.

I followed this advice during my work in London. And, I may say, not without success.

I left for my new post in London on 20 October or thereabouts. ... Agniya and I spent about two days in Berlin. We also stopped for a few days in Paris, where Agniya stocked up on essentials – when a woman decides to replenish her wardrobe, it always takes a good deal of time. In fairness, though, Agniya is a rather modest person in this respect.

We left Paris for London on the morning of the 27th. I had phoned London beforehand to ask Kagan[9] to meet me in Dover. Our journey between the two Western capitals passed without incident.[10] The sea was fairly calm. On the way

12. A victorious return to London.

---

[9] Sergei Borisovich (Samuil Bentsionovich) Kagan was first secretary at the Soviet embassy in London in 1932–35, but on Maisky's recommendation was raised to the rank of counsellor, 1935–36, and served as his right-hand man. Banished from Narkomindel in 1939 and employed as a financial worker in the party's municipal committee in Moscow.

[10] Twenty years earlier, Maisky had almost been denied entry at Folkestone, arriving on the ferry from France with a third-class ticket and failing to possess 'an immigrant's minimum' – the sum of £5. Only after producing from his pocket a crumpled letter from Chicherin, attesting to his status as a 'political refugee from tsarism', was he grudgingly allowed to proceed to London.

from Dover to London, Kagan briefed me on matters at hand. Nearly the whole colony was waiting for us at the station in London: some 300 people. Monck[11] was also there, representing the Foreign Office. There was an awful commotion on the platform. Our comrades crowded around us, cheering loudly, and there was a terrible crush. Newspaper photographers unleashed their own bombardment. ...

Led by a few gallant policemen we inched along the platform to the exit, surrounded by a noisy crowd of comrades. A moment later and we were in a stylish embassy car, speeding along familiar London streets towards our 'home' at 13 Kensington Palace Gardens, W8...

We slowly ascend the stone steps to the entrance hall... We climb to the first floor... Open our apartment doors, marked 'Private' ... Walk around the rooms... Look out the windows...

A new home, a new country, a new job. A thought runs through my mind, like lightning: 'How much time have I to spend here? What will I see? What will I live through? And what will the future bring me?...'

---

[11] John B. Monck, vice-marshal of the diplomatic corps, 1936–45.

13. Presentation of credentials at St James's Palace.

1934

[Maisky started writing his diary in earnest only in 1934, when relations between the USSR and Great Britain had reached rock bottom. In July 1933, six British engineers from the Metro-Vickers firm were arrested in London and charged with wrecking and espionage. The Metro-Vickers trial marked the high-point of an economic and diplomatic battle, which had been inflamed by the Labour government's conclusion in 1930 of an Anglo-Soviet trade agreement, the terms of which appeared to be detrimental to the British. The new National Government, effectively a Tory one, which came to power in 1931, forced the Russians into negotiations for a new, more equitable agreement; but the talks stalled following the conviction of the British engineers. The denunciation of the treaty by Lord Simon,[1] the foreign secretary, somewhat dampened the enthusiasm with which Maisky embarked on his mission.

With Hitler now firmly ensconced in power and unwilling to rekindle the Rapallo spirit, conditions seemed conducive for improving relations with Britain. Litvinov's presence at the World Economic Conference in London, in June 1933, led to a meeting with Simon and to the lifting of all punitive economic measures imposed on Russia, while the imprisoned British engineers were released. Fresh negotiations on a trade agreement were promptly resumed and a new agreement was signed on 16 February 1934, paving the way for Russia to join the League of Nations later that year.

In going about his ambassadorial duties in London, Maisky studiously followed the lead of Litvinov, who had spotted the Nazi threat as early as 1931. However, it took Litvinov almost a year to convince Stalin that Hitler's rise to power meant that 'ultimately war in Europe was inevitable'. The formal shift in Soviet foreign policy, from an isolationist militant 'class against class' position towards a system of collective security in Europe and the Far East, occurred in December 1933. Litvinov pressed for the conclusion of a regional pact of mutual defence within the framework of the League of Nations, in what he termed 'Eastern Locarno'.

---

[1] John Allsebrook Simon (1st Viscount Simon), secretary of state for foreign affairs, 1931–35; home secretary, 1935–37; chancellor of the Exchequer, 1937–40; lord chancellor, 1940–45.

Vansittart,[2] the permanent undersecretary of state, was the advocate of such ideas in Britain. He had been critical of Simon, Anthony Eden[3] and Neville Chamberlain,[4] who espoused bilateral agreements with rivals as the best means of preserving peace and stability – practices which eventually led to appeasement. His own strategic vision, in the wake of Hitler's rise to power, rested on the premise that Britain could preserve a local balance of power in both Europe and the Far East by allying with the Soviet Union, which could place a check on both Japanese and German expansion. A critic of emotional politics, he did not allow his abhorrence of communism to sway him from playing the vital Russian card in the power game. He thus gravitated towards European security based on the pre-1914 entente of Britain, France and Russia.

Consequently, Vansittart and Maisky assumed the Cassandra role, resolutely giving voice to premonitions about Hitler's intentions. The Vansittarts first encountered Maisky and his wife at a reception at Buckingham Palace in 1933. The couples were to end up meeting frequently, as Maisky and Vansittart not only shared a political outlook, but also went on to forge a literary and cultural bond based on a common admiration of Heine, Lermontov and Kant. Their conversation would drift to de Basil's Ballets Russes at Covent Garden or to the new production of Bernard Shaw's *Saint Joan* at the Russian embassy.[5] However, what really drew them close was the clairvoyant conviction that Nazi Germany posed a formidable menace to Britain and the Soviet Union. Both also shared a belief in the importance of personal relationship in diplomacy. This was manifested in Vansittart's practice, well recorded throughout Maisky's diary, of leaking information as a means of exerting public pressure – a method which Maisky soon mastered to perfection. 'Curious,' observed Dalton,[6] 'how these two very dissimilar witnesses corroborate each other's evidence on many points.' Chamberlain's rise to power, however, led to Vansittart's 'promotion' to the specially created new post of 'chief diplomatic adviser' at the beginning of 1938, effectively removing him from the process of policy-making and depriving Maisky, at a crucial moment, of an important ally within the Foreign Office.

Their first meeting of consequence took place during a lunch given by Vansittart in Maisky's honour on 21 June 1934, which was also attended by Simon. Referring to the secretary of state, Lady Vansittart whispered into Maisky's ear: 'I suppose it's my

[2] Robert Gilbert Vansittart (1st Baron Vansittart), principal private secretary to Lord Curzon, 1920–24, and to successive prime ministers, 1928–30; permanent undersecretary of state for foreign affairs, 1930–38; chief diplomatic adviser to the foreign secretary, 1938–41 (often referred to as V. in the diary).
[3] Robert Anthony Eden (1st earl of Avon), Conservative MP for Warwick and Leamington, 1923–57; undersecretary of state for foreign affairs, 1931–34; lord privy seal, 1934–35; foreign secretary, 1935–38, 1940–45 and 1951–55; dominions secretary, 1939–40; secretary of state for war in 1940.
[4] Arthur Neville Chamberlain, chancellor of the Exchequer, 1923–24 and 1931–37; minister of health, 1923, 1924–29 and August–November 1931; prime minister and first lord of the Treasury, 1937–40.
[5] George Bernard Shaw, the famous Irish playwright, dramatist, critic and socialist was a member of the Executive Committee of the Fabian Society, 1885–1911.
[6] Hugh Dalton, chairman of the National Executive of the Labour Party, 1936–37; minister of economic warfare, 1940–42; president of the Board of Trade, 1942–45.

14. Ballet for the young: the *vie quotidienne* for the children of the embassy staff.

neighbour on the left who is making difficulties?... why should you not have a frank talk
about this with Van?' Her indiscreet intervention led to a series of meetings on 3, 12 and
18 July (described in the diary), heralding a long-lasting association which introduced a
thaw in Anglo-Soviet relations, and in turn helped Litvinov push through the collective
security line in Moscow.]

12 July

Vansittart asked me over to brief me about the results of Barthou's[7] visit. The
British are very pleased with its outcome. The British Government has promised to support the Eastern Pact scheme, as well as the project for a supple-
mentary Franco-Soviet guarantee pact, but under the crucial condition that
Germany be allowed to participate in the pact on an equal footing with France
and the USSR. Simon will speak to this effect in the House tomorrow. The
British ambassadors in Berlin and Warsaw have been instructed to advise ('in
a friendly manner') participation in the Eastern Pact, while the British ambassador in Rome has been instructed to ask the Italian Government to support
the British move.

I expressed satisfaction with Vansittart's report and promised to inform the
Soviet Government of the British desire to draw Germany into the guarantee
pact. ...

---

[7] Jean Louis Barthou, French foreign minister, 1934. Visited London on 9–10 July.

18 July

I informed Vansittart today that the Soviet Government is ready to admit Germany as an equal member to the Franco-Soviet guarantee pact. Vansittart was very pleased and promised to take measures to secure wide coverage in the press. It would be good if the Soviet Government also made its decision public. Germany's sole objection to the Eastern Pact has now been removed. If Germany, nonetheless, once again declines the proposal, she will have only herself to blame when other countries become suspicious of her intentions.

I inquired about the reception of the British *démarches* in Berlin and Warsaw, of which Vansittart informed me on 12 July.

V. replied that Neurath's[8] attitude was cold and hostile, and Beck's[9] – chilly. Both, however, had promised 'to study the issue'. So far there has been no response from them.

V. then impressed on me once again the British Government's desire to improve Anglo-Soviet relations. 'A certain improvement is already apparent,' said Vansittart, 'but I can see no reason why this process should not go significantly further.' The USSR is concerned about Britain's attitude to Germany and Japan, but Simon defined the British Government's position towards the former country in the House on 13 July (I nodded and said that his speech went down well in our country). ...

V., however, has a complaint of his own to make concerning the conduct of the Soviet press, which not infrequently accuses Britain of setting Japan and Germany against the USSR. ... But it is desirable to avoid direct accusations that Britain is preparing for war against the USSR, which only serve the cause of elements hostile to Anglo-Soviet *rapprochement* in the press and in Parliament ('all the more so as such suspicions are absolutely unfounded').

I replied that although I could fully sympathize with V.'s feelings and intentions, the nineteenth century has undoubtedly left a burdensome legacy while the Soviet period has been characterized by Britain's unceasing struggle against the young workers' and peasants' state. Is it surprising that the Soviet masses have grown to regard Great Britain as their enemy? ...

9 August

I called on Vansittart to say goodbye before leaving for my holidays, and he used my visit for a serious political talk.

---

[8] Konstantin von Neurath, German ambassador in London, 1930–32; foreign minister, 1932–38; Reich protector of Bohemia and Moravia, 1939–41.
[9] Józef Beck, Polish foreign minister, 1932–39.

First of all, V. announced that in reply to our *démarche* of 3 August (made by Kagan during my visit to Scotland), the British Government would willingly support the USSR's admission to the League of Nations and approve the League of Nations' invitation. ...

'So,' V. continued, 'we shall soon be members of the same "club" (V. meant the League of Nations). I am very pleased. At the present time I fail to see a single major international problem that could seriously divide Britain and the USSR. The very course of events and the logic of things are pushing our countries towards each other, both in Europe and in the Far East. We take the same line on where the threat to the world is coming from – so our views on how to parry the danger should also concur in many respects. Our serious and frank discussions (particularly the first one, on 3 July) have greatly contributed to the elucidation of our reciprocal positions and to the growth of mutual understanding. But this is only the beginning. The fact that the British Government has supported the Eastern Pact and is now ready to support the entry of the USSR to the League of Nations is the best proof of a serious shift in Anglo-Soviet relations.'

... 'During your holidays,' said V., 'you will, of course, see Mr Litvinov. Tell him, please, that in order to improve our relations it would be desirable to avoid all vexatious incidents. Take, for example, the Metro-Vickers case or the dispute over Lena Goldfields.[10] These cases may not be that crucial *per se*, but the danger lies in arousing passions among the English masses that it would be better not to inflame. It is also important that the press of both countries should act with discretion. Now that Britain and the USSR are becoming members of the same 'club', it would be strange if we began to accuse each other of cheating or of pointing guns at one another under the table.[11] ...

In conclusion, I asked V. what he knew about the Eastern Pact. V. said that Germany and Poland were maintaining silence. This cannot last for long. Both governments have had enough time to 'study' the issue of the pact. A direct answer must now be demanded of them. If a response is not forthcoming, France and the USSR must act. It would be dangerous to delay the signing of the pact. In general, Hitler's position has become more and more enigmatic of late. Following the death of Hindenburg,[12] he has become Germany's true master. What does he want? War or peace? Austria ought to be the touchstone. Time will tell. So far, Hitler has stuck to the recipe of *Alice's Adventures in Wonderland*:

---

[10] A dispute over a concession given to a British firm and revoked by the Bolsheviks in the wake of the revolution.

[11] According to the British records, Vansittart was more blunt: 'What would be the position in any club card-room if members were continually accusing each other of having the fifth ace and a Thompson sub-machine gun under the table? ... I shall tell M. Maisky again the next time I see him.'

[12] Paul Ludwig von Hindenburg, field marshal during the First World War, 1916–18; president of the Weimar Republic of Germany, 1925–34.

'Jam tomorrow and jam yesterday – but never jam today.' That's just how Hitler is with peace. He always promises peace tomorrow, but not today.

We parted warmly and arranged to meet two months later, upon my return to London.

[A keen traveller, Maisky left England for an absorbing three-month journey through the much-admired cradle of Western civilization – Italy, Greece and Constantinople – before returning to the Soviet Union. Shortly before his return to London, Maisky had two days of intensive talks with Stalin and Litvinov on the future course of Soviet foreign policy which left him with a strong impression that Stalin 'had now established very nearly the same mental superiority over his colleagues as Lenin[13] once enjoyed'. Back in London, he fervently tried to convey the message that the Soviet Union had abandoned its dynamic revolutionary drive. Maisky's claims were, however, dismissed in the Foreign Office. They showed 'the length to which [the Soviet Government] was prepared to go to secure favour here ... it was more likely to have been dictated by expediency than by conviction'. Nonetheless, the fear that the Russians and the Germans might close ranks encouraged the Foreign Office to respond favourably to the Soviet overtures.]

31 October

I was told the other day that when the prime minister appears on the newsreel, the audience laughs.

MacDonald's[14] personal authority seems to be at very low ebb.

1 November

I am increasingly convinced that despite everything, Baldwin[15] is still the real leader of the Conservative Party and, consequently, the leader of England and the British Empire. But he is no ordinary leader. H. Macmillan[16] (Conservative) once told me that Baldwin 'is our Kutuzov' (he meant the Kutuzov of L. Tolstoy's *War and Peace*).

---

[13] Vladimir Ilyich Lenin (Ulyanov), founder of the Russian Communist Party (Bolsheviks), leader of the Bolshevik Revolution, 1917, and chairman of the Council of People's Commissars, 1917–24.
[14] James Ramsay MacDonald, prime minister of the first and second Labour governments of 1924 and 1929–31; prime minister of the National Government, 1931–35; lord president of the council, 1935–37.
[15] Stanley Baldwin (1st Earl Baldwin of Bewdley), British prime minister, 1923–24, 1924–29 and 1935–37.
[16] Harold Macmillan (1st earl of Stockton), Conservative MP, 1924–29 and 1931–64; parliamentary secretary to the Ministry of Supply, 1940–42; undersecretary of state for the colonies, 1942–45.

4 November

In today's *Observer* Garvin[17] sharply attacks Japan's demand for naval parity with Britain and the USA. Seen from the perspective of British imperialism, there is much truth in his arguments. Garvin draws the following conclusion: if an agreement between Japan, the USA and Britain proves impossible, then an agreement must be sought between the USA and Britain (against Japan). ...

The same issue of the *Observer* carries news from Calcutta that Gandhi,[18] tired and disillusioned, is retiring, and that the Indian Congress, which now consists almost exclusively of highly pragmatic political dealers, is ready to reconcile itself to the reform of the Indian Constitution being prepared by the British and to take full advantage of the positions and cosy jobs that it will make available. Gandhi's 'impractical idealism' merely inhibits these dealers. That's why they are glad to see him bowing out...

... Gandhi! I have Fülöp-Miller's book *Lenin und Gandhi*, published in Vienna in 1927. The author sketches the two leaders with considerable talent, juxtaposing them as the two equal 'peaks' of our time. Seven years ago this comparison seemed absurd only to communists, and perhaps to a few of the more perspicacious representatives of the European bourgeoisie. But now? Who, even among the ranks of bourgeois intellectuals, would dare equate Lenin and Gandhi? Today, any man, even an enemy, can see that Lenin is an historical Mont Blanc, who will forever remain a radiant guiding peak in the thousand-year evolution of humanity, while Gandhi is just a cardboard mountain who shone with a dubious light for some ten years before rapidly disintegrating, to be forgotten just a few years later in the dustbin of history. This is how time and events separate authentically precious metal from its cheap imitation.

[In what today would be a routine practice, but was in the 1930s quite uncommon, Maisky diligently cultivated relations with the proprietors and editors of leading newspapers, particularly the more Conservative ones. His intensive correspondence with Garvin, the associate of Lord and Lady Astor[19] and editor of the *Observer*, is a striking example. Maisky would brief Garvin, sometimes in a subtle way and sometimes quite bluntly, about issues which he deemed of sufficient importance to be raised in the paper.]

---

[17] James Louis Garvin, editor of the *Observer*, 1908–42.
[18] Mohandas Karamchand Gandhi, leader of the Indian nationalist movement against British rule. Maisky's evaluation of Gandhi reflects the official Soviet critical view of Gandhi, whose ideology of non-violent resistance was identified with the interests of the national bourgeoisie.
[19] Nancy Astor, Viscountess Astor, Conservative MP for Plymouth, 1919–45, and the first woman to sit in the House of Commons. A non-conformist politician, she accompanied Bernard Shaw on a tour of Russia and met Stalin, but diverted her sympathies to Hitler when she established the 'Cliveden set', a spearhead in the appeasement of Nazism.

9 November

Today I had a long meeting with Simon. ... He stated categorically that the British Government has no designs on Soviet territory, that the government has never supported advocates of the theory that Great Britain would profit from a *nice little war* in the Far East between the USSR and Japan ... At the same time, he made it clear that *rapprochement* with the USSR should not advance to the detriment of Britain's relations with any other third power (he obviously had Japan, and perhaps Germany, in mind) ...

Today's talk with S. may prove to be a soap-bubble, or it may become an important historical event. Everything depends on the Cabinet's judgement.

I'm sitting at my typewriter, wondering which of the alternatives will materialize.

Let's wait and see.

10 November

Last night I attended the lord mayor's[20] annual dinner. November 9th is a great day in the life of the City. Lord mayors have been inaugurated on this day since time immemorial. ... The *Lord Mayor Show*, a medieval ceremony, proceeds along the streets of the town and in the evening a sumptuous banquet is held at the Guildhall for London notables, attended by some 500–600 guests. Heads of mission are also included in the list of guests, but... first, they are invited without their wives (though the English notables come with their ladies) and, secondly, not all heads receive this honour – only the ambassadors and the two most senior heads of mission.

The evening ceremony is most curious. The newly elected lord mayor and his wife – the present lord mayor[21] is a widower and he was therefore accompanied by his daughter – stand on a small dais at the far end of the long hall of the Guildhall's library. A beautiful dark-red carpet, along which the newly arrived guests proceed, stretches from the hall's entrance to the dais. A herald clad in Tudor dress loudly announces the name of each guest. The guest should walk the length of the carpet at a stately pace, step onto the dais and shake hands with the lord mayor and his wife. Then he moves away to the right or to the left of the host, depending on his position and rank. Gradually, large crowds of guests gather on either side of the carpet, scrutinizing each new arrival. According to the custom, outstanding guests are greeted with applause. The volume of applause varies sharply in proportion to the guest's status and popularity. Once

---

[20] Sir Stephen Henry Molyneux Killik.
[21] Sir Percy Vincent.

the last guests have arrived, the ceremonial procession is formed. Trumpeters lead the way in medieval dress, followed by the City marshal and the lord mayor's confessor. Then comes the mace-bearer on the left, followed by the lord mayor, wearing a hat and a robe with a long train; then the prime minister (MacDonald) with the sword-bearer on the right and behind them the prime minister's wife (on this occasion his daughter Ishbel[22]) and the lord mayor's wife. ... The entire procession passes slowly through the Guildhall's picture gallery and moves around the banquet hall before its members finally take their places at the dinner table. The 'feast' then gets under way, beginning with the obligatory turtle soup, which I seem to find quite indigestible...

On the whole, the scene impresses one with the vividness of its colours and its medieval solemnity. No wonder: the programme and the banquet menu bear on their cover an engraving of the Charter of King John of 9 May 1215 that asserted the liberties of the City of London and granted the barons the right annually to elect their mayor, who should be loyal to the king, modest and fit to rule the city, and who should be presented to the king, or to his supreme judge in the king's absence, immediately upon election.

* * *

There were some interesting moments at yesterday's banquet.

... When, in search of my seat, I found myself two chairs away from my destination, I was suddenly struck by the sound of Russian speech. I raised my head and saw the following scene. On the other side of the table, directly opposite my seat, a tall grey-haired lady wearing a grey-blue silk dress and a yellowish brocade cloak was in quite a state and making gestures. Her face was quite pleasant, but now it was all blotched with red. Two young people hung about her, quite at a loss: a young girl in green and a respectable grey-headed gentleman wearing a velvet suit with a star on his breast. I heard the woman saying hysterically in Russian: 'I cannot sit here! I just can't!'

The respectable gentleman whispered something into the grey woman's ear in an attempt to calm her down, but without success. 'I won't sit here! I'm leaving!' the obstinate lady continued to yell.

The green girl rearranged the sets on the table and moved the lady two chairs away from me. The lady calmed down a touch, but she flared up again when she saw me on the point of taking my seat and shouted, her face aflame: 'Blood on your hands!'

I cast an ironic glance at the agitated lady and started talking calmly to my neighbour. The lady flopped into her seat and angrily shifted a vase so that I could not see her behind the flowers.

---

[22] Ishbel MacDonald, inn proprietor and daughter of former Prime Minister Ramsay MacDonald.

In the course of conversation I asked my neighbour, who turned out to be the wife of the senior alderman Twyfold, for the surname of the woman who had just made a scene.

'Oh,' she said, 'that's Lady Kynaston Studd.[23] Her husband, Sir Kynaston Studd (the gentleman in a velvet suit), was an alderman. He served as lord mayor for a year, then retired. He is rich, and she is a Russian princess. They married during the war.'

Then my neighbour added with a meaningful intonation: 'Lady Studd is a charming woman, but she is somewhat highly strung.'

What delicacy of expression! How very English! The husband of the Russian princess, evidently taken aback by his wife's behaviour, took pains to be especially nice to me (once again, in the English fashion) and even toasted my health. Meanwhile, his stubborn wife, a little flushed with wine, seemed to have 'tempered justice with mercy'. She pushed aside the vase that separated us and started to scrutinize me with unconcealed insolence...

15 November

Today I attended the dinner given by the ancient guild, the Worshipful Company of Stationers and Newspaper Makers (already 600 years old).

I had expected the dinner to be accompanied by some very old customs, but I was disappointed. It was a dinner like all the others, right down to the inescapable turtle soup, and only the painted arched windows of the dining hall suggested the past. I tell a lie: there was also 'The loving cup', but I had seen that already at the lord mayor's banquets. The guests, though – they really did bring the odd whiff of medieval times. To my right sat Lord Marshall[24] (a big publisher and a former lord mayor of London), who proudly declared that he had been in the guild for 55 years!

'Is membership hereditary?' I asked in some perplexity.

'No,' answered Lord Marshall, 'it is not. I joined the guild as soon as I became an apprentice in my profession.'

It turned out that my neighbour was already 70. To my left sat Lord Wakefield,[25] a major oil industrialist, prominent philanthropist and London alderman. He's also about 70 years old (a schoolmate of Marshall's!). This venerable notable of the British Empire told me that about 30 years ago (a truly English time span!) he had planned a visit to St Petersburg and had even booked the tickets when suddenly, at the last moment, he received a telegram,

---

[23] Sir John Edward Kynaston Studd, alderman of the City of London, 1923–42; lord mayor of London, 1928–29.
[24] Horace Brooks Marshall (1st Baron Marshall of Chipstead), lord mayor of London, 1918–19.
[25] Charles Cheers Wakefield (1st Viscount Wakefield), British businessman; lord mayor, 1915–16.

claiming 'plague in Russia'. Naturally, he decided not to travel. Perhaps now was the time to go?... I seconded his intention.

'Tell me,' he continued, wiping his brow and appearing to remember something. 'You seem to have a man... Lenin... Is he really terribly clever?'

'I can assure you he was,' I answered, smiling, 'but unfortunately he died back in 1924.'

'Died?' Wakefield sounded disappointed. 'Really?... I wasn't aware of that.'

See how well the cream of the English bourgeoisie is informed about Soviet affairs!

Truly it smacks of the Middle Ages!...

* * *

Since last year, the chairman (or Master) of the guild has been the Prince of Wales.[26] Our 'friend' the archbishop of Canterbury[27] made a witty toast in honour of the prince (the archbishop, it must be said, is an outstanding dinner speaker), and the prince responded in the customary manner. Then everybody moved to the smoking-room. Here the prince, who considered it his duty as host to exchange a couple of niceties with every diplomat present, quite unexpectedly engaged me in a long and inappropriately serious conversation. First, he asked me whether I have to deliver many speeches. When I complimented him on his speech he, somewhat embarrassed, started talking about the best English orators, past and present. He named the late Lord Birkenhead,[28] General Smuts[29] and Lloyd George,[30] but not MacDonald. He said of the premier, with a slight grimace: 'You know, he is not exactly...' ... He then moved on to international politics, speaking at length about the threat of war and the complicated international situation, before finally concluding: no one wants war – not England, not France ('she only stands to lose by war!') and not even Germany. I expressed my doubts as to the peaceful intentions of the latter, as well as of Japan. The prince did not object, but he began to argue emphatically that England strives only for peace, and that militarist ideas are alien to the spirit of the British nation. ... For my part, I stated that Soviet foreign policy was a policy of peace, and that I was glad to hear from the Prince of Wales that Great Britain seeks the same aim. This pleased the prince, who repeated that nobody really wanted war and that the forces of peace were far more numerous

---

[26] Prince of Wales, 1911–36; King Edward VIII of Great Britain, January 1936, becoming Prince Edward, duke of Windsor, after abdicating from the throne in December 1936.

[27] William Cosmo Gordon Lang, archbishop of Canterbury, 1928–42.

[28] Frederick Edwin Smith (1st earl of Birkenhead), secretary of state for India, 1924–28.

[29] Field Marshal Jan Christian Smuts, prime minister, foreign minister and defence minister of the Union of South Africa, 1939–48.

[30] David Lloyd George, Liberal MP for Caernarvon 1890–1945; prime minister of Great Britain 1916–22; leader of the Liberal Party, 1926–31.

and mightier than the forces of war. I remarked, however, that the forces of war were much better organized, especially arms manufacturers, so the threat of war was very serious indeed. ... Towards the end of our conversation he inquired about my past, so I described my career in diplomacy. He then asked: 'Where did you learn English?' I answered that for five years, between 1912 and 1917, I had lived in England as a political émigré. The prince laughed and exclaimed: 'And now you are the ambassador! It's a sign of the times. We are living in an astonishing epoch!'[31]

Our chat lasted for 10–15 minutes. The prince and I stood in the centre of the smoking-room, while a crowd of shocked diplomats and some 200 British notables, headed by the archbishop of Canterbury, stood around us, exchanging glances and whispers.

16 November

I visited Eden on returning from holiday. I hadn't meant to discuss serious matters, but our conversation seemed to veer of its own accord towards current political issues. The most important:

(1) Eden said, word for word: 'At the present moment, no conflicts exist between Great Britain and the USSR anywhere in the world. On the contrary, they have one common and highly important interest – the preservation of peace. You need peace to complete your great experiment, and need it for the development and flourishing of trade. This creates favourable conditions for improving Anglo-Soviet relations.'

(2) Eden was very glad to learn that we had not abandoned our efforts to conclude the Eastern Pact. He stated that he would discuss this issue with Beck in Geneva (Eden leaves for Geneva tomorrow to attend the session of the Council of the League of Nations).

(3) The talks between Eden and Ribbentrop[32] bore an entirely frivolous character. Eden is very sceptical about the likelihood of Germany's imminent return to the League of Nations. It is possible that Hitler himself does not want war, but everything that is now taking place in Germany clearly points towards it. That's why Germany is the main potential seat of war at the present time.

... Eden invited me to drop in when he returns from Geneva.

[The description of the meeting with Eden is typical of the subversive methods Maisky would adopt throughout his ambassadorship to convey to Moscow his own ideas, while attributing them to his interlocutors. It became the only effective way of operating,

---

[31] Maisky told Beatrice Webb (but did not report home) that the Prince of Wales had actually intimated his wish to visit the Soviet Union.

[32] Joachim von Ribbentrop, German ambassador to Great Britain, 1936–38; foreign minister, 1938–45.

with the Terror raging in the late 1930s. In this particular case, though he credited the idea to Eden, it was Maisky's own plea that Litvinov should attend the League of Nations session. He thereby hoped to secure a meeting between Eden and Litvinov and reinforce rapprochement by further driving a wedge between Eden and Simon.]

23 November

'Functions' linked to the royal wedding have begun. Today our doyen, the Brazilian de Oliveira,[33] held a reception for the diplomatic corps 'to meet the Duke of Kent[34] and Princess Marina'.[35] At around 6 p.m., all the heads of mission gathered in the doyen's relatively small residence, accompanied by their wives. ... The happy couple arrived at 6.30, accompanied by the parents of the bride. Excitement was growing in the hall. Silence, snatched whispers, ladies casting curious glances... Eventually the guests appeared, preceded by the doyen and his wife. Marina looked charming to me, much better than she did in the newspapers: a blonde with luxurious hair, a rosy complexion, bright eyes. Thin and refined. One diplomat later told me that her photographers should have been shot for ruining Marina. Right he was! The duke of Kent isn't bad either: tall, slender, with quite a pleasant face. He stoops a little and seems to be very shy. In any case, he is the most handsome of the king's sons. On the whole, seen from the physical and physiological point of view, they make a nice couple. The bride's parents – Prince Nicholas of Greece[36] and his wife (a Russian princess,[37] I believe) – resemble provincial landowners of middling means...

The doyen made a short welcome speech in English and presented the bride and groom with a large silver tureen and two silver salad bowls on behalf of the entire diplomatic corps. (Today, I received a letter from the doyen, notifying me that the cost of the present was 300 pounds, of which my share is 6.) The facsimile signatures of all the heads of mission who contributed to the gift are engraved on the inside of the tureen, and my name is among the first. It immediately catches the eye when one looks inside. Won't that be fun for Marina! It may spoil her appetite, I'm afraid. ...

27 November

The second 'function' concerning the royal wedding!

---

[33] Raul Regis de Oliveira, Brazilian ambassador in London, 1925–40; doyen of the diplomatic corps, 1933–40, succeeded by Maisky.
[34] Prince George Edward, duke of Kent, fourth son of George V.
[35] Princess Marina, duchess of Kent, wife of Prince George, duke of Kent.
[36] Prince Nicholas of Greece, father of Princess Marina, who in 1934 married the duke of Kent.
[37] Former Grand Duchess Elena Vladimirovna of Russia.

A grand evening reception in honour of Marina at Buckingham Palace. More than 800 guests, including all heads of mission. On top of that, a whole 'brigade' of royalties – the entire royal family (the king[38] and queen,[39] the prince of Wales, the duke of York[40] and his wife, the duke of Kent, the younger son John, the so-called 'princess royal', i.e. the king's daughter, together with her husband; only the duke of Gloucester[41] was absent – he's currently in Australia), as well as the king of Denmark[42] and his wife, the king of Norway[43] and his wife, Prince Regent Paul of Yugoslavia,[44] Princess Juliana of Holland[45] (the heiress), and so on. There was also a great quantity of grand princes of various nationalities, including Kirill Vladimirovich Romanov[46] ('Emperor of All Russia'!), accompanied by his wife and daughter Kira,[47] who was one of the eight bridesmaids. Add to that an endless number of princesses (Greek, Yugoslav and others)...

The procedure: all the ambassadors and envoys of the countries whose heads were present at the wedding formed a semicircle according to seniority in the round hall of the palace, while the remaining envoys and chargés d'affaires were put in the adjoining long hall. Representatives of the English nobility and the upper bourgeoisie were gathered in groups in the other rooms. A long and dazzling cavalcade of royalties emerged from the corner room adjacent to the round hall. First, the British king and queen passed along a line of ambassadors and wives, shaking hands with all of them and exchanging a few pleasantries with some chosen guests. Among the latter were our doyen (by virtue of his rank) and Matsudaira[48] (the English are scared of the Japanese!). The royal couple passed from the round hall to the adjoining room, where the envoys were, but they did not pause there before individual diplomats, confining themselves to general bows to the right and to the left. Foreign royal couples (Danish, Norwegian, etc.) followed their example, as did members of the British royal family. They all shook hands with us and smiled politely ... Actually, that's not quite true: there were exceptions. Marina's mother demonstratively walked past Agniya and me without greeting us. Well, we'll get by in this world without her handshakes! Two or three wizened old witches, ugly as sin, came out of the corner room and hesitated, whispering secretively and glancing in our direction,

---

38 King George V of Great Britain, 1910–36.
39 Victoria Mary, queen consort of King George V, 1910–36.
40 Later King George VI.
41 Prince Henry William, duke of Gloucester, third son of King George V.
42 King Christian X of Denmark, 1912–47.
43 King Haakon VII of Norway (born Christian Frederik), 1905–57.
44 Prince Paul of Yugoslavia, Prince Regent of Yugoslavia, 1934–41; was deposed in a coup d'état after he signed the agreement on Yugoslavia's access to the Axis in March 1941.
45 Princess Juliana van Oranje-Nassau. Queen of the Netherlands, 1948–80.
46 Kirill Vladimirovich Romanov, Russian grand duke; assumed the titular Emperor and Autocrat of All the Russias, 1924–38, being the next in line to the throne following the murder of the tsar's family.
47 Grand Duchess Kira Kirillovna, second daughter of Grand Duke Kirill Vladimirovich of Russia.
48 Tsuneo Matsudaira, Japanese ambassador in London, 1929–36.

before deciding to proceed directly to the envoys' room, bypassing the line of ambassadors. The Soviet ambassador had given them a fright! There were also some ladies and gentlemen decorated with ribbons and diadems, who stumbled at the sight of me and immediately backed off every which way. That must have been Kirill and his retinue. On the whole, my presence at the royal reception was an unpleasant disappointment for a certain group of guests. ...

* * *

I witnessed a curious scene at the end of the reception.

The king approached Baldwin and began to speak to him. I don't know what they were talking about, since I was standing too far away, but I couldn't help observing them. The king – short, balding, frail, his arms almost straight down by his sides – moved his lips slowly and, bending slightly forward, gazed ingratiatingly at the Conservative leader. Baldwin – solidly built with a paunch, red hair and a confident grinning face – was leaning back arrogantly and listening to the king in a calm and somewhat majestic manner. First he stood akimbo, then he unceremoniously scratched the back of his head, before finally folding his arms across his fat chest. The king just talked on and on... Observing the scene, one was apt to ask: 'Which of the two is the master?' It certainly didn't seem to be the king.

* * *

Lady Astor caught hold of me. Clad in a fine green velvet dress, as buoyant and ardently vigorous as ever, she made a very favourable impression against the general background of laxity and degeneration.

'I've just had a real fight with Kira!' she exclaimed with great enthusiasm.

'Over what?' I inquired.

'Well, naturally, over the USSR! I was trying to prove to her that she is wrong and that you, *bloody Bolsheviks*, are good people.'

'I can imagine the impression that made on Kira!' I chuckled.

'Don't laugh!' Lady Astor flared up. Whereupon, she took me by the arm and dragged me after her, saying: 'Come on, I'll introduce you to Kira. She wants to see you!'...

It was with some difficulty that I succeeded in extracting myself and vanishing in the crowd.

What a crazy woman!

[Maisky's memoirs, and particularly their Russian edition, geared as they were towards vindicating Soviet policies on the eve of the war, present a sinister and often factually inaccurate portrait of Lady Astor. They do reveal how intriguing Maisky found the strikingly glamorous and witty American, who in 1919 was the first woman to enter

Parliament – a Conservative MP who championed the Soviet cause (following a tour of Russia and a meeting with Stalin at the Kremlin in 1931). Maisky was clearly attracted, though not beguiled, by the 'small, thin, elegant lady with the slightly whipped dark hair, a minute expressive face and lively crafty eyes' which rendered her the 'absolute embodiment of eternal restlessness'. He remained a frequent visitor to her Versailles-modelled mansion at Cliveden, Buckinghamshire, even after 1937, when it became a Mecca for appeasers such as Chamberlain, Halifax,[49] Hoare[50] and others, who spent long weekends there.]

28 November

Between 3 and 5 p.m., Agniya and I were at St James's Palace, at a specially arranged viewing of the wedding gifts presented to the duke of Kent and Marina. A great mass of people. An incredible crush and confusion. There were so many presents that when we entered the hall with the tables, chairs, beds and others gifts presented to the bride and groom, you might have thought you were in a furniture store. The greatest attention was lavished on the items of jewellery, especially the three diamond diadems given to Marina by her fiancé, her father and the British queen. The diadems were kept under glass, and the wives of the ambassadors and British notables were simply dying of envy and rapture. Out of all the books presented to the duke and Marina, it was a thick leather-bound volume entitled *Russian Imperial Dinner Service* that caught my eye.

As we travelled from the embassy to the palace, a heavy black fog started descending quickly on London. It was a remarkable scene: in one direction the sky was already black and impenetrable, in the other it still glowed with rapidly fading lights of pink and straw-like complexion. There was something menacing and tragic in this rare combination of colours. As if some mighty natural calamity were taking place or drawing near, like the destruction of Pompeii or the great earthquake of 1923 in Japan...

29 November

The royal wedding finally took place today. From first light, and even from the previous night, London seemed to be overflowing its banks. Up to half a million

---

[49] Edward Frederick Lindley Wood (1st earl of Halifax), a prize fellow at All Souls College, Oxford, he went on to become the viceroy of India, 1926–32; Conservative leader of the House of Lords, 1935–38; secretary of state for war, 1935; lord privy seal, 1935–37; lord president of the council, 1937–38; secretary of state for foreign affairs, 1938–40; and British ambassador to the United States, 1941–46.

[50] Samuel John Hoare (1st Viscount Templewood), Conservative, minister for the affairs of India, 1931–35; secretary of state for foreign affairs, 1935; first lord of the Admiralty, 1936–37; secretary of state for home affairs, 1937–39; lord privy seal, 1939–40; secretary of state for air, 1940; ambassador to Spain on special mission, 1940–44.

people descended on the capital from all over the country. Many foreigners arrived from the Continent. The streets along which the wedding procession would pass were filled to bursting by an immense crowd that had gathered on the previous evening to occupy the best places. Typically, the crowd consisted almost entirely of women. I, at least, noticed barely a single man on my way from the embassy to Westminster Abbey. Some newspapers also noted this (the *Manchester Guardian* for one). Large platforms were erected at various points along the procession, with seats being sold for between one and ten guineas. The city, particularly its central part, was decked out gaudily with flags, festoons and banners showing portraits of the bridegroom and the bride; and in the evening, the town was lavishly illuminated. The full works, in other words. The wedding was turned into a real national event.

... On this occasion I was obliged to attend the wedding ceremony itself, in Westminster Abbey. That's what Moscow decided. It was the first time I had attended a church service since leaving school, 33 years ago! That's quite a stretch.

The diplomatic corps sat to the right of the entrance, and members of the government on the left. Simon was my partner on the opposite side. MacDonald zealously chanted psalms during the service, Baldwin yawned wearily, while Elliot[51] simply dozed. Churchill[52] looked deeply moved and at one point even seemed to wipe his eyes with a handkerchief. Henderson[53] sang *God Save the King* with an extraordinary display of energy. All the royalties gathered to the right and left of the pulpit, and the remaining space was crammed with representatives of the aristocracy and *big business*. A choir clad in white occupied the special seats upstairs, where the organ droned away, filling the high vaults of the cathedral with the sounds of Bach, Handel and Elgar.

My appearance in the church caused an exchange of glances and whispers among diplomats and members of the government. ... My neighbour, a Nepalese minister,[54] was very striking: on his head he wore a gold hat sprinkled with big diamonds and rubies, and topped by a huge 'cock's tail'. The general effect was rather amusing; but at that moment the Nepalese envoy was undoubtedly carrying tens of thousands of pounds on his head.

---

[51] Walter Elliot, Conservative MP, 1924–45; minister of agriculture, 1932–36, secretary of state for Scotland, 1936–38; minister of health, 1938–40; director of public relations, War Office, 1941–42.
[52] Sir Winston Leonard Spencer Churchill, Conservative MP for Epping, 1924–31 and 1939–45; chancellor of the Exchequer, 1924–29; the 'wilderness years', 1929–39; first lord of the Admiralty, 1939–40; prime minister, 1940–45 and 1951–55.
[53] Arthur Henderson, chairman of the Labour Party, 1908–10 and 1914–17; general secretary of the Labour Party, 1911–34; secretary of state for foreign affairs, 1929–31; Nobel Prize for Peace in 1934.
[54] General Bahadur S.J.B. Rana, first Nepalese ambassador in London, 1934–36. He was president of the 1947 Constitutional Reforms Committee, putting him two places below the maharaja; the Rana prime minister and effective ruler of the country. He disappeared from public life after the end of the Rana regime. I am indebted to Prof. David Gellner of All Souls College, Oxford, for the information. See a diary entry on the ambassador on 5 June 1935.

1 December

A terrible disaster! Comrade Kirov[55] has been killed in the Smolny in Leningrad. Who killed him? With what motives? Who sent him?... As yet, I know nothing. Fleet Street is thick with rumours and alternative versions. Some say that the assassin was an engineer with a grudge against Kirov. Others (the *Daily Express*) suggest that Alfred Rosenberg,[56] Hitler's aide-de-camp, had a hand in it. I know only one thing for sure: the obituary signed by Stalin, Molotov, Voroshilov[57] and others (I caught it on the radio) states that 'the assassin was dispatched by class enemies'.[58]

We got news of the assassination attempt at around 9 p.m. By 11.30 p.m. the Ozerskys,[59] Alperovich and Kagan had all gathered in my office. We all felt like being together, seeking sympathy in the collective and an outlet for our agitation. We talked, exchanging thoughts, suppositions and conjectures. ...

It's simply horrid! An entirely unexpected break in the path of development which our country has been following for the past year. The sooner I find out all the details, the easier it will be to judge the significance of this tragic event in the Smolny.

6 December

Today the urn with Comrade Kirov's ashes was immured in the Kremlin wall on Red Square. Hundreds of thousands of people were present, along with troops, members of the Central Committee and the Government. ...

Here, in London, we also remembered our departed leader. The embassy flag flew at half-mast. Our entire Soviet community gathered in the embassy. The hall was decorated with greenery and flowers. A bust of Lenin and portraits of Stalin and Kirov were placed near and along the walls. I made a brief speech

---

[55] Sergei Mironovich Kirov, first secretary of the Leningrad Regional Committee of the CPSU, 1926–34, member of the party's Politburo from 1930.

[56] Alfred Rosenberg, editor of the Nazi Party newspaper *Völkischer Beobachter*; foreign affairs secretary of the Nazi Party, 1933–45; minister for Eastern occupied territories, 1941–44.

[57] Kliment Efremovich Voroshilov, people's commissar for defence, 1934–40; marshal of the Soviet Union from 1935; commander-in-chief of the Soviet forces in the war against Finland, 1939–40; deputy chairman of the USSR Council of People's Commissars 1940–45; commander-in-chief of the northwest armies and of the Leningrad front, 1941.

[58] It has been frequently suggested, but never proven, that the assassination was related to the political threat Kirov posed to Stalin in 1934. At the 17th Congress of the CPSU, the so called 'Victory Congress', Kirov had delivered a fiery speech which was met with a tumultuous ovation – in contrast to the reception of Stalin's rather uninspiring oratory. There is little doubt, though, that Stalin exploited the event to unleash the Great Terror, issuing a directive on the day of the assassination advocating harsh treatment, including the death penalty, of suspected terrorists. It was typical of Maisky to initially take Stalin's account at face value and endorse it, but then later, perceiving the consequences, to simply maintain a low profile.

[59] Aleksandr Vladimirovich Ozersky, head of the Soviet trade mission in Great Britain, 1931–37. Recalled to Moscow, arrested and executed. Rehabilitated posthumously.

in memory of the deceased. Lazyan[60] (from the trade mission) shared with us his reminiscences of Kirov. We sang a funeral march to piano accompaniment. Then we parted, in a quiet and pensive mood. ...

I simply cannot come to terms with this awful tragedy. Only six weeks ago I was sitting in Kirov's office, deep in discussion with him about the international situation, and in particular Anglo-Soviet relations. Kirov had an excellent understanding of foreign affairs. His opinions were usually simple in form, but profound and vivid in substance. He viewed the British Conservatives as an extremely serious enemy. I remember visiting him in Leningrad on my way to Helsinki in the autumn of 1931, after the elections in Britain had handed the Conservatives a landslide victory. When our conversation touched on the elections, Kirov exclaimed: 'To win such a victory while fully retaining one's self-control – it's the highest manifestation of the art of governance! Only yesterday was there a mutiny in the navy.' (He meant Invergordon).[61] 'What would Mussolini have done after such a triumph? He would have crushed the mutineers into smithereens; he would have shot hundreds of sailors... And what did the Conservatives do? They kept their heads; they were not intoxicated by success. They won a tremendous victory and said to the mutineers: let's forget the past! Yes, these people know how to rule. They need to be taken seriously.'

Kirov's voice expressed deep loathing, mixed with deep respect.

... The assassination of Kirov comes at a very bad time for us politically. It runs counter to the general course of our internal and external development. It is impossible that it derived from some serious processes occurring in the depths of the Soviet system. Rather, it smacks of the dregs of the past, still not entirely expunged. But which?!...

In any case, the assassination will have some repercussions for us in Europe. Not major complications, perhaps, but complications nevertheless. Time will tell.

13 December

At M.M. [Litvinov]'s instruction, I acquainted Vansittart with the Franco-Soviet Protocol of 5 December.[62] V. was obviously flattered by our attention and

---

[60] I. Lazyan, a protégé of Mikoyan in the London trade mission.

[61] The sailors of the British Atlantic Fleet took industrial action, protesting against a 10 per cent pay cut.

[62] Following the refusal of Germany and Poland to participate in an Eastern Pact, the Russians reverted to a joint protocol with the French, signed in Geneva on 5 December 1934. France and the USSR vowed not to enter into negotiations with potential members of a pact that might lead to multilateral or bilateral agreements, which would thus undermine an Eastern Regional Pact. Czechoslovakia acceded to the protocol two days later. Litvinov instructed Maisky to inform Vansittart that the protocol was inspired by Hitler's attempt 'to sow mistrust' between the Soviet Union and France through rumours of separate negotiations, 'now with the USSR, now with France'. He shared Maisky's concern about a possible British overture to Germany which might tie French hands.

confirmed once again that the British Government remains in favour of the Eastern Pact, as it was in summer.

... We spoke about the current status of Anglo-Soviet relations. ... V. remarked that he thought 'our summer conversations were a turning point in Anglo-Soviet relations'. ... Now we could think of the next steps towards the further improvement of our relations.

I supported V. and proposed, as a sort of 'prelude', that we run our eyes over the map of the world, to see if we could find a single region where the interests of Britain and the USSR might clash. V. willingly agreed ... I expressed satisfaction with the results of our analysis and added that I had talked to Simon on the same subject some five weeks ago. Simon wanted to acquaint the Cabinet with the substance of our conversation. V. raised his eyebrows in astonishment. No, he knows nothing about Simon's *démarche*. But he will seek clarification...

I told V. not to worry himself, but decided for myself that Simon, in his usual two-faced way, had obviously not done what he promised. ...

17 December

I invited the Coles[63] over today and had a serious talk with them about the *Declaration of the 43.*[64] ... During their conversation with me, both were highly agitated, now turning pale, now turning red. Mrs Cole's hands even trembled nervously.

I gave my guests a stern ticking-off. I told them that over the last three or four months the Soviet authorities had established the existence of a large terrorist conspiracy against our Party leaders, beginning with Comrade Stalin. It is being organized and financed by the German 'Nazis'. Its agents are Russian White Guards and all those dissatisfied little groups which exist inside the USSR. The White Guards secretly cross the border in Poland, Latvia and Finland with the assistance of the authorities of the listed countries and, once in the USSR, enter into contact with conspirators of Soviet citizenship. Recent months have seen a series of attempts on the lives of Comrades Stalin, Voroshilov, Molotov, Postyshev,[65] Balitsky,[66] and others. Fortunately, such attempts have as yet proved unsuccessful, thanks to the vigilance of the NKVD.[67] The plotters got lucky with Kirov. The death of Kirov was striking

---

[63] G.D.H. Cole, Chichele Professor of Social and Political Theory and fellow of All Souls, Oxford, 1944–57; chairman of the Fabian Society (1939–46 and 1948–50) and its president, 1952–57.

[64] A protest by Labour and Trade Union Congress leaders about Stalin's secret trials and death sentences in the wake of Kirov's murder.

[65] Pavel Petrovich Postyshev, member of the Central Committee of the Communist Party of Ukraine, 1925–37.

[66] Vsevolod Apollonovich Balitsky, people's commissar for home affairs in Ukraine, 1924–30 and 1934–37.

[67] People's Commissariat for Internal Affairs.

proof of the gravity of the terrorist threat. In such a situation, the Soviet Government had no choice but to take tough measures against the plotters – not only those who were guilty of Kirov's death, but all those arrested at various times and in various places in recent months in connection with terrorism. We couldn't try the terrorists publicly without risking serious complications with Germany and other states that would undoubtedly have been implicated in this case. ... It is a hard and unpleasant thing to shoot 80–100 people, but it is still better than to risk the lives of millions of workers and peasants on the battlefield. Moreover, one should never forget the words of Mirabeau,[68] who said, some 140 years ago, that revolution cannot be made with lavender oil.

The Coles did not object. ... They were particularly troubled by the question: what were these executions? A return to the 'red terror' of the past or an isolated exceptional act of passing significance? I reassured them, saying that the 'new course' launched this spring is not being revised. The 'new course' continues. The measures taken against the terrorists represented an exceptional event brought about by exceptional circumstances. ...

19 December

Today, Vansittart and I concluded the conversation begun on 13 December.

V. began by expressing his satisfaction with the result of our joint 'survey' of Anglo-Soviet relations. I also expressed my satisfaction, but added that *rapprochement* between the USSR and Great Britain remained a very tender and delicate flower that required much attention and care to grow normally and develop. ...

We then addressed the question: what next? 'The current phase of Anglo-Soviet relations,' I said, 'brings the following picture to mind: after a long spell of stormy days, calm weather has finally arrived. It's a bit foggy. A bit chilly. The sky is overcast. The sun is not yet in sight. It is, of course, a great step forwards when compared with what went before...'

'But it's not enough, you wish to say,' V. exclaimed with a laugh. 'One needs a bit of sun, a bit of warmth...'

'And why not?' I replied.

'I couldn't agree with you more,' said V.

So we began to discuss practical steps for achieving a better atmosphere in Anglo-Soviet relations. ... At the very end of our conversation, we turned to the possibility of British ministers and major public figures paying visits to the USSR. 'Why,' I asked, 'do high-ranking Englishmen travel easily and freely over the entire world, with the exception of the USSR? Is this not also a form of entrenched

---

[68] Comte de Mirabeau, prominent figure in the period of the French Revolution, favouring a constitutional monarchy.

'discrimination'? Yet their visits could contribute greatly to the demolition of the Chinese wall that has risen between our countries since the revolution.'

V. tried to defend British ministers by referring to their extremely busy schedules. 'I hardly ever leave London,' he noted, by way of a telling argument. 'I've only been to America once, when I visited Hoover[69] with MacDonald in 1929.'

I smiled and remarked half-jokingly: 'But you spent your holidays in Italy! Why not spend them in the Caucasus?' ...

20 December

[Preceding the entry, a press cutting from the *Manchester Guardian*, 20 December 1934:

'The marriage of a Jew to a non-Jewish woman must be punished with death', said Herr Julius Streicher,[70] the Governor of Silesia, when he addressed 3,000 lawyers and judges of North Bavaria at a Nazi Bar Association meeting in Munich. And the words were greeted with cheers.

'The blood corpuscles of a Jew,' he added, 'are completely different from those of a Nordic. A non-Jewish girl is lost forever to her own people the moment she marries a Jew.']

Utter idiots! And blood-thirsty beasts to boot. The day of reckoning will come, and Hitler will pay for the suffering of millions.[71]

The kafuffle over the shootings does not abate. Barely have I liquidated the protests of the 'Left' Labourites than the Right appears on the horizon. It is mostly the work of Citrine.[72] Today, the *Daily Herald* published an indignant editorial.[73]

27 December

Vansittart unexpectedly asked me over, at the height of the Christmas season. I felt somewhat anxious on my way to the FO [Foreign Office]. In fact, however, there was no cause for concern. ...

V. ... informed me that he had given a lot of thought to our last conversations and had arrived at the conclusion that ministerial visits to the USSR would be one of the best ways of improving relations between our countries. ... I steered

---

[69] Herbert Hoover, president of the United States, 1929–33.

[70] Julius Streicher, founder and editor of the anti-Semitic weekly newspaper *Der Stürmer*.

[71] Relates directly to Maisky's own personal situation, were he to find himself in Germany.

[72] Walter McLennan Citrine, secretary of the General Council of the TUC, 1926–46; director of the *Daily Herald*, 1929–46. Opposed the alliance between the Soviet and British trade unions in 1925–27.

[73] The article under the headline 'Terror in Russia' concluded with the words: 'The Russian executions are barbarous and unworthy of a regime which professes to be the most advanced in the world.'

the conversation to the Pact of the Four proposed by Neurath to counterbalance the Eastern Pact, and declared plainly that the Pact of the Four is absolutely unacceptable to us in any form (e.g. as a pact of five or six powers), for it will only undermine the authority of the League of Nations. V. promised to inform the Cabinet of our attitude to the pact.[74]

When I was about to leave, V. took a very intimate and friendly tone and informed me, 'in absolute confidence', that if Soviet 'interference' in England's domestic affairs were to continue, all our efforts to improve Anglo-Soviet relations would go to rack and ruin.[75]...

31 December

Another year has ended, and I stand on the threshold of a new year! Involuntarily, my gaze is cast back over the twelve months that have passed...

Politically and economically speaking, this last year has been a success for us, although it was darkened at its end by the death of Kirov. We have grown stronger, grown up, and begun to play a major global role. Our trajectory has risen steeply all the time. In particular, the past year has marked a turning point in Anglo-Soviet relations: the signing of the trade treaty, my summer talks with Vansittart, the British Government's declaration in favour of the Eastern Pact, the astonishing debates in Parliament on 13 July, during which Churchill and Austen Chamberlain[76] declared themselves 'friends' of the Soviet Union and insisted on its admittance to the League of Nations – all this marks the onset of a new phase in relations between the USSR and Great Britain. Not that the English lords have suddenly developed an affection for us, the unwashed Bolsheviks – no, this is not the case and never will be. It's just that the moment arrived when the skill at 'facing the facts' (whether pleasant or unpleasant) which is so characteristic of British politicians finally overcame their enmity towards us on grounds of class and politics. We have now become such a major and stable international force that, willy-nilly, even the most incorrigible Conservative beasts can ignore us no longer and are forced to 'acknowledge' our existence and, as inveterate political operators, to derive from us whatever profit they can. ...

---

[74] Maisky had been instructed by Litvinov that any future agreement with Germany, France or Britain should be conditional on adherence to the 'Eastern Pact' and should exclude any revival of the 'Pact of Four', which had been signed by Britain, France, Italy and Germany on 15 July 1933 but which never came into force due to major disagreement between the signatories.

[75] Maisky's report home was extremely succinct and, as would become his practice, attributed to Vansittart initiatives of his own that clearly exceeded his authority. It was Vansittart, he claimed, who 'established' that no points of necessary friction existed between the Soviet Union and Britain, while in fact the undersecretary of state was only cajoled into confirming Maisky's long exposé.

[76] Joseph Austen Chamberlain, Conservative MP, 1892–1937; elder half-brother of Neville Chamberlain; secretary of state for foreign affairs, 1924–29; architect of the Locarno Agreement, for which he received the Nobel Peace Prize, 1925.

15. Agniya in the sanatorium in Sochi.

How has the year been for me personally? I mull it over, recollect, sort out facts and dates. Agniya and I are both quite well. Feka[77] stayed with us in London for a month and together we went on a very pleasant tour of England and Scotland ... Then we went on a two-and-a-half month vacation to the USSR, both ways via Berlin. We were in Moscow, Leningrad (just me, Agniya

---

[77] Feoktista (Feka) Poludova, Agniya's sister. Her husband Poludov signed the 'platform of 10' letter against Stalin, was arrested and shot, while she was banished to the gulag for eight years.

16. An obligatory visit to a kolkhoz near Sochi.

didn't travel), Kislovodsk, Sochi, Sukhumi, Gagra, and Novy Afon. We put on some weight and blew out the cobwebs. I left the spa weighing 69 kilos. ... And that, I think, is about it. Not all that much and not all that interesting. Pale when compared with those truly major events which 1934 witnessed in the political, social and economic life of the USSR. ... But why pale? It's how it should be: for Communists, the personal must dissolve in the general, or, at the very least, retreat far into the background. ...

1935

8 January

A fire at the embassy.

Tonight, at about 11 p.m., smoke suddenly appeared from under the floor near the fireplace in my study. There was a general agitation, the alarm was sounded, and when we raised the floorboards we found a flame in the wall near the flue. We doused the fire as best we could, but some smoke persisted all the same, albeit less than before. We spent a lot of time trying to locate the cause, but in the end I decided to call the fire brigade. Five lads arrived in copper helmets. They smashed apart the floorboards, fireplace and wall and found that a thick wooden joist adjoining the main flue under the floor was on fire. The firemen thought that the joist had probably been burning for several weeks or even months, but because there was no airflow the flame had remained low, smouldering away and charring the girder. Perhaps that was so, but that was no help to me. The fire was put out, the girder amputated, and at around 4 a.m. the firemen left, leaving the room in a terrible mess. ...

18 January

Mikhail Sholokhov[1] has left. He spent about a fortnight in London with his wife. They lived in the embassy. I arranged two receptions for him: one for journalists who interviewed Sholokhov (the interview was poorly covered in the press) and the other for writers. ... I liked Sholokhov very much. He is young (29) and full of *joie de vivre*. An ardent hunter and angler. Despite his fame, he has not been spoiled. He is modest and straightforward. Will this last? We'll see. He has a very good wife – intelligent, positive, pleasant. This is a great boon for him. A wife like her will keep him away from the many follies that our young writers are so prone to. Sholokhov has a very charming appearance: a

---

[1] Mikhail Aleksandrovich Sholokhov, Nobel Prize for literature in 1965, author of *And Quiet Flows the Don*, *Virgin Soil Upturned* and *They Fought for Their Country*.

well-proportioned, blue-eyed blond of medium height, with delicate features, a shock of curly hair over a large, open forehead and a pipe permanently stuck in his teeth. Just as you would imagine a poet. What a shame he saw so little of England. He spent most of his time meeting literary people, attending parties, and shopping (he had a lot of money – the fee he received for the publication of *The Quiet Don*[2] abroad).

25 January

... Yesterday I gave a lecture on planning in the USSR at Cambridge. ... After the lecture we had tea at Trinity College ... and chatted indefatigably about a great variety of topics. There were about 15 people, smoking, making a racket, knocking over cups – i.e. behaving just as one would expect at a noisy student gathering. My general impression is that young people in Cambridge are at the crossroads. They have serious qualms about the past, and they are seeking something new to meet the demands of the present. It is a condition full of promise and danger: who will catch the mood of the young? The Right or the Left? Fascists or communists? For the present, the fascists have the better chances, and that is where the main danger lies.

17. Maisky tries his hand at punting in the land of the 'Cambridge Five'.

---

[2] Normally known in English as *And Quiet Flows the Don*, this is what Maisky wrote in English.

4 February

I learned the following details about the meeting between the English and French ministers.[3]

MacDonald and Simon have always been advocates of Hitler, especially MacDonald. Baldwin and Eden cautiously supported the French. Vansittart stressed the particular importance of Italy's participation in all European combinations. MacDonald made every effort to convince the French of the unfeasibility of the Eastern Pact ('Germany doesn't want it, and it is impossible to impose anything on Germany'), recommending that they should not insist on it, but limit themselves to the organization of Western security, leaving Eastern Europe to follow the natural course of events.

MacDonald and Simon encountered stiff opposition from the French. True, Flandin kept silent for the most part, but Laval spoke at great length. ... The French ... favoured the advancing of the Eastern Pact. The English resisted, but a compromise was finally achieved: all problems included in the communiqué were to be resolved 'concurrently'. However, this method lacks all clarity. Germany is not present in Geneva, but where outside Geneva could one find a suitable venue for holding such complicated negotiations with the participation of so many powers? The English seem to be willing to play the part of honest broker in negotiations between Germany and other states, but the French don't like the idea at all. We'll see. ...

6 February

Masaryk[4] (the Czech envoy) informed me today that yesterday he had a frank talk with Vansittart. M. didn't hide his concern about the meeting of English and French ministers ... But V. assured him that Czechoslovakia had no reason to be afraid for her future. He said that England was extremely interested in Czechoslovakia's integrity and welfare. V. is rather sceptical about the upcoming talks with Germany and hardly expects a positive outcome. Yet such a step should be taken, if only for the sake of enlightening British public opinion. ...

I found out from a reliable journalistic source that Hoesch (the German ambassador) has advised Hitler, with Simon's consent, that in his reply to the joint English and French proposal he should place the issue of the Eastern Pact at the bottom of the negotiations agenda. Should agreement be reached on all

---

[3] Pierre Etienne Flandin, prime minister of France, 1934–35. Flandin and his foreign minister, Laval, visited London on 1–3 February and met MacDonald and Simon.

[4] Jan Garrigue Masaryk, Czechoslovak ambassador to Great Britain, 1925–38; minister of foreign affairs of the Czechoslovak Government in exile in London, 1940–45 and deputy prime minister, 1941–45.

preceding items, the Eastern Pact could easily be 'buried in the sand'. A crafty move! But will Hitler be smart enough to follow his ambassador's advice?

10 February

MacDonald and Simon ... are pursuing a systematic campaign to muzzle the Eastern Pact and divert attention entirely onto questions of 'Western security'. In other words, they are telling Hitler: 'Leave France and England alone and, by way of compensation, do whatever you like in Eastern Europe.' I am of the impression that Baldwin, Eden and Vansittart are aware of the impossibility and perils of a policy of aiding and abetting, yet for the time being they are giving MD and S. *carte blanche*. ...

Our Soviet activity is now an important factor on the international scene. I think that the time has come to clarify our Soviet attitude to the communiqué of 3 February.[5]

20 February

Yesterday I delivered my lecture at the League of Nations Union. I informed the London papers beforehand that I was planning to make an important political statement. As a result, the hall at the School of Economics was chock-full (some 600 people came), and correspondents from every newspaper and agency sat at the press desk, with many foreigners among them ... The final part of the lecture, dealing with the communiqué of 3 February, attracted particular attention. Excerpts from it were broadcast last night on the radio. ... Excellent! We've fired the first shot at MacDonald and Simon. The bullet seems to have hit the target. But we cannot rest on our laurels.

21 February

The second shot followed sooner than I had even imagined.

Early on the morning of 20 February I received from Moscow our evaluation of the London communiqué, with the request to hand the text over to Simon today.

... Simon received me in the Houses of Parliament. Eden was present throughout the meeting, but he spoke little. Simon began with my speech at the League of Nations Union, complimented me and asked me to explain various

---

[5] The Franco-British communiqué agreed to abolish the limitations set by the Versailles agreement on the German armed forces and called for a new arms agreement to coincide with Germany's return to the League of Nations, the conclusion of an Eastern Pact, and the preservation of Austrian independence.

points. Then I read our evaluation of the communiqué aloud and put the document on the foreign secretary's desk. ... I put before S. the question I had put
before Vansittart a few days earlier, namely, what would the British Government
do should Germany accept all the points of the London programme bar the
Eastern Pact? My question embarrassed my interlocutor and he began talking
through his hat, using high-flown but incoherent phrases. What they seemed to
amount to was this: if Germany were to resist our demand, the pact would be
'castrated' – instead of mutual assistance, we would have a straightforward pact
of non-aggression.

I began objecting fiercely; I confess that I did not mince my words. I stated
that mutual military assistance is the heart of the pact, that we could make no
concessions on this point, and that without an Eastern Pact of mutual assistance there will also be neither disarmament nor European security, even in its
limited Western form.

S. was clearly concerned. Massaging the bridge of his nose, he asked cynically: what are you ready to propose to buy Germany's consent to the Eastern
Pact? I replied that the guarantee of security which Germany would receive
along with the other powers if the pact were concluded would be sufficient
reward. S. raised his eyes to the ceiling and shrugged his shoulders in a rather
ambiguous manner.

I left with the very definite impression that Simon had finally understood
that the attempt to exclude the USSR from the resolution of the issue of
'European appeasement' had failed. If anything is to be achieved in this area,
the USSR needs to be brought in on equal terms with the other great powers.[6]

28 February

I've been in a very difficult situation this past week.

I never had the slightest doubt that the reports in *The Times* and the
Daily Telegraph about a British minister visiting Moscow were the work of the
Foreign Office and of Vansittart in particular. Over the course of the following
week, the press persistently and systematically inflated this topic in every way
possible. ... Vansittart told me, at about the time I was presenting Putna[7] to him,

---

[6] Simon left Maisky in no doubt that the main objective of the Eastern Pact was to 'give confidence
necessary to make an arms agreement possible'. While the British Government believed that a general
European arms agreement could still be achieved if Germany's legitimate grievances were addressed,
Maisky told Dalton: 'By all means talk with Hitler, and come to agreements and compromises. But talk
to him with a rifle in your hand, or he will pay no regard to your wishes.'
[7] Vitovt Kazimirovich Putna, who distinguished himself in the Civil War, sided with Trotsky's opposition in 1923. Between 1927 and 1931 he was Soviet military attaché in three countries – Japan, Finland
and Germany; and then in Great Britain, 1934–36. Recalled from London and arrested in summer 1936,
he was tortured and sentenced to death. Maisky was forced to denounce him in Moscow in 1938.
Rehabilitated posthumously in 1957.

that although the Foreign Office had nothing to do with the press campaign concerning a minister's visit, the idea itself deserved a very good hearing. In a word, it was absolutely clear that the British Government, having realized that it would be impossible to cobble together 'European security' without us, had decided that it could at least turn a profit from engaging the USSR in the organization of security – in particular, by playing the role of 'honest broker' (a role the English have always enjoyed) in seeking a compromise between Berlin and Moscow on the question of the Eastern Pact. ...

But our people in Moscow wouldn't yield. To my first request about the line I should adhere to, which I sent right after the first communications appeared in the press, I received the reply that newspaper reports lack authority, that I should remain calm, and that I was to inform Moscow if the Foreign Office approached me. Initially, it seems, the NKID even had the impression that Simon's visit to Moscow would serve to camouflage his visit to Warsaw (it was said in the press that the British minister would go to Warsaw from Berlin and then on to Moscow). I objected, referring to the material at my disposal, and asked whether the Soviet press could show, albeit cautiously, that it was well disposed to Simon's visit. But the NKID would not agree even to this, citing doubts about whether Simon really did want to go. Nevertheless, by 26 February I did manage to secure permission to at least encourage the idea of Simon's visit in the event of the Foreign Office, or circles close to it, approaching me on the subject. ... On 25 February, responding to a question in the House of Commons, Simon said that the government was considering the issue of his visit to Moscow. I appealed to M.M. again and today I at last received the instruction to tell Vansittart that I was authorized to extend an official invitation to Simon just as soon as the British Government had definitively resolved the question of an English minister's visit to the USSR. But the NKID wants to see Simon and nobody else... Hmm! Surely, considerations of prestige are playing their part here: if Simon is going to Berlin, then it is he who must also go to Moscow. Clear enough. But still, I would not make such an ultimatum about Simon. Actually, Eden would probably be more advantageous. Be that as it may, today came as a great relief...

29 February

Lloyd George's family and nearly his whole 'party' had lunch with us yesterday: the old man himself, his wife, Gwilym,[8] and Megan.[9] Also present were

---

[8] Gwilym Lloyd George, Lloyd George's son; Liberal MP and parliamentary secretary at the Board of Trade.
[9] Megan Lloyd George, Lloyd George's daughter; Liberal MP, 1929–51 and Labour MP, 1957–66.

Maitland[10] (a prominent Conservative), Jarvie (a banker),[11] the 'independent' Labourite Josiah Wedgwood,[12] and others.

I couldn't help but admire Lloyd George. He is 72 and still bursts with life. He looked magnificent after his recent vacation: a strong, tanned, fresh face under a shock of bright white hair. The old man was in a cheerful mood. He didn't drink wine at table, but he enjoyed the vodka and drank one or two more portions after the first.

L.G. said that he is not greatly interested in the German question at the moment. The fears aroused by German belligerence are highly exaggerated. Germany needs at least ten more years to restore her military, economic and financial might. Until then Europe can sleep easily.

L.G. is far more concerned about matters in the Far East. ... Japan, through the widespread use of carrot and stick, is clearly bent on establishing a powerful 'yellow' empire on the Asian continent.

... L.G. flared up and unleashed a torrent of criticism in the direction of the government. He was in his element here and he castigated the government venomously, calling them dunderheads devoid of the slightest imagination, with no policy worth the name. MacDonald and [Neville] Chamberlain were singled out for particular abuse.

4 March

As the senior lady guest, Lady Vansittart sat next to me at dinner in the embassy and described to me in the frankest terms the difficulties her husband is currently facing. ... The question of Simon's visit to various European capitals in connection with the Anglo-French agreement has turned Vansittart's life into absolute hell. The problems derive from Vansittart's and Simon's differing views on numerous matters. Moreover, Simon devotes little time to the Foreign Office and shifts the entire mass of routine business onto Vansittart. The latter is up to his neck in work from early morning till late at night, while Simon visits his country house every weekend and plays golf. ... After I told Vansittart about the Soviet Government's positive attitude to Simon's visit, Vansittart felt it essential to push this issue through as a matter of urgency. But he could not get in touch with Simon for several days since, after returning from his lecture in Paris, Simon did not even look in at the Foreign Office, but went straight to

---

[10] Arthur Maitland.

[11] J. Gibson Jarvie, chairman of United Dominions Trust, hailed Stalin's five-year plan in a major speech in Glasgow in 1932 which was then often quoted by Stalin, who omitted Jarvie's qualifying comment that although Russia was claiming 'to be a Communist State, nevertheless that country to-day was, unquestionably, practising state capitalism'.

[12] Josiah Clement Wedgwood (1st Baron Wedgwood), Labour MP, 1919–42; sought to become ambassador in Moscow in 1940, but Churchill opted for Cripps.

his country house to play golf. Vansittart tried to get hold of him, but Simon
was clearly doing his best to avoid meeting him. On Sunday, 3 March, his
patience exhausted, Vansittart set off by himself to see Baldwin and then
MacDonald. He had long talks with both and obtained their approval for
Simon's visit to Moscow. The final decision will most likely be taken at the
nearest Cabinet session, i.e. on 6 March. But all this has put extraordinary
strain on her husband and frayed his nerves terribly. ... I asked Lady V. whether
Simon would go to Berlin alone or with Eden. She answered with a sigh of
relief: 'Fortunately, together with Eden. Simon is easily flattered, and Hitler is
likely to be generous in this regard. This may prompt Simon to make some
careless statements in Berlin. Eden will restrain him and put him right.'

5 March

Vansittart and his wife dined with us in the embassy. I had a talk with V. after
dinner. ... I drew V.'s attention to the obsequious servility to Hitler shown by the
British press and some members of the Cabinet, Simon in particular. This is a
poor tactic. It only inflames the Führer's appetite and makes him still more
unyielding. Simon has not yet crossed the German border, but he has already
proposed, in his talk with Laval in Paris on 28 February, to replace the Eastern
Pact of mutual assistance with bilateral non-aggression pacts between Germany
and her neighbours. What use will that serve? I added that we could make no
concessions on the Eastern Pact issue.

... What an unfortunate coincidence: Simon in England and Laval in France.
One cannot think of worse foreign ministers from our point of view, and in
such a serious period!

7 March

The decision has been taken!

Vansittart phoned me today and said that the Cabinet has decided to
send Eden to Moscow. Simon will make an announcement after dinner in
Parliament.

... I made some complimentary remarks about Eden, but added that I had
been authorized to hand the official invitation to Simon or to Simon and Eden.
Now that the situation had changed, I would have to approach Moscow for
instructions once again. Vansittart did not object. In conclusion he made a
meaningful remark: he implores me to believe that the decision on sending Eden
is the maximum that could have been achieved at the current stage. I
understand.

So, Eden is going! Very good! There is no doubt that this is a historic step.

8 March

Undoubtedly, the decision to send Eden and not Simon is a mild form of anti-Soviet discrimination on the part of the British Government. ...

In actual fact, Eden is better for us than Simon, for Eden's star is rising, while Simon's is setting. Eden has been promoted by Baldwin, an influential Conservative, while Simon essentially represents no one. Compromised at home, he is liked neither by the Conservatives, nor the Liberals, nor Labour. Finally, Eden takes a tolerant attitude towards the USSR, while Simon is our inveterate adversary. Yes, Eden is much better!

... I sent a long telegram to Moscow today requesting that Eden be received courteously. We'll wait to see the reaction.[13]

[The idea of a ministerial visit to Moscow was first mooted by Maisky in autumn 1934. The plan had been cooked up with Vansittart, behind the backs of Litvinov and Simon, long before the foreign secretary's visit to Berlin was contemplated. Maisky, however, received little encouragement from Litvinov, who feared that any Russian initiative might be snubbed by the British or used as a card in their negotiations with the Germans.

Maisky, who had great faith in his ability to carry out a coup together with Vansittart and Eden, pursued his plans unabated. On 11 February, he pressed Litvinov to provide him with guidelines for a forthcoming meeting, which he claimed had been proposed by Vansittart, but in fact had been suggested by him. Litvinov reluctantly allowed Maisky to ascertain what the British attitude was, but remained highly sceptical of the outcome, complaining that even the Germans believed that the British 'were not in the least interested in the Eastern Locarno'. Maisky did not shy away from seeking backing from some unexpected quarters: he approached Molotov, chairman of the Council of People's Commissars and Stalin's right-hand man. When Simon's intention of meeting Hitler in Berlin came to light, Litvinov finally gave way to the pressure exerted by Maisky, allowing him a free hand to decide when the time was propitious to tender an invitation.]

9 March

Hurrah! Moscow seems to look favourably on Eden. M.M. has asked me to deliver an official invitation and suggests that Eden come to Moscow as soon as possible ... concurrently with Simon's departure for Berlin or after the Berlin talks. ... I've called Moscow to ask whether I should accompany Eden. It would be good if the answer were affirmative.

---

[13] In conveying the decision, Maisky pressed Litvinov to receive Eden, producing a misleading argument that 'at present the whole Berlin visit hangs in the air and it is not clear whether it will take place at all'.

11 March

... Ribbentrop met François-Poncet[14] in Berlin a few days ago and told him something to this effect: let us settle all controversial issues between ourselves. Forget Russia – it's an Asian power. Why should we, Europeans, allow it into Europe? François-Poncet replied that, according to physical and political geography, Russia is located in Europe.

　　Truly German gaucherie!

12 March

The Foreign Office is worried and perplexed at seeing no response to the decision on Eden's visit in the Soviet press. Indeed, it's not quite right. I'll have to push Moscow. ... We shall see what will come of it. It's a risk, but it's worth it ... M.M. is still sceptical about Eden's visit. He even thinks it might not happen at all, or not for a good while. For this reason he has put off deciding whether or not I should accompany Eden. He has another reservation: Eden is not a Foreign Office minister. But I'll still go. I'll arrange it.

13 March

Presumably as a result of yesterday's telephone conversation with Eden, Simon and Eden invited me to Parliament today. I arrived at 3 p.m. We talked for some 40 minutes. The subject of the talk was the timing of Eden's visit to Moscow. Simon spoke nearly the whole time, admiring himself and skilfully juggling words. Eden spoke little. ... S. raised his eyes languidly to the ceiling and suddenly asked: 'Excuse my asking you this question, which may seem strange to you: but might the lord privy seal have a talk with Mr Stalin?'

　　I was waiting for this question and answered calmly: 'I don't know. Mr Stalin is not a member of the Council of People's Commissars and does not usually meet with foreign ministers and diplomats.'

　　Once again S. set about trying to convince me. Oh, naturally he does not stipulate a meeting with Stalin as an indispensable condition of Eden's visit to Moscow. He knows Litvinov very well and respects and values him. Still, Stalin is the major Soviet figure for the British public. Attaching enormous importance to Eden's visit to Moscow, the British Government would like to arrange his visit in such a way as to make the greatest possible impression on British public opinion. As I must know full well, not all in Britain approve of the government's decision to send a minister to the USSR; some influential circles frown on this move. It is

---

[14] André François-Poncet, French ambassador to Germany, 1931–38, and to Italy, 1938–40.

important, therefore, to use this visit to effect a radical change in public opinion. For this it is highly desirable that Eden should meet with Stalin.

I promised to make the necessary enquiries in Moscow. ... At this point S.'s secretary rushed into the room to say that S. was expected in the House. ... Eden and I were left alone. Eden added in a very particular tone: 'I ought always to be near Sir John, both during the preparatory work and during the negotiations with Germany.'

This can be understood as follows: the Conservative Party adamantly refuses to let Simon go to Berlin alone. The 'party commissar' – Eden – must assist him.

14 March

M.M. called me at 1 p.m. from Moscow, as I had asked in the telegram I sent yesterday. He spoke directly from Comrade Stalin's office. The reply was as follows: let Eden come to Moscow on 28 March; Comrade Stalin will receive him; I should accompany Eden, from Berlin onwards; it is desirable that Simon should make a public statement on the equal importance of the Berlin and Moscow visits. ...

I was back in Parliament at 3 p.m., on this occasion in Eden's office. He asked me somewhat impatiently: 'So, what's the news?' I communicated to him the substance of Moscow's response. Eden was extremely glad. He remarked about the meeting with Stalin: 'You understand, of course, that I would hardly insist on this for my own sake. But for the British public, for the *man in the street*, such a meeting is very important.'[15] He was deeply moved on hearing that I would accompany him.

... Hurrah! M.M. has shown his charitable side: I have permission to go to Moscow together with Eden, or a day in advance – but on condition that Eden sets off soon. I don't understand this condition, but the main thing has been settled. Even if Eden sets off not so soon, I'll go with him all the same. It's a sure thing!

17 March

A great historic date: Hitler issued a new law yesterday: compulsory military service is being introduced in Germany, and the strength of the army has been set at 500,000.

---

[15] Maisky explained to Eden that Stalin was no longer only the secretary of the Communist Party, but now held a 'special position on the Executive of their elected Assembly. M. Maisky incidentally informed me with a grin that he himself was now an M.P.' Maisky had just been elected to the Central Committee of the Communist Party.

A major step on the road to a new world war!

So, the cards are on the table. The Versailles treaty has been openly and ceremoniously torn to pieces. Nazi Germany is turning into a formidable military power. Her army will now surpass the French army in number. The Anglo-French platform of 3 February has been effectively liquidated. There is no point in Simon going to Berlin – what can he negotiate there in the new circumstances?

The consequences of the latest German move will be immeasurable. The attempt at a Franco-German rapprochement, dreamt of by Flandin and Laval, has been cut short. Next comes the conclusion of the Eastern Pact without Germany and possibly without Poland. The French have hesitated and tacked about on this matter throughout – but now there must be an end to all uncertainty. The evening news announces Laval's forthcoming visit to Moscow. Very good. The Eastern Pact might well be signed in Moscow. The English, of course, will spin the thing out and play both sides, but the logic of things will not let them do it for long. ...

The seal of death shows through ever more clearly on the face of the capitalist world. The cruel and idiotic Versailles treaty, the idiotic post-war policy of France and Britain towards Germany, Hitler's idiotically provocative behaviour... As a result, the world rushes ever faster and more uncontrollably towards a military catastrophe, in the womb of which is borne the proletarian revolution!

19 March

... M.M. is very angry – and rightly so – with the English note to Hitler concerning the decree of 16 March.[16] He considers it a complete capitulation to Germany.

I shall add a few humiliating details. The note was delivered by Phipps[17] (the British ambassador in Berlin) at about 4 p.m. on the 18th. The reply was received at about 7 p.m. on the same day and sent to London by phone right away. At 9 p.m. the parliamentary session was interrupted (an unprecedented fact in history!) to let Simon communicate the joyous news: Hitler is prepared to grant the British ministers an audience after all!

How shameful! What degradation! See what hatred of the Soviet Union can lead one to...

---

[16] Without consulting the French, the British Government sent a note of protest to the Germans on 18 March over their unilateral action, ending, however, by asking whether the Germans were still interested in a meeting between Simon and Hitler.

[17] Eric Phipps, British minister in Paris, 1922–28, and in Vienna, 1928–33; ambassador in Berlin, 1933–37, and in Paris, 1937–39.

20 March

... Vansittart invited me to see him today. He was in a somewhat melancholy, even slightly despondent, mood, as if he had had a bout of illness the day before and had not yet fully recovered. V. spoke of the extreme importance of the improvement of Anglo-Soviet relations, of his own struggle for this improvement, and of his delight at Eden's forthcoming visit to Moscow. Yes, he regards Eden's visit as a major historic event, and it is crucial that his visit should have major historic consequences. ... In an almost trembling voice, V. added: 'For many months we have been working together in the cause of Anglo-Soviet rapprochement, and I have brought the matter to its present stage, at which you have initiated direct talks between ministers. Here, naturally, I had to efface myself and step back...'

I glanced at V. in some surprise, and my surprise only grew: it was obvious that he was jealous of my contacts with Eden or of the fact that the process of Anglo-Soviet rapprochement was progressing despite his playing a less active role than before! ...

21 March

I learned some curious things today from good sources. Simon, it seems, is obsessed with the quite fantastic idea of becoming prime minister after MacDonald, who, it has allegedly been decided, will step down immediately after the royal jubilee. Simon needs an impressive 'success' to achieve that. He has been planning to bring this 'success' back from Berlin. That's why, early in the year, he began 'secret' negotiations (unknown to the Foreign Office) with Hitler through Lothian,[18] Ribbentrop and others. During these negotiations, Hitler pulled the wool over Simon's eyes, refusing to commit himself definitively, but sending the vague message that, under certain conditions (which?), he might be ready to 'consider' the question of arms limitation, a return to the League of Nations, and the preservation of the demilitarized zone on the French border. Simon believed, with peculiar naiveté, that all these concessions were more or less in the bag, hence the blatantly pro-German line he has been espousing for the last three months. Hence also his craving to travel to Berlin, and his servile attitude to Hitler with regard to the latter's 'hoarseness' and to the decree of 16 March. At a conference on Sunday, 17 March, which was attended by Baldwin, MacDonald, Eden, Simon and Vansittart and had been held to discuss the reaction to the German decree, Simon and Vansittart argued so heatedly that Vansittart was on the point of declaring his resignation. ...

---

[18] Philip Kerr (11th marquess of Lothian), Lloyd George's private secretary, 1916–21; chancellor of the duchy of Lancaster, 1931–32; ambassador to the USA, 1939–40.

22 March

We had talks between the three of us today: Eden, Vansittart and I. ... Eden and Vansittart assured me that we had nothing to worry about [the Berlin meeting]. The British ministers have not been authorized to decide or agree anything; their task is to elucidate and investigate. They understand the role of Eastern security perfectly well. They will be firm with Hitler. I thought to myself: 'May your words come true. Let's see what comes of it...'

At 4 p.m. I saw Eden off at the Croydon Aerodrome. Kagan was with me. Strang[19] and Hankey[20] were accompanying Eden. Eden's wife, a tall, nice-looking woman, was there. So was Hankey's wife. We were photographed in various poses and combinations. ... Simon will be back in London on the morning of the 27th, while Eden will meet me at the railway station in Berlin on the evening of the 26th, and from there we shall travel to Moscow through Poland. ...

As Eden's airplane rose heavily into the air – roaring, buzzing, and generating a furious wind all around – I couldn't help thinking: 'This is the beginning of an important flight that may become truly historic... Will it?' ...

[Maisky accompanied Eden on his train journey from Berlin to Moscow. After a preliminary meeting with Litvinov, Eden was grudgingly shown the Pushkin Museum's prodigious collection of impressionists – 'bourgeois art' – which was closed to the general public. From there he was whisked off to Litvinov's dacha. A stiff walk on frozen ground in the surrounding woods was followed by a banquet-like lunch. Pats of butter were served in the form of rosettes; at the base of each appeared Litvinov's famous dictum: 'Peace is indivisible.' This evoked a wry warning from Strang when Maisky was about to help himself to a pat: 'Be careful how you cut that!' On his last day, Eden was taken for a ride on the first line of the spectacular underground railway, which had just been completed. He was unaware, of course, that it had been constructed by inmates of forced labour camps.

But the highlight of his visit was clearly the meeting with Stalin on 29 March. Preliminary conversations with Litvinov had given the Russians an accurate and detailed picture of the forlorn talks in Berlin. Indeed, on the way to Moscow, Eden had already cabled home his impression that Germany was unlikely to return to the League of Nations, but his recommendation to create a system of collective security under the umbrella of the League of Nations went unheeded. The meeting lasted for an hour and a quarter. Eden resorted to flattering rhetoric, which was interrupted rather brusquely

---

[19] William Strang, member of the British embassy in Moscow, 1930–33; head of the Foreign Office Department for the League of Nations, 1933–37; assistant undersecretary of state for foreign affairs, 1939–43.

[20] Maurice Hankey (1st Baron Hankey), secretary to the Committee of Imperial Defence, 1912–38, and to the Cabinet, 1916–38; minister without portfolio, 1939–40, and paymaster general, 1941–42.

18. Maisky's coup: Eden in Stalin's Office at the Kremlin (left to right: Eden, Stalin, Molotov, Maisky, Chilston and Litvinov).

by Stalin. It emerged, as Eden was forced by Litvinov to admit, that the main difference between the British and the Soviet points of view was 'that the former did not believe in the aggressiveness of German policy'. 'Compared, say, to 1913,' Stalin challenged Eden, 'is the situation better or worse?' He was hardly convinced by Eden's assurance that it was better. The aggressive postures of both Japan and Germany, Stalin argued, now posed an acute danger of war which could only be forestalled by a mutual assistance pact. Maisky was surely not amused at the metaphor Stalin chose to illustrate his point, after dismissing Eden's advocacy of bilateral agreements:

> Take the six of us present in this room. Suppose we concluded a mutual assistance pact and suppose Comrade Maisky wanted to attack one of us – what would happen? With our combined strength, we would give Comrade Maisky a hiding.
> Com. MOLOTOV (humorously): That's why Comrade Maisky is behaving so humbly.
> EDEN (laughing): Yes, I quite understand your metaphor.

Despite the efforts invested by Maisky and Litvinov, the visit made little headway in advancing the idea of an Eastern Pact; nor did it dramatically alter Eden's views. He found Stalin to be 'a man of strong oriental traits of character with unshakeable assurance and control whose courtesy in no way hid from us an implacable ruthlessness'.

In their memoirs, both Maisky and Eden hailed the visit to Moscow as the pinnacle of the diplomatic efforts to bring about a shift in Anglo-Soviet relations and to lay the foundations for an effective anti-Nazi coalition. Maisky's expectations of Eden, however, were clearly too high. He was neither the first nor the last politician to be beguiled by Eden's lofty demeanour, his charm and the respect which he seemed to command, as well as by his ability to convey authority and power (which he completely lacked). The 'Welsh wizard', Lloyd George, who formerly had great faith in Eden and in his courage, regarded him, according to Maisky, as 'a funk'. His verdict was harsh: 'They all call him a darling, they say his heart is in the right place but I doubt if his spine is!'

While the negotiations were still in progress at the Kremlin, Litvinov had been informed that the French had been discouraged by the British from making any tangible commitments in their pact of mutual assistance (signed with the Russians on 2 May 1935), which left the nature of military assistance wide open. Suspicion in Moscow was further aroused by the exclusion of Russia from the Stresa meeting in mid-April, when measures to check Germany were discussed by the Italians, the French and the British. An extraordinary session of the Council of the League of Nations on 17 April 1935 ended with a feeble denouncement of Germany's unilateral withdrawal from its international obligations. Maisky did not write in his diary until early June.

Rather than turning against Germany (as Maisky predicted), the hardliners in the Foreign Office were effectively prevailing on Cabinet to make further concessions to Germany. In his speech to the Reichstag on 21 May, Hitler rejected the Anglo-French proposals for disarmament and an Eastern bloc. During the meeting of the General Council of the League in Geneva, Eden deliberately avoided Litvinov, who came to realize the success of the strident and persistent Nazi campaign concerning the 'Bolshevik danger'.]

3 June

I attended the dinner of the 'dying swans', as the diplomats called it. Any day now there will be a Cabinet reshuffle, and MacDonald will retire as prime minister. Many other ministers will also be replaced. Tonight, though, the old members of the Government were still in their posts and they gave the annual dinner in the Foreign Office to mark the king's birthday. This time the celebration was on a larger scale than usual: the king has turned 70.

... To my left sat Halifax, former viceroy of India and presently the minister of education... He himself began speaking about the German threat and inquired about our attitude to Hitler, the Franco-Soviet pact, etc. Summing up, Halifax said: 'It's extremely irksome that the German threat has re-emerged in Europe. I'd give anything for someone to persuade me that there is no such

19. Eden given the honour of the first ride on the new Metro in Moscow.

threat. But facts are facts. Since Germany's intentions are unclear, you need to base your practical calculations on the worst scenario, not the best.'

5 June

A rather unusual neighbour moved in last year to house No. 12a (our embassy occupies No. 13), namely General Sir Bahadur Shamsher Jung Bahadur Rana, the Nepalese envoy extraordinary and minister plenipotentiary, together with his staff. I'd read in the papers that this Bahadur had arrived in London on a special mission, to bestow on the king the highest order of his country, and that he had fulfilled his mission successfully and with all due solemnity. Later, caught up in daily events, I forgot about Bahadur; I even thought that he had returned to his mountainous homeland.

Then it suddenly emerged that Bahadur was my neighbour! Taking into consideration the particular sensitivity of the English towards 'Indian affairs', I instructed the embassy staff to be reserved, even cold, with the neighbours, and not make friends with them. One fine summer's day, however, Bahadur himself paid me a visit. Even though our buildings stand side by side, he arrived in a car (oh, the Orient!). He wore national dress: a round lambskin hat, a long black caftan (something between a frock-coat and a lapserdak) on a short fat body, close-fitting black trousers tight at the shins, and soft white shoes with no counters. Bahadur did not remove his black hat even indoors. It was the time of afternoon tea. The maid carried in a tray with two cups, a teapot, hot water, and the other necessary ingredients. With a cordial gesture, I invited Bahadur to partake... And then! And then sheer horror appeared on his face and his hands convulsed as if he wanted to shield himself from a blow with a cudgel. I looked at my guest in bewilderment. He said in an apologetic tone: 'The law of my country forbids my sharing a meal with foreigners.'

... I looked at Bahadur in surprise and asked: 'How do you expect to work in London? Here, people are forever meeting over lunch, dinner or high tea.'

'Yes, I am aware of that,' my guest replied, 'but there's nothing I can do.'

The maid left and I closed the door behind her. Bahadur looked around cautiously and said: 'You can't imagine how hard it is for me here in London. I understand perfectly well that I can achieve nothing here if I don't share meals with foreigners, but what can I do? It is the law of my country. I have already appealed to His Majesty my sovereign with a letter regarding these difficulties and I am waiting impatiently for Him to resolve this serious problem.'

See what problems may occur in the epoch of socialist revolution and in the eighteenth year of Soviet rule in the USSR! To eat or not to eat – this is the question!

I sympathized with Bahadur and he, a little moved perhaps or with my Soviet origin in mind, said to me in a half-whisper, casting wary glances at the door: 'Here, in private, I can make a small exception, but let it remain strictly between ourselves...'

Bahadur shyly took a cup of tea from my hands, but he refused outright the offer of a pastry. Having drunk half of the cup, he put it on the table and pleaded: 'This is strictly between ourselves.' I solemnly vowed to keep his secret.

Then the conversation turned to other subjects. We talked about our homes, the conditions of life in London, the weather, etc. For some reason my guest was terribly interested in the question of whether or not I had a cowshed. Flummoxed, I replied that I had a garage but not a cowshed.

'But it's precisely a cowshed that interests me,' Bahadur repeated with obscure insistence.

I couldn't understand what he was on about. Why would a man in London suddenly need a cowshed? After some cautious interrogation, it emerged that Bahadur really did need a cowshed. In accordance with native customs and religious laws, he had brought with him from Nepal not only his national dress, interior decor and servants, but also his very own Nepalese cow. Upkeep of the cow has been causing my neighbour no end of difficulties. With no cowshed at home, he has had to rent separate premises for his four-footed friend, and this has proved highly inconvenient. That is why he was so keen to know whether or not I had a cowshed.

... Something mysterious happened to Bahadur's wife. He arrived married in London. His wife fell ill and died, but from what I don't know. I only know that she fell ill during her husband's visit to Italy, where he bestowed the highest order of his country on Mussolini and the Italian king. Anticipating her death, Bahadur's retinue took his wife out into the country, to a clearing, and there she eventually died. Apparently this was done because, according to Hindu laws, it is bad for the deceased if his body is kept between stone walls. Out of concern for their mistress, the servants moved her away from stony London in good time. Once I happened to visit Bahadur when he was in mourning. He received me dressed in what seemed to be white pyjamas beneath a light summer coat, soft white shoes without counters, and a small white cap. It was quite an amusing sight (as if the man had just jumped out of bed at night), but it turned out to be Nepalese mourning dress.

A few months later Bahadur left London and returned with a new wife, who never leaves the house. She does not even venture into the embassy garden.

6 June

I called on Vansittart. He met me cordially, but looked somewhat worn out and upset. Paler than usual. He took me aside and informed me on an entirely confidential basis (but with the request that I tell the Soviet Government!) that Samuel Hoare had been appointed foreign secretary. He had hoped for better, but this wasn't too bad. ... Vansittart fears, however, that the name Hoare might make an unfavourable impression in Moscow, and that the Soviet press might give him a hostile reception. One should not jump to conclusions... I replied that we view the restructuring of the British Government with equanimity, and that we will judge the new Foreign Office, and indeed the new government as a whole, not by their words but by their deeds.

* * *

We had a grand dinner in honour of Eden tonight. Twenty-seven guests were present. The atmosphere was not bad, even though Hoare had been appointed foreign secretary. Eden and Lord Cecil[21] assured me that Hoare was a convinced

---

[21] Robert Cecil (Gascoyne-Cecil) (1st Viscount Cecil of Chelwood), president of the League of Nations Union, 1923–45; winner of the Nobel Prize for Peace in 1937.

advocate of collective security and that he would make a good foreign secretary. We'll see!

[Vansittart assisted Maisky in setting up a powerful lobby within Conservative circles. The introduction of Maisky to the Fleet Street magnate Beaverbrook[22] resulted in the first favourable mention of Moscow in the *Daily Express*, which, according to Maisky, hitherto had printed only 'obvious libels'. Maisky was further invited to a dinner *en famille* at Vansittart's home, where he met Churchill. 'I send you a very strong recommendation of that gentleman,' wrote Beaverbrook to Maisky. 'In character he is without a rival in British politics. I know all about his prejudices. But a man of character who tells the truth is worth much to the nation.' Churchill indeed told Maisky that, in view of the rise of Nazism, which threatened to reduce England to 'a toy in the hands of German imperialism', he was abandoning his protracted struggle against the Soviet Union, which he no longer believed posed any threat to England for at least the next ten years. He fully subscribed to the idea of collective security as the sole strategy able to thwart Nazi Germany. But the tide was turning against the rapprochement embarked upon by Maisky and Vansittart in 1934. The Franco-Soviet Pact offered the Germans a convenient excuse for finally burying the idea of an Eastern Pact. Under the circumstances, in late autumn the Foreign Office rejected both the 'policy of drift' (waiting for events to occur) and the policy of 'encirclement' (the creation of an anti-German military alliance with France, Russia and the Little Entente), preferring the third option of 'coming to terms with Germany' – a policy that would signal the transition to 'appeasement'.]

12 June

Just back from my first meeting with S. Hoare. He invited me according to the custom of receiving all diplomatic representatives accredited in London, but our conversation, which lasted some 40 minutes, far exceeded the bounds of mere etiquette. What first impression did I gain of 'my' new foreign secretary?

First, the external details. The desk in the office has been moved – a new broom sweeps clean. What next, I wonder? Will H. limit himself to furniture rearrangement?... Time will tell.

H. is dry, elegant and quite short. His face is sharp, intelligent and guardedly attentive. He is very courteous and considerate, but cautious. He still feels unsure of himself in his new position, is unfamiliar with the current problems, and is afraid most of all of committing himself in any way to anybody. He wants to keep his hands free and to have room to manoeuvre in all directions.

---

[22] William Maxwell Aitken (1st Baron Beaverbrook), Canadian-born British politician, financier and newspaper proprietor; publisher of the *Daily Express* group of newspapers from 1916; founder of the *Sunday Express* in 1918 and proprietor of the London *Evening Standard* from 1923; minister for aircraft production, 1940–41; minister of supply, 1941–42; minister of war production and lord privy seal, 1943–45.

... I asked H. how he envisaged that peace could be secured in Europe. H. gestured his ignorance and refused to answer, emphasizing that he had only been foreign secretary for three days. ... Then H. started 'thinking aloud', and I soon had sufficient grounds to establish that my misgivings had not been unfounded. H.'s 'thoughts' boiled down to the following. The English are tired of endless, futile conversations. They want action, not talk. A small practical success is better than a truck-load of eloquent chatter. The disarmament conference failed because it set itself tasks that were too broad and all-embracing. If, 15 years ago, the powers had embarked on arms limitation via separate categories and not in general terms, we would currently be facing a very different situation. The British public now wants 'something, somehow, somewhere to be done'.

I replied that I found H.'s theory very dangerous. Disarmament cannot be fulfilled piecemeal, while the term 'somewhere' might easily be interpreted in the spirit of Hitlerite notions: 'security' in the West and a free hand in Eastern Europe. Does H. support such notions? Does he think that peace is divisible? H. replied that the British Government would of course take our point of view into account in developing its foreign policy, but he again dodged my direct question. ...

What are my conclusions?

I'm somewhat alarmed. Although Vansittart reassured me that H.'s views basically coincided with his own, I think nevertheless that H. might prove more dangerous than Simon in the next few months. He is a novice, he underestimates the difficulties, and is prone to experimentation. He wants quick, concrete, demonstrable successes to justify his appointment in the eyes of the English public. He wants to oppose his 'sober', 'concrete', 'practical' policies to the 'foggy', 'baggy', 'spineless' policies of Simon. This is dangerous. Simon, for all his negative traits, had some experience. He had been bested more than once, and received many bloody noses in his attempts to regulate various international problems. ... H. obviously wants to experiment in the sphere of Anglo-German relations – what will come of it? H. will learn, of course, but let's hope this process doesn't come at too great a price.[23]

We must be doubly vigilant! France, the Little Entente and the USSR must demonstrate maximum activity!

19 June

I've learned (admittedly, from a third party) some details of Stalin's meeting with Laval.

---

[23] Maisky reported home that he had gained a 'strong impression' that Hoare would strive to achieve a quick agreement with Germany. Indeed, five days later the naval agreement was signed.

Having exchanged greetings, L. declared, with the utmost French parliamentary courtesy, that he was delighted about the very recent signing of the Franco-Soviet Pact, which, he said, was not directed against any particular country. S. replied: 'What do you mean? It is absolutely directed against one particular country – Germany.'

L. was somewhat astonished, but he immediately tried to right himself and, with the same charming courtesy, expressed his pleasure at S.'s frankness. Only real friends could speak to one another like that.

Then S. asked him: 'You're just back from Poland. What is happening there?' In reply, L. fell into lengthy, polite and ornate explanations about how, despite pro-German attitudes remaining strong in Poland, there are signs of improvement that will eventually lead to a change in Polish policy, etc. S. interrupted L., declaring tersely, 'To my mind, there are no signs at all!' Then he added: 'You are a friend of the Poles, so try to persuade them that they are playing a game that will bring disaster on themselves. The Germans will trick them and sell them short. They will involve Poland in some adventure and when she weakens, they will either seize her or share her with another power. Is that what the Poles need?'[24] L. was again shocked by S.'s directness and frankness.

Referring in the course of their conversation to the power and influence of the Catholic Church, L. asked S. whether reconciliation could not be sought between the USSR and the pope,[25] perhaps by concluding a pact with the Vatican... S. smiled and said: 'A pact? A pact with the pope? No, that won't happen! We conclude pacts only with those who have armies, and the Roman pope, as far as I know, does not have an army.'

2 July

Abyssinia is the focus of attention today.[26] The English are in a bit of a fix. Yesterday's parliamentary session was interesting. The project of ceding to Abyssinia a tiny piece of British Somalia, including the port of Zeila, caused an absolute uproar in Parliament! Yells from the members' benches when Hoare said that Parliament should 'trust' the Executive! Someone even shouted: 'Hitler!'

---

[24] Maisky's diary is a vital source for the meeting. Stalin's clairvoyant comment, suggesting a possible deal between Germany and the Soviet Union at Poland's expense, may have discouraged the Russians from declassifying the official report.

[25] Pope Pius XI, 1922–39.

[26] Mussolini sought to restore the fallen Italian Empire in North Africa and Ethiopia, after securing a tacit agreement from Laval. In September 1935, Italian troops invaded Ethiopia. The League of Nations condemned the invasion and imposed economic sanctions on Italy, which were frustrated by Germany and the United States. The results exposed the bankruptcy of the League of Nations and hastened the rapprochement between Hitler and Mussolini, which finally led to the formation of the 'Axis'.

I don't know how the British Government will extricate itself from this difficult situation, but if the genius of British diplomacy has not yet died, then Baldwin, taking his cue from long-distance imperialist policy, should have drawn up and implemented approximately the following plan: ... Great Britain agrees to form a united front with France and the USSR. Then the three governments immediately bring it to Mussolini's notice (while the war in Africa has not yet begun) that if the League of Nations declares Italy an aggressor, they will be forced to impose economic sanctions on her. ... If Great Britain and France were to find the strength and resolution to implement a plan like this, not only would the Abyssinian problem be settled for many years to come, and not only would the prestige of the League of Nations be considerably raised, but the united front of Great Britain, France, Italy and the USSR against the German threat would be consolidated, and the paths to relative calm in Europe would be opened. Can Britain and France find the requisite strength and determination? I doubt it. But time will tell.

9 July

Vansittart asked to see me in order 'to state his case' ... Naturally, V. defended the naval treaty.[27] He remarked in passing that he himself was also in favour of signing it. The reasons? There are two: (1) Better something than nothing ... (2) If agreement had not been achieved and the British Government, spurred by the inevitable naval arms race, had to raise taxes in a year or two, there would be a great uproar in England and accusations that the British Government had rejected Germany's promising proposal just to please France. ...

In my view ... (1) the Conservatives and Labour are desperately scrapping for the pacifist vote, and the naval treaty can be presented to the electorate as the first real step on the way to cutting or limiting arms in a sphere as important to England as that of the navy; (2) declining belief in the effectiveness of collective security and the ensuing desire 'to seize the moment' by concluding advantageous bilateral agreements ... (3) the anti-Soviet factor: why not strengthen Germany in the Baltic just in case? Why not tie up the 'Soviets' in Europe? Who knows, perhaps one day they will want to bring the Communist Manifesto to the peoples of the West at the point of the bayonet?...

[Before departing for a protracted summer holiday at a sanatorium at Kislovodsk, Maisky took his leave of Samuel Hoare. Their conversation left him with a grim

---

[27] The Anglo-German naval treaty of 18 June 1935 sanctioned the building of a German fleet up to 35 per cent of the tonnage of the British navy. It was abrogated by Hitler on 28 April 1939. Maisky remarked that 'In signing the naval agreement with Germany, Great Britain had snatched at an apparent advantage, as a greedy boy will snatch at a cake on the table; the result is likely to be an attack of indigestion.'

impression that Hoare was 'fully prepared to reach a compromise with Germany on the basis of European Security'. While in Moscow, Maisky found the Kremlin 'greatly perturbed' by rumours about French and British attempts to reconcile with Germany. It had become convinced that Germany was intent on breaking up Czechoslovakia and on bringing about *Anschluss* with Austria. Maisky now feared that circumstances were propelling the Russians into an isolationist position. He felt that the ground was quickly shifting under his feet. In a strictly personal letter to Litvinov, he expressed fears that he might be asked to take the embassy in Washington, and raised fierce professional and personal arguments against his transfer:

> From the business point of view it would be completely irrational for me to leave England. I know well the country, the people, the mores and the customs. I have many varied connections here, accumulated over ten years. ... As far as I can tell and judge, I have succeeded in winning a decent position here in governmental, public and political circles. ... It is only now, as plenipotentiary in England, that I am fully in my element ... and I am in a position to give the maximum diplomatic benefit to the USSR. ... From a personal viewpoint I prefer England to any other country except the USSR. ... I would really not want to go to the USA: I have never felt any sympathy for that country, Washington's foreign policy is of little interest, it's deeply provincial, and it doesn't promise us anything positive in the near future.]

6 November

Following my absence of nearly three months from England, I visited Hoare to renew contact. Hoare was so very polite that I began to feel somewhat ill at ease. There's too much sugariness and formality in this civility. You can't help being on your guard...

We spoke, of course, about the Italo-Abyssinian conflict.

Hoare started complaining about the French: they are far too optimistic in thinking that the conflict can be settled in a trice. The untangling of the African knot, alas, will be a lengthy process, to judge by the evidence. The Italian demands remain absolutely unacceptable to Abyssinia, as they do to the League of Nations and England. It would be best of all to end the war without winners and losers; peace in the future would be more stable.

... I briefed H. on our position. We have no quarrels with Italy. The political and economic relations between the USSR and Italy have been good for the last ten years. We have no interests in Africa. If we are currently taking a stand against Italy, it is only as a loyal member of the League of Nations and because we want to teach a lesson to serve as a warning for any future aggressors. Italy is not a very serious aggressor, but there are more dangerous candidates in the world, particularly in Europe. An appropriate precedent must be set for them.

H. assured me that the British position is exactly the same. England also has no interests of its own in the conflict. She is guided, he claims, purely by loyalty to the League of Nations and the desire to admonish a more dangerous potential aggressor who might appear in three, five or ten years (H., like me, does not regard Italy as a terrifying aggressor). H. formulated his thought in such a way that it was clear he had Germany in mind.

15 November

So, last night the five of us (Agniya, I, the Kagans and Mironov) sat in the Royal Automobile Club and listened to radio broadcasts about the election results until 2 a.m. We walked for a while along streets that were unusually calm for an election night. Today, we've learned the basic outcome of yesterday's voting. Well, the results are not bad, though they differ from my expectations. ... The National Government will have to pursue a more careful policy towards the USSR and it will have to emphasize its loyalty to the League of Nations. It will be more difficult for it to engage in any anti-Soviet intrigue. The chances of improving Anglo-Soviet relations are greater. If only Labour would not spoil everything with their absurd Germanophilia! We shall see.[28]

14 December

The situation becomes more and more mysterious.

On 11 September, Hoare made his famous speech in Geneva, in which he resolutely stated that from now on British foreign policy would be the policy of the League of Nations. His speech was received here and abroad as a great, almost historic milestone in the sphere of international politics. For the next two months, Baldwin, Hoare, Eden and all the other members of the British Government declared, emphasized and trumpeted their loyalty to the promise made on 11 September.

... I had assumed that loyalty to the League of Nations remained very much in the interests of the British Government. And, all of a sudden, the Hoare–Laval 'peace plan'[29] appears in Paris! A plan that marks the most brazen, most impudent betrayal of the principles of the League of Nations! And when? Three weeks after the election! And at what precise moment? The moment of the

---

[28] The Conservative Party won 432 seats in Parliament; Labour 154; and the Liberals 21.

[29] The Hoare–Laval plan of 8 December 1935 proposed a settlement of the Italian–Ethiopian conflict, whereby the Ethiopian Government would cede large parts of its territory to Italy, in return for the sea port of Aseb in southern Eritrea and a narrow corridor connecting it with the mainland. The League's defiance prompted Mussolini to occupy Addis Ababa on 5 May 1936. Indignation in Britain led Baldwin to replace Hoare with Eden, an advocate of the League of Nations.

manifest failure of the Italian army in Abyssinia and of ever-increasing problems for Mussolini at home!

It's beyond understanding! What's it all about? Who is to blame?

Knowing the political and diplomatic customs here, I can easily imagine the following course of events... After the election contact with Laval was established ... the potion was brewing in the imperialists' infernal kitchen. When Hoare went to Switzerland 'on holiday', he was given merely the most general instructions: do your best to end the conflict as soon as possible, even by 'correcting' Abyssinian frontiers and offering Italy some economic privileges in Negus's[30] empire (after all, something must be given to Mussolini!). Hoare arrived in Paris. Laval pressed him, making it clear that England could not count on France in an armed conflict with Italy. He categorically refused to support oil sanctions... What was to be done? Hoare felt a surge of imperialist sentiments (which came so naturally to him) and decided to show that he was not some Simon or other, capable only of babbling on. He could be an Alexander the Great of British foreign policy.

... Meanwhile, a real political crisis has erupted in England. Today's newspapers report that Hoare is hurrying home and will speak in the House on 19 December. While skating in England, Hoare managed to break his nose. For this reason, he will not leave his home for a few days. How symbolic! Yes, Hoare has broken his nose politically as well as physically. Will he and will the Government draw the proper conclusions? Will Hoare resign? We shall see. To tell the truth, I doubt it.

---

[30] Haile Selassie, emperor of Ethiopia, 1930–74.

1936

20 January

Wickham Steed[1] lunched with me. ... We talked about the king's illness, and Steed related some interesting details concerning George V and his predecessors. ... On King Edward VII: Steed once found himself among the royal retinue in Karlsbad, where the king had gone for a cure. King Edward had to send a complimentary telegram to the Boy Scouts in England. The king's secretary asked Steed if he would write the draft. Steed did so. The next day the secretary ruefully informed Steed: 'Nothing doing, I'm afraid. The king read your draft and said: these are not the words of a father-king to his children, but an editorial from *The Times*. This won't do for me.' Edward composed the telegram himself; according to Steed, it really was much better than the one he had written.

King George also wrote most of his own speeches and addresses to the nation. A few years ago, when Steed was still working at *The Times*, the king's secretary asked him to send a man to draft the monarch's speeches. Steed sent a brilliant journalist. A month later the journalist returned to Steed in disappointment and said: 'I am not needed there at all. Whatever draft I tried to write, the king would rewrite it from scratch and barely a sentence of my own would remain. I resigned my post in the palace.' Steed claims that in 1928, shortly before his illness, the king was in a very depressed frame of mind. He felt that he was coping poorly with his duties and steadily losing authority and respect among his subjects. He even toyed with the idea of abdication. Baldwin, who was prime minister at the time, tried to reassure the king and resolutely opposed abdication. In December 1928, George fell seriously ill. The general sympathy displayed by the public during his illness impressed the king deeply. He became calmer, having decided that the Empire needed him; his will to live came sharply into focus. This psychological state greatly facilitated the king's

---

[1] Henry Wickham Steed, a BBC foreign correspondent and former editor of *The Times*, who endorsed 'The Protocols of the Elders of Zion', but despite his notorious anti-Semitism was early to warn of Hitler's intentions.

almost miraculous recovery seven years ago. 'Perhaps the same will to live will save the king even now,' Steed concluded. 'Who knows?...'

21 January

King George V died yesterday.

Rumours about his illness were already circulating at Christmas. They were officially denied. The king even broadcast his Christmas appeal to the Empire and many, including Bernard Shaw, complimented the king publicly on his skill at speaking over the radio. Then all the rumours faded. Not until the evening of 17 January did a medical bulletin appear dedicated to the state of the king's health. Listeners were informed that the weakening of the king's cardiac activity 'gives cause for concern'. That was a very serious symptom and a serious warning. Things went from bad to worse. A prominent cardiologist was summoned to Sandringham, bulletins began to come out more often and their contents were ever more disquieting. On Sunday, 19 January, I notified Moscow by telegram of the possibility of the king's death and requested that condolence telegrams be sent in that event to the queen and the royal family from Kalinin[2] and to Baldwin from Molotov. On 20 January, Agniya and I went to the cinema. On leaving the cinema at about 11 p.m., we saw on newspaper posters: 'The King is Dying.' When we got home, we tuned into the radio and began listening. There was a bulletin every quarter of an hour. The Kagans came over to listen with us. At 12.15 a.m. the radio announcer said with emotion: 'It is with deepest regret...' All was clear. The king had died at 11.55 p.m. on 20 January.

We woke up Falin (our chauffeur)[3] and ... drove into town to see what was happening. The traffic was unusually heavy. There was a long black queue near Buckingham Palace, which was slowly passing the gates, on which hung a notification of the king's death. The square in front of the palace and the adjacent streets were crammed with cars. A large body of policemen had a hard time trying to keep order. There was a restrained, intent silence, but there were no tears or hysterics – or perhaps these were concealed by darkness. We drove on to Fleet Street, which was noisy and lively. Newspaper boys carrying huge piles

---

[2] Mikhail Ivanovich Kalinin, member of the Politburo, 1926–46, and chairman of the USSR Supreme Soviet, the titular head of state of the Soviet Union, 1938–46. Although he survived the purges, his wife was arrested, tortured and sent to a gulag, from which she was released in 1945, a year before his death.

[3] Maisky's driver was clearly charged with surveillance of his movements. Beatrice Webb recalls a party attended by Maisky and a certain Captain Bennett, who had been taken captive by the Bolsheviks in the Civil War, but who escaped. When Maisky's chauffeur was summoned to drive him home, 'there was an instantaneous recognition between former gaoler and escaped prisoner', Beatrice Webb recorded in her diary, 'the Soviet chauffeur turning out to be a GPU [Soviet Secret Service] official. They chummed up and were joined by Dick and Lord William Percy – both of whom were connected with the British Secret Service – whereupon the four "mystery men" strolled off together for a friendly glass and a smoke – much to the astonishment of Their Excellencies and the other guests!'

of fresh print were running in all directions, shouting: 'The king is dead!' The passers-by stopped them and hastily bought newspapers still smelling of ink. We also bought some. They were the next day's issues of all the major papers (*Daily Herald*, *Daily Express*, *Daily Mail* and others) and were almost entirely given over to the king's death. They already carried editorials on the subject, lengthy surveys of the king's reign, character sketches of George V as monarch and man, and salutations to the new king, Edward VIII. I checked my watch: the time was not yet 1 a.m. The king's heart stopped beating only an hour or so ago. London journals work fast! There is no doubt that the editorials, recollections and salutations were written in advance, and that the printing presses were just waiting for the signal to unleash millions of copies on the world, but all the same

I sent a telegram to Moscow suggesting that Litvinov, who is nearby in Geneva, should attend King George's funeral. Will they consent? We'll see. They ought to, otherwise it will look like a demonstration of deliberate coldness on our part, which politically would be highly undesirable for us right now.

[When Maisky first met King George in November 1932, he was astounded by the king's resemblance to his cousin, Tsar Nicholas II.[4] 'I thought he would look upon me as a ... murderer,' he confessed, 'but it was quite different from what I had expected.' Maisky resented it when such insinuations were made. 'After all, if we are regicides,' he told Lady Vansittart, 'if we killed Tsar Nicholas, you killed King Charles and the French sent Louis XVI to the guillotine.' 'Yes,' retorted Lady Vansittart, 'but that was two centuries ago and more, and you killed the entire imperial family.' As Maisky recalled, she then added, in a characteristic English reflex: 'Why! You even killed their dog!' The observant Lady Vansittart noticed tears in the eyes of Maisky as he walked behind the coffin of the tsar's cousin.]

26 January

M.M. [Litvinov] has just arrived. I travelled to Dover to meet him.

Concurrent with my telegram of 21 January, supplemented by another the next day, M.M. sent his own telegram, advising Moscow to send a special delegation to the funeral consisting of himself and someone from the top ranks of the Red Army. We had had the same thought...

---

[4] Nicholas Aleksandrovich Romanov, cousin of George V, he was the last Russian emperor, 1894–1917, forced to abdicate after the 1917 February Revolution and shot with his family by the Bolsheviks in July 1918.

20. Maisky welcomes the Litvinovs to the Soviet embassy in London.

Agniya is very busy with the wreath we shall lay on the king's coffin. The wreath is very fine: white lilies and lilies of the valley, with red orchids in the centre. The black-and-red ribbon bears the inscription: 'From the Central Executive Committee of the USSR'. The papers have noted both the beauty of the wreath and the very fact of its laying. ...

28 January

The king's funeral finally took place today. It was all most solemn and imposing, but I will not give a detailed description of the ceremony, which can be found in the newspapers. I would like to record something else here, which was not mentioned in the press and probably never will be.

We've seen a right old mess here over the last eight days!

The king died the night of 20 January. I expected the Foreign Office and the doyen to inform all diplomats the next morning what they were to do. Nothing

21. Mourning the death of King George V, cousin of Tsar Nicholas II.

of the sort! Nobody told us a thing. ... Next came the question of the embassy's flag: for how long should it be kept at half-mast? Again, neither the Foreign Office nor the doyen could give exact advice. I decided that I should keep it that way till the day of the funeral, and that also proved correct: the other diplomats did the same. On 23 January, the king's body was brought from Sandringham to London and the coffin was placed in Westminster Hall in Parliament. Hundreds of thousands were filing past the coffin. Should diplomats take part in the procession? Neither the Foreign Office nor the doyen knew.

... We arrived in Windsor at 12.05. The funeral service was to begin at 1.15. Thus, there was a one-hour gap. Why? What for? From the station we walked directly to St George's Chapel, sat down in pews before the altar, and waited. It was cold and uncomfortable. The ladies sat huddled up tight and shivering, wrapped in overcoats and capes. We spoke in half-whispers to our neighbours ... The organ was playing, and from time to time dark female figures in long veils would appear, taking their seats in the pews. Like spectres from the other world. It was tedious. Time dragged on intolerably. I examined the faces opposite me, of members of government and their wives. There were Baldwin, Simon, Halifax, Duff Cooper,[5] Elliot, Stanley,[6] and others. Eden sat somewhere behind me where I couldn't see him. The clock struck one, then quarter past. No coffin. Half past one, a quarter to two... Still no coffin. What was the matter? We began feeling uneasy. After a long time, at around two o'clock, there came the loud tramp of thousands of feet, the noise of trumpets and commands, and the king's coffin, upholstered with violet velvet, was brought into the chapel. Why the delay? On the way to Paddington, it emerged, crowds had broken through the police cordons and filled up the streets and squares. It took about 40 minutes to clear the route. ...

The coffin was placed on a pedestal before the altar. The royalties all took their seats behind the coffin, and behind them the military, courtiers and numerous others. Final prayers, parting words, and all was over. The pedestal started its slow descent. The coffin sank further and further into the crypt. Now it was already at the bottom. The queen (I had a good view of her from my seat) shuddered and shrank into herself, but she held her nerve. No tears. But the duchess of Athlone[7] wept openly. The new king threw pinches of earth into the open crypt three times. Then the royalties began a slow procession past the crypt. The diplomats and the government did not join and, turning away, left

---

[5] Duff Alfred Cooper (1st Viscount Norwich of Aldwick), financial secretary to the Treasury, 1934–35; secretary of state for war, 1935–37; first lord of the Admiralty, 1937–38; minister of information, 1940–41; chancellor of the duchy of Lancaster, 1941–43.
[6] Oliver Stanley, Conservative MP, 1924–45; president of the Board of Education, 1935–37; president of the Board of Trade, 1937–40; secretary of state for war in 1940; secretary of state for the colonies, 1942–45.
[7] Alice, duchess of Athlone, the last surviving grandchild of Queen Victoria.

through another door. The Spaniard came up to me and asked: 'Can you tell me why they kept us in that cold for a whole two hours?' My thoughts precisely.

We returned to the railway station. One train left, then another, and a third... After a 40-minute wait, we boarded the diplomatic train, where lunch had been promised (we were all hungry by then). 'Lunch', though, consisted merely of tea and sandwiches. We reached London at four and got home half an hour later.

Such mess and confusion! I am sure the Germans would have organized everything infinitely better in a similar situation. Even we in Moscow would probably have avoided many of the *gaffes* committed by the English. I'm becoming more and more convinced that the English are good at managing events that come round every year (for instance, the air shows in Hendon). They accumulate experience and make good use of it. But when it comes to arranging something from scratch and – above all – in haste, you may confidently expect a flop. ...

29 January

A day of appointments and meetings.

Yesterday evening Eden invited Litvinov, Agniya and myself to have lunch with him today at 1.30. This morning the marshal of the diplomatic corps (Sir Sidney Clive[8]) informed me that the king was granting a private audience to Litvinov at 2.30 in the afternoon. Then Baldwin's secretary phoned to say that the prime minister was expecting Litvinov today at 3.30. I had to phone Eden and ask him to shift our lunch to one o'clock.

We had lunch in Eden's private apartment. It was my first visit to Eden's home. Nothing special or splendid. An ordinary middle-class English house, rather cold, with second-hand furniture and a faintly Bohemian flavour. A pile of gramophone records lay on the floor of the drawing-room: waltzes, foxtrots and polkas. There were a few fine pictures on the walls and a couple of Vigeland[9] prints in the dining-room. We arrived a little bit early: Eden was still at a Cabinet meeting, and Mrs Eden was busy with housework. Eden arrived with Duff Cooper, the war minister. We sat down in a small dining-room downstairs, at a table which could accommodate no more than ten. For some reason I found myself to the right of the mistress of the house, and Litvinov to her left. Duff Cooper's wife, an exceptionally beautiful and impressive lady, floated in half an hour late. There were no serious conversations. ... On parting, we arranged with Duff Cooper to have lunch in our embassy, where he could meet

---

[8] Lieutenant General Sir Sidney Clive, marshal of the diplomatic corps, 1934–45.
[9] Adolf Gustav Vigeland, Norwegian sculptor.

Tukhachevsky.[10] As he said goodbye from the staircase, Eden told Litvinov: 'If you would like to have a talk with me, I am at your service.'

Litvinov headed straight to the palace, while Agniya and I went home. The reception given by the king was very courteous and amicable. ... Their conversation lasted 50 minutes instead of the normal 15 or 20 – at the king's will. It was a very wide-ranging dialogue. Edward skipped from one topic to another, asking questions and waiting for Litvinov to answer them. Some were of a very delicate nature. For example, Edward asked why and under what circumstances Nicholas II was killed. Was it not because revolutionaries feared his reinstatement? ... Then Edward mentioned Trotsky[11] and asked why he was deported from the USSR. M.M. again gave the required explanation, stressing the debate about the possibility or otherwise of building socialism in one country. The king listened to him attentively and then said, as if the penny had dropped: 'So Trotsky is an international communist whereas you are all national communists.' In the sphere of foreign policy, the king was interested in our relations with Germany and Poland. M.M. said that we want good relations with both countries and work in that direction but, unfortunately, without much success so far. The USSR's policy is a policy of peace. 'Yes,' Edward responded, 'all nations want peace, nobody wants war.' In the course of conversation he also remarked: 'Germany and Italy have nothing at all. They are dissatisfied. Something should be done to improve their condition as far as raw materials, trade, etc. are concerned.' ... As to the League of Nations, Edward had some doubts: he was afraid that the League might spread war all over Europe as a result of its efforts. There was the sense that Edward regretted the failure of the Hoare–Laval plan.

... On the whole, the king impressed M.M. as a lively and spirited man, with a keen interest in world affairs.

After his talk with the king, Litvinov went to see Baldwin. Their conversation was brief, lasting 15 or 20 minutes, and rather trivial. Litvinov later referred to it as an *innocent talk*. Baldwin told M.M. ... that he had studied Russian at the beginning of the war, that he was fond of Russian literature ...We went to the cinema in the evening. A bad idea. We saw *Top Hat*[12] – a very silly comedy,

---

[10] Mikhail Nikolaevich Tukhachevsky, marshal of the Soviet Union and a brilliant innovative military theoretician. deputy and then chief of staff of the Red Army, 1924–28; deputy to the people's commissar for defence, 1934–36. A victim of the military purges, he was arrested, tortured and sentenced to death in June 1938; rehabilitated posthumously.

[11] Leon Trotsky (Lev Davidovich Bronshtein), second only to Lenin in his stature as a revolutionary in 1917, he went on to become the first commissar for foreign affairs, 1917–18, followed by a career as the commissar for military and navy affairs, before being chased out of politics, and of Russia, by Stalin in 1927. The most severe critic of Stalinism, in 1940 he was assassinated in Mexico, where he had sought refuge.

[12] The quintessential Fred Astaire and Ginger Rogers film.

which M.M. did not enjoy. After the movies we dined at Scotts, a restaurant, opened in the 1850s.

30 January

... Prior to Litvinov's arrival in London, I hinted to Vansittart that it might be good for him to meet with Litvinov in private. I proposed lunch at the embassy. V. declined my offer and insisted on lunch at his home. I did not object. ... The lunch felt like a family affair. ... The entire conversation was dominated by the spectre of Hitler. Speaking about the German danger and how to rebuff it ... I related my recent conversation with Austen Chamberlain and emphasized the latter's idea that peace could be preserved only with the backing 'of a strong League of Nations', and that the League of Nations could be strong only if its great powers – Britain, France and the USSR – had a uniform policy and worked in close cooperation with one another. ... 'I subscribe entirely to Chamberlain's prescription,' echoed M.M.

... At 5.30 p.m. M.M went to the Foreign Office to talk with Eden. ... His general impression after the talk was as follows: Eden was quite satisfied with the political line set forth by M.M., but did not want to draw any concrete inferences from the appraisal of the situation on which they were in agreement.

[If Maisky expected Eden to have been won over by his Moscow visit, he was to be disappointed. 'I have no sympathy to spare for Mr Maisky,' Eden minuted. 'I hope that next time M. Maisky comes with complaints he will be told that our goodwill depends on his Government's good behaviour; i.e. keep their noses and fingers out of our domestic politics. I have had some taste of the consequences of this lately ... I am through with the Muscovites of this hue.'

Eden's appointment as foreign secretary now put Maisky's expectations to the test, particularly against the backdrop of the swift British move towards appeasement. On 6 January, Maisky met Eden briefly, as part of the foreign secretary's introductory round of meetings with foreign ambassadors. Reporting home, Maisky emphasized Eden's commitment to the stand he had taken in Moscow and his adherence to the Eastern Pact. A different picture emerges from the British records describing how desperate Maisky was to bring about a movement in relations. He did not conceal from Eden that 'it would be a great grief to him personally ... as well as a misfortune for Europe' if the opportunity was missed. Eden, however, briefed his officials at the Foreign Office that 'while I want good relations with the bear, I don't want to hug him too close. I don't trust him, and am sure there is hatred in his heart for all we stand for.'

It was becoming increasingly apparent that Maisky's own personal safety was intertwined with the success of collective security. He could not afford to remain passive. On 11 February, he went on the offensive, confronting Eden with a long survey of the international scene. To his chagrin, he found Eden determined not to undertake any further commitment in Central and South-East Europe, expecting France to do 'the dirty work'. Whatever hopes Maisky may have entertained of stopping the drift towards appeasement were dashed when Eden, siding with the Foreign Office officials, warned: 'Let us beware of Mr Maisky, he is an indefatigable propagandist.' The sobering moment came on 7 March, when Hitler abrogated the Locarno Treaty and moved into the demilitarized Rhineland, justifying the advance by the supposed incompatibility of the Locarno Treaty with the Franco-Soviet Pact, ratified on 27 February. Baldwin conceded in Cabinet that, with Soviet help, France could possibly defeat Germany, but he feared it would lead to the Bolshevization of Germany. His heart, he asserted, would not break if Hitler went to the East.]

8 March

I don't like the British response to Hitler's '*coup*' in the Rhineland. Today's Sunday press is appalling. In the *Observer*, Garvin chides Hitler mildly for his bad manners, then insists on the need to pay due attention to 'the Führer's brilliant and timely proposals' and to do so 'in a spirit of sympathy and good will' ... I haven't met with any influential people about this (the 'weekend!'), but I sense a new and very dangerous turn towards Germanophilia in British policy. ...

9 March

I was unable to meet Eden, who flew to France at four o'clock, so I spoke with his deputy, Cranborne.[13] The mood of the English? They are in the mood to negotiate, of course. It is clearly a national English disease: negotiations, negotiations, negotiations... Therefore, the British Government is prepared to begin *exploration* (what a lovely word!) ...

10 March

The directives arrived from M.M. They coincide entirely with what I told Cranborne yesterday. M.M. maintains that the British standpoint signifies a reward for the aggressor, the break-up of the collective security system, and the end of the League of Nations. Talks with Hitler on the day after his speech will have more harmful consequences than the Hoare–Laval plan. Trust in Britain

---

[13] Robert Arthur James Gascoyne-Cecil (Viscount Cranborne, later 5th marquess of Salisbury), parliamentary undersecretary of state for foreign affairs, 1935–38; secretary of state for the dominions, 1940–42 and 1943–45; secretary of state for colonies, 1942; lord privy seal, 1942–43 and 1951–52.

will be undermined for good. The League of Nations will lose its importance as an instrument of peace. The USSR is ready to support any action of the League of Nations adopted collectively. Quite right!...

... Eden and Halifax invited representatives of the Locarno powers to come to London on 12 March, and, on the 14th, the entire Council of the League of Nations. So, I'll see M.M. here in London soon. He left Moscow yesterday.

3 April

A new memorandum from Hitler, brought by Ribbentrop from Berlin! The British response to it is a bit better. ... Almost the entire press favours negotiations, but in a far calmer spirit than before. ... Eden is clearly playing for time. Just today he told Ribbentrop that Hitler's proposals needed a certain period of 'calm deliberation'.

... My personal opinion is that temporary isolation of Germany is a minimum requirement, as is the working out of a 'peace plan' (either within the League of Nations or outside it) by the other Europeans powers for the whole continent. This should then be offered to Hitler. Moscow is thinking along the same lines.

8 April

Agniya and I lunched at the Vansittarts. I thought I would have an open talk with V. about the current situation, but he seemed to want to avoid this. ... V. is in a sour mood. He gives the impression of a man who is not quite himself. ... V. thinks it impossible to avoid negotiations: the British public would not comprehend a refusal to talk. The negotiations should be used for exposing Hitler. This is the easiest way of educating public opinion.

... We are leaving for France tomorrow for ten days: Easter. Time to blow away the cobwebs.

[In a strictly personal letter, Maisky urged Litvinov on 24 April to take the lead in a European conciliation, redressing what he recognized to be Germany's justified grievances. 'If we do not wish to severely weaken our authority and our influence among the democratic elements of Europe,' he suggested *inter alia*, 'then we should, alongside offering the severest possible criticism of Hitler's method of foreign policy, promote ... our own "peace plan", under the auspices of which we can begin the mobilization of the democratic and pacifist elements of the East and the West.' 'It seems to me,' he wrote to Bernard Shaw, that 'the greatest sin of modern statesmen is vacillation and ambiguity of thought and action. This is the weakness which before long may land us into war. Happily Stalin is possessed, in the highest degree, of the opposite qualities!'

Paradoxically, his only solace came from the champions of the British Empire, Beaverbrook and Churchill. Maisky invited Churchill for 'lunch à deux', and found out that he shared the Soviet view both that peace was 'indivisible' and that the German danger was an immediate one. 'We would be complete idiots,' Churchill told Maisky, 'were we to deny help to the Soviet Union at present out of a hypothetical danger of socialism which might threaten our children and grandchildren.']

3 May

Yesterday the Abyssinian Negus fled the capital. ... He plans to cross over into Palestine. ... The war has ended, Abyssinia is conquered, Mussolini triumphs. This is also the final nail in the coffin of the League of Nations; and Europe is at a fateful junction. You can smell the gunpowder! A terrible storm is approaching at full speed!

I spent the whole morning in the garden thinking how and when to build a shelter under the embassy against gas attacks. We shall need it soon. I'll have to ask the commissariat for special credits and directions.

10 May

On 5 May, I presented new credentials to the new King. The ceremony was simplified and conducted in full accord with former precedents ... and certainly with the precedent created by the late George V. No court carriages were sent for me, and my 'retinue' did not accompany me: I just drove to the palace in my own car. All heads of missions gathered in the Bow Room and in order of seniority presented their credentials to the king, who was in the adjoining room. The doors to the hall were open and those awaiting their turn could hear snatches of the king's conversation with the head of mission who was presenting his credentials.

... I entered the room and handed the envelope with my credentials to Eden, who was standing to one side and who placed it on top of similar packets already lying in a small basket. Meanwhile, Edward shook my hand and began asking questions befitting the occasion. ... At the end, the king said: 'In January I had a long and interesting conversation with Mr Litvinov.' I replied that I had heard about the conversation and that Mr Litvinov was *delighted* with his meeting with the king. That was all. It seemed to me that the king was chillier towards me than during our previous meetings when he was still the Prince of Wales. Why? Was it the result of a general *muddle* in the sphere of British foreign policy? Or the reflection of Edward's allegedly growing Germanophilia? Or maybe I am mistaken and there was no particular coldness in the king's manner?

Leaving the palace, I met Monck, the Foreign Office chief of protocol, and told him that I was going to present new members of my diplomatic corps to the king at the nearest levee.

'Yes, of course!' replied Monck.

'But you know,' I continued, 'one of the new members is a woman: the deputy of trade, Mosina.'

The expression on Monck's face changed. Trying to conceal his embarrassment with a laugh, he exclaimed: 'Oh, that's a quite different matter!'

He hesitated for a moment before continuing: 'Maybe it would be better to present the lady not at the levee but at the summer *garden party*? What do you think?' ...

My conversation ... reminded me of Kollontay's[14] story about the commotion caused by her appointment in the Swedish court and the protocol. .... The presentation of credentials takes place in the morning. Ambassadors who do not have uniform usually wear tails, that is, evening dress. What dress should she wear? An evening dress? It does not befit a lady to wear an evening dress in the morning. An afternoon dress? The chief of protocol was frightened. Then A.M. took matters into her own hands and announced: I'll wear a black long-sleeved dress with a white lace collar. The chief of protocol frowned but gave his consent.

Furthermore, according to Swedish etiquette, nobody may appear before the king with their head covered. Men present their credentials bareheaded. What was A.M. to do? She is a lady, and ladies wear hats on their daily business. A long and lively discussion followed. A.M. was for a hat and the chief of protocol against. Finally, the poor chief of protocol asked in exhaustion: 'What kind of hat do you have?' A.M. said: 'A small black brimless hat.' The chief of protocol raised his hands and cried: 'All right, all right! A small black brimless hat. But a very small one, please!' So, agreement was reached on this issue of global importance as well.

... One more 'problem'. After the presentation of credentials, the king converses with the envoy. Both should be standing. But, in Swedish society, when a man converses with a lady, he offers her a seat. What to do with A.M.? On the chief of protocol's insistence, it was decided that A.M. should talk while standing, like a male envoy.

---

[14] Aleksandra Mikhailovna Kollontay (*née* Domontovich) was born into a wealthy family. The daughter of a colonel on the tsarist general staff, she turned out to be an eminent pioneer of women's equality. A militant revolutionary, she was first a member of the Mensheviks but sided with Lenin and the Bolsheviks at the outbreak of the First World War. In 1917, she became people's commissar for social welfare, but her political career was nipped in the bud due to her association with the Workers' Opposition. She was then side-tracked to ambassadorial posts in Norway, 1923–26 and 1927–30, Mexico, 1926–27 and Sweden, 1930–45. She was recalled to a non-active role as a counsellor at the Soviet Ministry of Foreign Affairs, 1945–52.

In the event, nothing came out quite as planned. When A.M. appeared in the doorway with her credentials, the king, twitching in obvious embarrassment, made a couple of hesitant steps in her direction. They met halfway. When the credentials had been presented and the conversation began, the king became twitchy once again and said in some confusion, 'Now, it seems, I should ask you to be seated.' A.M. sat down and the king sat next to her, and it was from their armchairs that they conducted the rest of their conversation. ... Thus, the gentleman won out over the man of the court...

26 May

J. Cummings[15] told me about his conversation with Churchill. Churchill is ranting and raving at the government's spinelessness and indecision. Baldwin bears the brunt of the blame. Cummings asked when Baldwin would retire, and Churchill exclaimed irritably: 'He will never retire of his own accord! He wants to stay not only until the coronation but afterwards too, if he can. Baldwin must be *kicked out* – this is the only way to get rid of him.' Then Churchill added: 'Baldwin reminds me of a man who has held on to the gondola of a rising balloon. If he lets go of it when the balloon is only 5 or 6 metres above ground, he will fall, but he won't break his bones. The longer he hangs on, the surer he is to die when he does inevitably fall.'

Well put, in a true Churchillian manner. It reminded me how, some three months ago, Churchill answered a colleague's question as to why Baldwin had delayed the appointment of a defence minister with the following devastating witticism: 'Why, Baldwin is looking for a man smaller than himself as defence minister, and such a man is not easy to find.' ...

28 May

Yesterday Sir Edward Grigg[16] and General Spears[17] came to lunch, where they cursed and swore (insofar as this is possible in English and at the table of the ambassador of a great power) in the direction of Baldwin and the government. The Cabinet lacks spine, is unable to take decisions on serious matters, and has no policies, especially foreign policies. It has lost its way in broad daylight and

---

[15] Arthur John Cummings, editor of the liberal *News Chronicle*, 1920–55; reported among other notable events the Metro-Vickers trial of British engineers (Moscow 1933) and the Reichstag fire trial (Leipzig 1933).

[16] Edward Grigg (1st Baron Altrincham), director of Reuters, 1923–25; Conservative MP, 1933–45; parliamentary secretary to the minister of information, 1939–40; joint undersecretary of war, 1940–42.

[17] Sir Edward Louis Spears, Conservative MP, 1922–24 and 1931–45; Churchill's personal representative to French prime minister, May–June 1940, and to General de Gaulle, June 1940; British minister to Syria and Lebanon, 1942–44.

is rapidly driving the country to disaster and Europe to war. But when I tried to discover my guests' political line, embarrassment followed: they, too, were confused and unable to make any definite statements. In Grigg's words, the masses ... need the government's guidance. There is none. For this reason, if Hitler attacks Czechoslovakia, 'England will be unable to do anything – unless perhaps the USSR will help her?' ...

[There follows a long gap in the diary at a rather crucial moment, marked by a swift deterioration in relations between the two countries and the unleashing of the political trials and terror in Moscow. The Anglo-French debacle in handling Mussolini, Maisky lamented, was leading the Soviet Government to doubt 'whether it was worthwhile binding themselves up with such half-hearted partners as the British Government'. Despite recurring setbacks, Maisky, unlike Litvinov, remained convinced – right up until the outbreak of war – that Anglo-Soviet interests were in harmony and that gradually the British were bound to seek Soviet assistance. For the moment, however, he obviously had to toe the Kremlin line, though he would make persistent subversive attempts to prepare the ground for an approach by Britain.

The swift turn of events, however, made it difficult for the Soviet Union to sit on the fence while Hitler appeared to be effectively wooing British politicians, largely by whipping up the 'red scare'. Despite Hitler's virulent response to tentative Soviet feelers, Stalin opted for further futile negotiations in Berlin. It took a while for the repercussions of the horrific Spanish Civil War, which erupted on 17 July when General Francisco Franco[18] led a military revolt against the Spanish Popular Front government, to be fully registered in Moscow. The war undermined Litvinov's efforts to restore the First World War coalition against Germany. He was coming under increasing criticism, while his personal life was in turmoil. His decision at the end of July 1936 to have Zina, a 17-year-old girl – described (by Litvinov's wife) as 'nubile ... decidedly vulgar, very sexy, very sexy indeed' – accompany him 'as his daughter' to the sanatorium at Kislovodsk led Ivy[19] to pack and leave for remote Sverdlovsk. There, heedless of his distraught entreaties, she remained teaching schoolchildren English for three years, until his demotion. A large part of Litvinov's melancholy and resignation – often ascribed to the failure of collective security and the mortifying purges in his ministry – should clearly be attributed to personal aspects of his life.[20]

---

[18] General Francisco Franco, chief of general staff, 1935; commander-in-chief Canary Islands, 1936; commander-in-chief and head of state of Spanish Nationalist regime, 1936–39.
[19] Ivy Litvinov, British wife of Maksim Litvinov.
[20] Litvinov was crushed by Ivy's decision to leave. 'Like most men', Ivy wrote, 'he desired a wife and a mistress.' 'I used to go about the town,' she recalled, 'walking about the streets, and suddenly our enormous Cadillac would dash by with Zina sitting beside the chauffeur, she'd gone out shopping ... she turned up at the Foreign Office to fetch him in full riding kit.' Coming back into town from their dacha, Litvinov 'would have his arm round her, shrieking with laughter and giggling, tickling ... people in trams gazing down'.

Off to Kislovodsk, Litvinov encouraged Maisky to take early summer leave, but continued to fend off his efforts to rekindle the intimacy of their exile days, while reiterating his position as *primus inter pares*. 'It would be difficult,' he responded to Maisky's pleadings to attend the September Assembly of the League, 'to swap you for Potemkin[21] or Shtein[22] for no good reason, as they have developed very good personal contacts over there.' Maisky left England for the Soviet Union on 11 August, first for Sochi and then – blissfully cut off from the world – for a delightful tour of the Caucasus. Harsh reality awaited him on his return to Moscow. He was urgently summoned to the Foreign Ministry, briefed about the war in Spain and rushed to a nocturnal meeting with Stalin and instructed to return to his post right away.

In London, Maisky faced a grim situation which would trouble him for the next three years. During his absence, Britain and France had formed a 'non-intervention' committee, which the Soviet Union joined on 23 August. The scores of meetings of the committee over the next three years not only sapped his energy, but exposed even more the helplessness of Russia, which became increasingly alienated from the West. Much of this was due to Hitler's success in wrapping the Civil War in an ideological mantle, harping on British fears that communism would spread from Spain to France, whose prime minister, the socialist Léon Blum,[23] headed a Popular Front government. At a stroke, the war in Spain stripped Maisky of the limited success he had enjoyed in England. Alarmed at the harsh British reaction, the French threat to abrogate the mutual assistance pact, and the precarious situation on the battlefield, Litvinov succeeded in convincing Stalin that Soviet assistance should gradually cease. 'The Spanish question has undoubtedly significantly worsened our international position,' he explained to the defiant Maisky. 'It has spoiled our relations with England and France and sown doubt in Bucharest and even in Prague.']

1 December

Lothian lunched with me today. Despite some wobbles along the way, we meet and talk from time to time. It's interesting. He is a bright representative and

---

[21] Vladimir Petrovich Potemkin, a pedagogue, embarked on a career devising a revolutionary curriculum for schools in the People's Commissariat of Education of the RSFSR. Success in political agitation during the Civil War led to a diplomatic career in 1922. He was Soviet ambassador in Italy, 1932–34, and in France, 1934–37, and deputy people's commissar for foreign affairs, 1937–40. Survived Litvinov's demise in 1939, but a year later was removed from office and diverted to his former field of education, being entrusted with the revival of the traditional Russian national-cultural values in Soviet schools.

[22] Boris Efimovich Shtein, general secretary of the Soviet delegation at the Geneva Disarmament Conference, 1927–32; chief of the Second Western Department in the NKID, 1932 and 1934; member of the Soviet delegation to the League of Nations 1934–38; ambassador to Finland, 1933–34, and to Italy, 1934–39; demoted to a lecturer position at the diplomatic academy of the NKID in 1939.

[23] André Léon Blum, member of the French Socialist Party from 1904 and of the Chamber of Deputies, 1919–28 and 1929–40; premier of France, 1936–37, 1938 and 1946, and vice-premier, 1937–38 and 1948.

ideologist of the imperialist wing of the English bourgeoisie *par excellence*, and his pronouncements often reflect its latest moods...

Today the mood was vague and alarmed. Lord Lothian's Germanophilia has faded, owing especially to Hitler's colonial demands. 'I emphatically warned my German friends against raising this issue, for it can sow discord between Germany and England, but they just will not listen,' he said. L. criticized the German–Japanese pact, and the Franco-Soviet Pact, too, saying that the latter had led to the former. ... As for the Spanish question, L. seems to be closer to us than I expected. Proceeding from the imperial interests of Great Britain, L. prefers the victory of the Spanish Government. For this reason, he severely criticized the position of the British Government. 'All intelligent people under-stand,' L. said, 'that we are currently seeing in Spain the first serious duel between the USSR on the one side and Germany and Italy on the other. Much depends on the outcome of this test of strength, including the future orienta-tion of British policy. The English always gravitate towards the victor. If the fascist powers prevail in this conflict, England may ultimately, and very reluc-tantly, join them. If the USSR wins, an Anglo-Franco-Soviet alliance will become a *fait accompli* in the near future.'

1937

10 January

The last two or three months have seen unmistakable shifts in British foreign policy. These have been suggested first by Eden's four speeches last November and December, and secondly by the change in the British Government's attitude towards the Spanish question.

... Appraising Eden's speeches, I would define the current position of the British Government in the following way: England's prolonged retreat in the face of aggression has ended, at least for as long as the guidelines announced by Eden remain in force; but there has been as yet no counter-offensive against the aggressors.

... Now a few words on the Spanish question. Last October, the British Government clearly gambled on Franco winning. This was all too obvious in the notorious Non-Intervention Committee. Moreover, Eden himself ventured a rash statement against the USSR in Parliament. ... It is said that Eden's words slipped out at a moment of extreme vexation, under harassment from Labour MPs, and that afterwards he greatly regretted his lack of restraint... Perhaps.

The British Government's attitude has certainly changed for the better. ... Of course, any illusions here would be dangerous. The English are infected to the core with the poison of 'compromise' and 'balance-of-power politics'. Besides, class hatred towards the USSR remains a fixed reality. Also, the current situation deters the City from effecting any drastic changes in the political and economic spheres. I do not know whether British policy will remain at its present level (if not above it), yet the aforesaid shifts are certainly interesting and cannot be ignored.

16 January

The Japanese ambassador, Shigeru Yoshida,[1] paid me an unexpected visit. ... Yoshida had evidently come to provide some reassurance about the impact of

---

[1] Shigeru Yoshida, Japanese ambassador to Great Britain (1936–39) and prime minister (1946–54).

the German–Japanese pact and, while he was about it, to demonstrate that he did not belong to the aggressive school of Japanese political thought. Certainly, Y. was very candid. He was sharply critical of the actions taken by the army and navy of his country, and said that the Japanese people had to pay heavily for their 'stupidities'. ...

12 March

On 4 March, all heads of diplomatic missions submitted their credentials to the new king, George VI.[2] The procedure was simplified and carried out *en masse*. All the ambassadors and envoys were lined up in order of seniority in the Bow Room of Buckingham Palace. They were admitted one by one to the neighbouring room, where the king was expecting them, submitted their credentials to him, exchanged a few remarks as demanded by protocol, and left, giving way to those still waiting. The king devoted two or three minutes to each diplomat. Eden was present at the ceremony and gave some assistance, as the king is taciturn and easily embarrassed. He also stammers. The entire ceremony went smoothly. The only shock, which caused quite a stir in the press and in society, was Ribbentrop's 'Nazi salute'. When the German ambassador entered the room to meet the king, he raised his right hand in greeting, rather than making the usual bow. This 'novelty' offended the English deeply and triggered an adverse reaction in conservative circles. Ribbentrop was accused of tactlessness and was compared with me – a 'good boy' who greets the king properly, without raising a clenched fist above his head.[3]

To meet the diplomats' wives, the king and queen also gave a five o'clock tea party today, inviting the heads of missions and their spouses. Ribbentrop again saluted the king with a raised hand, but he bowed to the queen in the normal manner. The little princesses were also present: Elizabeth[4] and Margaret Rose,[5] both wearing light pink dresses and, it was clear, terribly excited to be present at such an 'important' ceremony. But they were also curious in a childish way about everything around them. They shifted from one foot to the other, then they began to giggle, and then to misbehave, to the considerable embarrassment of the queen. Lord Cromer[6] led my wife and me to the royal couple and we had quite a

---

[2] King George VI, 1936–52.
[3] Maisky summed up his impression of Ribbentrop: 'Since I sat for a whole year diagonally opposite the German ambassador at the table of the Committee for "Non-intervention", I had the opportunity of studying him at close quarters. And I must without mincing words say that this was a coarse, dull-witted maniac, with the outlook and manners of a Prussian N.C.O. It has always remained a mystery to me how Hitler could have made such a dolt his chief adviser on foreign affairs.'
[4] Queen Elizabeth II of Great Britain and Northern Ireland since 1952.
[5] Princess Margaret Rose Windsor (countess of Snowdon), daughter of George VI.
[6] Rowland Thomas Baring (2nd earl of Cromer).

long chat – I with the king and Agniya with the queen. The ladies were, for the most part, discussing children, whereas the king inquired about the state of our navy and the White Sea–Baltic Canal. The king expressed great satisfaction when I informed him that the battleship *Marat* would arrive for the coronation.

16 April

My wife and I were invited by Eden to lunch at the Savoy. The guests were a mixed bunch: Minister for the Coordination of Defence Inskip,[7] Marshal of the Diplomatic Corps Clive, the Chinese ambassador, the Austrian, and others, all in all 25 people. I was the senior guest.

At lunch, Eden's wife couldn't stop complaining about how busy she was and, most of all, about the haste with which everything had to be done. Not a moment to reflect, or to catch one's breath. Everything moves at breakneck speed, and you find yourself caught in a maelstrom from which there is no escape. Truly, our fathers and grandfathers lived in better times! Everything in the world was quieter, calmer and steadier then. There was time enough for taking a walk, reading a book or having a think. 'Why wasn't I born in that time?' Mrs Eden sighed.

After lunch I talked with her husband. Our conversation revolved around Spain. ... So far Eden is succeeding in preserving the British Government's current position, which does not recognize Franco's belligerent rights.

Eden's position on the Spanish question is, in essence, rotten: on the face of it, England does not care which side wins, because Spain will be extremely weakened at the end of its civil war and it will have to start looking for money, which it can find only in London or Paris. The pound is more powerful than the cannon. Therefore, the British Government does not worry too much about the outcome of the Spanish war. On the other hand, Eden is terribly afraid that England might get trapped in the Spanish events, since Spain, according to Eden, is a death-trap for anyone who tries to poke their nose into its affairs. Take Napoleon, Wellington, and now Mussolini. Mussolini's prestige was much higher prior to his Spanish adventure than it is at the moment. And unless he hastens to leave Spain, he is headed for a bad end.

Here Eden added with a cunning smile: 'You are conducting your Spanish campaign brilliantly: you are doing whatever you consider necessary without getting bogged down. You even preserve the appearance of complete inno-cence.' I replied in the same tone: 'Now even Ribbentrop has stopped yelling about the fact that there is a large Soviet army in Spain.' 'An army, you say?' Eden exclaimed. 'You've given the Spaniards something far more important than an army, particularly an army like the Italian one.' I grinned and said: 'The

---

[7] Thomas Inskip (1st Viscount Caldecote), minister for coordination of defence, 1936–39.

Non-Intervention Committee deemed the USSR's participation in the war in Spain to be unproven.'

18 April

The Vansittarts came to us for lunch. The lunch was *à quatre* and our conversation was quite frank. Vansittart is certain that the Cabinet will be restructured after the coronation, with Baldwin resigning, Chamberlain taking his place, and Simon most probably becoming chancellor of the Exchequer. Eden will remain in his post. When I inquired about Chamberlain's foreign policy, V. said that its general character would not change, but that it would become somewhat better defined. As regards Germany, Chamberlain is considered *all right*. Well, we shall see. I'm somewhat sceptical about V.'s assurances. I recall how, in the spring of 1935, he also tried to set my mind at rest concerning Hoare, and we know how that turned out...

According to V., anti-German and anti-Italian sentiments are growing in England. A change in the position of *The Times* is particularly telling in this respect. Even Lothian treats Germany with increasing suspicion. The prospects for a new Locarno pact are very faint. ...

21 April

Eden and his wife came to dinner at the embassy. There were many diplomats, public figures and other guests. On the whole, it went off well.

After dinner I had a long talk with Eden. ... Spain, naturally, occupied most of our discussion, and Eden, to my mind, displayed unjustified optimism. Germany is increasingly inclined to leave Spain. The same tendency is growing in Italy, where the 'Spanish war' is becoming less and less popular.

... If Eden's expectations were to materialize (and he hopes they will), the ground would be cleared for the major European issues to be addressed by early winter. All the more so as British armaments will have increased considerably by that time, whereas the internal difficulties of Germany and Italy will have intensified.

I objected to this and criticized Eden's conception. In particular, I expressed my utter conviction that Mussolini was not going to leave Spain so easily. I sense this at every session of the Non-Intervention Committee. Eden stuck to his guns and finally said: 'You Soviets are eternal pessimists. You see dangers everywhere, even where there are none.'

'But don't you find that nine times out of ten we turn out to be right?' I retorted.

Eden laughed, but at that moment his wife came up to say goodbye.

24 May

The battleship *Marat*, which had arrived to take part in the coronation festivities, left yesterday. She was docked at Spithead for a week. The effect of her appearance was certainly positive. First, it was a sort of official recognition of the Soviet navy on the part of England. Soviet ships had never participated in naval parades in Great Britain before. Second, it was a good display of the efficiency of our navy. Two things particularly impressed the English: (a) during that week there was not a single case of drunken misbehaviour, a single fight or a single scandal involving sailors from the *Marat*. So the 'jail' prepared for Soviet sailors just in case remained empty, whereas similar 'jails' prepared for sailors from other countries had no lack of clientele; (b) on entering Spithead, the *Marat* moored in the space of 55 minutes, whereas warships of other nations spent several hours on this operation, while, at the previous coronation in 1911, it had taken a Russian battleship a whole 15 hours. Third, the arrival of the *Marat* was interpreted in court and political circles as a sign of the USSR's friendly disposition towards England. Churchill told me that the king and the government were particularly impressed by the 'Hurrah!' with which the *Marat* sailors greeted the passing royal yacht, as custom demands. It was an ordinary Russian 'Hurrah!', broad, booming and repercussive. However, compared to

22. The sailors of the battleship *Marat* being greeted by the ambassador, having impressed Churchill and the king with their 'Hurrah!' and exemplary behaviour.

the short and abrupt hurrahs of the English and most other nations, which sounded rather like the barking of dogs...

9 June

I went to see Vansittart. ... I said that I had observed a certain shift in Anglo-German relations lately. I listed a number of facts: the transfer of Phipps from Berlin to Paris; the appointment of Sir Nevile Henderson,[8] a fervent Germanophile, as ambassador to Berlin instead of Phipps, whom Hitler dislikes; a change in the tone of the British Conservative press with regard to Germany; the broad coverage in the English press of the dispatching of medical personnel by air to Gibraltar to render aid to the wounded sailors of the *Deutschland*;[9] and, finally, Henderson's speeches in Berlin, during the presentation of credentials and especially at the dinner arranged by the Anglo-German Society.[10] All this induced certain thoughts. I stressed, in particular, that Henderson's last speech had caused 'amazement' in Moscow, not to mention other more definite emotions.

V., of course, tried to persuade me that nothing had changed, that everything remained as before. Mere 'running on the spot'. ... As for Henderson, his Berlin speech at the English–German dinner was entirely his own creation ... but he pleaded 'mitigating circumstances': Henderson's inexperience and his poor knowledge of current European politics – he has been in South America until now. V. expressed the hope that Henderson would be more careful in future. ...

[The drift towards 'appeasement' became the subject of conflicting appraisals in Narkomindel and the London embassy. Litvinov held on to his belief that the British Government was intent on washing its hands of Spain, while Maisky was 'not inclined to attach much significance' to the overtures made to Berlin. He expected Hitler to produce 'new tricks' which would bring rapprochement to an end.]

16 June

Today I called on Titulescu,[11] who is staying, as always, in the Ritz Hotel and who is his usual noisy, dazzling, confident and even impudent self.

---

[8] Sir Nevile Henderson, British ambassador to Germany, 1937–39.
[9] The cruiser was shelled by the Republican forces on 29 May 1937. Maisky warned Moscow on 3 June that the British were seeking to bypass the Committee for Non-Intervention by making separate arrangements with Germany, Italy and France, a 'four-power pact in practice'.
[10] A society set up by various bankers in the City in conjunction with the Imperial Policy Group, aimed at drawing Great Britain closer to Nazi Germany and Japan.
[11] Nicolae Titulescu, Rumanian foreign minister, 1927–28 and 1932–36, and permanent representative at the League of Nations, 1920–36.

Titulescu has been in London for about a week. He has managed to see Chamberlain, Eden, Vansittart, Churchill and many others in high places.

... . Titulescu has been saying more or less the same things to everyone: peace in Europe and the integrity of the British Empire depend on whether *a peace front led by England, France, and the USSR can be set up in good time*. If this happens, everything will be fine. If not, mankind in general and Great Britain in particular will have to endure a two-act tragedy: Act 1 is the forging of *Mitteleuropa* by Germany, and Act 2 is the destruction of the British Empire by *Mitteleuropa*. The British should make their choice and do so urgently.

... . Titulescu also observed that Germanophile sentiments have grown considerably in England since his last visit to London in March 1936.

In reply to my question about his plans for the near future, Titulescu first told me the story, at very great length, of how the Germans have attempted to poison him three times in Switzerland and Bucharest. Then he said that he would return to Rumania in October. It was dangerous, of course, but he had to do it. He did not want to become a defector, as it would mean the end of his serious political activity and struggle. Titulescu, after all, is full of fire and determination. He dropped a typical remark on parting: 'If I am not assassinated within the first six months after my return home, Rumania will be mine!'[12]

1 July

Conversation with Lloyd George

... The moment I mentioned the word 'government', Lloyd George all but leapt out of his seat. 'Government?' he asked sarcastically, 'Is it really a government? It's rather an assembly of mediocrities, a group of hopeless milksops. Do they have will? Or courage? Can they guard our interests? They inherited a rich legacy from their ancestors, but they are managing it very badly, and I am afraid they will squander it. They are all wretched cowards. It is not cowardice, but daring that is needed to build and protect our Great Empire!'

I observed that very few major figures could be seen on the European democratic horizon at the moment.

'You are absolutely right,' Lloyd George exclaimed. 'Where are they, the major figures? European democracy is in famine. ... There's no point looking in England or France. Baldwin, Chamberlain, Blum or Chautemps[13] – what are

---

[12] Titulescu, who had floated the idea of a mutual assistance pact with the Russians, had been removed from office by King Carol at the end of 1936. His support of an agreement was not based on any liking for Moscow, but on 'a desire to keep Russia sweet, and prevent her from claiming Bessarabia'.

[13] Camille Chautemps, French socialist prime minister, February 1930, 1933–34, and 1937–38.

any of them good for? They have to deal with genuinely significant and powerful individuals – Hitler and Mussolini. Those fascist dictators are no fools. They are made of rough stuff and they use rough methods: force, impertinence and intimidation. But they act, they are vigorous and energetic, and their countries follow after them. Are our ministers good enough to stand up for our interests in the face of dictators? Are they capable of that? Not a bit of it! If Winston Churchill were prime minister, he would know how to make the dictators reckon with him, but the Conservatives are terrified of admitting Churchill to the government. As a result, we have milksops dealing with men of action – Hitler and Mussolini. What a shame that both are fascists and opponents of democracy. But one has to admit that they are men of strength. Can you imagine what could happen if, say, Eden had talks with Mussolini? Mussolini would be sure to wipe the floor with him. That is exactly what happened at the time of the Abyssinian war. Your Stalin is a quite different matter. He is a big and very decisive man. He has a strong grip, he can impress dictators and he is capable of successfully repulsing Hitler and Mussolini. Ours are a sheer misfortune. Take Chamberlain – a narrow, limited and fruitless individual. A fish with a cold head – that's how I described him during the recent debates in Parliament. ... Chamberlain's "master plan" amounts to the following: to make peace with Germany and Italy within the next year and to conclude a pact of four. As to Central and South-East Europe, Chamberlain is ready to rest satisfied with the dictators' vague pledges of non-aggression. Your country is to be shut out of the European mix and be left to its own devices. After achieving all this, Eden wants to go to the polls. He will tell the voters: "The insoluble problem of European appeasement has been resolved by me and my government. Now everything is all right. Vote Tory!" Having won the election, he'll secure his party's rule for another five years. The invitation to Neurath to visit London was his doing. ...'

'However,' Lloyd George went on, 'I'll tell you frankly that our opposition, Labour in particular, is scarcely better than the Government. It's worse and weaker in fact. The opposition has neither leaders, nor programme, nor energy, nor fighting spirit.'

... I asked Lloyd George about his impressions from his visit to Germany last year. Lloyd George livened up and said: 'I went to see Hitler and had a long talk with him. He struck me as a very unpretentious, modest and quite well-educated man. One can discuss things with him and exchange opinions calmly. Yet, he has a sore point – communism. Every time Hitler mentioned communism or communists he immediately became deranged and his very face suddenly changed: his eyes flashed with sinister fire, and his lips began to twitch convulsively. Several times I tried to bring it home to him that unhealthy relations with your country could only put Germany at a disadvantage. But that made no impression on Hitler. He would begin shouting again, all but foaming at the mouth, about communism and the communist menace. He really believes that he was called to this world to accomplish a special mission: to save Western civilization and crush the hydra of communism. After all I saw at this meeting, I am entirely convinced that he will never agree to sign any sort of treaty with the Soviet Union, nor will he ever put his name to an international document alongside the signature of Stalin.'

27 July

Conversation with Eden

Eden invited me to come to see him in the House of Commons. He told me that he was about to take a three-week vacation (but without leaving the country). Lord Halifax would act for him while he was absent.

... Eden began with the Far East. Just this morning he received alarming news from Peking. His initial optimism, it seems, has proved unjustified. The events in China are taking a very serious turn and the Japanese may enter Peking any day now.

Then Eden asked for our evaluation of the events in China. I replied that their true nature was hardly in doubt any longer. Japan is trying to repeat the 'Manchurian incident' that happened six years ago. In other words, Japan is aiming to establish a second Manchukuo in northern China. Her technique is identical to that employed in 1931. In her attempts to expand, Japan, like any aggressor, will be guided primarily by empirical, opportunistic considerations. She will probe how far she can go with impunity. Therefore the success or failure of the new Japanese venture will depend greatly on two factors: (1) the strength of Chinese resistance, and (2) the behaviour of the great powers with interests in the Far East.

... I asked Eden how other great powers planned to react to this prospect. Eden shrugged his shoulders and said: 'I don't know.' He told me that he had tried twice to draw the USA into a united front of three powers (Britain, the United States and France) against Japanese aggression, but without success. ...

[After his appointment as prime minister in May 1937, Chamberlain hastened to seize the initiative from Eden and pursue his own foreign policy. He hoped to restore good relations with Italy by recruiting her to a four-power pact together with Germany and France. Maisky first met Neville Chamberlain, then chancellor of the Exchequer, on 16 November 1932. Though scornful of the 'revolting but clever little Jew', Chamberlain's early contacts with Maisky did not betray the animosity which would settle in later.

The contrast between Chamberlain's attitude to the Italian ambassador, Grandi,[14] and Maisky – both of whom he met on the same day – set out in a letter to his sister, is most telling: 'My interview with Grandi seems to have made a very good impression in Italy and I see they have now "revealed" that I sent a personal letter to Mussolini ... My interview with Maisky was at his request and no doubt was intended by him to be a counter demonstration. But he hadn't really anything to say.']

29 July

Conversation with Chamberlain

1. Following the English custom, I had long been planning to pay an official visit to the new PM.[15] ... He received me in his office in the House of Commons on 29 July. Knowing that he was very busy, I decided not to waste time and to take the bull by the horns. I already had information before visiting Chamberlain that the conclusion of a four-power pact, and especially the improvement of relations between Britain and Germany, represented the general line of his foreign policy. I wanted to check whether this was true and asked him straightaway: which in his view are the best methods to achieve the 'appeasement of Europe'?

2. Chamberlain, who clearly hadn't been expecting a question of this sort, hesitated and looked at me either in surprise or embarrassment. Then he began his reply, articulating his words slowly and occasionally faltering: 'I cannot suggest a shortcut to achieving this result. The appeasement of Europe is a complicated and lengthy business. It demands great patience. Any means and any methods that might prove effective are good. Any available opportunity should be exploited.' The PM paused for a moment, pondered and continued: 'I think that a successful settlement of the Spanish question could be the first direct step towards the appeasement of Europe.' ... Does Chamberlain think that the Italians and the Germans are really ready to withdraw their so-called 'volunteers' from Spain? I doubt it. Chamberlain did not answer at once. He first looked out the window, then at the ceiling, before beginning slowly: 'There is no doubt that Mussolini is very keen to see a fascist Spain. ... In Mussolini's opinion, Franco's victory is needed to avoid Spain turning into a "Bolshevik state". If Franco fails, the triumph of communism in Spain is, he says, inevitable, and that is something Italy cannot accept.'

... Then the PM inquired what we think about the Spanish conflict and what position the USSR holds in the matter. I provided the requisite explanations and underlined our desire to eliminate intervention and turn the Spanish

---

[14] Dino Grandi, Italian minister of foreign affairs, 1929–32; ambassador to Great Britain, 1932–39; minister of justice, 1939–43.
[15] Maisky had been laid low by a severe bout of malaria.

conflict into a purely Spanish affair. True to our common principles, we, too, are striving to secure 'the right to national self-determination' for the Spanish people. We do not aim to establish a communist or any other system in Spain. ... Chamberlain listened to my account with great attention and evident sympathy, but afterwards it immediately became clear that he had understood it in his own way. The PM said: 'Mussolini wants to establish a fascist state in Spain, and you do not want this to happen. We are facing two extremes. Britain tries to hold an intermediate position between you and Mussolini.' I objected that he was giving a false picture of the actual state of affairs. In fact, Mussolini wants to establish a very definite regime in Spain – a fascist one – while the USSR is not striving to establish some particular regime there, whether socialist, communist or other.

... The PM paused again and turned to another subject. 'I am constantly troubled by one particular thought: today's Europe is full of fear and suspicion. Countries and states do not trust each other. As soon as one power begins to arm, another instantly begins to suspect that these arms are set against it and also starts to arm to parry the real or imaginary threat. ... Years and years will be needed to appease Europe. But at least the first step could be taken towards creating a more benevolent atmosphere in our part of the globe, could it not?' I asked Chamberlain what exactly he had in mind. The PM answered: 'Alongside the Spanish question, there is a second, very important and urgent question – the German one. I consider it very important to make the Germans move from general phrases about the "haves" and "have nots", the true meaning of which nobody understands, to a practical and business-like discussion of their wishes. If we could bring the Germans to the negotiating table and, with pencil in hand, run through all their complaints, claims and wishes, this would greatly help clear the air or at least clarify the current situation. We would then know what the Germans wanted and we would also know whether it would be possible to satisfy their demands. If it were possible, we would go as far as we could to meet them; if not, we would take other decisions.'

... The conversation left me with the general impression that Chamberlain is seriously entertaining the idea of a four-power pact and of organizing Western security, and is prepared to make considerable concessions to Germany and Italy in order to attain his goal. However, if it were to transpire in the course of events that an agreement with those two countries was impossible or that the price England had to pay for the agreement was unacceptable, he would take a far firmer stand towards the fascist powers than was taken by Baldwin.[16]

---

[16] Maisky remembered Chamberlain saying: 'Oh, if we could sit down with Hitler at the same table with pencils in our hands and go over all the differences between us, I am sure that the atmosphere would clear up immensely!'

1 August

The Far East is on fire. The consequences are hard to foresee, but they may be immense.

As soon as the Japanese launched an offensive near Peking in mid-July, the Chinese ambassador in Moscow asked what we were planning to do. He was particularly interested to know whether we were ready to interpose separately or together with other powers. M.M. [Litvinov] answered that we would not interpose separately, but that if a joint démarche were proposed to us, we would discuss it.

... Chinese Minister of Finance K'ung,[17] who recently arrived in England from the USA, visited me on 23 July, accompanied by Quo Tai-chi.[18] K'ung, a thickset vigorous man of about 50 with sharp gestures and rough manners, lost no time in demanding our aid to China, stressing rather clumsily that the seizure of Peking by the Japanese would be merely a prelude to an attack on the USSR. ... K'ung also said that in Germany, before his visit to the USA, he spoke

23. Struggling with Chinese food at the house of Quo, the Chinese ambassador.

---

[17] Hsiang-hsi K'ung, Chinese minister of finance, 1933–44, and governor of the Bank of China, 1933–45.
[18] Quo Tai-chi, Chinese ambassador to London, 1932–41; Chinese delegate to the League of Nations, 1934–38; minister of foreign affairs, April–December 1941.

with the leaders of the regime and found Göring to be utterly anti-Soviet and Schacht,[19] on the contrary, to be a 'Sovietophile', while Hitler, allegedly as the result of a two-hour talk with K'ung, began to yield to the thought that the normalization of relations between Germany and the USSR was *perhaps* possible.

... Quo Tai-chi visited me today. He told me that he had seen Eden twice and had insisted on the USSR being brought into a joint action in the Far East. Eden declined his request, however, arguing that this would only have complicated the situation. Quo is of the impression that Eden is simply afraid of Germany and Italy. ... According to Quo, the British ambassador in Berlin, Henderson, is trying to talk Dodd,[20] the American ambassador in Germany, into raising a joint Anglo-American loan for Hitler. Also, in his talks with the Nazi leaders he expressed the opinion that Britain would easily be reconciled to the annexation of Austria and Czechoslovakia by Germany on 'federal terms'. Son of a bitch!

10 August

Masaryk called on me. I'll note the following from his accounts. (1) He asked Vansittart bluntly the other day: what is the British attitude to Czechoslovakia's 'Russian policy', and particularly to the Czecho-Soviet pact? There is a widespread opinion in Europe that England disapproves of this policy and, in particular, of the pact. Is this true? Vansittart replied that it was absolutely untrue. Taking into consideration the current situation in Europe, Britain quite understands and even approves of the present relations between Czechoslovakia and the USSR. (2) Masaryk defines Britain's attitude to Czechoslovakia in this way: Britain is not indifferent to the fate of Czechoslovakia; it even sympathizes with Czechoslovakia as the outpost of democracy in Central Europe; but its sympathy is lukewarm and one can hardly count on an energetic response from London, were Czechoslovakia to be endangered. It seems to me that Masaryk's description of the situation is correct. (3) Vansittart and the Foreign Office in general are unhappy about the PM's flirtation with Mussolini. They think that the ground is not yet ready for an agreement and, above all, they are annoyed by the fact that Chamberlain has completely ignored the FO in his attempts to reach an understanding with Italy.

23 August

I visited Vansittart ... In general, V. was in a very pessimistic frame of mind, particularly with regard to the Far East and the Mediterranean. Things are

---

[19] Hjalmar Schacht, president of Reichsbank, 1923–30 and 1933–39; minister of economics, 1934–37; minister without portfolio, 1939–43.
[20] William Edward Dodd, American ambassador in Germany, 1933–37.

getting worse and worse, the danger is ever nearer, yet no real measures are taken to fight it. Where is the world headed?

V. spoke bitterly about the fact that international complications have spoiled everybody's vacations this year. He himself has to remain in London permanently. Eden is having a holiday, but within England and for just three weeks – with trips to the capital every now and again. Even the PM had to interrupt his holidays and convene an extraordinary meeting of the Cabinet. This is the first time since the war that the PM has not been able to spend his holidays in peace.[21] This is what we have come to!

I listened to V. and smiled to myself: if only the spoilt vacations were the only trouble!

27 October[22]

The first 'five-year plan' of my ambassadorship in England has come to an end! ...

Five years have passed since then. What years they were! ... A thought runs through my mind, like lightning: 'How much time have I to spend here? What will I see? What will I live through? And what will the future bring me?...'

16 November

Today Agniya and I attended the 'state banquet' given by George VI in honour of King Leopold of Belgium, who has arrived on a four-day visit. It was a banquet like any other: 180 guests, the entire royal family, members of government, ambassadors (but not envoys) and various British notables. We ate from gold plates with gold forks and knives. The dinner, unlike most English dinners, was tasty (the king is said to have a French cook). Two dozen Scottish 'pipers' entered the hall during the dinner and slowly walked around the tables several times, filling the palace vaults with their semi-barbarian music. I like this music. There is something of Scotland's mountains and woods in it, of the distance of bygone centuries, of man's primordial past. Pipe music has always had a strange, exciting effect on me, drawing me off somewhere far away, to broad fields and boundless steppes where there are neither people nor animals, and where one feels oneself young and brave. But I saw that the music was not to the taste of many guests. They found it rough, sharp and indecently loud in

---

[21] Chamberlain exploited Eden's absence to embark on negotiations with the Italians behind his back, aimed at liquidating the conflict over the Abyssinia crisis.
[22] This entry has been moved to the prologue in this diary.

the atmosphere of palatial solemnity and refinement. Leopold was one of the disgruntled diners...

After two speeches made by George VI and Leopold, who proclaimed unbreakable friendship between their states, the guests moved to the adjacent halls and we, the ambassadors, were gathered in the so-called Bow Room, where the two kings, ministers and some high-ranking courtiers were located. The ladies were in a neighbouring hall with the young queen and the old queen mother. Here, once again, everything was as it always is at 'state banquets': first the kings talked between themselves while the ambassadors propped up the walls like expensive 'diplomatic furniture'. Then Lord Cromer and other courtiers began buzzing among the guests and leading the 'lucky few', who were to be favoured with the 'very highest attention', to one or other of the kings. Leopold conversed with Chamberlain, Hoare, Montagu Norman (governor of the Bank of England) and, from among the ambassadors, with Grandi, Ribbentrop and Corbin.[23] There was an obvious orientation towards the 'aggressor' and the aggressor's collaborator.

Naturally enough, I was not so honoured: the USSR is out of fashion today, especially in the upper echelons of the Conservative Party. Japanese Ambassador Yoshida, who skulked in a corner, was not invited to pay his respects either. No wonder: Japanese guns are currently firing on British capital and British prestige in China!...

I eventually tired of this dull spectacle and I was already planning to slip out to the other rooms, where I could see many interesting people I knew. But at that moment there was a sudden commotion in the Bow Room. I looked up and realized what was happening. Lord Cromer, emerging from a neighbouring room, led Churchill to Leopold and introduced him. George soon joined them. The three of them carried on a lively and lengthy conversation, in which Churchill gesticulated forcefully and the kings laughed out loud. Then the audience ended. Churchill moved away from the kings and bumped into Ribbentrop. Ribbentrop struck up conversation with the famous 'German-eater'. A group immediately formed around them. I did not hear what they were talking about, but I could see from a distance that Ribbentrop was, as usual, gloomily pontificating about something, and that Churchill was joking in reply, eliciting bursts of laughter from the people standing around. Finally Churchill seemed to get bored, turned around and saw me. Then the following happened: in full view of the gathering, and in the presence of the two kings, Churchill crossed the hall, came up to me and shook me firmly by the hand. Then we entered into an animated and extended conversation, in the middle of which King George walked up to us and made a comment to Churchill. The

---

[23] Andre Charles Corbin, French ambassador in Great Britain, 1933–40.

impression was created that George, troubled by Churchill's inexplicable proximity to the 'Bolshevik ambassador', had decided to rescue him from the 'Moscow devil'. I stepped aside and waited to see what would happen next. Churchill finished his conversation with George and returned to me to continue our interrupted conversation. The gilded aristocrats around us were well-nigh shocked.

What did Churchill have to say?

Churchill told me straight away that he considers the 'anti-communist pact' to be directed against the British Empire in the first place and against the USSR only in the second. He attaches a great deal of importance to this agreement between the aggressors, not so much for the present as for the future. Germany is the chief enemy. 'The main task for all of us who defend the cause of peace,' Churchill continued, 'is to stick together. Otherwise we are ruined. A weak Russia presents the greatest danger for the cause of peace and for the inviolability of our Empire. We need a strong, very strong Russia.' At this point, speaking in a low voice and as if in secret, Churchill began asking me: what was happening in the USSR? Hadn't the most recent events weakened our army? Hadn't they shaken our ability to withstand pressure from Japan and Germany?

'May I reply with a question?' I began, and continued: 'If a disloyal general commanding a corps or an army is replaced by an honest and reliable general, is this weakening or strengthening an army? If a director of a big gun factory, engaged in sabotage, is replaced by an honest and reliable director, is this the weakening or the strengthening of our military industry?' I continued in this vein, dismantling the old wives' tales which are currently so popular here about the effect of the 'purge' on the general condition of the USSR.

Churchill listened to me with the greatest attention, although he shook his head distrustfully every now and again. When I had finished, he said: 'It is very comforting to hear all this. If Russia is growing stronger, not weaker, then all is well. I repeat: we all need a strong Russia, we need it very much!' Then, after a moment's pause, Churchill added: 'That Trotsky, he is a perfect devil. He is a destructive, and not a creative force. I'm wholly for Stalin.'

I asked Churchill what he thought about Halifax's forthcoming visit to Berlin.[24] Churchill pulled a wry face and said that he regarded the trip as a mistake. Nothing will come of it; the Germans will only turn up their noses even more and treat the visit as a sign of England's weakness. This is no use either to

---

[24] Halifax accepted an invitation to Germany in his capacity as the 'Master of the Middleton Hunt' to attend an international hunting exhibition in Berlin, in the course of which he had a lengthy talk with Hitler. In the meantime, Maisky had gleaned from Lloyd George that the reconciliation with Germany had become Chamberlain's main goal, even if it meant sacrificing Spain, Austria and Czechoslovakia and was pursued against Eden's specific will.

England or to the cause of peace. But at least Halifax is an honest man and will not succumb to any 'disgraceful' schemes, such as betraying Czechoslovakia or giving Germany a free hand in the East. All the same, they should never have bothered with this visit!

Churchill shook my hand and proposed that we should meet more often.

[The three waves of purges at Narkomindel commenced at the end of 1937, gathered momentum after the Munich Conference, and peaked with the dismissal of Litvinov in early May 1939 and the subsequent cleansing of the Commissariat for Foreign Affairs. Stalin was determined to break up the old cliques and, above all, to stamp out the prevailing dual allegiances – to him and to patrons in the various party and state institutions. The Commissariat for Foreign Affairs was especially vulnerable, as the recruitment of key personnel was conducted personally by Chicherin and Litvinov from a cosmopolitan, polyglot and independent-minded retinue, in many cases members of the revolutionary intelligentsia from the tsarist days. Cosmopolitanism in particular implied contamination through direct contact with the seductive bourgeois environment. The old cadres were to be replaced by a new generation of leaders, devoid of an 'inflated sense of their own worth, due to revolutionary service', who owed their promotion to Stalin personally.

At least 62 per cent of top-level diplomats and officials among the old guard at the commissariat were wiped out, while only 16 per cent remained in post, as Narkomindel was infiltrated by NKVD officials. The all-consuming purge and basic survival instincts set diplomats against each other both secretly and publicly. Second, and just as significant, was the ravaging image of the Terror abroad. Maisky was alarmed by the execution of Litvinov's deputy, Krestinsky,[25] who was replaced by Potemkin, a cunning and ambitious diplomat who was 'wriggly, adulatory' in Litvinov's presence, but out of his superior's sight left no one in any doubt that he could be at least as good a commissar for foreign affairs.

'The past winter and the current summer,' Maisky lamented to his brother, 'have been very agitated in the sphere of international affairs, and this has significantly affected my health. What is more, I have been on average 50% busier this year than before. ... With time this has had a significant effect on my nerves, my attention, and – taken together – my day-to-day work.' His oblique reference above to the trying situation is typical of the mood of subdued depression which had enveloped the Soviet diplomatic corps throughout Europe as the wave of repressions started to lap at Narkomindel's door. Circumspection had clearly become the order of the day, as is well illustrated by the paucity of entries in Maisky's diary for the second half of 1937. An

---

[25] Nikolai Nikolaevich Krestinsky, deputy commissar for foreign affairs 1930–37; shot in 1938; rehabilitated posthumously.

indiscreet comment or an emotional outburst could be fatal for a diplomat in the event that he was indicted; yet the need for self-expression and empathy was nigh irresistible. A love letter written by Maisky to Agniya on their wedding anniversary is drenched in allusions to the fragility of the future and the need to celebrate the fleeting moment – and above all the past. It is prefaced by two lines from Anatoly Nekrasov's portentous poem 'A New Year':

... And what has once been taken from life
     Fate is powerless to take back.
     Dear, beloved and ever-so-slightly-crazy Agneshechka! The poet's right. The future will bring what it brings, but the 15 years we have spent together are ours, and nobody can do a thing to change that. In memory of these 15 years, which, despite the occasional shadow, were years of love, life, fight and movement ... please accept this modest gift from me. As for the future ... let us stride on, in friendship and good cheer, towards our 'silver wedding'.
     Mikhailych

No wonder, therefore, that when the time arrived for his summer vacation, Maisky was determined to avoid Moscow on his way to the sanatorium. Litvinov, too, was cracking under the pressure: he relished the cure he took in Czechoslovakia, and even more so the five days he could spare before the Assembly of the League met, when he toured Austria and Switzerland and tried to avoid thinking about the gathering clouds on the international scene 'and other unpleasant things'. He now protected his ambassadors by conferring with them in Geneva. Maisky, who a year earlier had been discouraged from attending the Assembly, was now welcomed, but at the same time was instructed to defer his holiday in Russia and remain at his post. Two prominent members of the Soviet delegation in London, the military attaché Putna and Ozersky, the head of the trade delegation, had been recalled and executed. The veteran first secretary at the embassy, Kagan, had also been recalled to Moscow, like so many other experienced diplomats – ostensibly to prevent them from 'being too acclimatized to particular countries'. Rumours were rife in the London press about Maisky's own imminent withdrawal.

It was hard enough to pursue level-headed policy at the time of the purges; but just as testing for Maisky were the constant demands from friends and foes alike to come up with explanations for them. He would, Beatrice Webb noted, be 'reserved about the arrests and rumours of arrests; justifies some, denies the fact of others'. She found Agniya, whose brother-in-law had just been arrested and sent to a gulag, to be 'tired and I think, depressed' and wondered 'whether Maisky will last long as ambassador in England ... The poor Maiskys, what a life they must be leading!' Agniya indeed suffered a nervous breakdown, from which she partially recovered only at the beginning of 1938.]

n.d. circa 20 November[26]

... Although the reaction to the anti-communist pact in England has been sharply negative, this does not mean that the immediate practical conclusions drawn by the ruling elite of the Conservative Party follow a course close to that of our policy. I have informed you more than once about Chamberlain's foreign policy plans: he wants to reach an agreement at all costs with Germany and Italy over some form of 'Western security', and then go to the polls in the role of 'appeaser of Europe' so as to consolidate the power of his party for the next five years. Eden is against this policy, finding it short-sighted and an affront to all the principles of the League of Nations. That discord exists between the PM and the foreign secretary about the general line of British policy is beyond doubt. However, Eden is not a sufficiently major, independent and resolute figure to be in a position to defeat Chamberlain's line. He is supported by 'young' Conservatives. ... Chamberlain, in turn, finds support among the more influential 'old men', like Halifax, Simon and Hoare. Concerning the latter two, their political considerations are mixed with considerations of personal animosity towards Eden. As a result, Chamberlain's line prevails, but its practical implementation is held back to a certain extent by the opposition provided by Eden's group. I take the rumour that Chamberlain is going to replace Eden, possibly with Halifax, with a grain of salt. It is hard to believe that Chamberlain would part with Eden in the capacity of foreign secretary, since Eden is very popular in England and is held in respect by the opposition. Besides, the London diplomatic corps treats him very well, and he has an excellent reputation among the French. To throw Eden out would be to deliver a blow to the Cabinet's prestige and to make it appear utterly reactionary, which would increase the chances of the opposition. And what would be the point? In spite of his disagreements with the foreign secretary, the PM knows full well that Eden wants a career for himself and that, in the final analysis, it is possible to 'get on' with him. Eden is not made of iron, but rather of soft clay which yields easily to the fingers of a skilful artisan.

Now, to turn back to Chamberlain's plans, I am more and more convinced that he is ready to go a long way to implement them. He is ready, for instance, to sacrifice Spain. He is ready to accept German hegemony in Central and South-East Europe, provided the forms it takes are not too odious. It goes without saying that he would not move a finger to help the USSR in the event of an attack on it by the fascist bloc. In general, Chamberlain would be glad to pay a very high price in Europe for the organization of 'Western security'. ...

---

[26] This entry comprises excerpts from a draft letter to Litvinov included within the diary.

1 December

In October, the 'Cliveden Set' proved especially lively and active. It is grouped around Lady Astor's salon and it has *The Times* and the *Observer* as its mouthpieces. The key figures in this clique are Lady Astor, Garvin, Geoffrey Dawson[27] (editor of *The Times*) and Lothian. The latter appears to have been wavering recently, but he has not yet broken with the Cliveden Set. Dawson is particularly energetic.

Lady Astor's group has a powerful representation in Cabinet: the majority of the 'old men', including Hoare, Simon, Halifax, Kingsley Wood,[28] and Hailsham.[29] Hoare plays the most active role among the 'Cliveden' ministers. He hates Eden and wants to take his place. Chamberlain, as PM, tries to be neutral, but he basically shares the attitudes and views of the 'old men'.

The 'old men's' programme roughly boils down to the following.

A deal with Germany and Italy (at least in the form of a four-power pact), even at the cost of great sacrifices: Germany will be given a free hand in Central, South-East and Eastern Europe; Spain will lose out; certain colonial compensations will be granted to Hitler.

... Next comes that which many call, with a smile, the Cliveden Conspiracy.

Here are the stages of the 'conspiracy'.

The 'conspirators' gather in Lady Astor's country estate in Cliveden throughout October. They work out a 'plan' of major action in order to change the general line of British policy in a decisive manner, shifting it towards a four-power pact and rapprochement with Germany. Hoare plays the leading role. Halifax and Kingsley Wood are active participants.

The Field journal sends Halifax an invitation to attend the world hunting fair in Berlin that will be held in November. The 'conspirators' decide to seize the opportunity and organize a 'private meeting' between Halifax and Hitler. Simon and Hailsham are all for it. Chamberlain gives his blessing without himself getting involved. Nevile Henderson (the ambassador in Berlin) tests the ground in Hitler's company. Hitler agrees to meet with Halifax. Eden and Vansittart are bluntly against the venture from the very beginning, but cannot prevent it.

In early November, prior to the signing of the tripartite anti-communist pact in Rome (6 November) a preliminary platform for the discussions,

---

[27] George Geoffrey Dawson, prize fellow of All Souls College, 1898; editor of *The Times*, 1912–19 and 1923–41; a proponent of appeasement.

[28] Sir Howard Kingsley Wood, minister of health, 1935–38; secretary of state for air, 1938–40; lord privy seal April–May 1940; chancellor of the Exchequer in Winston Churchill's Cabinet, 1940–43.

[29] Douglas Hogg (1st Viscount Hailsham), attorney general, 1924–28; lord chancellor, 1928–29 and 1935–38; secretary of state for war, 1931–35.

evidently drawn up by Göring, arrives from Berlin via Henderson. The following is the essence of the 'platform'.

Eden and Vansittart once again categorically object to Halifax's trip, especially in the light of the 'platform'. Chamberlain finds that German demands 'go too far', but thinks that Halifax should still go: why not talk to Hitler all the same? No harm can come of it. A lengthy struggle ensues in Cabinet. Eden, who left for the Brussels conference on 1 November, returns on the 5th for the weekend and tries once again to hinder Halifax's visit. He goes back out to Brussels on the 8th. The question of Halifax's visit remains undecided.

On 10 November, in the absence of Eden, the 'big four' (Chamberlain, Halifax, Hoare and Simon) rush the decision on Halifax's visit through Cabinet and Halifax goes to Germany on 16 November. Eden protests and threatens his resignation (but he does not resign).

... Hitler and Halifax meet in Berchtesgaden. Hitler lectures Halifax and Halifax listens, only occasionally asking questions or making a remark. Hitler speaks in general and relatively modest terms. He asks for the recognition in principle of Germany's right to have colonies without any compensation and the right to adjust relations with Central European countries bilaterally, and intimates that he would be ready to return to a 'reformed' League of Nations under certain conditions. Halifax states that the British Government is not antagonistically disposed to Germany and that it admits the possibility of certain changes in Central Europe, but only by peaceful means and with the consent of France. Practically no mention is made in the conversation of the USSR and communism.

Halifax returns to London on 22 November, rather disheartened. Chamberlain is also disappointed. But Eden rejoices and puts on a feast for a few of his friends in a restaurant on the evening of the 22nd (as Masaryk told me). Mrs Eden is delighted and joyfully announces that the dark clouds looming over her husband have dispersed. In our conversation of 26 November, Harold Nicolson[30] confirms that the outcome of Halifax's visit strengthened Eden's position. However, the danger has not passed, since Chamberlain will certainly try again to come to an understanding with Germany.

... What are my conclusions? Here they are.

The 'Cliveden Conspiracy' has evidently suffered defeat. The attempt to change the course of British foreign policy failed. The policy remains as it was before: that is, weak, vacillating, zigzagging, retreating before the aggressor; but not, at least, a policy of alliance with the aggressor at the expense of third countries.

---

[30] Harold George Nicolson, Foreign Office official, 1909–29; National Labour MP, 1935–45; parliamentary private secretary to the minister of information, 1940–41; society figure and diarist.

Chamberlain was taught a good lesson. Eden's position has been greatly strengthened. The PM will clearly have to 'straighten' his line in the near future.
... The final conclusion: we must be on the alert!

[The ferocious purges meant that Maisky's personal survival had become bound up with the success of collective security, for which the extraordinary connections he had forged in London were vital. This was an extremely delicate balancing act: he had to manoeuvre between the need to provide Moscow with objective evaluation and the need to keep alive the prospects of an alliance with the West. Maisky by no means shared the view that isolation was being forcibly imposed on the Soviet Union. He pleaded with Litvinov to seek compromise. Whether intimidated by Stalin or, more likely, following his own convictions, the defiant Litvinov waved away Maisky's appeals, arguing that: 'We sometimes prefer to be isolated rather than go along with the bad actions of others, and that is why isolation does not scare us.' However, when Maisky resorted to the 'isolation' card to raise concern in London over the plans for a four-power pact, he was severely reprimanded for causing 'unnecessary nervousness and distress'. For the moment Maisky persevered in his efforts to seek collaboration with Eden, and even obtained Stalin's personal approval.]

4 December

Good riddance! Ahlefeldt[31] is a typical diplomat of the pre-war generation, obsessed with etiquette and clueless in politics. Over five years I have failed to observe any real intelligence in him. Only *bonhomie*.

But his wife! Good grief! Tall as a pole, flat as a plank, with a neck so long and dismal that she always had to keep it propped up with a high collar made of spangles, stones and celluloid. The countess was truly hideous. A nose a yard long, eyes like a frog's, and skin that had darkened from decay and spite. Every time I had to look at her I started feeling sick.

In addition to all these charms, Countess Ahlefeldt was from the Russian White Guard. She had once been a maid of honour in the court of Mariya Fedorovna[32] and lived in the Anichkov Palace. Then she fled the revolution and married her splendid 'consort'. Of course she hated us with a visceral loathing, and this was the seed of conflict between the Soviet embassy and the Danish mission; it has lasted throughout the five years of my time in London.

---

[31] Count Preben Ferdinand Ahlefeldt-Laurvig, Danish envoy to Great Britain, 1921–37.
[32] Mariya Fedorovna, wife of Tsar Alexander III.

12 December

Today, spending the weekend with the Webbs.

... Beatrice told us the amusing story of Bernard Shaw's marriage.

The year was 1908. Shaw was earning no more than six pounds a week and living in the countryside with the Webbs. He had a rakish temperament, his affairs never ceased, and the writer's 'girlfriends' made scenes that gave the Webbs no end of trouble. For instance, some of Shaw's jilted girlfriends blamed Beatrice for their frivolous lover's betrayals. They were jealous of her and pestered her with scenes of indignation and despair. Finally Beatrice got bored of all that and decided to have Bernard married.

At that critical juncture, Beatrice's old school friend, Charlotte Townsend, came to visit her. Charlotte was not married and she had a yearly income of some 5,000 pounds following her father's death. Charlotte decided to move in with the Webbs. Beatrice warned her that two men were living there, Shaw and Graham Wallas[33] (the well-known Fabian writer). Charlotte had nothing against it. Beatrice, discussing her matrimonial projects with Sidney, told her husband regretfully about her apprehension that Charlotte, with her character and tastes, would get along better with Wallas (he was a bachelor, too) than with Shaw. To her great surprise and joy, Charlotte and Bernard became the closest of friends in three days. They had a stormy and fast-paced affair, but Shaw did not want to marry, for how could he, a pauper, marry a wealthy woman?

At this time, the Webbs were about to go to America. Beatrice summoned Shaw and told him bluntly: either get married immediately or leave my house. If you stay here without us, your relationship will become too obvious to everyone and it will bring a great deal of trouble.

Shaw refused to marry, moved out on the next day and settled in a garret in London. Charlotte also left. She went to see Rome. The Webbs departed for America.

Sometime later, when they were already in America, the Webbs received a telegram from Wallas saying that Shaw was dying (Shaw had tuberculosis and life in the garret was taking its toll). The news shocked the Webbs and they were about to return to England. However, on the next day they received a second telegram from Wallas that greatly surprised them: Bernard had married Charlotte.

The Webbs were perplexed. Clarification came later. Wallas had first sent a telegram to Charlotte, notifying her that Shaw was ill. Charlotte rushed to

---

[33] Graham Wallas, political psychologist and educationalist, dominant during the Fabian Society's early years along with Sidney Webb and Bernard Shaw.

England and lodged Shaw in a splendid villa. She summoned doctors and a serious course of treatment began. Then Bernard told Charlotte: 'If this is how it is, then we have to marry. It must be fate.' They married the same day. Bernard and Charlotte still live together now. Shaw is 80 and Charlotte 82.

24. Bernard Shaw entertained at the embassy.

1938

4 January

I found Vansittart's name in the New Year's Honours List. But what kind of an 'honour' is this? As yet, it's hard to tell.

V. has been accorded a lofty award and a new position to boot: he ceases to be permanent undersecretary (a most important post as effective head of the Foreign Office staff and thus, to a significant extent, head of the FO itself) and becomes 'chief diplomatic adviser' to the foreign secretary. What does this mean? ... If V. succeeds in working his way into the PM's entourage (like Horace Wilson,[1] chief industrial adviser to the British Government) and in gaining the latter's trust, then the new appointment will represent a major promotion for him, and his influence will grow. If, however, V. fails in this and remains in the capacity of 'adviser' only to the FO, the new appointment will have to be regarded as a demotion or, more precisely, as a retirement ticket, only with uniform, decorations and a pension. We shall see what we shall see. ...

27 January

I visited Vansittart and inquired about his new position and duties.

Judging by what V. told me, matters stand as follows. He remains in the Foreign Office, keeps his old office and reads all the correspondence, but is no longer involved in administrative affairs. ... V. will focus wholly on drawing up and giving advice on the main issues of foreign policy. What will the relations between V. and Cadogan[2] in the sphere of 'advice' be like? ... V. could not clarify this issue at all. The problem evidently persists both for him and for Cadogan. Friction and conflicts are possible. But V. does not intend to surrender. He told me with a laugh: 'I have always given advice, both when I

---

[1] Sir Horace John Wilson, permanent secretary in Ministry of Labour, 1921–30; chief industrial adviser to the British Government, 1930–39; seconded for special service with Chamberlain, 1937–40.
[2] Alexander Cadogan, permanent undersecretary for foreign affairs, 1938–46.

was asked and when I wasn't but thought it necessary. I intend to do the same in the future, too.'

[The Soviet Government, Maisky disclosed to the Webbs, 'was tending towards isolation and though she will not leave the League she will cease to be interested in it. Collective security must be applied everywhere or nowhere – to Germany in the west as well as to Japan in the east.' He was obviously attentive to Zhdanov's[3] frontal attack on Litvinov, during which he had castigated Narkomindel's policies. Zhdanov now chaired the Foreign Affairs Commission of the Supreme Soviet, which gradually took over the formulation of foreign policy from the deflated Politburo and Narkomindel. In his despair, Litvinov had composed, but not sent, a letter of resignation addressed to Stalin.

On 24 January, Maisky begged Litvinov confidentially to allow him to proceed to Geneva within days to discuss 'a highly important personal question'. If it could not be justified as a business trip, he was even prepared to make the journey as 'a private one'. Though there are no reports of what transpired in Geneva, corroborative evidence seems to confirm Maisky's growing concern about the future of Litvinov, his guardian and mentor, no less than about his own continued stay in London. Life had become unbearable, with rumours of his imminent withdrawal circulating widely in the press and with the intrusion of the NKVD into the embassy.]

7 February

So, Hitler has struck a blow at his army![4] The legal 'opposition' to the dominance of the 'party', which grouped around Reichswehr and included big industrialists, landlords, old-school diplomats and so on, has been broken for good. The removal of Schacht was a sign of the approaching climax. Blomberg's[5] marriage to a plebeian was the last straw. Is the 'purge' over? Hard to tell. I am inclined to think that the disgraced military will come in for more exiles, arrests, and so on. To give Hitler his due, he carried out the operation very skilfully and with lightning speed. Even if this is only a 75% victory, it is a victory none the less. ... In general, the army was a restraining factor in German policy: it opposed the occupation of the Rhineland, and it was very

---

[3] Andrei Aleksandrovich Zhdanov, replaced Kirov, after his murder in 1934, as general secretary of the Communist Party in Leningrad; chairman of the RSFSR Supreme Soviet, 1938–47; member of the Politburo, 1939–48. Actively involved in the purges of the thirties, he introduced the *Zhdanov Doctrine* – the rigorous communization of East Europe, as well as the cultural purges of the post-war era.
[4] On 4 February, Hitler concentrated power in his own hands, replacing Werner Fritsch, the army's commander-in-chief, with General Keitel and assuming command of the Wehrmacht, while abolishing the Defence Ministry. Whether or not inspired by Stalin, Hitler went on to purge the Foreign Ministry of its hard core of professional diplomats, replacing Neurath with Ribbentrop at the head of the office.
[5] Werner Fritz von Blomberg, German minister of defence and later minister of war, 1933–38 and commander-in-chief of the German armed forces, 1935–38.

unenthusiastic about the Spanish adventure. The army believed that Germany was not ready for a big war and, for this reason, should not take excessive risks.

What can we expect now, after this crackdown on the military? Increasing aggressiveness in German policy (not for nothing has Ribbentrop been appointed foreign minister), the strengthening of the Axis and the anti-communist bloc and, as a result, the accelerated formation of two fronts, although the latter process may not be a linear one. More purposeful attempts to seize Austria and, perhaps, Czechoslovakia are also very probable, as are a more contentious approach to the issue of colonies and more active support for Japan in the Far East and for Italy in Spain.

The events of 4 February have made a profound impression in England. ... I have no doubt that the British Government's first response will be to expedite Anglo-German negotiations. Chamberlain & Co. will argue that the last chance must be taken to avoid a war. Oh, these eternal appeasers! Is there any end to their short-sightedness and cowardice?

... If Hitler manages not to behave like a bull in a china shop, and particularly if he says a few encouraging words in his speech on 20 February,[6] Chamberlain will be just dying to meet him halfway. The slow pace of the Anglo-German talks, which Vansittart recently spoke to me about, will then speed up and the outline of a four-power pact at the cost of Central, South-East and Eastern Europe will loom clearly on the horizon.

11 February

Went to see Eden. ... I had hardly crossed the threshold when Eden began firing questions at me: what do I think about the German developments? What will be the effect of Goga's[7] resignation? Is Mussolini really going to withdraw from Spain? etc. Eden was in such an animated, even excited state that I had to ask him what he was so pleased about.

Eden confessed that he had not been so happy for quite a while. ... Germany is bound to become weaker for a while due to the latest events. True, the party had won out over the 'moderate' elements, but the newly created 'balance' is by no means fixed and various unexpected things may happen. Eden then listed the various branches of government activity in Germany and, after indicating the changes in personnel since 4 February in the army, economy, foreign ministry and so on, concluded that smaller, less experienced men had replaced

---

[6] Hitler in fact announced his intention of redressing the grievances of the German population in Austria and Czechoslovakia.

[7] Octavian Goga, Rumanian prime minister, 1937–38.

figures of greater weight. This cannot but affect the efficiency of the machinery of the state. When Eden mentioned the foreign ministry, he made a startled comic gesture, as if he were fending off a ghost that had suddenly appeared before him, and exclaimed with a laugh: 'For reasons of diplomatic etiquette I must be silent, but you know what I think!' I laughed out loud. Ribbentrop's shade was hovering over us at that moment. I sharply refuted Eden's optimism and said that, on the contrary, I was now expecting an intensification of German aggression in various directions. Specifically, what would happen to Austria and Czechoslovakia? Eden tried to defend his case, but he was not particularly successful. Eventually, he said that Germany would probably behave more scandalously than ever, but that it would actually become less dangerous. I shook my head distrustfully.

... I criticized Eden once again for his complacency. I would like him to be right, but I do not see sufficient grounds for that to be the case. ... Eden is definitely competing with M.M.! Or, more precisely, at every political turn he wants to remain in contact with the USSR. This is very reassuring. It is this new quality which I have been observing in him recently and which was expressed so vividly during our meeting just before the New Year.

But relations between Eden and Chamberlain are not improving at all. I've learned from various sources that Eden regards settling the Spanish question as a basic prerequisite for an agreement with Italy, while Chamberlain is prepared to give up Spain as a last resort. So far, Eden has evidently succeeded in convincing the Cabinet to back his point of view, but there is no guarantee that tomorrow Chamberlain might not get his revenge.[8]

25 February

After the disturbances and worries of the past few days, life is returning to its normal course. Chamberlain got his way after all, and Halifax was appointed foreign secretary, but it is the PM who will be speaking in the Commons on all the more important foreign policy issues. A certain Butler,[9] former parliamentary assistant minister of labour, has replaced Cranborne. ...

[Maisky penned a portrait of Halifax following his appointment, describing him as 'a typical representative of the old generation of Conservatives'. While praising his

---

[8] Chamberlain's decision to pursue negotiations with Mussolini behind Eden's back led to the latter's resignation on 20 February. Chamberlain confided to his sister that he had gradually reached the conclusion that 'at bottom Anthony did not want to talk either with Hitler or Mussolini, and as I did he was right to go'.
[9] Richard Austen Butler, undersecretary of state, India Office, 1932–37; undersecretary of state for foreign affairs, 1938–41; minister of education, 1941–45.

intellectual and administrative abilities (he had been a prize fellow at All Souls College, Oxford), Maisky dismissed his outlook on foreign policy, which was geared towards achieving a 'balance of power and Western security ... an indifference to Anglo-French cooperation and a proclivity towards a rapprochement with Germany and Italy. His attitude to the Soviet Union is hostile but so far he has made no anti-Soviet appearance.' Once in office, Halifax, who was 'particularly averse to conversations with Russians and Japanese', tended to delegate such meetings to Butler, his parliamentary undersecretary of state.]

1 March

Today Halifax received all the ambassadors, one after the other. Monck met them in the lobby and supervised the visits, notifying each ambassador that he would have 10 to 15 minutes with Halifax.

'Well, that'll be enough,' I remarked jokingly, 'to put some questions to the foreign secretary that will spoil his mood.'

'Alas! Alas!' Monk answered with a touch of melancholy. 'In the old days, it was not the done thing to touch upon serious matters during one's first visit to a newly appointed foreign secretary.' ... Conscious of having so little time at my disposal, I asked Halifax just two questions:

(1) What is Britain's stance towards Central Europe? The answer was barely intelligible: Britain considers itself an interested party in this region, but cannot take on any commitments in advance. Everything will depend on the circumstances. This attitude seems almost deliberately designed to excite Hitler's appetite and provoke him into aggression.

(2) What is Britain's stance towards Spain? More specifically, is an agreement between London and Rome, which would ignore the 'resolution' of the Spanish question in terms of the evacuation of foreign troops from Spain, conceivable?

The answer was again vague and evasive. ...

My questions certainly spoiled Halifax's mood, but at least I now know *where we are.* The new leaders of British foreign policy will not move a finger in regard to either Central Europe or Spain. I even have the feeling that Chamberlain has already decided in his soul to 'sell' Spain to Mussolini for whatever price he deems fair.

Halifax's manners are those of a well-bred English lord. He is polite, almost friendly. Talks little and uses platitudes. Likes to appeal to exalted feelings and noble principles, in which he half believes and, playing the hypocrite, half pretends to believe. He is always mindful of his own interests. Let's see how we get on. ...

8 March

Neville Chamberlain. In order to better understand the origin and significance of the ministerial crisis that ended in Eden's resignation, we must have a clearer understanding of the personality of the current prime minister – Neville Chamberlain ... he is certainly not a man of great stature. He is narrow-minded, dry, limited, lacking not only external brilliance but also any kind of political range. Here, he is often called the 'accountant of politics': he views the whole world primarily through the prism of dividends and exchange quotations. It is for this reason that Chamberlain is a darling of the City, which places implicit trust in him. At the same time, Chamberlain is very obstinate and insistent, and once an idea has lodged in his mind he will defend it until he is blue in the face – a rather dangerous quality for the prime minister of a great power nowadays, but such is his nature. A particularly important trait of Chamberlain's character is his highly developed 'class consciousness', which, of course, is the 'class consciousness' of a great-power British bourgeois.

... Accepting that capitalism's disintegration and the creation of a new social system on its ruins might be inevitable, Baldwin prayed to God for just one thing: 'Let it happen after me! I want to die under capitalism. I'm accustomed to it and I haven't fared so badly under its conditions. The new generation can do what it wants.' Chamberlain is different. He believes in capitalism devoutly. He is firmly convinced that capitalism is not just the best, but also the only possible socio-economic system, which was, is, and will be. Capitalism for Chamberlain is as eternal and unchanging as the principle of universal gravitation. This makes him a vivid and self-confident representative of bourgeois class consciousness, which in our days, as we know, can come decked only in deeply reactionary colours.

Indeed, Chamberlain is a consummate reactionary, with a sharply defined anti-Soviet position. ... He both acknowledges theoretically and <u>feels with his every fibre</u> that the USSR is the principal enemy and that communism is the main danger to the capitalist system that is so dear to his heart. ... Such is the prime minister we have to deal with now in England.

<u>The gathering crisis.</u> ... From the very first days of his premiership, Chamberlain took the following course in regard to Eden: either to 'tame' the foreign secretary and make him an obedient tool of his policy or (if this failed) to get rid of him as quietly as possible. ... The foreign secretary, however, turned out to be a much tougher nut than the PM had expected. Attempts to control Eden ended in failure. ... In the PM's own office, something like a parallel FO was formed, headed by Chamberlain's first secretary Sir Horace Wilson, who acted independently of, and even against the wishes of, the real Foreign Office. Chamberlain acquired his own 'unofficial' and unaccountable agents in various

countries, who supplied him with information contradicting that of the ambassadors and envoys; but the PM trusted this intelligence more than he did Foreign Office reports. ... The relationship between PM and foreign secretary thus grew more strained with every passing month, and their disagreement over the Italian negotiations was merely the straw that broke the camel's back.

The crisis. ... The widow of the late Austen Chamberlain went on holiday to Rome a while ago. Mussolini decided to 'conquer' her, and did so. He showered kindnesses and attention on the honourable Lady Chamberlain and managed to convince her that he was ready to sell Great Britain his 'friendship' for a very modest price. At the same time, however, Mussolini told Lady Chamberlain outright that he could not conceive of an agreement with Britain while Eden remained foreign secretary. Lady Chamberlain assailed her brother-in-law with letters demanding quick and resolute action. Her message to Chamberlain from Mussolini was that the question of reconciliation between Britain and Italy was at the point of 'now or never'. ... Despite Italy's violation of yet another international agreement, Chamberlain did not even frown, but made a renewed and more resolute statement to Grandi that serious talks in Rome were highly desirable. After Grandi's departure, Eden pointed out to the PM the danger of such an approach vis-à-vis the Italians and added that if Chamberlain was intent on sticking to his guns, he, Eden, would have to resign. This was beginning to look like a crisis. So Chamberlain, sidestepping hallowed British tradition, convened a special Cabinet meeting after lunch the following day (19 February), a Saturday, where he raised the question of the immediate commencement of negotiations between Britain and Italy. A great battle followed, in which, as was to be expected, most of the ministers, headed by Chamberlain, Hoare and Simon, spoke against Eden. ... At the end of the meeting, Eden left for the Foreign Office, across the road from the PM's residence, and returned a quarter of an hour later with his letter of resignation. Eden then went home, but there was great agitation among the members of the government. Fearing the repercussions of Eden's resignation, Chamberlain implored several of Eden's closest friends in the Cabinet to persuade him to revoke his resignation. I know that, throughout the evening of 19 February and the morning of 20 February, Elliot, Morrison[10] and young MacDonald[11] went to great lengths to try to keep Eden in the Cabinet, but Eden would not budge. On Sunday, 20 February, another special Cabinet meeting was set for 3 p.m., at which Chamberlain himself, supported by a large number of his colleagues, tried to get Eden to reverse his decision. This attempt also ended in failure. Eden was adamant.

---

[10] Herbert Stanley Morrison, Labour MP, minister of supply, 1940; home secretary and minister of home security, 1940–45; member of War Cabinet, 1942–45.
[11] Malcolm John MacDonald, secretary of state for dominion affairs, 1935–38 and 1938–39; secretary of state for colonies, 1935 and 1938–40.

What prospects are now in store? ... The events of the next six to eight months will prove critical, and future historians may one day mark 1938 as a decisive year in the development of foreign politics in our era. Meanwhile, we should prepare ourselves for a spell of deterioration in Anglo-Soviet relations, the duration of which will depend directly on the fate of the four-power pact.

[The resignation of Eden, whom Maisky had been meticulously cultivating, was yet another blow to collective security. This was further undermined by the muzzled reaction in Britain to Hitler's annexation of Austria on 12 March – a precursor to the Czechoslovak debacle six months later. 'Extremely pessimistic', Maisky expected Chamberlain to resuscitate the four-power pact, 'excluding the Soviet Union'. He had no high hopes of Chamberlain, who, he assumed, was guided exclusively by his ideological bent. Maisky's main concern was that the crisis might reinforce the drift towards isolation which had 'already been discerned in Moscow for quite some time'. Had it been possible to bring about a closer and more effective alliance between the USSR, France and Britain, he told the French ambassador in London, 'his government would certainly have engaged in a more active policy of European collaboration. The successive disappointments inflicted on her led to the gradual turnabout.' Chamberlain, Maisky told Lloyd George, 'was playing with one card, on which he had put all his money'. Indeed, Chamberlain confided to his sister on 18 March that he had 'abandoned any idea of giving guarantees to Czecho-Slovakia or to France in connection with her obligations to that country'.

Although Litvinov had succeeded in convincing Stalin not to remain 'completely passive', he hardly anticipated a favourable response to his 'final appeal' to Europe for collective action. The appeal was aimed as much at exonerating Russia of possible accusations of isolationism as it was at scotching the widespread rumours that the purges had rendered her militarily weak. Maisky had also to protect himself against the storm brewing in Moscow, where the third public trial of former Trotskyists, accused of plotting with the Germans and Japanese to topple the Soviet regime, had just commenced. Among the accused were the 70-year-old Christian Rakovsky, the first Soviet ambassador to Britain, and Arkady Rosengoltz, who was Maisky's superior in London in 1926. Both were convicted and eventually shot.]

22 March

Today I returned a visit to Kennedy,[12] the new US ambassador to Great Britain. He is quite a character: tall, strong, with red hair, energetic gestures, a loud

---

[12] Joseph Patrick Kennedy, American financier and a heavy contributor to Roosevelt's presidential campaign; American ambassador to Great Britain, 1937–40.

voice, and booming, infectious laughter – a real embodiment of the type of healthy and vigorous *business man* that is so abundant in the USA, a man without psychological complications and lofty dreams.[13]

When Kennedy came to visit me, he stayed for a full hour and exclaimed on leaving: 'Just give me a chance to cope with all these visits and formalities and I'll come and see you. We can spend a couple of hours together discussing all the questions I'm interested in. I like you. You know your business. None of the diplomats here in London have talked to me in such plain, human language. I value that. I'm not really a diplomat. I like to have real conversations.'

Today I visited Kennedy in his new office on Grosvenor Square. It's a four-storey office-type building which houses not just the US embassy, but also all its affiliates: the air and naval attachés, commercial and agricultural counsellors, and others. The entire staff of the embassy, including service personnel, totals 170 employees. Not bad!

Kennedy was roaring with laughter again and, by the by, told me a very interesting thing.

'Tell me something,' he exclaimed. 'All the Brits keep assuring me that, according to the most reliable sources, a profound domestic crisis has taken over your country (which is why trips to the USSR have lately become so complicated for foreigners) and that your army is falling to pieces and is unfit for serious military operations. So, the Brits claim, you would not be able to help Czechoslovakia if it were attacked by Germany, even if you wished to. They are saying the same to the French and asking them: in these circumstances, is it worth you running risks by following to the letter your agreement with Czechoslovakia?'

I ridiculed the English insinuations and clarified the true state of affairs to Kennedy.[14] He thanked me and confessed that he knew virtually nothing about the USSR. He hoped that one day he would visit our country.

So that's what the English are like! Chamberlain wants to tear France away from its Eastern allies and to that end he is exploiting our recent trials. That won't work.

---

[13] 'The Americans', Maisky told Beatrice Webb, 'had no civilisation of their own: they were first rate as mechanics, good organisers, open and alert minded; but fundamentally without a national culture or traditional background, in the sense that these are present in Great Britain, France, Germany and Scandinavia.'

[14] Kennedy wrote to Roosevelt that Maisky, who gave him a long explanation of the trials, 'look[ed] scared to death himself'. Kennedy's impression was that 'if the telephone had rung and said "Come back to Russia", Maisky would have died right on my hands', to which the president responded: 'Poor old Russian Ambassador! I hope he will not die of fright if he is sent for.'

23 March

Conversation with Churchill.

(1) Randolph Churchill[15] rang me up and said that his father wanted very much to see me. We agreed to meet at Randolph Churchill's apartment for lunch. I found Winston Churchill greatly agitated. He took the bull by the horns and addressed me with the following speech: 'Could you, please, tell me frankly what is going on in your country? ... You know my general standpoint. I deeply detest Nazi Germany. I believe it to be an enemy not only of peace and democracy but of the British Empire, too. I think that the only reliable means to restrain this beast could be a "grand alliance" of all peace-loving states within the framework of the League of Nations. Russia should occupy one of the most prominent positions in this alliance. We badly need a strong Russia as a counterweight to Germany and Japan. I have been working, and continue to work, on bringing about an alliance, despite the fact that I often find myself in a minority in my party. But lately I hear from all quarters, particularly from Conservative friends, and from ministers and officials close to them, that Russia is currently experiencing a grave crisis. They say, referring to supposedly reliable sources, that a bitter domestic struggle is under way in Russia, that your army is on the verge of degeneration as a result of recent events and has lost its fighting capability, and that Russia, broadly speaking, has ceased to exist as a serious factor in foreign politics.' ...

Churchill's look, tone and gestures left no doubt of his sincerity. I had to take the floor and lecture my interlocutor at some length on elementary politics, providing him with the clarifications of recent events that he had requested. Churchill listened to me most attentively, occasionally interrupting me with brief remarks and questions. When I had finished, Churchill seemed to brighten up a bit, gave a sigh of relief, and exclaimed: 'Well, thank God. You've reassured me a little.' Then he continued with a crafty grin: 'Of course, you are ambassador and your words have to be taken *cum grano salis*; yet much is becoming a great deal clearer to me and I'm beginning to grasp what is going on in your country.' Then, after a minute's pause, Churchill went on: 'I hate Trotsky! I've kept an eye on his activities for some time. He is Russia's evil genius, and it is a very good thing that Stalin has got even with him.' Another minute's pause and Churchill, as if answering his own thoughts, exclaimed: 'I am definitely in favour of Stalin's policy. Stalin is creating a strong Russia. We need a strong Russia and I wish Stalin every success.'[16] ...

---

[15] Randolph Churchill, son of Winston Churchill; Conservative MP, 1940–45.

[16] In the succinct report to Moscow, Maisky, rather cunningly and with great circumspection, exploited Churchill in order to convey the damage inflicted by the trials on Soviet interests, while at the same time going a long way to praise Stalin's leadership.

(2) When we had finished discussing the USSR's domestic situation, I decided to pay Churchill back in his own coin, and asked him: what was happening now in England? In the course of my professional duties, I have been keeping close track of foreign and domestic policy in my country of residence throughout the last five years, and I have to say that with every year I have been growing increasingly pessimistic about everything connected with British foreign policy. ... The feebleness and indecision of the British Government and its continuous yielding to the aggressor greatly diminish Great Britain's prestige and raise the stock of Germano-Italian fascism. What is more, all this is very damaging to the cause of peace and gives rise to isolationist sentiments in other countries, including the USSR. I do not mean that the Soviet Government is embracing a policy of isolationism. It certainly is not. The Soviet Government adheres, as before, to the principles of collective security and to the Covenant of the League of Nations. ... Yet I have to say that more and more people in the USSR have begun asking themselves the question: are the 'Western' democracies capable of any kind of energetic response against the aggressors?

(3) ... I had anticipated protests and objections from my interlocutor, but I was mistaken. He responded quite differently. Churchill admitted that there was much truth in my critique of the Tories, and his face reflected his bitterness. Over the last five or six years, the leading group of the party had indeed displayed cowardice and short-sightedness on a scale with few, if any, precedents in history. ... I asked who could become prime minister in a reorganized Cabinet. Chamberlain? Churchill shrugged his shoulders and replied: 'Things become very complicated at this point. The Conservative Party won't let anyone tell it who should be its leader. On the other hand, the opposition simply cannot accept Chamberlain. The idea has been floated of bringing Baldwin back.' ... I should note in passing that I had already heard about this suggestion a few days ago, and that the supporters of this alternative named Churchill as the real head of the government, representing the Cabinet in the House of Commons. As if reading my thoughts, Churchill began to ponder aloud about how much he enjoyed his position as a 'freelance Tory' who could afford to criticize the government, and said he would not exchange it for a Cabinet post.

'It is far more pleasant,' Churchill remarked venomously, 'to read books or write articles than to try to convince ministerial nonentities that twice two is four.' But it was clear that he was merely showing off and being coy. I inquired about Eden's intentions. Churchill replied that it was too early to tell. He has the impression that Eden won't want to clash with the Conservative Party. Quarrels like that are always unpleasant. It causes the 'rebel' no end of difficulties. Besides, Eden has already grown used to power and his high standing.

This can spoil a man. Therefore, in Churchill's opinion, Eden will sit this out. When the time comes for the anticipated restructuring, Eden will undoubtedly return to the Cabinet and take up a major post. ...

(4) Our conversation moved on to international questions. Churchill sees the general situation in a menacing light. Where is Hitler headed? Churchill is in no doubt that Hitler's dream is a 'Central Europe' extending from the North Sea [*sic* – Maisky possibly means the Baltic Sea] to the Black and Mediterranean Seas, possibly as far as Baghdad. He has an excellent chance, unless he meets proper resistance from the other great powers. ... However, Churchill is not inclined to think that Hitler will attack Czechoslovakia in the nearest future. What good would it do him? Open aggression against Czechoslovakia might bring France and the USSR onto the scene, which would be undesirable, since Hitler is not yet ready for a full-scale war. ... Churchill finds the isolationist sentiments which, by my account, can be observed in certain quarters of Soviet public opinion to be rather dangerous. For Churchill thinks it nearly inevitable that Hitler's next step after setting up a 'Mitteleuropa' would be an eastward attack against the USSR, with its vast territories and immeasurable resources.

(5) I objected by saying that I had a rather different picture of the prospects for the more distant future. Even if we assume that Hitler will succeed in creating a 'Mitteleuropa', I do not believe that he would then focus his aggression on the East. ... If Churchill is correct in his calculation that Hitler would need four or five years to set up 'Mitteleuropa' (provided he meets with no resistance from other great powers), it means that peace for the USSR would be guaranteed during this period. In turn, this means we would manage to fulfil our third five-year plan. ...

(6) My reasoning seemed to impress Churchill, because he replied: 'Let's assume that a "Mitteleuropa" is equally dangerous to both of us. Doesn't this suggest that we should join forces in the struggle against Hitler's Germany?' I answered that we had always been and remained active supporters of the collective struggle against aggression, wherever it might be committed, and that we had joined the League of Nations for this very purpose. It's up to his country now, not ours. As far as I can judge, Chamberlain intends not to fight aggression, but to make a deal with the aggressors in the form of a 'four-power pact' at the expense of Central and South-East Europe, and also of the USSR, which would be isolated. ... Churchill gestured in annoyance and replied contemptuously: 'A four-power pact? What nonsense! What sort of four-power pact could there be? ... Chamberlain is a complete ignoramus in matters of foreign policy, and that is why he can talk in all seriousness about a four-power

pact.' Churchill began to elaborate his idea. At present he advocates the idea of a 'grand alliance' within the frame of the League of Nations. It would be intended, first and foremost, to unite Great Britain, France, the Little Entente and the USSR.

(7) 'But this,' Churchill continued, 'is of course only the very worst, the very last solution. Less a solution, in fact, than a dire necessity. I still haven't given up the hope of something better. I believe that the time of the grand alliance will come. ... Today, communism does not represent such a danger to the Empire. Today, the greatest menace to the British Empire is German Nazism, with its idea of Berlin's global hegemony. That is why, at the present time, I spare no effort in the struggle against Hitler. If, one fine day, the German fascist threat to the Empire disappears and the communist menace rears its head again, then – I tell you frankly – I would raise the banner of struggle against you once more. However, I don't anticipate the possibility of this happening in the near future, or at least within my life-time.' (Churchill is 63.) 'In the mean-time, we are walking the same path. That is why I am advocating the idea of a "grand alliance" and perhaps of closer cooperation between London, Paris and Moscow.' Finishing his speech, Churchill asked me with a subtle grin: 'Tell me, what do you, the USSR, demand from us?' I answered: 'We do not demand anything; but we would just like you, Great Britain, to be a good member of the League of Nations.' Churchill exclaimed: 'That's my wish too. And it's the wish of many of my friends.'

29 March

I attended a session of the House of Lords for the first time ever during my life in England – whether in exile or after the revolution.

Foreign policy issues were on the agenda. There were at most 100 or 120 people sitting on the red leather benches. They looked like flies in milk, since the chamber can house three times as many. But today was a 'big day'! Normally, no more than 30 to 40 peers are present, while the quorum in the House amounts to... 3!...

But what a session it was! It was opened by the leader of the Labour opposi-tion, Lord Snell,[17] with an attack on the government's foreign policy. I had heard more or less the same things a few days ago from Attlee[18] and Noel-Baker[19] in

---

[17] Henry Snell (1st Baron Snell), chairman of London County Council, 1934–38.
[18] Clement Richard Attlee (1st Earl Attlee), Labour Party leader, 1935–55; lord privy seal, 1940–42; deputy prime minister and secretary of state for dominion affairs, 1942–43; lord president of the council, 1943–45; prime minister, 1945–51.
[19] Philip John Noel-Baker, Labour MP, 1929–31 and 1936–50.

the House of Commons. But what a difference, what a terrific difference in presentation! The speaker's voice was subdued, his appearance expressly respectable, his gestures almost those of a preacher, and his words as though rolled in cotton. Snell was followed by a Liberal lord, who spoke so quietly that I couldn't understand a thing. He looked around 80. Then the archbishop of Canterbury took the floor and... gave his full and unconditional backing to Chamberlain! What had become of his old loyalty to the League of Nations? What had become of his anti-German tendencies? In his white mantle, which looked crumpled and unkempt from afar, the archbishop resembled a large bird with a hooked beak. After him spoke other lords, whose names I do not know, claiming that Hitler was a wonderful man who did the right thing by occupying Austria: after all, by doing so he saved the world from another 'civil war' in Europe – incredible! One speaker called for the publication in English of an unabridged translation of Hitler's *Mein Kampf* at the price of no more than a shilling per copy – so impressed was he by the profundity and foresight of the Führer's writings. To unstinting cheers from the government benches, Ponsonby[20] explained why England should not worry itself about the League of Nations, and why it was against her interests to assist Czechoslovakia, a country whose whereabouts are unknown to 99% of her people. ... How can I sum up my impressions?

Never in my life have I seen so reactionary a gathering as this House of Lords. The mould of the ages lies visibly upon it. Even the air in the chamber is stale and yellow. Even the light through the windows is gloomy. The men sitting on these red benches are historically blind, like moles, and are ready to lick the Nazi dictator's boots like a beaten dog. They'll pay for this, and I'll see it happen! ...

12 April

A very interesting conversation with Sun Fo. (Incidentally, he is not the son of Sun Yat-sen,[21] as many believe. The only connection is that his second wife is the daughter of the great Chinese revolutionary's sister.)

Sun Fo has spent six weeks in Moscow, seeking an agreement with the Soviet Government on aid to China. He left content and he expressed his gratitude for our thorough implementation of the agreements reached in Moscow. Initially, however, Sun Fo was not quite so pleased with the Moscow negotiations. As far as I could understand from his rather foggy explanations (he

---

[20] Arthur Ponsonby (1st Baron Ponsonby of Shulbrede), Labour MP, 1922–40; leader of the opposition in the House of Lords, 1931–35.

[21] Sun Yat-sen, Chinese revolutionary; founder of Kuomintang (National People's Party) in 1912, and leader of the Republic of China, 1921–22 and 1923–25.

usually speaks clearly, precisely and frankly), he had hoped to convince the Soviet Government of the necessity of joint military action with China against Japan. The Soviet Government declined the proposal, but it did promise active assistance to China by sending arms, aircraft, etc. The results have been obvious in military operations in China. There is no doubt that the Chinese successes of the past three weeks have been due in no small measure to the arrival of our planes, tanks, artillery, etc. No wonder Sun Fo feels almost triumphant.

The details of his crucial meeting with Stalin are interesting. 'I was told the date of my meeting with your leader,' Sun Fo said, 'but not the time of day. I got ready. I sat at the embassy and waited. Evening came: eight o'clock, nine o'clock, ten o'clock, eleven o'clock... Nothing! Somewhat disappointed, I decided to call it a day. I got undressed and went to bed. Then all of a sudden, at a quarter to midnight, people came for me: "Please, you are expected." I jumped up, got dressed, and set off. Molotov and Voroshilov were with Stalin. Towards the end of the meeting, Mikoyan[22] and Ezhov[23] also arrived. The conversation lasted from midnight until 5.30 in the morning. That's when it was all decided.'

According to Sun Fo, it was during that conversation that the Soviet Government dismissed the idea of direct military involvement in the war against Japan. The reasons given by Stalin to justify this line of behaviour boiled down, in Sun Fo's account, to the following: (1) Military action by the USSR would immediately rally the entire Japanese nation, which at present is far from unified in its support of Japan's aggression in China. (2) Military action by the USSR, on the other hand, might well frighten right-wing elements in China and thereby split the United National Front which has recently emerged there. ... (4) Military action by the USSR, and this is particularly important, would be exploited by Germany for an attack on our country in Europe, and that would unleash a world war. For all these reasons, Stalin considers open military action against Japan by the USSR to be inexpedient. But he is quite prepared to render assistance to China by providing it with arms and so on.

[The time had arrived for Maisky's obligatory summer vacation and, far more terrifyingly, the newly instituted procedure of annual hearings for ambassadors at the ministry.[24] Maisky's gloomy reports to Narkomindel on appeasement were now

---

[22] Anastas Ivanovich Mikoyan, Politburo member, 1935–52; people's commissar for external trade, 1938–49; member of the State Defence Committee, 1939–45.

[23] Nikolai Ivanovich Ezhov, people's commissar for internal affairs (NKVD) and general commissar of state security, 1936–38, who oversaw the 'Great Terror'. He was demoted to the position of people's commissar for water transport, 1938–39; arrested in April 1939, charged with conspiracy and espionage; convicted and shot in February 1940.

[24] Kollontay wrote a morbid farewell letter – practically a will – to an intimate friend, entrusting her with her diary and personal correspondence 'in the event of my death (something can always happen while travelling)'. She then confided in her diary: 'The world is now so terrible, tense. It is frightful for many friends. I worry, my heart is torn for them ... If I don't fall "underneath the wheel [of history]" it

tempered by an illusory conviction, largely sustained by conversations with members of the opposition, such as Churchill, Lloyd George and Beaverbrook, that 'the ground was systematically shifting under the English Government's feet, though that process does not make headway fast enough'. As insurance, before he left for Moscow Maisky extracted from Lloyd George 'a warm message of admiration to Stalin, as the greatest statesman alive!' At the same time, he did not fail to keep the elderly Liberal informed of his whereabouts in Russia and, though well aware that it was monitored, kept up a constant flow of correspondence while he was away. By the same token, in a report to Narkomindel, Maisky highlighted 'the Soviet demonstration' by Chamberlain, who, at the royal reception on 11 May, made a point of approaching him and of displaying interest in his vacation plans, allegedly eager to find out when he could be expected back in London. The unusual approach, Maisky hastened to add, was well covered by journalists, who had been ringing the embassy since the early hours of the morning.

Unlike on his previous vacations, Maisky was confined to a sanatorium outside Moscow, from where he was indeed summoned to Narkomindel and forced to compose a confessional autobiographical sketch, in which he admitted to political short-sightedness and failure to recognize the 'enemies of the people' within his embassy. He was confronted with testimonies extracted from his former subordinates, Putna, the military attaché at the embassy, and Ozersky, the head of the trade delegation in London. Both had apparently given compromising evidence against him before being shot. Together with Litvinov, he was then rushed to the Kremlin on 1 June, where, in the presence of Molotov and Voroshilov, Stalin urged them to keep a low profile and act prudently. Consequently, he was let out 'on parole', well aware of the vulnerability of his situation.

Maisky and Agniya returned to London at the end of July, disclosing to the Webbs the Kremlin's 'coldness towards Great Britain, hatred of Chamberlain as their enemy, concern about Czech-Slovakia and coolness towards the present French Government'. In further candid talks with Harold Nicolson and Vansittart, Maisky warned of 'the incipient movement towards isolation in Russia', which he attributed to the West's intention of keeping Russia 'at arm's length', but which 'he hoped would not go too far'. He vowed, though, as he had done at his meeting with Halifax a few days earlier, that 'If France and Great Britain, in the event of an invasion of Sudetenland, came to the armed support of Czechoslovakia Russia would come in on our side.'

Maisky's personal salvation lay in the success of collective security. With Litvinov increasingly hamstrung by the vacillating and sceptical attitude of the Kremlin,

---

will be almost a miracle.' Litvinov explained to the wife and daughter of the ambassador in Italy, Shtein, who were pleading with him to allow the ambassador to return to Moscow for a vacation, that it was 'better for him to sit in Rome than to be here'. Shtein, whose nerves were cracking, was advised by a private doctor he saw in Geneva to let off steam by 'destroying a dinner service once a month, powerfully and angrily crashing it on the floor'.

crippled by the purges in his ministry, and plagued by domestic problems, Maisky would henceforth become the sole driving force in trying to bring about a change in British policy. This he hoped to achieve by resorting to unconventional methods. Throughout the following year, the sharp discrepancies between his reports to Moscow and the British records (as well as his misleading and tendentious memoirs) reveal painstaking efforts on his part to attribute his own ideas to his interlocutors. In so doing, he hoped to elicit from Moscow a positive response, which might spark a chain reaction that would advance the ideas of collective security and extricate the Soviet Union from its increasingly forced isolation. Perhaps as striking was his unabashed interference in British domestic politics, as he incited the anti-Chamberlain opposition in wishful anticipation that the worsening international situation would encourage it to overthrow the prime minister and install either Eden or Churchill in his stead.]

10 May

Sir Horace Wilson came over for lunch. ... I was acquainted with him in late 1932 on my arrival in Britain as ambassador. ... He always struck me as a clever, cunning and somewhat cynical fellow, well versed in the politics of trade, a dab hand at formulating compromises, and an ardent defender of the interests of British industrialists and traders. I never saw him display an understanding of international politics, still less a desire to be engaged in those complex and sensitive matters.

... Today Wilson and I had lunch *tête-à-tête*. We spoke, of course, about international affairs. I advanced and substantiated the thought that Hitler's immediate objective was to set up a 'Mitteleuropa' and that Chamberlain's policy only facilitated his attainment of this aim. Meanwhile, 'Mitteleuropa' would, it seems, threaten the interests not only of the USSR, but also, and perhaps to an even greater extent, of Britain.

In a subtle but perfectly clear manner, Wilson suggested that Hitler's next blow after 'Mitteleuropa' would be directed eastward, against the USSR, and this would accord with British interests. ... 'I confess that your considerations have a sound basis. There is a possibility that Hitler may not move eastward. Still I am not inclined to think that even in this case "Mitteleuropa" would pose such a terrible threat to Britain. You see, today Germany is a monolith: one nation, one state, one leader. That is her strength. "Mitteleuropa" will be different: a conglomerate of nationalities, state organizations and economic regions. Internal contradictions, friction, struggles and conflicts are inevitable. All these mitigating factors shall certainly come into play. As a result, "Mitteleuropa" may prove weaker than present-day Germany. And I have no doubt that it will be less aggressive. Germany's empty stomach will be filled. She will grow heavy and calm down...'

So this is what Wilson's, or for that matter Chamberlain's, 'philosophy' amounts to!

4 August

... I have received interesting information about the Anglo-French talks held during the king's visit to Paris. ... On the issue of Czechoslovakia, Halifax maintained the following: Czechoslovakia is an artificial state incapable both of defending itself and of getting assistance from the outside. Great Britain will not detach itself from Central European developments, but France should exert greater pressure on Prague, demanding more serious concessions to Henlein.[25] The Czechs must be made to come to terms with the Germans. ...

6 August

Masaryk had much of interest to tell me.

The British démarche in Berlin on 21 May[26] was accompanied by moments of high drama. First, under strict instructions from London, Henderson (the British ambassador to Germany) pointed out to Ribbentrop that the concentration of German troops on the borders of Czechoslovakia might have grave consequences for the world; that Czechoslovakia would respond to any German aggression with armed resistance, which would entail military interference by France and the USSR; that in this case the war would assume European dimensions; and that Britain would not be able to stay out of the conflict. Let Hitler consider whether it would be in his interests to see the British Empire among Germany's enemies and, in the light of this prospect, assess his subsequent moves.

Henderson's words enraged Ribbentrop, who, with characteristic tactlessness, screamed: 'Your British empire is an *empty shell*. It is rotten and decaying. It would have collapsed long ago were it not for Germany's support. What right have you to come here with your advice and to interfere in affairs which do not concern you?'

It was Henderson's turn to fly into a rage and, banging his fist on the table, he exclaimed that he would not tolerate language of this kind against his country. He then grabbed his hat and made for the door. Ribbentrop shouted after him: 'Britain is governed by Jews, ha-ha-ha! Isn't it so?'

---

[25] Konrad Henlein, leader of the fascist Sudeten-German Home Front Party in Czechoslovakia, 1933–38; Gauleiter of Bohemia and Moravia, 1939–45.

[26] The démarche was prompted by erroneous information which had led the Czechoslovak Government to partially mobilize in order to counter a reported concentration of German troops on the country's border.

Stunned, Henderson paused on the threshold, turned round and cried: 'We, at least, are governed by gentlemen!'

Slamming the door, the British ambassador left Ribbentrop's office.

Upon receiving Henderson's report about his talk with the German minister for foreign affairs, Halifax felt somewhat embarrassed and approached Lothian with a request to inform Hitler privately that the British démarche on 21 May was not meant to insult him, that the British Government believed in his peaceful intentions, and that Britain was not going to defend Czechoslovakia with arms in hand. Halifax was extremely shaken when Lothian not only categorically refused to carry out this mission, but also expressed his disapproval of the British Government's capitulatory policy.

... Heavens above! The zigzags and shifts of British policy! Masaryk also told me the following: ever since the Austrian *Anschluss*, Halifax has ceaselessly demanded that Czechoslovakia should grant maximum concessions to the Sudeten Germans, and that she should do so as soon as possible.

... Just imagine how shocked Masaryk must have been when Halifax invited him over in mid-July and began singing a quite different tune. Speaking on behalf of the British Government, he expressed his concern that the talks between the Czechoslovak Government and Henlein were moving too fast, given the very serious issues at hand; that there was no need to rush; and that it would indeed be a very good thing if the Czechs could drag out the talks till late autumn. At first Masaryk failed to understand a thing, but shortly afterwards the mystery cleared up. The British Government had learned that Hitler was preparing an open assault on Czechoslovakia and that he intended to exploit the breakdown of talks between the Czechoslovak Government and Henlein as a pretext. The British Government was frightened. ... Chamberlain hit upon 'the brilliant idea' of dragging out the talks and buying time.

Hence Runciman's[27] mission. The mission was thought up by Chamberlain himself (or, as seems to me more probable, Horace Wilson). Neither Halifax, the Foreign Office, Corbin, Masaryk nor the Czechoslovak and French governments had the vaguest inkling about the PM's 'genius plan'. All rumours and claims to the contrary are false. Half an hour before Halifax's departure, together with the king, for Paris, Chamberlain told his foreign secretary, 'By the way, could you sound out the French Government's attitude to this project...', and proceeded to outline his plan for Runciman's trip to Czechoslovakia. That is how foreign policy is carried out now in England! ...

---

[27] Walter Runciman (1st Viscount Runciman of Doxford), British politician and shipping magnate; National Liberal MP, 1931–37; president of the Board of Trade, 1931–37; lord president of the council, 1938–39.

10 August

Resuming contact after my vacation, I visited Oliphant.[28] He's just the same. Hasn't changed a bit.

I asked him about the meaning of Runciman's mission. Oliphant gave me a caustic glance, pulled at his long red moustache and said with a tone of barely perceptible irony: 'What is Runciman doing in Prague? He is taking in the atmosphere.'

I couldn't help laughing. According to Oliphant, Runciman will spend four to six weeks in Czechoslovakia. He has no fixed plan, just a few ideas. Of course, regardless of all the denials, Runciman is in essence a representative of the British Government. But, in the end, what's wrong with that? If Runciman succeeds in reconciling the Czechs with the Germans, then wonderful. If he fails, that's also no reason to cry: at least we'll have gained some time.

'Are you displeased? I can see by your face that you resent our policy in Czechoslovakia. Why?'

'Yes, we are dissatisfied with your policy,' I agreed, 'for you are constantly striving to restrain not the aggressor, but the victim of aggression. Runciman's mission serves the same end.' ...

17 August

Bidding farewell to me before my vacation, Halifax asked me to visit him as soon as I got back from Moscow.

... The meeting took place today. Halifax asked what I thought about the problem of Czechoslovakia. I took the opportunity to discuss the matter at length. I told Halifax that on my arrival in the USSR I noticed great disappointment in the policies of Britain and France. In the opinion of my Moscow friends, these policies demonstrate the weakness of 'Western democracies' and thereby encourage the aggressors. The governments pursuing such policies are making themselves responsible for unleashing a new world war. Czechoslovakia is a fine illustration of the view I have just expressed. It seems to us that the course pursued by Britain and France on this issue represents an unhealthy distortion. Britain and France strive to restrain the victim of aggression rather than the aggressor. In Prague they raise their voices to such an extent that the Czechs feel offended, whereas in Berlin their voices are so soft that Hitler pays no heed to them. What's happened to impartiality and justice? It is quite understandable that the Soviet Government cannot sympathize with policies of this kind. The Soviet Government maintains that the fate of Czechoslovakia is in

---

[28] Lancelot Oliphant, deputy undersecretary of state for foreign affairs, 1936–39.

the hands of 'Western democracies'. If Britain and France are willing and able to take a firm stand with regard to Germany, Czechoslovakia will be saved and a lasting peace in Europe will be secured.

My words were hard, almost harsh, and I had expected Halifax to respond with a vigorous defence of British government policy. But I was mistaken once more. Halifax had no thought of remonstrating. His whole bearing and behaviour, his gestures and rare remarks showed quite clearly that a significant part, if not all, of what I had said met with his approval...[29]

24 August

Nicolson confirms that Eden is aiming for the post of prime minister, yet he may need some time to realize his ambition. He also confirms that Chamberlain is still strong ('he saved us from war!'), although so-called 'solid Conservative opinion' is turning against his foreign policy more and more. But it is considered unpatriotic to challenge the PM openly...

26 August

What an awful life!

Masaryk came to impart the latest news to me. It is distressing. The anti-Czechoslovak campaign in Germany is growing daily. Henlein rejects all concessions. For his own part, he would certainly agree to a compromise, but Hitler does not allow it. Runciman's mission is on the brink of collapse. ... The only bright spot in this gloomy picture is today's communication from Moscow, relayed to Masaryk from Prague. The German ambassador, Schulenburg,[30] made a statement to Comrade Litvinov ... stressing Germany's neutral conduct in the recent Japanese–Soviet conflict in Manchuria, expressing the hope that the USSR would reciprocate if Germany had to take the settlement of the Sudeten problem into her own hands. M.M., however, replied that the USSR would not be able to stand aside in this case, that the USSR would meet all its commitments under the Czechoslovak–Soviet Pact, that France would also have to interfere, and that in the long run Britain would be drawn into the war, too. ...

Masaryk asked if Litvinov could make a similar statement in public, before the press. It would be of great significance and would greatly reinforce France's

---

[29] The British records show that in reality Maisky was rebuffed by Halifax, who bluntly informed him that there was 'no question' of Britain shifting its policy. To facilitate Litvinov's attendance in Geneva, which could no longer be taken for granted, Maisky further manipulated Halifax so that he apparently expressed a great wish to meet Litvinov and exchange views on current affairs at the Assembly.

[30] Friedrich-Werner Graf von der Schulenburg, German ambassador to the USSR, 1934–41.

resolve to come to the aid of Czechoslovakia. I promised to convey his request to Moscow.

I asked Masaryk: what was the stance of the British at present?

Masaryk waved his hand in despair and said: 'Well, you know the English! Just yesterday Halifax said to Cambon[31] that although the British Government deemed the situation in Central Europe to be very serious, it would hardly go beyond its declarations made on 24 March (Chamberlain's speech)[32] and on 21 May (Henderson's démarche in Berlin).' Simon is going to speak in the same vein tomorrow. Curses! What's the use of ambiguous gestures and slippery half-promises? Today, when one must bang one's fist on the table to avert the disaster? ...

29 August

Vansittart invited me to a lunch *tête-à-tête*. We talked with complete frankness.

At first the host inquired about my impressions of the general mood in Moscow. I replied in the same vein as in my talk with Halifax on 17 August. Vansittart was apparently alarmed at the growing disappointment in Moscow over Anglo-French policy and our shift towards isolation. He began arguing passionately that we should not despair and that major processes were unfolding in the thick of British life and would soon produce concrete results. He concluded: 'For Britain and the USSR to pass to an isolationist policy means to serve Europe to Germany on a platter.'

I answered that I had to agree with his formula. Yet if, contrary to our will, we had to face this eventuality, Great Britain would bear the brunt of the responsibility. It was Great Britain that for the last three years had been delivering blow after blow to the League of Nations and collective security. ...

30 August

The Cabinet held its meeting today, and the Government took one really 'important decision': to do nothing. Nevile Henderson attended the meeting to shed light on some issues. Tomorrow he is returning to Berlin, but contrary to yesterday's rumours he is not carrying a 'personal letter' from Chamberlain to Hitler. He is not even meant to seek a meeting with Hitler or Ribbentrop.

---

[31] Roger Cambon, counsellor at the French embassy in London. Cambon stayed on as chargé d'affaires after the resignation of Ambassador Corbin on 26 June 1940, before resigning himself on 5 July 1940.
[32] Chamberlain announced that Britain had no obligations towards the region, where she did not have such vital interests as she had in France and Belgium.

So, *'wait and see'.* England's favourite policy!

* * *

An acquaintance of mine passed Halifax's words to me: even though no decisions were taken at today's Cabinet meeting, it was ascertained after three hours of debate that all ministers except one (who could it be? Kingsley Wood?) consider it impossible for Britain to stand aside if war breaks out over Czechoslovakia.

Very good. But what practical conclusions can be drawn from the above? There may be two possible conclusions. The <u>first</u> is to provide effective support to Czechoslovakia now, scare Hitler, and thus avert a war. The <u>second</u> is to exert 'friendly' pressure on Czechoslovakia to the extent that it would surrender entirely to Hitler without fighting, and thus avoid war. I have a strong suspicion that the Cabinet might draw the second conclusion.

[Unbeknownst to Maisky, Chamberlain had just come up with the most 'unconventional and daring' plan 'Z', which 'took Halifax's breath away': if the crisis in Czechoslovakia continued, he proposed to fly to Germany and meet Hitler to avert war. On the eve of his departure for Geneva on 2 September, Litvinov asked Payart,[33] the French chargé d'affaires in Moscow, to convey to Bonnet,[34] the French foreign minister, that the Soviet Union stood steadfastly by its contractual commitments to Czechoslovakia in the event of an attack on her by Germany. He called for an immediate conference between Great Britain, France and the USSR to coincide with consultations between the representatives of the Soviet, French and Czech armed forces. Payart, however, concealed the essence of the message (which he considered, without any reason, to be insincere) from his superiors. Briefed by Litvinov, Maisky followed his own counsel, disclosing to wide circles the content of the proposals made to Payart.]

31 August

Sir Horace Wilson visited me today and we had lunch together. ... Wilson's mood was completely different from how it had been four months ago. Then he had been full of energy, self-confidence and optimism. He believed that, together with Chamberlain, he was about to inscribe a new and glorious page into the book of European 'appeasement'. Now W. looked somewhat gloomy, anxious and faded. And conversations with him assumed a despondent, almost panicky tone.

---

[33] Jean Payart, French first secretary at the Moscow embassy, 1931–38 and 1939–41.
[34] Georges-Etienne Bonnet, French ambassador to the United States, 1936–37; finance minister, 1937–38; minister of foreign affairs, 1938–39; justice minister, 1939–40; member of the National Council, 1941–42.

Indeed, the flowers have shed their petals and the fires died out...

... Hitler clearly inspires panic in him. He expects little but trouble from him. The four-power pact has retreated to a hazy distance. Czechoslovakia is the key problem today. If it is lost, the creation of 'Mitteleuropa' will be inevitable. ...

'But if you are so well aware of the paramount importance of the Czechoslovak problem,' I remarked, 'why is Britain unwilling to take a clear and resolute stand? It could indeed restrain Hitler and prevent war.'

In reply, W. began to harp on the usual English tune. Public opinion 'won't understand' a war over Czechoslovakia, the dominions are against the interference of their mother country in European affairs, the British rearmament programme is far from being completed (the production of aeroplanes only began to accelerate last July). France, Britain's closest ally, is internally weak in financial, political and military terms (French aviation is not up to the mark, etc.). If only the conflict could be postponed for twelve or at least six months, Britain would feel stronger and everything would be different.

This familiar tune drove me out of my wits and I took the bull by the horns: 'Let us assume,' I began, 'that public opinion won't agree "to fight for Czechoslovakia", as you say, though in fact the matter concerns not so much Czechoslovakia as the future of the British Empire. Let us assume this is really so, but isn't it possible to put forward a slogan that is more comprehensible and closer to the ordinary Englishman, such as, "We will back France under any conditions"?' ...

W. shrugged his shoulders and began thinking aloud. Of course, a resolute statement like that could, quite probably, forestall a war. But that means challenging Germany! What for? To avert a hypothetical danger that will not become pressing for a few more years? How can one take responsibility for this? Fine if Hitler becomes scared. But what if he doesn't? What if he charges on? It's terrifying! No, better to wait and see. Maybe things will sort themselves out one way or another.

This is how the chief adviser to the prime minister feels today. ...

1 September

Yesterday Winston Churchill invited me for dinner. We met in the apartment of his son, Randolph.[35]

Churchill-*père* took the bull by the horns right away. The situation in Europe is exceptionally serious. War could break out any day now. Should

---

[35] Hitherto no such meeting was known about; it sheds fresh light on their following meeting on 3 September.

Czechoslovakia resist German invasion with arms, France shall undoubtedly come to her aid. Even Britain will have to interfere, though not, perhaps, from the very beginning. ...

But the most important thing is to prevent war. How? Churchill has such a plan. At the critical moment, when the Prague talks eventually reach a dead end and Hitler starts rattling his sabre, Britain, France and the USSR should deliver a collective diplomatic note to Germany – it must be collective, Churchill emphasized – in protest against the threat of an attack on Czechoslovakia. The exact wording of the note is not so crucial, and could even be toned down if necessary. It is the very fact of a joint move by the three powers that is crucial. A démarche of this kind, which would undoubtedly receive the moral support of Roosevelt,[36] would scare Hitler and lay the foundations for a London–Paris–Moscow axis. Only the existence of such an axis can save humanity from fresh carnage. ...

What do I think of his plan? What would the Soviet Government make of it?

I replied that it's not for me to speak for the Soviet Government. As for me personally, I think the plan is a good one, but it has no chance of being implemented. I simply can't believe that Chamberlain would agree to join with the USSR in standing up to Germany. ...

2 September

... A visit from Corbin, who has just returned from holidays in Évian-les-Bains. In Paris he met Daladier[37] and Bonnet. The situation in Europe is critical, according to them, and Corbin wants to be in as close contact with me as possible. Simon's speech in Paris is considered insufficiently clear and firm. France itself will fulfil its obligations to Czechoslovakia.

Very good. Yet there was something I didn't quite like. I asked Corbin what the French Government would consider to be an act of aggression sufficient to oblige it to stand up against Germany? ... Corbin was confused and began 'treading water'. He eventually announced that it was hard to discuss hypothetical situations in detail. ...

---

[36] Franklin Delano Roosevelt, governor of New York, 1928–32; 32nd president of the United States, 1933–45.
[37] Edouard Daladier, French minister of defence, 1932–34, 1936–38, and September 1939 to March 1940; prime minister, January–October 1933, January 1934 and April 1938 to March 1940.

3 September

An exceptionally important conversation took place yesterday in Moscow between M.M. [Litvinov] and Payart, the French chargé d'affaires.

Payart came at Bonnet's behest with an official inquiry: how could the USSR come to the aid of Czechoslovakia in the event of German aggression, given the reluctance of Poland and Rumania to allow Soviet troops and aircraft to pass through their territory?

M.M. noted with typical acidity that in fact the USSR should pose a similar question to France, since France's obligations to Czechoslovakia are unconditional, while those of the USSR would come into force only once France implements hers.

Payart either could not or would not give a clear answer to M.M.'s question, but M.M. continued unperturbed.

Provided France fulfils its obligations, <u>the USSR is also determined to carry out its obligations under the Soviet–Czech pact</u>. Rumania's unwillingness to let Soviet troops pass through its territory could, most probably, be overcome, should the League of Nations recognize Germany as the aggressor and Czechoslovakia as the victim of aggression. To Payart's comment that the League of Nations could hardly be expected to reach a unanimous decision on this issue, M.M. noted that even if only a majority of League members voted for this formula (especially if they included the great powers), the moral effect of the decision would be immense and would exert the necessary influence on Rumania, which, he hoped, would itself vote together with the majority. In view of the sluggishness of the machinery of the League of Nations, M.M. would consider it desirable to start preparing for such a move as soon as possible, using provisions of Article 11 of the Covenant.

M.M. further suggested that it was senseless to speak of the military defence of Czechoslovakia by three countries (France, the USSR and Czechoslovakia) without preliminary preparation of the respective military plans. This requires negotiations between the general staffs of the three armies. The USSR was prepared to take part in such negotiations.

The crucial thing at the moment, however, was to prevent the outbreak of war. In this regard, M.M. thinks that the proposals made by him in his interview of 17 March, right after the *Anschluss* of Austria, are now assuming particular significance. All peace-loving powers of the world are to get together to consult and seek measures against aggression. A joint declaration made by Great Britain, France and the USSR, with the guaranteed moral support of Roosevelt, could do more than anything else to prevent violent acts on the part of Hitler.

Unfortunately, we have very little time, and we must act quickly.

... So, our position in the Czechoslovak crisis has been set out with absolute clarity. We are ready to offer armed assistance to Czechoslovakia, if the others are ready to fulfil their duty. Will they rise to the demands of this terribly serious historical moment? We'll see. But in any case, even if Czechoslovakia should still suffer ruin and Germany becomes the hegemonic power in Western Europe, responsibility for this cannot be laid at the door of the USSR.

4 September

I visited Churchill on his country estate.

A wonderful place! Eighty-four acres of land. A huge green hollow. On one hillock stands the host's two-storey stone house – large and tastefully presented. The terrace affords a breathtaking view of Kent's hilly landscape, all clothed in a truly English dark-blue haze. On the other hillock is a beautiful wood. There are ponds in three tiers down the slope of the hill, all with goldfish of varying size: in the upper pond they weigh up to 3–4 pounds, in the next they are somewhat smaller, while the really tiny ones are in the lowest pond at the bottom of the hollow. Churchill is fascinated by his big and small fish; he happily holds forth on their every detail and obviously considers them to be one of England's most characteristic attractions.

The estate also contains an artificial pool for swimming and bathing, a fine garden, an abundance of fruit (plums, peaches, etc.), a tennis-court, cages with blue birds that can speak in human voices, and a great deal else besides. Churchill took me to a pavilion-cum-studio with dozens of paintings – his own creations – hanging on the walls. I liked some of them very much. Finally he showed me his pride and joy: a small brick cottage, still under construction, which he was building with his own hands in his free time.

'I'm a bricklayer, you know,' Churchill said with a grin. 'I lay up to 500 bricks a day. Today I worked half the day and, look, I've put up a wall.'

He slapped the damp and unfinished brickwork with affection and pleasure.

It's not a bad life for the leaders of the British bourgeoisie! There's plenty for them to protect in their capitalist system!

Churchill must have guessed my thoughts because, taking in his flourishing estate with one sweeping gesture, he said with a laugh: 'You can observe all this with an untroubled soul! My estate is not a product of man's exploitation by man: it was bought entirely on my literary royalties.'

Churchill's literary royalties must be pretty decent!

Then the three of us had tea – Churchill, his wife and I. On the table, apart from the tea, lay a whole battery of diverse alcoholic drinks. Why, could Churchill ever do without them? He drank a whisky-soda and offered me a Russian vodka from before the war. He has somehow managed to preserve this rarity. I expressed my sincere astonishment, but Churchill interrupted me:

'That's far from being all! In my cellar I have a bottle of wine from 1793! Not bad, eh? I'm keeping it for a very special, truly exceptional occasion.'

'Which exactly, may I ask you?'

Churchill grinned cunningly, paused, then suddenly declared: 'We'll drink this bottle together when Great Britain and Russia beat Hitler's Germany!'

I was almost dumbstruck. Churchill's hatred of Berlin really has gone beyond all limits!

His wife made a good impression on me. I'd barely known her before now. A lively, intelligent woman who was interested in politics and understood it. With a glance at his wife, Churchill genially remarked: 'I tell her everything. But she knows how to keep mum. She won't spill a secret.'

Randolph Churchill wasn't present. He's doing three months' training in the army.

[The diary does not reveal the main purpose of this second meeting with Churchill in two days: to disclose to him 'in detail' Payart's statement to Litvinov and to prod him to relay the information to Halifax. Maisky was acting on his own initiative. Churchill recalled how Maisky asked to come down to Chartwell to see him 'at once upon a matter of urgency'. Churchill attached such significance to the meeting that a whole chapter – 'The Maisky Incident' – appeared in an early draft version of his war memoirs and was later dropped, while the final account of the meeting was criticized by his literary agent for lacking colour.]

5 September

Today I saw Corbin and was surprised to find out that he still knew nothing about Litvinov's conversation with Payart on 2 September. I had to relate it to him in its every detail. Strange! Such an important talk at such a crucial moment should, it seems, have been conveyed to the French ambassador in London right away, and yet... Something is wrong here! Equally strange is the fact that, despite the talkative nature of the French, not a word has been written about the Moscow conversation in the French press. Bonnet, it seems, is trying to hush up the news. ...

7 September

... I have seldom felt such indignation as I did reading the above citation[38] ... Hitler wrinkled his nose – so let's throw him yet another bone... Vile betrayal

---

[38] *The Times* leader of 7 September floated a *ballon d'essai* on behalf of the inner Cabinet. It urged the Czechoslovak Government to cede the Sudetenland, as 'the advantages to Czechoslovakia of becoming

not only of Czechoslovakia but of the whole European world! A stab in Czechoslovakia's back at the most critical moment in her history! That's English politics.

... Halifax sent over the main points of his upcoming speech in Geneva concerning the reform of the League of Nations. Very nice of him. But the things he's planning to come out with! I can hardly believe my eyes. Halifax intends to make Article 16 optional and turn Article 19 into a 'reality'. To come forward with such a proposal right now, when Czechoslovakia is in mortal danger – isn't this just another flagrant betrayal of Czechoslovakia and the European world as a whole?

8 September

An unexpected invitation to see Halifax.[39] It turned out that he wanted to ask me to convey his apologies to Litvinov for not being able to meet him in Geneva on account of the European crisis. He is really very sorry, he was greatly looking forward to meeting and speaking to M.M., but sadly there is nothing to be done. The British delegation to the League will be headed by Lord De La Warr.[40]

Then Halifax turned to current affairs, expressing his concern that Henlein might reject the fourth plan. I noted with some irritation that the editorial in yesterday's *Times* would surely contribute to Henlein's decision. Halifax suddenly became animated, even turned a little pink in the face, and said that the editorial was a regrettable fact, that it did not express the opinion of the British Government and that both Prague and Berlin had already been informed about this. 'Unfortunately,' Halifax added somewhat naively, 'nobody believes our denials.'

I made no comment, but I didn't believe them either. And I was right. Because when I asked Halifax whether the British Government considered the fourth plan to be Czechoslovakia's absolute limit, the foreign secretary seemed confused and merely said that it represented a 'big step forward'. ...

11 September

Here we are, in Geneva at last.

We left London on 9 September at about nine in the morning. At noon, we boarded the ferry in Dover. The sea was *rough*, but Agniya bore it bravely. In

---

a homogeneous state might conceivably outweigh the obvious disadvantages of losing the Sudeten German districts of the borderland'.

[39] This is misleading. The meeting had been engineered by Maisky but failed to produce the desired results.

[40] Herbrand Edward Dundonald Brassey Sackville (9th Earl De La Warr), parliamentary undersecretary of state for the colonies, 1936–37; lord privy seal, 1937–38; president of the Board of Education, 1938–40; chairman of the National Labour Party, 1931–43.

Calais, against our expectations, we had a rather unpalatable lunch in the restaurant at the railway station. We were in Paris by 11 p.m., with little to report about the journey. What surprised me was the emptiness of the French roads: very few cars, and we rarely had to overtake. Quite different from England.

The embassy was empty, too. Surits[41] and his family have already left for Geneva. Hirschfeld is on leave in the USSR and will stay to work in Moscow. A number of the embassy staff are away, either on holiday or on business. ... On the morning of the 10th we walked around the city and did some shopping. At about three o'clock, having lunched in a restaurant we found on our way, we set off. We wanted to get to Dijon before nightfall, but the evening was dark and wet, so we decided to make a stop in Avalon. We put up in a small and primitive hotel on the way to this little town, where they served us a magnificent supper. I am fairly indifferent to the qualities of food, but on this occasion even my taste buds were astonished by the exceptional quality of the *poulard* which we were served. At eleven in the morning we were back on the road. Lunch in Dijon, the capital of Burgundy. Excellent yet again. The French are simply geniuses in matters culinary. We had a fantastic Burgundy with our meal. Whether because of the wine or for some other reason, I left my Baedeker to France in the restaurant. ... In a good mood (improved further by the fine

25. The warrior's respite on the way to Geneva.

---

[41] Yakov Zakharovich Surits, like Maisky, joined the revolutionary movement in 1902. He was arrested and exiled first to Tobolsk and eventually to Berlin, where he studied political science. Recruited to NKID in 1918, he served as Soviet ambassador in Turkey, 1923–34, and in Germany, 1934–37. He was a member of the Soviet mission at the League of Nations, 1937–39 and Ambassador to France, 1937–40. Declared *persona non grata* by the French in March 1940, recalled to Moscow and diverted to the backstage of diplomacy until his retirement in 1948.

weather) and with a pleasant weight in our stomachs, we left Dijon at about three and, after crossing the Jura, reached Geneva at about seven that evening.

We found the Richmond empty. It was Sunday and M.M., accompanied by the whole delegation and 'undersecretary' Sokolin,[42] had set off in the morning, as always, for an outing to France. They were expected to return late in the evening. After settling in at the hotel, Agniya and I quickly toured the town. We dined at the Bavaria.

13 September

Taking advantage of the fact that the commissions had not yet started working in earnest, Agniya and I drove out to Montreux. The weather smiled on us: the Lake of Geneva shone in its dazzling way, but a light haze, unfortunately, covered the French shore. We visited the Castle of Chillon. I'd been there during the emigration years and it had struck me as gloomy, menacing and majestic – perhaps I was under the fresh influence of the famous poem by Byron, whom I'd been so fond of in my childhood and youth. The castle now seemed much less impressive, something between a museum and a hotel made out to look old. The romanticism had gone, leaving only the prose of life. I even felt bored. Or maybe it's the years that have taken their toll? After all, 30 years have passed since I first set foot in the castle of Chillon – and what 30 years they've been!

On our way back from Montreux we stopped to have lunch in Ouchy (Lausanne). I found the Hotel d'Angleterre, where Byron, so impressed by his visit to the Castle of Chillon, wrote his famous poem in 1816.[43] A metal plate on the wall of the hotel recalls this fact...

* * *

The situation is becoming increasingly acute. After Hitler's speech yesterday, Henlein announced today that ... plebiscite was now the order of the day. Disturbances and provocations have begun in the Sudetenland. The tension grows with every passing hour. Attlee has again been to see Chamberlain and said that a plebiscite in the present situation would mean a partition of Czechoslovakia, which is why the British workers' movement was against it. The PM replied that he, too, was against a plebiscite, but he did so in such a manner that Attlee departed full of suspicion...

I have the impression that the world is sliding uncontrollably towards a new world war ... The only uncertainty is when it will begin.

---

[42] Vladimir Aleksandrovich Sokolin, counsellor at the Soviet embassy in Paris, 1936–39.
[43] *The Prisoner of Chillon.*

14 September

The day was spent in boring committees. ... Late in the evening K.[agan] telephoned from London with the latest sensation: it has been decided at today's Cabinet meeting that Chamberlain will fly out tomorrow for a meeting with Hitler in Berchtesgaden.[44]

Incredible! The leader of the British Empire goes to Canossa cap in hand to the German 'Führer'. This is how low the British bourgeoisie has sunk!

[Rab Butler, whose support for appeasement and the Munich agreement exceeded even that of Chamberlain, suggested in his memoirs that he 'was left in no doubt that the Russians did not mean business' and that 'Litvinov had been deliberately evasive and vague'. However, the diary and corroborative material sustain the argument that Stalin's caution and Litvinov's vague public statements reflected a Soviet dilemma. Any public statement might be provocative towards Germany and have unimagined repercussions if the Anglo-German negotiations did indeed reach a positive conclusion, as was anticipated. While unilateral assistance was therefore not on the cards, the Soviet Union's commitment to its contractual obligations, provided the French first fulfilled their obligation, remained unshaken. Such an outlook, a precursor to the following year's negotiations on a triple alliance, drew on the lasting and clear lesson of the failure to turn the 1934 agreement with France into a full-blown military alliance and the dismal experience of acting alone in Spain while appeasement of Germany was in full swing. It was one thing fighting the Germans and Italians on the edges of Europe, but quite another having to face Germany alone on the Soviet border, with an insouciant Western Europe looking on. What Litvinov vainly sought in Geneva, therefore, was the inception of military talks in London and Paris (which might have deterred Hitler), rather than negotiations with Beneš[45] at the Castle in Prague.

The session of the morally bankrupt League, which practically ignored the Czech crisis, coincided with Chamberlain's negotiations with Hitler leading to the Munich Conference. It turned out to be Litvinov's swan song. Kollontay bumped into Litvinov as he emerged from his meeting with Bonnet, 'waving his hand impatiently and with obvious irritation: "Results? None ... The French don't intend to fulfil their obligations to Czechoslovakia. When it comes to our Soviet proposal, Bonnet dodges and prevaricates, claiming he needs to consult London first. A delaying tactic, in other words. And right now every hour counts."' At the meeting with the British delegation on 23 September, Litvinov 'reiterated the firm resolve of the Soviet Government to fulfil all

---

[44] 'I fear,' Lloyd George warned Maisky from London, 'that the Czechs are being betrayed by Neville and Daladier.'

[45] Edvard Beneš, Czechoslovakia's representative at the Paris Peace Conference, 1919–20; foreign minister of Czechoslovakia, 1918–35; president of the Czechoslovak Republic, 1935–38 and 1946–48; president-in-exile of the Provisional Czechoslovak Government in London, 1940–45.

her obligations under the Soviet–Czech Pact'. However, his demand for an emergency meeting of the powers involved, either in Paris or London, to coordinate military plans against the backdrop of the collapse of the Godesberg talks, was dismissed out of hand by the Foreign Office as being 'of little use', since it was bound to 'certainly provoke Germany'.]

15 September

In the morning, Agniya and I drove to Lac de Lucerne and on the way back stopped in Lausanne. Lunched again at Hotel d'Angleterre. Then we had a good long stroll around town. I found the street and the house where I lived in the summer of 1908, right after my emigration from Tobolsk province. The house is 17, Avenue Eduard Dapples. ... Thousands of reminiscences crowded in my mind. How much water has flowed under the bridge since then! How the times have changed! How I, too, have changed! 1908 and 1938 – they are like two quite separate worlds, divided by centuries.

* * *

... Chamberlain's visit to Hitler is the focus of attention.

Attlee and Greenwood[46] met Chamberlain, and he explained to them the purpose of the trip. It's necessary, don't you see, to find out what Hitler wants on the Sudeten issue, and at the same time to inform him of 'England's intentions'. The PM has no concrete proposals. He will take no binding decisions in Berchtesgaden. Typical English tricks. Smells fishy.

Kagan informs me that London is greatly alarmed, and that the British Government is gradually mobilizing its army and navy. Live ammunition has even been loaded onto the vessels on the open sea.

16 September

M.M. [Litvinov] told me about his meetings with Bonnet in Geneva (11 September) and Herriot[47] (somewhat later).

Bonnet was, as always, mischievous and evasive. He wanted to know our position concerning Czechoslovakia. M.M. repeated what he had said to Payart in Moscow on 2 September, but much more decisively. I am not sure what impression it made on Bonnet. Probably not a very good one. Bonnet is doing whatever he can to avoid fulfilling the obligations under the 1935 French–Czech

---

[46] Arthur Greenwood, deputy leader of the Labour Party, 1935–54; member of the War Cabinet, and minister without portfolio, 1940–42.

[47] Edouard Herriot, leader of the Radical Party, 1919–35; premier of France, 1924–25, 1926 and 1932; deputy premier, 1934–35; president of the Chamber of Deputies, 1936–40.

26. Maisky and Kollontay mourning the fate of their colleagues near Geneva.

agreement. Our resolute stance spoils his plans. He may well try to muddy the issue...

* * *

So, Chamberlain is in Berchtesgaden today. According to the press, he will be Hitler's guest for one or two days at least.

The Times, of course, is quick to put a fly in the ointment ... insinuating that the intentions of the USSR are unclear and that Czechoslovakia can hardly expect any real help from it. An ulterior motive must exist. Yesterday, Mander[48] said ... that, according to his information, Britain and France would exert strong pressure on Czechoslovakia: she should abrogate her pact with the USSR, which in fact is more a *liability than* [an] *asset*. It seems that this process has already begun: today, the Czechoslovak Government addressed the Soviet Government with an official request – can it count on the local fulfilment of the Soviet–Czechoslovak pact by us?

---

[48] Geoffrey Le Mesurier Mander, Midland industrialist, an art collector and impassioned Liberal parliamentarian, 1929–45; an anti-appeaser and a crusader for the League of Nations in the thirties; parliamentary private secretary to Sir Archibald Sinclair (minister for air), 1942–45.

18 September

Sunday. The whole delegation headed by M.M. [Litvinov] went to the French Savoy. We ate well, had a walk, talked and were home in the evening.

Events keep developing at breakneck speed. Contrary to all expectations, Chamberlain had only one meeting with Hitler, on 16 September, and then decided on an immediate return to London. Yesterday, on the 17th, he landed in Croydon. ...

Late in the evening, the first news arrived from London. Chamberlain has put forward a proposal at the meeting to cede to Germany the Sudetenland areas where the German population exceeded 50% ... and to provide guarantees for the rest of the Czechoslovak territory on the part of the four Western powers. ...

Kagan informs us that he has been visited, at Layton's[49] request, by a very worried Cummings. A member of the Cabinet told Layton that even if France came out to protect Czechoslovakia with arms in hand, the USSR would do nothing more than raise the question of German aggression in the League of Nations. Is this true? Kagan, of course, ridiculed and refuted this canard. But where has it flown in from? ...

19 September

What a dead place Geneva is today! The Assembly, the commissions, the meetings, the protocols, lunches and dinners, the political gossiping in the corridors... Who needs all this right now? And does it really matter? Events of the greatest importance are unfolding in the world, events on which the future of Europe and perhaps all humanity depends in the most literal and immediate sense; yet here, in bourgeois, obtuse, dull Geneva we wander like sleepy flies along the corridors of the League of Nations and our hotels, waiting for news from that big and real (even if vile and repulsive) life, which tears along like a violent stream somewhere beyond these beautiful, hidebound mountains. What a pity that I'm here, in Geneva. ... I'm fed up to the back teeth with Geneva and I'm simply desperate to be in London. Well, we'll just have to stick it out...

News from London that the meetings of the English and French ministers have produced a so-called three-point 'Anglo-French plan' to settle the Sudeten problem. ... It is rumoured that Osouský,[50] the Czechoslovak envoy in Paris, was in tears after his meeting with Bonnet. In London, Masaryk was cursing

---

[49] Walter Layton, editor of *The Economist*, 1922–38; director-general of programmes, Ministry of Supply, 1940–42.
[50] Štefan Osouský, Czechoslovak ambassador to France, 1920–39.

obscenely (he knows Russian all too well!) after receiving the text of the plan from Halifax.

... The Labour delegation had a stormy talk with Chamberlain. It demanded that Hitler be met with a decisive rebuff, declaring: 'Now or never!' The PM agreed that, sooner or later, a fight with Germany was inevitable, but he deemed the present moment unsuitable. ... Dalton (one of the three members of the delegation) interrupted Chamberlain, saying that, according to information in his possession, the Soviet position was quite clear, while the readiness of the Soviet Government to fulfil its obligations under the Soviet–Czechoslovak pact was beyond any doubt.

Chamberlain was slightly embarrassed and said that he had received his information on the Soviet position from Bonnet, who recently met with Litvinov in Geneva. ... Bonnet! So he's the source of all the fabrications about the USSR's position! A despicable individual. ...

21 September

M.M. [Litvinov] delivered a major speech at the Assembly today. A forceful, venomous, terrific speech! The audience listened with bated breath. The house was packed for the first time during the entire Assembly. I watched their faces: many expressed sympathy and many could not conceal their smiles at those points where M.M. gave free rein to his malicious wit. ...

The baseness of the English and the French knows no bounds! Yesterday evening, after receiving the Czechoslovak reply with its proposal to settle the German–Czech dispute through arbitration, Chamberlain contacted Daladier and late at night (at 3 a.m., I'm told) the two premiers, without even informing their Cabinets, sent an ultimatum to the Czechoslovak Government: <u>either Czechoslovakia accepts the 'Anglo-French' plan, or London and Paris leave Czechoslovakia to the mercy of fate in the event of a German attack</u>. The French even announced that in such a case they would no longer consider themselves bound by the terms of the Czech–French treaty. <u>The Czechs were given six hours to respond</u>. ...

22 September

The Czechoslovak Government has resigned. ... Jubilation and festivities in Germany. Entirely merited. It's not just that Hitler is getting the Sudetenland without a fight, but that it's being handed to him on a plate by the British and the French. ...

Today, Agniya left for a tour of Switzerland by car. Why shouldn't she see a bit of the country? Who knows whether we'll have occasion to be here again?

After all, tomorrow Hitler might extend his paws to Switzerland with equal right and with equal success. ...

According to De La Warr, tension in England is growing by the day. The 'Anglo-French plan' is extremely unpopular. Unfortunately, the French are taking a stance of complete capitulation. The conduct of Daladier and Bonnet during the recent meetings in London was a savage blow to the hopes of English supporters for a more active policy. The crucial thing now is to boost Czechoslovak morale for at least the next couple of days and to lean on France to rectify its position. Then there will be a great swell in Britain and everything will sort itself out. Frankly speaking, De La Warr's reasoning seemed too optimistic to me, but ... after all, he'd just returned from London, where he is a member of the Cabinet! ...

23 September

... I attended the 6th Commission, where the discussion of Article 16 continued. ... Just before the meeting came to a close, a secretary of the British delegation approached M.M. and said that De La Warr and Butler would like to have a talk with him and me right away. A quarter of an hour later we all gathered in the office of the British *sous-secretaire*. It was about eight in the evening, and a somewhat romantic semi-darkness filled the room.

De La Warr spoke first. He had just received instructions from London to see Litvinov and me as soon as possible. Things are bad in Godesberg.[51] The collapse of negotiations can be expected any hour. The British and the French governments have already informed Czechoslovakia that they no longer believe they have the right to prevent her from mobilizing. Prague will probably declare mobilization tonight. Germany will certainly not tolerate such a situation. So we can expect an armed move by Hitler against Czechoslovakia. What then? What would be the position of the USSR in these circumstances?

M.M. answered that he would like to know the facts first. What is happening in Godesberg? What are they talking about there? What difficulties have they met?

De La Warr and Butler, however, didn't know much (or pretended not to know). They explained this by saying that the Godesberg–London telephone line was tapped by the Germans, so the British delegation in Godesberg had to be very careful. Sheer nonsense! But I certainly do not rule out the possibility that London is deliberately keeping De La Warr and Butler in the dark about what is really happening. Such are the methods of foreign policy work

---

[51] At the second meeting between Chamberlain and Hitler at Bad Godesberg, on 22 September, Hitler ruled out further negotiations and threatened an invasion of the Sudetenland the following week.

introduced by Chamberlain. But the two Englishmen did say that Hitler had put forward a series of new and unacceptable claims, and that the PM was returning to Britain tomorrow. Most likely, a new meeting of British and French ministers will be immediately convened in London. But what do we think of the situation?

M.M. answered that our position was stated with sufficient clarity in his speeches at the League of Nations on 21 September and today. We are sincerely prepared to meet our obligations under the Soviet–Czechoslovak pact. It's up to France. England's position is also important.

De La Warr tried to find out whether the Soviet Government has already taken some military measures. Has the army been mobilized, at least partially? Have the troops been moved to the border?

M.M. avoided answering these questions directly, saying that he had been abroad for almost three weeks. ... Butler, for his part, said he would like to clarify the question of when and under what conditions the USSR would be ready to *move*. Only after France moves? Or earlier?

M.M. replied with absolute clarity that this was the case: only after France. Those were the obligations undertaken by the USSR under the Czechoslovak–Soviet pact.

'What then should be the next practical step?' asked De La Warr.

'If the British Government has seriously decided to intervene in the developing conflict,' M.M. answered, 'then the next step, to my mind, should be an immediate conference of Britain, France and the USSR with the aim of working out a general plan of action.'

De La Warr agreed with this and asked M.M. where this conference might be held.

M.M. observed that the choice of place was of secondary importance, with one reservation. The conference should not be held in Geneva. Hitler is so accustomed to identifying Geneva with irresponsible talk that any conference convened there would fail to make an adequate impression on him. And this impression is now more important than anything.

De La Warr and Butler conceded the truth of this observation, and De La Warr asked M.M. whether he had any objections to holding the conference in London. M.M. replied that he did not.

'Who could represent the USSR at the conference?' continued De La Warr. 'Would you be able to attend yourself?'

M.M. replied: 'If the ministers of other countries are present at the conference, then I am ready to come to London.' ...

On parting, De La Warr and Butler said a few times, with emphasis: 'Let us consider today's meeting as the first "*informal step*" on the way to establishing contact between the two governments. "*Informal*", of course! Only "*informal*"!'

On the way home, M.M. and I exchanged views about our meeting with the British. M.M., as usual, was most sceptical. I am also not in a very optimistic mood, but one thing is clear to me: if London is so eager to seek at least *informal contacts* with the Soviet Government, then Chamberlain must be having a very hard time of it.

Late in the evening De Valera,[52] president of the Assembly, gave a big reception in the hotel Les Bergues. Up to a thousand people gathered, of every appearance and rank. It was hot, stuffy and crowded, but nobody seemed to notice. Everyone's thoughts were elsewhere. News of mobilization in Czechoslovakia had arrived late in the afternoon. Godesberg was being spoken of as a complete failure.

... All evening I myself could not get rid of the thought that there was no longer a way out, and that war was inevitable. ... Hitler, of course, will use force. Czechoslovakia will respond by resorting to force as well. War will break out and France will have to come to Prague's aid. We shall follow France. And then events will run their inevitable course.

24 September

A lovely, bright, sunny day. From the windows of our hotel we can see the cumbersome dark mass of Le Salève; the green fields and trees; the blue lake that seems to be laughing; the yellow anthill of the town drenched in the cheerful, spring-like sun...

In this magical setting you can hardly believe that the world is on the brink of a great catastrophe. Or maybe it isn't?

It's Saturday. Very few League commissions hold their sessions today. M.M. [Litvinov] and I devote the morning to strolling and shopping. ... We wandered about for quite a while, buying barometers, thermometers, envelopes, paper and other small things. Crossing the bridge and looking down at the clear blue water foaming along noisily beneath us, I couldn't help remarking: 'What a glorious day. Such fine weather.'

'Stop it,' M.M. grumbled back. 'You're inviting bad weather for tomorrow.'

Tomorrow, Sunday, he plans his usual jaunt into the countryside by car.

'When Surits plays cards, he always begins by yelling, "Wonderful cards! Beautiful!", and then, as a rule ends up with nothing.'

M.M. was half-grumbling, half-laughing. But still! ... Even he is not immune from something like superstition.

---

[52] Eamon (Edward) De Valera, president of the Sinn Fein party in 1917; prime minister of Ireland, 1932–48 and 1951–54.

* * *

Chamberlain was back from Godesberg in time for lunch in London. The details are gradually emerging.

In Godesberg, it transpires, Hitler presented the British prime minister with a series of new and unexpected demands. ... Appetite comes with eating. After Berchtesgaden, it would seem, Hitler's appetite grew considerably. That's no surprise, given Chamberlain's conduct there. But will even Chamberlain be able to swallow Hitler's impertinent demands? And will the French swallow them? This is the crux of the matter now. It would seem that London and Paris ought to choke on the Godesberg ultimatum. But who knows? ... Halifax handed the memorandum to Masaryk today. The following conversation took place:

Halifax. Neither I nor the prime minister thinks it possible to advise you on Mr Hitler's memorandum. But I would like to tell you man to man: think well before giving a negative answer. The prime minister is convinced that Mr Hitler desires only the Sudetenland and that, if he receives it, he won't make any more demands.

Masaryk. And you believe this?

Halifax (sharply). I told you, the PM is convinced of it.

Masaryk. If neither you nor the prime minister wants to give us advice on the memorandum, what then is the role of the PM?

Halifax. The role of a postman, and nothing else.

Masaryk. Should I understand that the British prime minister has become an errand boy for that killer and brigand, Hitler?

Halifax (embarrassed). Yes, if you so wish.

* * *

News from Moscow that Potemkin summoned the Polish chargé d'affaires yesterday and made an official statement to him that if Poland crossed Czechoslovakia's border, the Soviet Government would view it as an act of aggression committed by Poland and would instantly renounce the Soviet–Polish non-aggression pact of 1932. ...

25 September

Sunday. The League of Nations is not working. Indeed, outside Geneva, in the great world where ominous events are unfolding, the thermometer still shows 40°. In Prague, people are getting ready to die for the freedom and independence of their country. In London, the British Cabinet was in session yesterday for many hours, while today a fresh meeting of British and French ministers is to be held on the subject of the Godesberg ultimatum. But here in Geneva it is Sunday: silence, calm and rest from toil, as once we sang as children.

We all, excepting A.M.,[53] make another trip to France. M.M. wants to find some new, as yet untried restaurant somewhere in Doucier (Jura). On the way we get out of the car, stroll, talk, and make bets. M.M. asks me: 'Well, what do you think: will there be a war or won't there? Yesterday at Lac Léman our views diverged. I believe that the English and the French will yield again and that there won't be a war. Yakov Zakharovich [Surits] agrees with me; Boris Efimovich [Shtein] and Vladimir Aleksandrovich [Sokolin] hold the opposite view. And what do you say?'

Shtein barges into the conversation and starts arguing that the Czechs will reject the ultimatum, the English and the French will not be able to exert pressure on them in such a situation, the Germans will attack, the Czechs will resist,

27. With the League of Nations paralysed (during Chamberlain's visit to Hitler at Godesberg), the survivors of the purges (right to left) Maisky, Litvinov, Surits, Shtein and Kollontay, find refuge in the French Alps.

---

[53] Aleksei Fedorovich Merekalov, deputy people's commissar for foreign trade, 1937–38. Stalin's personal appointee as ambassador to Berlin in April 1938, he initiated rapprochement with Germany a year later, but was recalled to Moscow in May 1939 and side-tracked to direct the country's meat industry.

the French will have to support the Czechs, and then the course of events will resemble a spontaneous avalanche. I listen to Shtein and his logic seems irrefutable. Yet a voice deep in my soul tells me: 'Will Chamberlain and Daladier stand their ground when the time comes to say plainly: war? I doubt it.' So, answering M.M.'s question, I say: 'Knowing my English friends, I'm inclined to agree with you. Yet there are other factors in the current situation which have not been taken into account and which are capable of playing a great role: for instance, the Czechs' behaviour at the moment of danger. Therefore, I can't make a bet.'

The restaurant in Doucier was superb. The food was heavenly. After lunch, Agniya and I asked for tea. The owner, who was attending our table himself (and why not? M.M. was immediately recognized and an atmosphere of amicable sensationalism constantly surrounded us), grimaced in horror and disbelief. 'Tea?' he asked, almost dumbstruck. 'You would like tea?'

We realized we had committed a sacrilege. The owner went on: 'I have first-class coffee!... Wonderful coffee... You won't find such delightful coffee anywhere else!'

We were defeated. They brought us fragrant black coffee...

Late at night, when we returned to Geneva, the news came that Czechoslovakia had rejected the Godesberg 'memorandum'.

26 September

Moscow instructed us today that Surits, Merekalov, and I should be back in our places. Surits has already been in Paris for five days. After consulting M.M., Merekalov and I decided to leave tomorrow. I shall go by train in order to arrive by 28 September, when a session has been planned in Parliament, at which Chamberlain will make a statement about his talks with Hitler and at which, who knows, a decision might be taken about war. Agniya will return by car one or two days later. ...

* * *

When Chamberlain returned from Godesberg, Attlee and Greenwood went to see him. Halifax was also present at the meeting.

Chamberlain began with lengthy deliberations on the theme that Hitler is 'an honest man', and that, having received the Sudetenland, he would be appeased. The speech bored Greenwood, who interrupted the prime minister and asked him: 'Have you read Hitler's *Mein Kampf*?'

Chamberlain got angry and answered irritably: 'Yes, I have, but I have conversed with Hitler and you have not!' ...

28. Maisky with Surits in Geneva – the former Menshevik survivors in the London and Paris embassies.

27 September

I started preparing for the journey in the morning. Agniya and I did our last bits of shopping and paid our last visits. A grey and foggy day. Some occasional drizzle. In the evening a *blackout* was enforced in Geneva. The city was plunged into complete darkness. The cars moved about with their lights a deep shade of blue. Despite the fact that it was a trial alarm or, perhaps, precisely because of that, the streets quickly filled with people. You could hear footsteps every-where, along with the sound of restrained laughter and people talking. Young people came out in particularly large numbers. For them this was such *fun*!

It was pitch-black at the railway station. I had some trouble finding a porter and then my carriage. I said goodbye to Agniya and the train moved off. Louis Fischer[54] turned out to be my travelling companion. We had a long talk about Spain and European affairs. He told me, among other things, that

---

[54] Louis Fischer, American journalist who gained access to the Soviet leadership in the post-revolutionary years.

Chamberlain had spoken on the radio that evening. The prime minister was almost weeping, his voice trembled, and he couldn't reconcile himself to the thought that the war could begin any moment now. That's bad. A speech like that augurs ill. ...

28 September

The train arrived in Paris on time. It was around seven o'clock in the morning. I was met at the station and went to the embassy for half an hour. In view of the early hour, I decided against waking Surits. I saw only one or two employees at the chancellery. My train for London was leaving at 8.20. I had deliberately chosen an early train, arriving in London at 3.21 p.m., as I planned to go straight from the station to the Parliament session where Chamberlain was expected to speak at 3.30. ...

The journey from Paris to London passed without incident. The sea was calm. ... A great disappointment lay in store for me on the British shore. The 'war alarm' of the last few days had already affected the regularity of the trains. Our train from Dover to London was one hour late. This had very unpleasant consequences for me. I had hoped that, with nine minutes at my disposal, I would have got from Victoria station to Parliament in time for the beginning of Chamberlain's speech. But I arrived in London at 4.25 p.m., instead of 3.21 p.m. At the station, I couldn't help wondering: wasn't it too late to go to Parliament? But I dismissed the thought, jumped out of the carriage and rushed to Westminster.

When, panting for breath after a brisk walk along the Parliament corridors, I ran up to the entrance to the diplomatic gallery, the fat, good-natured policeman at the door, who knew me well by sight, broke into a happy smile and said hastily: 'Have you heard the good news? The prime minister has just informed the House: Mr Hitler has invited him to a new conference in Munich. Tomorrow.'

I ran upstairs. Not only all the galleries, but even all the approaches to them were crammed with people. With great difficulty I pushed my way to the front row, but there was no way of getting through to the diplomatic gallery. To make it worse, there were no vacant seats there. I stood where I was and focused my attention on my surroundings. Down below, the chamber was black with MPs. Not only were all the benches taken, with no room left to swing a cat, but thick crowds of MPs thronged the gangways. You could sense a tremendous tension. It seemed unbearable, as if on the brink of a spontaneous explosion.

Chamberlain was speaking. When I entered, he was coming to the end of his speech. He had just announced Hitler's invitation and his consent to fly to Munich the following day. ...

29 September

Halifax invited me over. He began with justifications. The British Government fears that the conference of the four which convened today in Munich could arouse certain suspicions in the Soviet Government, for it is very familiar with our attitude towards anything resembling a 'four-power pact'. Halifax wants to dispel our suspicions. Although only four powers are meeting in Munich, the British Government has always desired and still desires to maintain good relations with the USSR and fails to understand why this should not be possible.

Then Halifax moved on to an account of the circumstances under which the Munich Conference originated. In his desperate attempts to avert war, the prime minister made a final appeal to Hitler and Mussolini on the morning of 28 September. At 4 p.m., while speaking in Parliament, Chamberlain received Hitler's invitation to come to Munich on the 29th for a conference that would be attended by Mussolini and Daladier as well. Chamberlain gave his consent without consulting the French, as the matter seemed absolutely clear to him. Daladier also gave his consent to come to Munich without consulting the British. The British Government did not raise the question of sending an invitation to the USSR because, first, time was terribly short, with not a minute to spare, and, secondly and most importantly, it knew beforehand the reply that it would get to such a proposal from Hitler. The last chance to preserve peace could not be wasted because of an argument about the composition of the conference.[55] ...

After hearing all this, I asked about the programme of the conference. Halifax threw out his hands and said they had had no time to work out a programme and that the agenda would depend to a great extent on the intentions and mood of the 'Führer'. In any case, Halifax does not rule out the possibility that questions may be raised in Munich regarding not only Czechoslovakia, but also other problems, such as Spain, general European 'appeasement' and so on. ...

30 September

... Yesterday I didn't go to bed until almost 4 a.m., and sat listening to the radio. At 2.45 it was finally announced that an agreement had been reached in Munich and the peace of Europe had been secured. But what an agreement! And what peace!

Chamberlain and Daladier capitulated completely. The conference of the four essentially accepted the Godesberg ultimatum with minor and negligible

---

[55] Halifax, as his report attests, was indeed apologetic, explaining to Maisky that 'We all had to face facts, and one of these facts was, as he very well knew, that the heads of the German Government and of the Italian Government would not be willing ... to sit in conference with a Soviet representative.'

WHAT, NO CHAIR FOR ME ?

29. A cartoon by David Low.

adjustments. The one 'victory' won by the British and the French is that the transfer of the Sudetenland to Germany will take place not on the 1st but on the 10th of October. What a tremendous achievement!

I paced the dining-room for a long time, lost in thought. My thoughts were distressing. It is difficult to grasp at once the true meaning of all that had just happened, but I feel and understand that a landmark of enormous historical significance was passed last night. In one bound quantity became quality, and the world suddenly changed...

I woke up in the morning with a headache and the first thing that occurred to me was that I should immediately visit Masaryk. When I entered his reception room there was no one there. A minute later I heard someone's hurried steps on the stairs and the host sidled in. There was something strange and unnatural about his tall, strong figure. As if it had suddenly iced over and lost its habitual agility. Masaryk threw a passing glance at me and tried to make polite conversation in the usual manner: 'What fine weather we are having today, aren't we?'

'Forget the weather,' I said, with an involuntary wave of my hand. 'I have not come here for that. I have come to express my deep compassion for your people at this exceptionally hard moment and also my strong indignation at the shameful behaviour of Britain and France!'

A kind of current seemed to pass through Masaryk's tall figure. The ice melted at once. Immobility gave way to quivering. He rocked rather comically on his feet and fell all of a sudden on my breast, sobbing bitterly. I was taken aback and somewhat bewildered. Kissing me, Masaryk mumbled through his tears: 'They've sold me into slavery to the Germans, like they used to sell Negroes into slavery in America.'

Little by little, Masaryk calmed down and began to apologize for his weakness.

I shook his hand firmly. ...

I had a long talk with Churchill yesterday. This was before the news came from Munich, and Churchill expressed his almost total confidence that this time Chamberlain would not be able to make any serious concessions to Hitler. In any event, Chamberlain would not be able to retreat from the Anglo-French plan of 18 September! How terribly mistaken Churchill was! ...

In conclusion, Churchill told me about the campaign against the USSR being conducted in London. It transpires that the *Cliveden Set* and other related elements have been busy spreading rumours that Soviet aviation is weak; that the recent 'purges' have deprived it of nearly all its qualified personnel. ... Churchill learned from Cabinet circles that the British Government has received a document confirming that between 60 and 70% of the officers in our air forces have been 'liquidated' in some form or another. When relating all this, Churchill tried to smile sceptically, but I could see that the 'information' he had received worried him. I scoffed at the *Cliveden Set*'s idle talk and tried to reassure Churchill. I don't know to what extent I succeeded.

1 October

I visited Lloyd George in Churt. We had a long talk about the crisis. Among other things, Lloyd George told me an extraordinary story. A week ago, Baldwin came to Chamberlain and said: 'You must do everything in your power to avoid a war, however humiliating the cost. Just think what will happen if it comes to war! Our complete unpreparedness will immediately become apparent and then the indignant public will have us both hanging from the street lamps.' Lloyd George is convinced that this consideration played a major role in the capitulation in Munich. ...

Lloyd George was interested in the Soviet response to the Munich Conference. I replied that I had not been fully informed as yet, but I had no doubt that the response would be sharply negative. Disappointment and irritation with Britain and France would undoubtedly grow and isolationist tendencies would inten-sify among the general population. Of course, the Soviet Government, with its inherent realism (far removed from that of Chamberlain), will hardly take any serious decisions in a hurry. Most likely, it will wait, think things over, weigh up the current situation and examine subsequent developments before undertaking any changes in our foreign policy. But I am speaking now not about the Soviet Government, but about the mood of the general public.

[For the Soviet Union (and for Litvinov and Maisky personally), the Munich agreement was a horrific setback. Litvinov's 'year-long and untiring efforts to realize his policy of collective security against Germany,' reported the British ambassador from Moscow, 'would appear ... to have fallen into the water'; he 'has scarcely been visible since his arrival' from Geneva. Maisky was severely reproached for the failure to respond critically to the 'deceitful inventions' of Halifax and others regarding presumed 'cooperation' and 'consultation' with the Soviet Union prior to the Munich agreement. 'One gets the impression,' he was reprimanded, 'that you seriously accept this eyewash, which, however, should have been all too obvious to you.' It is hardly surprising that Maisky appeared henceforth to be 'vague, mordant, and ominous', barely concealing his 'unutterable disgust with the Chamberlain policy', which he feared would spawn a four-power pact leading to the institutionalized isolation of Russia. He now regarded Chamberlain as 'The Enemy', while he nicknamed Halifax 'The Bishop' who 'retires to pray and comes out a worse hypocrite than before'.

The Soviet Union's raging denunciation of the Munich agreement should have alerted Chamberlain to the likelihood of Soviet reclusion and possibly its corollary, an accommodation with Hitler. However, in the absence of an alternative policy, Stalin was, for a while, dissuaded by Litvinov from withdrawing into isolation, particularly after Hitler's seizure of Prague in March 1939. Maisky's existentialist need to preserve collective security led to an ambivalence, whereby ominous threats about isolation were combined with assurances that isolation was not likely.]

11 October

In the morning papers today I came across an account of the speech delivered by Lord Winterton[56] (member of the Cabinet and chancellor of the duchy of Lancaster) in Shoreham on 10 October. 'Russia,' he stated there, 'had offered no aid during the crisis over Czechoslovakia and, as a result of its military weakness, had confined itself merely to promises of a vague and general nature.'

I decided to act immediately, without even making preliminary contact with Moscow. First of all, I sent off my reply to Winterton's slander to the press, and then I asked Halifax for a meeting. ... I made the following statement:

... 'The purport of the slander being disseminated by the persons I have mentioned is absolutely clear. They simply wanted to shift the blame from the sick to the healthy party and make it seem as if the responsibility for the

---

[56] Lord Edward Winterton, chancellor of the duchy of Lancaster, 1937–39; deputy to secretary of state for air, March–May 1938; member of the Cabinet, March 1938 to January 1939.

systematic retreat of Britain and France before the aggressors, culminating in Munich, lies with the USSR.' ...

I was already preparing to leave, thinking that my mission had been accomplished, when Halifax, apparently provoked by my last remark, stopped me and began to speak: 'It seems to me that you, like many others in Europe, do not understand England's position clearly enough. We think that nowadays the world is witnessing the struggle of two ideological fronts – fascism and communism. We, the English, support neither one nor the other. Moreover, we dislike both. We have our own notions and institutions, developed over centuries. We do not want to change them for anything else. In the struggle between the two fronts, we occupy a neutral or, if you please, a middle position. It is precisely for this reason that we are misunderstood so often on the Continent and attacked so frequently from both sides.'

I have heard this 'philosophy' of the cowardly Brits a thousand times already, and I had little difficulty finding the necessary arguments in reply. I remarked with a hint of mockery that the notorious 'anti-Comintern pact', which was supposedly geared primarily against the USSR, was so far operating against China, Spain, Czechoslovakia, Abyssinia, and against the interests of the British and French empires.[57] ...

25 October

War Minister Hore-Belisha[58] came over for lunch. ... Hore-Belisha was jovial, drank Russian vodka at a gulp, and said some quite interesting things. The German to British aircraft ratio is 3:1. The production capacity of German aircraft factories is 800 units a month, while the British plan to increase their output to 700 aircraft a month no earlier than the end of 1939. ... I then asked whether the Cabinet was at least planning to set up a ministry of supply in the near future and to mobilize industry.

'Not yet,' answered Hore-Belisha.

'Why?' I insisted.

'Why?' Belisha shrugged his shoulders and said in a sarcastic tone, 'Have you been to 10, Downing Street lately?'

'No, I haven't.'

'There you are. Had you been there, you'd have seen that the PM's apartment is strewn with flowers sent to him by female admirers from all over the country. The PM seriously considers Munich a victory, and is convinced that if

---

[57] Maisky's ironic comments were later adopted by Stalin in his famous 'chestnuts' speech of March 1939, see pp. xxv and 163.
[58] Leslie Hore-Belisha (1st Baron Hore-Belisha of Devonport), secretary of state for war, 1937–40; member of the War Cabinet, 1939–40.

he takes a delicate approach towards Hitler and Mussolini he will succeed in appeasing Europe.'

Translated into the language of politics, this means that Chamberlain intends to retreat even further. Hore-Belisha confirmed this: although no official Cabinet decision has been taken, the general opinion of the majority of ministers is that a 'colonial deal' should be struck with Hitler.

3 November

Halifax invited Agniya and me to lunch. ... Apart from the hosts, there were Inskip, De La Warr and Butler with their wives. The food was good and homely. Nothing serious was discussed. After lunch, Inskip had me in hysterics with his sudden complaints about his inability to grasp military terminology: 'What is a division? There is a peacetime division and a wartime division, a continental division, an imperial division, a stationed division and a territorial division, and in every division there is a different number of men. Sometimes, the difference is as much as 50 or 60%! Or take air squadrons. How many planes are there in a squadron? Nine? Twelve? Fifteen? You can never tell. Or the navy. How many vessels are there in a flotilla? I'm completely lost in all these terms. Why can't the military make its terms more simple and specific?'

That is how the minister for [the coordination of] defence of Great Britain speaks! Is it any wonder that the defence of his country is in such a poor state?[59] ...

9 November

Once again I attended the traditional banquet of the lord mayor of the City of London.[60] For the sixth time. It's becoming boring, as the same ceremony is repeated every year.

... At the table I was seated between the Hoares, husband and wife, and I had a very interesting conversation with Sir Samuel. At first, I avoided politics on purpose, and spoke mainly about literature. Hoare said he reads a lot, in Russian, too. He enjoys Stendhal and Mérimée. He lavished praise on Alexei Tolstoy's *Peter the First*, which he read in translation. Hoare is also a passionate admirer of Pushkin – he has read all his works in the original.

... Little by little, however, our conversation shifted to political themes, and what I heard from Hoare was highly characteristic and instructive.

---

[59] Churchill revered the position. The appointment of Inskip evoked comments such as: 'This is the most cynical appointment since Caligula made his horse a consul.'
[60] Sir Frank Henry Bowater, sheriff of London, 1929–30; member of London County Council, 1934–37; lord mayor of London, 1938–39.

According to Hoare, home secretary and member of Chamberlain's 'inner Cabinet', it transpires that the prospects for peace in Europe are better today than they were six or twelve months ago. Why? Simply because the Czechoslovak question, the only one that could have been the cause of a European disaster, has been settled. The German expansion to the south-east is a 'natural process' and cannot lead to a European war. Spain is no longer a threat to peace in Europe. So there are no more political entanglements which might erupt in a European war. ...

I concluded from my talk with Hoare that the British Government is not planning to arm in earnest and has evidently reconciled itself to the prospect of German air supremacy. What lies behind this?

The main reason, it seems to me, is that Chamberlain has not yet lost hope of 'coming to terms' with the aggressors at the expense of third countries and of setting them, especially Germany and Japan, against the USSR.

25 November

Eden and his wife came for lunch. They examined the walls of the yellow drawing-room and the upper dining-room with a connoisseur's eye. They were very complimentary about Kustodiev's[61] and Grabar's[62] paintings, as well as the furniture. They praised some other pictures and engravings as well. I recalled that when Eden was planning his trip to Moscow, he asked me to include in his schedule a visit to the museum of Western painting. His artistic background shows!

There were four of us at the table. The conversation was very frank. Far more so than when Eden was foreign secretary.

I asked Eden what he thought about England's immediate prospects? Will Chamberlain and his policy of 'appeasement' hold out for long?

Eden shrugged his shoulders and answered that the current situation is very unclear. Chamberlain certainly enjoys his party's support and can hold out until the next election. ...

'It follows,' I reasoned, 'that there is no hope of a change in British foreign policy as yet?'

'What can I say?' Eden responded. 'A change in policy is conceivable even without elections. Events might force the hand even of the present Government.'

---

[61] Boris Mikhailovich Kustodiev, Russian painter and stage designer, best known for portraits and scenes from traditional country life.
[62] Igor Emmanuilovich Grabar, Soviet painter of landscapes of ancient Russian or old country estate architecture. Head of the Tretyakov Gallery, 1913–25; director of the Scientific Research Institute of Art History, 1944–60.

Eden stopped for a moment before continuing: 'If I were in Chamberlain's shoes, I would do the following. I would address the party and the nation and say: I have done everything in my power to reach an agreement with Germany and secure the "appeasement" of Europe. I have made every kind of concession for the sake of this. I have made many sacrifices. I have been ready to forgo my own and my country's pride, to endure assaults, criticism and accusations for the sake of achieving the goal... But now I see that all my efforts have been in vain: Germany does not want an honourable peace for both sides, it wants a *pax germanica*. I cannot agree to this. That's the limit. We can do no more. We must defend ourselves. If the prime minister put the question like that, he would have a united country behind him and could carry out a firm and dignified policy of genuine peace.'

'And you think that Chamberlain is capable of performing an about-turn of this kind?'

Eden grinned: 'No, of course he won't do that.'

'So how do you expect a change in foreign policy under the present PM?' I went on.

'I'm speaking about the Government, not about the PM,' Eden replied. 'Of course, a change in policy is possible only if the present Cabinet is substantially refreshed.'

... The trouble is that the power of the party machine has increased immensely and terrorizes many MPs. Some 25 years ago there were many Conservative MPs with their own private means, who felt independent and paid little attention to the instructions given by the *chief whip*. They spoke and voted as they wished. Nowadays the overwhelming majority of Tory MPs are subsidized from party funds at election time, so they seek to ingratiate themselves with the *chief whip*.

'Isn't that so, Beatrice?'[63] Eden concluded, turning to his wife.

Beatrice agreed with her husband and cited her late father as a characteristic example. For the remainder of our talk, Eden would repeat, after stating his opinion: 'Isn't that so, Beatrice?'

Evidently, Beatrice is not only Eden's wife, but also his adviser.

... Eden condemned Chamberlain's foreign policy most harshly. It is leading directly to the downfall of the British Empire. The PM's policy on rearmament is virtually criminal. The immediate prospects in France worry Eden greatly. He is very interested in our stand on international affairs and was clearly glad to hear that we are not hurrying to make definitive conclusions, but are merely following the course of events in Europe. He repeated that in his opinion salvation lies only in the London–Paris–Moscow axis, and added in this connection

---

[63] Beatrice Eden, Anthony Eden's wife.

that he was including the speech he gave at the dinner in Moscow during his 1935 visit in a collection of speeches to be published imminently.

During our conversation, I remarked in passing that capitalism was a spent force. I was surprised to hear Eden reply: 'Yes, you are right. The capitalist system in its present form has had its day. What will replace it? I can't say exactly, but it will certainly be a different system. State capitalism? Semi-socialism? Three-quarter socialism? Complete socialism? I don't know. Maybe it will be a particularly pure British form of "Conservative socialism". We'll see.'

18 December

... Masaryk, whom I saw two days ago, told me that during his farewell audi-ence, the king complained to him at length about the difficulties which Chamberlain faced in trying to carry through his policy of 'appeasement', while dealing with people such as Hitler and Mussolini. Then the king said *verbatim*: 'These people (i.e. Hitler and Mussolini) were once useful to their nations. They united them and inspired them with courage and confidence. But the useful mission of Hitler and Mussolini is over. Everything they do now is directed against us and against civilization.'

And Halifax asked Masaryk, during his farewell visit, to convey to Roosevelt, whom Masaryk hopes to meet on his trip to the USA, that 'neither the prime minister nor I cherish any illusions about Germany'.

Symptomatic.

19 December

Today we had a farewell dinner for Masaryk. ... The number of defecting ex-diplomats is rapidly growing: Franckenstein,[64] the Austrian, now naturalized and bearing the title Sir George Franckenstein; Martin, the Abyssinian, who has not been invited to a single official reception since 15 November (the date when the Anglo-Italian agreement came into force); and now Masaryk. All this in the course of just one year! What speed! The question arises: who next?

In his endearing but very muddled speech, Masaryk uttered: 'I'll fight for the "Lorelei" to be sung in Germany again!'[65]

[Munich had confirmed for Litvinov how futile it was to try and recruit Britain and France to collective security. His outlook now conformed very much to the isolationist

---

[64] Georg Freiherr von und zu Franckenstein, Austrian envoy in London, 1920–38.
[65] During the Nazi period, the popular 'Die Lorelei', written by Maisky's favourite Jewish poet Heinrich Heine, was attributed to 'an unknown poet'.

views held in the Kremlin, but his paralysis reflected his association with the discredited idea of collective security and his apparent refusal to consider the obvious alternative of reconciling with Germany. Maisky, whose room for manoeuvre had been significantly narrowed, retained some vestige of hope that the damage could be repaired. He tried relentlessly to galvanize into action oppositional elements inside government circles.

He went on wooing his collaborators with gifts of caviar and vodka as the year drew to a close. However, attuning himself to his master's voice, Maisky conveyed to Litvinov his conviction that Chamberlain's policy would be aimed 'not at resistance but at a further retreat in the face of the aggressor'. He had heard from Chamberlain's entourage the following remark: 'What sense is there in feeding a cow which Hitler will slaughter anyway?' Litvinov was glad to observe that Maisky did not 'overrate the successes of the English opposition'.

The year 1938 thus ended miserably for Maisky. He had become somewhat estranged from Litvinov, his sole remaining succour in Moscow – himself teetering on the edge of the abyss. Earlier in the year, Maisky had – tongue in cheek – welcomed Narkomindel's infusion of 'new blood' to the embassy and promised to 'help these new people stand on their own two feet'. However, in what seems likely to have been a move aimed at self-preservation, he warned that the new cadre 'had no experience of diplomatic work, particularly considering the difficult and sensitive work which takes place in centres such as London'.

His private sphere was now increasingly invaded, culminating in a harsh report by an investigation committee concerning the décor and workings of the embassy. The precarious and degrading position of a Soviet ambassador at the time is well reflected in Maisky's rebuttal:

... Over the last few years I have tried to augment and renew the embassy's collection of paintings in order to represent suitable works by old and new artists. Thus I have added ... a few paintings by contemporary Soviet artists, some portraits of Comrade Stalin ... a bust of Lenin and other works. ... The way in which clause 7 [of the report] is formulated might lead one to think that there are no portraits of the leader in the embassy. The truth is entirely the opposite. In the very reception room under discussion there is a large, life-size, well-executed portrait of Comrade Stalin by Sokolov,[66] so displayed as to dominate the room. ... There are many further portraits of the leader in other rooms and areas of the embassy.]

---

[66] Mikhail Ksenofontovich Sokolov started his career as a prolific innovative suprematist painter and ended up painting in a socialist realist fashion as a member of the Moscow Institute of Painters and Graphic Artists (1936–38). It was during this time that Stalin commissioned from him the portrait, as well as a painting of Lenin's arrival at the Finland Station to take charge of the revolution in Russia in 1917. Stalin is depicted disembarking the train, following Lenin, although he had actually not been present. In 1938 Sokolov was arrested and banished, imprisoned for seven years in Siberia.

30. Victims of the Munich meeting: Maisky consoling Masaryk.

31. Maisky: 'In the very reception room ... there is a large, life-size, well-executed portrait of Comrade Stalin by Sokolov, so displayed as to dominate the room.'

1939

10 January

A new year. What will it bring?

I anticipate a stormy and difficult year, perhaps even a decisive one for our epoch. We shall see...

We celebrated the New Year in Paris. Agniya and I got away for five or six days to have a change of scene. We were sick and tired of our customary London surroundings. We had a good time. Spent much of it wandering around Paris – a wonderful city! What a shame that it is the capital of a country in deep decay. We visited museums, picture galleries and theatres – we saw nearly all the fashionable plays – and, of course, I chatted a lot with S[urits] about various political topics. ...

32. Before the storm: a break in Paris.

19 January

I congratulate you, Ivan Mikhailovich, on an important birthday: today you are 55 years old!

I've lived more than half a century. And what a time to live! The thread of my life has stretched along the boundary of two great epochs: the end of capitalism and the beginning of socialism. ... What does the future hold?

... Leaving aside unpredictable and unexpected events, which our time has more than enough of, I am mapping out the following tentative 'plan for the end of my life' (the end, after all, is not so far off).

Judging by my current state of health (and leaving aside, once again, unforeseen incidents and circumstances), I can hope to live to about 75. So I have about 20 years at my disposal. I am dividing this period into two more or less equal parts. The next ten years, until I turn 65, can be devoted to active work in the service of the party and the state; that is, in the service of socialism. Considering my experience, knowledge, training and so on, it would be most expedient for me to remain in the sphere of foreign policy. The following ten years, between the ages of 65 and 75, should be devoted to summing up and 'rounding off' my life, and specifically to writing my memoirs, which I may choose to entitle 'The Novel of My Life'. ...

26 January

Barcelona has fallen. The very thought of it makes my heart bleed. Over the past two and a half years, when fate has bound me so closely to the fortunes of Spain, I identified with the heroic struggle of the Spanish Republic. Its victories were my victories, and its defeats my defeats. Strange as it may seem, it's as if we, in the Soviet Union, suddenly rediscovered the Spanish people afresh. Never in the past have the destinies of Spain and Russia intersected. We knew little about this country and her people. We never took an interest in them. It is only now, in the din and thunder of the Spanish war, that we have suddenly come to understand and feel how wonderful, proud and heroic the Spanish nation is and what reserves of revolutionary energy it has accumulated over long years of oppression and suffering. ...

Barcelona has fallen. I fear that this is the beginning of the end. ...

3 February

Visited Butler. Total chaos in the corridors of the Foreign Office: filing cabinets, boxes, heaps of files, bundles of documents, etc. Virtually impossible to get through. I asked the attendant what the matter was. It turns out that the

Foreign Office is building an anti-gas shelter and the basement has to be temporarily cleared. ...

[The ill winds of isolation blowing from the Kremlin in the wake of the Munich agreement, further accentuated by Litvinov's depression, disillusion and exclusion from the formulation of policy – increasingly firmly in the hands of Stalin and Molotov – drove Maisky into reclusiveness. But he was himself partly to blame: in his efforts to keep pace with the Kremlin, he had inflamed suspicions in Moscow by suggesting that Chamberlain was 'deliberately promoting the "Ukrainian direction" of German aggression, in an attempt to prompt Hitler to embark on precisely such a course'. At the same time, Maisky blatantly ignored his instructions to stay out of things, and instead tried to prod the British into action by sounding the alarm. Litvinov did not subscribe to Maisky's appraisal that the Conservatives were undergoing a 'sobering' process, that 'Chamberlain's road of "appeasement"' could not be pursued indefinitely, and that the moment was approaching 'when one will have to say in all firmness: "So far and no further!" ']

4 February

I learn from a good source that Hitler's general policy amounts to the following.

His long-range objective is to dismember the USSR and set up a number of 'independent' states which would maintain 'friendly' relations with Germany.

However, prior to carrying out 'this large and complicated task', Hitler considers it necessary to secure his rear in the west by obtaining 'real guarantees' from Britain and France that they will not attack him while he is implementing his eastern plans. ...

13 February

Samuel Hoare came over for lunch. Unless I am mistaken, it was his first visit to the Soviet embassy. In the short period he headed the Foreign Office he did not manage to visit. Hudson,[1] the vigorous and clever secretary of the Department of Overseas Trade, was also present. ...

The way Hoare spoke about the USSR was entirely unexpected. He lavished praise on our air force and mocked those who speak of the weakness of the Red Army. He said: 'You are a country which can never be defeated. We, too, are a country which can never be defeated. Both our countries, unlike others, are capable of taking a long-term view when assessing events. It doesn't matter if

---

[1] Robert Spear Hudson (1st Viscount Hudson), parliamentary secretary to the Ministry of Labour, 1931–35; minister of pensions, 1935–36; secretary in the Department of Overseas Trade, 1937–40; privy counsellor, 1938.

things go badly for six weeks or six months; ultimately, both you and we will emerge on top.'

He added: 'The crucial thing at present is that both you and we are arming.' What's more: 'Our enemies are exactly the same.'

Goodness gracious, what a turnabout! I've never heard anything like that from the lips of Samuel Hoare. There must be something behind it. ...

20 February

We had Halifax, Churchill, Dawson of Penn,[2] the Rothensteins (father and son),[3] Balutis[4] and some others for dinner, all accompanied by their wives. It was the first time Winston Churchill had crossed the threshold of the Soviet embassy. He had always avoided doing so and we usually met on neutral ground.

Halifax told me, *inter alia*, that following our conversation on 27 January he had made a careful study of Anglo-Soviet trade relations and had reached the conclusion that renouncement of the current trade agreement would be undesirable. However, since the British industrialists have been complaining about a number of difficulties in trade relations between the two countries, the best solution, in his view, would be a visit by a British minister to Moscow in order to try to settle contentious issues through amicable talks. Such a visit, furthermore, could have a certain political effect, which would be particularly desirable in the current situation. Hence Hudson's mission, announced in Parliament today. ...

27 February

This day will go down in the history of Britain and France as a day of disgrace and folly: London and Paris recognized Franco *de jure*...

It took Britain and France seven years to recognize the Soviet Government. And it took them barely seven days to recognize Franco. These facts reflect the true essence of 'capitalist democracies' just as a drop of water reflects the sun.

28 February

Azcárate[5] came to see me at around 6 p.m. Inside he must be deeply perturbed or even shaken, but outwardly he retains his usual restraint and composure.

---

[2] Bertrand Dawson (1st Viscount Dawson of Penn), physician to the British royal family.
[3] William Rothenstein, principal, Royal College of Art, 1920–35; trustee, Tate Gallery, 1927–33; director, Tate Gallery, 1938–64.
[4] Bronius Kazys Balutis, Lithuanian ambassador in Washington, 1928–33, and in London from 1934.
[5] Pablo de Azcárate y Flórez, Spanish ambassador in London, 1936–39.

Yesterday Azcárate received a note from the Foreign Office in which Halifax informed him in refined and courteous language that the British Government had taken the decision to recognize Franco, and consequently 'your name can no longer appear on the list of foreign representatives at this court, as a result of which your diplomatic privileges must come to an end'. However, the note mercifully promised to extend Azcárate's personal privileges – tax exemption, in particular – for another three months, so that he could wind up his business without undue haste.

Unwilling to hand over the embassy to Alba[6] in person, Azcárate agreed with the Foreign Office that it would take the building from him and put Alba in possession at a later date. ...

[Maisky had been at odds with Litvinov about the Civil War from the outset. Temporarily enjoying Stalin's backing, he was later forced to repent for 'this interference in a sphere which is not entirely within [his] competence'. The Non-Intervention Committee was dissolved on 20 April, following the British recognition of Franco's government.]

2 March

Yesterday, as today's English papers pompously put it, we had a 'historic reception' at the embassy. In fact, there was nothing special about the reception as such, just the usual evening for 'friends' and 'acquaintances' which we hold every year...

But as for the guest list... Yes, that was exceptional!

I'll start at the beginning. When, at the end of January, I was sending out invitations for the 1 March reception, I sent cards to all the Cabinet members, as custom dictates. I expected all the ministers to decline politely, or for just two or three of them to accept and then not actually turn up. That's how it has always been.

Imagine my amazement when, on 1 February, I received a long letter from the prime minister's office informing me that Chamberlain would attend the reception, and that his wife, who unfortunately was due to attend a charity ball that evening where she was to meet the duchess of Gloucester,[7] would nevertheless do her best to put in an appearance and would let Mme Maisky know her final answer at a later date. After reading this missive, I said to myself: 'Aha, there is something behind this! Not a single British prime minister (even a Labourite) has ever crossed the threshold of the Soviet embassy during the

---

[6] Jacobo Fitz-James Stuart (17th duke of Alba), Spanish foreign minister, 1930–31; Spanish ambassador to Great Britain, 1939–45.
[7] Princess Alice Christabel, duchess of Gloucester.

entire period of Soviet rule, and now look: not only the 'man with the umbrella' himself, but also his spouse, is desperate to attend our reception!' ... What was most important was <u>who</u> accepted the invitation. All the pillars of society: major MPs and businessmen, bankers, lords, diehard Tories, high-born aristocrats, members of government... Well, well, well! Thirteen members of Cabinet, i.e. more than half, promised to come, and most of them did. It's quite unheard of in the six-and-a-bit years of my employment in London. That's what a shift in the international scene means! That's what the growth of Soviet might means!

I nonetheless had my doubts until the very last minute whether or not Chamberlain himself would make an appearance. I rather expected something 'unforeseen' to hold him back at the eleventh hour. ... It's hard to describe the stir created among the guests by the prime minister's appearance. Nobody knew about it in advance, and nobody (of the more than 500 invitees) had expected such a 'daring step' from him. There was a general commotion and agitation. People stopped in the middle of their sentences and rushed childishly to have a look at Chamberlain in the interior of the Soviet embassy. I first led him to the white ball-room and then to my office, where I offered him and his daughter *refreshments*. Chamberlain declined vodka, but had nothing against mulled wine. The office soon filled with people. I tried to keep the crowd back, but I didn't always succeed. Standing by the sideboard, the PM and I discussed various topics.

Chamberlain first broached the matter of Hudson's forthcoming trip. Its aim is to settle various trade disagreements and prepare the ground for expanding Anglo-Soviet trade. Unlike Halifax and Vansittart, Chamberlain said not a word about the political aspect of the visit.

... I asked the PM what he thought of Europe's immediate prospects.

Chamberlain replied that he remained an 'optimist' despite everything. The general situation is improving. The German and Italian people do not want war. Both Hitler and Mussolini gave Chamberlain their personal assurances that their task was the peaceful development of the resources at their disposal. Chamberlain was left with the definite impression that Hitler and Mussolini are afraid of war.

I smiled and said that I quite agreed with him on one point: Hitler and Mussolini are indeed afraid of any serious war. The danger of the situation, however, lies in the fact that they are firmly convinced that they can gain <u>bloodless victories</u>, victories based on bluffing and on holding their nerve better than other world leaders.

Chamberlain suddenly darkened and seemed to stretch another inch in height. He uttered testily: 'The time of such victories has passed!'

Our conversation moved away from this subject and somehow alighted on Chamberlain's father. The PM instantly brightened up and seemed to become more cordial.

33. Chamberlain entering the lion's den.

'You know,' he said, 'my father never thought that I would go into politics. When he died in 1912 (correct date is 1914), I myself had no idea that I might become a parliamentarian and minister.'

'And how did it happen?' I inquired.

'It happened this way. In 1911 I was elected to the city council of Birmingham. In 1915 and 1916 I was lord mayor of Birmingham. Lloyd George, then prime minister, invited me to take the post of director-general of national service. I agreed and resigned as lord mayor. I soon discovered, however, that Lloyd George was not giving me the support to which I was entitled, so half a year later I resigned.' (Lloyd George, in his turn, once told me that Chamberlain had turned out to be a quite useless director-general.) 'I could not return to my post as lord mayor of Birmingham as it had been filled. So I had a long think and decided to try my luck at politics. I entered Parliament and began to occupy myself with affairs of state. I can say with some justification that I became a politician thanks to Lloyd George.'

Then, with a somewhat spiteful expression and with obvious sarcasm in his voice, Chamberlain added: 'Lloyd George may regret it, but now it's too late!'

There's no love lost between Chamberlain and Lloyd George. None at all!

... I gained the impression from our talk that the PM considers himself a 'man of destiny'! He was born into this world to perform a 'sacred mission'.

A dangerous state of mind.

8 March

(1) My wife and I had lunch with the Hudsons. We were alone and were therefore able to have a detailed and uninhibited discussion about Hudson's forthcoming visit to Moscow. At first we talked about trifles, such as what Muscovites wear, what the weather is like, what sights should be seen in the city and its environs, etc. ...

(2) Hudson directly posed the following question: does 'Moscow' seriously want to talk about a meaningful improvement of relations with Britain? He has heard more than once in London that this is very doubtful. He was told that after Munich, Moscow had decided to retreat into its borders, to break with the West and pursue a policy of isolation, and that for this reason it was useless to seek a common language with Moscow. The main objective of Hudson's visit – and this is much more important than the trade talks themselves – is to gauge Moscow's frame of mind in this respect through contact with the leading figures of the Soviet Union. Very much will depend on this because, as Hudson sees it, the next six to twelve months will be crucial in determining British foreign policy for many years, if not for a whole generation. Indeed, he said, a most serious change has occurred in the mood of the country (viz. England,

viz. the Conservative Party) in the past two or three months, as I too must have had occasion to observe. ... 'The prejudice against communism that hampered cooperation between our countries has been almost entirely overcome. However, doubts exist in London as to whether or not we desire such cooperation.' Hudson's key task is to clarify this point and report to the Cabinet. ... Hudson leaves for Moscow with his hands untied. ...

(3) I told him that he could, of course, expect a very friendly reception in Moscow, and that representatives of the Soviet Government would indeed be willing to talk with him about the matters that concerned him. ...

9 March

Beaverbrook told me that Chamberlain had a talk with Churchill the other day and was forced to admit that the policy of 'appeasement' had failed. Chamberlain will, of course, make every effort to defer conflict and alleviate the tension through various manoeuvres, but the PM can see now that lasting peace and genuine friendship between Britain and Germany are impossible. This, in Beaverbrook's opinion, explains the prime minister's marked turn towards the USSR, which he demonstrated by attending our reception. In this connection, Beaverbrook inundated me with a stream of rather heavy compliments: 'Stay here for another two or three years and you'll be able to reap the rich harvest in the sphere of Anglo-Soviet relations which your work will have prepared over preceding years.'

Beaverbrook also told me that Germanophobia was spreading rapidly among the general public and that, in the contrary direction, sympathy towards the USSR was clearly on the rise. ... Sinclair[8] told me that mention of the USSR and of the urgent need for a joint struggle for peace had been met with stormy applause at every meeting he had spoken at up and down the country. ...

15 March

I had lunch at Randolph Churchill's. Also present were his father, Lord Dufferin[9] (deputy minister for colonies), the son of Lord Camrose (publisher of the *Daily Telegraph*),[10] and the American correspondent Roy Howard,[11] who was granted the celebrated interview with Comrade Stalin in March 1936 which stopped Japanese aggression against the M[ongolian] P[eople's]

---

[8] Archibald Sinclair (1st Viscount Thurso), secretary of state for Scotland, 1931–32; secretary of state for air, 1940–45; leader of the Liberal Party, 1935–45.
[9] Basil Hamilton-Temple-Blackwood (4th marquess of Dufferin and Ava), lord-in-waiting, 1936–37; parliamentary undersecretary of state for the colonies, 1937–40.
[10] The son was John Seymour Berry (2nd Viscount Camrose).
[11] Roy Wilson Howard, editor and president of the *New York World-Telegram* and the *Sun,* 1931–60.

R[epublic]. We spoke, of course, about the international situation, first and foremost about Czechoslovakia.

Winston Churchill expressed his view that Hitler's move against Czechoslovakia by no means signified a turn towards the East. Before striking a serious blow to the West, Hitler simply had to secure his rear, i.e. liquidate the Czechoslovak army, the Czechoslovak air force, etc. Moreover, Hitler was very keen to reinforce himself with Czechoslovak weapons, ammunition, aircraft and excellent armaments factories.

Winston Churchill inquired with great anxiety about the meaning behind Stalin's speech.[12] Was it a refusal to cooperate with the democracies?

I replied that such an interpretation would be incorrect. We have always been and remain advocates of collective retaliation against aggression, but it is essential that the 'democracies' should also be prepared to fight against the aggressors and not just chatter about it.

Churchill attaches great significance to Hudson's visit. This is a manifest sign of change in the sentiments of the ruling circles. Even if Chamberlain conceived Hudson's visit as merely a tactical manoeuvre (I raised this possibility), the logic of events will give it a far more serious tone. ...

19 March

The atmosphere in Europe is becoming increasingly heated. On the evening of 17 March, in a speech in Birmingham, Chamberlain was sharply critical of Germany for its latest actions, but he did not risk drawing all the important logical conclusions. The front pages of yesterday's papers brought sensational news about 'Germany's ultimatum to Rumania'. ... As I have learned, this news was given to the press by Halifax himself on the same evening. The 'German ultimatum' made a deep impression in England and France.

Halifax, however, did not limit himself to publication of the 'ultimatum'. On the same evening of 17 March, Halifax sent out urgent inquiries to Paris, Moscow, Warsaw, Ankara and possibly some other capitals, asking the respective governments what their response would be to German aggression against Rumania.

Seeds[13] presented M.M. with this inquiry on the morning of 18 March. M.M. inquired in his turn about the British Government's position and added

---

[12] In his speech to the 18th Party Congress, on 10 March, Stalin had defended Russia's isolation and urged the party 'to be cautious and not allow Soviet Russia to be drawn into conflicts by warmongers who are accustomed to have others pull the chestnuts out of the fire'. Here Stalin had appropriated a metaphor employed by Maisky a couple of months earlier.

[13] Fulfilling a lifetime's ambition, William Seeds, who had studied Russian and spent time in St Petersburg at the turn of the century, was appointed ambassador to the Soviet Union in 1938, conducted the negotiations on the triple alliance in Moscow, and returned to London disillusioned by the politics of both sides in the wake of the Soviet invasion of Finland in December 1939.

that Rumania itself had not sought assistance from us. He nonetheless promised to report Seeds' inquiry to the Soviet Government, and the same evening
he communicated our proposal to Seeds: to convene immediately a conference
of the six powers which were most concerned with the matter (Britain, France,
USSR, Poland, Turkey and Rumania), and to discuss measures by which to
confront the imminent danger. It would be advisable to hold the conference in
Bucharest. But this could be negotiated.

While Seeds was paying his first visit to M.M. in Moscow, here in London I
was summoned by Halifax. He first spoke about Hudson (who was about to
leave London, at 2 p.m. on 18 March) and asked that he be given a warm
welcome. ...

I met Halifax at 12.45. Earlier, at eleven in the morning, I had a conversation with Vansittart, who spoke heatedly and at length about the importance of
making Hudson's visit a 'success'. British sentiments are rapidly changing,
owing to the latest events. Leadership in foreign policy is returning from *10,
Downing Street* to the Foreign Office. Halifax now shares Vansittart's view of
things.

... At 3 p.m. today I saw Halifax, to inform him of our answer to the
British inquiry (although Seeds had certainly notified him about it through
his own channels, there was no harm in my repeating it just to make sure)
and, most importantly, to find out what the British Government thought
of it. It was Sunday, but Halifax was in the Foreign Office. Moreover, he had
already exchanged opinions with the PM earlier in the morning, concerning
our proposal for a six-power conference. Halifax finds the proposal 'premature': if the conference is not prepared properly in advance, it could culminate
in failure, with a negative political effect. Besides, we must act quickly, whereas
the convening of a conference will take some time. So, instead of a conference,
the British Government suggests the prompt issuing of a 'declaration of the
four' (Britain, France, USSR and Poland) to the effect that the said powers
will respond to the threat of aggression by immediately organizing a consultation on measures of resistance. This is the first step. Then, after the four
powers sign the declaration, the remaining peace-loving countries will be
invited to join, and a conference of the respective countries may be convened,
where the methods and forms of fighting aggression will be discussed.
Of course, agreement must be reached primarily by the *big boys*, i.e. the
'big four'.

I began to object. I said that the conference could be convened in a few days
if there was a desire to do so, that an announcement of the date and venue
could be published tomorrow, that this alone would have a far-reaching
political effect, and that if Britain really *means business*, the risk of the
conference failing was very small. But Halifax stuck to his guns. He informed

me that the text of the declaration was being worked on. It will be adopted by the Cabinet tomorrow morning and immediately sent to the capitals concerned. ...

It is clear that Chamberlain does not want a genuine struggle against aggression. He is still working for 'appeasement'.

34. Maisky bids farewell to Seeds on his appointment as ambassador to Moscow.

22 March

Today we gave our reply to the British: we are prepared to sign their 'declaration of the four' if France and Poland sign it, too. To add weight to the declaration, we propose that it be signed not only by the foreign ministers of the four countries, but also by their premiers.

So, Britain, France and the USSR have given their consent. But what about Poland? Yesterday, at a banquet at the palace in honour of Lebrun,[14] I questioned Raczyński[15] (the Polish ambassador) about this. He said that he approved of the declaration personally and would willingly sign it, but he wasn't sure that Warsaw shared his attitude. Raczyński is a poor representative of Beck. He is a Westernist and a League of Nations man, and you can hardly use him to judge what the Polish Government is thinking. We will see. ...

[Maisky admitted to Dalton that the object of the Soviet proposal was 'to test British and French intentions of which they were suspicious'. Litvinov, who remained highly sceptical, forbade his diplomats from taking any initiative. 'If Britain and France genuinely change their line,' he instructed them, 'they should either make their views on our former proposals known or else offer their own. The initiative must be left to them.' Maisky, who found it difficult to abide by Litvinov's instructions, continued to use his old method of inciting his interlocutors to come up with ideas which, unbeknownst to the Kremlin, often originated with him.]

25 March

... My general impression is that the PM still believes in *appeasement* and still hopes to push Hitler towards the Ukraine. But the public's mood is rapidly hardening. England sees again in its mind's eye the phantom of a great power striving for hegemony on the Continent. This phantom has awoken past fears and mighty passions in the English soul. Philip II of Spain, Louis XIV, Napoleon I, the Kaiser! England has waged stubborn and destructive wars against the 'hegemons' of the past. She has satisfied herself only with their complete annihilation. The same feelings and moods are elicited by the name of Hitler today. Of course, were Hitler to move East, decisive steps against Germany could be postponed. But most Tories are far from convinced about Hitler's 'eastern aspirations'. Very many of them fear the opposite: that Hitler, having secured Balkan and Baltic resources of raw materials and food, and having immobi-

---

[14] Albert Lebrun, 14th and last president of France's Third Republic, 1932–40.
[15] Count Edward Bernard Raczyński, Polish delegate to the disarmament conference in Geneva, 1932–34; ambassador to Great Britain, 1934–45.

lized Poland by one method or another, will bring his colossal, newly acquired might to bear on France and England.

[On the afternoon of 29 March, Chamberlain was alerted by Halifax to intelligence reports from Berlin about an impending German attack on Poland. The two decided 'then & there' to issue a guarantee declaration, promising Poland assistance 'in the event of any action which clearly threatened Polish independence'. Chamberlain deliberately opted for Poland rather than Russia as an ally, against the firm advice of the chiefs of staff. By so doing, he not only pushed the Russians further into isolation, but also inadvertently set the scene for a Soviet–German rapprochement (dictated by a suspicious Kremlin's wish to steal a march on Britain).]

29 March

I visited Cadogan.[16]

First of all, I requested an explanation for the strange incident that occurred regarding the communiqué which concluded Hudson's visit to Moscow.[17] ... Cadogan asked me whether I had read yesterday's statement by the PM in Parliament. I replied that I had and, moreover, had been greatly surprised by it. Chamberlain said that the British Government's intentions 'go significantly farther than mere consultation' and that 'the powers, with which we are in consultation, have been given to understand clearly what actions we are ready to undertake under certain circumstances'. Until now I've had every reason to believe that the Soviet Union is one of the powers with which Britain is in consultation, but I am as yet aware only of the draft 'declaration of the four' that stipulates 'consultation', and nothing more. Is it any surprise that I was somewhat taken aback yesterday by the prime minister's revelation?

In saying this, I intentionally went a little over the top: I had already gleaned something of the British Government's new plans from unofficial sources, but the Foreign Office had not said a word about it to me.

Cadogan was a bit embarrassed and started explaining the current situation. It turns out that 'the declaration of the four' is now in the past. The view that has come to dominate British Government circles at present is as follows: as an

---

[16] Maisky had been trying in vain to meet Halifax. He was finally diverted to Cadogan, who had been instructed 'to stall him'.

[17] Hudson had arrived in Moscow, complained officials at the British embassy in Moscow, with 'an anodyne message of encouragement' from Halifax and a vague promise of a political deal. A few hours before leaving Moscow, a telegram arrived from London instructing him 'to stick to commercial negotiations and in no circumstances to broach any political matters whatever'. Litvinov was hauled back to Moscow from his dacha complaining 'acidly that he had thought he was dealing with a plenipotentiary, but now found that he was a second-rate office boy'. He informed Maisky on 28 March that 'the visit had no political or economic repercussions whatsoever'.

initial stage it is necessary to build a four-power bloc of Britain, France, Poland and Rumania, with the former two committing themselves to armed defence of the latter two in the event of German aggression against them. The USSR remains to one side for the time being, but it will be drawn in at the second stage. ... Listening to Cadogan, I did not hide my deep mistrust. Knowing the English and the traditions of British foreign policy, I could not accept that Chamberlain would make any firm *commitments* in Eastern Europe.[18] ...

31 March

Poland is the centre of attention. The German press is waging a rabid campaign against Poland. German troops are concentrated on the Polish border. Hitler is expected to strike any moment now, but in which direction? That is not quite clear as yet. Most probably, Danzig or Silesia. Or maybe in both directions at once.

In view of the current situation, the British diplomatic machinery has been working at a quite uncharacteristically frenzied pace for the last seven or eight days. When it transpired that 'the declaration of the four' was not viable due to Poland's objections, the British Government, without breathing a word to us, stepped up its search for other means *to stop aggression*. As usual, the English took the path of creeping empiricism, i.e. the method of the rule of thumb. They decided: since at this precise moment it is Poland that faces acute danger, let's think how to help Poland. And only Poland. Fighting aggression in Europe in general does not interest us. Two days ago already, Cadogan informed me of the direction which the British Government's thinking was taking. By the way, no decision was taken in the end at the Cabinet meeting on 29 March. But on the same evening and yesterday, 30 March, there was an almost unbroken flow of meetings of the Cabinet and of its foreign policy committee (Chamberlain, Halifax, Simon, Hoare and two or three more ministers) in attempts to find the best way of helping Poland. It was only today that the results of all this unusual activity on *Downing Street* became known. ...

On the 29th, after lunch, I received a call from the Foreign Office asking me to visit Halifax at seven in the evening. I accepted. But at 6 p.m., Halifax's secretary phoned me again to say that, unfortunately, the minister couldn't receive me today and asked me to come at 4 p.m. the following day. Once again I accepted. On 30 March at 3 p.m. there was another call from the Foreign Office: it turned out that the foreign secretary couldn't receive me on this day either

---

[18] According to Cadogan, Maisky was astounded by the new plan, which he thought tantamount to 'a revolutionary change in British policy' and might have 'far-reaching results'. His positive response was in brazen defiance of the reserve advocated by Litvinov.

and wished to postpone my visit to the following morning at 10.30. I agreed to that as well. On the 31st, at 10 a.m., yet another call came from the FO: Halifax was unable to keep his last promise. He would let me know when he could see me. Finally, at noon on the same day, 31 March, Halifax's secretary asked me to come to the FO at 12.45. Only then did my meeting with Halifax take place.

It began with much bowing and scraping on the part of the foreign secretary. He was terribly sorry that he had had to postpone our meetings again and again, but during the past two days he had been holding endless meetings. 'It is not so easy to edit a document that would mean a revolution in our foreign policy,' Halifax said by way of self-justification.

He then gave me a sheet of paper with the text of the speech the prime minister was to make in Parliament at 3 p.m. I quickly skimmed the document. Halifax watched my face attentively, and when I had finished reading, asked me anxiously what I thought about it. I replied that it was difficult for me to formulate a considered opinion since I had only just seen the text of the prime minister's statement, but my first reaction was that the document lacked precision. ...

Halifax started to defend the text of the statement, though it was clear that my words had somewhat confused him. He then asked: 'But generally speaking, the statement is in line with your aims, is it not?'

'Perhaps,' I said, 'but it is not firm and consistent enough.'

Halifax was silent for an instant, before blurting out: 'What would you think if the prime minister told Parliament that the Soviet Government also approves of his statement?'

And then, after a little hesitation, he added, as if forcing the words out against his will: 'If the prime minister could say this, it would greatly alleviate the situation... This would prevent unnecessary arguments and discord in our midst...'

I immediately realized what was behind it: Chamberlain wanted to use us as a shield against the opposition's attacks. Affecting great surprise, I replied: 'I don't quite understand you, Lord Halifax. You did not consult us while preparing your Polish action. The Soviet Government has not seen the present statement. I myself had the opportunity to familiarize myself with it just a few moments ago. How could the prime minister say that the Soviet Government approves of his statement under such circumstances? I think it would be rather awkward.'

Halifax was embarrassed and hastened to say: 'You may be right.' ...

[Rather than the Munich agreement, Stalin's 'chestnuts' speech or the dismissal of Litvinov in May, the guarantees given to Poland appear to have been the crucial event paving the way to the Molotov–Ribbentrop Pact, and the opening salvo of the Second World War. By guaranteeing Poland, Chamberlain to all intents and purposes abandoned Britain's traditional position as arbiter in the European balance of power, and instead confronted Germany head on. The guarantees had two potential major effects. Beyond redressing the humiliation inflicted on him by Hitler's brazen abrogation of the Munich agreement, what was uppermost in Chamberlain's mind was the deterrent effect: the guarantees (he hoped) would check Hitler and bring him back to the negotiating table. The second possible repercussion was overlooked by Chamberlain: if Hitler persevered with his territorial claims against Poland, the military axiom of avoiding war on two fronts would make it imperative for the Nazis to seek agreement with the Soviet Union. Consequently, the hitherto inaccessible German option suddenly opened up for the Soviet Union. Conversely, once it did dawn on Chamberlain that the path to a 'second Munich' was not plain sailing and that the possibility of war had become real, he would reluctantly be forced to secure at least a measure of Soviet military commitment, vital for the implementation of the guarantees. In this manner, and without prior design, the Soviet Union now became the pivot of the European balance of power.]

1 April

Yesterday, after the statement had been read in Parliament, Chamberlain invited Lloyd George to his office to exchange views on international affairs. An unprecedented event, since Chamberlain and Lloyd George hate each other.

During their conversation, Lloyd George raised the issue, in the sharpest terms, of engaging the USSR in security guarantees in Europe. Chamberlain replied, as always, that he was only too willing to do so, but that Poland and Rumania were making things difficult. Lloyd George then asked: 'But if the question of engaging the USSR is still hanging in the air, how could you risk giving Poland Great Britain's unilateral guarantee? That's damnably dangerous.'

Chamberlain parried Lloyd George's remark by declaring that, according to the information available to the government, Hitler would never risk a war on two fronts.

'And where is your second front?' Lloyd George snapped back.

'Poland,' answered Chamberlain.

Lloyd George roared with laughter and started mocking the prime minister: 'Poland! A country with a weak economy and torn by internal strife, a country that has neither aviation nor a properly equipped army ... And that's your second front! What nonsense! There cannot be a second front without the USSR. A guarantee to Poland without the USSR is an irresponsible gamble that may end very badly for our country!'

Chamberlain did not have an answer.[19]

---

[19] Chamberlain's circle found Maisky's extra-parliamentary activities during the debate repulsive. 'I saw [Churchill] with Lloyd George, Boothby and Randolph, in a triumphant huddle surrounding Maisky. Maisky, the Ambassador of torture, murder and every crime in the calendar,' recorded Sir Henry Channon in his diary.

6 April

Today I saw Halifax, who briefed me on the results of his talks with Beck. According to Halifax, the three days Beck spent in London have been very profitable. The main achievement is the bilateral agreement on mutual assistance against aggression which the prime minister announced in Parliament today. In this way, the unilateral guarantee which Great Britain gave to Poland on 31 March is now transformed into a pact of mutual assistance between the two countries. ...[20]

On parting, Halifax expressed the ardent hope that he would be able to get away at Easter to his estate for five days. Just think: he has not been 'home' for a whole six weeks!

Will he leave? I don't know. Dark clouds are gathering on the Albanian horizon.

[Cautiously steering a course through the rather schizophrenic Soviet policy, Maisky admitted to the Webbs that, like other Soviet diplomats, he had become increasingly isolated, hardly in touch with any of the leaders and 'kept out of the Molotov–Stalin government circles'. Moscow, he confided, 'did *not* trust [Chamberlain] and it was doubtful whether they would join a pact if he remained Premier'. He continued cautiously to challenge Moscow's dithering, urging Litvinov to provide him with instruction concerning 'the direction our work here should take', particularly if the Western powers were to offer a pact of mutual assistance. The response, however, was a harsh accusation levelled at Maisky for having inadvertently become putty in the hands of Chamberlain and Vansittart. Determined 'to keep quiet, and not show any nervousness or impatience' he could not refrain from coaxing intermediaries (provided his name was not mentioned) to encourage the Foreign Office to invite Litvinov to London. 'I regard association with the Soviet,' Cadogan sealed the debate (echoing Chamberlain), 'as more of a liability than an asset.']

11 April

Halifax didn't manage to get away to his estate after all! The Italians attacked Albania on the morning of the 7th, and as of today King Zog[21] is already a refugee in exile.

---

[20] Chamberlain felt in tune with Beck's views on Europe. He was, as he confided to his sister, 'very anxious not to be tied up with Russia ... because of the effect on German opinion & policy'. 'I confess', he concluded, that 'I very much agree with him for I regard Russia as a very unreliable friend with very little capacity for active assistance but with an enormous irritative power on others'.
[21] Ahmet Muhtar Bej Zogolli, King Zog I of Albania, 1928–39.

I visited Halifax at his request.[22] We talked at length about the spread of aggression in Europe and the need to take urgent measures against it. Halifax wanted to know whether we would agree to give Poland a guarantee in the forms that would make Soviet aid acceptable to Warsaw (arms, ammunition, aviation, etc., but not large land forces). I declined to give him a direct answer. Halifax further let me understand that the British Government was preparing guarantees for Greece and possibly for Rumania too. He tried to argue that Britain, like the USSR, was thinking about the organization of security all over Europe, only our methods were different: Britain wants to build security 'from the bottom', laying one brick on another, whereas the USSR wants European security to be built 'from the top', by setting up an all-embracing peace bloc. In Halifax's view, the British path is more practicable.

I objected, arguing that aggression is like water: if you block it in one direction, it finds another. We should not split hairs and set about this like amateurs. We must stop the spread of aggression across Europe right away, and the only way of doing that is to form a 'peace bloc' around 'the big troika': Britain, France and the USSR. Our exchange came to nothing, of course, but I think I managed to put some useful ideas into Halifax's head. ...

[Litvinov took a dim view of the line adopted by Maisky in his conversations with Halifax. He took the unusual step of seeking Stalin's approval to reprimand Maisky, and instructed him to 'assume a more reserved attitude in his conversations with representatives of the British Government'.]

14 April

Following instructions from Moscow, I went to see Halifax today. I referred to the interest he displayed in our previous talks about the forms of aid which the USSR could grant Poland and Rumania, and said that the Soviet Government was in principle prepared to help Rumania, but that first it wished to hear the opinion of the British about the best way of organizing this assistance.

Halifax was very glad to hear this, but at the same time he was somewhat upset. It transpired that just before my visit he had finished writing instructions to Seeds. He advised Seeds to ask the Soviet Government whether it would consent to give unilateral guarantees to Poland and Rumania, similar to the guarantees Britain and France had given to Rumania and Greece, on condition that the USSR would render assistance to Warsaw and Bucharest only at their request and in forms that had been agreed with them. Halifax thought that in this way it would be possible to avoid the difficulties that had sunk 'the

---

[22] Halifax summoned Maisky to 'keep him in touch', but deliberately concealed from him any details of the agreement being worked out with the Poles.

declaration of the four'. These instructions were meant to go out to Moscow that night. But what should he do now, on hearing my news? Send the instructions as they were, or not send them at all?

Halifax stopped talking and started thinking it over. At last he said: 'Your communication does not contradict my instructions. Therefore I'll send them as they are and add that I got your communication after the instructions had already been drawn up.'

Halifax expressed his hope that our reply to the British inquiry would come soon, by 17 April if possible. He wanted to know my opinion about the British proposal, but I evaded discussion of this topic. ...

[Halifax proposed that the Soviet Government should make a 'unilateral public declaration on its own initiative', to be carefully hedged around by such qualifications as 'that in the event of any aggression against any European neighbour of the Soviet Union which was resisted by the country concerned, the assistance of the Soviet Government would be available, if desired, and would be afforded in such manner as would be found most convenient'. A 'positive declaration' by the Soviet Government, Halifax believed, 'would have a steadying effect upon the international situation'. This idea of a 'steadying effect' reflected the deterrent element in British policy, which always sought reconciliation.]

15 April

Yesterday, late at night, I received the order to proceed immediately to Moscow for consultation on Anglo-Soviet negotiations. Very good. This will significantly clarify to me the tasks ahead.

Today is Saturday, so it will be impossible to complete all the formalities before Monday, the 17th. I'll leave on the 18th. To save time, I'll fly to Helsinki via Stockholm, and from there I'll take a train for Moscow via Leningrad. I've never flown before. Let's try. It's high time I got used to the most modern means of transport.

16 April

[Maisky describes his visit to Hudson's country house.]

... Far more interesting was my conversation with Elliot, whom I met at Hudson's. He pulled me aside and, strolling with me in the park, disclosed a good deal of intriguing information.

I asked Elliot: 'The British Government seems to be changing tack in its foreign policy – is this a serious change or not?' ... Yes, said Elliot, the turn in English policy is serious. The desire to cooperate with the USSR is entirely sincere. ... Chamberlain? A strange figure! Until now he has placed sincere faith in Hitler, thinking he had only one goal in mind: to unite all Germans within a single state. Prague was a terrible catastrophe for Chamberlain, both politically and psychologically. The PM is certainly undergoing a profound change in his outlook, but this change is not yet complete. Echoes of the past still linger – for instance, in Chamberlain's attitude to Italy. He is grossly disappointed in Hitler, but he still retains some trust in Mussolini. This will eventually pass, too.

Chamberlain understands that cooperation between Britain and the USSR is inevitable. He is moving in this direction, but at a slow and faltering pace. It is not easy for him to make this change. At present, the prime minister has two gnawing doubts: (1) Is the Red Army effective? Like a true merchant he wants to try the goods before he buys them. (2) What are the true intentions of the USSR? ...[23]

35. David Low, 'Chamberlain's gallant effort to acquire Soviet culture, under the guidance of M. Maisky'.

---

[23] Maisky's redeeming picture of Chamberlain is hardly borne out by the prime minister's own admission, in a letter to his sister, 'of being deeply suspicious of [Russia] ... Her efforts are devoted to egging on others but herself promising only vague assistance ... Our problem therefore is to keep Russia in the background without antagonising her'.

[Maisky's dogged determination to open an active dialogue with the British finally resonated with Litvinov. Challenged openly by Stalin and Molotov, Litvinov now strongly recommended making a proposal to London whereby the unilateral guarantees would be replaced by a full-blown binding triple pact. The offer was made on 17 April. Hoping to maintain control over the conduct of Soviet foreign policy, fast slipping out of his hands, Litvinov attempted in vain to shield Maisky and prevent his recall. Were Maisky to leave London, warned Litvinov, the embassy would 'cease to function, for there is no one who could conduct serious diplomatic negotiations or whom the English would take notice of'. Surits, who was recalled as well from Paris, had been warned by Potemkin, in a handwritten message, to be vigilant, as 'the slightest lapse is not only recorded but also provokes a swift and violent reaction'. Merekalov, the third ambassador recalled for the meeting, never returned to Berlin and was banished from Narkomindel.]

17 April

The press has already made a first-class sensation out of my trip to Moscow, and today all the papers have been ringing the embassy non-stop to find out the particulars and to learn when I'm leaving and from which station. So far we have managed to keep everything secret.

The day was spent in the usual bustle before any trip. I paid a short call on Cadogan to settle a minor routine matter and to inform him of my departure. I could hardly disappear without warning when difficult diplomatic negotiations were in full swing. Then I attended a bankers' lunch, which was arranged by Brendan Bracken,[24] editor of *Financial News*, and attended by Anselm Rothschild, the heads of Lloyd's Bank, and others. Then I had a talk with our staff.

At around eleven at night, Sir Walter Layton, editor of the *News Chronicle*, suddenly called. He apologized for disturbing me at such a late hour and asked if he could visit right away, as he simply had to see me before my departure. He arrived at 11.30. He immediately directed the conversation to the current state of Anglo-Soviet relations. He insisted that public opinion in England had undergone radical change in the last four or five weeks, that England had taken a new course in earnest and for the long term, and that she sincerely wanted to repel aggression, and to achieve agreement and cooperation with the USSR. It was evident from the tone and nature of Layton's speech that he was paying me this late visit not on his own initiative, but on somebody's

---

[24] Brendan Rendall Bracken, editor of *The Banker*, chairman of the *Financial News*, and managing director of *The Economist*; parliamentary private secretary to the prime minister, 1940–44; minister of information, 1941–45.

instructions... Whose? I can't say with any certainty, but it's possible that he acted on the instructions of the PM, for I know that Layton has access to Chamberlain and that during the September crisis Chamberlain personally 'briefed' Layton more than once.

The British Government seems greatly concerned about my being summoned to Moscow and wants to convince me before I leave, and the Soviet Government through me, of its sincere wish to work together with us on the establishment of a peace front.

18 April

Yesterday M.M. handed Seeds our reply to the British proposal of 14 April. Here is the essence of our reply.

Following the British inquiry about the Soviet Government's readiness to render assistance to our immediate European neighbours in the face of aggression, Moscow received a French proposal to enter into bilateral commitments for mutual military assistance against aggressors. Accepting the French proposal in principle and following its spirit, as well as wishing to lay a firm foundation for relations between the three states, the Soviet Government seeks to combine the British and French proposals in the following points offered for consideration by the British and French governments:

(1) The USSR, France and Britain sign an agreement for a term of 5 to 10 years, mutually committing themselves to provide immediate assistance in all forms, including military aid, in the event of aggression in Europe against one of the three contracting states.

(2) The USSR, France and Britain undertake to provide every kind of assistance, including military aid, to the Eastern European states located between the Baltic and Black seas and bordering on the USSR in the event of aggression against these states.

(3) The USSR, France and Britain shall, at the earliest possible date, discuss and establish the forms and extent of military aid to be rendered by each of the said states in compliance with Paras. 1 and 2. ...

28 April

The ten days that have passed since my last entry seem almost like a fairy-tale to me now... So, at about a quarter past nine on the morning of 18 April I took the plane from Croydon. ... I boarded the plane with my chin held high but, I admit, not without some anxiety in my heart: what if I turned out to be a bad flier after all? The last farewells... The last blown kisses... The last fussing of the service personnel... The propeller starts its noisy whirring, and the huge

Douglas, capable of carrying 21 passengers, sets off heavily down the runway...
Then it suddenly detaches itself from the ground and begins its climb... A green
field, hangars, little houses with red roofs – everything starts to fall away rapidly
and unexpectedly... deeper and deeper ... Obeying some conditioned reflex, I
cast around for cork lifebelts, before I suddenly realize: what's the use of them?
If something happens to the plane, cork lifebelts won't help. You'll die while
you're still in the air or when the plane hits the surface of the sea. ... Suddenly,
the huge steel body of the plane shudders several times. Its long powerful wings
bank sharply now left, now right. The shaking is so strong that the passengers
jump in their seats and grab feverishly at their seat belts. Thick white fog on
both sides of the plane. Nothing to be seen through the windows. We're in the
clouds. The pilot gains height again. The pointer on the altimeter is spinning
round... Upwards and upwards... Two and a half thousand metres already... The
fog has vanished, we're out of the clouds... Above us only the bright but somewhat cold sun and the endless blue sky. Below us once again the mighty fields
of white, curly cotton wool, and upon them, like an evil bird of prey, the
speeding shadow of our plane, black and shaped like a cross...

Aleksandra M. Kollontay and the first secretary meet me at the aerodrome.
Another swarm of photographers and reporters. We get into a car and drive to
the embassy...

I make a telephone call to London to tell Agniya about my safe arrival and
my victory over the airways.

* * *

I spent the night in Stockholm and at 9 a.m. on the 19th flew out to Helsingfors.
... The hours before evening flew by. Journalists besieged me, of course, eager
to find out what 'proposals' I was bringing along with me. I brushed them off
with a laugh: 'my pockets are empty'. This only made the reporting brethren
even more curious. I didn't pay visits to any of the ministers. Just sent my
visiting cards. Then I wandered about the city and bought a few things. I took
the train from Helsingfors at 11.20 at night. The train was just the same as
before. I slept like a baby and in the morning stepped off in Rajajoki to stretch
my legs and have a drink. Here, too, nothing had changed. We crossed the
Sestra River... My native land! Beloostrov! I drew a deep breath and listened to
my inner voice: yes, the air was different! Strong, bracing, resonant and above
all ours!..

... In Leningrad I was met by A.V. Burdukov.[25] Natasha[26] had been hospital-
ized with pneumonia. That was an unpleasant surprise for me. I saw my

---

[25] Aleksei Vasilevich Burdukov, Soviet explorer of Mongolia.
[26] Maisky's only daughter from his first marriage.

grandson – a wonderful little boy with blue eyes and fair hair. His favourite amusement is to take a toy and hurl it on the floor. I visited Natasha in the hospital and left for Moscow in the evening.

I spent four days in Moscow (my bosses did not allow me more), which passed like a kind of dream. I stayed in Hotel Moskva. For 47 roubles a day I had a fairly decent room on the third floor with a bathroom, but, alas, the bathtub was in such a state that I had no desire to use it. I saw a great many people, attended various meetings concerning Anglo-Franco-Soviet negotiations, dropped in to my apartment, chatted with my relatives, and ... failed to visit the theatre even once. There just wasn't enough time.

On April 24 I took the *Krasnaya strela* back to Leningrad and spent half a day there. I visited Natasha in hospital, played with my grandson, and talked with A.V. I also saw some Leningrad officials. At 6.25 p.m. I left for Helsingfors. ... This time I couldn't avoid meeting the Finnish ministers. Erkko[27] expressly asked me through Derevyansky[28] to pay him a visit, and it would have been inappropriate to decline. So here I was again in the very familiar building of the Foreign Ministry, sitting in the very familiar office of the foreign minister in a very familiar armchair.

... At 5.30 I flew out of Helsingfors, and at 8 p.m. I was already sitting in A.M. Kollontay's cosy flat in Stockholm. It was a smooth flight, in spite of a very dense fog over the Baltic Sea.

At 9 a.m. on the 27th I left Stockholm and landed safely in Paris at four in the afternoon. There was only one stop in Copenhagen, where I was totally besieged by photographers and reporters, who would later spread absurd canards all over the world. I spent the entire evening talking with Surits. Afterwards we strolled for hours around the old quarters of Paris, and Y.Z. Surits related to me, with love and considerable knowledge, the history of many buildings associated with the events of 1789–93. He spoke engagingly and with real feeling.

Today, at 10.30 a.m., I left Paris by train for Boulogne–Folkestone and arrived in London at about five in the afternoon, without particular incident.

I'm back home. It seems I never left.

['The unforgettable meeting in Moscow' on 21 April is summed up in the diary in a single, rather muted paragraph. Molotov, Mikoyan, Kaganovich[29] and Voroshilov – the

---

[27] Juho Eljas Erkko, Finnish foreign minister, 1938–39; ambassador to Sweden, 1939–40.
[28] Vladimir Konstantinovich Derevyansky, an electrical engineer and devout Bolshevik, he was recruited to the diplomatic service, but after serving as ambassador in Helsinki, 1938–39, and Latvia, April–October 1940, sank into oblivion.
[29] Lazar Moiseevich Kaganovich, a member of Stalin's inner court; people's commissar for transport, 1935–44, and of heavy industry, 1937–9; deputy chairman of the Council of People's Commissars, 1938–44 and 1944–47; member of the State Defence Committee, 1942–45.

entire Politburo *chetverka* in charge of foreign affairs – were present, as were Litvinov and Potemkin. At the end of a thorough debriefing on the general mood in Britain, the political perspectives, and the balance between the supporters and opponents of a pact, Maisky was asked to evaluate the prospects for a positive response to the Soviet proposals. His succinct account in his memoirs fails to convey how shocking it was for him to observe for the first time the relationship between Litvinov, Stalin and Molotov – 'strained to the extreme'. When later Beatrice Webb asked Maisky about the encounter with Stalin, she gathered from 'his sullen expression and monosyllabic reply' that he had 'no particular liking for the idolised leader of the masses'. Maisky found the mood in Moscow to be 'disturbingly troubled' by news that Hitler was seriously preparing for war. Stalin, who outwardly looked calm, was 'manifestly dissatisfied with England' for having left the Soviet proposal 'hanging in the air'. Molotov apparently 'turned out violent, colliding with Litvinov incessantly, accusing him of every kind of mortal sin'.

The prevalent concern, which – judging by his memoirs and diary – Maisky obviously failed to allay, was that 'there might be a plot in London or Paris to involve Moscow in a war and then leave her in the lurch'. Nor does Maisky mention either Molotov's insistence that alternative options, including an improvement in relations with Germany, should be considered, or Litvinov's dramatic apparent offer of resignation, which was rejected (for the moment) by Stalin. Since 1934, Molotov had consistently given collective security a lukewarm reception, and he was behind the various attempts to reopen negotiations with Berlin.

In his memoirs, Maisky's fleeting account of the meeting conceals the fact that once he had acquainted himself with the prevailing mood in the Kremlin, his optimistic outlook on the eve of his departure for Moscow gave way to a 'not very consoling' report. This turned out to be a devastating prognosis of the prospects for negotiations between Germany and the appeasers, and obviously heightened Stalin's obsessive concern about a possible 'Danzig agreement', which would give Germany a free hand in the East. His report contrasted sharply with Litvinov's refusal to subscribe to the view that Britain and France were diligently trying to embroil Germany in war with the Soviet Union – a standpoint which contributed to his downfall a fortnight later.

Maisky's survey at the Kremlin certainly encouraged Stalin to probe further into the German option with Merekalov, who was now hastily summoned to the Kremlin for the last hour of the meeting. After the customary exchange of greetings, Stalin asked Merekalov point blank: 'Will the Germans advance on us or won't they?' In his incomplete memoirs, Merekalov (like Maisky) misleads his readers into believing that, regardless of what Stalin expected to hear, he took the 'bold step' of telling the *vozhd* that Hitler was bent on attacking the Soviet Union, probably in 1942–43. In reality, still under the impression of a meeting he had had with Weizsäcker, the German state secretary, on 17 April, Merekalov actually proceeded to linger on the prospects for at least a short-term rapprochement with Germany, for which – for as long as she was preoccupied with France and Poland – the neutrality of the Soviet Union was indispensable.

36. Maisky recalled to Moscow, April 1939.

Though Maisky hailed Stalin for his decision to give the negotiations with the West another chance, he was left in no doubt that the talks were 'on probation' and were to be based firmly on the Soviet proposal. In a handwritten enclosure to the entry of 28 April, Maisky scribbled a rough outline of the directives handed to him in Moscow, which continued to give priority to a grand alliance with France and Britain, for a duration of at least five years, on condition that there was: a clear definition of aggression; a right for Soviet troops to transit through foreign territory; the conclusion of a simultaneous political and military agreement; a settlement regarding spheres of influence on the Black Sea littoral; and an undertaking not to conclude separate negotiations 'once an agreement is reached'. And yet, given the British procrastination, it was clear to Litvinov and Maisky that they were now working on borrowed time.]

29 April

Halifax's invitation to visit came a few hours before I even returned from Moscow. I went to see him today. He first inquired if my trip had been interesting, obviously expecting me to indulge in revelations. I only said 'yes, very interesting', before turning to the question of our 17 April proposals, to which the English had so far not responded at all.

37. Relieved, Maisky returns from Moscow, April 1939.

Halifax apologized for the delay, which he attributed to the fact that the British Government had been preoccupied with the conscription problem during the last fortnight, but then he set about cautiously criticizing our proposals. True, they were 'very logical and well put together', but great difficulties would arise in their practical implementation. Then he started harping on that old tune about Poland and Rumania.

A few minutes later, however, Halifax started contradicting himself. Speaking about the visit of Gafencu[30] (the Rumanian foreign minister) he said that, according to Gafencu, Rumania would need Soviet assistance in the event of war, but until that happened Rumania feared that open association with the USSR might 'provoke' Germany. Rumania wished for the time being to maintain a certain 'balance' between the Soviet Union and Germany. So it seems that Rumanian objections to the inclusion of the USSR in the security guarantee are a matter of tactics. not principle.

---

[30] Grigore Gafencu, Rumanian foreign minister in 1932 and 1939–40; minister to Moscow, 1940–41.

... Towards the end, we touched upon Hitler's speech of yesterday.[31] Halifax believes it changes nothing in the present situation. He does not anticipate any new negotiations with Germany in the near future, notwithstanding Hitler's indirect invitation. Halifax was less sure about specifically naval negotiations (the old 'appeaser'!).

With a little embarrassment, Halifax (in response to my question) explained the reasons for the return of the British ambassador to Berlin.

The thing is, you see, that if you are maintaining diplomatic relations with a country, then you need an ambassador there. So Henderson could only be recalled for a short time. Hitler was about to make a speech – what should have been done? If the speech had turned out 'sharp', it would have been awkward for Henderson to return immediately. But his return would also have been awkward if the speech had turned out 'soft', for such a move could well have been interpreted as proof that the British Government believed Hitler's promises, when the man should never be trusted. Faced with that dilemma, Halifax decided to cut the knot by sending Henderson back a few days before Hitler delivered the speech. Henderson had only one assignment: to inform the German Government of the British Government's decision about conscription before it was announced officially in Parliament. All other rumours were sheer speculation unworthy of attention.[32]

[The Foreign Policy Committee, discussing the 'extremely inconvenient' Soviet proposals, subscribed to Chamberlain's delaying tactics of repeating the original offer of unilateral guarantees, while denying accusations that its policy was motivated by ideological aversion. 'Read between the lines', it was commented in the Foreign Office, the real motive for the Cabinet's attitude was 'the desire to secure Russian help and at the same time to leave our hands free to enable Germany to expand eastward at Russian expense'.]

2 May

What is the current situation in England?

Summing up all the material at my disposal, I would describe it as follows.

The attitudes of the broad masses of the population are sharply anti-German everywhere, except for a part of Scotland. ... The situation in government is somewhat different.

---

[31] In response to the introduction of compulsory military service in Great Britain, Hitler announced the abrogation of the naval agreement with Britain, concluded on 18 June 1935; claiming Danzig, he also tore up the Polish–German non-aggression pact of 1934.
[32] Aware of the deadline set by Stalin, Halifax's response had the effect on Maisky 'of a bucket of cold water'. He pressed Halifax to send a reply to the Soviet Government 'in the course of next week'.

... Reconstruction of the Government. This is considered absolutely inevitable now, and even the Beaverbrook press has started a campaign to this effect. But Chamberlain is stubbornly postponing the entry of such figures as Eden, Churchill and others into the Cabinet until the very last moment.

... Our proposals. There can be little doubt that the British Government will eventually accept them. Its situation is desperate. Yet Chamberlain stubbornly resists and has kept us waiting for the English answer for over two weeks now. Moreover, at first he even tried to hush up the Soviet proposals and conceal them from the public. However, thanks to the supporters of an Anglo-Soviet military alliance in government circles, our proposals were leaked bit by bit to the press and by the time of my arrival from Moscow their essence had become public knowledge. The opposition started exerting pressure in Parliament, and a lively debate got going in the press. So the British Government will have to respond to the Soviet proposals one way or another in the very nearest future. It may not wish to accept them immediately, but will have to do so sooner or later. ... That is why, leaving insignificant, everyday details to one side, I am inclined to take an optimistic view of the 'general line' in the development of Anglo-Soviet relations.

3 May

Attended an Anglo-Chinese dinner where Quo Tai-chi, Lord Chatfield[33] and Lord Snell spoke and where mention of the Soviet ambassador among the guests was greeted with loud and unanimous applause.

When the speeches were coming to an end, Vernon Bartlett[34] came up behind me and hurriedly thrust a piece of paper into my hand. The note read: 'News just in from Moscow that Litvinov has resigned.'

[Litvinov's dismissal on 3 May had colossal repercussions on the international scene and for Maisky personally. A protégé of Litvinov, at a stroke Maisky lost his sanctuary. It is easy to imagine his shock when he read the telegram, unusually signed by Stalin personally, informing him and other key ambassadors of the 'serious conflict' between Litvinov and Molotov 'ensuing from the disloyal attitude of Comrade Litvinov to the Council of Commissars of the USSR'. Considered to be a relic of the past, Maisky was gradually ostracized. He now remained practically the sole genuine exponent of a pact with the West. Despite Molotov's reassurances that the resignation implied no change in Soviet foreign policy, a great deal of anxious speculation circulated in the West.

---

[33] Admiral Alfred Ernle Montacute Chatfield (1st Baron Chatfield), minister for coordination of defence, 1939–40.
[34] Vernon Bartlett, a leftist anti-appeaser correspondent of the *News Chronicle*.

THE DANCING BEAR — CHANGE OF PROGRAMME

38. A caricature by David Low.

Maisky himself would claim in retrospect that it was the British failure to pay heed to the Soviet proposals which delivered the 'smashing blow to the policy of effective collective security, and led to the dismissal of Litvinov'. Pinning the blame for the ousting of Litvinov and the shift towards Germany entirely on British 'appeasement' is, however, becoming an increasingly hard position to sustain.

The ousting of Litvinov steered Soviet foreign policy in a new direction. The shift should be examined within the wider context of the construction of the Stalinist edifice. This process led to the removal from Narkomindel of the cadre of the first generation of Soviet diplomats, most of whom were intellectuals drawn from the revolutionary intelligentsia of the tsarist period. They were rapidly replaced by diplomats who were perhaps inexperienced, but were zealous and educated young Stalinists who could be trusted to follow the Kremlin line, particularly at such a crucial moment. The novices were deliberately denied access to policy-making and their room for manoeuvre was restricted. In her diary, Kollontay conceded that somewhere in the depths of her consciousness, 'there [had] been a feeling for a long time that Moscow was unhappy with Maksim Maksimovich ... the symptoms were invisible, but they were there'. Ivy Litvinov later reminisced that the 'writing on the wall' had become increasingly 'legible' by the end of 1938, when 'more and more people closely connected with L[itvinov]' had been persecuted. Litvinov himself had complained to the French ambassador in Moscow at the end of 1938: 'How can I conduct foreign policy with the Lubyanka across the way?'

The breach was accentuated by the personal antipathy and jealousy that character-ized the two types of revolutionaries. 'You think we are all fools!' Molotov shouted at Litvinov as the latter was leaving Stalin's office following his dismissal. At a meeting of the commissariat in July 1939, Molotov charged Litvinov with failing to toe the party line and with 'clinging to a number of people alien and hostile to the party and to the Soviet state'. The continued presence of independent-minded ambassadors would no longer be tolerated at Stalin's court. Henceforth Maisky would find it extremely hard to abide by Molotov's perception of the ambassador's role, which was 'simply to transmit what they are told to pass on'. A 'centralized diplomacy' guaranteed that 'it was impos-sible for the ambassador to take any initiative ... it was Stalin, not some diplomat, who played the decisive role in it'. The removal of 'that astute cosmopolitan, M. Litvinov', Seeds reflected a year later, left Soviet policy in the hands of Stalin and his inner circle, who were 'provincial' and regarded compromise as a 'sign of insincerity'.

What may have further precipitated Litvinov's dismissal was the verbatim report of the interrogation of Ezhov,[35] conveyed to Stalin by Beria,[36] his successor, on 27 April. This report would lead to a preliminary investigation by the NKVD into Litvinov's 'high treason' which was dropped later in June. Ezhov, *inter alia*, recalled how he had unex-pectedly found himself spending an evening with Litvinov at a sanatorium in Merano. After dancing a foxtrot, Litvinov teased him: 'Here we are relaxing, going to restaurants, dancing, but if they found out about it in the USSR they'd really kick up a fuss. Nothing particularly terrible is happening here, but, you see, we have no culture, our statesmen have absolutely no culture whatsoever ... If our political leaders established personal relationships with European political figures, a lot of sharp corners in our relations with other countries could be smoothed off.'

Maisky's position had become most perilous, as the repressions in Narkomindel continued unabated. Molotov was instructed by Stalin to purge the ministry of the 'semi-party' elements, particularly Jews. Moreover, the NKVD tightened its direct control over embassies, and practically the entire cadre of ministry workers was replaced. Maisky was alienated from those newly arrived diplomats, who were attracted to the more popular and friendly style of Molotov's leadership, which seemed to reju-venate Narkomindel. However, the acute fear of a 'second Munich' rendered Maisky's continued presence in London indispensable.]

---

[35] Nikolai Ezhov, 'Stalin's Loyal Executioner', was the head of the NKVD from 1938–40, at the pinnacle of the great terror, only to become its victim in 1940.

[36] Lavrentii Beria, succeeded Ezhov as the head of the NKVD, until his own execution in December 1953, in the wake of Stalin's death, charged with planning to overthrow the communist regime. One of the hidden chapters in Maisky's life had to do with the subversive ties he was compelled to establish with Beria in the latter's bid for power: see the chapter 'The Price of Fame'.

6 May

Halifax summoned me and asked straight out: Litvinov has retired – is our old policy still valid? In particular, do our proposals of 17 April remain intact?

The British Government has prepared its reply to our proposals, but before sending it to Seeds, Halifax would like to hear my response to his questions.

I laughed and said that I didn't understand his doubts. Of course, both our policy and our proposals remain in force.

Halifax was visibly relieved on hearing my answer.

Then he set out the gist of the British reply. Far from reassuring. The British Government does not deem it possible to accept our proposals concerning a tripartite pact because it believes that such a pact would only scare off other powers whose participation in the 'peace front' is very important. ... Consequently, the British Government decided to forward to us once more its formula of 14 April. ...

I expressed great disappointment. It took the British Government three weeks to consider our proposals, at the end of which the mountain has given birth to a mouse. ... It goes without saying that the British Government has the right to send whatever formula it wishes to Moscow, but I could tell Halifax in advance that Moscow would reject this formula.

9 May

Yesterday the British Government finally gave its reply to our 17 April proposals. An unsatisfactory one.[37] ... A rather long, confusing, and clumsy statement, and, above all, even worse than what Halifax told me on 6 May. I went to see him in order to find out the reason for this discrepancy, but the foreign secretary could tell me little beyond the fact that the British formula had not yet been definitively worked out at the time of our conversation. This means that the prime minister must have made changes to the formula prepared by the Foreign Office. I recalled, incidentally, that as I was leaving Halifax's office on 6 May his secretary entered the room and informed him that the PM was expecting him at *10, Downing Street* after my visit.

... Halifax assured me that the British Government was eager to negotiate with us as soon as possible and reach an agreement.

I remained cool and critical throughout. Numerous indicators lead to the conclusion that Hitler's speech on 28 April has caused a temporary recurrence of 'appeasement' in government circles. *The Times* wrote the other day that 'one more attempt' should be made to seek reconciliation with Germany, so this

---

[37] Lloyd George, who had lunch with Maisky at the embassy, found him to be 'very depressed, and feared that his country might return to a policy of isolation'.

must be the view of the prime minister, or at least Sir Horace Wilson. It won't wash! The time for 'appeasement' has come and gone. Whether Chamberlain wants to or not, he will have to make major concessions to our point of view. For such is the logic of the current situation.

11 May

... When I called on Halifax today on another matter (more on this below), his first question was: 'Have you been instructed to communicate anything to me from the Soviet Government?'

The foreign secretary was greatly disappointed when he learned that I had brought no news on this subject.

On Monday, 15 May, the Council of the League of Nations will convene, chaired by the USSR. Surits asked Moscow to adjourn the session until 22 May so that Potemkin, who is only today returning to Moscow from his three-week trip around the Balkans and the Middle East, could also be present at the session. This certainly makes sense. An adjournment of the Council session, however, requires the unanimous agreement of all its members (and primarily of the great powers). Surits had already gained the consent of the French. I had to obtain the consent of the English.

Halifax opened his diary and started thinking aloud: 'The week beginning 22 May is already very full for me... But... but the decisive consideration here should be the possibility of your government representative coming to Geneva... So, although this is rather difficult for me, I agree to the adjournment.'

Then Halifax asked me who exactly would come from Moscow. C[omrade] Molotov? Or C[omrade] Potemkin?

Out of prudence I did not give a name, merely saying that 'a representative of the Soviet Government' would come.

Halifax had obviously made his mind up that C[omrade] Molotov would not go, for he suddenly asked whether C[omrade] Potemkin spoke English. And in general, would Halifax be able to converse in English with the Soviet delegation in Geneva?

I answered half in jest: 'If a common political language is found, linguistic problems will be easily overcome.'

15 May

I have been appointed USSR representative at the forthcoming session of the Council of the League of Nations. Comrade Potemkin is not coming to Geneva. There will be nobody except me in the Soviet delegation. This means, then, that I will also be chairing the Council session.

It's an awkward situation. We asked for the Council session to be adjourned to enable a Soviet delegate from Moscow to come to Geneva. Now, with the session adjourned at our request, nobody from Moscow is actually coming. The English and French will certainly be offended and annoyed, all the more so as Halifax was placing great hopes on the possibility of coming to a final agreement with the Soviet Government on the question of 'European security'.

... In Geneva there will be Maisky, that same Maisky whom Halifax can meet in London any day of the week. What cause can there be for further delays? The answer will have to be given fast and straight.

[The idea that Halifax should proceed to Moscow for 'a straightforward' discussion with Molotov originated with Maisky. Halifax, however, preferred the meeting to take place at the forthcoming session of the Council of the League of Nations in Geneva, to be presided over by the Russians. He looked forward to a conversation with Molotov or Potemkin, 'who could speak with full knowledge of the mind of the Soviet Government'.]

16 May

On 14 May in Moscow our reply to the British proposals of 8 May was handed to Seeds. It boils down to the following:

The proposals of the British Government of 8 May cannot serve as the basis for organizing a peace front to counter the further expansion of aggression in Europe. ...

17 May

Yesterday the Vansittarts came over for an 'intimate' lunch. We discussed international affairs at length, and above all the Anglo-Soviet negotiations. Vansittart expressed the view that the second point of our most recent proposals (military negotiations) was easy to implement, but that the first (a tripartite mutual assistance pact) and the third (guarantees to Central and Eastern European countries) would be more difficult. I, in turn, made it quite clear to Vansittart that the three points of our proposals were the minimum, and that if the British Government was not inclined to accept them, I saw no chance of reaching an agreement at all.

Today, at 12.30 in the afternoon, Vansittart urgently summoned me to the FO. He received me not in his office, but in his secretary's office next door. He apologized, saying that an important meeting was currently under way in his room. Indeed, during my talk with Vansittart, the door to his office opened for a split-second and I caught a glimpse of several Foreign Office officials amid clouds of tobacco smoke.

Vansittart looked highly agitated. He said that yesterday, after our lunch, he had had the chance to speak to Halifax, after which he decided to try 'on his own initiative' to hasten the process of finding a basis for agreement between our governments. To this end he had drafted a formula, but before sending it to Moscow he wanted to hear what I thought about it. ... I replied that there was no need to send the formula worked out by Vansittart to Seeds. It would inevitably be rejected.

... This evening, at seven o'clock, Vansittart invited me once again to the FO. This time he received me in his own office. He looked even more agitated than in the morning and, handing me a sheet of the bluish paper which is so often used by the FO, he asked me to treat the document he had prepared without prejudice and with an awareness of the responsibility that lay on us all in these critical days. Perhaps the document was not ideal, but it was the most he could get the Cabinet to accept at the moment. ... I skimmed Vansittart's new formula and raised my head. Vansittart was looking at me with bated breath, waiting for my response.

I shook my head doubtfully.

'Your new formula,' I said, 'is composed skilfully, but in essence it differs little from what you showed me in the morning. This fact determines my attitude towards it.' ... Vansittart insisted on asking me to forward the formula to Moscow and to recommend it to the Soviet Government. He also wished to receive our reply as soon as possible, preferably the following day, 18 May. ...

18 May

Walking in the embassy garden this morning, I pondered Vansittart's move yesterday. I think it can be explained in the following way.

The Soviet Government's reply of 14 May put the British Government in a tight spot. Our proposals are clear, simple, reasonable and capable of appealing to the consciousness of the *man in the street*. They have already leaked out to the press, and were the Anglo-Soviet argument over the terms and conditions of agreement to be judged by the British public, Chamberlain would most definitely lose.

On the other hand, the British Government's commitments towards Poland, Rumania and Greece render a quick deal with the Soviet Union absolutely essential from the British point of view. For, without us, those commitments cannot be made good. What, in fact, can England (or even England and France together) really do for Poland and Rumania if Germany attacks them? Very little. Before the British blockade against Germany could become a serious threat, Poland and Rumania would cease to exist. So British guarantees in the east without an agreement with us will inevitably mean military defeat for Britain, with all the ensuing consequences. That's assuming England honours its word. Should it break its word and avoid giving assistance to Poland and Rumania under some pretext, then it would be signing its own death warrant as a great power. Not only would this entail a catastrophic loss of global credibility – political and economic – but the rapid disintegration of its Empire.

All these considerations – domestic, imperial and international – are undoubtedly occupying the minds of Chamberlain and his ministers. They are especially concerning at the current time, as the House is scheduled to have a debate on foreign policy on 19 May, in which Churchill, Eden, Lloyd George and other 'stars' will speak, and which will essentially boil down to the question: why has a pact with the USSR not been signed yet?[38] Meanwhile, for psychological reasons, the prime minister is still unable to swallow such a pact, since it would throw him into the anti-German camp once and for all, thus putting an end to all projects aimed at reviving '*appeasement*'. That's why Chamberlain keeps bargaining with us like an old gypsy, trying to foist a bad horse on us instead of a good one. It won't work! Yet he still hasn't lost hope...

19 May

To my surprise, the reply from Moscow arrived on the 18th at 5 p.m. ... As I expected, the reply was brief and unambiguous: unacceptable.

I visited Vansittart in his flat today at 10.30 a.m. He did not seem surprised by our reply. It seems that he was fully prepared for it after our conversation in the evening of 17 May. He merely sighed and uttered, as if to himself: 'Well, it can't be helped. Looks like we'll have to get down to work again and think up something new.'

... At 7 p.m. Vansittart asked me to drop by at his flat for a few minutes. When I entered the hall, he rushed to greet me and announced excitedly that he had good news to communicate. The decision had just been taken to ask Seeds to inform the Soviet Government that as a result of the recent exchanges (the British proposal of 8 May and our counter-proposal of 14 May, and my talks with Halifax, Vansittart and others) the positions of the parties have been definitively clarified and the existing difficulties accurately identified. The British Government would make every effort to overcome these difficulties

---

[38] In his speech to the House, Churchill, briefed in detail over the phone by Maisky about the state of the negotiations, reproached Chamberlain for being guided rather by emotion than by state interests, which called for an alliance with Russia. Maisky, 'the smirking cat', observed Sir Henry Channon, was 'leaning over the railing of the ambassadorial gallery and sat so sinister and smug (are we to place our honour, our safety in those blood-stained hands?)'.

and hoped to find the appropriate means to do so. However, the new proposals required a special decision by the whole Cabinet and would be adopted at its meeting on 24 May. ... Vansittart hopes that agreement will be reached next week.

I shook my head doubtfully and, taking my leave, teased Vansittart in a now entirely unofficial manner: 'Admit it, Sir Robert, deep down you are pleased we have taken a firm stand!'

Vansittart burst out laughing and exclaimed: 'Perhaps!'

We parted till the end of the month. Agniya and I are taking the night train to Geneva.

21 May

Here we are in Geneva.

We arrived in Paris yesterday, at 9 a.m., and wandered about the city until evening. Talked a lot with Surits. Did a bit of shopping.

... It so happened that Halifax and I travelled from Paris to Geneva in the same train and even the same carriage. Photographers at the station made our life hell: they were dying to take a photograph of me next to the British foreign secretary. But I managed to avoid that.

When the train moved off, Halifax met me in the corridor of our carriage and said that he would like to see me in Geneva the following day for a thorough discussion. He promised to call me immediately after our arrival. He has yet to call.

The Paris train arrives in Geneva devilishly early, at 7.13 in the morning. We all crawled out of the carriages sleepy, gloomy and peeved. For some odd reason, Halifax decided to walk from the station to the hotel. It was a grey, drizzly morning, and his long, lean figure striding through Geneva under a black umbrella seemed to have leapt from a cartoon by Low.[39]

* * *

Halifax called, and we met in his hotel at 11.30 a.m. Strang was also present during the conversation, which lasted nearly an hour and a half.

Halifax began by asking me to explain our resolute opposition to the British formula of 8 May.

Emphasizing that this was my personal reply, I indicated the reasons underlying our position.

The Soviet Union can pursue one of two courses today:

---

[39] David Low, British political cartoonist and caricaturist in *The Star*, 1919–27, *Evening Standard*, 1927–50, *Daily Herald*, 1950–53, and *Manchester Guardian* from 1953. Was a frequent visitor at the Soviet embassy.

(1) A policy of isolation and freedom of movement in international affairs. This could ensure its <u>relative</u> security (considering its might, its abundant resources, the size of its population, etc.). I say 'relative' because such a policy would not be able to stave off a world war, with all the ensuing consequences.

(2) A policy aimed at building a peace bloc, primarily with Britain and France, which would impose heavy military obligations on the Soviet Union and limit its freedom of action in international affairs, but which would promise greater security, for by taking this route one could hope to avert a world war.

The USSR prefers the second course and wishes to pursue it. ... Yes, the Soviet Union is prepared to abandon freedom of action and assume heavy obligations, but only on condition that the British and the French *mean real business*. Otherwise it makes no sense for the USSR to refuse the opportunities offered by the first option.

... Halifax replied that the British Government had two principal motives.

First, the Baltic states, in their fear of Germany, do not want to be guaranteed by a tripartite pact. In the end, one cannot impose guarantees on others by force.

Secondly – and this is far more important – many in Britain think that a tripartite pact may push Hitler to unleash war straight away, and therefore, rather than preventing war, the pact will hasten it. Halifax made a point of emphasizing that this was not his own opinion, but the opinion shared by influential British circles, including some of his colleagues.

I replied that I found both arguments unconvincing. ... The gravest mistake made by certain leading English figures is their complete failure to grasp the psychology of such men as Hitler and Mussolini. These Englishmen perceive them as they would a *business man* from the City or an English *country gentleman*. They could not be any more mistaken! Aggressors have an entirely different mentality! Those who would like to understand the aggressor *mentality* would do better to look to Al Capone as a model. ... Only force will make them doff their cap! That is why I am absolutely convinced that the creation of a tripartite pact would not only not lead to war, but would make Hitler and Mussolini retreat.

23 May

In my role as Council chairman I gave a lunch today in Hotel de Bergues for all members of the Council and Secretariat of the League. I'd brought caviar and vodka for this occasion from London. We had traditional Russian hors d'oeuvres, the kulebyaka pie, pickled mushrooms, and other delicacies for which Soviet lunches have long been renowned in Geneva thanks to M.M. [Litvinov].

During lunch, I spoke a lot with Halifax, who sat on my right as the senior guest. Halifax questioned me about the status of religion in the USSR (he is a

39. Bonnet and Halifax reluctantly consider negotiations for a triple alliance in Geneva, May 1939.

very religious man, one of the senior representatives of Anglo-Catholicism). The talk then somehow turned to the fall of the Romanov dynasty, and I related many curious details to Halifax about the last period of tsarist rule in Russia. He displayed great interest in Rasputin[40] and in the correspondence between the tsar and tsarina, published in the early years of the revolution.

We spoke little about current issues. I merely asked Halifax whether he had reached any conclusions, following our talk of 21 May. Halifax didn't give a straight answer, and asked in return: 'So you are quite sure that a tripartite pact could avert the threat of war?'

'Yes, I am,' I answered.

Halifax had nothing to add, but he gave the impression that he was mentally underscoring some paragraph or other in the speech he'll be giving tomorrow to the Cabinet. ...

---

[40] Grigory Efimovich Rasputin, Russian mystic who served as personal and domestic policy adviser to Tsarina Aleksandra Fedorovna. Murdered in December 1916 following a monarchist conspiracy suspicious of his intentions.

40. Maisky replacing the absent Molotov as chairman of the Council of the League of Nations, May 1939.

25 May

On instructions from Halifax, Butler met me this morning at the L[eague] of N[ations] and handed me a memorandum, whose essence was the following:

His Majesty's Government, having given careful consideration to the matter, is now disposed to agree that effective cooperation against aggression in Europe between the Soviet, French and British governments might be based on a system of mutual guarantees which should be in general conformity with the principles of the League of Nations. The guarantees in question would cover direct attack on any of the three governments by a European state, and also the case where any of the three governments was engaged in hostilities by the attacking state in consequence of aggression upon another European country. The conditions of the last mentioned eventuality would need to be carefully worked out.

... The memorandum ended by indicating that in the nearest future the Soviet Government would be offered 'a formula that gives expression to the above-mentioned principles'.

'Well, what do you think?' Butler asked me after I had run my eyes over the memorandum.

'It is undoubtedly a step forward,' I answered, 'but I'll withhold my final judgement until I see the promised "formula" in black and white.'

'You are very cautious,' Butler said with a laugh.

'I learned to be so in London,' I responded in the same spirit.

[Maisky tailored his report home from Geneva to suit the views of Molotov and Stalin with which he had become acquainted during his latest sojourn in Moscow. It was 'perfectly obvious', Maisky wrote, that the British Government was 'avoiding a tripartite pact purely out of a desire not to burn its bridges to Hitler and Mussolini'. He emerged from the talks optimistic, however, convinced that Halifax had appreciated his arguments and would make 'a favourable report to the Cabinet'. Journalists expected an agreement to be concluded within a week or two.

Chamberlain was disappointed by Halifax's failure to 'shake Maisky' from his demand for an alliance. However, guided by domestic considerations, he 'very reluctantly' conceded that it would be most difficult to reject the Soviet proposal. He remained, however, deeply suspicious of Soviet aims. As Maisky had correctly surmised, above all he was concerned lest an alliance 'make any negotiation or discussion with the totalitarians difficult if not impossible'. Such considerations, however, were outweighed by the grim realization in the Cabinet that an alliance had become indispensable if Hitler was to be deterred.]

28 May

It was with great relief that I left Geneva today. I took away with me a vague, unpleasant aftertaste. The weather had been foul throughout. The League of Nations smelled of carrion. But what repelled me most of all about Geneva was the fact that I witnessed at first hand the staggering might of the legal-procedural chicanery which has built its nest in the 'Palace of Nations'.

... Yesterday, 27 May, Seeds presented proposals to Comrade Molotov in Moscow. They represent a concrete expression of the 'principles' discussed in the memorandum which Butler gave to me in Geneva on 25 May.

30 May

In the absence of Halifax and Cadogan, who have left town for Whitsun, Oliphant invited me to see him. He met me somewhat sullenly, with the air of someone who had been unfairly insulted.

He began by reading out to me numerous ciphered messages exchanged over the past 4–5 days between London and Moscow. ... Halifax had fully expected us to accept the proposals at once, instead of which Molotov had greeted Seeds with an avalanche of unpleasant comments: that the British Government was dragging out the talks, that it did not in fact desire effective resistance to aggression, that the League of Nations was included in the British proposals simply for the purpose of creating impediments to a fast reaction to an attack by an aggressor, etc. Seeds and Payart tried to dispel Molotov's suspicions, but had obviously failed.[41]

Oliphant finds all this very distressing. The British Government, he says, wishes to reach an agreement as early as possible. In order to overcome the new difficulties, Oliphant sent fresh instructions yesterday to Seeds. ...

Having familiarized me with these instructions, Oliphant asked whether they would dispel the doubts of the Soviet Government and lead to an early conclusion of the talks.

I replied that I could not give a definite answer to his question. The instructions are certainly intended to dispel some of our doubts, but will they succeed? I am not sure. The Soviet Government is used to believing deeds, not words.

Personally, I could only say that, after familiarizing myself with the British proposals, I too was disappointed. Following my talk with Halifax in Geneva, I had expected the proposals to be clearer, simpler and more definite. In fact, they contained many ambiguous statements allowing for varied interpretations. Since I was fully aware of the high calibre of the Foreign Office staff, and in particular of those who took part in formulating these proposals, I could hardly attribute the flaws to negligence. Some objective must have been concealed beneath the deficiencies of wording. And this could not but render me, and everyone else on the Soviet side, suspicious. We were conducting negotiations about a document of paramount political and military importance, on which literally millions upon millions of lives would depend – so it was only to be expected that we would carefully weigh every word and clause of the document. Halifax had no reason to be either surprised or disappointed. ...

[The Kremlin's policy continued to be driven by a deep-seated suspicion of Chamberlain. The Franco-Soviet Pact – which, as Molotov reminded Seeds, had 'turned out to be merely a paper delusion' – had taught the Russians the 'absolute necessity' of concluding 'simultaneously, both a political and a military agreement'. In his speech to the Supreme Soviet on 31 May, Molotov found it hard to shake off the suspicion that the 'authoritative representatives' in Britain, who were 'glorifying the success of the ill-fated Munich agreement', betrayed 'a sincere desire to abandon the policy of non-intervention, the policy of non-resistance to further aggression'. He feared that Britain was trying to divert the aggression and confine it to 'certain areas'. The crack opened up by Stalin in his 'chestnuts' speech was further widened when Molotov declared that there was 'no necessity for refusing to have commercial relations with such countries as Germany and Italy'.]

---

[41] In Moscow, Seeds and Payart, too, were taken aback by Molotov's fierce reaction. Seeds tried in vain to convince Molotov that the decision of the British Government 'marked a radical turning point in English foreign policy'.

3 June

[Included without commentary is a satirical verse, 'Decameron', by Don-Aminado (Aminad Shpolyansky), an émigré poet, published in the Russian émigré newspaper *Poslednie novosti* on 2 June 1939. The satirist scoffs at the Anglo-Soviet alliance: the 'spousal' ends with the adultery between the 'Russian lady' and Hitler, and the 'English lord' and 'the Italian lady'. The matchmakers Potemkin and Maisky find themselves in prison.]

Decameron

They differed like June and December,
And both had quite high self-regard.
The bride was a Komsomol member,
The groom was an English milord.

This contrast they could not address,
Yet still they decided to wed.
She sported a cotton-print dress
While he wore a tail-coat with velvet.

And so at the registry office,
Performing her citizen's duty,
She offered her husband a kiss
And shone with quite magical beauty.

A telegram came from Kalinin,
And Halifax sent one soon after.
Our couple set out on their journey,
Put one foot in front of the other.

They tried, and they strove, and they suffered.
Out walking in various cemeteries,
They sang of hard labour and workers,
And hoped they could make life more merry.

But soon their neighbours did whisper:
The bloom of their love it is fading,
The lady is visiting Hitler,
The lord his Italian plaything...

The rulers, like angels of Sinai,
Delivered them straight into hell.

The brokers Potemkin and Maisky
Were rapidly sentenced to jail.

D. Aminado [translated by Oliver Ready]

8 June

Halifax invited me to see him today and informed me of the British Government's decision to send Strang to Moscow. The motives for the decision are as follows: Seeds has been *out of touch* with the Foreign Office for many months and is poorly informed about the present mood and wishes of the British Government. Halifax wanted to summon him to London for instruction, but Seeds went down with the flu. It was therefore decided to send Strang to Moscow to assist and brief Seeds. Besides, the British Government finds that the method of exchanging notes which has been practised hitherto leads to misunderstandings and wasted time. Meanwhile, the dangerous international situation renders haste essential. For this reason, the British Government would like to have a 'round-table conference' in Moscow. The British representative at the conference will be Seeds, while Strang will prove a good assistant. Out of all this *eloquence*, one thing was clear to me: the Foreign Office considers Seeds poorly qualified for serious negotiations and is sending Strang as reinforcement. Well, let them!

[Ironically, Maisky would henceforth be increasingly removed from the negotiations, warily conducted by Molotov in Moscow at the same time as feelers were put out to Germany. Halifax was reluctant to have the talks in London, as he doubted whether Maisky 'would be given any latitude in negotiating'. A noticeable dissonance could now be felt. While Maisky evinced confidence in the prospects for concluding an agreement, Molotov remained sceptical and his attitude hardened. Maisky played down the obstacles and was 'inclined to think', as he wrote to Kollontay, that the alliance would be formed 'in the not-too-distant future'. The agreement, he told the Webbs, would be 'settled and signed this week or next'.]

12 June[42]

... Strang was present during this part of our conversation. Halifax wrote down everything I said. He appeared to be pleased and asked whether an identical statement had been made to the French Government in Paris. As I could not give him a definite answer, Halifax said he would himself communicate my

---

[42] Maisky transmitted to Halifax on 12 June a message from Molotov restating the Soviet insistence on binding the political and military agreements and 'taking note' of the decision to send Strang to Moscow.

ALL YOU HAVE TO DO IS TO SIT DOWN

41. A caricature by David Low.

message to the French. ... [Strang] and Seeds have been given full authority to find ways of reaching an agreement with the Soviet Government on the spot, while taking into account the general British standpoint. Halifax hopes that they will succeed. Secondly, might our doubts about paragraph 6 of the most recent Soviet proposals (whereby the pact and the military convention will enter into force simultaneously) possibly be dispelled if a definite date is set for the opening of military negotiations?

I didn't take Halifax up on these points and merely noted that all these questions would probably come under discussion in Moscow.

... Then I remarked, as if in passing, that I did not quite understand why Halifax had deemed it necessary to deliver Thursday's speech (8 June) at this particular time.[43] It struck me as premature.

Somewhat embarrassed, Halifax defended himself by claiming that his speech was well balanced, that its harsh and soft notes were distributed more or less fairly, and that its main purpose was to counter Goebbels'[44] propaganda about the alleged 'encirclement' of Germany, propaganda which had unfortunately struck a chord in German hearts. There could be no question of returning

---

[43] Halifax said that if Germany was prepared to discuss 'a real settlement', the British Government 'would advocate it' so long as it was achieved through negotiations and without recourse to force.
[44] Paul Joseph Goebbels, Nazi Reich minister for propaganda and national enlightenment, 1933–45.

to appeasement. ... 'Your last speech,' I concluded, 'has already given rise to all manner of speculation which it would have been wiser to avoid.'

... Before leaving, I dropped a gentle hint that it would be good for Halifax to visit Moscow and that a warm welcome would be waiting for him there. My hint fell on fertile soil. True, Halifax began making conventional excuses to do with the international situation, which ties him to London, but I could see that he liked my idea. He promised to think it over.[45]

The British were obviously offended by Potemkin's no-show in Geneva. Voroshilov's refusal to come over to attend the British manoeuvres also stung them. Halifax's speech on 8 June was undoubtedly motivated by the desire to shake a fist at us for our unyielding approach in the negotiations. But I still think that, barring extraordinary circumstances, Halifax will go to Moscow.

[Maisky exceeded Molotov's strict but laconic instructions 'to drop a hint' that Halifax would be welcome in Moscow. In fact the British records show that he pleaded with Halifax at length 'that a great deal depends on you personally ... If you were to agree immediately, this week or at latest next, to go to Moscow, to carry the negotiations through to the end there and sign the pact, peace in Europe would be preserved.' By now, however, Chamberlain had dampened Halifax's initial positive response to the suggestion that Churchill or Eden might proceed to Moscow, arguing that 'to send either a Minister or an ex-Minister would be the worst of tactics with a hard bargainer like Molotoff'. Chamberlain's genuine concern, though, was that the opposition, which he knew was constantly plotting with Maisky, might use the mission to topple him.]

17 June

The talks in Moscow started only on 15 June. It is a real 'round-table conference': Comrades Molotov and Potemkin on the one side, and Seeds, Strang and Naggiar[46] (the French ambassador) on the other. But as yet there is nothing to show for it.

In the first meeting (15 June), the British and the French set out their views and proposed several possible solutions. Despite the warning I gave on 12 June, their rough drafts were such that TASS[47] published a communiqué in the late afternoon describing them as 'entirely not satisfactory'. The heart of the matter is that the British and the French refuse to satisfy our demands fully concerning guarantees to the Baltic states.

---

[45] Maisky believed that the stiff demands of Molotov were 'an "acid test" of the bona fides' of the British Government, which could be restored if Halifax were to proceed to Moscow. On Eden's testimony of Halifax's reluctance to go to Moscow, see diary entry for 13 October 1941.

[46] Paul-Emile Naggiar, French ambassador to Yugoslavia and China, 1932–39, and to Moscow, 1939–40.

[47] Telegraph Agency of the Soviet Union.

On the 16th another meeting was held at which C[omrade] Molotov said that, as the talks had shown, the problem of guarantees to small countries from the tripartite bloc was not yet ready to be resolved. Therefore the Soviet Government proposed that the problem of guarantees to other countries should be postponed and that for now we should conclude only the tripartite pact between Britain, France and the USSR on mutual assistance in the event of direct aggression against one of these countries.

The British and the French were shocked and wished to consult their capitals. I think ours was the right move to make, and an ingenious one at that. Of course, the solution proposed by C[omrade] Molotov does not suit our partners at all, but we are right in terms of tactics and substance.

23 June

Halifax invited me over and started complaining bitterly: we were creating unnecessary difficulties, we were absolutely unyielding, we were using the German method of negotiation (offering our price and demanding 100% acceptance), and as a result we were delaying the conclusion of the agreement and dealing a heavy blow to the cause of European peace. Halifax ended his bitter outburst with a direct question: 'Do you or don't you want an agreement?'

I looked at Halifax in astonishment and replied that I did not find it possible even to discuss such a question. The foreign secretary's complaints struck me as entirely unfounded. ... 'Excuse me, Lord Halifax,' I retorted, 'the Soviet Government did not just say "no" to you; it also submitted three detailed drafts of counter-proposals.'

Halifax ... confessed that, despite the large quantity of telegrams he had received from Seeds and Strang, he couldn't quite grasp what the problem was. Why weren't we satisfied with the last British formula which, in his view, covers all possible cases of aggression in the Baltic? Why did we insist on naming the three Baltic states in the agreement? Could I not clarify in greater detail the Soviet point of view?

I answered that negotiations were being held in Moscow, and that I was not up to date with their every detail. If Halifax was perplexed or had doubts, the best approach was to seek clarification in Moscow. Halifax obviously did not like my reply, but there was nothing he could do. ...

At every step of the conversation I could sense Halifax's annoyance and displeasure.

[Maisky's claim in his memoirs that the triple alliance was a viable alternative to the Molotov–Ribbentrop Pact should be examined against the backdrop of the ongoing German–Soviet negotiations, about which he was ill informed. A study of the protracted Soviet–German negotiations of 1939 casts doubt on the notion that the Molotov–Ribbentrop Pact was signed under duress, in the absence of any alternative, at the twelfth hour. True, on his appointment as foreign minister, Molotov does not seem to have received any explicit instructions to change the course of policy and seek political rapprochement with Germany. For the moment, the alternatives remained a full-fledged agreement with the West or isolation. Both policies had been endorsed by Litvinov. The obvious advantage of isolation for the Soviet Union was its ability to preserve its newly acquired position as holder of the balance of power by delaying choosing for as long as possible. And yet a retreat into 'isolation' was also a convenient cloak under which alternatives could be cultivated. By the time of Molotov's appointment, the bankruptcy of collective security had been conceded and the new prospects in Germany recognized.

Soviet policies were examined by the 'men of Munich' through an ideologically tinted prism. Likewise, Stalin's decision to consider the German option emerged from an obsessive suspicion that Britain and France were resolved to divert Hitler eastwards. The decision was further sustained by cold calculations concerning the economic and military benefits to be reaped from such an agreement. In early May, Hitler issued Operation Weiss, the directive for the attack on Poland. Within a week, Stalin was given detailed information about the German designs by military intelligence. However, suspicion persisted of collusion between Britain and Germany. It is discernible in a twelve-page detailed memorandum (which had hitherto eluded historians) submitted to Molotov on 15 May. Bearing the title 'English diplomacy's dark manoeuvre in August 1914', it sought to demonstrate how the events of that period 'resemble very closely the manoeuvre of May 1939'. While scanning it attentively, Molotov underlined numerous references to the alleged British consent in 1914 to remain neutral and to guarantee France's passivity if Germany diverted the war eastwards. His misgivings and scepticism concerning the 'humiliating' British proposals for a triple alliance were apparent in correspondence with both Maisky and Surits. It seems that the main reason for the Politburo's decision to pursue the negotiations was a fear of facing Germany in the future, allied to Poland, and with Britain and France neutralized.

The Russians did not hide their deep-seated suspicion that the German overtures were 'a kind of game' aimed at driving a wedge between Moscow and London. The way to overcome this mistrust, Molotov told Schulenburg, the German ambassador in Moscow, was through the construction of a proper 'political basis'. At the end of May, the Russians were reassured that Germany harboured no aggressive intentions towards Russia and that ideological differences should not be an obstacle to the normalization of relations. They were even led to understand that if the Soviet Union were to dissociate itself from Britain and France, the Germans might be prepared to come to an arrangement concerning 'a division of spheres of influence'.

In early June, while the Soviet draft treaty was being submitted to London, Stalin sent Molotov handwritten instructions to find out whether the Germans were serious, as he could 'not accept that negotiations were again interrupted unexpectedly by the Germans and for unknown reasons'. Stalin set guidelines for the negotiations and supplied a list of required commodities, including vital military items, which was obviously aimed at testing German intentions. On 19 June, Stalin received an intelligence report emanating from General Kleist's headquarters that Hitler was determined to solve the Polish question at all costs – even if he risked fighting on two fronts. The report further confirmed the information provided by Merekalov at the crucial Kremlin meeting on 22 April, that Hitler was counting on Moscow to 'conduct negotiations with us, as she had no interest whatsoever in a conflict with Germany, nor was she anxious to be defeated for the sake of England and France'. Hitler, it concluded, now believed that 'a new Rapallo stage should be achieved in German–Russian relations', at least for a limited period of time.]

29 June

[The diary carries, without comment, an article by Zhdanov, published in *Pravda* on that day under the title 'The British and French Governments Do Not Want an Equal Agreement with the USSR'.]

1 July

We spent yesterday in Canterbury as guests of the *Dean of Canterbury* (Dr Hewlett Johnson).[48]

His 65 years notwithstanding, the dean recently married a young artist aged 35, his student. True, the dean is still full of life, energy and panache, even though he is nearly bald and the hair that remains (down the sides) is the bright colour of senile silver. But the English take a different view of such things from us Russians. Just the other day I read in a newspaper that an 89-year-old lord has married a widow of 45. And such an occurrence is no exception.

The deans of English cathedrals don't do too badly! Dr Johnson has a splendid house, servants, a car, a wonderful garden and, of course, a quite 'decent' income. There is a Roman wall in the garden, which is about fifteen hundred years old and along which we walked calmly and comfortably with our hosts. The Romans really knew how to build!

The surroundings of the dean's residence are steeped in history. The cathedral dates back to the twelfth century and its construction was definitively completed in the fifteenth century. Since then there have been no major changes. The dean's house is nearly 700 years old. It was 'modernized', the dean

---

[48] Hewlett Johnson, the 'Red Dean' of Canterbury, 1931–63.

told me, in the year 1583! With a wide sweep of his arm, the host pointed to a portrait on the wall in the living room – it depicted the notorious sixteenth-century 'modernizer' in the attire and regalia of his time. All the walls in the house are covered with portraits of the dean's predecessors: following established tradition, each new dean adds his portrait to the ancient collection. Dr Johnson has already done his duty: his portrait, done by his own wife, already hangs in the stairway on the second floor. In the garden we came across a small fountain of unusual design, and I asked the dean whether it had been there a long time. Dr Johnson shrugged his shoulders and replied almost apologetically: 'Oh, no more than two hundred years.'

In spite of all this antiquity, the dean is a perfectly contemporary man. Strolling about the garden we chatted on various philosophical subjects, and the dean confessed to me that the question of the afterlife was unclear to him: maybe it exists, or maybe it doesn't. An equal number of arguments can be adduced for and against, so the dean considers the issue a moot point.

What he is in no doubt about is that our life on earth must be made better, more beautiful and noble for as many people as possible. Such, in his opinion, is the true essence of true Christianity. This, too, is Dr Johnson's personal aim in life. Seen from that perspective, not only Germany and Italy, but also England and the United States are not Christian countries. In general, the true essence of true Christianity cannot be realized under capitalism. This is possible only under socialism or, still better, under communism. That is why Dr Johnson considers the USSR to be the only truly Christian country in our day. That is why he is so well disposed to the Soviet Union and admires it so much. That is why he makes every effort to disseminate the truth about the USSR among the English masses and, incidentally, devotes so many of his sermons in the cathedral to the USSR. The archbishop of Canterbury told his dean more than once that he 'speaks too much about Russia', but Dr Johnson sticks to his guns...

Such is the philosophy of the current *Dean of Canterbury*.

Dr Johnson has indeed long been a great friend of the USSR. He spoke in our favour even during difficult times, such as the Metro-Vickers case. He visited the USSR in 1937 and has since made hundreds of enthusiastic speeches about the Soviet Union at hundreds of meetings all over England. He has just finished writing a book about the USSR which is to be published by Gollancz,[49] with illustrations by the dean's wife. ... Dr Johnson is certainly a very interesting and typically English figure. Listening to him you begin to understand better

---

[49] Victor Gollancz, educated at St Paul's and New College, Oxford, Gollancz went on to establish a most profitable and successful publishing house bearing his name. His flair for political agitation and publishing found its expression in the promotion of the Left Book Club. A close friend of the Maiskys, he founded (in 1941) and presided over the Anglo-Soviet Public Relations Committee.

the role of religion in English life, along with such whims of history as, for example, Reverend Stephens, the famous leader of the Chartists.

4 July

My scepticism concerning the Moscow talks has proved justified.

... On 3 July C[omrade] Molotov gave our reply to the proposal made by our partners.

We agreed to name the guaranteed countries in an appendix, but expressed our surprise at the fact that, while all previous negotiations had been based on there being only eight 'children', the number had now suddenly leapt to eleven. Being willing to compromise, we were ready to include Holland and Switzerland in the list of guaranteed countries, but on one condition: since the inclusion of the latter meant an extension of our obligations, we considered ourselves justified in demanding a corresponding extension of the guarantees of our security, in the form of mutual assistance pacts to be concluded between the Soviet Union on the one side and Turkey and Poland on the other. In addition, we proposed, without detriment to the immediacy of aid in the cases stipulated by the pact, to hold a consultation of the 'big three' whenever the probability arose of the obligations of mutual assistance needing to be implemented. ...

[Molotov, now more resolute, told Maisky that the British proposals were 'a repetition of the previous proposal', and had to be 'rejected as unacceptable'. To allay the Soviet fear that the main British object was 'to trap them into commitments and then leave them in the lurch', Halifax swayed the Committee on Foreign Policy on 26 June to accept the Soviet demands to extend guarantees to all the Baltic states. 'We are going to the furthest limit,' observed Cadogan in his diary, 'without any very sure hope – on my part – that the dirty sweeps will respond.' At the other end, Molotov referred to the British negotiators as 'crooks and cheats' who were resorting to 'clumsy tricks'. He was set on extracting a watertight agreement from either the British or the Germans.]

5 July

For the past couple of weeks, a major campaign for an immediate government reshuffle has been waged behind the scenes in Parliament. ... I remain rather sceptical about the prospects of this campaign (how many have there been now?) despite the 'brilliant' names of its leaders. I've heard so many times that 'it can't go on like this', that 'Chamberlain is skating on thin ice', that a reshuffle is already well under way, that a list of new ministers is being compiled somewhere in some decision-making centre – and yet nothing has changed. Chamberlain doesn't care a straw, and Churchill is still in his favourite corner *below the gangway*. I'm afraid the same will happen this time, too: people will kick up a fuss, talk a lot, get worked up, and the Government will remain as it was. I am more and more convinced that the English elite will grant Churchill power only on the day after war is declared. It is not without reason that Mrs Chamberlain told her husband the other day that 'an invitation to Churchill to enter the Cabinet would be tantamount to your political suicide'.

It's a pity, for were Churchill to enter government today, war could still be averted.[50]

6 July

Halifax invited me over.

He began, of course, with complaints about the slow pace of the talks, obviously hinting that we were principally to blame. I parried his objections with little difficulty. ... Halifax said that the British Government wished to make yet another, final attempt to reach agreement with us on the question of guarantees. If this attempt should fail, the British and the French would confine themselves for the present to a simple tripartite mutual assistance pact, effective in the event of direct aggression against one of the signatories.

Halifax is trying to scare us. A simple tripartite pact suits neither Britain nor France. London is bargaining. We shall bargain, too.

12 July

Meetings were held again in Moscow on 8 and 9 July, but their details are still a little unclear to me. ... Halifax summoned me again today. In the process of 'informing' me about the course of negotiations he said that ... as far as 'indirect aggression' was concerned, the British Government would adhere to its former formula. Otherwise it 'fears driving the Baltics into the Germans' embrace'. With regard to the simultaneous implementation of the pact and the military convention, the British Government would most probably raise no objections. ... Later, Halifax added that the British Government did not oppose opening military negotiations immediately. Couldn't the dispute on this matter be resolved by setting dates for both the opening and the closing of military negotiations?

---

[50] Chamberlain was convinced that the 'drive' to include Churchill in the government was a conspiracy 'in which Mr Maisky has been involved'.

I replied that it was difficult for me to answer his question and that he had better address Moscow on this matter.

13 July

The British Government is currently conducting a major campaign: rumours are being spread far and wide in the press, Parliament, and public and political circles that the Soviet Government is acting stubbornly on trifling matters and thereby deliberately dragging out the negotiations; that it is simply 'playing' and does not actually wish to conclude a pact. As if the Soviet Government were flirting with Hitler and were ready to form a bloc with Germany.

The purpose of the campaign is clear. By sabotaging the talks, Chamberlain wants to make a scapegoat of us. We'll do our best to ruin his ploy.

In fairness, however, it must be said that the campaign has had a demoralizing effect even on some of our 'friends' in Labour and Left circles.

18 July

Only yesterday did Seeds and Co. deign to pay a visit to C[omrade] Molotov. Thus, the fresh instructions of which Halifax informed me on the 12th travelled for a whole five days from London to the British embassy in Moscow! To judge by our negotiations, British diplomacy must use oxen as its means of transportation.

... No progress has been made on the issue of indirect aggression. ... Indeed, the meeting on 17 July left such an unpleasant aftertaste that our people in Moscow have started wondering whether anything will come of these never-ending talks. Judging by some indicators, one cannot exclude the possibility that they may be broken off in the very near future. For now, let us wait and see.

[At the Cabinet meeting of 19 July, Halifax sided with Chamberlain, preferring 'a breakdown of the negotiations' to acceptance of the Soviet terms. Having succeeded in warding off the pressure for a treaty with Russia, Chamberlain reverted to attempting to deter Hitler from resorting to force by offering him various economic incentives. A series of intermediaries who had received Halifax's blessing paved the way for a meeting of prominent British industrialists with Göring. Though the negotiations never really got anywhere, they did succeed in fuelling Soviet suspicion and may well have contributed to the *volte face* in Maisky's critical assessment of British intentions in the fortnight preceding the conclusion of the Molotov–Ribbentrop Pact. Maisky – who, as the following entry shows, continued to believe in an agreement right up to, and even after, the outbreak of war – was now attuned to Moscow.]

25 July

Halifax invited me to see him and said that at the last meeting in Moscow, on 23 July, Comrade Molotov proposed opening military talks immediately, emphasizing again that the Soviet Government would not sign the pact without a military convention. Comrade Molotov further let Seeds and Co. understand that should the question of the military convention be resolved favourably, the remaining political difficulties (indirect aggression) would cease to be insuperable. Since Seeds had not been authorized to decide the matter raised by Comrade Molotov, he appealed to London. Today, the British Government took an extraordinarily important decision: it accepted Comrade Molotov's proposal and is prepared to begin military negotiations right away, parallel to the political ones. The pact and the military convention will be signed concurrently. The British and French military missions will leave for Moscow in seven to ten days. The composition of the missions is yet to be decided. ...[51]

28 July

Back home at last! We were away for a mere 36 hours, but how many interesting, vivid and unforgettable impressions were amassed in such a short interval!

It all began in a very simple, even prosaic way. About a month ago, the Cardiff branch of the Society for Cultural Relations with the USSR invited Agniya and me for *lunch* in Cardiff, to present us with a collection of gramophone records of Welsh folksongs. ... We were met at the railway station in Cardiff by the local SCR representatives, and also by Mr W.G. Howell,[52] the lord mayor of Cardiff, in full dress and with gold chains around his neck, together with his wife. ...

On the way there, W.G. Howell remarked, as if in passing: 'Last week the duchess of Kent was our guest.'

I smiled to myself.

When we were driving past the *City Hall* I noticed, with some surprise, a big red hammer-and-sickle flag on top of the building. In answer to my inquiring look, the lord mayor explained that the flag had been hoisted in honour of the Soviet ambassador. Indeed, the red flag fluttered on the mast of the Cardiff City Hall throughout the 24 hours I spent in the city. Nothing like that had ever occurred in the history of Anglo-Soviet relations.

---

[51] In his memoirs, Maisky gives a distorted account of the meeting, claiming (in clairvoyant fashion) that he left Halifax 'with a feeling of great alarm'. Both the full diary entry and the succinct telegram he sent to Moscow show a guarded optimism. According to Halifax, Maisky thought the arrangement 'was a good one'; Moscow considered that 'real progress had been made ... and hoped that we were now approaching the end of our negotiations'.
[52] William Gough Howell, lord mayor of Cardiff, 1938–39.

In the evening, the lord mayor gave a grand official reception in our honour at the *City Hall*, at which some 900 people were present – a gaudy mixture of suits, political parties and social groups from this crisis-ridden black-coal region. From dyed-in-the-wool conservatives to communists – such was the range of the political spectrum. The lord mayor and his wife, together with Agniya and me, welcomed the guests. Our hands became swollen from endless handshakes. While the guests were coming in, a young woman in Welsh national costume played folk tunes on the harp. It was a little exotic, but beautiful and pleasant.

The reception began with a concert given by the best Welsh workers' choir – the *Pendyrus Male Choir*. A hundred and fifty singers, of whom 90 turned out to be miners and 60 unemployed. The choir was truly superb. The solo performances were good, but the Welsh folk songs sung in chorus were best of all. Most remarkably, however, the concert opened with a wonderful rendition of the 'Internationale'. It ended, of course, with '*God Save the King*', but this was mere custom: this was, after all, an official reception given by the official lord mayor in the official *City Hall*. ...

Early the next morning we began a long and wearying schedule.

First up was the '*Temple of Peace*', the brainchild of Lord Davies,[53] on which he spent about 50 thousand pounds. It's a beautiful building with marble columns, a large hall and dozens of smaller rooms – the headquarters of the local friends of the League of Nations. ... Then came the Welsh National Museum. We were taken round by its director and his assistants. ... There is no question that the Welsh are different from the English: lively, talkative, merry, melodious, artistic. Welsh songs rather recall those of the Ukraine.

... The '*Nine Mile Point Colliery*', belonging to Lord Davies. We are welcomed by a huge crowd of miners, women and children. Greetings, friendly cheers, clapping, fists raised in salutation. We put on miner's overalls and pick up miner's lamps. Newspaper photographers snap away. We descend 1,200 feet. Accompanied by the mine director, administrators and trade-union men, we, together with Lord Davies, walk for two hours in the underground galleries, touch the timbering with our own hands, break off pieces of coal, stroke the *pit ponies* (which turn out to be huge horses) and on the whole do everything that should be done on such occasions. Agniya is in high spirits – excited and cheerful. But the mine makes no particular impression on me. It's not the first time I've been underground. Besides, I'm sure that this dry, well-timbered and highly mechanized mine is to some extent a 'model mine' to be shown to 'eminent travellers'.

---

[53] David Davies (1st Baron Davies), founder and trustee of the League of Nations Union.

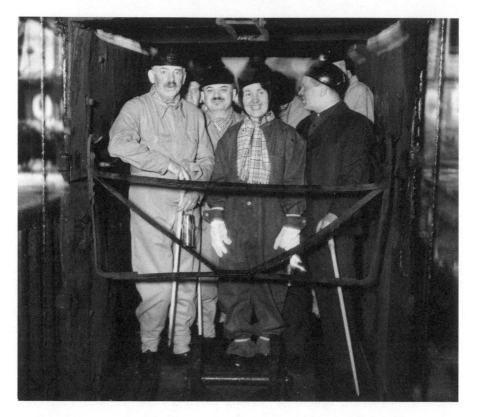

42. In their element: the Maiskys are welcomed for a tour of a mineshaft in Wales.

We climb back up. Inspect the coal washing and the scales for weighing the mine cars. Then we go to clean ourselves. I have a shower in the well-equipped *pithead bath*. Then we drink tea in the pit's office and get ready to return to Cardiff in order to catch the 6.36 train to London. ...

* * *

Sitting in the lord mayor's dining-room after supper, shortly before our departure for London, I conversed with Lord Davies.

'What you've told me about the Anglo-Soviet negotiations saddens me greatly,' said Lord Davies. 'When I see what's happening in my country now, when I see Chamberlain and his Government meekly making one crucial concession after the other to the aggressor, when I see how this stupid and narrow-minded policy is paving the way to the downfall of our Empire, I can feel my heart breaking. I often ask myself: why was I not killed by a German bullet in France in the last war? That would have been easier.'

Such are the feelings evoked by the current decline of the British bourgeoisie among its most honest and far-sighted representatives! ...

4 August

... The members of the military mission to Moscow – Admiral Drax[54] (head), Air Marshal Burnett[55] and Major General Heywood[56] – came for lunch. The guests were highly reserved in conversation and preferred to discuss such innocuous topics as partridge hunting, the season for which they will clearly have to spend in Moscow.

During lunch, however, I did learn one thing which seriously alarmed me. When I asked Drax, who was sitting on my right, why the delegation was not flying to Moscow by plane to save time, Drax drew in his lips and said: 'You see, there are nearly 20 of us and a lot of luggage... It would be uncomfortable in the plane...'

I can hardly say that I found his response convincing. I continued: 'In that case, why not travel by warship... On a fast cruiser, for example... It would look impressive and it would hasten your arrival in Leningrad.'

43. The Anglo-French military mission about to embark on a freight steamer on the way to Russia.

[54] Admiral Reginald Aylmer Ranfurly Plunkett-Ernle-Erle-Drax, commander-in-chief at Plymouth, 1935–38.
[55] Charles Stuart Burnett, air officer commanding Iraq Command, 1933–35; Training Command, 1936–39; inspector-general of the RAF, 1939–40.
[56] Major General Thomas George Gordon Heywood; brigadier, Royal Artillery, Aldershot, 1936–39.

Drax sucked his lips again and said, deep in thought: 'But that would mean kicking 20 officers out of their cabins... That would be awkward...'

I couldn't believe my ears. Such tender feelings and such tactful manners!

The admiral hastened to gladden me, though, with the news that the military delegation had chartered a special vessel, *The City of Exeter*, which would take them and the French mission to Leningrad. At this point Korzh[57] intervened in the conversation, remarking pointedly that he had heard from the owner of this ship earlier today that her maximum speed was 13 knots an hour. I cast a look of surprise at Drax and exclaimed: 'Is that possible?'

Drax was embarrassed and mumbled: 'The Board of Trade chartered the ship. I don't know the particulars.'

So, the English and the French military missions are travelling to Moscow by freight steamer! It must be a freighter, to judge by its speed! And this comes at a time in Europe when the ground is beginning to burn beneath our feet! Incredible! Does the British Government really want an agreement? I'm becoming more and more convinced that Chamberlain is pursuing his own game regardless: it's not a tripartite pact that he needs, but talks about a pact, as a trump card for cutting a deal with Hitler. ...

[Bar the occasional lapse, right up until the very day the Molotov–Ribbentrop Pact was concluded, Maisky maintained that an agreement with the Western powers was inevitable. In his apologetic memoirs, he puts a misleading gloss on the narrative, whereby Halifax's refusal to proceed to Moscow and the bizarre episode of the military mission startled and convinced him that an agreement was doomed. This narrative, meticulously constructed and widely disseminated by Maisky to justify the pact, was later adopted by Stalin. Halifax's refusal to travel to Moscow and the arrival of the forlorn military mission in Moscow had supposedly left him with no choice but to conclude the pact. Maisky's narrative is refuted by the following diary entry – a telling exposition of his inner thoughts at the time. Moreover, visiting the Webbs at their cottage two days later he was certain that 'Great Britain will be *forced* to come into alliance' with the Soviet Union.]

5 August

Went to *St Pancras* railway station to see off the British and French military missions. Lots of people, reporters, photographers, ladies and young girls. I met General Doumenc,[58] head of the French mission, and a few of his compan-

---

[57] Mikhail Vasilevich Korzh, first secretary of the Soviet embassy in Great Britain, 1937–42.
[58] Joseph Édouard Aimé Doumenc, French general in command of the 1st Military Region, 1937–39; member of the Supreme War Council, 1939–42.

ions. The heads of the British mission – Admiral Drax (head), Air Marshal Burnett and Major General Heywood – were my guests for lunch yesterday and we greeted one another like old acquaintances.

On my way home, I couldn't help smiling at history's mischievous sense of humour.

In subjective terms, it is difficult to imagine a situation more favourable for an Anglo-German bloc against the USSR and less favourable for an Anglo-Soviet bloc against Germany. Indeed, the spontaneous preferences of the British 'upper ten thousand' most definitely lie with Germany. In his sleep, Chamberlain dreams of a deal with Hitler at the expense of third countries, i.e. ultimately at the expense of the USSR. Even now the PM still dreams of 'appeasement'. On the other side, in Berlin, Hitler has always advocated a bloc with Britain. He wrote about this fervently back in *Mein Kampf*. Highly influential groups among the German fascists, bankers and industrialists also support closer relations with England. I repeat: the subjective factor is not only 100%, but a full 150% behind an Anglo-German bloc.

And yet, the bloc fails to materialize. Slowly but unstoppably, Anglo-German relations are deteriorating and becoming increasingly strained. Regardless of Chamberlain's many attempts to 'forget', to 'forgive', to 'reconcile', to 'come to terms', something fateful always occurs to widen further the abyss between London and Berlin. Why? Because the vital interests of the two powers – the objective factor – prove diametrically opposed. And this fundamental conflict of interests easily overrides the influence of the subjective factor. Repulsion is stronger than attraction.

The reverse scenario holds for Anglo-Soviet relations. Here the subjective factor is sharply opposed to an Anglo-Soviet bloc. The bourgeoisie and the Court dislike, even loathe, 'Soviet communism'. Chamberlain has always been eager to cut the USSR's throat with a feather. And we, on the Soviet side, have no great liking for the 'upper ten thousand' of Great Britain. The burden of the past, the recent experience of the Soviet period, and ideological practice have all combined to poison our subjective attitude towards the ruling elite in England, and especially the prime minister, with the venom of fully justified suspicion and mistrust. I repeat: the subjective factor in this case is not only 100%, but a full 150% against an Anglo-Soviet bloc.

And yet the bloc is gradually taking shape. When I look back over the seven years of my time in London, the overall picture is very instructive. Slowly but steadily, via zigzags, setbacks and failures, Anglo-Soviet relations are improving. From the Metro-Vickers case to the military mission's trip to Moscow! This is the distance we have covered! The abyss between London and Moscow keeps narrowing. Field engineers are successfully fixing beams and rafters to support the bridge over the remaining distance. Why? Because the vital interests of the

two powers – the objective factor – coincide. And this fundamental coincidence overrides the influence of the subjective factor. Attraction proves
stronger than repulsion.

The military mission's journey to Moscow is a historical landmark. It testifies to the fact that the process of attraction has reached a very high level of
development.

But what an irony that it should fall to Chamberlain to build the Anglo-
Soviet bloc against Germany!

Yes, mischievous history really does have a vicious sense of humour.

However, everything flows. The balance of forces described above corresponds to the present historical period. The picture would change dramatically
if and when the question of a proletarian revolution outside the USSR becomes
the order of the day.

[Negotiations with the British and French were now being conducted in parallel to
those with the Germans, even if the latter had lost some steam since April. Maisky, like
the other Soviet plenipotentiaries, was oblivious to their existence. On 10 July, the
Germans acquiesced to the procedure proposed by the Russians to link the economic
and political negotiations, eliciting from Stalin an immediate reaction: 'we are ready to
move ahead'. Further negotiations, however, stalled until 26 July, when the Soviet
chargé d'affaires in Berlin was informed that Ribbentrop had been displaying a personal
interest in the improvement of Soviet–German relations.

Given Maisky's warning that the British were still trying to agree terms with the
Germans, Stalin was resolved to steal a march before the military negotiations got
under way with the democracies. On 2 August, Astakhov[59] was given the green light to
meet Ribbentrop. He found the German foreign minister eager to conclude a trade
agreement, which might 'signal an improvement in political relations'. Ribbentrop
impressed on him that no conflict existed between the two countries 'from the Black
Sea to the Baltic' and that 'all related issues were open for discussion'. On 12 August,
Astakhov relayed from Berlin that, in anticipation of a conflict with Poland, the Germans
were eager to enter economic as well as political negotiations.

Hardly had the military talks got under way in Moscow than Schulenburg suggested
to Molotov on 15 August that Ribbentrop should come to Russia. Though welcoming
the idea, Molotov, who was always suspicious of behind-the-scenes intrigues,
wanted more precise information on the nature of the German proposals. Moreover,
he obviously wished to extract the best terms from the Germans while military negotiations with the democracies were on. It was not until 17 August, following the collapse

---

[59] Georgy Aleksandrovich Astakhov, counsellor at the Soviet embassy in London, 1934–35; chief of the
Press Department of NKID, 1936–37; counsellor and temporary Soviet chargé d'affaires in Germany,
1937–39. Regarded as a Litvinov disciple, he was banished from the Foreign Ministry in 1939, accused
of treason and sent to a labour camp, where he died in 1942.

of the forlorn military negotiations, that Molotov raised with Schulenburg the idea of a non-aggression pact and a 'special protocol', addressing the mutual interests of the two countries. The text of such an agreement was ironed out by both sides on 19 August.

Two days later, Hitler addressed Stalin personally, in what was tantamount to an ultimatum, demanding that Ribbentrop be received in Moscow in the next couple of days to sign the agreements. Stalin responded within two hours. The negotiations at the Kremlin were brief. Stalin predicated the signing of the non-aggression pact on an agreement in principle for a secret protocol governing the division of Central and Eastern Europe into 'spheres of influence'. He arranged for the startled Ribbentrop to have a direct phone link to Hitler, who gave his consent on the spot.]

20 August

We got away for a week and spent it at the Malvern drama festival. Eleven years ago, Barry Jackson, the prominent and wealthy Birmingham patron, and Bernard Shaw decided to put on the first-ever drama festival in England. ... We saw all six [plays], including Bernard Shaw's *In Good King Charles's Golden Days* and Vansittart's *Dead Heat*.

Apart from going to the theatre, we drove around the wonderful Malvern countryside, scrambled up and down the beautiful but modestly sized mountains which surround it, walked, rested and read. We had been invited

44. Agniya cherishing the newly arrived ZIS-101 (Zavod imeni Stalina), modelled on Buick's limousine of the time.

to Malvern by Shaw and Vansittart. We met a few diplomats there and others from London 'society'. We were guests at the estate of Sir Sidney Clive, marshal of the diplomatic corps. Most of the talk at the tea table was about the threatening international situation. One of the guests from the City asked me what was to be expected in the upcoming week. Not wanting to embark on a lengthy analysis, I just said: 'I fear that next week will be very difficult.'

I think I was right. But we shall see.

21 August

It seems that our negotiations with the British and the French have collapsed. Already in July there had been a strong desire in Moscow for their termination. Now things have gone from bad to worse. To judge by information received from various sources, the situation is roughly as follows.

When negotiations between the military delegations opened in Moscow on 12 August, the Soviet side inquired about the British and French missions' letters of credentials. It turned out that they had not brought any with them. Naturally, this produced a very bad impression. The Soviet side asked the British and the French to get the required letters from London and Paris. A few days later these were received and presented, but... they turned out to be so general and vague that it became clear to us that London and Paris had no serious intention of concluding an agreement.

Next came the issue of Poland. When the British and the French, having set forth their considerations concerning the assistance they could provide to Poland in case of need, asked the Soviet side what it could do for Poland, Comrade Voroshilov outlined our plan. Since the USSR does not have common borders with Germany, it could of course offer effective aid to Poland, France and Britain only if Poland were to let the Red Army pass through its territory. ... The Polish Government refused categorically to let the Soviet troops pass through its territory and even announced that it did not need any assistance from the USSR. Poland would manage by itself if Britain and France fulfilled their duty. What shocked the Polish most was the prospect of the Red Army marching through Wilno, Piłsudski's[60] birthplace. 'The shade of Piłsudski,' they exclaimed theatrically, 'will rise from his grave if we allow the Russian troops to pass through Wilno.'

... The negotiations stalled on this issue. Deadlock had been reached. Indeed, what's the use talking to the British and the French if the Poles refuse categorically to accept the only plan that could save Poland?

---

[60] Józef Klemens Piłsudski, Polish prime minister, 1926–28 and 1930; minister for war, 1926–35.

Once again it has become clear that London and Paris are not serious about an agreement. Or, perhaps they even incited the Poles to reject our proposal?

Some major decisions, one feels, are in the offing...

[Although the British Government accepted the Soviet wish to embark expeditiously on military negotiations, the delegation was instructed to 'go very slowly with the conversations', treat the Russians 'with reserve' until a political agreement was reached and 'await authorization from London before dealing with the core issues'. General Doumenc, Surits alerted Molotov from Paris, was not pleased with the instructions, which were 'nothing more than general and stereotyped phrases and remarks'. Embarking on the mission, he could not avoid thinking that there was something symbolic in 'the old cargo ship ... representative of the old British commercial fleet. Sturdy, somewhat dated, with an entirely Indian crew carrying the testimony of the Empire'.

By 16 August the negotiations had reached stalemate, while the German pressure was mounting. Marshal Voroshilov warned that 'a definite' response to the Soviet request to enter Poland 'as soon as possible was of cardinal importance'. In conversations with the American ambassador, Molotov insisted that he attached 'great significance' to the negotiations and was 'counting on their success', so long as they were concluded with 'concrete obligations' for mutual assistance, rather than with 'general declarations'. Doumenc duly informed his government that the Russians 'clearly expressed the intention not to stand aside ... to act in earnest'. Impressed by the Soviet 'precise' statement regarding their potential military assistance, he estimated it to be 'considerable ... between 70 and 100 per cent of the forces we would put up'. A partially positive French response was conveyed to Voroshilov on 22 August; however the nature of such assistance was to be decided by 'the course of events'. By now, however, the dramatic news was released that Ribbentrop and a large retinue of advisers were flying to Moscow the following morning to sign a non-aggression pact.]

22 August

Last night, at around 12, I got a telephone call from Hillman of the International News Service, who shouted down the phone, in great alarm and agitation, that the following news had just come in from Berlin: Germany and the USSR were signing a non-aggression pact. Ribbentrop would be flying to Moscow for that purpose tomorrow. Was this possible?

Involuntarily, I threw up my hands.

This was quickly followed by calls from various newspapers and agencies. That was just the start of it. Within half an hour taxis lined up in front of the embassy and a few reporters tried to force their way in, demanding a *statement* from me. Needless to say, I avoided speaking to the press. The doorman told the reporters that I was out. They decided to wait until I returned, got into taxis and sat there. A few journalists, however, headed off to Korzh's apartment. The siege of the embassy lasted until two o'clock. Worn out, the journalists left soon after two, satisfied that they wouldn't catch me there.

Since early morning there has been a great commotion, almost panic, in town today. Telephone calls. Visits. Requests to see me. Lloyd George came specially from Churt, and invited me for lunch in his office. The old man is anxious, but he fully understands us. He told me plainly: 'I've been expecting this for a long time. I'm still amazed at your patience. How could you negotiate with this Government for so long?'

We had a long talk about the current situation and discussed the position that the old man would take on the issue. Finally, he stated directly: 'While Chamberlain remains in charge, there will be no "peace front". This man will destroy the Empire.'

Later, the duchess of Atholl[61] paid me a visit. Worried and confused. What is this? The complete neutrality of the Soviet Union? A free hand for Germany in Europe? We had a long talk. The duchess left somewhat reassured.

Greenwood and Dalton came to see me in the evening. They are also worried, bewildered, and unable to understand anything. ...

[Dalton and Greenwood found Maisky 'as much surprised as we were by the latest turn'. In Stockholm, Kollontay was 'annoyed and irritated' when she learned of the pact, going through the newspapers in the embassy. Litvinov, hidden away in his dacha, 'went almost crazy: "what do they mean? What do they mean? Do they really intend to link up with the Germans?"' For Maisky, as Agniya indiscreetly admitted to Eden over lunch, 'the recent events had been a disappointment'. Out of touch since the negotiations were moved to Moscow in mid-June, Maisky still clung to his belief – even after the pact was signed – that an agreement with the Western powers would be concluded. 'Apprehensive' about the likelihood that the military mission might be withdrawn from Moscow, he pleaded with Dalton and Greenwood to 'hurry up and finish the political and military conversations', as Russia would 'be neutral if there is a war'.]

23 August

Nevile Henderson has been to Berchtesgaden and handed Hitler a personal letter from Chamberlain, in which the latter brought it to the Führer's notice that, in the event of German aggression against Poland, England would fulfil

---

[61] Katharine Marjory Stewart-Murray (née Ramsay) (duchess of Atholl), Conservative MP for Kinross and West Perthshire, 1923–38.

the pledges she had undertaken. Hitler replied in the sharpest terms that no British letter would stop Germany securing her 'vital interests'.

Ribbentrop has flown in to Moscow surrounded by 32 attendants! That's just like him. I remember that when he was ambassador in Britain he travelled between London and Berlin accompanied by no fewer than 30–40 adjutants. The negotiations have already begun.

... Preparations for an *emergency* are in full swing in the city. Shelters are being dug, piles of sandbags are being heaped up in front of buildings, windows are being blacked out, museums and picture galleries are being emptied, the evacuation of schools, women and children is being organized, and instructions are being given over the radio about what to do with... cats and dogs.

Tension is growing, along with the expectation of something frightful, menacing and unavoidable. Is this serious? Or are these just psychological preparations for a new Munich? We'll see. There's no doubt that Chamberlain would like a second Munich very much. The trouble is that Hitler's appetite is growing fast, which makes a repeat of Munich more difficult. ...

24 August

Yesterday, late at night, the non-aggression pact between the USSR and Germany was signed in Moscow, and today Ribbentrop is flying back. The pact stipulates consultations between the governments on matters of mutual interest, and does not contain an *escape clause*. The duration of the pact is ten years.

Our policy is obviously undergoing a sharp change of direction, the meaning and consequences of which are not yet entirely clear to me. I must wait for further information from Moscow. ...

29 August

A day of anxiety and suspense.

The fates of war and peace are being weighed on unsteady, quivering scales, and who can tell what the next day will bring?

... Parliament met. Chamberlain made a short announcement, in which he said that nothing had changed since the session of 24 August, and that the threat of war had not diminished. The prime minister further noted the most important events of the last few days, such as Henderson's arrival and the British reply to Hitler's proposal, and once again emphasized that Britain would honour its obligations towards Poland. On the whole, the prime minister's speech sounded quite resolute. ... Planes are constantly buzzing in the air. At night the searchlights' flashing swords furrow the sky, 'catching' enemy bombers.

In Moscow, a quite different mood clearly reigns: they are not expecting war, and are counting on a new Munich. Here are the facts.

A few days ago I asked NKID whether it was safe to send confidential materials by diplomatic mail, in view of the possible disruption of the railways or even the opening of hostilities between Germany and Poland in the nearest future. I received the reply: send mail in the normal fashion – and in such a tone that Moscow clearly wished to tell me: 'Don't panic!' Nevertheless I did not send confidential materials with the couriers. And I was quite right not to do so. Today I learned that these couriers have got stuck in Berlin.

On 27 August, NKID informed me that I have been appointed head of the Soviet delegation to the League of Nations Assembly scheduled for 11 September. Thanks for the vote of confidence. I doubt, however, whether the Assembly will take place in the present situation.

Today, 29 August, the *Kooperatsiya* set sail from Leningrad with members of the Red Banner Song and Dance Company on board. Tomorrow, the 30th, the *Mariya Ulyanova* should leave with the others.[62] In Southampton, the Company is to board the *Aquitania*, bound for America. I fear, however, that this may not happen: new events may force the Company to return to the USSR.

31 August

Another day of tension and suspense. ... At about five o'clock, Agniya and I got into a small car and drove around town to see what was going on. It was the end of the working day. The usual hustle and bustle in the streets, on the underground, and on the buses and trams. But no more than usual. All the shops are trading. The cafés are open. The newspaper vendors shout out the headlines. In general, the city looks normal. Only the sandbags under the windows and the yellow signs with arrows pointing to the nearest bomb shelters indicate that England is on the verge of war.

In the evening, Agniya and I went to the Globe to see Oscar Wilde's delicious comedy *The Importance of Being Earnest*. The actors were superb. An image of the 'good old times' – without automobiles, radio, airplanes, air raids, Hitlers and Mussolinis – seemed to come alive. People were funny and naive then, to judge by today's standards. We laughed for two hours. That's something to be grateful for.

When we got back from the theatre, the radio brought sensational news: the 16 points which Hitler demands from Poland. The immediate return of Danzig,

---

[62] The ship was named after Lenin's sister, Mariya Ilyinichna Ulyanova.

a plebiscite in the 'Corridor', an international committee made up of Italian, British, French and Soviet representatives, a vote in 1940, and so on and so forth.

What's this? A step back? Slowing down?

I doubt it. It's too late for Hitler to retreat. It's almost certainly a manoeuvre. Is it an attempt to hoodwink the world's public and perhaps the German people as well before a decisive 'leap'?

1 September

Yesterday's doubts have been fully justified. Today, early in the morning, Germany attacked Poland without any prior warning and began bombing Polish cities. The Polish army and air force are putting up strong resistance everywhere.

So, war has begun. A great historical knot has been loosened. The first stone has rolled down the slope. Many more will follow. Today, the world has crossed the threshold of a new epoch. It will emerge from it much changed. The time of great transformations in the life of humankind is nigh. I think I'll live to see them unless, of course, some crazy incident cuts my days short...

Parliament met at six in the evening. As I drove up to Westminster, photographers began snapping away. And why not? What a sensation: the Soviet ambassador at a parliamentary session on the matter of war. And this directly after the signing of the Soviet–German pact!

A nervous and panicky mood reigned in the Parliament corridors. A motley crowd of every age and status had gathered. There were many rather young women and girls, gesticulating frantically and speaking in raised voices. I walked down the corridors, saluted in the usual manner by the Parliament policemen, and approached the entrance to the diplomatic gallery. It was quite jammed with ambassadors, envoys, high commissioners and other 'notables'. As soon as the door attendant caught sight of me, he pushed back a few 'ministers' to clear a narrow path for me to the staircase. On the way, I greeted the Rumanian, the Dane, the Egyptian, the Finn and a few other diplomats. I immediately sensed the atmosphere: an attitude of restrained hostility, but with a hint of deference.

The same was repeated upstairs, where I squeezed past some *distinguished strangers* and sat down on the front bench next to Quo Tai-chi. We greeted each other in a friendly fashion, as we always do. Raczyński, who sat down on the other side of Tai-chi, shook my hand and did so, it seemed, with a certain feeling. As for Cartier[63] (the Belgian) and Corbin, who has turned quite grey over these past few weeks, they barely stretched out their hands. I responded by

---

[63] Baron Emile de Cartier de Marchienne, Belgian ambassador to London, 1927–46.

offering just a couple of fingers. Kennedy immediately leapt out of his seat when he saw that we would be neighbours, made a clumsy gesture, and took a seat in the second row (the 'envoys' row'), his great vanity as American ambassador notwithstanding. The events of recent days have certainly affected the mood in diplomatic circles.

I looked down. The small chamber of the Commons was full to bursting with agitated, tense MPs. They were packed in like sardines. The Government bench was just the same. All the stars – if there are any – were present: Chamberlain, Simon, Hore-Belisha, Kingsley Wood, Brown,[64] Inskip and the rest. All the opposition 'stars' were also in attendance on the front bench, minus Attlee, who has not yet fully recovered from a recent operation. The atmosphere was heavy, menacing and oppressive. The galleries of the Lords, the press and guests were jam-packed. Near the 'clock', wearing plain grey suits, sat the duke of Gloucester and the duke of Kent. A few MPs were in khaki, among them Captain Macnamara,[65] who has paid me several visits on Spanish matters. All eyes were trained on me. The mood was the same: restrained hostility, but with a hint of deference. I calmly endured this bombardment of glances. Then I began to make out individual faces. Lady Astor, as is her custom, seemed to be sitting on needles, and looked at me as if she meant to grab me by the hair. Mander, Nicolson and Ellen Wilkinson[66] looked at me with friendly, sparkling eyes. I had the impression that Eden also cast a quick, and not remotely hostile, glance at me, but I can't say for sure.

The speeches were brief and failed completely to rise to the great historical level of the occasion.

Chamberlain, looking terribly depressed and speaking in a quiet, lifeless voice, confessed that 18 months ago (when Eden retired!) he prayed not to have to take upon himself the responsibility for declaring war, but now he fears that he will not be able to avoid it. But the true responsibility for the unleashing of war lies not with the prime minister, but 'on the shoulders of one man – the German Chancellor', who has not hesitated to hurl mankind into the abyss of immense suffering 'to serve his senseless ambitions'. ... Chamberlain declared that today the British and French ambassadors in Germany handed Ribbentrop a note demanding that the German Government stop Germany's aggression against Poland and withdraw German troops from her territory. Should this not be done (and the PM, of course, did not expect the demand to be fulfilled), the British and French ambassadors would have to ask for their passports, and Britain and France would come to the aid of Poland using all the means

---

[64] Ernest Brown, minister of labour, 1935–40; minister of national service, 1939–40; secretary for Scotland, 1940–41; minister of health, 1941–43.

[65] John Macnamara, Conservative MP, 1935–44.

[66] Ellen Wilkinson, Labour MP nicknamed 'Red Ellen' for her militant and activist role in the trade union movement; parliamentary secretary, Ministry of Home Security, 1940–45.

available to them. This would mean war, a long and hard war, but 'it only remains for us to grit our teeth and see it through to the end'.

Strong and serious words. At times, Chamberlain even tried to bang his fist on the famous 'box' on the Speaker's table. But everything cost him such torment and was expressed with such despair in his eyes, voice and gestures that it was sickening to watch him. And this is the head of the British Empire at the most critical moment in its history! He is not the head of the British Empire, but its grave-digger! ...

Unless an extraordinary miracle happens at the very last moment, Britain will find itself at war with Germany within the next 48 hours.

3 September

Today, the denouement really did take place.

At 9 a.m. Henderson, acting on instructions from London, handed Ribbentrop the 'final note', in which the British Government asked the German Government to present by 11 a.m. its final response to the note of 1 September, which contained the demand to withdraw German troops from Polish territory. In addition, the British Government warned that if the German Government failed to present its reply before eleven o'clock, this would signify the breaking-off of relations and the beginning of war.

It goes without saying that no reply followed from Hitler. As a result, the prime minister went on air at 11.15 a.m. and declared that, as of then, Britain was at war with Germany.

Half an hour later the air filled with the bellowing sounds of the siren. People scampered off to their houses, the streets emptied, and cars stopped in the road. What was it? A drill? Or a genuine raid by German bombers?

Fifteen minutes of tension and anxiety – then we heard the prolonged siren wail: '*all clear*'! It had been just a drill. There were no enemy planes.

I got to Parliament by midday. I was a couple of minutes late because of the alarm.[67] I took the first available seat in the second row. Chamberlain was already speaking. A darkened, emaciated face. A tearful, broken voice. Bitter, despairing gestures. A shattered, washed-up man. However, to do him justice, the prime minister did not hide the fact that catastrophe had befallen him.

'This is a sad day for all of us,' he said, 'and to none is it sadder than to me. Everything that I have worked for, everything that I hoped for, everything that I have believed in during my public life – has crashed into ruins.'

---

[67] The view of Maisky in Chamberlain's circles was best recorded by Sir Henry Channon in his diary: 'A little later Maisky dared to appear, and he beamed his Cheshire-cat smile. No wonder. It is the moment he has long intrigued and hoped for.'

I sat, listened and thought: 'This is the leader of a great Empire on a crucial day of its existence! An old, leaky, faded umbrella! Whom can he save? If Chamberlain remains prime minister for much longer, the Empire is ruined.' ...

5 September

Chamberlain has carried out a 'reconstruction' of his Cabinet. Everything was done the Chamberlain way, i.e. halfway and with much splitting of hairs. His former Cabinet has swollen a bit in quantity, but has altered little in quality. A few ministers have swapped places. 'Fresh blood' was added in the persons of Churchill (first lord of the Admiralty) and Eden (secretary for the dominions).

... If the 'reconstruction' goes no further, Churchill and Eden will find themselves hostages, and Britain will surely lose the war. But I think that the 'reconstruction' cannot end at this point. This is just the beginning. Further steps will follow. ...

[Once again, Maisky's survival was hanging by a thread. The *Daily Herald* suggested that he was being recalled to Moscow to report. Beatrice Webb felt sorry for him, as his friends were bound to 'fall off'. She was wondering whether their forthcoming encounter was 'a farewell visit? I fear so ... Poor Maiskys, we shall never see them again ... With their friend, Litvinoff, they will disappear, let us hope safely, somewhere in the background of that enormous and enigmatic territory.' In no time, however, Maisky bounced back, hoping that the inclusion in the Cabinet of Eden and Churchill, whom he had been cultivating for years now, would still bring the countries together. 'I earnestly hope,' Churchill wrote for the first time on Admiralty notepaper, 'all will go well between our two countries, and I am sure you will do all in your power to that end.' 'Winston Churchill,' Maisky told the Webbs, 'would be trusted by the Kremlin.']

8 September

Just back from the *Kooperatsiya*. It was late in the evening when we drove back. An incredible sight.

The giant city was in pitch darkness. No street lamps (all removed!). No lights in the houses. No sparkling restaurant or café windows. No brightly lit signs or advertisements. Everything had gone dark, as if by the waving of a magic wand. Only the stars shone in the sky, along with the blind winking of the automatic traffic lights. But they, too, were on the wane: instead of the usual bright lights of red, yellow and green, little crosses, pale and slender, hung pensively on the sombre garments of the night.

Gloomy, darkened and lifeless buildings looked like menacing cliffs. The streets between them were black gorges. Cars moved slowly in the thick darkness, like ghostly shadows. Like magic birds with a red eye on their tail. Quiet. Gloomy. Watchful. Fantastical. A scene from Dante's *Inferno* ...

That is how London lies low, waiting for the raids of the German bombers.

13 September

'Well hello, my neutral!' said Lloyd George with a smile as I shook his hand in Churt today.

The old man wanted very much to see me. I came for *lunch* and we spent two hours in lively conversation.

Naturally, we spoke mostly about the war and related matters. I asked Lloyd George whether Britain would fight in earnest.

'Yes, it will,' Lloyd George replied with a shake of his grey mane. 'Chamberlain, of course, wants peace. He'd be ready to make peace with Hitler tomorrow and pull off a second Munich. But he can't do it. The country is against him.'

I pointed out the absence of military enthusiasm or of a visible patriotic surge such as had occurred at the beginning of the last war, but Lloyd George demurred: 'Yes, that's true. Today, you'll not see that somewhat light-headed military enthusiasm which was so striking in 1914. ... But do not delude yourself: there is a *grim determination* in the masses – among workers, farmers, shopkeepers, intellectuals and the "middle class" – to carry the war to the end. A government that decided to ignore this would not last a fortnight.' ...

17 September

Today, at 6 a.m., Potemkin handed a note to the Polish ambassador, Grzybowski,[68] in which the Soviet Government declared that since the Polish state has disintegrated and the Polish Government has gone into exile, the Soviet–Polish non-aggression pact is null and void. Under these conditions, Poland in general, and especially its eastern part, has become a land where anything can be expected. In its eastern part there live 10–11 million Belorussians and Ukrainians, oppressed by the Polish state and Polish landlords. The conclusion: the Red Army is crossing the Polish border and occupying Western Belorussia and Western Ukraine in order to protect the population's lives and property.

---

[68] Wacław Grzybowski, Polish ambassador to the USSR, 1936–39.

... All this struck London like a bolt from the blue. True, there has long been talk and suspicion here of a German–Soviet agreement to 'partition Poland', but the crossing of the Polish border by the Red Army has come as a real shock. A shock so great that today in the late afternoon Greenwood issued a 'declaration' sharply attacking the USSR and affirming that Poland must be restored.

What will be the response to our actions in England? ... I expect a note of protest, an angry speech in Parliament by the prime minister, and campaigns in the press, but nothing more.

19 September

My expectations are beginning to be fulfilled. Yesterday, late in the evening, the British Government made a toothless statement, not even a protest, concerning our actions in Poland, and reaffirmed its determination to fight the war to the end. We shall see what Chamberlain says in Parliament tomorrow.

... The events of recent weeks have wreaked havoc with people's minds. Gollancz is in despair: in his view, the Soviet–German pact killed off communism. Strachey,[69] in connection with the same pact, came to Harry[70] with tears in his eyes. Cummings, writing in the *News Chronicle* (19 September), simply cannot make sense of things. Duff Cooper published an article in today's *Evening Standard* about 'Two Breeds of Bolshevism' – communism and fascism. Every day I receive many letters – anonymous and otherwise – which show their authors to be in a quite incredible state of shock. Yes, the general muddle is on a colossal scale. And it is not easy to combat: there's a lack of information and materials for that purpose. ...

21 September

Now that Poland no longer exists, it is entirely reasonable to ask: will England fight in earnest or will she not?

History has played a cruel joke on the elite of the British bourgeoisie. Today, they really do find themselves *between the devil and the deep [blue] sea.*

If Britain refuses to fight and agrees to a new Munich (Chamberlain's constant dream), the consequences will be not only direct losses in territory, capital and so on, but even greater indirect damage. ... On the other hand, fighting would mean facing the gravest military difficulties, sustaining colossal

[69] Evelyn John St Loe Strachey, a militant communist and Marxist theorist, he was editor of the *Socialist Review* and *The Miner* from 1924. Broke away from the Communist Party of Great Britain (CPGB) in 1940 and became a leading Labour politician in the post-war era.
[70] Harry Pollitt, one of the founders of the CPGB in 1920 and its general secretary, 1929–39 and 1941–56.

human and material losses and, in the end, coming round to 'socialism'. The conviction that 'socialism' would be the inevitable result of a major war is now universal – even in bourgeois circles. Of course, everyone has his own idea about what kind of 'socialism' this would be, but all are convinced that there is no getting round it. So, to fight is also very dangerous.

No wonder the bourgeois leaders are in two minds. How will the war problem be resolved? It's too early to say. But the possibility of a serious war cannot be excluded. Yesterday in Parliament, Chamberlain stated once again, absolutely categorically, that the Government was braced for a war that would last at least three years. ...

23 September

Today, quite out of the blue, Halifax invited me over. I hadn't seen him for almost two months, since 25 July. Total chaos reigned in the familiar corridors of the Foreign Office: tables, bookcases, files, boxes, papers – all piled up in complete disorder. They must have been making some additional arrangements in the event of air raids.

My talk with Halifax lasted 20–25 minutes. The atmosphere was tense and unnatural throughout. Halifax spoke slowly and chose his words carefully. He often paused, sighed and stared at the ceiling. He was excruciatingly polite, but I felt all the time that looking at me he was thinking: are you an enemy or not?

In essence, Halifax called me over to probe our mood and intentions. He beat about the bush for a good long while, saying that the international situation had changed beyond recognition in recent weeks, that one had to find one's bearing anew, and that he would be extremely grateful to me and the Soviet Government if we could enlighten him as to our views about the present situation and the immediate future.

... My general impression: the British Government is very anxious about our relations with Germany and wishes to glean how far they have advanced. At the same time, it is plainly considering the resumption of contact with us, but hesitates to make a corresponding démarche, not knowing how we would receive it.

27 September

Today I conveyed to Halifax the following answers given by the Soviet Government to the questions raised by Halifax during our conversation of 23 September.[71]

---

[71] The succinct response conveyed the Soviet intentions of adhering to neutrality. It also indicated that the demarcation lines in Poland were 'provisional' and that the Soviet Union was prepared to pursue trade negotiations.

... Halifax was not fully satisfied. He asked whether we intended to form a buffer Polish state, but I was unable to satisfy his curiosity on this score. In addition, he was obviously bewildered by the statement that the USSR would remain neutral only so long as England did not force her to intervene in the war, and asked me anxiously: 'Have we done anything to you?'

... At Halifax's request, I gave a brief description of Polish landownership and the poverty and exploitation of the Polish, Ukrainian and Belorussian peasantry.

'And what do you do with the landlords' land?'

'It is confiscated without exception and distributed among the peasants.'

Halifax shook his hand and uttered gloomily: '*A grim tale.*'

His landlord's heart couldn't bear it.

... At the end, Halifax touched upon the first point.

'Still,' he remarked, 'I just can't reconcile the events of recent weeks with the foreign policy principles proclaimed by Mr Stalin at your last party congress.'

I looked at Halifax with half a smile and replied: 'There's this folk tale we have. A peasant fell ill and took to his bed. While he lay there helpless, one of his neighbours took his horse, another stole his cow, and a third grabbed his plough. When the peasant recovered and went back to work, he saw that he had been robbed. He went to the house of the first neighbour, punched him in the face and took his horse back. Then he came to the second and third neigh-bours, and got his cow and plough back in the same way. Can the peasant's actions be qualified as "an act of aggression"? No, they can't. He simply retrieved that which his neighbours had illegally appropriated when he was weak.'

'So you think that this Russian tale has relevance to recent events?' Halifax asked.

'Undoubtedly,' I replied, 'with the sole difference that in this case the USSR didn't punch anybody in the face.' ...

29 September

Another day of excitement and sensations. Journalists have been calling all day on the telephone.

Communications about the outcome of Ribbentrop's visit to Moscow have come in. A friendship and boundary treaty, an exchange of letters concerning the strengthening of trade relations, and a joint declaration about peace in Western Europe. In addition, a Soviet–Estonian pact of mutual assistance.[72] ...

---

[72] Ribbentrop, who visited Moscow on 27 September, signed the final secret protocols concerning the division of spheres of influence in seven separate documents.

[The narrative of the events leading up to the pact, assiduously composed by Maisky and adopted almost verbatim by Stalin, maintained that the Soviet Union was left with no choice but to sign an agreement with Hitler. It comes as a startling revelation, however, that – contrary to the accepted wisdom – Stalin believed he could success-fully avoid war altogether. The German–Soviet collaboration was not, therefore, tran-sient and precarious, but appeared to have long-lasting prospects. Stalin was bent on exploiting the new opportunities to redress the grievances which, he felt, had been inflicted on Russia not only at the Versailles peace conference, but also during the nineteenth century – specifically by the humiliating Paris Peace Treaty of 1856 (following the Crimean War) and at the Congress of Berlin (following the Russo-Turkish wars of 1877–78). His gaze, like that of the tsars, was fixed on the Balkans, the littoral of the Black Sea and the Turkish Straits.

Rather than being a manifestation of defeatism, motivated by ideological expecta-tions of the outbreak of revolution, the 'peace campaign' served more mundane Soviet interests. It was to be instrumental in efforts to bring the war to a rapid conclusion. That was to be followed by a peace conference, probably in 1941–42. The main thrust of Stalin's policies in 1939–41, therefore, was to gather together the best cards he could, ahead of the anticipated peace conference. He expected the conference, which would be attended by a debilitated British Empire, to topple the Versailles Agreement, acknowledge the new Soviet security arrangements in Central and Northern Europe, and extend them to the south.]

3 October

Today Chamberlain gave his appraisal in Parliament of the German–Soviet agreements. Nothing sensational, just as I'd thought. The PM did not declare war on us. He did not even risk expressing disapproval of the Moscow treaty.

... [Lloyd George's] speech, as ever, was a model of oratorical mastery. He spoke very cautiously, for the subject was a very hazardous one, and it was as if he was constantly probing the atmosphere in the chamber with invisible hands. Lloyd George's feel for Parliament is astonishing. It derives from talent and 50 years' experience. The chamber listened to him tensely, with bated breath, even though he was clearly going against the stream. Only the occasional weak hissing could be heard from the Labour benches, and even these sounds merely accentuated the dense hush which had filled the House.

Lloyd George said that the anticipated peace proposals should be carefully studied and discussed by Parliament before the British Government responded. Then he said that Hitler was of course not to be trusted, but that if the great neutral powers – the USSR, Italy and the USA – could be involved in resolving the question of peace, a different situation would emerge. The terrible blood-shed that threatened Europe might possibly be avoided.

... Eventually I tired of all this dawdling and went to see Lloyd George. He received me in his room in Parliament. We drank tea and spoke about the current situation.

'Winston is awfully angry with me,' the old man said with a chuckle. 'Did you see how he was behaving while I was speaking?'

I had seen Churchill turn various shades of red and white during Lloyd George's speech, shake his head in agitation, and generally express his disagreement with the speaker through gestures and glances.

'Winston is insanely determined to fight to the end! He is enraged and thinks of nothing else but how to throttle Germans... But that doesn't bother me. I always say what I think. During the Boer War I was against the war...'

6 October

Churchill's secretary called and asked me to come to see him at the Admiralty at 10 p.m.[73] Not exactly the ordinary hour for receiving ambassadors in England, but the present situation is far from ordinary, and the man who invited me is also far from ordinary!

It's dark and misty tonight. The clouds are low and gloomy. It's pitch-dark on the streets. I reached *Horse Parade* [*sic*], where the Admiralty is located, with some difficulty. We had to stop the car frequently to check our bearings. We eventually arrived. The familiar square seemed quite unfamiliar. The Admiralty building rose darkly out of the swirling fog like a fairy-tale fortress. Not a single light or human being in sight. I knocked and rang at the various doors and gates – silence. Were they all asleep in there? Or had this huge institution, which governed the movement of the British navy all over the globe, 24 hours a day, given up the ghost?... I was beginning to lose my patience. At last I saw a pale ray of light in the archway of the gates, and behind it there appeared a sleepy watchman. I explained my business. A few minutes later I was already sitting in the office of the 'first lord of the Admiralty'.

Churchill greeted me with a welcoming smile. The walls of his office are covered with a collection of the most varied maps of every corner of the world, thickly overlaid with sea routes. A lamp with a broad, dark shade hangs from the ceiling, giving a very pleasant soft light. Churchill nodded to the lamp and, pouring whisky and soda, said with satisfaction: 'The lamp was here 25 years ago, when I was naval minister for the first time. Then it was removed. Now they've put it up again.'

---

[73] A meeting which was clearly initiated and motivated by Maisky, probably triggered by Churchill's famous radio broadcast on 1 October, in which he described Russia as 'a riddle wrapped in a mystery inside an enigma', but then provided the key of 'Russian national interests', which could not allow Russia to see Germany 'plant herself upon the shores of the Black Sea'.

How very English!

Then Churchill led me over to a wide, folding door in the wall and opened it. In the deep niche I saw a map of Europe with old, faded small flags pinned onto it in various places.

'It's a map of the movements of the German navy in the last war. Every morning, on receiving the naval reconnaissance information, the flags were moved, meaning that we knew the location of each German ship at any given moment. I ordered this map 25 years ago. It's still in good condition. Now we will need it again. We just have to bring the flags up to date.'

I looked at Churchill with a smile and said: 'So, history repeats itself.'

'Yes, it repeats itself, and I'd be only too happy to philosophize about the peculiar romance of my returning to this room after a quarter of a century, were it not for the devilish task at hand of destroying ships and human lives.'

We returned to the present and I asked: 'What do you think about Hitler's peace proposals?'

Churchill sprang to his feet and, quite abruptly, began pacing the room: 'I've just looked them through and haven't had time to exchange views with my colleagues in the Cabinet. Personally, I find them absolutely unacceptable. These are the terms of a conqueror! But we are not yet conquered! No, no, we are not yet conquered!'

Churchill once again set about pacing the room in vexation.

'Some of my Conservative friends,' he continued, 'advise peace. They fear that Germany will turn Bolshevik during the war. But I'm all for war to the end. Hitler must be destroyed. Nazism must be crushed once and for all. Let Germany become Bolshevik. That doesn't scare me. Better communism than Nazism.'

But all this was just an opening flourish. The main story which Churchill wanted to discuss with me so late at night was the state of Anglo-Soviet relations.

Churchill asked me how we define the present state of our relations. I repeated to him what I had told Halifax on 27 September. Churchill listened to me attentively and then spent nearly an hour relating to me the British Government's view of Anglo-Soviet relations. The essence of this view is as follows.

Anglo-Soviet relations have always been poisoned by the venom of mutual suspicion, today more than ever before. What are these suspicions? Britain suspects the USSR of having concluded a military alliance with Germany and that it will openly come out, one fine day, on Hitler's side against the Western powers. Churchill himself does not believe this, but many (including some in government circles) do. This circumstance cannot but affect the general tone of Britain's attitude to the USSR. On the other hand, the USSR suspects Britain of pursuing a hostile policy against the USSR and of various machinations against it in the Baltic, Turkey, the Balkans and elsewhere. This condition cannot but affect the general tone of the Soviet attitude to Britain. Churchill understands why our suspicions are especially acute today. The Anglo-Franco-Soviet Pact negotiations were conducted in a repulsive way (I know his view on this matter) and have left bad memories in Moscow's mind. But let the dead bury the dead. The present and the future are more important than the past. And the present and the future are precisely what Churchill wants to talk about.

His starting-point is that the basic interests of Britain and the USSR do not collide anywhere. I know this to have been his view in the past, as it is in the present. It follows that there is no reason why our relations should be poor or unsatisfactory. ... We should not take too much to heart the criticism and indignation with which the Soviet–German non-aggression pact and the subsequent moves of the Soviet Government have been met in Britain. This was due to their unexpectedness. The initial shock, however, has now passed, and people are beginning to see things in a more accurate perspective.

The Baltic states. The Soviet Union is going to be master of the eastern part of the Baltic Sea. Is this good or bad from the point of view of British interests? It is good. ... In essence, the Soviet Government's latest actions in the Baltic correspond to British interests, for they diminish Hitler's potential *Lebensraum*. If the Baltic countries have to lose their independence, it is better for them to be brought into the Soviet state system rather than the German one. ...

Finally, the Balkans and the Black Sea. Churchill walked up to a big map of Europe and drew a sweeping line which approximately traced the new Soviet–German border and northern Rumania and Yugoslavia. He then exclaimed: 'Germany must not be allowed any further! It is especially important not to let Germany reach the Black Sea.'

He set about arguing, with some feeling, that if Germany were to reach the Danube estuary, it would not only seize the Balkans, but would inevitably extend itself also to Asia Minor, Iran and India. It would want to possess the Ukraine and Baku. Neither Britain nor the USSR can allow this to happen. Here, too, their interests coincide rather than clash. The Soviet Government is greatly mistaken if it thinks that Britain is plotting against it in Turkey and the Balkans. Britain is interested in one thing only: not to let Germany reach the Black Sea. ...

What conclusion can be drawn from the above? ... The British Government treats our declaration of neutrality as a positive fact, merely wishing for it to be friendly neutrality.

... Churchill asked me what could be done to improve relations between the two countries. Were there no useful steps or measures that I might recommend?

I refrained from offering advice. Churchill himself thought that the best way of alleviating tension would be to expand trade operations. Then, as though summing up his thoughts, he noted with a sly smile: 'Stalin is playing a big game at the moment and is doing so felicitously. He can be satisfied. But I fail to see why we should be dissatisfied.'

We parted 'like friends'. Churchill asked me to keep in close touch and to turn to him without ceremony whenever the need arose. I'll keep this in mind. ...

12 October

Today in Parliament, Chamberlain delivered his long-awaited statement on Hitler's 'peace proposals' (of 6 October). The meaning of the statement is clear: No!

'Hitler's proposals,' the prime minister said, 'are unacceptable in themselves. What's more, we don't believe a single word spoken by this man. If Hitler really wants peace, he must first prove it in deeds, not words. Then we can start talking in earnest. It all depends on Hitler.'

... So, if Hitler makes no concessions in the next few days and suggests no new, more acceptable conditions of peace – directly or through neutrals (Mussolini, Roosevelt, etc.) – the war will start in earnest.

13 October

The Edens came to us for lunch. There were four of us and we conversed candidly. Eden was in a good mood. He is clearly delighted about returning to the bosom of government. His light grey suit and colourful tie gave him a cheerful, almost vernal appearance. His 'Beatrice', though, was all in black and unusually stern and silent.

We spoke, of course, about the burning issue of the moment – the war. Eden confessed that he was quite *puzzled* by our change of policy. He was in the camp with his battalion when news arrived of Ribbentrop's trip to Moscow. An officer woke him up in his tent at 6 a.m. to inform him. Eden exclaimed 'nonsense!', turned onto his side, and wanted to go back to sleep. So the officer thrust a fresh paper with the news under his nose. That made Eden jump out of bed right away. He was wide awake. And although subsequent events clarified a great deal for Eden, he still hasn't understood everything.

I explained to Eden in a few words the meaning and causes of the Soviet actions, beginning with the Soviet–German non-aggression pact. He listened to me attentively and seemed to display understanding.

Then it was his turn to speak. He believes, just as he did four years ago, that British and Soviet interests do not seriously collide anywhere, on any issue or in any part of the world. What we observe today is a temporary and transient tension. It must be eased. How? Eden, like Churchill and Elliot, began sounding me out: might not an authoritative delegation be sent to Moscow? A trade delegation, perhaps? Or a delegation dealing with some other affairs? Or a member of government? What if Seeds were replaced with a more suitable person? Whom would we like: a diplomat, a politician, a public figure, a writer, Bernard Shaw? Mentioning Shaw, Eden openly smiled, but in essence he was dead serious.

Since I didn't know Moscow's feelings on the matter, I preferred to refrain from giving advice.[74]

As far as war is concerned, Eden strongly supported the official point of view. War is inevitable and must be fought to the end.

16 October

Halifax summoned me today and said that the British Government would like to improve Anglo-Soviet relations. It is ready to discuss all possible measures with this end in view, but thinks it best to begin with trade (truly: a *nation of shopkeepers*!). On 27 September, in response to his inquiry, I had informed Halifax that the Soviet Government did not object to the opening of trade negotiations.[75] ...

* * *

Went to see the Webbs yesterday. ... How much snobbery there is even in the best English people! In conversation with the Webbs, I mentioned what Churchill said to me the other day: 'Better communism than Nazism!' Beatrice shrugged her shoulders and noted that such a statement was not typical of the British ruling elite, and I would tend to agree. But then, for some reason, she found it necessary to add: 'Churchill is not a true Englishman, you know. He has negro blood. You can tell even from his appearance.'

Then Beatrice Webb told me a long story about Churchill's mother coming from the South of the USA and there being some negro blood in her family. Her sister looked just like a 'Negroid'.

---

[74] Maisky, who, according to Eden, 'talked almost the whole time', advised him that the Kremlin would prefer to see someone who enjoyed the British Government's confidence, and that it would 'probably always be doubtful of this if they were dealing with a Left Wing politician while the Government of this country was Right Wing'.

[75] According to Halifax, it was actually Maisky who initiated the idea of a trade delegation to Moscow; however, in his report home, Maisky (as was his wont) attributed it to Halifax.

Then I happened to mention the famous African explorer Henry Stanley.[76]
... Beatrice Webb suddenly became agitated: it transpired that she had known
him in her youth. She described Stanley as a rather unpleasant man – and I am
quite prepared to believe her – but one thing shocked me. Relating the elderly
Stanley's marriage to a beautiful young girl, who was a friend of hers, Beatrice
said with a certain distaste: 'At the time everyone was astonished by this match.
She came from a very good family, an educated, considerate and beautiful girl,
while he was a real upstart, a coarse, uncouth fellow.'

Beatrice appealed to her husband, whose expression and gestures indicated
full assent.

The crux of the matter is that Stanley was ... a true plebeian, and that
matters, even to the Webbs.

17 October

I had a telling conversation today with Butler. ... We lunched *tête-à-tête* and he
spoke very candidly. First and foremost I was interested in the prospects of
Hitler's 'peace offensive'. Butler replied: 'None for the moment. Not because we
are against peace – on the contrary, we very much wish to avoid war, and that is
why we need a solid and lasting peace and assurance about this peace. We need
the assurance that if we conclude peace today, it will not be broken in six months'
time. We are ready to pay a high price for a solid and lasting peace of 20–25 years.
We would not even refuse Germany substantial colonial concessions. We have a
large Empire and we do not need every part of it. Something could be found for
the Germans. Not Tanganyika, of course, which could easily be turned into a
naval and air base on the Indian Ocean, but perhaps Togo, Cameroon, etc.'[77] ...

24 October

A strange war!

It's as if you were on the western front. The bulletins of the French general
staff contain phrases such as: 'the night passed uneventfully', 'the day was
marked by patrol operations', 'German forces about the size of a single company
mounted an offensive', etc. The bulletins of the German general staff are in the
same vein.

---

[76] Henry Morton Stanley, commanded the search expedition for the missionary David Livingstone,
1871–72, and traced the course of the Congo River.
[77] Molotov queried Maisky whether he thought Butler had been hinting at a possible Soviet mediation
'with a view of concluding peace with Germany on particular terms'. Maisky had not gained any such
impression, but thought Butler did subscribe to the idea.

In the skies, we also see only minor advance guard operations, with no serious consequences. The Germans announced proudly over the radio not long ago that they had shot down 37 French and 12 British planes over the course of almost an entire month. The English, in their turn, boasted some three days ago that of the 30 German machines that recently raided Scotland, 25% were destroyed! What astonishing successes!

The war at sea is a bit more serious. The British blockade is being conducted in earnest, and the Germans feel it. More than 20 submarines have been sunk by the British and the French. One hears that this represents between a quarter and a third of the German submarine fleet. This might be possible, were it not for the fact that the Germans have begun manufacturing submarines as quickly as they produce aircraft. Germany, in turn, has delivered a number of impressive blows to Britain at sea, of which the most painful was, of course, the loss of the *Royal Oak* at Scapa Flow. This was a truly superb strike on the part of Germany and a shameful failure for Britain. Still, even at sea 'real' war has not yet begun.

A strange war! One gains the impression that everything that is being done today is just an opening flourish: the main story is still ahead of us.

... There is no shortage of symptoms to indicate that the ruling elites on both sides of the front are trying even now to find a modus for a deal, an agreement.

Will they succeed? I doubt it. The imperialist contradictions within the dying capitalist system are so deep that constructing a bridge between them is difficult even for Chamberlain and Daladier. Barring a truly extraordinary turn of events – some sort of real political 'miracle' – a terrible, bestial, blind slaughter will begin in the very nearest future.

28 October

'How old are you, if you may excuse such an indiscreet question?'

'Why indiscreet? I'm 55. And you?'

'Oh, I'm significantly older than you... I'm 57.'

'You surprise me! What does a two-year difference mean for men of our age?'

Horace Wilson (for it was he) shrugged his shoulders and said: 'Perhaps you are right. But that's not the point. The point is that you belong to the same generation as I and must remember the time when only one event happened at any given moment, not a hundred, when one could live, breathe, move without haste, make plans for the future and, most important, *ponder*. Are you familiar with this English word?'

'Yes, I am.'

'Well, I like to "*ponder*" on life, people and events. But now I have absolutely no opportunity to do so. Events are unfolding at such a frenzied, unstoppable pace that one barely has time to breathe. So what chance does one have of controlling events? You can count yourself lucky just to flow with the current and avoid the most overpowering blows coming from right and left.'

I gazed at this unprepossessing, skinny man with his calm, somewhat feline movements, a face both intelligent and sly, the man into whose hands capricious fate had placed the future of the British Empire, and found myself wondering: 'Is this true or not? Is he speaking sincerely or playing some premeditated role?'

We sat down to table and moved on to other topics. The war, of course, immediately became the focus of our attention. I asked Wilson what he thought about the prospects for peace.

... 'In theory, the question of peace can still be raised. For war has not yet begun in earnest. Bombs are not yet falling on London and Berlin. The warring passions of the masses are still dormant; they have not yet reached boiling point. The people are still able to think calmly and to reason.' ...

Wilson took a sip of soda water (he firmly declined the offer of wine) and continued: 'Where can peace come from? ... A conference requires careful preparatory work, but there are no signs whatsoever of such work being done. Add to this the fact that we would have to talk with Hitler! We don't believe a single word from this man's mouth!'

'Does it mean,' I asked, 'that the precondition for any talks about peace is the disappearance of Hitler? And even, perhaps, of all his closest associates?'

'Yes, we would like to deal with a different government in Germany,' Wilson answered. 'The disappearance of Hitler alone would be sufficient.'

... When Wilson spoke of Hitler, I discerned personal hostility, almost hatred, in his tone of voice and in his eyes. Clearly, he is unable to forget how Hitler '*let him down*' with such contempt and cruelty. I've heard that Chamberlain now bears the same personal malice and hatred towards Hitler. ...

13 November

I lunched with Winston Churchill and Brendan Bracken at Bracken's flat in Westminster (*8, Lord North Street*). From the outside, a very plain, small house; on the inside, a superbly furnished modern apartment fit for a representative of the bourgeois intelligentsia.

Churchill arrived slightly late from a meeting of the War Cabinet. He is in fine fettle: fresh, younger, full of energy, with a spring in his step. He is pleased with his power, pleased with his ministry, and pleased at the opportunity to bring his strengths to bear on matters of great consequence. Another source of satisfaction, it seems to me, is the awareness and expectation of historical possibilities unveiling themselves before him...

I mentioned Moscow's wish to improve relations with England (such was the latest information I had received). Churchill's face lit up and he exclaimed: 'That's very good! The desire is the main thing. If there's a will, ways and means will also be found.'

... Then, at Churchill's initiative, the conversation moved on to Finland. Churchill asked me about the details of our negotiations and also about our further intentions. I complained to him once again about the conduct of British diplomats: they incite the Finns to resist, promising them Britain's 'moral support', and the Finns – those true provincials in politics – imagine that this 'moral support' will make the walls of Soviet Jericho fall and stubbornly refuse to recognize our utterly lawful claims. As a result of London's interference, the prospects for an agreement between Moscow and Helsinki are reduced. Why is British diplomacy doing this? I don't know. ... 'My view on the issue you have raised is as follows,' replied Churchill. 'Russia has every reason to be a dominant power in the Baltic, and should be one. Better Russia than Germany. That's in our, British, interests. I don't see why we should put a spoke in your wheel as you build naval and air bases on the Baltic coast. I consider your claims towards Finland to be natural and normal. It's truly ridiculous that Leningrad should find itself in the firing-line of long-range guns on the Finnish border, or that the Finnish isles should block the entrance to the Gulf of Finland. You have every right to demand that the Finns rectify the frontier on the Karelian Isthmus and give you a few isles in the Gulf of Finland.'

... And then, pulling on his cigar – we had already finished lunch – Churchill added thoughtfully: '... Were it not for Russia, the Battle of the Marne would have ended in our defeat and the entire outcome of the war would probably have been different. That is why I think that Britain and France owe Russia in general a historical debt, whatever Russia that may be – Red or White – and we now have a moral obligation to help Russia strengthen her position on the Baltic Sea. ... Finland should not impede rapprochement between Britain and the USSR, which is my chief political objective.'

Churchill added: 'I would hope, however, that the USSR will not resort to force to resolve its dispute with Finland. If the USSR chose to follow such a path, as I'm sure you understand, it would make a most painful impression here in England and would render the improvement of Anglo-Soviet relations impossible for a long period of time.'

... We turned to the war. Churchill exclaimed: 'Your non-aggression pact with Germany triggered the war, but I bear you no grudge. I'm even glad. For a long time now I've felt that a war with Germany is <u>necessary</u>. Without your pact, we would have hesitated and drawn things out, until we procrastinated to the point when we could no longer win the war. But now we will win it, even though it will cost us dearly.'

Churchill set out his thoughts about the war. Peace is impossible in the near future. In peacetime the British often look like pampered, gluttonous sybarites, but in times of war and extremity they turn into vicious bulldogs, trapping their prey in a death grip.[78]

15 November

Beaverbrook lunched with us. I hadn't seen him since that memorable lunch in the embassy in early July. Since then he has managed to make two trips to America and, as ever, was full of news, primarily from overseas. His most interesting revelation was that, in Beaverbrook's words, Roosevelt is quite definite in his support of war and the participation of the USA in the war on the side of the 'Allies', because he believes that 'fascism' must be crushed once and for all. Of course, the isolationist sentiments of the American masses hinder the realization of Roosevelt's intentions, but he will still do everything in his power to help Britain and France win the war. Under certain conditions (if, for instance, the Germans attacked Holland and Belgium) Roosevelt could even draw the United States into the war.

Beaverbrook himself opposes the war.

'I'm an isolationist,' he fretted. 'What concerns me is the fate of the British Empire! I want the Empire to remain intact, but I don't understand why for the sake of this we must wage a three-year war to crush "Hitlerism". To hell with that man Hitler! If the Germans want him, I happily concede them this treasure and make my bow. Poland? Czechoslovakia? What are they to do with us? Cursed be the day when Chamberlain gave our guarantees to Poland! A peace conference must be convened immediately, without any preliminary conditions. Were this to be done, I'd support the move with all the means at my disposal, even if I had *to ruin my papers* to do so.'

... Beaverbrook is sure that Chamberlain will retire soon for reasons of ill-health. He thinks that either Hoare or Halifax will succeed him. Churchill, apparently, has no chance at all. Even Eden is more likely to become prime minister. We shall see, however, whether Beaverbrook's forecast proves correct, particularly as far as Churchill is concerned. I've noticed that Beaverbrook's attitude to Churchill is very changeable: one day he might praise him as Britain's greatest statesman, on another he might call him a 'swindler', 'turncoat' or 'political prostitute'. Today he is madly annoyed with Churchill – isn't that the

---

[78] Maisky's detailed report home avoided the important prediction that Churchill would become the next prime minister, as well as his own advocacy of improved relations, which clearly exceeded the mandate he had from Molotov.

real reason for his extreme pessimism about Churchill's chances of becoming prime minister? Time will tell.

[While making his unauthorized overtures to his former allies in Britain, Maisky toiled hard to pacify Molotov. In a tedious eight-page report, he addressed the crucial issue of whether Britain was heading towards war or peace. Contradicting what he entered in his diary, Maisky, who had been reprimanded by Molotov, affirmed that Chamberlain was firmly in the saddle, having successfully created a 'united national front' and having mobilized the Empire. He expected him to 'emerge victorious' over the Churchill group and to seek an end to the war through a dignified compromise. In the same breath he warned that Chamberlain's policy remained hostile to the Soviet Union and 'at the end of the day he might somehow succeed in diverting Hitler to the East'.]

27 November

Halifax invited me over to discuss the trade negotiations. He began, however, with Finland.

Expressing his great concern about the aggravation of the Soviet–Finnish conflict, Halifax began interrogating me in detail about the Moscow talks. I told him as much as I knew, stressing the uncompromising and even provocative behaviour of the Finnish Government, particularly that of Erkko and Cajander.[79] I also pointed out that the Finns refuse to come to terms with reality and inhabit a world of incomprehensible fantasy. ... It is quite clear that there is someone behind them, encouraging them and pushing them towards their insane policy. I say 'insane' because, although the USSR would like nothing better than to settle the present dispute in neighbourly fashion, it has to consider its own security interests and those of Leningrad in particular. It is beyond doubt that influence is being exerted on the Finns from abroad.

Halifax interrupted me at this point and asked with an air of angelic innocence: 'And where might those influences come from? America?'

I replied that the USA in general and Roosevelt in particular bear some responsibility for the aggravation of the Soviet–Finnish conflict, but there are some countries 'closer to home' whose responsibility is even greater. I named Scandinavia (especially Sweden) and... England. Halifax was evidently shocked at this mention of his motherland. ...

... As he was seeing me out of his office, Halifax returned once again to the question of Finland. Appealing to me as president of the Council of the L[eague] of N[ations], he asked me to bring all my influence to bear on warding off an acute conflict with Finland. ...

---

[79] Aimo Kaarlo Cajander, Finnish prime minister, 1937–39.

28 November

... I went to lunch with Butler. He received me not at his place (he was afraid I might catch the 'flu from his father, who was ill), but at the home of his *parliamentary secretary*, a beautiful mansion with numerous paintings, luxurious furniture and a handsome dining-room in the style of the Alhambra. The host was absent. We ate alone.[80]

For no less than an hour and a half, Butler, swearing on his honour, deployed every means possible to persuade me that the British Government was not engaged in any kind of diplomatic game against the USSR (Butler obviously knew about my conversation yesterday with his boss). Our suspicions about the intentions of the British Government are absolutely unfounded. The British policy is not as Machiavellian as some assume it to be. It is simple, and is currently defined by the basic and decisive fact that Britain is at war with

45. Outcast after the Molotov–Ribbentrop Pact, Maisky has to make do with 'Rab' Butler, parliamentary undersecretary of state for foreign affairs.

---

[80] Vansittart had advised ministers to give Maisky 'a rather wide berth ... for he derives some illusions from his imaginary successes'. Butler, who regarded Maisky as an 'agreeable scoundrel', politely turned down Maisky's invitations to the embassy and preferred to lunch with him in the privacy of the home of Henry Channon, his parliamentary secretary, so as not 'to be seen with him in public'. The host, on his return, did not forget to 'check up on the snuff-boxes ... but did not notice anything missing'.

Germany. Britain has its hands full. ... Hence the proposal for trade negotiations, which are important not so much *per se* but as a first step on the way to a general settling of relations. Unfortunately, nothing has been heard from the Soviet Government for more than a month in response to the British proposals. A great pity. Halifax is particularly vexed by our silence: he was fighting energetically in government for negotiations to be opened and now finds himself in a foolish position. ...

29 November

Yesterday evening the Soviet Government denounced the Soviet–Finnish non-aggression pact in view of its violation by the hostile actions of Finland. Diplomatic relations with Finland were broken off tonight. ... At the same time, Molotov has said, in a speech which I heard over the radio, that had Finland been an amicably disposed country, it would have been possible to discuss the issue of the reunification of Soviet Karelia with Finland.

... When I signed the agreement on 21 January 1932 with Yrjö-Koskinen, Finland's foreign minister at the time, it never crossed my mind that the pact would meet such an end. ... I can't understand the present position of the Finnish Government. Of course, the British, French and Scandinavians have all been meddling there, confusing the Finns and drastically exacerbating a conflict which could have been settled in a neighbourly way. Still... don't the Finns understand that, if trouble comes, they can't count on anyone to help them? Who will help them? The Swedes? The British? The Americans? Like hell they will! A racket in the newspapers, moral support, oohing and aahing – yes. Troops, airplanes, cannons, guns – no. Butler told me plainly yesterday: 'Should anything happen, we wouldn't be able to send a single warship to Finland.'

What are the Finns counting on?

[As early as February 1939, Stalin had unsuccessfully sought to persuade Finland to cede territories which he deemed to be essential for the defence of Leningrad, a mere 33 kilometres away from the Finnish border. Haunted by the still vivid memory of Western intervention in that region during the Civil War, Stalin feared that Finland might serve as 'a springboard' for an Anglo-Franco-German attack on the Soviet Union. After subjecting the Baltic states to similar arrangements, negotiations with Finland were resumed in Moscow on 12 October and limped on until 9 November. The Finns rejected the Soviet offers, and a border incident on 30 November served the Russians as an excuse for unleashing a full-scale war. In the early stages of the 'Winter War', the Russians faced unexpectedly stiff resistance, which exposed the fragility of the Red Army in the wake of the purges. Only in March 1940 did the Russians break through the

Mannerheim Line and force a peace treaty. The unpopular task of blaming the war on the stubbornness of the Finns, allegedly encouraged by the British, fell to Maisky.]

1 December

So, we too have our own 'war'. Cajander, Tanner[81] and Co. finally brought things to a head. On the morning of 30 November the Red Army was forced to cross the Finnish border and move deep into its territory. ...

The British have reacted with fury. The press, the radio, the cinema, Parliament – everything has been mobilized. ... The British Government's position is to wait and see. It wants to observe which way the wind is blowing. There are no signs of active British intervention in Finnish affairs so far. But I can't say for sure how the British Government will act if the events in Finland drag on. I doubt, however, that Chamberlain will give open military assistance to Tanner, Kajander and Co.: he won't want to have the USSR as an enemy in the European war, in addition to Germany.

3 December

Three months of war.

Much has changed in British life over this short period of time. More than a million have been called to arms, with some being deployed on the French front, and the greater part training at home. On the street, on the omnibus, on the underground, in the theatre, at the skating rink – everywhere there are military uniforms. And not only men's. A great number of women are to be seen in khaki: rugged boots, short skirts and perky caps from which clumps of unruly hair stick out. They are members of the women's Auxiliary Territorial Service. There are relatively few cars on the roads and in the city: petrol is rationed and the rations are far from generous. Sandbags are piled up high in front of buildings, shops, institutions and monuments. The monument at Piccadilly Circus is shielded by an entire pyramid of sandbags. In parks, gardens and on public squares there are gas-proof shelters, bomb shelters and antiaircraft batteries. The air is filled with hundreds of balloons, their silver scales sparkling in the sun (on the rare occasions when it shines). Strict black-out is enforced in the evenings. It's pitch-black, especially in our Kensington Palace Gardens. It's difficult, dangerous and cheerless to move around after sunset. The theatres and picture-houses are open, but not all of them, and those that are open close early. *Social life* has come to a stand-still: no grand receptions, no banquets, no *diplomatic functions*. Even the lord mayor

---

[81] Väinö Alfred Tanner, Finnish social-democrat foreign minister, 1939–40.

cancelled his annual banquet scheduled for 9 November. Food prices are rising, while the quantity and choice of products shrink. Rationing is being introduced for butter, bacon and sugar. There are complaints of food shortages in certain regions. A series of restrictions has been imposed on the freedom of movement, the press, correspondence, etc.

Yes, there are many changes. But <u>so far</u> the basic patterns of English life have not been disturbed too much. Parliament functions normally, albeit with a few restrictions. The old party system is also functioning, although an electoral truce has been concluded between the parties for the duration of the war. The old government is also working as before, although it has been somewhat 'freshened up' with the introduction of Churchill and Eden. Chamberlain is stronger than before: all rumours and discussions of his retirement have subsided.

... London itself has changed little in appearance. It's the same old London – true, it has furrowed its brow, tightened its belt and put on its work clothes for a dirty job, but it's still the familiar London. Even the places of amusement are chock-full, regardless of the darkness and the bleakness of the 'black-out'.

12 December

The Red Army is advancing relatively slowly in Finland. The nature of the terrain, the climate, the season (short days, low cloud cover, lakes and marshes not yet properly frozen) – everything is against us. In such conditions, the mechanized forces of the Red Army cannot be fully effective. Moreover, the Karelian Isthmus is strongly fortified by the Finns, who have exploited the numerous rivers, lakes and marshes. All these difficulties will be overcome, of course, but for now what's needed is patience. ...

The slow development of events in Finland is helping to fan a frenzied anti-Soviet campaign in Britain. The campaign began almost a fortnight ago, and there are no signs of it subsiding. If anything the tension is growing.

The press is still raging, and the 'Left' (*Daily Herald* and *News Chronicle*) turns out to be even worse than the 'Right' (*The Times, Daily Telegraph*, etc.). All sorts of slanders, lies and nonsense concerning the USSR are published under foot-long headlines on the front pages of the London papers. The press simply excels itself when it comes to 'the bombing of women and children' and 'the use of gas' by the Red Army. We have already issued official denials, but to no avail.

... The British Government has clearly decided against shyness. *Gloves off!* Otherwise, this whole frenzied campaign would be inconceivable. Halifax's speech in the House of Lords on 5 December is very indicative in this respect. Similarly indicative is Butler's belligerent activity in Geneva, where he supports the proposal to expel the USSR from the League of Nations. Equally interesting is the fact that the British Government has decided to publish a 'White Book' on the summer negotiations in Moscow. The Foreign Office had until now been against publishing it, arguing on more than one occasion that 'it could have an unfavourable effect on Anglo-Soviet relations'. Now this consideration has been dropped. One can easily imagine the content of this 'White Book'! The British Government will exploit the opportunity to justify its conduct during the talks and to accuse the USSR. Lies, slander, distortion – everything will be used for this purpose. Not blatant lies, in all probability, but (which is far more dangerous) a crafty mixture of truth and deceit.

... As for the anti-Soviet campaign, one thing is particularly striking. In the campaigns connected with events in Poland and then in the Baltic, the USSR was accused of 'imperialism'. Now emphasis is placed on 'world revolution' and 'communism'. The question: who is the No. 1 enemy? – Germany or the USSR? ... However, in spite of the anti-Soviet frenzy dominating the social and political atmosphere in the country, there is no talk here (unlike in France) of severing diplomatic relations with the Soviet Union. The English are cleverer than the French. Moreover, they have already tried it once and do not wish to repeat the unfortunate experience. However, I cannot vouch for the more distant future. Anything may happen in times of war.

... I'm an old bird, and this isn't the first storm I've had to face. As soon as the events in Finland come to an end, it will blow over. The British are past masters at accepting the 'fait accompli'.

15 December

Yesterday the League of Nations expelled the USSR from its ranks.

... Britain and France directed everything in Geneva. The USA backed them up by exerting pressure on the South Americans. A US representative attended the LN meetings as an 'observer'. It is said that Paul-Boncour,[82] who headed the French delegation in Geneva, was personally against the expulsion of the Soviet Union, but it was Daladier who took the decision. As for Butler, he was clearly unhappy with the role assigned to him, but he conscientiously pursued the Cabinet's line. The result: Britain and France have played in Geneva the unenviable role of organizers of a new 'anti-Comintern bloc'. I don't think they will have any more luck in their enterprise than Germany.

... When I was leaving Geneva in May, I hoped I would never again have to honour the grand rooms of the Palais des Nations with my presence. Seems

---

[82] Augustin Alfred Joseph Paul-Boncour, French premier, 1932–33; minister of foreign affairs, 1932–34, 1936 and 1938; French permanent delegate to the League of Nations, 1932–36.

that my hope has been fulfilled. At any rate, never again will I have to deal with this League of Nations!

[The Maiskys tried to put on a brave face. They, however, were clearly being ostracized by foes and former friends alike. Cut off from news from Moscow, as he complained in a private letter to Litvinov, Maisky feared that Britain and France 'had become definitely hostile to the USSR and were planning a peace with a defeated Germany and then an anti-communist alliance!' The mask slipped, though, at Christmas, when rumours started circulating of a breakdown in relations and of his recall. He was little encouraged by a rather acrimonious exchange of telegrams with Molotov. Maisky's distress is discernible in his desperate attempts to persuade Molotov that his continued stay in London was indispensable to prevent the outbreak of hostilities.]

31 December

In view of the current situation, we cancelled the New Year's celebrations for the whole colony in the embassy. We decided to greet the New Year individually or in groups at home. Agniya and I did so as if we were in Moscow, at nine o'clock London time. Then we dropped in for a moment at the L.'s upstairs, where a small group of embassy personnel were celebrating with their wives, singing and dancing. After that we drove around the city to see how the English were seeing in the New Year. The streets were shrouded in the usual black-out gloom. The pavements were white with snow: the week has been uncommonly cold and snowy for England. There were people in the streets, but immeasurably fewer than in former years. At Piccadilly, where huge, noisy crowds, singing and dancing, always flood the square on New Year's Eve, there were now only a few sparse, silent groups. At St Paul's Cathedral, where there is always a sea of human beings, shouting, laughing and dancing, there was nobody to be found. It was the same all over. Only Whitechapel was noisier, but perhaps that was due to the character of the locals.

War! Its deadly breath has frozen the New Year celebrations of 1940.

Now, back at home, I sit and ponder: what does tomorrow have in store? ... Here I am, seeing in the year 1940 in London, in circumstances of war and 'black-out', entirely uncertain of the near future – not only of my personal future (what would that matter?), but of the future of Europe and all mankind. ... The greater part of my life is behind me. Even in the best scenario, only a short period lies ahead. But as yet I have no fear of death, nor sharp regret for the fact that three quarters of my life have already passed.

1940

3 January

The curve of Anglo-Soviet relations continues to drop.

The 'White Book' about the summer negotiations in Moscow is to be published in a fortnight or less. Rumours keep circulating that it will be prepared in such a way (unless something unexpected happens at the last moment) that it will inevitably result in the severance of diplomatic relations between the two countries, or at least the mutual recall of ambassadors.

The *Daily Worker* raised the alarm back on 27 December, giving the first warning about the danger of a break in relations. On the same day, the Foreign Office refuted the newspaper's report through Reuters and interviews with foreign correspondents.

Nevertheless, yesterday, 2 January, Seeds left Moscow 'on leave'. Before his departure, he visited Comrades Potemkin and Molotov for discussions about the state of Anglo-Soviet relations. He was given to understand that the Soviet Government harboured no hostile intentions towards England but was resolutely determined to eliminate the danger to Leningrad presented by hostile, bourgeois Finland. ... Seeds' departure merely confirms the rumours that the publication of the 'White Book' will preclude his continued presence in Moscow. The same rumours say that my stay in London will also become very precarious after the appearance of the Book, although I confess that it is not entirely clear to me how this might happen. Time will tell.

Today's newspapers report that Naggiar, the French ambassador in Moscow, is also soon to depart on 'extended leave'. The Italian ambassador in Moscow, Rosso,[1] has also received instructions from his government to go 'on leave'. ...

So, three great powers are recalling their ambassadors from Moscow. This is no coincidence. It is part of the plan presented by Daladier at the last meeting of the Inter-Allied Supreme War Council on 19 December. ... It was eventually decided to pursue a wait-and-see policy and to use various means to provoke

---

[1] Augusto Rosso, Italian ambassador in Moscow, 1936–40.

Moscow to sever relations: by lending assistance to Finland, by recalling ambassadors, by publishing the 'White Book', and so on. ...

4 January

On New Year's Eve, Beaverbrook unexpectedly called me to extend his good wishes, and yesterday Agniya and I went to his place for lunch. There were only three of us, so the conversation was quite frank.

Beaverbrook, who has told me before that he sees no sense in the current war, is now most interested in the prospects for peace. ... What is the alignment of forces in the British ruling circles? The 'big four' (Chamberlain, Simon, Hoare and Halifax) are ready to conclude peace without crushing Germany, if an acceptable basis is found. Churchill, who relies on the Labour–Liberal sector and certain Conservative circles, believes that, before discussing peace, Germany must be crushed.

What are the prospects? Beaverbrook believes that if Hitler were to agree to the minimal acceptable conditions, including Poland and Czechoslovakia – conditions, in other words, which could be presented to the nation as a fulfilment, albeit not absolute, of the 'war aims' – the 'big four' would immediately conclude a peace. Should Hitler not agree, Churchill will triumph and the war will continue.

I asked Beaverbrook: what position would England take should Scandinavia be drawn into the war? Beaverbrook answered without hesitation: 'We would most certainly fight for Scandinavia, especially for Norway.'

... Beaverbrook is extremely worried about Anglo-Soviet relations. He himself is definitely against a rupture, and certainly against waging war with the USSR. He thinks therefore that the British can 'applaud Finnish bravery', but should not send arms and ammunition to Finland. Unfortunately, there are notable elements among the general public and in government who favour meddling in Finnish affairs, even at the risk of provoking the USSR to break off relations. ... If the USA severs diplomatic relations with the USSR, the British advocates of a 'resolute policy' on the Finnish question will gain the upper hand. ... He is consoled by Churchill's support for a 'cautious' line regarding the Soviet Union. This is important because Churchill's influence at the present time is great. As a result, Beaverbrook has not yet lost hope that a rupture in Anglo-Soviet relations may still be avoided, but he deems the situation dangerous. ...

[Beaverbrook's attitude was an exception. Maisky had become a pariah in London. He found most doors bolted, while his invitations were politely turned down. George Bilainkin, a journalist for whom the doors of the embassy were always open, noted in his diary 'the deep lines' under Maisky's eyes 'when the clamour rose' for a declaration of war against the Soviet Union: 'As I walked away, along the icy cold and ice-covered "Millionaires' Row", I thought of its principal tenant, who had so eagerly striven for success in his mission, had nearly won it in the middle of last year, and then watched triumph being taken from his grasp.'

Maisky barely recovered his social standing after the conclusion of the Winter War. As late as May, an invitation for Eden and his wife to come to lunch at the embassy 'quite privately' drew the lukewarm response 'I will, if I may, let you know later about my wife as she is away in the country at present'. Dalton likewise describes in his diary a luncheon he attended on his own at the embassy, as his wife 'would sooner be found dead than in [Maisky's] Embassy'.]

5 January

A remarkable incident happened today.

Strang dropped in unexpectedly. I hadn't seen him for a long time, since early August, when he had just got back from his unsuccessful visit to Moscow.

I asked him to sit down and offered him a Russian cigarette. Strang took a deep drag before declaring that he had come 'on the instructions of Lord Halifax, but in a private capacity'. In mid-January the 'Blue Book', devoted to the Moscow negotiations on the pact, is to be published (it turns out to be a 'Blue', not a 'White' Book, the difference being that the 'White Book', which has no dustcover, is usually smaller than the 'Blue Book', which does have one). This Book will contain, among other materials, records of a few conversations which Halifax once had with me. As a point of courtesy and on a private basis, Halifax would like to offer me the opportunity to acquaint myself with the passages that relate to me before the Book is published, should any corrections be required. After all, records of conversations are made after the fact, and one can never be entirely sure of their accuracy. Having said this, Strang took the proofs from his pocket (a sizeable parcel) and pushed them towards me, suggesting that he was prepared to leave them for me to peruse and correct as required.

I confess that I was sorely tempted to take the Book into my hands at once. But I immediately checked myself, for the thought suddenly flashed across my mind that 'honourable' Halifax had laid a trap for me. ... So I replied to Strang in the politest of tones that I was grateful to Halifax for his courtesy, but that unfortunately I could not take advantage of it. The publication of the Blue Book had not been agreed with the Soviet Government. The latter had not even been informed of the decision to publish the Book. ... And, without a glance at the proofs of the 'Blue Book', I pushed them nonchalantly back to Strang.

Strang was clearly nonplussed, but assured me that he quite 'understood' me and would convey my exact words to Halifax, who would, of course, also 'understand' everything. Then, returning the proofs of the Book to his pocket, Strang added: 'Lord Halifax thought it his moral duty to make you this offer... Now he may consider his conscience to be clean.'

That's Halifax to a tee! Pritt[2] once told me that, according to Butler, Halifax used to say to the latter at the beginning of each working day: 'Mind, Butler, we mustn't sacrifice a single principle today!'

And, having sent up this 'prayer' to God and put his soul at ease, Halifax would apply himself to the next intrigue being cooked up in the dirty kitchen of British foreign policy.

They are dangerous, these men of God! Halifax has now made two cynical attempts to deceive me: the first on 31 March, in connection with last year's guarantee to Poland, and the second today. He has failed, but I must be vigilant!

Strang also declared during our conversation today that the British Government was not planning to break off diplomatic relations with the USSR ('provided, of course, that the Soviet Government does not intend to do this,' he added rather pointedly) and that Seeds was indeed taking the two months' leave due to him for rest and medical treatment.

8 January

Although I politely refused Strang's offer to acquaint myself with the text of the 'Blue Book', I came to learn of its contents all the same. ... It seems that the object of the British Government's selection and arrangement of the materials was to create the impression that the summer negotiations collapsed owing to the USSR's 'duplicity'. This is illustrated in two ways: (1) the Soviet Government held parallel negotiations throughout the summer with the British and the French on the one hand, and with the Germans on the other, without really wishing to conclude an agreement with the British and French but merely manoeuvring so as to lay the blame for the break on the 'Allies'; (2) declaring through C[omrade] Stalin its duty to assist victims of aggression, the Soviet Government was itself occupied solely with thoughts of aggression and eventually committed it in Finland. The reader of the Book is therefore meant to draw the conclusion that the Soviet Union is in essence a 'wolf in sheep's clothing' and that the British Government was very wise to avoid concluding a pact with such a dangerous partner.

The division of roles between C[omrade] Molotov and me during the negotiations is given as further evidence of Soviet 'duplicity'. In Moscow C[omrade] Molotov was stubbornly sabotaging any progress in negotiations by piling one

---

[2] Denis Pritt, radical British lawyer and Labour MP, 1935–50.

obstacle on another. Meanwhile I in London was weakening the vigilance of the British Government, using nice words to assure its members of the USSR's desire to maintain friendship with Britain, and praising British moves and proposals. And so it went on until the very moment the talks were broken off.

[The draft White Book contained 150 pages of documents conveying the official British version of the 1939 triple negotiations. Its publication would certainly have exposed Maisky's autonomous initiatives (by revealing discrepancies between his and Halifax's records of the meetings) and his dissension from Molotov's line. This was particularly true about the thread running through the long, analytical introduction by the distinguished All Souls' scholar Llewellyn Woodward, who had been entrusted with the editorial work. He particularly dwelt on Maisky's assurance to Cadogan at the end of March that the guarantees to Poland 'would be a revolutionary change in British policy' and 'would increase enormously the confidence of other countries'. Maisky was terrified that the appearance of the White Book would lead to his recall.

It is hardly surprising, therefore, that Maisky remained obsessive about the incriminating document. He was, however, saved by the bell. The idea of publishing a White Book invited opposition from the outset, as it exposed not only what was assumed to be Russian treachery, but also the reluctance of Chamberlain to reach an agreement and the conflicting French and British positions. On 6 March, Chamberlain announced in Parliament that publication of the White Book was to be dropped. In due course, Maisky succeeded in obtaining a microfilm of the scrapped book, from 'friends of the USSR', most likely through intelligence channels (thereby exceeding his own authority), which he concealed from his superiors. The microfilm was the main reason for his indictment in his trial in 1955. Seeking a full rehabilitation, Maisky made the dubious claim that it was a mere case of negligence and a 'slip' of his memory.][3]

21 January

I've been receiving information in the last few days that a dispute has emerged in Labour circles concerning Finland and the Soviet Union. There was a long and confusing debate on this matter at the meeting of the executive committee of Parliamentary Labour on 16 January. ... Today, meanwhile, Lord Strabolgi[4] arrived unexpectedly, in sports clothes, straight from the skating rink. After emphasizing that he was acting in a private capacity, Lord Strabolgi (formerly Kenworthy) first began asking whether the Soviet Government might wish to invite a trade union–Labour delegation like the one which had left for Helsinki

---

[3] On his arrest and trial, see the chapter 'The Price of Fame'.
[4] Joseph Montague Kenworthy (10th Baron Strabolgi), opposition chief whip, House of Lords, 1938–42.

on 19 January at the invitation of Finnish trade unions and cooperatives (Citrine, Noel-Baker and Downie[5])? Labour would like to be entirely 'impartial' and hear out both sides. I expressed my astonishment at his suggestion and made it clear to him that there were no chances whatsoever that it might be accepted. ...

26 January

About a month ago (24 December) I established in my diary the state of Anglo-Soviet relations at the time. Today, I can summarize the processes that have unfolded since then. There's nothing to celebrate!

The general curve of Anglo-Soviet relations continues its downward path. ... In this connection, the matter of Finland acquires special significance for British ruling circles. By helping Mannerheim,[6] they hope to kill two birds with one stone. First, they hope to raise the spirits of the small neutral countries (the 'Allies' do not leave them to the mercy of fate in their hour of need!) and thus draw them into the war more easily. Second, they hope to prolong the war in Finland, weaken the USSR, tie us hand and foot in the north and thus reduce our freedom of manoeuvre in other directions, and, finally, deprive the Germans of the possibility of getting raw materials, food and so on, from the USSR.

This plan is particularly attractive to the British Government. ... But it is still too early to say whether the British Government will succeed in realizing its plan, and to what extent. Any number of obstacles could get in the way: military, international, domestic. The reaction of the neutral countries to Churchill's speech[7] is a useful reminder in this respect. But we must be doubly vigilant. Should the British Government fulfil even 60 or 70% of its intentions, the rupture of Anglo-Soviet relations would be most likely inevitable.

[This entry dovetailed with a long letter sent to Molotov on the same day. Convinced that the severance of relations was imminent, Maisky depicted in sombre colours the state of Anglo-Soviet relations which, he warned, posed 'a serious danger' to the Soviet Union. The object of his apocalyptic letter was to impress on Molotov that the sooner the war in Finland was concluded 'in terms favourable to us the better are the chances for Anglo-Soviet relations to survive the present crisis'. It was entirely clear to the Labour leadership that Maisky was conscious of the danger that the Finnish war might

---

[5] John Downie, representative of the cooperative movement.
[6] Baron Carl Gustaf Emil Mannerheim, commander-in-chief of the Finnish army, 1939–40 and 1941–46; Finnish president, 1944–46.
[7] In a speech broadcast on 20 January, Churchill suggested that the extension of hostilities was likely to draw more states into the war.

lead to British involvement, but he was forced to defend it, otherwise 'he would be recalled & liquidated'.]

29 January

What a journey!

Yesterday, Agniya and I went to see the Webbs after lunch. The weather this January is unusually cold and snowy. As we were leaving, it was getting a little warmer. The snow began to melt and, even on the way to the Webbs, the car was occasionally sliding. We set off back home at about midnight. It was very dark. A very unpleasant surprise awaited us on the main road: it was just like an ice-rink. Driving was nearly impossible. The car slid from one side of the road to the other. The wheels would not bite. At times the car threatened to turn over. After driving for an hour and a half and covering barely 7–8 miles, we decided to stop somewhere for the night. With the greatest difficulty we reached a tiny roadside *inn* bearing the resonant name *Red Lion Hotel, Thursley*. Unfortunately, the inn was already crammed with fellow travellers stranded like us. Like everywhere now, there were many sailors and soldiers. A room was out of the question. We had to content ourselves with two armchairs at the fireplace in the dining-room and two fascinating novels borrowed from the hosts' library. So Agniya and I spent the whole night reading by the fire. We set out again this morning. It had snowed overnight and our car, which had been parked outside (the inn had no garage), was completely frozen up. White had a big job to start the engine. We saw dozens of fallen trees, torn telegraph wires, and broken-down cars on the way to London. In town we learned that the railway had been disrupted overnight: many trains had got stuck *en route*, trains from Scotland were running 8–9 hours late, etc.

Well, such a thing has never happened to me before in England! ...

Beatrice Webb told me yesterday that in her opinion the capitalist system has only 20–30 years left to live, and no more. Real progress! ... Brendan Bracken came to lunch today. In spite of his Conservative parliamentary mandate and his proximity to Churchill, he, too, is unsure about capitalism's future. He expounded his thoughts at length, arguing that the world is heading for the triumph of socialism, but not exactly the socialism we have in the Soviet Union. Just like Gretchen in *Faust*. Bracken is not opposed to socialism in principle. But he would like it to establish itself in a 'respectable' manner, without smoke and powder, and without financial collapse and economic chaos. In his opinion, the best way to 'bring about socialism' is through the inheritance tax. By raising this tax to 80–90%, all capitalists will be gradually 'expropriated' and socialism will become inevitable. ...

30 January

I went to see Butler. ... He asked me what I thought about the state of our relations. I shrugged my shoulders and said that he surely knew as much about it as I did. There were no acute, concrete conflicts between us, but...

'You mean to say,' Butler interrupted, 'that the sea is calm, but the water temperature is very low.'

'Yes, you may well be right.'

Butler asked if anything in particular could be done to improve our relations, or at least prevent their further deterioration. I retorted that he was in a better position to know: all our difficulties derive from British policy, and in particular from the British Government's desire to interfere in affairs that are of no concern to her.

Butler objected that the Government was doing all right, but that 'public opinion' was very worked up and was exerting pressure on the Government. ... Butler continued: 'The main difficulty in Anglo-Soviet relations is that you support our deadly enemy. Many in England are convinced that you have a *cast-iron* agreement with Germany which practically makes you a single bloc.'

Referring to C[omrade] Molotov's speeches, I advised Butler not to heed idle gossip. Butler listened to me with obvious satisfaction, but with little trust. Then he exclaimed: 'If only we knew for sure that your hands really are untied and that you are pursuing your own, independent policy, so much could be different.'

As far as I could understand, he meant that much could be different in England's behaviour on the Finnish question, too.

I laughed and said that the Soviet Union had always pursued and continues to pursue only its own independent policy. ...

[Maisky had assured the Webbs that he was complying with the 'orders from Moscow to *stay put*', in a 'jovial defiant manner'. And yet his diary and his report to Molotov deliberately conceal the grave concerns he felt for his own survival and his repeated pleas to Butler 'not to be too spectacular ... and maintain our diplomatic relations'. Moreover, he was apologetic about the Molotov–Ribbentrop Pact, lamenting that 'we lived in a period of change, that anything might happen, that in the jungle the strangest of animals got together – if they felt their joint interests made this advisable'.

Woodward, the editor of the White Book, was the first to record Maisky's meeting with Butler, in his 1962 official history *British Foreign Policy in the Second World War*. Maisky was furious, and in his memoirs, vehemently denied using the jungle metaphor. But according to Alexander, first lord of the Admiralty,[8] the following exchange with

---

[8] Albert Victor Alexander, Labour's first lord of the Admiralty, 1929–31 and 1940–46.

Maisky took place a couple of months later: 'I said in a casual way: "We live in strange and rapid times", to which he answered, "Yes, this is the period of the jungle."]

8 February

The Inter-Allied Supreme War Council met in Paris on 5 February. ... The French continued to insist on severing relations with the USSR ... but the British adhered to their former position in respect of the USSR (not to break off relations themselves, but to provoke the USSR into doing so).

... As far as Finland is concerned, the parties agreed to 'speed up' and 'increase' material aid to Finland and 'stimulate' the 'volunteer' movement.

On the day of the Supreme War Council meeting, the French police arranged a brazen raid on our trade mission. A true *Arcos Raid*,[9] if not worse. Evidently, the French wanted to create a favourable 'atmosphere' in which the decision about breaking with the USSR could be taken, and wished to tie the hands of the British in advance. For now, it seems, they have failed. ...

11 February

Visited the *Old Wizard* in Churt. It is always pleasant and salutary to talk with him, especially in difficult times. He has an exceptional brain: a sort of clot of high-voltage intellectual energy. He catches your meaning at once and responds with a cascade of brilliant thoughts and comparisons. Yet he also possesses in abundance that supreme wisdom which sees through things, is not distracted by glittering appearances, does not lapse into indignation, does not shout, weep or become agitated, but simply understands and takes everything into account, drawing the appropriate inferences. Whenever you converse with Lloyd George, you immediately sense that you are dealing with a man of the highest calibre, a cut above all around him – ministers, parliamentarians and public figures. The difference between Lloyd George and every other contemporary 'leader' is like that between Kreisler[10] and a violinist from a provincial orchestra. One may say without hesitation: he is an astonishing person.

We talked for about three hours today. Leaving my own arguments and considerations to one side, I'll try to convey the gist of what the 'Old Wizard' told me.

'If it comes to war between England and the USSR,' Lloyd George exclaimed, with a toss of his pince-nez, 'this would be the greatest catastrophe. It's terrifying even to contemplate. But one shouldn't close one's eyes to the facts.

---

[9] A raid of the London offices of the Soviet trade delegation in May 1927 which led to the severance of Anglo-Soviet relations.
[10] Fritz Kreisler, Austrian-born American violinist and composer.

46. With Lloyd George, 'the Old Wizard'.

Anglo-Soviet relations have been deteriorating since the beginning of the Finnish war and are in a precarious state today.'

... The situation is very serious but not entirely hopeless. Chamberlain, Hoare, Halifax and Kingsley Wood are against war with the USSR. Simon, as usual, is hedging his bets. This group may indeed be able to withstand French pressure. But the Soviet Government must show flexibility as well. First of all, it mustn't yield to provocation. It's very good that the Soviet Government responded calmly to the farce in Geneva and to the raid on the trade mission in Paris. And it's very good that the Soviet Government did not recall me in response to the departure of Seeds ('a big fool'). Surits mustn't be recalled from Paris.

21 February

Our undeniable successes at the front (breakthrough in the western section of the Mannerheim Line) have made a powerful, but double-edged impression in Britain.

Our successes have made <u>more reasonable</u> people – among whom should be numbered Chamberlain's group in the government, Beaverbrook, Labourites like Hicks,[11] Tom Williams,[12] Strabolgi and others – more restrained and circumspect on the matter of aid to Finland. They are less inclined than ever to risk the possibility of war with the Soviet Union.

<u>Less reasonable</u> people, including certain ministers who appear to be led by Churchill (though I have no definite information about the latter's stance on the Finnish question), supporters of Hore-Belisha, Liberals headed by Sinclair, and various newspapers – *News Chronicle*, *The Star*, *Sunday Times* and others – draw the reverse conclusion. Sensing Mannerheim to be weakening, they have launched a frenzied campaign in London to provide energetic support to the Finns on the broadest scale, *including the sending of troops*, while ignoring the risk of open war with the USSR and the transformation of Scandinavia into a field of battle between the 'Allies' and Germany.

Calmly assessing all these factors, I'm inclined to think that the people in the first group outweigh those in the second group by a significant margin, since England itself is at stake here. ... On the whole, the situation has to be recognized as dangerous and fraught with any number of surprises. One might easily be drawn into a major war. The best means of avoiding this danger is speed on the Finnish front. The Anglo-French calculations are based on the assumption that the decisive phase in Finland will not begin until May. If we

---

[11] Ernest George Hicks, Labour MP, 1931–50; Trades Union Congress (TUC) leader involved in the formation of the TUC's Anglo-Russian Joint Advisory Committee, 1925–27.
[12] Tom Williams, member of the Anglo-Russian Parliamentary Committee.

could upset these calculations and bring the war to an end within a few weeks (or, if not end the war completely, at least deliver a decisive blow to the Finns, after which the hopelessness of their position would be obvious to all), we would exit the danger zone.

The root of British activism is the widespread conviction that the USSR and Germany are 'allies' – if not yet formally, then in the near future. Hence the tendency to make no distinction between Germany and the USSR and to label both as 'enemies'. This is where explanations must be sought for Churchill's and Hore-Belisha's change of tack. ... I try proving to everybody that talk about a Soviet–German 'alliance' is absurd. But since nobody believes a word anyone says in the world of diplomacy at the moment, I have no illusions about the effectiveness of my refutations on this issue. Moscow ought to have demonstrated this in a more obvious manner.[13]

13 March

I barely slept last night. Moscow radio announced in the evening that an important communication would be transmitted after midnight. I immediately understood that this was about the peace treaty with Finland and sat down by the radio to await news. It was a long wait. It was only at 3.30 a.m. Moscow time that the end of the Soviet–Finnish war and the conclusion of peace between the belligerents was finally announced.

Hurrah! I was ready to hurl my hat into the air.

We have emerged from a very great danger. We have preserved the possibility of staying out of an imperialist war. And we have gained what we wanted: Leningrad and our north-western borders are now secure.

In the afternoon I went to Parliament, where Chamberlain was due to make a statement about the conclusion of peace. The diplomatic gallery was practically empty. There were only myself, the Bulgarian and... the duke of Alba (the Spaniard). But the House was packed to the rafters and the air was humming, as before a storm.

Chamberlain made a brief statement consisting of little more than formalities. ... I can't recall seeing [the Parliament] in such a state of excitement and fury. Indeed, the only word to describe the mood of the majority of all the MPs, with only a few exceptions, was <u>fury</u>. Impotent fury, but fury nonetheless – vivid, seething, overflowing fury...

---

[13] This entry was sparked by Molotov's telegram to Maisky upbraiding the British Government for spreading the 'ridiculous and slanderous' rumours about a military alliance between Germany and Russia. Maisky had prompted Butler to raise the possibility of British mediation in the negotiations with the Finns. Molotov gave it his full blessing and produced the peace terms, which were, however, turned down by the Cabinet. It was, as Channon wrote in his diary after meeting Butler, 'A diabolically clever scheme, but Maisky's dove is clearly a vulture.'

'It's fallen through! What a pity, it's fallen through,' were the words that seemed to hang in the air.

This frenzy was expressed in the House's reactions to the various anti-Soviet volleys by ministers and MPs. When Chamberlain referred to 'aggression' in reference to the Finnish events, the House shook with shouts of approval. When the 'Independent' McGovern[14] took aim at the USSR and C[omrade] Stalin, the hall resounded for an entire minute with deafening yells, 'Hear! Hear!'

Looking down from the diplomatic gallery, I watched that vile display of angry impotence with a sense of superiority. And at the same time it was clearer to me than ever that peace had been concluded at just the right time.[15] ...

16 March

I visited Lloyd George in Churt. The old man has a cold and is not in the best of health, but he is alive and looking as bright as ever.

He congratulated me on the timely conclusion of peace.

'I won't touch upon the *merits of the case*,' he said. 'I think we might disagree on this point, but I'm very glad about the peace. The danger of war between England and the USSR was quite real. I had much evidence of this in recent weeks, since our last meeting. Had the war dragged on till May, I can assure you that conflict between our countries would have become unavoidable.'

... In the course of our conversation L-G asked when I had last seen Halifax. I said I saw him three and a half months ago, on the eve of the Finnish war. Lloyd George raised his hands to the heavens in a comic gesture of despair and exclaimed: 'I say! If I were in Halifax's place, I'd summon you at least twice a week to try to influence you and keep the USSR from getting too close to Germany. Three and a half months! Good heavens!'

A mischievous twinkle sparkled in L-G's eyes, and he said with his infectious laugh: 'I have plum trees in my garden. The short ones yield a lot of fruit. The very tall ones devour a ton of fertilizers but bear no fruit at all. They're absolutely barren. My gardener says about the tall ones: "They're nice to look at, but don't go expecting any fruit from them." The same with Halifax: he is tall and good-looking, but barren as a fig-tree.'

The old man roared with laughter once more.

---

[14] John McGovern, Scottish MP, 1930–50, and chairman of the Independent Labour Party, 1941–43.

[15] A feeling shared by Halifax: 'I can't myself resist some feeling of thankfulness at not having got an Expedition bogged where it could not be maintained, and I don't believe anything in the long run would have made much difference. But I certainly shall not say this in public.' He was surely influenced by Eden's rather cynical (but pragmatic) long letter to him earlier in the month questioning whether it was 'a world-rocking tragedy' for the Allies if 'the Finns go under'.

[The diary entry of 18 March (not reproduced here) is Maisky's official record of his meeting with Butler. Ironically, Butler, who would now replace Vansittart as Maisky's 'ally' in the Foreign Office, had been the quintessential appeaser and an arch opponent of a triple alliance prior to the conclusion of the Molotov–Ribbentrop Pact. He advocated moderation in relation to Russia with the same dogged determination that had characterized his support for appeasement. 'There is a certain noble purity about British policy,' he minuted, 'which tends – provided right is on our side and the human brain dictates the logic of an action – to add one enemy after another to those opposed to us.' His views now paradoxically coincided with the Kremlin's new policy of seeking a peace agreement that would bring the war to an early conclusion and establish a new European order, in which the Soviet Union would share with a battered Britain and Germany hegemony over Europe.

Maisky impressed on Butler that he had little doubt that 'it was not in Herr Hitler's interest for the war to continue'. Butler emerged from the talk convinced that Maisky was eager to leave him with 'the idea that we should satisfy the Germans that we were not interested in the complete destruction of the German people'. Maisky had already told Bernard Pares, the outstanding historian of Russia, that his country was 'above all things, against an extension of the war ... Russia would prefer a negotiated peace to a vindictive one, which would follow the triumph of either side and would bring more wars.' Maisky reasserted that although the USSR did not 'wish to come under the heel of Germany or to be dragged into further complications with her', it 'might be possible to make a bargain with [Hitler] whereby the German colonies were restored and in return a certain freedom was given to the Poles and the Czechs'.]

19 March

... I lunched at Beaverbrook's today. I found him in a state of sheer fury: he is outraged by the '11 points' for peace that have been published in the newspapers. According to Beaverbrook, these points are that very basis upon which Hitler and Mussolini agreed in Brenner.[16]

'This is a conqueror's peace!' Beaverbrook huffed. 'We shall never agree to such conditions!'

Beaverbrook thinks that England could wash its hands of Poland and Czechoslovakia, and it could even sacrifice some of its colonies, but it will never recognize Hitler's right to establish the 'economic empire' in Europe about which he spoke with Sumner Welles[17] and which is outlined in the eleven points.

'You know, I was against war,' Beaverbrook went on. 'I wanted an early peace. But now I'm all for the war! I'm in favour of an intensification of the

---

[16] The humiliating peace offer was made by Hitler during his brief meeting with Mussolini in his train carriage at the Brenner Pass on 18 March.

[17] Benjamin Sumner Welles, American under secretary of state, 1937–43.

blockade and of the war in the air! I'm ready myself to be a gunman on a plane piloted by my son!'

Beaverbrook is against all sentimentality in war. International law is irrelevant. An eye for an eye, a tooth for a tooth!

I have never seen Beaverbrook in such belligerent mood. ...

23 March

The Finnish war is over and it seems that things have returned to normal. ... Yes, normality in this strange *Sitzkrieg* has undoubtedly returned.

And yet, I am increasingly gripped by a vague sense of the illusoriness and unreality of everything I see around me.

Parliament sits three times a week... The MPs ask questions, as usual... The ministers read out their answers, as usual... The Speaker nods away, as usual, as he sits there in his wig... The departments arrange their *conferences* and do their paperwork, as usual... The newspapers invent sensational stories and spread high-society *gossip*, as usual... Shops sell their goods... Bankers count money and deliver their annual reports... Courting couples hide in the parks... Throngs of children play rowdily in the playgrounds... The taxis line up at the cab-stands... Newsboys, shouting at the tops of their voices, sell the evening papers, as usual...

Everything is as it always is. Everyone lives for today, for the petty interests of the hour, the minute. No one thinks of the future, no one tries to look ahead. One's instinct is to avoid doing so, even if a capricious thought happens to bring one to the verge from which vistas open up into the future. All are especially keen to emphasize that everything is happening in the normal, customary, traditional manner. No novelties. No excesses.

But to me it all seems temporary, unreal, fantastic...

Perhaps I'm wrong, or, at least, not entirely right, but one and the same picture keeps appearing before my mind's eye.

A gigantic wave. It grows, swells, rises higher and higher. Its dark depths conceal powerful turbulence. Immeasurable forces are gathered and concentrated there. Any moment now and the forces will break through in a catastrophic, irrepressible torrent. Yet while the surface of the wave is still relatively smooth and calm, tiny boats full of passengers sail to and fro over this surface in their normal, habitual order, or rather disorder. The boats make intricate patterns as they come together and drift apart, as the passengers shout out to each other, laugh and argue. Gentlemen court ladies, and the ladies flirt and paint their faces. Coloured handkerchiefs flutter, carefree voices are carried on the breeze. Everything seems eternal, normal, immutable, ordinary... No one thinks of the storm that is ready to strike...

And then, a sudden crash and roar!...
The catastrophe arrives.

27 March

[A cutting from *The Times* of 27 March 1940, entitled 'Soviet Union Recalls its Ambassador', is attached to the diary. It surely alarmed Maisky. It alleges that Surits, the Soviet ambassador in Paris, had sent Stalin a telegram concerning the French position in the Finnish war which had been intercepted by the censor and was regarded by the French Government as interference in its domestic affairs. The French Government declared Surits *persona non grata*. In order to deprive the French of their pretext for severing relations, Molotov (who had always regarded Surits – and Maisky – as accomplices of Litvinov's) reprimanded him and relieved him of his duties as ambassador in France.]

An absolutely idiotic story! I don't know any details about the sending of the telegram (here we never send such things as telegrams *en clair*) but the French are obviously spoiling for a fight. I can't understand their policy. What are they counting on?

I spoke to Surits by telephone today. He is going to leave Paris in a few days. It's not yet been decided who will stay on there. ... It was said today in the press department of the Foreign Office that the recall of Surits is a purely French affair, that the British Government has absolutely nothing to do with it, and that Anglo-Soviet relations continue as they were. We shall see.

[A second entry for 27 March is a long report to Molotov on a barren meeting with Halifax. Maisky had been instructed by his government to propose the reopening of trade negotiations, in order to counter the pressure exerted by the French to bomb the Baku oilfields. Halifax, who recognized that any such operation 'would almost certainly lead to a definite alliance between Germany and the Soviet Union', instructed the Foreign Office to conduct the negotiations 'with a stiff upper lip', in a manner which would not 'prevent us at a later stage from taking action in the Caucasus, should the Turks agree to cooperate with us there'. Finally, it was only the German attack on France that put a seal on the operation, which might indeed have culminated in Britain finding itself at war with Germany and Russia.]

28 March

... Sylvester, Lloyd George's personal secretary, told me the following story.

In 1917 (Sylvester was already working for Lloyd George at that time) Lloyd George appointed Neville Chamberlain as director of the department responsible for conscription. The army needed men badly. Great hopes were pinned on the department. Chamberlain approached the task with the methods and horizons appropriate to a lord mayor of Birmingham, such as he had just been. Chamberlain chose as his *permanent undersecretary* a Birmingham *town clerk*, a certain Smith. Smith was a man of little calibre who had not the slightest idea of London life, the machinery of government, the methods of work essential in wartime, etc. But Chamberlain acted wholly in compliance with the *advice* of his *permanent undersecretary*. It quickly transpired that the department was unable to provide the army with the necessary number of conscripts. Lloyd George was greatly displeased and asked Bonar Law[18] and Austen Chamberlain to exert their influence on Neville Chamberlain. They tried several times, but to no avail. Neville would invariably answer that he should be guided in his job 'by the counsels of Mr Smith'. Lloyd George finally lost his patience and yelled at Neville: *'Get out! Get out you and your Mr Smith!'*

Chamberlain had to leave the department in disgrace. He has not forgotten it to this day. That is why Sylvester thinks it improbable that Lloyd George might enter a Cabinet headed by Chamberlain. Nothing less than absolutely extraordinary circumstances would force Chamberlain to allow this. ...

Randolph Churchill is one of those who have recently reappeared on my horizon. His visits used to be a frequent occurrence, and his telephone calls even more so. After the war began, when he became an officer in a tank battalion stationed in the countryside, Randolph would drop by every time he visited London. But after the beginning of the Finnish war he disappeared and I had no news of him for three and a half months. Last week, once peace had been concluded with the Finns, Randolph called on me out of the blue. Just the other day he visited me again, and brought his young wife to me (he married at the very start of the war). This is significant. Even more telling is the change in Randolph's mood: when hostilities began he boasted of an easy victory, but now he displays great anxiety about the course and outcome of the war.

2 April

The effect of C[omrade] Molotov's speech at the Supreme Soviet on 29 March will, without doubt, be a positive one.[19] His statement will certainly make life

---

[18] Andrew Bonar Law, Conservative prime minister, 1922–23.

[19] Molotov restated the USSR's firm determination to pursue a policy of neutrality and to ensure the restoration and maintenance of world peace. The speech may have been prompted by Maisky, following the advice he had received from Sir Charles Trevelyan, the Labour Member of Parliament who had advocated a popular front in the 1930s, that it was 'a matter of quite first-class importance that, as soon as the settlement with Finland has been reached, a full statement should be made to the world by the Soviet Government ... The more frank and far-reaching that statement the greater would be its value for preventing any later extension of the war into an attack on Russia.'

harder for those elements abroad opposed to us, especially in England and France. Beaverbrook is simply delighted. He called me and shouted down the telephone: 'Molotov is for isolation! Wonderful! This conforms with British interests.'

The meaning of Beaverbrook's words is clear. Over the last couple of months the general consensus in England has been that the USSR is an 'ally of Germany'. Even Butler has expressed such fears. In the past few weeks, the press has kicked up a lot of fuss about a 'tripartite totalitarian bloc' (Germany, Italy and the USSR) on the Balkan question. The 'Allied' countries have interpreted C[omrade] Molotov's speech in the following way: no 'alliance' exists between Moscow and Berlin; the USSR maintains its independent policy, and this independent policy is neutrality. What could be better?... The nightmare oppressing the souls of London and Paris is no more.

There are, however, sceptics. Some say: 'Neutrality... hmm... What sort of neutrality? There are many sorts of neutrality.'

These people think it better to wait and see than to start clashing cymbals. ...

5 April

The Shaws came to lunch with us today. We hadn't seen the old couple for several months. They are still vigorous, especially he, but their health is beginning to fail them. No wonder: he is 83 and she is even older. But Shaw's verve, memory and interest in events are still amazing. There were just the four of us at the table (which, we discovered at the end, pleased the old couple). These were the best circumstances for a talk and Shaw plunged into reminiscences of the distant past. He accompanied his vivid account with much gesticulation.

'In the eighties, after we had just set up the Fabian Society, a May Day meeting was arranged in Hyde Park. I was the chairman and the speaker. When the meeting was over I set off across the park through the crowd. Suddenly, I was stopped by a bearded man of medium height in a brown suit. Congratulating me on the successful meeting, he asked: "Do you know me?" I had the feeling that I had met him before, but could not recall where and when. I responded with the customary banality that his face was very familiar to me but that I couldn't remember the circumstances of our meeting. The bearded man laughed and said in a genial voice: "No, you don't know me. I'm Friedrich Engels." So that's what Engels looks like, I thought. I had heard a lot about him, but we had never met. The next May Day I spoke in Hyde Park again. And again Engels came up to me and asked jokingly: "Well, do you recognize me now?" "But of course I recognize you! You are the great Engels!" I cheerfully exclaimed and shook his hand firmly.'

... From Engels the conversation turned to Marx. Shaw had never met Marx. He died before Shaw joined the socialist movement. But he knew Marx's daughter Eleanor, called Tussy in the family.

'She was a striking blonde,' Shaw recounted, 'lively and extremely intelligent. She knew several languages to perfection. Often used to interpret at international conferences and congresses. But she was a very "partial" interpreter: she translated the speeches of "her people" with a brilliance lacking in the original versions (she was a superb speaker herself), but made her "adversaries" seem like fools, which they were not. I noticed this and began insisting on paid and "non-party" translators for our congresses.'

Shaw's face clouded over briefly and he continued in a more subdued tone: 'Eleanor became involved with Aveling.[20] Have you heard the name?'

I nodded.

'I don't know what they had in common. Aveling was a strange man. I have no doubt that he was a convinced socialist and atheist who would go to the scaffold for his convictions, but he was a man of rather low morals in ordinary life.' (A *scoundrel*, Shaw added). 'A university professor, he coached university entrants, preferring girls (women had just been admitted to study at universities). Aveling usually took payment for twelve lessons in advance, borrowed more money from his students, and gave them one lesson only. When the students lost patience there were scandals, but Aveling never returned their money. Once he came to me and asked me for five pounds. As I knew Aveling well, I refused to lend him so much as a penny. He tried every means of persuading me and finally declared: "You may be quite sure you'll get my debt back. If you present my receipt to Eleanor two months from now and tell her that I'll end up in prison if she doesn't pay, she'll immediately give you the money." I was quite disgusted and threw Aveling out of the house.'

Shaw paused and then continued: 'Poor Eleanor! She committed suicide. It happened like this. Eleanor and Aveling lived together without ever being wed in church. Aveling had a lawful wife, with whom he didn't live, and this made a formal marriage with Eleanor impossible. When Aveling's wife died, her family, who hated Eleanor, did all they could to hurt her even after the wife's death. In the obituary which they published in the newspapers it was mentioned that the deceased was Aveling's lawful wife, in order to emphasize Eleanor's unlawful status. Be that as it may, Aveling was now a free man. Eleanor, being a woman of progressive views and noble character, did not insist for a moment on legalizing their long relationship. She was quite happy for them to continue as they were. And do you know what Aveling did? Now that he was free, he deserted

---

[20] Edward Aveling, a prominent 'Darwinist' he was a founder of the Socialist League and the Independent Labour Party.

Eleanor and married another woman. Eleanor, who had already suffered greatly from Aveling's behaviour in the past, could not endure this final blow and took her own life. When I wrote my play *Doctor's Dilemma*, I used much of what I knew about Aveling's character and escapades.'

Shaw paused again before adding: 'There was also that wonderful woman, Helene...[21] You know about her, I'm sure. She worked as a sort of maid in Marx's house. It always made me laugh that Marx, who devoted his entire life to the proletariat, actually knew only one proletarian, Helene, whom he didn't even pay!... Yes, Marx's finances were nearly always in an awful state. It was a real tragedy. Marx's wife was at times driven mad with despair. But even though Helene did not receive a salary, she was eventually rewarded: her name is inscribed on Marx's tomb.'

... Shaw then turned to reminiscences of the more recent past.

Shaw visited the USSR with the Astors and Lothian in 1931, and they were received by C[omrade] Stalin. Louis Fischer was their interpreter. M.M. [Litvinov] was also present.

Nancy Astor was, of course, the first to attack C[omrade] Stalin. Lady Astor tried to prove to him that children were brought up in the wrong way in the USSR. She gave an example. She had just visited a kolkhoz school. She didn't like it: the children were dressed too finely and they were too clean. That's unnatural. Children should be dirty – that's how they're meant to be – except at table. And they should be dressed very simply: just a piece of cloth that can be washed and dried in half an hour. Highly agitated, Nancy said to C[omrade] Stalin: 'Send a sensible woman to me in England and I'll teach her how to treat children.'

C[omrade] Stalin smiled and asked her to give him her address. Nancy gave it. Shaw thought this was mere courtesy on C[omrade] Stalin's part, so he was greatly astonished when he later discovered, once he was already back home, that not one but twelve women had visited Lady Astor from the USSR.

Lothian, in his turn, started explaining to C[omrade] Stalin that the British Liberal Party had split in two. The part led by Simon had sided with the Conservatives, while the other part was at the crossroads. In Lothian's view, that second faction, led by Lloyd George, might, after the necessary schooling, become the British party of scientific socialism.

... Lord Astor[22] was next. He delivered a reconciliatory speech, stating that in general British public opinion was not hostile towards the Soviet Union. Lord Astor was in a very radical mood in Moscow. He felt almost as if he were

---

[21] Helene 'Lenchen' Demuth.
[22] Lord Waldorf Astor, politician and newspaper proprietor who, with his wife, Nancy Astor, shared a deep reverence for the Empire and for social reform; chairman of the Royal Institute of International Affairs, 1935–49.

a 'Bolshevik', and wore shirts with short sleeves. He wanted to say something that would please C[omrade] Stalin.

C[omrade] Stalin turned to Shaw and asked him what he thought of Astor's statement. Shaw laughed and said: 'In my country, Ireland – I'm Irish, not English, you know – they still sing a song which Cromwell is alleged to have sung: "*Put your trust in God, But keep your powder dry.*" So I'd say: I don't know whether you trust in God – I think not – but I advise you from the bottom of my heart: *Keep your powder dry!*'...

6 April

Another Cabinet reshuffle! Same old, same old. It's been done on the principle of Krylov's 'Quartet'. I can't help quoting that writer of fables:

> My friends, you can change places all you want,
>   But you'll never make musicians.

Yet, there is one noteworthy thing about the reshuffle, which is significant not so much for the present as for the future: a trend that might have great consequences. I mean the new role of Churchill. He has been appointed president of a committee consisting of the war, naval and air ministers and the chiefs of staff. Churchill is thus theoretically responsible now for the conduct of war. But... Hoare has been made secretary of state for air in the latest *reshuffle*. That is, Chamberlain is putting his own man in the committee to sabotage Churchill's activity. Yet the trend remains, and it will probably manifest itself fully earlier than we expect. In times of war all processes develop at a feverish pace. We shall see. ...[23]

[Maisky's standing had hit rock bottom not only in England but – far more alarmingly – also in Moscow. The dismissal of Surits encouraged Molotov to clip Maisky's wings. A series of harsh letters from Fedor Gusev[24] severely criticized Maisky's diplomatic work. He was instructed to restrict his encounters to top officials, and to obtain all necessary information from the media. Fulfilment of those instructions would have robbed Maisky of his trump card – his prolific circle of interlocutors. Finding himself

---

[23] Maisky was actively engaged in restoring Churchill's standing in Moscow after his Finnish 'relapse'.

[24] The archetype of Stalin's and Molotov's new diplomat, Fedor Tarasovich Gusev graduated from the Institute of Soviet Construction and Law and worked in the Economic Planning Commission of the Leningrad region. With the repressions in Narkomindel in full swing, he underwent a crash course in diplomacy. His party loyalty landed him a brilliant career in Narkomindel, where, by 1938, at the age of 35, he had become the director of its West European Department. He was appointed the Soviet ambassador in Canada in 1942 before replacing Maisky in London in 1943. Sir Archibald Clark Kerr, the British ambassador in Moscow, characterized him as 'a rude, inexperienced and bad-mannered fellow'.

up against the wall, Maisky resorted not to his customary survival strategy of intricate manoeuvring and flattery, but rather to confrontation. What follows are some very intriguing excerpts from a nine-page visionary 'lecture' to Gusev on diplomacy in general, and on its peculiarities in England. Though an apologia, it was just as much a lament on the vanishing vision of modern diplomacy, of which he was now virtually the sole survivor:

> ... The most important and substantive element in the work of every ambassador is the *actual contact* he has with people. It is not sufficient to read the newspapers – that can be done in Moscow. It is not enough to work with books and statistical reports – that, too, can be done in Moscow. ... An ambassador without excellent personal contacts is not worthy of the name.
>
> Every country has its peculiarities. The nature and number of the contacts differ in accordance with the varying political, economic and individual conditions of each state. There cannot be a single template in such matters. What is acceptable in Paris may be completely unsuited to Tokyo, and vice versa. ... In the case of England, the creation of these vital personal contacts is extremely difficult and requires a great deal of the ambassador's time. ... In order to be *au courant* with what is happening in different areas of English life, it is not enough to know one or two people in each group. ... It is quite simply not enough to have contacts with, for example, the secretary for foreign affairs and his deputy, but also one needs to know the head of the Northern Department of the FO, for the USSR falls within his sphere of competence. ... It is necessary to maintain contact with around 15–20 people in the FO alone, and of course our work requires us to have business with other ministries: the Ministry of Trade, of Finance, of the Economy, of Defence and so on.
>
> Or else, to take another example, consider Parliament and the political parties. This is an extremely important element of English political life. It is most useful to attend the more important sittings of Parliament (which works for about eight months of the year): you get an exceedingly accurate impression of the current mood of the country. But this is not enough. If you wish to be well informed of the different areas of interior and exterior policy, then you need to be in personal contact with a significant number of Members of Parliament. Of course, it is inconceivable, as well as unnecessary, to maintain relations with all 615 MPs. But let us say that you do need to know around a hundred MPs from all the different parties.
>
> Here is yet another example: the press. This is an extremely complex and active group, with an immense number of people belonging to it. The people are capricious and don't stand on ceremony. They come to you with all manner of questions, surveys and clarifications – personally, or else by telephone, at any hour of the day or night. ... In order to maintain normal contacts with the press, one needs to know about 50 people. ... I have made the calculations and come to the conclusion that, if the ambassador wants to fulfil his duties as they should be fulfilled, then he needs

to maintain contact with *at least 500 people* (if we include the representatives of all the groups mentioned above).

Now, as for the nature of these contacts. What does it mean to maintain a contact? Certainly it is not enough to have a nodding acquaintance with a man, and to meet him once or twice a year at some official function or in the corridors of Parliament. You will get precisely nothing from such contacts. The sort of contact which can be useful from our point of view must be a much *closer* contact. This means that you must meet the person more or less regularly, invite him to breakfast or dinner, visit him at home, take him to the theatre from time to time, go when necessary to the wedding of his son or his daughter, wish him many happy returns on his birthday, sympathize with him when he is ill. It is only when your acquaintance has come a little closer to you (and Englishmen need to scrutinize someone for quite some time before they count him among their 'friends') that his tongue starts to loosen, and only then may you start to glean things from him, or else start to put the necessary ideas into his head.

... How should an embassy work to maintain contacts? ... Every comrade will be expected to maintain and widen his knowledge of the sector, to meet the relevant people, to have breakfast or dinner with them (in England, all meetings usually take place at table – over breakfast, at tea, at dinner, etc.), to give them the information it is decided to give them, to nudge them in a direction favourable to us. But this work does not have any clear boundaries.

... I repeat that all our contacts have been in the hands of two people – myself and Comrade Korzh. We have had to run like hamsters in a wheel. It has been an advantage that, thanks to my old acquaintances built up in the years of Anglo-Soviet 'friendship', I have been able to behave 'simply' with many people (Lloyd George, Leighton, Beaverbrook, Churchill, Eden, Butler, Vansittart and others): it has not been necessary to throw them a breakfast or a luncheon every time I have needed them, and sometimes I could just call them on the phone, or meet them in the corridors of Parliament and so on. However, even with these advantages it has sometimes been physically impossible to maintain an active relationship with various individuals with whom we should have kept in contact, and we have had and still have many gaps.

The programme you have set out, if we are to take it seriously (and of course, this is how we should take it), is extremely complex. It will require qualified workers with a great deal of time to devote to this project alone. And whom do we have in the embassy at the moment? Comrade Korzh, whom you wish to control the information gathering, has, as well as a complete lack of time for such work, no experience of literary or scientific research. In the past he was a sailor, then he commanded a charter ship, and for the last two years he has been carrying out current diplomatic duties as a first secretary. The intern Comrade Krainsky[25] has a technical

---

[25] Anatoly (Ariel) Markovich Krainsky, secretary at the Soviet embassy in Great Britain, 1939–44.

education, was a security officer in Washington for two and a half years and has only just now started embassy work. I have deputed him to watch the English economy. He is a keen worker, but it is a new area for him and he is unaccustomed to it, and it is difficult at the moment for him to orientate himself. The other intern, Comrade Mikhailov, still does not know English and has an incomplete degree from an agricultural academy. Before joining the NKID, he worked at a tractor station, and has never done any sort of either diplomatic or research work. ...

I will conclude with a couple of words. ... In the state of spy mania in which England exists at the moment, we have to be extremely careful with any observations, so as not to give our enemies an excuse for anti-Soviet provocation. On this note, I will bring this letter to an end, and I hope that the department and the embassy will now work more cohesively together.

The German Blitzkrieg in the West, however, would play into Maisky's hands, again rendering him indispensable and ensuring his continued stay in London on his own terms.]

9 April

What a sharp and unexpected turn of events!

Only yesterday the British were planning for a lengthy *Sitz-Krieg*; today, the Germans have made *Blitz-Krieg* the order of the day.

German troops invaded Denmark and Norway this morning. Denmark, it seems, is putting up no resistance and, if German communications are to be believed, the whole country will be occupied within the next 48 hours. Copenhagen is already in German hands. ...

In Parliament the prevailing mood today was one of confusion, anger and chauvinism. All had one and the same question on their minds: where the devil was our navy? How could our navy let the Germans reach not only Oslo, but also Norway's Atlantic ports? However, as soon as Mander set about posing this question to the prime minister, an animal-like roar erupted on all sides of the House against the excessively daring MP. Chamberlain's speech was weak and colourless. He had once again been taken by 'surprise'. ... Only one thing was clear from the PM's words: the Allies had taken the firm decision to provide Norway with military assistance. ...

11 April

Today Churchill made a speech giving more detailed explanations about the events in Norway. I had never seen him in such a state. He clearly hadn't slept for several nights. He was pale, couldn't find the right words, stumbled and kept getting mixed up. There was not a trace of his usual parliamentary brilliance.

In its essence, his speech was unsatisfactory. Its running thread was a tone of apology. Churchill produced rather lame arguments to explain the German breakthrough: bad weather, the vastness of the sea, the impossibility of controlling it all, and so on. ... But Chamberlain, sitting on the front bench next to Churchill, was clearly pleased. No wonder: Churchill's failure is Chamberlain's success.

13 April

Great excitement in political circles. A German attack on Holland is expected imminently. The British, French and Belgian military staffs are holding urgent conferences. Contact with Holland is being maintained. One often hears the following opinion. The Germans want to strike in the west in order to divert the Allies' attention from Norway – so be it. That's even better. It is easier for the Allies to wage war in the west than in Scandinavia. Here, they are better prepared. ...

15 April

Diplomatic relations between the Labour Party and the embassy have been restored. ... Attlee and Greenwood finally paid me a visit today.

We mentioned neither the 'quarrel' nor Finland. Our conversation focused on Anglo-Soviet relations in general and trade negotiations in particular. I informed the Labour leaders about the present state of affairs. They expressed their ardent desire to improve our relations and promised their assistance. Greenwood did most of the talking, constantly addressing Attlee with the words: 'Isn't that so, Clem?'

To which Attlee kept answering: 'Oh yes, absolutely.'

On the whole, I got the impression that Attlee's attitude was more favourable than Greenwood's. Greenwood drank a lot, as is his wont, while Attlee merely sipped his cherry brandy.

And so, diplomatic relations are restored!

Facts are stubborn things, and the power of the USSR is undeniably one of them.

2 May

During the last two or three days the press has patently been preparing public opinion for the evacuation of Norway. And today Chamberlain declared this plainly in Parliament. The PM's speech had an oppressive effect. The MPs were gloomy, and the question of an inevitable government reshuffle was openly

47. 'Diplomatic relations are restored' between Attlee and Maisky.

discussed in the corridors. Chamberlain is clearly bankrupt. But there were no debates today. They have been postponed until 7 May, when important developments can be expected.

On 29 April I handed Halifax our reply to the British memorandum of 19 April. Halifax told me that he had to delay his response until he had studied it with the experts. It was already past 6 p.m. when I met Halifax.

On 30 April, at noon, a representative of the Foreign Office press department declared at a press conference that our reply had been deemed 'unsatisfactory' in 'authoritative circles'. This was repeated over the radio a little later. So, in less than 24 hours the 'authoritative circles' had succeeded in 'studying' the Soviet reply and pronouncing their verdict! ...

7 May

Beaverbrook came for lunch. He is in a resolute and belligerent frame of mind. The Allies will fight to the end! Let it take three, five or seven years – so be it. Both sides will be ruined by the end. Civilization will collapse. So be it. England will not yield! England cannot yield!

Yes, Norway is a failure. But failures occur in every war. He who laughs last, laughs best.

... I asked Beaverbrook about the state of the Government. Should one expect any changes in this sphere in view of the parliamentary debates that will begin today?

With a dismissive wave of his arms, he asserted with confidence that the Government would of course be criticized during the debates, but no serious consequences would follow. Chamberlain's position is secure. ...

Brendan Bracken spoke to me about this yesterday in equally confident terms. And he, after all, is Churchill's *alter ego*, with an excellent knowledge of all the goings-on in the kitchen of politics.

It's strange. Beaverbrook and Bracken are to all appearances exceptionally well-informed individuals. And yet, I have the feeling that England has approached a crucial boundary; that these debates ought to yield something; that change is in the air...

We'll see.

8 May

My intuition didn't fail me! Following two days of debates, the Chamberlain Government has fallen... The Government has not yet formally resigned, but this is merely a matter of time, and will happen sooner rather than later. The fatal blow has been struck.

How did it happen?

It happened like this. The MPs spent the weekend in their constituencies, put their ears to the ground, and were back by Tuesday, 7 May, as quite different people from those who had left on the 3rd. For the 'ground' – the country and voting public – is deeply unhappy with the way the war is being conducted, and agitated and alarmed about the future of England. These feelings found vivid expression in the debates of the past two days, and led to Chamberlain's downfall.

The chamber presented a very curious spectacle yesterday and today.

Chamberlain, Hoare, Stanley and, last of all, Churchill spoke on behalf of the Government. The first three were very weak. Chamberlain's speech was simply rot.[26] Hoare, jerking his leg, related in a thin, sharp voice various trivial details about the raids, landing and take-off of British aircraft in Norway. Hoare is the air minister, and all these details would be of interest to specialists, who might even find them inspiring. But to devote his whole speech to such things at such a moment (when the fate of the Government hangs in the balance and the entire conduct of the war is the object of the sharpest criticism) – does this not show him up as a political pygmy? Stanley (the war minister) was a bit better, but only relatively so. Taken together, their speeches, far from raising the reputation of the Government, did it significant harm. Churchill's speech made some amends. It was interesting and brilliant, but unconvincing. ...

The attack on the Government was, on the contrary, exceptionally sharp, brilliant, and at times simply devastating. Lloyd George was his inimitable self. When Churchill made an attempt to shield the Government, Lloyd George remarked, to the raucous laughter of the chamber, that Churchill 'must not allow himself to be converted into an air-raid shelter to keep the splinters from hitting his colleagues'.

Turning to Chamberlain, the old man concluded his speech with the words: 'there is nothing which can contribute more to victory in this war than that he should sacrifice the seals of office!' Morrison's attack on the Government, and on Chamberlain personally, was astonishingly fierce and ended with a call for the resignation of the prime minister, Simon and Hoare. Duff Cooper spoke brilliantly and was the first among the Government's supporters to declare that he would vote against it. His speech made a great impression. Amery[27] also demanded the resignation of the Government. Admiral Keyes,[28] who arrived in Parliament in full-dress uniform with all his decorations, spoke to exceptional effect on behalf of the navy. Keyes is a poor speaker and practically read out his lines. He stumbled, got confused and agitated, and for precisely those reasons produced a very moving speech. ... Keyes' words had the effect of shells fired from 16-inch guns. Almost all MPs present who were connected with military affairs – representatives of the naval, air and land branches – spoke against the Government and its conduct of the war. It was very significant.

Yesterday, on the first day of the debates, it was still unclear whether Labour was going to request a vote of no confidence. ... Not only Labourites and Liberals, but also many, many Tories had reached breaking point. The iron was hot, and Labour declared that it would demand a vote.

---

[26] Even the sympathetic Geoffrey Dawson described it as 'a lame performance'
[27] Leopold Amery, Conservative MP, secretary of state for India and for Burma, 1940–45.
[28] Admiral Roger Keyes, director of combined operations, 1940–41.

Churchill's concluding speech and his fiery exchange with Labour had raised the temperature in the chamber considerably. The no-confidence vote demanded by Labour added more fuel to the fire. When the voting began and the MPs started walking out through two doors, the Chamber buzzed like a disturbed bee-hive. The tension reached its peak when the tellers came in, approached the Speaker's chair, and announced in the dead silence of the House: 'The vote of no confidence is rejected by a majority of 281 to 200.'

Triumphant roars erupted like a storm from the opposition benches. Chamberlain sat in his place, white as chalk. For although the vote of no confidence had been rejected, the Government's majority had never fallen so low.[29]

... I met Lloyd George in the Parliament restaurant before the vote. The old man was very excited and in high spirits. 'Well, Chamberlain is done for,' he exclaimed. 'He might hold on for a few weeks... You know, a duck with a broken leg still flutters its wings, but its fate has been decided. The same with Neville.'

He changed the subject abruptly and asked me: 'Where will Hitler go next? What do you think?'

'No one can vouch for Hitler,' I replied, 'but I think the Balkans are the least probable direction for him now.'

'I say the same,' Lloyd George responded with feeling. 'Hitler will now attack Holland!'

'Very possibly,' I agreed.

13 May

And so, England is ruled by a new government – the Churchill Government!

The duck with a broken leg passed away sooner than Lloyd George predicted. Hitler is to blame for that. But, rather than run ahead of myself, I'll relate the facts as they happened.

The day after the fatal vote, at nine in the morning, Chamberlain summoned Amery and told him that he thought a serious government reshuffle was in order. Measures should be taken, however, to prevent Labour from coming to power. The Government must remain in Tory hands. The prime minister went on to offer Amery any portfolio he wanted (except the PM's), including those of chancellor of the Exchequer or foreign secretary. He also promised to do the Conservative 'opposition' a good turn by offering ministerial posts to its more prominent members. Amery, however, categorically refused the offer. He said that it wasn't a question of his portfolio. It was a question of the composition of

---

[29] Kennedy, who sat next to Maisky in the gallery, noted in his diary: 'The Prime Minister looked stunned and while he appeared to carry it off, he looked to me like a definitely beaten man.'

the Government and above all its leadership. Amery thought it impossible for Chamberlain to remain prime minister.

Having failed to 'buy' Amery, Chamberlain invited Attlee and Greenwood to see him after lunch and inquired about the possibility of including Labourites in a government headed by himself. ...

Wilson and Margesson[30] set their machinery in motion and were preparing to launch a large-scale campaign to 'rescue Chamberlain' by sacrificing some of the most unpopular ministers. But then Hitler unexpectedly intervened and turned everything upside down.

In the night between the 9th and the 10th the Germans attacked Holland and Belgium. This fact had a tremendous effect in England. The temperature immediately shot up. The whole country became tense. Events developed at breakneck speed. Wilson's and Margesson's plans, which required a certain amount of time to be put into practice, fell by the wayside.

It was clear to all that the reconstruction of the Government should be carried out immediately and in a far more radical way than conceived before.

On the morning of 10 May, the Labour executive committee, excluding Morrison, left for Bournemouth, where Labour delegates had gathered for their annual conference. As head of the London County Council and antiaircraft defence, Morrison stayed in London, in the event of a German air raid on the capital. The executive committee reached Bournemouth in time for lunch, after which they immediately opened the conference in order to work out their answers to Chamberlain's questions. The executive committee's mood was fairly well unanimous. They refused categorically to serve under Chamberlain, but agreed to be a part of a government under another prime minister, on condition that Labour be 'sufficiently represented' in the key positions. ... Attlee and Greenwood were just getting into the car when there was a telephone call and Chamberlain's secretary enquired about Labour's decision. Attlee answered the call and informed him. Then the Labour leaders set off for London. It took them about two and a half hours to get to London, and when they arrived at seven o'clock the Chamberlain Government was no longer in existence. In the time they spent travelling, Chamberlain managed to submit his resignation to the king, and the king managed to appoint Churchill as the new prime minister.[31] ...

---

[30] David Reginald Margesson, chief whip of the Conservative Party, 1931–40; secretary of state for war, 1940–42.

[31] According to Halifax, the king told him that he 'had hoped if Neville C. went he would have had to deal with me'. Halifax, however, feared that Churchill, as minister of defence, would be the effective leader, while he, having no access to the House of Commons, would 'become a more or less honorary Prime Minister, living in a kind of twilight just outside the things that really mattered'. Churchill 'with suitable expressions of regard and humility', told Halifax 'he could not but feel the force of what I had said, and the P.M. reluctantly, and Winston evidently with much less reluctance finished by accepting my view'.

Directly upon their arrival in London, Attlee and Greenwood were invited to meet Churchill at the Admiralty. There they conferred with the new prime minister for about two hours. They had no difficulty in agreeing on a common policy. The allocation of portfolios was a trickier matter, but agreement was soon reached on that as well. ...

The hardest thing was to agree with Churchill about Chamberlain. As Attlee and Greenwood travelled from Bournemouth to London, Chamberlain not only resigned but also received a proposal from Churchill to join the new Government as a member of the War Cabinet. In doing so, Churchill was guided mainly by consideration of the large group of Chamberlain's supporters among Tory MPs: Chamberlain would be less harmful inside the Cabinet as a 'hostage' than outside as the instigator of all manner of intrigues. ...

After lunch on the same day, a short closed session of Parliament was convened, at which Churchill presented his new Government. When Chamberlain entered the hall, most of the Conservatives greeted him with such a storm of fervent applause that it could only be viewed as a demonstration of hostility towards Churchill. This was rendered even more emphatic by the fact that Churchill's entry into the House was met with relatively feeble applause: the opposition is not in the habit of cheering Conservative leaders, and most Tories remained silent. But Churchill didn't seem to mind. Presenting the Cabinet, he uttered only a few, forceful words. He said he could offer his new colleagues nothing but 'blood, toil, tears and sweat'. But he is sure of eventual victory.[32]

This is how a new chapter has opened in the history of this war and in the political history of England.

15 May

Visited Lloyd George in his office in Thames House.

He is greatly alarmed. He thinks Belgium is lost. However, what happened yesterday at Sedan is much more serious. There were signs of a breakthrough there. If that happens, the situation will become really ominous. Sedan is located at the juncture of the Maginot Line and the lighter fortifications running along the Belgian border towards the sea. After breaking through the French line, the Germans would be able to reach the rear both of the Maginot

---

[32] Maisky has more empathy towards Churchill in his memoirs. While recognizing that in Churchill's nature 'there was always something of the actor', he describes how on this occasion 'he was genuinely moved. Even his voice broke from time to time.' As for the drama, visiting Churchill at his 'dugout', Halifax, too, commented that 'he was exactly like a thing on the stage in what I understand nurses are accustomed to call "a romper suit" of Air Force colour Jaeger-like stuff ... I asked him if he was going on the stage but he said he always wore this in the morning. It is really almost like Goering.'

Line and of the Anglo-French army deployed along the Belgian border. It's terribly dangerous. It could decide the outcome of the war in France. That is why Lloyd George's attention is now fixed on Sedan.

... I asked directly: 'So you think France and England will lose the war?'

Lloyd George waved his hand and said: 'You put the question too brutally. I don't want... I can't answer it.'

He hesitated for an instant, then added: 'The Allies cannot win the war. The most we can think about now is how to hold the Germans back till autumn and then see.'

Can even that be achieved?...

Lloyd George made a vague gesture. I was left with the definite impression that the old man fears that the Allies may be defeated, and especially France. He was silent for a while and then exclaimed bitterly: 'How terribly unfortunate that we failed to conclude a pact with you last year!'

Lloyd George asked me if I had met with Churchill since his appointment as prime minister. I said I hadn't. Lloyd George insisted: 'And Winston didn't invite you to see him?'

'No.'

Lloyd George raised his hands in despair: 'Incredible! If I were in Churchill's place, the first thing I would do would be to summon you and have a serious *heart-to-heart talk*.'

Then Lloyd George began to criticize Churchill. Churchill invited him to join the War Cabinet, but Lloyd George declined. He considers the present Cabinet utterly useless and does not wish to bear responsibility for its work. Why have Chamberlain and Halifax been admitted to the War Cabinet? They can do nothing but harm. What kind of a War Cabinet is it? Churchill, Chamberlain, Halifax, Attlee and Greenwood. Leaving Churchill aside, what are the rest good for? Chamberlain and Halifax are simply poisonous, and Attlee and Greenwood are nonentities. What can these men bring to the Cabinet? How can they help Churchill? ...[33]

---

[33] Churchill's Machiavellian move was aimed at harnessing Lloyd George's energies by putting him in charge of a Food Council. He assured Halifax, though, that he 'meant to put [Lloyd George] through an inquisition first' to ascertain 'that any Peace terms now, or hereafter, offered must not be destructive of our independence'. Lloyd George made his acceptance conditional on the removal of Chamberlain from the Cabinet, which was rejected by Churchill. In December, Churchill tried in vain to divert Lloyd George to the embassy in Washington. In fact, as the latter confided in his secretary, he 'preferred ... to await his country's summons a little longer ... until Winston is bust'.

20 May

The Anglo-French bourgeois elite is getting what it deserves.

If one reflects on what has happened in the European arena over the last 20 years, it becomes entirely clear that the main cause of the Allies' current plight is the <u>bourgeois elite's mortal hatred of 'communism'</u>.

This hatred has prevented this elite from establishing any sort of stable, friendly relations with the USSR over these 20 years. There have been ups and downs but, on the whole, our relations have been unsatisfactory throughout. After all, there are only a few major pieces on the international chessboard, and if a player discards even one of these, for whatever considerations, he considerably weakens his position.

Owing to that very hatred, the ruling elite of England and France systematically supported the Japanese warmongers, Mussolini and Hitler. What's more, it's that same elite which nurtured Hitler – in the hope that one day he would march east and wring the Bolsheviks' necks. But the 'Bolsheviks' proved too strong and too skilful. Hitler headed not east but west. The ruling elite of England and France fell into the same trap they had set for us. ...

We are witnessing the fall of the great capitalist civilization, a fall similar in importance to that of the Roman Empire. Or, perhaps, even more important...

22 May

Cripps[34] spent the whole evening with me. He told me over dinner that he was making meticulous preparations for his visit to Moscow. He has been to all the ministries concerned: the Foreign Office, the Board of Trade, the Ministry of Economic Warfare, the Ministry of Supply and others, collected much material, and received instructions. He told me, among other things, that all notes and memorandums relating to trade negotiations which had been handed to me in the last two months should be considered null and void. The British Government wishes to make a fresh start. ...

So far there has been no response from Moscow concerning the arrival of Cripps as a *special envoy*. Cripps expressed some anxiety on this score. I tried to reassure him, while cautiously intimating that the reply might indeed not be entirely favourable. I explained that on a personal level the Soviet Government was well-disposed towards Cripps, as he could see for himself in February (when he flew to Moscow from Chungking), but when it comes

---

[34] Richard Stafford Cripps, radical left-wing British intellectual; Labour MP, 1931–50; British ambassador to Russia, 1940–42, member of the War Cabinet, February–November, 1942; minister of aircraft production, 1942–45.

to trade talks the Soviet Government would rather deal with a negotiator who represents the British Government. Does Cripps represent the British Government?...

There can be only one answer to this question. And Cripps understands this all too well.

25 May

I went to see Dalton. His ministry is like a fortress: barricades of sandbags at the entrance and men with rifles inside. Dalton welcomed me most cordially. He shook my hand, seated me in the best armchair, and beamed with pleasure. Dalton is terribly happy to be a minister and to be able to receive me in this capacity.

... [Dalton] assured me that the new Government has drawn a line under the Anglo-Soviet relations of the past and wants to establish genuinely friendly relations with the Soviet Union. ... Dalton hopes that Cripps, whom the British Government is sending to Moscow, will be able to conclude a trade agreement or at least pave the way for one.

26 May

I heard the following colourful story from a reliable source.

Churchill was appointed prime minister on 10 May. On the morning of 11 May, Sir Horace Wilson (now referred to by all and sundry as Sir Horace Quisling), clean-shaven and impeccably dressed as usual, came to 10, Downing Street and, as if nothing had happened, proceeded to his room next to the PM's office (under Chamberlain, Wilson had offices both in the Treasury, where he is permanent undersecretary and *Head of the Civil Service*, and in 10, Downing Street). However, when he opened the door, he found 'German paratroopers' inside, who had descended and occupied his room at night: red-headed Brendan Bracken was sitting at his desk and Randolph Churchill had made himself comfortable on the couch. The two 'paratroopers' looked meaningfully at Wilson, and Wilson looked meaningfully at the 'paratroopers'. Not a single word was uttered. Sir Horace *withdrew*.

Then Wilson was invited to see the new prime minister. Churchill asked him to sit down and said: 'Sir Horace, I've heard you have plenty of work in the Treasury.'

Churchill paused and added even more emphatically: 'Yes, Sir Horace, plenty of work!'

Wilson kept a respectful silence, studying his fingertips.

Churchill sighed and continued with a threatening note in his voice: 'If I learn that you, Sir Horace, are engaged in anything other than Treasury business... a different job will be found for you, say... as governor of Iceland!'

The audience was over. And Wilson's career as the British prime minister's 'chief adviser' on all matters, particularly matters of foreign policy, was over, too. ...

20 May

Leopold of Belgium has negotiated a ceasefire with the Germans behind the Allies' backs, and even let the German troops pass through Belgian lines towards the British and the French. The Allies' left flank was thus exposed and they had to regroup speedily and start a full retreat towards Dunkirk. Hopes of closing the German breach, if anyone still entertained them, had to be abandoned. The Allies must concentrate simply on saving their skin. They will do well to withdraw at least part of their troops from Flanders, but even that is far from guaranteed. ...

Dark clouds hung over Parliament today. Churchill made a brief statement about the current situation which he concluded with the following words: 'The House must steel itself for grievous and painful news.' A single question was asked over and over again in the lobbies: how could this happen?

Afterwards, I went to see Lloyd George in his office. He was very worked-up and upset. I had never seen him so alarmed. ... I asked Lloyd George what he thought about the possibility of a German invasion of England.

The old man lifted his hands and said: 'A fortnight ago I would still have said that it was absolutely impossible. However, Hitler has succeeded in doing so many things which used to be considered impossible, that I refuse to make any forecast concerning an invasion.'

4 June

Churchill's speech in Parliament today made a powerful and favourable impression on MPs. This is understandable. On 28 May, the prime minister asked his colleagues to steel themselves for grim news from Flanders. Today he confessed that a week ago he had little hope that 30,000–40,000 men would be successfully rescued. Reality proved more merciful. Thanks to a tremendous effort, the valour of the troops, efficient transportation and excellent weather, 80% of the expeditionary corps trapped in Flanders (about 200,000 men) plus more than 100,000 Frenchmen were evacuated – in all, 335,000 men. An undeniable success, and one which supplied Churchill with an appreciative audience.

But that was not all. Everyone was pleased that the prime minister did not try to conceal the gravity of the current situation. He frankly stated that the Allies had sustained 'a colossal military disaster' in Flanders, that the situation at the front was very dangerous, and that, no matter how skilfully the evacuation had been carried out, evacuations do not win wars. At the same time, Churchill firmly declared that the struggle would continue and that England would even fight on her own if she had to!

... After Churchill's speech I went to drink tea on the Parliament terrace, where I met Randolph Churchill and Brendan Bracken. The latter has now become Winston Churchill's private parliamentary secretary. We spoke about the military situation and the immediate prospects. Where will Hitler move next? ...

[The following entries focus on Maisky's role in the appointment of Stafford Cripps as the British ambassador to Moscow. Churchill has often been credited with the appointment. In retrospect, he would regret not realizing sufficiently that 'Soviet Communists hate extreme Left Wing politicians even more than they do Tories or Liberals'. In May, however, he was preoccupied with the disasters inflicted on the French army and the British Expeditionary Force in France. Following a familiar pattern, it was Maisky who broached with Butler the idea of conducting negotiations 'by word of mouth and not by notes' and who mentioned *en passant* Cripps's desire to act as a go-between. On 16 May, Butler conveyed the message to Halifax and urged him to 'really move a little more quickly' by appointing an ambassador to Moscow. That evening the foreign secretary had Cripps to dinner. The odd collusion between Halifax and Cripps dated back to their association with the World Alliance of Christian Churches movement, which had been inspired by Cripps's father Lord Parmoor. Cripps outlined his views on India and Russia, and offered to proceed to Moscow and exploit the changing circumstances.

Next morning, Halifax consulted Butler, who enthusiastically endorsed Cripps. Butler suggested that Cripps should be allowed 'latitude to discuss over a reasonably wide field with the Soviet authorities'. 'After the Cabinet meeting,' Halifax's diary records, 'I talked with [Churchill] in the garden for a few minutes, partly about an idea I had had to send Stafford Cripps on an exploratory mission to Moscow, and partly about future prospects of the war.'

Visiting the Webbs on 20 May, Maisky, oblivious of the turnabout, appeared 'angry and contemptuous of Halifax – "the pious old fool"'. Earlier in the day, Maisky had been seen in the corridors of the Foreign Office 'much perturbed' by the news just coming in of the collapse of the French defence and the advance of the Wehrmacht as far as the Channel. He could not know that at that very moment Cadogan was breaking the news to Seeds that he 'would not go back to Moscow but that Sir Stafford Cripps, the extreme Left-Winger M.P., is to go there on a Special Mission' and that it was 'hoped that the Kremlin may prove more amenable than it was to [Seeds] as representing the infamous (!) Chamberlain'.

Summoned to Whitehall in the evening, Maisky was therefore pleasantly surprised to find Halifax amenable, 'concerned at the unnecessary misunderstandings which seemed to have developed' and proposing to send Cripps 'to explore' with the Soviet Government how to advance the trade talks. Maisky was assured that not only would Cripps be equipped with full authority, but would 'of course enjoy full liberty to explore in discussion any other question which he or the Soviet Government wished to raise'.

Stalin was shaken by the sweeping success of the Wehrmacht's Blitzkrieg in France. He now feared that a special mission by Cripps might provoke Hitler, who would see it as an attempt to cement an alliance between Russia and Britain in an effort to thwart further German expansion. The solution he sought was to ensure that Cripps arrived in Moscow as a normal ambassador, replacing Seeds in a routine diplomatic procedure. Maisky returned to Halifax with Stalin's qualified acceptance on 26 May. 'The Soviet Government agrees to Cripps,' Halifax entered in his diary, 'but wants him to be an Ambassador. I told Maisky we meant to send an Ambassador, and hardly supposed the Soviet Government claimed to choose him for us.' As it turned out, that is precisely what transpired.]

5 June

At last, Cripps's fate has been decided! But what a story it's been!

It all began on 20 May, when Halifax summoned me and said that the Cabinet had decided to send Stafford Cripps to Moscow as *special envoy*. For about a week leading up to this, I heard 'rumours' from all sides that the new Government wanted to turn a new leaf in its relations with the Soviet Union. It was being said that the prime minister would invite me for a *heart to heart talk*, that the question of the British ambassador in Moscow would be settled, and that the absurd 'correspondence' concerning trade negotiations would be annulled. Personally, I thought that the question of the British ambassador in Moscow should come first. And when Halifax began speaking to me about improving Anglo-Soviet relations, I expected to hear that either Seeds would be returning to Moscow or that the British Government was going to request an *agrément* for a different ambassador. Halifax's news concerning a *special envoy* greatly disappointed me and I inquired rather coolly about the purpose of this envoy's mission. Halifax sighed, pondered for a moment, and said: '*To explore the possibilities.*'

'*What kind of possibilities?*' I asked.

Halifax replied that he meant the 'possibilities' of a general improvement in Anglo-Soviet relations, in particular the 'possibility' of a trade agreement with the USSR.

I expressed my surprise that even now the British Government was planning merely to 'explore possibilities', instead of getting down to practical matters, but promised to convey Halifax's message to Moscow.

As was to be expected, the British scheme did not appeal to Moscow. Indeed, what need have we of some astral *special envoy*, whose obscure mission is *to explore the possibilities*? Moscow, however, took some time over the reply and finally sent it to London on 26 May. The answer was that the Soviet Government was prepared to receive Cripps, or any other person authorized by the British Government, only not in the capacity of a special envoy, but as an ordinary ambassador accredited on the same basis as I was accredited in London.

... I received the aforesaid reply from Moscow on the morning of 26 May and delivered it to Halifax that very evening (even though it was Sunday). The foreign secretary was confused and unpleasantly surprised. He told me that the issue of a British ambassador in Moscow had only just received the attention of the Government. Four days earlier, it had been decided to recall Seeds and replace him with someone else. Halifax was just about to inform me of the decision and request *agrément* for the new ambassador. Unfortunately, not all the procedural details had been arranged, so Halifax would only be able to inform me of the name of the new ambassador in a few days' time. But what should we do with Cripps in the meantime? After all, he had already left and was probably halfway there, perhaps even in Athens.

Halifax sighed again, pondered, and proposed a solution: let Cripps go as a *special envoy*, and in a couple of days the British Government would announce the appointment of a new ambassador, who could arrive in Moscow in three or four weeks' time.

I objected, saying that the Soviet Government was ready to receive one, not two, representatives, and this sole representative must be the ambassador.

Halifax began fidgeting and tried to convince me that his proposal was highly practical. As a last resort, the British Government would be prepared to give Cripps the rank of ambassador for the period of his mission in Moscow, though such a solution did not appeal to Halifax personally: the rank of ambassador is usually given in cases when the *special envoy* intends to stay in the country to which he is sent for a long period of time (like Hoare, who has just been appointed 'Ambassador Extraordinary and Plenipotentiary on a Special Mission' to Spain), while Cripps's mission was conceived as only a short-term measure. ...

My meeting with Halifax occurred between six and seven in the evening. At 9 p.m., when I was at home, the telephone suddenly rang and to my very great astonishment I heard the following words: 'Cripps speaking.'

'Where are you calling from?' I asked in bewilderment, thinking that perhaps he was calling from somewhere in France.

I was wrong. Cripps was in England and was calling me from the aerodrome he was meant to have left from the previous day. But for various reasons the plane was still there and take-off was only expected the next day. On Saturday morning I had been looking for Cripps and rang him at home. Cripps had been informed of my call and now wanted to know what the matter was. I laughed to myself about the coincidence and replied: 'Two hours ago I gave the Soviet Government's reply concerning your visit to Halifax. I advise you to get in touch with him before leaving.'

'What is the nature of the response?' Cripps asked.

I briefly related the key points to him. Cripps thanked me and hung up.

An hour had not passed before the telephone rang again. It was Cripps: 'I've just spoken to Halifax. Everything has been arranged. I'll receive the proper appointment. Halifax will summon you to see him on this matter tomorrow.'

'I shall be waiting,' I said. 'I wish you a good journey and a successful trip.'

Cripps thanked me and hung up once more.

The following day, 27 May, I waited in vain for Halifax's invitation. Butler finally called at about seven o'clock in the evening and asked me to come to his apartment right away. I thought he wanted to inform me of Cripps's appointment as ambassador, but that turned out not to be the case. Butler started questioning me once again about the nature of the Soviet Government's reply which I had conveyed to Halifax the day before, and tried to clarify whether there was any hope of the Soviet Government agreeing to receive not one but two British representatives: the ambassador and the *special envoy*. I left Butler in no doubt. On parting, Butler told me that the matter of Cripps's status would probably be resolved the following morning.

... Nonetheless, when the next morning, 29 May, Butler informed me officially that Cripps had been appointed ambassador, it appeared that his rank was that of 'Ambassador Extraordinary and Plenipotentiary on a Special Mission'. Butler justified this by the fact that according to British law a Member of Parliament could not occupy a post whose salary was paid for by the government (the division of legislative and executive power!). Therefore, a member of the House of Commons could not be an ordinary ambassador, but only an ambassador 'on a special mission'.

... Le Rougetel[35] was received by C[omrade] Molotov on 31 May and requested *agrément* for Cripps. Surely, C[omrade] Molotov told him that the Soviet Government wanted an ordinary ambassador, not one 'on a special mission', adding that it was ready to receive Cripps or any other person authorized by the British Government. C[omrade] Molotov also noted that the British

---

[35] John Helier Le Rougetel, First Secretary at the British embassy in Moscow.

Government evidently desired to send a person of leftist leanings to Moscow. The Soviet Government, however, thinks that it is not the personal convictions of the ambassador that matter, but the fact that he represents his Government. If that condition is satisfied, we are indifferent to the ambassador's party affiliation.

C[omrade] Molotov's reply reached London on the evening of 1 June, and the Cabinet decided at once to satisfy our wishes and appoint Cripps ambassador without a 'special mission'.

... The Foreign Office mandarins are furious at Cripps's appointment. ... I fear that the sabotaging of Cripps will not stop at that. The Foreign Office machine is too strong, while Butler, who seems to sympathize with Cripps, is not firm or influential enough to restrain the 'experts'.[36]

14 June

Paris has fallen. German troops are parading down the Champs-Élysées and the Grands Boulevards. Hitler has ordered flags to be hoisted and bells to be rung all over Germany. No wonder! Even Bismarck[37] never saw such a victory in 1871.

... Agniya and I went to the Keyneses[38] for lunch two days ago. We found them in a state of extreme pessimism. Lopukhova is utterly lost and stunned, and told Agniya of her feeling that the old world is dying and a new one is being born. The new world obviously frightens her and she doesn't know what to do. She repeated several times: 'If the British and the French were not ready for war, then why did they declare it?'

Keynes himself tries to behave in a manner befitting an economist and philosopher, but he confessed to taking a very gloomy view of the future. The ruling classes of England have gone to seed. That is now absolutely clear. New forces ought to take their place. Which forces? Keynes does not have a clear answer to that question. But he is convinced that England will fight long and hard, even if she is on her own. Keynes discards the possibility of a German invasion of the Isles.

---

[36] Cadogan indeed warned that Cripps had 'not yet won his spurs in diplomacy'. It was assumed in the Foreign Office that Cripps would not remain in Moscow as ambassador 'for more than a brief period'.

[37] Otto von Bismarck, German chancellor, 1871–90. The reference is to the Franco-Prussian war of 1870–71.

[38] John Maynard Keynes (Baron Keynes of Tilton), British economist, author of *The General Theory of Employment, Interest and Money* (1936) and editor of the *Economic Journal*, 1911–44. Married the ballerina Lidia Lopukhova of the *Ballet Russe*. An agnostic and liberal, he deplored Marxism, which he argued rested on erroneous economic premises. If one needed religion it could hardly be found 'in the turbid rubbish of the red bookshop'.

17 June

... France has capitulated. Why?

Undoubtedly, Germany proved incomparably more powerful than France in terms of army strength, mechanization and aviation. But that is far from all; it may not even be the main thing. I'm growing more and more convinced that France capitulated because of its internal disintegration. The rule of the '200 families' had its effects. It split France, poisoned its political atmosphere, emasculated it militarily, and paved the way for its present defeat. More than that, it introduced elements of decay into the French army and undermined its combat efficiency.

... What will England do now?

Clearly, she will fight alone. There is nothing else for it. I remember what Randolph Churchill told me a couple of weeks ago: 'Even if the worst comes to the worst, France can survive without its Empire. ... England's position is different: if we lose our Empire, we shall become not a second-rank, but a tenth-rank power. We have nothing. We will all die of hunger. So, there is nothing for it but to fight to the end.'

In England, news of France's capitulation was received with dismay and shock. In the street today one could often hear talk of the impossibility of fighting alone. Politicians and journalists sighed voluptuously: 'Ah, if only a revolution would break out in France and the Pétain Government could be overthrown!'

Even the Tories have been speaking in a similar vein. No wonder! Some have hinted rather openly that a revolution in France is needed as a bait to draw the USSR into the war. 'Paris is well worth a mass,' said Henry IV. 'The participation of the Soviet Union in the war against Germany is well worth a revolution in France,' say British Tories today. ...

18 June

I spent the afternoon in Parliament. Today's speech by Churchill has lifted morale. His firm statement that England, regardless of France's defeat, will fight to the end was met with loud applause from all the benches. The prime minister's arguments about the impossibility of a German invasion of the Isles made a great impression. This was the only subject of conversation in the lobbies.

... The end of today's sitting was marked by a rather unusual demonstration. The Labourite John Morgan[39] took the floor and suggested that the House should mark the fact of Cripps's arrival in Moscow and his accession to the post

---

[39] John Morgan, Labour MP for Doncaster, 1938–41.

of ambassador. The suggestion was welcomed with cheers from all sides. Furthermore, Members of Parliament turned their faces to the diplomatic gallery, where I was sitting in the front row. Morgan then wished Cripps every success in his new job. Friendly approval echoed round the chamber once more and Churchill, half-rising from the government bench and looking in my direction, waved his hand in salutation. Other ministers followed the PM's example. Evidently, this was a sudden demonstration which had not been prepared in advance, since my presence in the diplomatic gallery at that moment was a matter of sheer chance. ...

23 June

Today it is already clear that the decision of the British Government to continue fighting, notwithstanding the capitulation of France, has proved popular among the masses. It has gone down particularly well among the workers. The initial perplexity and confusion have passed. On the contrary, a surge of cold, stubborn, truly British fury is gathering momentum. The English, it seems, will resist to the end.

Such is the general backdrop. Upon it, some very significant patterns can be discerned.

... There is a clear split in the attitudes of the ruling classes. Churchill's group stands for war to the end, for the sake of which it is ready to meet many of the workers' demands in the sphere of domestic and economic policy. Chamberlain's group, on the contrary, is scared stiff about the social and political consequences of the war and is ready to conclude a 'rotten peace' at any given moment in order to retain its capitalist privileges. They produce a simple argument: better to be 'rich' in a small Empire than 'poor' in a big one. This group has not given up hope of diverting Hitler to the east at some point in the war. Naturally, these people are keeping silent. ... So, war to the end. But what is the general strategic plan of the British Government? Summing up the information available to me, I can venture the following.

The British Government plans to remain on the defensive until about the end of this year: there are not enough men, arms and aircraft. By the beginning of 1941, the British Government hopes to have overcome these difficulties, to gain superiority over the Germans in the air, and to move on to the offensive. Until then, England must be turned into an unassailable fortress, capable of repelling every German assault.

25 June

American Ambassador Kennedy lunched with me today. He takes a gloomy view of British prospects. He doubts that England will be able to wage a long war single-handedly. He accepts the possibility of a German invasion of the Isles. He thinks it utterly inevitable that England will be almost completely destroyed by air raids. Kennedy says the United States will be helping England in every way, with arms, aircraft, etc., over the next few months, but will hardly enter into the war before the presidential election, unless something extraordinary happens, such as the Germans using gas. Kennedy scolded the British Government for failing to come to an agreement with the Soviet Union last year and said that the upper classes of British society are *completely rotten*. A rather unexpected judgement from a man of his status! ...[40]

28 June

Little by little many, very many people's gazes are turning towards the Soviet Union.

The ill-fated 'Polish Government' recently came running to London together with its president. Polish Premier Sikorski[41] met with Churchill and assured him, first orally and then in writing, that the Polish Government did not wish to impede in any way the improvement of Anglo-Soviet relations. Governmental circles here interpreted this to mean that the 'Polish Government' is ready to formally relinquish its claims on Western Ukraine and Belorussia. We hardly need this renunciation, if truth be told; but as a symptom of the Polish mood, it is very interesting.

In less official Polish circles the following notion is gaining ground: if the Germans hold Poland, Polish nationality itself will eventually be eliminated. If Poland goes over to the USSR, Polish nationality will survive and even develop. Hence the conclusion: 'Let it be a Soviet Poland, but still Poland!'

4 July

Churchill's speech in Parliament today was a personal triumph and, at the same time, a significant display of patriotism.

Initially, the mood in the House was hard to determine. Churchill's appearance was welcomed with noises that were encouraging without being particularly impressive or unanimous. As usual, most of the cheers came from the opposition benches, while the greater part of the Conservatives held a

---

[40] Maisky told an acquaintance that 'Kennedy was sceptical about Britain's chances of resisting attacks on the island'. He, on the other hand, 'was not pessimistic; everything depends on whether you use your cards, of which you have so many, in the right spirit, with resolution'.
[41] Władysław Eugeniusz Sikorski, Polish prime minister, 1922–23; prime minister of the Polish government-in-exile and commander-in-chief of the Polish armed forces, 1939–43. Unsubstantiated conspiracy theories claim that Maisky, whose plane happened to be on the tarmac next to Sikorski's in Gibraltar airport in July 1943, was involved in Sikorski's death when the plane crashed during take-off.

gloomy silence. This pattern was repeated when Churchill rose to make his speech.

But the longer this brilliant and skilful performance continued, the more it affected the mood of the MPs. Churchill's topic, of course, was a sure winner. He said that the British navy had scored a great success, that the greater part of the French fleet was either in British hands or out of action, and that consequently the chances of a German invasion had fallen steeply... How could the House refrain from rejoicing? How could it fail to greet each rousing sentence of the PM's speech with boisterous applause?

It could not. The House exulted and gave vent to its elation.

Then Churchill spoke about the future. He firmly and categorically refuted all rumours of a possible peace. He vowed to fight to the end. At this point the outburst of patriotism reached its peak, and when Churchill finished his speech and sank into his seat, the whole House, irrespective of party affiliation, jumped to its feet and applauded the prime minister for several minutes – a loud, powerful and unanimous ovation. Sitting on the Treasury bench, the tension draining from his body, Churchill lowered his head and tears ran down his cheeks.

It was a strong, stirring scene. 'At last we have a real leader!' was the cry echoing through the lobbies. Curiously, it was Labour which pronounced these words most often. For the time being, at any rate, talk of a 'rotten peace' can be put to one side. ...

[The collapse of France induced a dramatic change in the Soviet attitude to the peace offensive. Complacency gave way to profound concern, leading to the hasty occupation of Bessarabia and the annexation of the Baltic states. Ever since the shift in Soviet policy following the conclusion of the Molotov–Ribbentrop Pact, Maisky had found himself in a perilous state. He was barred from the Kremlin's decision-making process, at the same time as being socially and politically ostracized in Britain. He seldom received a diplomatic bag or newspapers from Moscow. Being of Jewish origin, he could hardly watch with equanimity the blooming romance between Moscow and Berlin. Later on, he was indeed to find himself at the top of Hitler's publicized list of those to be shot after the occupation of Britain. Maisky certainly reckoned with 'the possibility of a temporary appearance of the Germans in London. ... I even inquired of Moscow how I should conduct myself if the Germans were to occupy the district in London in which our embassy is situated.' The turn of events, however, meant that the persisting threat of a severance of relations was lifted as 'the prolonged "winter of discontent"' came to an end.

Maisky's relief concerning the German threat to the Soviet Union was replaced by a serious worry about the British ability to withstand a German onslaught and the probability of a peace agreement. On 28 June, Alexander, the first lord of the Admiralty, returning from a meeting with Maisky, alerted Churchill to the Soviet apprehension about a peace agreement modelled on the French surrender. It was most telling that Maisky – who had little patience with Alexander's ironic comment that, until recently, the British communists 'had been leaders of a peace offensive' – insisted that 'the present attitude of the CPGB. was to organize resistance against the invader' and reiterated that the situation was 'full of danger'. Briefed by Alexander, Churchill, who had not seen Maisky since taking office, met him on 3 July. The meeting (for which there is no entry in the diary) was, according to Maisky's memoirs, 'brief, but most significant'. It was a relief for him to learn that Churchill 'categorically and forcefully denied rumours on possible peace negotiations' and explained that his present strategy was 'to last out the next three months' before moving on to the offensive. Churchill had been advised by the Foreign Office to avoid any discussion of political value with Maisky, as 'he was not in confidence of his own Government and is therefore useless'. 'You don't doubt Maisky being pro-British, do you?' Randolph Churchill asked Beaverbrook, encouraging him to draw Maisky closer to his circle. 'I don't doubt this at all, Randolph,' replied the press baron, 'but I very much doubt whether Stalin is pro-Maisky.']

5 July

A visit from Pierre Cot,[42] who has been swept onto British shores by the tide of events. ... Cot told me many interesting things about France. His account fully corroborates what Negrín[43] told me. At the heart of France's crushing defeat lies the internal degeneration of the ruling elite. Cot drew a most vivid picture of this process. He spoke at some length about 'female influences' in politics. Every major French figure has a wife or, more often, 'Madame de Pompadour', engaged in politics. In the overwhelming majority of cases these are extremely reactionary politics. One should be thankful, Cot says, if the mistress is stupid, for then she can do less harm. But if she is a clever woman, she presents a very grave danger. Daladier's mistress (Madame Crussol[44]), for example, isn't the brightest and could be tolerated. But Reynaud's[45] mistress (Madame de Portes[46]) is very intelligent and witty, and she has played a fateful role in Reynaud's life

---

[42] Pierre Cot, radical French MP, 1928–40; minister for air, 1933–34 and 1936–38; minister for trade, 1938–39; in exile in Great Britain, 1940–44.

[43] Juan Negrín, Spanish minister of finance, 1936–37; premier of the Republican Government, 1937–39; following Franco's victory in 1939, he fled to Paris, where he tried to organize a government-in-exile; found refuge in England when the Germans invaded France in 1940. Maisky was a frequent weekend guest at his country house in Bovingdon.

[44] Marquise Jeanne de Crussol.

[45] Paul Reynaud, minister of justice, 1938; minister of finance, 1938–40 and 1948; prime minister, 1940.

[46] La Comtesse Hélène de Portes.

and in the history of the French Government as a whole.[47] Reynaud is not bad in himself. He has good intentions and a good grasp of the situation, but he is not strong enough: he is in the hands of his entourage, in which Madame de Portes plays the leading part. She is an extremely reactionary lady. She is on friendly terms with Madame Bonnet, Madame Aletz and other ladies who not only share utterly retrograde views, but also maintain close ties with the Germans.

By way of illustration, Cot referred to the case of his failed visit to Moscow. When he returned in April from his meeting with me in London, Cot had a serious conversation with Reynaud about relations with the USSR. Reynaud was entirely reasonable. He understood that relations with Moscow should be resumed, and even outlined a few measures in this direction in his conversation with Cot. Cot was pleased. A few days passed, but no practical steps had been taken. Cot visited Reynaud again and was confronted with a completely different scene: the prime minister hummed and hawed, spoke of difficulties and recommended caution. What had happened? Madame de Portes and other persons from Reynaud's retinue had intervened, and the PM's good intentions had faded. ...

6 July

Paid a visit to Eden at the War Office. I hadn't seen him for some time and I wanted to gauge his mood.

... I posed Eden the same question that I put to Churchill a few days ago: what is the *major strategy* of the war, how does the British Government understand it?

Eden's answer came down to the following.

The first and most urgent task is to repel any attack on England. Every effort should then be made to achieve superiority over Germany in the air. Eden believes this can be done in approximately six months. At the same time, it is necessary to prepare a large, well-trained and well-equipped army, and also maintain a strict economic blockade of Germany and the countries it has occupied. Later, beginning in the first months or the spring of 1941, the British should move on to the offensive by air and by land. The British offensive ought to be facilitated by the fact that the blockade and its consequences should help undermine Germany from within.

---

[47] Daladier and Reynaud were neighbours, and their mistresses were not only acquaintances but also old social rivals. Halifax noted in his diary that the French minister Georges Mandel had asked George Lloyd, Churchill's special envoy to Paris, whether he could come away to London with him 'but said that he had also "des bagages"', which the ambassador interpreted as Mandel's mistress. 'At this George drew the line.'

I asked Eden whether he was thinking of concluding a peace agreement in the near future, and, if so, what kind of peace?

Eden categorically rules out the possibility of peace. The war will be fought 'to the end'. The operation with the French fleet has clearly demonstrated England's determination to fight.[48] England's intentions are serious and unshakeable.

7 July

Agniya and I visited the Webbs. As usual, Beatrice expressed a thought worthy of further consideration. Here it is.

England will undoubtedly be able to repulse a German attack on its islands. But it will not be able to win back France, Denmark, Norway, Holland and Belgium from Germany. As a result, a situation might emerge whereby Germany, depending on the European continent it has conquered, will not be able to defeat England, while England, depending on its Empire and possibly part of the French Empire, will not be able to defeat Germany. A *stalemate* will ensue. The Soviet Union and the United States might act as mediators and achieve a decent peace in Europe.

I learned the following details of Cripps's conversation with S[talin] in the presence of M[olotov] on 1 July.

Cripps raised four issues on behalf of the British Government:

(1) General policy. Germany has seized the greater part of Europe and is about to establish its supremacy in Europe. It is swallowing up one nation after another. This is dangerous for both England and the Soviet Union. Couldn't the two countries establish a common line of defence to restore equilibrium in Europe?

Stalin's reply: The Soviet Union is following the development of the European situation with the keenest interest, as it is the key issues of international politics which should be resolved in Europe in the near future as a result of the hostilities. However, the Soviet Government does not see any danger in the hegemony of a single state in Europe, still less in Germany's ambition to absorb other nations. ... These cordial relations are based not on transient, opportunist considerations, but on the vital national interests of both states. As far as the restoration of 'equilibrium' in Europe is concerned, that 'equilibrium' was suffocating not only Germany, but the USSR as well. That is why the Soviet

---

[48] Churchill's decision to sink the French fleet, under the command of the Vichy Government, at the port of Mers-el-Kebir outside Oran on 3 July.

Government will do all it can to ensure that the former 'equilibrium' is not restored. ...

(3) <u>The Balkans</u>. The British Government believes that the Soviet Union should assume control of the Balkan countries in order to maintain the status quo in the Balkans.

S.'s reply: It is the opinion of the Soviet Government that no single power can claim an exclusive role in the unification and control of the Balkans. The Soviet Union is certainly interested in the Balkans, but it does not claim an exclusive role in this part of the globe.

(4) <u>The Straits</u>. The British Government is aware that the Soviet Union is dissatisfied with the situation in the Straits and the Black Sea. It believes that the interests of the Soviet Union in the Straits should be secured.

S.'s reply: The Soviet Union is against Turkey taking unilateral control of the Straits, just as it is against Turkey dictating conditions in the Black Sea. The Turkish Government has been informed of the USSR's attitude.

8 July

Now that Cripps is finally settled in Moscow as ambassador of Great Britain I am trying to recover his true image in my mind. Who is he really? What are his most characteristic features?

... Cripps is undoubtedly a very intelligent and well-educated man. He is an English intellectual of the Left who considers himself a radical socialist, but who has never had anything to do with Marxism. Cripps's socialism is of a particular, English breed – a mixture of religion, ethical idealism and the practical demands of the trade unions. Cripps is a republican, which is a rather rare phenomenon in England. In recent years he has spoken out sharply against royal authority, and for a while his name was 'taboo' in Buckingham Palace. Cripps is very emotional, hence his instability and the frequent contradictions in his speeches of different periods. What is especially valuable about Cripps is the fact that he has <u>convictions</u> and is ready to stand up for them. He has proved his honesty and courage in deeds on more than one occasion, especially in connection with the propaganda of a 'united front', for which he had to pay a heavy price.

Despite being, by British standards, a man of the far Left, Cripps is deeply religious (not, of course, in a formal, churchly sense). He is a confirmed teetotaller and vegetarian, and even prefers to eat raw rather than boiled vegetables. Yet Cripps is a heavy smoker. He is exceptionally interesting to talk to. He is a fine orator, whose speeches are greatly influenced by the context in which he finds himself. In Parliament and in court, Cripps is a model of logical, juridical eloquence. But at mass meetings he is transformed beyond recognition: the sight of a crowd goes to his head and he becomes a tribune of the people. His excited imagination carries him farther and farther afield and he skips his habitual 'buts' and 'ifs', becoming more left wing than he actually is. That's why he has often found himself in awkward predicaments. Cripps is a very feeble tactician. He does not know how to manoeuvre, how to wait for an advantageous moment, or how to handle people. It was only because of these shortcomings that he was expelled from the Labour Party.

Cripps is a typical political individualist, such as may be found in England fairly often. He is akin to Lloyd George in this sense. Cripps enjoys great popularity in the thinking strata of the proletariat and among more enlightened Conservatives like Churchill, Eden and others. Labour, the Transport House, dislikes him. Butler and, strangely enough, Halifax think highly of him. Perhaps it is religion that unites Halifax and Cripps. It is difficult to foretell Cripps's future, but he will probably play a major role in the political events of the next few years. I've heard it said several times that Cripps is a future 'left-wing' minister of foreign affairs or 'left-wing' prime minister. Even such a man as Lloyd George, upon learning of Cripps's appointment as ambassador to Moscow, told me: 'I almost regret it. We need Cripps here more than in Moscow. He is the only major figure on the opposition bench.'

Cripps's attitude towards the USSR is entirely cordial. I remember the courage and skill with which he defended us on behalf of Labour during the debate on the embargo in connection with the Metro-Vickers case. No doubt, he still has very good intentions in respect of Anglo-Soviet relations. But will he be able to improve these relations significantly? I don't know. All will depend on the policy of the British Government, which is much further to the Right than Cripps on this matter. ...

[A member of a minority left-wing faction in Parliament, Cripps now found himself in a crucial role as British ambassador to the sole major power in Europe which still retained its independence, even as he remained an outspoken opponent of the prime minister. Convinced that Russia would eventually find itself at war with Germany, Cripps hoped to lay the foundations for an alliance during the war which could pave the way to a post-war agreement. Hardly had he settled in Moscow than he advocated an agreement with Russia that would recognize part of her acquisitions (mostly in the Baltic states) and lead to the establishment of a South-Eastern Alliance with Turkey. His detailed plan for post-war reconstruction – a premonition of things to come – contained some very radical thinking: in the wake of the war, which was bound to lead to significant social changes on the home front. Great Britain must, he argued, 'be prepared to regard herself as an outpost' of the United States. Cripps presented his ideas in a letter that he addressed to Halifax and which was shown to Churchill.

Churchill's own message, which Cripps delivered to Stalin on 1 July (at their only meeting before the German invasion of Russia), was confined to a general declaration of a desire to maintain 'harmonious and mutually beneficial' relations between the two countries, regardless of their 'widely differing systems of political thought'. The concrete proposals which Cripps made to Stalin were aimed at establishing a bulwark against Nazi Germany in the Balkans. The timing, however – just a week after the fall of France – was inauspicious. Stalin feared that Britain, under siege and with no apparent prospect of victory, might try to embroil Russia in a war with Germany. He was as suspicious that Britain might sign a peace agreement with Germany. The 'scramble for the Balkans' that followed best illuminates the nature of Stalin's frame of mind, as well as his *modus operandi* following the Molotov–Ribbentrop Pact. The annexation of Bessarabia in June 1940 was motivated by a need to improve the strategic position of the Soviet Union in the Black Sea area by securing control of the mouth of the Danube.]

10 July

Quite unexpectedly, after a six-week break (I last visited him on 26 May) Halifax invited me round. I arrived at six in the evening.

Halifax began with a semi-apology: he had nothing particular to tell me, but simply wanted to see me and have a chat. We hadn't been in touch for so long, and the times are so complex and unstable.

I bowed to him and replied with a half-smile: 'I'm entirely at your service.'

Halifax moved in his chair, crossed his long thin legs, and said: 'Cripps has had a talk with Mr Stalin. A very useful and interesting one. They spoke quite frankly. I attach great importance to this exchange of opinions. We shall draw the appropriate conclusions.'

As the content of the talk was not known to me, I considered it best to maintain a polite silence and allow the foreign secretary to speak.

... Halifax then asked whether I believed the landlords in England to be as bad as they were in Russia, and whether they could expect the same fate. I replied that I was insufficiently familiar with the English conditions to take a definite view, but that I felt it was wrong to draw excessively literal parallels. Russia was an agrarian country, so the question of landlords was central to our revolution. England is an industrial country, so here it is not the landlords but the bankers and industrialists who play the key role. My remark seemed to flatter Halifax and he added with relief: 'Our landlords will be *taxed out of existence*, but I don't think we'll have an agrarian revolution... I'm sure, for instance, that everybody in my village would be sorry if something happened to my family.'

I looked at Halifax and recalled that I had heard the same words from many landlords in Saratov before the 1905 revolution. But in the year of the revolution, furious peasants burned down their estates. Does history really repeat itself?

That was the end of our philosophizing. Halifax moved on to current events.[49]

... Halifax asked whether the new border between the Soviet Union and Rumania had been definitively fixed. I answered in the affirmative. ... 'How do you see it?' Halifax continued. 'Is the population of Bessarabia content with the changes that have befallen it?'

'That depends who you mean,' I answered. 'The Bessarabian landlords, of course, are not best pleased, but the Bessarabian peasants are, just as obviously, quite content. For them, transferral to the USSR signifies national freedom and the improvement of their material well-being.'

I told Halifax that the Soviet Government had already passed a resolution to establish the thirteenth Union Republic – that of Moldavia – and that the reforming of Bessarabian agriculture according to the Soviet model had already begun.

'Don't you think,' Halifax continued, 'that the Balkans might be drawn into the war in the near future?'

I expressed my doubts about this. Halifax also admitted that he is not expecting a military conflict in the Balkans at present: Germany and Italy are against it.

Then he asked: 'Imagine that Hitler is run over by a bus tomorrow or that he is forced to quit the stage for some reason or other: would the present German regime be able to hang on? I doubt it. Neither Göring, nor Goebbels nor Hess,[50] nor anyone else would be able to preserve it.'

I objected that this was too simplistic.

... Halifax wanted to say something more when his secretary entered the room and reported that Lord Lloyd (the minister for the colonies) wished to see him urgently. Halifax's face clouded over and he said, rising from his chair: 'We must meet again and have a chat... It is so important to share our thoughts at this time: after all, we are entering a new world.'

We parted.

My conclusions:

---

[49] Halifax entered in his diary: 'With Maisky I had a general talk in order to keep relations warm. He was quite interesting from his beastly Bolshevik point of view about the Russian land system.'
[50] Rudolf Hess, deputy Nazi Party leader, 1933–41; flew to Scotland on 10 May, on his own initiative, with a peace offer. See pp. 351 and 355.

(1) In general, Halifax, like many other representatives of the ruling upper crust, is full of dark forebodings and understands that the war will deprive the elite of its privileges. At a certain point, this could push him towards a 'rotten peace' with Hitler.

(2) In particular, as a consequence of the growing swell of opinion against Chamberlain, which this time is also hitting Halifax hard, the latter has to manoeuvre, and considers it profitable to demonstrate his contact with the Soviet ambassador. I doubt that this will help him.

12 July

Eden and his wife came for lunch with the two of us, Agniya and myself. We were sitting in the winter garden. It was a beautiful day, and Eden was in a good mood. Looking through the garden's open door, he said with a grin: 'One could come to your place just to rest.'

'You are very welcome!' I responded in the same tone.

Eden asked me about our position, and reminisced about the past, his visit to Moscow, and our meetings and conversations during his stint at the Foreign Office. He remarked: 'You know, the hardest thing for me during that time was to convince my friends that Hitler and Mussolini were quite different from British *business men* or *country gentlemen* as regards their psychology, motivations and modes of action. My friends simply refused to believe me. They thought I was *biased* against the dictators and refused to understand them. I kept saying: "When you converse with the Führer or the Duce, you feel at once that you are dealing with an animal of an entirely different breed from yourself." Some of our statesmen subsequently tried to approach the dictators in the same manner as they would approach *business men*. The results are well known.'

Then we discussed current events. According to Eden, the British Government is in a state of great bewilderment. Numerous symptoms and pieces of information clearly foretold the beginning of a German onslaught on England on 6 July. Today is the 12 July, but there has been no attack. Why not? Members of the Government are speculating, but are unable to reach any definite conclusion.

I suggested that the attack may have been deferred because of the fate of the French fleet. What if the initial plans for an attack had been based on the assumption that the Germans would have the French fleet in their hands, and now, after the events of 2–3 July, all these plans had to be revised. Such a process requires time.

Eden found my idea most interesting and, on the assumption that it was correct, began to develop it. He said, among other things, that whatever the reasons for the delay may be, the British Government was very glad about it. It has more time to prepare. From the sea, England is now fully protected. The situation in the air is more complicated. True, the airfields are properly guarded, but there are too many natural landing strips in the country. An intensive effort is under way to 'spoil' them. All available digging machines in England have been recruited for the task. Teams of volunteers are also helping out. The outskirts of most big cities are already fairly 'spoiled', but two more weeks are needed to complete the destruction of natural landing strips all over the country. It would be good if the Germans gave the British this fortnight.

... The causes of the France defeat were the last topic of conversation. In general, Eden has a fair grasp of these causes. I asked whether anything similar could happen in England, too.

Eden categorically rejected this possibility.

'Yes,' he said, 'we too have such men as Laval, but they do not play a major role and carry no weight in government. Besides, our army, or at least the greater part of it, has already fought with the Germans and found that "the devil is never so black as he is painted". This is terribly important. On the whole, army morale is high, and I do not expect any unpleasant surprises on this score.'

[Eden was impressed enough by Maisky's analysis of the prospects for a German invasion to send Churchill a personal brief:

> Monsieur Maisky commented several times upon the manifest difficulty which confronted Hitler in any attempt to stage a sea-borne invasion. He seemed to have a surer grasp of this aspect of the problem than I would have expected. In his view a sea-borne offensive could not be expected to achieve anything unless together with an air-borne invasion ... Monsieur Maisky admitted that even so he did not see how the problem of communications could be dealt with.

A prominent American journalist observed that 'Maisky, with his practical grasp of day-by-day changes in thought and emotion, his genial but unruffled contemplation of the whole war in all its details, seemed to me one of the most thoroughly competent observers I had the fortune to meet in England.']

22 July

Nearly a month has passed since the French surrender, and what was already obvious then has now become even clearer. England is resolutely determined to fight Hitler 'to the end' on her own (who will define what 'to the end' means?).

... This is how things stand. In these circumstances it is hard to conceive of the possibility of peace in the near future. Hitler's speech on the 19th, in which he enjoined England 'for the last time' to 'recover its common sense' and conclude peace, produced not the slightest effect here. Earlier still, the Germans and the Italians sent 'peace feelers' via the pope and Franco, but the British Government replied with a terse 'No!' On the whole, it is difficult to imagine a 'deal' between England and Germany so long as Churchill remains prime minister. ...

It is, of course, difficult to vouch for the future. It is hard to say what will happen if massive air raids begin, if the tension of waiting drags on and on, if things start going badly in the Empire, or if the British capitalist elite comes face to face with the threat of serious curtailment of its rights and privileges. But for now it is quite obvious that England is not like France. It will put up a tough fight against German invaders.

25 July

... And here is one more story Prytz[51] told me. A fortnight before the abdication of Edward VIII in December 1936, he was in London on business (at that time he did not yet hold an official post) and was invited to a lunch arranged by his predecessor, Palmstierna.[52] The lunch turned out to be thoroughly 'political'. The Swedish crown prince[53] was the main guest, but also present were Eden, the archbishop of Canterbury and other distinguished figures. The issue of Edward's abdication was in the air. Some persons close to the Court were asking the Swedish crown prince to use his influence on Edward to persuade him, in the interests of the 'monarchic idea', to sever all ties with Mrs Simpson[54] so as to remain on the throne. The crown prince agreed in principle, provided the British Government did not object. In fact, it was precisely in order to discover the Government's attitude that the lunch had been arranged. But as soon as the guests sat down to table and exchanged initial remarks on the subject in question, it became perfectly clear that there was nothing for the crown prince to do: the English guests immediately let it be understood that they desired Edward's abdication, and did not wish him to remain on the throne. The archbishop of Canterbury was especially categorical. He told Prytz, who was sitting next to him, with a laugh: 'I'm a very small and unknown man in the Empire, but do you think that even I could retain my *job* if I married Mrs Simpson?'

The Swedish prince did not have to save the crown for Edward VIII after all.

---

[51] Björn Prytz, Swedish ambassador to Great Britain, 1938–47.
[52] Baron Erik Palmstierna, Swedish ambassador in London, 1927–37. He stayed on in England, actively involved in the World Congress of Faiths.
[53] Gustaf VI Adolf, Swedish crown prince; married to Lady Louise Mountbatten, sister of Lord Mountbatten and aunt of Prince Philip.
[54] Bessie Wallis, duchess of Windsor.

27 July

Dalton lunched with me yesterday. ... Dalton told me an amusing story about Hoare. Hoare is in a state of permanent panic. He has got the idea into his head that Hitler dreams of capturing him and holding him as a hostage, threatening to lop off his head should circumstances demand it. That's why Hoare has been inundating the British Government with desperate telegrams of the 'Munich' type. In particular, Hoare protested against Dalton's intention to make a statement in Parliament yesterday, 25 July [sic], about the decision of the British Government 'to put Spain on rations'. Dalton has had to postpone this statement until 30 July. Hoare also insisted that Negrín should leave England.

The British Government, according to Dalton, wants to settle the question of the Straits; apparently, Cripps has even discussed this issue with the Turkish ambassador in Moscow.

31 July

This is what happened yesterday at a secret session of Parliament.[55]

... Butler spoke for about 50 minutes, mostly about Burma. He said that the Japanese navy was strong, while England could not send even a single ship from Europe to the Far East. The British Government had consulted with the A[merican] G[overnment] and it had emerged that although the Am. Gov. sympathized with England, it would not be in a position to do anything practical in the event of an armed conflict between Great Britain and Japan.

... He then turned to the USSR. Butler declared on behalf of the British Government that England wishes to maintain and develop cordial relations with the Soviet Union and that Cripps has succeeded in establishing useful contacts with members of the Soviet Government, but pointed out the difficulties standing in the way: the Soviet Union is, says Butler, akin to Peter the Great, in that it is at present disposed to pursue purely 'realistic' policies. In particular, the USSR is currently busy swallowing up the Baltic states. The British Government does not intend to engage in pettifogging politics, yet it cannot recognize the recent changes in the Baltic. ... All the same, the age-old 'struggle between the Teuton and the Slav' and conflicts between Germany and the Soviet Union are objectively advantageous to England.

---

[55] Maisky takes a particular pleasure of relating the content of the secret session. An American journalist who was present recalled that he saw that 'Maisky and the duke of Alba, Franco's ambassador, were the only foreign representatives of high rank there. The session was short, for Mr Churchill had decided upon a secret meeting. When he delivered the time-honoured formula for the exclusion of visitors he looked up at the diplomatic gallery and delivered it plain: "I spy strangers." As we walked out, I said to Maisky: "Which is the stranger in this place, you or Alba?" He smiled his inscrutable smile, famous in London (we used to call him Il Giocondo), and said "Who can tell?".'

6 August

Randolph Churchill turned up unexpectedly in his splendid hussar uniform. It turns out that he has been transferred from his tank battalion to the newly formed 'mobile units',[56] whose task is to 'wage partisan warfare' in the event of a German invasion. Randolph said many interesting things.

He says that the military are very put out: they are ready for an invasion, they are desperately eager to give the Germans a 'warm welcome', but the Germans just won't arrive. British air reconnaissance surveys the shores of France, Belgium and Holland every day: not the slightest sign of an imminent invasion. Can Hitler really have abandoned his idea?

... Nobody really has a clue, but the British Government wants to be ready for every eventuality. It is, for example, currently massing forces in the Middle East. Australians, incidentally, are being transferred there from England. Why Australians in particular? There are two reasons. First, they are good fighters. Second, no one knows how to deal with them in England: they are just too 'free-spirited'. They disregard discipline, disobey their officers, fail to salute and constantly quarrel with the British soldiers. The War Department is only too glad to get them off its hands and is sending them to Egypt and Palestine.

I asked what the British Government presumes *the major strategy of the war* to be?

Randolph replied that the immediate objective of the British Government is to eliminate the threat of invasion. After which come the following aims: to attain air superiority by the end of this year or the beginning of the following; to form a 3 million-strong land force by spring; and to move onto the offensive in 1941.

... We turned to internal affairs. I expressed my doubts about the ability of the British elite to pursue the war 'to the end': for this would raise, in the sharpest terms, the question of the preservation of their present privileges! Are they ready to make such a sacrifice? Hardly. Randolph, however, grinned and replied with a contemptuous wave of his arm: 'Are they ready? Father will make them do it!'...

And he added with undisguised hostility and irritation: 'My father will find it a particular pleasure to shatter the privileges of our upper crust. Oh yes! He'll gladly disperse that vile, decaying gang!'

What does this mean? Randolph's opinions always reflect those of his father. In which direction is the prime minister prepared to 'liquidate' the privileges of the English upper crust: to the Right (towards fascism) or to the Left (towards socialism)?

---

[56] The Special Operations Executive (SOE).

7 August

I saw Attlee in Parliament and had a serious talk with him on the Baltic question. Attlee behaved very strangely. At first he cast doubt on the freedom of the peoples of Estonia, Latvia and Lithuania in expressing their will to join the Soviet Union. So I asked him directly: 'Does this mean you don't wish to recognize the changes that have occurred in the Baltic states on considerations of principle?'

Attlee took fright and hastened to answer: 'No, no! You've misunderstood me.'

He then changed tack, arguing that it was not a matter of principle but of compensation: British citizens had investments in the Baltic states which they will now lose. If the matter of compensation is settled, there will be no complications. ...

15 August

Saw Lloyd George yesterday, who passed on some interesting news: Chamberlain has bowel cancer and although, formally speaking, he remains in the Cabinet, he is to all intents and purposes *done for*. This should have various political repercussions. One is already known: Beaverbrook has been brought into the War Cabinet. Further changes are to be expected. Churchill once again invited Lloyd George to join the War Cabinet (through Beaverbrook), but the old man declined the invitation because he disagrees with the Government on two matters: foreign policy and India.

Lloyd George maintains that the main issue in the sphere of foreign policy is the Soviet Union. But the Cabinet is gambling on the United States. That's a mistake. Even if the United States does enter the war, its participation will not have a practical effect for another two to three years, for the USA has neither an army nor an air force. All this still needs to be created. ...

[Cripps, complained Cadogan to Halifax on 17 August, 'argues that we must give everything – recognition [of the Baltic states], gold, ships and trust to the Russians loving us. This is simply silly. Agreed to tell him to sit tight. We will see what we can do here with Maisky. Exactly nil, I should say. However H. proposes to begin by asking Maisky and Madame to dine – and threatens to ask me too! Extraordinary how we go on kidding ourselves. Russian policy will change exactly when and if they think it will suit them. And if they *do* think that, it won't matter whether we've kicked Maisky in the stomach. Contrariwise, we could give Maisky the Garter and it wouldn't make a penn'orth of difference.']

17 August

The duke of Windsor has arrived with his Mrs Simpson in the Bahamas, where he has been appointed governor. Essentially, of course, this is exile. Why has the former king been treated so harshly?

I've heard from excellent sources that Queen Elizabeth[57] is behind it all. She is 'master' of the house and has the king under her thumb. She is awfully jealous. She has set herself the task of bringing popularity and splendour to the royal family. She sends the king everywhere – to camps, factories, the troops, the frontline – so that he should appear everywhere, so that people should see him and grow used to him. She never rests either: bazaars, hospitals, telephone operators, farmers, etc. – she visits them all, gives her blessing, graces with her presence, parades. She even pulled off the following, highly unusual stunt recently. The queen's brother, who serves in MEC,[58] arranged a private tea party, to which a dozen prominent American journalists were invited. The queen attended the party, too, and for an hour and a half she 'chatted graciously' to the correspondents, together and individually. But not, of course, for the papers. The queen is terribly afraid that the duke of Windsor might return home and 'steal' his brother's popularity, which required so much effort to achieve. That is why the duke of Windsor was exiled to the Bahamas.

20 August

From a purely oratorical point of view, Churchill was not at his best today, speaking in Parliament on matters related to the war and foreign policy. ... On the whole, Churchill's entire speech expressed growing confidence in England's fighting efficiency and a belief that the worst had already passed.

... After Churchill's speech I went into the lobbies. I saw many people ... all share the same mood of high, new-found confidence, and ecstatic admiration of the British air force. People are literally *crazy* about their pilots.

Megan [Lloyd George] expressed interest in the state of Anglo-Soviet relations. There was nothing I could say to reassure her. She was sorry, scolded Halifax, and gave the following explanation for the deadlock in relations between our countries: 'I've known Churchill for many years, ever since I was a small girl. He came over for lunch or dinner to our house on countless occasions, discussing various matters with my father... What always appealed to him most was war. He studied the wars of the past and contemplated the wars of the future. He always imagined himself a military leader, destroying armies, sweeping through Europe, overthrowing his enemies or putting them to flight. Military terms were

---

[57] Wife of King George VI.
[58] Middle East Command.

always on his lips, and his head was forever full of military plans and projects. I'm sure that today he is wholly absorbed and intoxicated by the war. He thinks only of that, is interested only in that. Everything else is secondary to Churchill, Foreign Office included. There he's given Halifax the reins... Ah, that man! I think Halifax is now far more dangerous than Chamberlain.'

There is, I sense, much truth in Megan's words.

22 August

Lunch with Sir Walter Monckton.[59] An idiosyncratic, thoroughly English type. Officially a Tory, but in actual fact an extreme radical to whom even revolutionary ideas are not alien. Legal adviser to the duke of Windsor and a close friend of Cripps. Currently occupies the post of chief censor and thinks about revolution in Europe.

... The conversation then turned to Churchill's role in this war. As leader of the military offensive, Monckton said, Churchill is good. But can he become leader of a political offensive as well? Monckton can't yet say, but he doesn't rule out the possibility that Churchill's romantic affection for Empire plus his love of power might make him such a leader. How far would Churchill go in this direction? This is also unclear to Monckton as yet. Churchill would probably be inclined to curtail sharply the privileges of the capitalist upper crust, but would he do so sufficiently *to win the war*? Of course, everything in England will be done the English way. The introduction of a Soviet system may not be necessary here in order to achieve 'victory'. The introduction of a particular, intermediary form of socialism may be enough. Perhaps Churchill will prove capable of 'accepting' or 'creating' such a form: he is, after all, neither a banker nor a businessman – he is not a man of the City. Churchill is a politician and a writer, who makes his living with his pen. He is not as steeped in the capitalist system as, for example, Chamberlain. He does not depend on shares, interest, landed property, etc. He will earn his 'crust' with literary labour whatever the circumstances. Why, then, should he not become the leader of a political offensive? If this happens, England's transition to a new system will proceed more or less peacefully and calmly. But if Churchill were to oppose the transition to a new system, then major domestic complications would be inevitable.

I listened to Monckton and thought to myself: which way will Churchill go? To the Left or to the Right? Towards socialism or towards fascism? What role is he destined to play in the impending events? In what shades will he be recorded on the pages of history?

---

[59] Sir Walter Turner Monckton, an outstanding radical barrister, he was director general of the Ministry of Information, 1940–41, and later minister of defence under Eden during the 1956 Suez Crisis.

1 September

The Germans have been carrying out mass air raids on England for three weeks now. ...

The daytime raids bring fewer planes than in the first phase, but they are more concentrated and focused. The Germans mainly target the London–Dover–Portland triangle. Their main objectives are ports, airfields, industrial facilities and railways – all in this area. They are obviously paving the way for an invasion. The attacks are frequent, several times a day. At night very few machines fly over England, especially over London. But they go round and round in circles for several hours on end and occasionally drop bombs. This is evidently a form of 'psychological attack' against the broad masses of the population. So far the night raids have not made a major impression on the English.

Of course, this is not the end. We'll see what happens next.

[The 'Battle of Britain' was the prelude to Operation Sealion, the plan for the invasion of Britain earmarked for mid-September. It was adopted in Berchtesgaden on 31 July by the naval and army chiefs, who, however, had serious reservations over what seemed to be insurmountable obstacles. Greatly impressed by the public spirit and resilience displayed by the residents of London, Maisky had become convinced 'that Great Britain will not be invaded by the German army, and that by next year she will be superior in the air ... the air raids in Great Britain will dwindle, and air raids in Germany and her occupied territories will increase in destruction and effect'. He was further convinced that Britain would preserve its stronghold in the Mediterranean, but he could not see how she could possibly dislodge the Germans from the territories they had gained in Europe.

The two alternatives he saw then were a negotiated peace or for Great Britain to become 'a socialized community, not necessarily on the Soviet model, but practically emancipated from capitalism and landlord control. There could be a real and lasting Soviet and British pact to free Europe from Hitler's dominance.' These views certainly were not in conformity with Stalin's outlook – to which Maisky was not privy – of extending the Molotov–Ribbentrop Pact to cover the Balkans and bring the war to an end, with the Soviet Union and Germany sharing dominance in Europe.]

8 September

It seems that the Germans themselves have realized the futility of their former tactics, because just yesterday they switched to new techniques of air warfare.

The Germans undertook a massive and intensive air raid of London yesterday afternoon. It was the first raid conducted on such a scale and with such intensity since the beginning of the war. The British were evidently shocked by the surprise attack and responded rather weakly. As a result the Germans succeeded in setting the dockyards on fire and demolishing many buildings and workers' houses in the East End. The fire is still raging today. I drove around the East End and stood on the hill in Greenwich Park from where I could clearly see columns of fire and clouds of smoke rising from various locations in the port. They say as many as 400 have been killed and 1,500 wounded.

Raids continued throughout the night of the 7th to the 8th. German planes went on pounding the city, taking their bearings from the tongues of fire. The workers' districts – the East End and Kilburn – suffered most of all. Many proletarian shacks have been destroyed. Industrial facilities, power stations, gas plants and so on have escaped serious damage. The Finnish embassy, though, has been wrecked. I don't know whether or not the Germans are targeting military objects; if they are, they are doing a bad job of it. It's hardly surprising: yesterday and today the German planes have been flying at an altitude of about 7 kilometres.

British resistance last night was very feeble. The sky was ablaze with searchlights, but they rarely picked out the enemy planes. The antiaircraft guns were mostly silent. Strange. The people are greatly alarmed at the absence of any proper retaliation. The Government will face serious difficulties if this continues.

9 September

Subbotić[60] visited me a couple of days ago. He arrived in quite a state: he had just received news from Belgrade claiming that the Soviet Union and Germany had reached or were about to reach an agreement about the 'division of spheres of influence' in the Balkans and the Middle East.[61] The Balkans would allegedly fall into Germany's 'sphere of influence' and Iran into the Soviet sphere. The question of Turkey remained undecided. If all this was true, was it not possible to arrange for Yugoslavia to be included in the Soviet 'sphere of influence'?

I set about ridiculing Subbotić, saying that one should not believe any old rumour, particularly now. The Soviet Union is not trying to carve out 'spheres of influence'. The Soviet Union pursues a policy of peace, using the means dictated by the given situation, and it takes a negative view of any widening of the current conflict. The Soviet Union has interests in the Balkans, and certainly does not want to see this part of the world ablaze with the flames of war.

---

[60] Ivan Subbotić, Yugoslav ambassador to Great Britain, 1939–41.
[61] The Russian expression Maisky uses translates as 'Near East'; however, that expression is now little used in English, 'Middle East' being preferred.

Subbotić left somewhat reassured, but not fully convinced.

Today I visited him and managed to dispel his suspicions completely. I assured Subbotić on behalf of the Soviet Government that no agreement exists between the Soviet Union and Germany about the division of 'spheres of influence' in South-East Europe and the Middle East, and that the matter has not even been raised in talks between the USSR and Germany.

Subbotić brightened up, shook my hand firmly and said he would wire this exceptionally important news to Belgrade right away. On parting, he said: 'We shall feel ourselves to be, as it were, under the invisible protectorate of the Soviet Union.'

10 September

Today, we made our first acquaintance with the bombs. It was about one in the morning. German planes were constantly buzzing about over our heads. Agniya and I were in the shelter and were about to go to bed. Suddenly the shelter shook from a heavy blow, the lights went out, and there was a terrible crash very close by, in the very building, it seemed, of the embassy itself...

My first thought was that a bomb had fallen on our house.

I grabbed the telephone and asked Krainsky, who was on guard at the entrance, what had happened. Krainsky, his voice shaking, replied that bombs had fallen somewhere nearby. Our building had not been damaged, apart from the knocked-out window-panes. He couldn't see much in the dark, but it seemed that the house across the street had been shattered to its foundations and had collapsed.

Agniya and I came up from the shelter to the embassy, walked around the building, and looked into our flat. Everything seemed all right except the panes and electric cable. Feeling a little calmer, we returned to the shelter and lay down to sleep.

At six in the morning, when the *all clear* was sounded, we got up and went out into the street. It was growing light. Pieces of asphalt from the road were scattered over our yard. The Lithuanians' house opposite was in one piece, but it gazed vacantly at us from the cavities of its shattered windows. We learned that three small bombs had been dropped two houses down from us (opposite No. 11). There were shell craters there. People were rummaging about. Workers were hammering away at something. I came closer and picked up a piece of shrapnel. The asphalt was still smouldering.

The house diagonally opposite from us was also intact; only two window panes needed replacing.

We returned to the embassy and went to the flat to catch up on our sleep.

48. The embassy's 'luxurious' shelter.

13 September

The seventh day of concentrated air attacks on London.

Once a German, always a German. A German acts according to a meticulous, fixed plan. That's what's happening now. Every day the same pattern is repeated. During the daytime – two, three or four short raids. Each raid generally lasts no more than an hour, sometimes only 15–20 minutes. Mass columns of bombers accompanied by fighters arrive from the French coast. British fighters and antiaircraft guns usually intercept them at the shore, before they approach London. Only small groups of German planes manage to break through to the capital. British fighters meet them again over London. The contest begins and the raiders either plummet or turn back (antiaircraft guns operate very rarely during the daytime for fear of harming the population with splinters). These day raids do little to disturb the city's ordinary life, but cost the Germans dear: they lose 60–80 machines a day, and sometimes more, in daytime combat, as against 20–30 British fighters. Pilot losses are even more disproportionate: the English lose single-pilot fighter planes, in which 40% of the pilots manage to save themselves one way or another, while the Germans lose a significant number of bombers with crews of 4–5 men plus a quantity of fighter planes, some of which carry two men.

... We pay little attention to air raids by day and try to work as usual. We generally succeed. In the evenings it's a different picture. The whole embassy relocates to the basement and we stay there from the beginning of the first raid until bedtime. If bombs start exploding in very close proximity, we move to the 'shelter'. Agniya and I have a special room down below, where we live like students. At night we sleep in the shelter, which is relatively safe, and hear neither the bombs nor the antiaircraft batteries. We sleep like soldiers, of course, dressed or half-dressed. The duty officer wakes us at 5 or 6 a.m., once the 'all clear' has sounded, and all of us – sleepy and dishevelled – return home to sleep in our own beds for the remaining three or four hours. That's how we live. It's more or less tolerable (leaving aside the squabbles among the staff over places in the shelter). But can one live like this for long? We'll see.

How London has changed over these past few days! Beyond recognition. Only a week ago everything looked relatively normal. London still resembled itself. And now?

Now the 'front' has come to London. Many streets are closed to traffic. At every step there are wrecked buildings, cracked pavements and broken windows. Most of the theatres and picture-houses are closed, and those that are open give only matinee performances. The evening black-out brings pitch darkness. Deserted streets. Omnibuses, trams and taxis caught in a raid stand rooted to the spot. Only the underground functions, along with military machines rushing at full pelt through the city. The antiaircraft guns roar, while bombs fall silently from the sky. Blazes flare up in one spot after another, and fire engines tear along the streets with a rumble and a rattle...

Yes, little is left of the old, familiar London. Still less will remain with each passing day.

... As far as transport is concerned, the Germans can only boast of very insignificant successes. True, the London dockyards have been partially burned and destroyed, but the London port continues to operate. True, Waterloo station has been closed and the Charing Cross and Victoria stations have been slightly damaged, but the railways still function normally, albeit with a few interruptions (delays, crammed carriages, etc.). All London's bridges are intact. Omnibuses, trams and taxis are in good order, as are the underground and the aerodromes. A remarkable thing: the Germans bomb the most important London stations intensively every night, but without any serious consequences. ...

And how is morale?

In the first 2–3 days of the current assault, the population, particularly in the East End, was confused, alarmed and nervous. What troubled them most was the total impunity experienced by the Germans and the feeble English response to the night raids. Tens of thousands of people were evacuated from the East End to other parts of the city between 7 and 9 September. However, this mood soon passed. Naturally enough, people are still full of concern and uncertainty about what the coming day will bring. Everybody curses and grumbles about the inconveniences caused by the air raids, but there are no signs of defeatist sentiments. On the contrary, feelings of anger and animosity towards Hitler and Germany are on the rise. And when an Englishman is driven to frenzy, he becomes a very dangerous animal.

The Government's mood? Oh, quite unshakeable: war 'to the end'! Churchill's speech of 11 September made this quite clear. It's precisely the resolute and definite character of the British Government's stance which has done so much to help the masses overcome their initial fright. There is no panic in the country and Churchill intends to fight tooth and nail. ...

14 September

Eden lunched with me yesterday. He looks fine: fresh, tanned, full of energy. His mood is confident and resolute. We spoke, of course, about the war.

Eden holds that the next ten days will be decisive: either Hitler will attempt an invasion over this period or he will have to put it off for a good while, if not indefinitely. After September there are storms at sea, rain and fog, and the difficulties which the German forces will face on landing will increase considerably. Besides, at least half of the German soldiers will be unfit for action when they reach English shores because of sea sickness (the average German is 'a poor sailor'). But even if Hitler decides to try his luck and invade, England is ready.

'Many people here,' said Eden, 'hope he does try. They are sure we will manage to beat off the Germans and the war might thus be brought to an early end.'

'And what do you think?' I asked the war secretary.

'I am also convinced we will manage to repel the Germans,' Eden replied, 'but I would prefer to avoid an invasion: it will come at too great a cost to the civilian population.'

'But still, do you think Hitler will decide to invade?' I continued.

Eden thought for a moment and said: 'I think he will. He likes to do what nobody has done before, what everyone considers impossible. An invasion of England?... This hasn't happened for nearly a thousand years. It's a terrible temptation for Hitler. That is why we are prepared.'

... Eden expressed interest in the condition and prospects of Anglo-Soviet relations.

'Personally, I take the view I took five years ago, when I visited Moscow. I think there are no critical, insurmountable contradictions between England and the Soviet Union in any part of the globe, so relations between our countries can and must be good.'

'Tell me frankly,' I replied, 'do many of your Conservative colleagues think the same?'

Eden admitted that a significant number of people in his party think differently.

'That is the whole problem,' I said. 'That is why I have lost confidence in the possibility of a serious improvement in Anglo-Soviet relations.'

12 October

What a tour that was yesterday!

A bit of history first. During the lunch which the Halifaxes arranged for Agniya and me on 10 September, we spoke at length about air raids and bomb shelters. Some three days earlier, the Germans had launched their air offensive against London. I made a tour of the East End and saw the fires and destruction in the port area. I was struck by the paucity of shelters in this part of London, fewer than in other districts with which I am more familiar. I related this impression during the course of the lunch. About two and a half weeks later, I received a long letter from Halifax where, referring to relevant statistical data, he declared that my impressions were mistaken.[62] In conclusion, he suggested I make a tour of the bomb shelters in the East End. Halifax promised

---

[62] Halifax's figures proved that in the East End boroughs, where the estimated population was 520,930, there were 328,913 private shelters and 81,821 public ones, while in the West End boroughs, where the estimated population was 462,520, there were 128,744 private shelters and 70,109 public, the comparison being 'definitely favourable towards East London'.

to organize the tour. I decided to accept the invitation and visited the East End yesterday with Agniya.

Our 'guide' was Admiral Evans,[63] who has just been appointed 'dictator' of the London bomb shelters. His chief of staff, Colonel [name missing in diary] accompanied us. ... We chatted with the admiral as we drove from one shelter to another. He turned out to be a very cheerful and talkative man. He looks astonishingly young for his 60 years. Evans told us his story.

'I'm an adventure-seeker by nature!' he exclaimed with a charming laugh. 'Much like our prime minister. Oh, Mr Churchill is a great adventurer! That's why I believe he'll win the war.'

Evans' career bears out his self-portrait. His father was a lawyer. At the age of eight the boy ran away from home, headed for 'the West Indies'. He was caught outside the London suburbs and returned to his parents. He did not calm down, however: he ran away for a second, and then a third time. In the end he was tried for 'vagrancy' and put in a workhouse. Then Evans felt drawn to the sea. He entered nautical school and joined the navy at 18. At the age of 21 he sailed with Scott[64] on board the *Discovery* to the Antarctic, where he spent two years. At 28, he set off with Scott again to the South Pole as his second-in-command. Spent three years on the ice. After Scott's death, Evans led the surviving members of the expedition back to England. He captained a destroyer during the last war. In 1917, the destroyer [name missing in diary][65] under the command of Evans, together with another destroyer, the *Swift*, sank six German destroyers. ... In general, Admiral Evans cuts an extraordinarily colourful figure. What's more, he is a first-class demagogue, of the classically English variety.

... I saw this for myself when we arrived in Tilbury. ... By this point the assembled public already knew who had come. They greeted us with loud cheers: 'Hurrah! Long live the Soviet Union!'

Agniya and I were surrounded on all sides. People shook our hands, shouted enthusiastically, punched the air, and embraced us. But the admiral kept his head. He took us by the arm and the three of us, accompanied by a local *warden* and a single policeman, proceeded to the tunnel.

We walked around the shelter for 15–20 minutes. Had a look at the medical aid post, where they asked us to sign the visitors' book. We observed the primitive – very primitive – sleeping arrangements which the East Enders had devised for themselves. The place was crowded and filthy, with wretched

---

[63] Admiral Edward Evans, a naval commander and Antarctic explorer; commander-in-chief, The Nore, 1935–39, he took part in the Norwegian campaign. Retiring from the navy in 1941, he was appointed London's regional commissioner for civil defence.

[64] Robert Falcon Scott, British Royal Naval officer and explorer.

[65] HMS *Broke*.

49. The Maiskys with Admiral Evans.

bedding on the stone floor, heaps of junk, and hundreds of children of all ages and appearances. The variety of individuals, and the variety of their conditions, was astonishing. I saw emaciated and hungry faces, and next to them red, well-fed physiognomies which belonged, I reckon, to the category of Whitechapel shopkeepers. Tall phlegmatic Englishmen jostled with rowdy Irishmen and nervously mobile Jews. Yes, the whole ethnographic spectrum of the East End was there.

Suddenly the admiral turned to the *warden* accompanying us and exclaimed: 'Gather the people! I want to say a few words to them.'

The *warden* jumped on a platform of sorts and set about shouting at the top of his voice, waving his arms: 'Over here! Over here! Admiral Evans will speak!'

The people quickly hurried over to the platform, onto which the admiral, with a lightness unusual for his age, had also managed to jump. A big, tightly packed, steaming crowd was soon assembled. Men, women and children. Hats, caps and bare heads. About two thousand people. Agniya and I stood at the foot of the platform, trying to keep in the shadows, and waited with curiosity to see what would happen next. Suddenly the admiral bent down towards us and, gesturing emphatically, addressed me: 'And what about you? Over here please! Over here!'

The admiral started tugging me and Agniya onto the platform. Someone helped us from behind and a moment later we were standing side by side with the admiral, who was waving his arms about energetically and shouting to the crowd: 'Come closer! Closer! Don't be shy!'

The people moved closer, bunching up tight. Evans took off his cap, waved it and exclaimed: 'Our country is the country of *fair play*! Am I right?'

An uncertain rumble passed through the crowd. One could interpret it as a sign of approval or as a mark of disapproval. The admiral continued unabashed: 'A few days ago the king and queen visited you here!'

The same uncertain rumble passed through the crowd, and someone in the back row cried out: 'What about it?'

The admiral went on without batting an eyelid.

'And today,' he shouted with sudden emphasis, 'I've brought you a different guest! I've brought you the Soviet ambassador!'

And with a wide sweep of his arm, Evans gestured towards Agniya and me.

Unrestrained cheering among the crowd. Everyone started shouting: 'Hurrah! Long live the Soviet Union! Long live the Soviet ambassador!'

Then Evans moved on to other topics. He said he sympathized with the people of the East End with all his heart. He couldn't promise them miracles, but he was doing all he could to improve the situation. Half of the tunnel had been freed to turn it into a shelter. It had been cleansed of rubbish and stench. That was progress, but it was just the beginning.

...The admiral mopped his forehead, put on his cap, and we all moved to the edge of the platform in order to get down. I already considered myself 'saved': given my delicate diplomatic status, it would have been a bit *embarrassing* for me to speak at this improvised meeting in the East End. So I hastened to get down, when I was suddenly met with deafening cries: '*Maisky! Speech! Speech!*'

Smiling broadly in all directions, I did my best to get out of it, but the shouts grew louder and louder and the people standing in the front rows rushed towards the platform to prevent my descent. The admiral spread out his arms, and giving me a friendly slap on the shoulder exclaimed: 'And really, why not say a couple of words? Speak! You must speak!'

All escape routes had been cut off. Standing on the edge of the platform, I gestured for silence and said: 'On behalf of my wife and myself I thank you kindly, friends, for the cordial welcome which you have given us here today.'

My voice was too weak for the gigantic space, but the crowd responded with frenzied shouts: 'Hurrah! Hurrah!'

'I'm especially touched by this welcome,' I continued, 'because I well understand that your greetings are addressed not so much to me and my wife as to the country I represent.'

The shouts grew even wilder. A section of the crowd started singing the 'Internationale'.

'Let me thank you once more, with all my heart!' I concluded and began getting down from the platform.

A few seconds later and we were all on the ground. The crowd was delirious. A path opened for the three of us – myself, Agniya, and the admiral. Agniya and I were once again squeezed on all sides, embraced, and shaken by the hand. An elderly woman with light brown hair and a face webbed with deep wrinkles cried out in Russian: 'Our Russia is still alive!'

Hundreds of people on both sides raised their clenched fists in salutation. The 'Internationale' sounded louder and louder.

'What are they singing?' asked the admiral naively. '"*Red Flag*"?'

'No,' I replied, 'they are singing the "Internationale". It's our Soviet national hymn.'

'Is that right?' The admiral was surprised. 'I had never heard it before.'

We arrived, at last, at our cars and climbed in, to the accompaniment of loud shouts: 'Long live the Soviet Union!'

Once again, the 'Internationale'. Once again, raised fists.

The admiral was somewhat amazed. He had hardly expected the Soviet ambassador to be accorded such a warm welcome. But he lost neither his presence of mind nor his good cheer. We headed off to the embassy for a cup of tea. And on the way I thought: 'This is how the East End greets the Soviet ambassador today. If the war lasts two more years, Piccadilly will greet him in a similar way.'

* * *

... Randolph Churchill dropped in. He assured me that *invasion is off*. He outlined the prospects for the winter in the following way.

An Anglo-German air war and defensive operations in Egypt. The British Government is certain it can repulse the Italians there. By spring 1941, England will achieve air superiority over Germany. It will be followed by British offensives against Germany in the air and against Italy in the air, by land and at sea – in Africa and in Europe. England will not yet be ready for an offensive against Germany by land in 1941. The blockade of Germany, of course, will continue unceasingly and implacably.

I wonder how events will develop in reality.

[In his diary, Bilainkin describes a tour he was given of the £1,500 (approximately £65,000 in today's money) air-raid shelter constructed 'many feet below garden level' at the Soviet embassy (still *in situ* today!):

The tube, of reinforced concrete, is the size of that in London's underground railways; it is covered by a foot of reinforced concrete, earth, more reinforced concrete, more earth, yet more reinforced concrete and yet much more earth. The whole is well ventilated and has several compartments. One is for the Ambassador and Mme. Maisky; here I saw a portable wireless set (house manager promptly obtained Moscow on the short-wave), a house telephone, a central exchange telephone, two forms of lighting, good bedding (tasteful blue satin). Embassy has special plant for cleaning air in shelter; pick-axes are in position, shovels, impressive boxes full of meat in tins, sardines, peaches; also soda water, knives, forks and spoons.

The families and children of the Soviet personnel at the embassy were evacuated in early October to 'a fairly large and comfortable house' in a village near Cheltenham. Agniya categorically refused to leave London. 'Her presence by my side,' recalled Maisky, 'was a serious support for me. And for political reasons it was more to our advantage that the British should see the wife of the Soviet Ambassador "in the front line", not in the rear.' To catch up on their sleep, they tended to spend the weekends out of London at the house of their close friend, Juan Negrín, the former prime minister of the Spanish Republican government. Maisky hinted a couple of times to Molotov that the Germans could perhaps be asked to spare the embassy. He was convinced, as he cabled Molotov, that it was no coincidence that the Soviet embassy was particularly targeted by the Germans. He attributed it to Ribbentrop's 'extreme hostility' towards him personally, dating back to the German foreign minister's time as ambassador to London. 'It may seem a fantasy,' he concluded, 'but we now live in fantastic times.']

22 October

On behalf of the British Government, Cripps has asked C[omrade] Molotov for an audience on a matter of 'paramount political importance'. C[omrade] Molotov could not receive Cripps, so instead Cripps met C[omrade] Vyshinsky,[66] to whom he submitted a special memorandum. Its concluding part contained three points:

(1) The British Government announces its readiness to recognize 'de facto' the changes in the Baltics so as to settle 'de jure' the whole issue later, probably after the war.

---

[66] Andrei Yanuarievich Vyshinsky, a former Menshevik, he was prosecutor general of the USSR, 1935–39, in charge of the rigged political trials, most of which ended in death sentences being handed down. Deputy chairman of the Council of People's Commissars, 1939–44; first deputy to people's commissar for foreign affairs, 1940–46; minister for foreign affairs, 1949–53.

(2) The British Government declares itself prepared to ensure the participation of the USSR, on an equal basis, in the settlement of European affairs after the war. (3) The British Government promises not to participate in any military actions against the USSR.

C[omrade] Vyshinsky told Cripps that he would report the matter to the Soviet Government.

29 October

Cripps submitted a note of protest to NKID against the Soviet Government's decision to take part in the Danube commission, accusing the USSR of violating neutrality.

2 November

C[omrade] Vyshinsky handed Cripps the response of the Soviet Government concerning the Danube question, which boiled down to a request to the British Government not to meddle in matters which don't concern it. ...

[The British initiative came five days after the invitation for Molotov to meet Hitler in Berlin on 11 November had reached the Kremlin. 'It looks,' Lloyd George wrote to Maisky, 'as if once more we have been too late.']

4 November

Conversing with Churchill on 3 July, I asked: what does the *major strategy* of the British Government consist of?'

Churchill grinned, shrugged his shoulders, and said: '*Major strategy*? First of all, to survive the next three months, and then we shall see.'

Four months have passed since then. England has not only survived: she is stronger than she was at the time of my talk with the prime minister. German plans for an invasion have fallen through. The famous *Channel* has saved Great Britain once more, as it has on more than one occasion down the ages. Hitler's weakness at sea, together with the failure to secure air supremacy over the Channel, wrecked Germany's only chance of overcoming the resistance supplied by a strip of water 40 kilometres wide. Hitler experienced the same fate as Napoleon 135 years ago: he lost the *Battle of Britain*. It is still too early to review all the consequences of this fact, but they must be serious.

As far as one can judge on the basis of all the information available in London (which tallies well with the facts), Hitler's *major strategy* offered the following picture: a triumphant conclusion of the war before the onset of winter. ... All Hitler's plans and hopes came unstuck. England's resistance, which Hitler did not expect, and the increasingly active role of the USA in the war, upset all his calculations. ...

But for England an extremely difficult situation is now emerging. Its official goal is 'to crush Hitlerism', which amounts to crushing Germany. All, on both Right and Left, swear to do this. Very well... But how? It is one thing to avoid defeat – England may assume it has achieved this. But winning the war is a very different matter. And it is not clear how this may be achieved in the foreseeable future.

... A prolonged war of attrition over many years bears huge revolutionary potential – not only for Germany, but for England and the British Empire as well. There can be no doubt that the English elite will set about seeking a 'compromise' with 'Hitlerism' long before these possibilities become realities.

That is why it seems to me that the ruling classes here are faced with an acute dilemma: either to find new allies who could help England 'settle' this war by purely military means with their authority and might, or, should this prove impossible, to seek a compromise peace...

The hunt for allies is now on, with the United States to the fore. But in the long run the ruling circles also dream of an alliance with the Soviet Union, in spite of all our refutation, explanation, etc. ...

This is what I can see now from my 'London window'.

Much will depend on various other factors that are difficult to take into account at present: on Germany – its military and diplomatic actions and its internal condition; on the sentiments of the broad European masses; and on the activity and consciousness of the proletariat...

Who can foresee all this?[67]

11 November

A huge bomb fell near the trade mission building on the night of the 10th to 11th, causing massive damage. The building still stands, but all the windows are smashed, the inner walls and partitions have collapsed, the furniture is broken, etc. The building has become uninhabitable, and much money and time will be needed to repair it. Our economic planners will have to move. Fortunately, no one was hurt. Everyone was sleeping in the mission's shelter and escaped with nothing worse than a fright. ...

---

[67] Maisky's evaluation (based on the diary entry) which he sent to Moscow evidently left a mark on Stalin's directive to Molotov for the negotiations with Hitler in Berlin.

12 November

Subbotić came to see me. He is terribly alarmed and concerned about C[omrade] Molotov's visit to Berlin.

'The Italo-Greek war,' said Subbotić, 'Graziani's[68] plans in Egypt, and British operations in the Mediterranean – all that completely pales in comparison. The outcome of the war, maybe the fate of the world, will be decided at that meeting in Berlin!'

Naturally enough, Subbotić worries most of all about the possible connections between the Berlin meeting and the events in the Balkans, primarily in Yugoslavia and Turkey. He hopes that 'Russia will not forget Yugoslavia', and that the interests of his country will not suffer as a result of the meeting in Berlin. Clearly, C[omrade] Molotov's visit to Berlin has caused great unease in Belgrade.

I told Subbotić that I was not privy to the agenda of the Berlin meeting but, judging by the persons accompanying C[omrade] Molotov, economic issues will be the focus of attention. I could also assure him in advance that the Berlin meeting would not bring about any changes whatsoever to our policy of neutrality.

[Since the fall of France, Hitler had been facing the dilemma of whether to attempt to bring the Molotov–Ribbentrop Pact up to date through arrangements in South-East Europe or, alternatively, to proceed with vigorous preparations for war. The realization that Russia had no intention of retreating from the Balkans prompted Schulenburg, the German ambassador in Moscow, to seek a four-power pact between Germany, Russia, Italy and Japan, in order to delineate spheres of influence. Hitler's expectations of the meeting did not tally with those of his ambassador: he assumed that, after his general idea for the 'new Europe' was outlined, the negotiations would gradually crystallize into a rigid proposal for delimitation that would exclude Russia from Europe and the Balkans and reflect German military supremacy. He had no intention of accommodating the Russians, beyond forcing Turkey to yield to some guarantees in the Straits and security arrangements in the Baku region. There is little to support the prevailing view that, during his visit to Berlin, Molotov conspired with Hitler to divide up the entire world – and more specifically to carve up the British Empire.

The directive for the talks, dictated to Molotov in Stalin's dacha and taken in longhand, was confined to intrinsic Soviet interests in the Balkans and the Turkish Straits, and was dominated by considerations of security. Foremost were repeated demands for the establishment of Soviet control of the mouth of the Danube and involvement in the

---

[68] Rodolfo Graziani (marquess di Neghelli), Italian viceroy of Ethiopia, 1936–37; chief of staff of the Italian armed forces, 1939; governor of Libya, 1940.

decision on the 'fate of Turkey'. Bulgaria, as in the war of 1877–78, was to be 'the main topic of the negotiations' and was expected to fall into the Soviet sphere of influence. In order to mitigate German influence, Stalin sought to include even a battered Britain in a peace conference, which he expected to be promptly convened. Maisky's assertion that Britain could not be written off and might even emerge victorious at the end of a slow and arduous process was of cardinal importance for the objectives sought at the Berlin meeting. A telegram from Stalin caught up with Molotov on the train as he was *en route* to Berlin. This reaffirmed the instructions not to broach with Germany any issues concerning the British Empire. Indeed, in Berlin Molotov endorsed Maisky's view that it was 'too early to bury England'.]

19 November

... Kennedy came by to pay a farewell visit. True, formally he is leaving for 'consultations' with Roosevelt, but he did not conceal the fact that he will not be returning.

Needless to say, we spoke about the war and about the prospects for England. Kennedy is still a 'pessimist': of course, the threat of an invasion has passed, but what will happen in Egypt? Judging by the US ambassador's reliable and very accurate information, defeat looms for the English there.

I replied that although I have no grounds to be an Anglophile, in my duties as ambassador I try to be 'objective' and weigh every 'for' and 'against' dispassionately, in order to provide my Government with correct information. Taking this approach to the question of war in Egypt, I must repeat what I said about the invasion in June: the British have enough cards in their hands to preserve their position in Egypt and in the Middle East in general – everything depends on whether they manage to play their cards well. I can't say whether they will or not, but the conduct of the English when faced with possible invasion inclines me to think they will probably be able to play their cards well in Egypt, too. But time will tell.

I asked Kennedy what he thought about the possibility of the United States entering the war.

Kennedy ducked the question, saying he had not been to his homeland for a long time and was not aware of the sentiments prevailing there. He personally thinks that the United States should not enter the war and that direct US participation in military operations would be less advantageous to the British than US non-interference. Then Kennedy said, as though in self-justification: 'I've never advocated appeasement as a matter of principle. Everything I said could be summed up in the following way: if the British Government has succeeded through its policies in dispersing all its friends, both former and potential, then it's senseless for it to risk a war.'

Taking his leave, Kennedy exclaimed with his loud, braying laugh: 'It's easy to be an American ambassador here in England, but devilishly difficult to be a Soviet one! But by God, you cope with your job superbly.'

I thanked Kennedy for his compliment (he likes to shower compliments left, right and centre), but I could not return it even out of courtesy. For although it is indeed easy to be an American ambassador in England, Kennedy has not been up to the job at all. Roosevelt, Churchill and the English political world – all are dissatisfied with him.[69] That is the cause of his dismissal, not his desire to return to his 'business affairs', as he told me today. At the bottom of it all lies the fact that Kennedy is a wealthy, orthodox Irish Catholic who has a mortal terror of revolution and would like to live in harmony with 'fascist dictators'. That explains his dislike of the Soviet Union, his liking of Chamberlain, whom he has always supported, and his fear of a war which may, under certain circumstances, unleash revolutionary potentialities.

C[omrade] Molotov's visit to Berlin has made a big splash in England.

At first, everyone got terribly frightened. The Germans were inflating the importance of the visit and predicting a decision of 'world-historical' significance. They let it be known that an exceptionally significant document was in preparation, and hinted at a 'division of the world' between the 'Axis' and the USSR: Europe would go to Germany, Africa to Italy, China and Eastern Asia to Japan, and India and Iran to the USSR. People in London only half-believed all this, but they got themselves into a state about it all the same. The initial response in political circles was: 'Look where Halifax has led us! Instead of tearing Russia away from Germany, he made Molotov's visit to Berlin possible.'

Rumours of Halifax's imminent dismissal have been doing the rounds again. The *News Chronicle* and the *Daily Herald* published sensational reports to this effect: Halifax would leave the FO within a fortnight. This was officially denied, but rumours and speculation continued. ...

30 November

Agniya and I went to the countryside to visit the young Churchill couple.[70] They live in the village of Ickleford, Herts, by the church, in the rectory, which has been empty for over half a century. The big house – 15 rooms – is too expensive for the local rector. So the clergymen live in a little cottage nearby, paying a small rent for it. The rectory is rented out to interested parties for 100

---

[69] Halifax entered in his diary: 'In the afternoon I saw Joe Kennedy, who told me he had decided to chuck up his job the week after next, and seemed in very bad temper with his own Administration. I don't think he is a very good fellow.'

[70] Randolph and Pamela Churchill were divorced in 1945, and she later married Averell Harriman, Roosevelt's personal envoy to Europe and US ambassador to Moscow.

pounds a year (the sum has not changed for 50 years – that's British conservatism for you!) and the rector uses the money to cover his current expenses.

Randolph and his wife are awfully proud of their seven-week-old heir, whom they have called Winston.[71] They showed us their treasure: a wonderful boy and, for his age, a very sentient being. He somewhat resembles his grandfather. I liked another of the prime minister's grandsons even more – Julian Sandys, a red-haired boy of three, vigorous, agile and cheerful. Sandys[72] married the prime minister's daughter, and his family shares the house with Randolph and his family. The PM's other daughter [Sarah], who is unmarried and a film actress, also lives there. On the whole, Ickleford is a 'Churchill commune'. Randolph will soon depart for the Mediterranean. He and his 20-year-old wife were a bit on edge today, maybe because of his forthcoming departure.

Randolph was very talkative. We argued at length about the war prospects. He, of course, could not accept anything other than complete 'victory'. When I asked him 'How?', he started mumbling something incoherent. Randolph's calculations are based on the following: if England delivers a *knock-out* blow to Italy next summer, and the United States enters the war after that, German 'morale' will crack.

'What if it doesn't crack? What then?' I queried. Then, Randolph thinks, the war will continue for one, two, three, even ten years, until the superior British resources and manpower (including the Empire) eventually produce the desired effect. Childish reasoning!

I expounded my thoughts about a 'political offensive' being the sole condition that would permit England 'to win the war'. Randolph brushed aside my arguments, saying: 'There will be no such offensive under the present prime minister! My father is not a socialist.'

I asked why the prime minister had agreed to lead the Conservative Party. His position may constrain him in the domestic and external manoeuvring that is inevitable during a war.

Randolph said his father is not afraid of that eventuality. He is confident that he will be the boss, not a hostage, of the Conservative Party. I have serious doubts on this account as well. Well, we shall see.

12 December

I visited Vansittart today. I hadn't seen him for several months and I was struck by his appearance: he looks emaciated, much older, and has become very highly

---

[71] A Conservative MP from 1970 to 1983.

[72] Edwin Duncan Sandys (Baron Duncan-Sandys), Conservative MP from 1935, was married to Churchill's daughter Diana. Wounded in action in Norway in 1941, he became a junior minister in his father-in-law's Cabinet and in various Conservative Cabinets after the war.

strung. The wrinkles on his face are deeper. His hands tremble. Although he is only 59, he is almost an old man. He has a cold. His wife is losing weight and is confined to her bed. In general, his life has not been a bed of roses recently.[73]

... Vansittart spoke eloquently and at length about the misunderstanding and underestimation of the English character abroad. It has been so since time immemorial. Napoleon, Bismarck, the Kaiser, and now Hitler, Ribbentrop and Mussolini – they all were and are grossly mistaken in fancying the English to be a 'nation of shopkeepers', 'degenerate gentlemen', 'depraved plutocrats', etc., who cannot and will not fight whatever the circumstances. A profound mistake. True, in peacetime the English like comfort, convenience, sport, travelling. They dislike drills, gaudy uniforms, goose-step and spurs. They give the impression of being a deeply 'civilian', pampered nation. And a little too much fat has grown on their bones in recent decades.

However, if their backs are against the wall and their lives are endangered, if they are irritated or enraged, they change beyond recognition. They become malicious, stubborn, ready to fight like animals and sink their fangs into the enemy. That is why the English, despite entering every war unprepared, with scarce forces and often with poor leaders, never lose wars. This leads Vansittart to the conclusion that England will defeat Germany in 1942 or 1943.

Such is now the typical philosophy of the ruling class, and not of the ruling class alone. ...

16 December

... I walked home through *Kensington Gardens*. It was damp and slightly foggy. The park was empty. On the shore of the little lake I observed an almost biblical scene: a young bespectacled soldier in crumpled, filthy uniform was feeding the swans and gulls. He had a big bag under his arm from which he was taking the crumbs and throwing them to the birds. Three big swans climbed out of the water and, gracefully bending their necks, took the crumbs straight from the soldier's palm. Hundreds of gulls surrounded the soldier, crying wildly and violently flapping their wings. They rushed about him as if possessed, plucked pieces of bread out of the air, and landed on his shoulders and arms, even on his head. And he, a puny, clumsy and pensive little soldier, peered through his spectacles with a certain surprise at this kingdom of birds, as if wishing to say: 'Yes, man and nature are one.'

---

[73] Maisky's unflattering description might have been triggered by a harsh private letter he had received from Vansittart, warning him that 'an increasing number of complaints are being made against your Embassy for offences against the black-out. I am sure that you personally must be unaware of what is going on, but it is evident that a firm hand on your part is required. I hope you will see to this at once.'

29 December

To Churt to see Lloyd George. I found the old man lucid, vigorous and in good spirits. An astonishing individual: after all, he will be 78 in three weeks!

Lloyd George related to me the particulars of Churchill's proposal to appoint him ambassador in Washington. On 16 December, the PM invited him to lunch and made his proposal (I recall how, while I was talking to Lloyd George in his office, Sylvester hurried into the room and whispered to the old man that there had been a call from 10, Downing Street asking him to be there by 1 p.m.).

But Lloyd George refused the offer. Why?

'To start with,' the old man explained, 'an ambassador has no control over the policy he must represent. I don't want to find myself in such a position. That's the main thing. Secondly, the post in Washington would be beyond me, physically speaking. Poor Lothian, during his last visit to London, complained bitterly that he had turned into a talking machine...'

... 'Well, the political result is positive: Eden is in the Foreign Office and Halifax goes to America. Strangely, he did not want to go and Lady Halifax was simply *furious*. The Court did not like it either: Lady Halifax, as I'm sure you know, is one of the queen's ladies-in-waiting. But Churchill dug in and got his way.'

Lloyd George lunched with the prime minister again on 20 December. They discussed matters of war and politics.

I asked Lloyd George about Churchill's present attitude to the Soviet Union. Lloyd George replied that in general the PM is in favour of improving Anglo-Soviet relations and will support Eden in that respect, but he is hardly prepared to go as far as Eden. For Churchill would like to 'win the war' without Soviet aid, so as not to have any obligations towards the Soviet Union. Besides, he counts on receiving active support from the United States.

Then we spoke about the Government's situation. Lloyd George says that Churchill's position is very secure, but quite a few of his ministers are 'a disappointment'. Bevin[74] is one of them.

'On the whole,' Lloyd George resumed, 'we have a good old Tory Government, even though there are several Labourites in it, who are sometimes more conservative than the Conservatives themselves.'

The old man burst into infectious laughter and added: 'They genuinely believe that they can win the war by military means alone. True capitalist idiocy!'

... I asked what Lloyd George himself thought of the war. His reply boiled down to the following: Lloyd George does not believe it possible for England to 'win the war' solely by force of arms. ... England can achieve a true 'victory' only

---

[74] Ernest Bevin, member of the General Council of the TUC, 1925–40; minister of labour and national service, 1940–45; fierce opponent of appeasement as well as of communism. Foreign secretary in the post-war Labour Government.

if the military offensive is backed up by a political offensive and even overshadowed by it at a certain point; that is, if England can, like a snake, cast off its capitalist skin in the course of the war and become an *essentially* socialist state. ... Be that as it may, the old man is very sceptical, and not without reason, about the British Government's readiness 'to cast off the capitalist skin'. So what can be expected? ... A situation conducive to the opening of peace negotiations may take shape next autumn or winter. That is when the Soviet Union and the United States could play a major role as mediators and builders of the future world.

[Though Maisky did 'not expect miracles', Eden's return to the Foreign Office on Christmas Eve raised new expectations. There was, as he wrote to Eden, 'a lot of debris to be cleared away, and the sooner it is started so much the better'. Shortly after the holidays, Maisky paid a visit to the Foreign Office, to find Eden beaming with excitement. The gloom which had pervaded Halifax's office had been replaced by a bright and orderly atmosphere. Eden projected the image of a triumphant return. He wished to convince Maisky that no major conflict of interest in foreign policy existed between the two countries. The ambassador did not beat about the bush, explaining to Eden that only British recognition of the Soviet absorption of the Baltic states could lead to an improvement in relations. Soon enough it became obvious that the change in scenery did not entail a change in policy. Like those of his predecessor, Eden's interests remained tactical, aimed at detaching Russia from Germany. However, Maisky, who was eager to exploit the change, deviated from the canon, admitting to Eden that Russia certainly did not wish to see Germany emerge as the victorious power in Europe. Soviet foreign policy, he explained succinctly, rested on three principles:

> First, they were concerned with promoting their own national interests. Secondly, his Government wished to remain out of the war. Thirdly, they wished to avoid the extension of the war to any countries neighbouring Russia. In general Soviet policy was not expansionist: the Soviets had already enough territories.

Maisky certainly did his utmost to impress on his superiors at home the significance of the change.]

30 December

Focused air raids have arrived, at last, in London, or more precisely its centre – the City.

On the night of the 29th, between 7 and 10 p.m., about 150 German bombers showered the City with incendiary bombs. The German planes are said to have dropped tens of thousands of bombs. As the City is empty at night (its daytime population is 500,000, but only 20,000 at night), there were no people there to deal with the bombs. The flames spread to a great many buildings and streets before the fire-fighters arrived. It was a terrible and beautiful spectacle. In the east, half the sky was aglow as we watched from the embassy. The City burned all night and throughout the day today. Even now, the fires have not been completely extinguished.

... Usually, a shower of incendiary bombs is followed by a shower of high-explosive bombs. This time, however, there were only incendiary bombs. But even without them the destruction in the City is immense. True, the Bank of England and the Stock Exchange have remained intact (how symbolic!), but the famous Guildhall has been reduced to ashes, and nearly a dozen ancient churches (the works of Wren) of great historical and architectural value have been destroyed. Many offices, stores, small shops, etc. are wrecked. All Moorgate Street, where our trade mission was located before 1927, lies in ruins and has been closed. As for 'military targets', only the Central Telegraph, located in the City, has suffered badly, while the Waterloo Bridge has been lightly damaged. Few human casualties.

50. The sanctuary of Maisky's private study, watched over by the *vozhd*.

1941

1 January

The New Year, 1941. What will it bring us?

My hypothetical forecast is the following.

This will be the decisive year of the war. Hitler must make a *supreme effort* (most probably in spring or in summer) in order to bring the war to an end this year – in his own favour, of course. It would be catastrophic for him to prolong the war into 1942 and subsequent years because in that phase of the war time will be on the side of England (and the USA). By the beginning of 1942, British military production will be at its peak, while the US military industry will be entering the phase of full-scale production. Then England and the USA will be capable of simply raining bombs and shells on Germany. By that time the British Empire will also have sufficiently mobilized its human and material resources. In a word, from 1942 onwards there will be no hope for Germany to tie the war, let alone win it, since the world remains on the plane of 'normal' capitalist relations. ... So a final, decisive *knockout blow* becomes all the more imperative.

But where? In which direction?

I think it will be directed against England, for a blow in any other direction cannot produce a decisive effect. ...

12 January

Yesterday evening at around 8.30 I was sitting at my typewriter and had just begun the third chapter of my memoirs about emigration. Suddenly I heard the rattle of a machine-gun outside. I raised my head. What was it? A diving German plane?...

At that same moment Agniya ran into the room. She was excited and out of breath, and shouted: 'Bombs! Fire...The street's as light as day!'

Together we ran to the bathroom window. Indeed, all was ablaze outside. Hundreds of bright white fires sparkled under the trees in Kensington Gardens:

incendiary bombs. Two firebombs were also burning in the garden of our Nepalese neighbours. The same in the courtyard of the house adjacent to the Nepalese. As far as we could see, the courtyards of all the houses in Kensington Palace Gardens were lit by the bluish-white flames of burning bombs.

We rushed to another window that overlooked our garden. Several bombs were burning below in various spots near the shelter and near the staircase that descended from the white hall.

I raced downstairs and began mobilizing our people. There were two more bombs outside the front porch, and further bombs by the garage and in the passage between our house and that of our Nepalese neighbours. Firebombs sparkled opposite in the yard of the Lithuanians and farther along the street. It was light enough to read a newspaper. But our thoughts were not set on reading.

Our people assembled. Some ran to put out the bombs at the front of the building and others rushed to the garden. I was with the second group. We took sandbags and poured sand over the flames. The bombs were extinguished fairly quickly. I put out one bomb; Agniya came running down to put out another. All our bombs were extinguished in about 15 minutes. Luckily, not a single one fell on the roof. ...

3 February

A few days ago I had an unexpected visitor: the well-known Zionist leader Dr Weizmann.[1] He is a tall, elderly, elegantly dressed gentleman with a pale yellow tinge to his skin and a large bald patch on his head. His face is very wrinkled and marked by dark blotches of some kind. His nose is aquiline and his speech calm and slow. He speaks excellent Russian, although he left Russia 45 years ago.

Weizmann came to discuss the following matter: at present Palestine has no market for her oranges – would the USSR take them in exchange for furs?

... In the course of the conversation about oranges, Weizmann talked about Palestinian affairs in general. Furthermore, he spoke about the present situation and the prospects for world Jewry. Weizmann takes a very pessimistic view. ... Weizmann spoke about Soviet Jews in particular: 'I'm not worried about them. They are not under any threat. In 20 or 30 years' time, if the present regime in your country lasts, they will be assimilated.'

'What do you mean, assimilated?' I retorted. 'Surely you know that Jews in the USSR enjoy all the rights of a national minority, like the Armenians, Georgians and Ukrainians and so on?'

---

[1] Dr Chaim Weizmann, President of the World Zionist Organization and the Jewish Agency for Palestine, 1921–31 and 1935–46; president of the State of Israel, 1949–52.

'Of course I know that,' Weizmann answered, 'but when I say "assimilated",
all I mean is that Soviet Jews will gradually merge with the general current of
Russian life, as an inalienable part of it. I may not like this, but I'm ready to
accept it: at least Soviet Jews are on firm ground, and their fate does not make
me shudder. But I cannot think without horror about the fate of the 6–7 million
Jews who live in Central or South-East Europe – in Germany, Austria,
Czechoslovakia, the Balkans and especially Poland. What's going to happen to
them? Where will they go?'

Weizmann sighed deeply and continued: 'If Germany wins the war they
will all simply perish. However, I don't believe that the Germans will win. But
even if England wins the war, what will happen then?'

Here he began to set out his fears. The English – and especially their
colonial administrators – don't like Jews. This is particularly noticeable in
Palestine, which is inhabited by both Jews and Arabs. Here the British 'high
commissioners' undoubtedly prefer the Arabs to the Jews. Why? For one very
simple reason. An English colonial administrator will usually get his training
in British colonies like Nigeria, the Sudan, Rhodesia and so on. These places
have a well-defined pattern of rule: a few roads, some courts, a little missionary
activity, a little medical care for the population. It's all so simple, so straightforward, so calm. No serious problems, and no complaints on the part of the
governed. The English administrator likes this, and gets used to it. But in
Palestine?

Growing more animated, Weizmann continued: 'You won't get very far
with a programme like that here. Here there are big and complex problems. It's
true that the Palestinian Arabs are the kind of guinea pigs the administrator is
used to, but the Jews reduce him to despair. They are dissatisfied with everything, they ask questions, they demand answers – and sometimes these answers
are not easily supplied. The administrator begins to get angry and to see the
Jews as a *nuisance*. But the main thing is that the administrator constantly feels
that the Jew is looking at him and thinking to himself: "Are you intelligent? But
maybe I'm twice as intelligent as you."'

... And then, taking all these circumstances into account, Weizmann
anxiously asks himself: 'What has a British victory to offer the Jews?' The question leads him to some uncomfortable conclusions. For the only 'plan' which
Weizmann can think of to save Central European Jewry (and in the first place
Polish Jewry) is this: to move a million Arabs now living in Palestine to Iraq,
and to settle four or five million Jews from Poland and other countries on the
land which the Arabs had been occupying. The British are hardly likely to
agree to this. And if they don't agree, what will happen?

I expressed some surprise about how Weizmann hoped to settle 5 million
Jews on territory occupied by 1 million Arabs.

'Oh, don't worry,' Weizmann burst out laughing. 'The Arab is often called the son of the desert. It would be truer to call him the father of the desert. His laziness and primitivism turn a flourishing garden into a desert. Give me the land occupied by a million Arabs, and I will easily settle five times that number of Jews on it.'

Weizmann shook his head sadly and concluded: 'The only thing is, how do we obtain this land?'

[In October, Ben-Gurion[2] met Maisky and, like Weizmann before him, tried to win him over by emphasizing that, although Zionism was 'a matter of life and death' for the movement, they were also 'most serious' about their socialist aims, and the proof was the successful construction in Palestine of a 'nucleus of a socialist commonwealth'. But behind the ideological lip service, Ben-Gurion tried to enlist Maisky's support for the Zionist aspiration in Palestine, hailing the role of the Soviet Union, which he expected to be 'at the least one of the three leading powers which would determine the fate of the new world'. The efforts culminated in Maisky's visit to Palestine on his way back from Russia in 1943.[3]]

11 February

Subbotić came by, extremely troubled by the latest news about increasing German pressure on Bulgaria.

He says the atmosphere in Belgrade is still tranquil. Three days ago he even received from there a reassuring telegram: the German troops were said to have temporarily halted their advance towards Bulgaria's borders. However, he was in the Foreign Office yesterday and the FO confirmed the statement made by Churchill over the radio on the 9th, concerning the rapid 'infiltration' of Germans into Bulgaria. Subbotić's first move in this difficult situation was to see me and exchange views, as well as to ask me to convey to the Soviet Government his fervent hope that the Soviet Union would interfere in Balkan affairs and prevent the capture of the Balkans by Germany.

[The left-wing leanings of Jacob Epstein[4] encouraged Victor Gollancz to arrange for Maisky and his wife to visit the artist's studio. Agniya was particularly struck by Epstein's *Madonna and Child* and suggested that the Russians might be interested in it 'although the title did not accord with the Soviet "Ideology"'. Maisky, who had learned from

---

[2] David Ben-Gurion, chairman of the Jewish Agency Executive in Palestine, 1935–48.
[3] See pp. 542–4.
[4] Jacob Epstein was born to Polish-Jewish parents in New York. He studied with Rodin in Paris before settling in London in 1905, establishing himself as a revolutionary and controversial sculptor. Some of his Strand statues were officially and publicly defaced.

Agniya that Epstein had displayed an interest in doing a bust of him, hastened to invite the artist for a luncheon with the Edens at the embassy on 12 February. He was much flattered by the offer, finding the time for the sittings, despite his many commitments.]

14 February

Jacob Epstein has convinced me to permit him to make my bust. I warned the sculptor that the USSR is a country of genuine democracy, so Soviet ambassadors are not able to pay artists of the capitalist world the fees they are accustomed to. Epstein was insistent. ... I was intrigued by the very process by which a major artist works and creates. For whatever one may say, Epstein and Vigeland are the greatest contemporary sculptors.

... The second sitting was today. Very interesting. I'm sitting on a soft, faded chair placed on a small platform. The sculptor's 'easel' stands in front of me. It is a small table on three legs with a half-metre iron rod in the centre. My head slowly grows out of the grey clay on the upper end of the rod. Epstein pinches pieces of clay mixed with water in a zinc washtub and rolls them in his palms into thick and thin sausages, from which he moulds my portrait. Much has been done already during two sittings: one can see the contours of my head, face, eyes, moustache and beard... Epstein himself keeps murmuring: 'This is just the beginning... A rough primitive sketch.'

Let's see what happens next. I'll have five or six sittings in all. With such original artists as Epstein, you never know what will come out in the end – you yourself or a monster. We'll see. I'm prepared for the worst.

The set-up is interesting. Epstein has been living for twelve years in a typical English house not far from us: 18, Hyde Park Gate. A long corridor leads from the porch to his studio behind the house. A large, bright room with two enormous windows, one above, the other on the left. Astonishing artistic chaos. Scattered over tables, chairs, benches and the floor are statues, heads, arms, legs and other parts of the human body in clay and plaster of Paris. In the corner stands a blackened and rusted small stove, which burns but doesn't warm. The figure of the sculptor himself moves quickly and deftly amidst the vast chaos. He is dressed in a shabby ginger jacket, over a torn grey shirt. His grey baggy trousers are stained with clay and plaster of Paris.

Epstein is a quite charming man. He is 60, but his blue eyes have a special sparkle, that of a genius and a child. For some odd reason his face, figure and manners remind me very much of M.M. [Litvinov] – especially when in the course of his work he sticks out his lips like a child. I told Epstein that he resembles M.M. He was pleased to hear this and said: 'One and the same type, one nation and birthplace: my parents, after all, were Polish Jews.'

51. Epstein admiring his bust of Maisky.

When Epstein works, the inspiration is palpable. He steps aside and gazes with absent, wild eyes. He runs to his 'easel' and feverishly flings a clay sausage onto the moist grey mass of clay that will be my head. Or he suddenly drops to his knees and examines the gradually developing oval of the face with a crazed look. Or he throws off his ginger jacket as if he is hot and starts pasting small pieces of moist clay onto the bust. ...

23 February

Epstein has sculpted quite a lot of heads – or 'portraits', as he calls them – of prominent literary figures: Tagore,[5] Bernard Shaw, Priestley[6] and others. His efforts were not always successful. Bernard Shaw's wife did not like her husband's head. Shaw himself thought his 'portrait' a success, but Mrs Shaw declared that if her husband took the portrait, she would leave the house. Under such a threat, Bernard was, of course, forced to capitulate. His portrait remained in Epstein's studio. He showed it to me. I commended the sculptor's

---

[5] Sir Rabindranath Tagore, Calcutta-born poet and educationalist; Nobel Prize for Literature, 1913.
[6] John Boynton Priestley, English novelist, playwright and broadcaster.

work (the bust was made masterfully), but thought to myself that this 'portrait' of Bernard Shaw did not quite catch the man. Something was missing.

'Mrs Shaw very much liked Rodin's[7] bust of her husband,' Epstein said. He grunted, shrugged his shoulders, and added: 'I don't know what she found in it. In my opinion the portrait is no good, although Shaw paid Rodin a heap of money for it. Women always have their fantasies, you know.'

Epstein's impressions of Tagore are interesting. Tagore used to arrive at Epstein's studio escorted by a group of young Hindus, his pupils. He would seat himself on the chair and not utter a word during the sitting. He behaved as if he were a saint. He maintained a meaningful silence and gazed into space with an air of profundity. Tagore's haughty treatment of his 'pupils' bordered on cruelty, while they looked at him in ecstasy, anticipated his every desire, and marvelled at his every gesture. Tagore paid not the slightest attention to them: he did not seem to notice them at all, looked over their heads and gave abrupt orders in a sharp dictatorial tone. He would, for instance, descend from the studio to the reception room where his pupils were waiting and bark in vexation: 'Taxi!'

The 'pupils' would rush to the door and scatter through the neighbouring streets to hail a car for him.

Once the following incident occurred. It so happened that a small Indian boy was living in Epstein's house at the time when he was doing Tagore's bust. He was the son of Epstein's friend and model (she sat for some of Epstein's best sculptures, such as *Mother and Child*). A brave and progressive woman, she left her husband and went to England, despite being a Muslim! Subsequently she returned to India and died in peculiar circumstances. Epstein suspects something tragic. Anyway, that small boy, the son of Epstein's friend, came running cheerfully into the studio one day when Tagore was there. Epstein patted the boy's head and said to his guest: 'Let me introduce a little compatriot.'

Tagore looked at the boy with a kind smile, but then, as if he had suddenly recalled something, asked curtly: 'Is he a Hindu or a Muslim?'

'He is a Muslim,' Epstein replied. 'Does it matter?'

Tagore stiffened. The smile instantly left his face. He turned away and fell into his saintly pose and displayed no further interest in the boy. He simply did not see him. The boy had ceased to exist for him.

Epstein was shocked. Tagore had revealed his true face.

25 February

Attended the reception given by Sklyarov[8] (the military attaché) to celebrate the Red Army anniversary. ... During the reception I spoke with Butler. ...

---

[7] François-Auguste-René Rodin, French sculptor (1840–1917).
[8] Major General Ivan Andreevich Sklyarov, Soviet military attaché in London, 1940–46.

Butler is very pleased with Cripps's trip to Ankara to meet Eden. He twice asked me most emphatically to inform Moscow that if the Soviet Government wanted to communicate something to Cripps in his absence, this must be done through the British embassy in Moscow, which would be in direct contact with Cripps all the time. The English are a naive lot. Do they really expect us to show particular interest in the talks between Cripps and Eden in Ankara, given the present state of Anglo-Soviet relations? ...

[Shortly after his appointment as foreign secretary, Eden, together with General John Dill,[9] chief of the general staff, left for the Middle East in a last-ditch attempt to reassemble the shattered remnants of the Balkan bloc, comprising Turkey, Greece and Yugoslavia. In Moscow, Cripps was fully aware of the anxiety which seized Stalin when Bulgaria – historically considered to be the pillar of the Russian security system in the Black Sea and the approaches to both the Danube and the Turkish Straits – joined the Axis on 1 March. He was therefore extremely eager for Eden to use the opportunity of his Middle Eastern tour to visit Moscow, 'flatter' the Russians and dispel suspicion. Churchill rejected the idea, stating that he did not trust the Russians as regards Eden's 'personal safety or liberty'. Eden, absorbed in his attempts to forge a Balkan bloc, remained noncommittal in his relations with the Russians.]

27 February

To Subbotić and his wife for lunch with Agniya. Also present were Aras, the Turkish ambassador, Sargent[10] from the FO and one or two others. Owing to the latest news from the Balkans, the atmosphere at lunch was like at a funeral. The wife of Subbotić remarked, somewhat coquettishly: 'The Balkans are in their death-throes.'

Subbotić himself was gloomy and let it be understood quite clearly that the USSR had failed to live up to the hopes placed in it by the Balkan states.

... After lunch I asked Aras about his last meeting with Churchill (24 February). Aras said the prime minister had no concrete proposals or demands towards Turkey. He merely informed Aras that Eden was flying to Ankara, where he would raise the question in all seriousness of Turkey's position in the war. Then Churchill assured Aras that the British Government had not the slightest desire to open a new front in the Balkans, and that if the Balkans did nevertheless become a theatre of war, there would only be Germany to blame. Churchill also expressed the thought that 'Russia's real interests' in this part of the globe lie on the English side. The current Soviet stance can be explained by

---

[9] Sir John Greer Dill, commander of 1st Army Corps in France, 1939–40; vice-chief of Imperial General Staff, 1940; aide-de-camp general to the king and chief of Imperial General Staff, 1940–41.
[10] Sir Orme Sargent, deputy undersecretary of state at the Foreign Office, 1939–46.

Russia's desire to avoid a conflict with Germany. This is understandable, but 'Russia will have to change its policy' sooner or later. ...

2 March (1)

We visited Lloyd George. When his wife died, Agniya and I sent him a warm telegram. He responded recently with a warm and friendly letter. I wrote a few words in reply, asking the old man to tell me when he would feel *fit* enough to see people. Three days ago, Lloyd George invited Agniya and me for lunch and today we visited him in Churt.

Lloyd George doesn't look too bad. But some kind of shadow seems to have fallen over his features. On top of that he has a cold: he coughs and blows his nose, pulling a handkerchief from his pocket every other minute. His hands tremble, especially when he pours water into his glass. The irrepressible *Welshman* is growing old. I wonder whether he will hold out much longer...

Lloyd George does not believe in the likelihood of an *invasion*. He waves his hand scornfully and utters with a sneer: 'It's impossible!'

But the situation at sea troubles him. ... 'Frankly speaking,' Lloyd George concluded, 'I see a serious danger to England here. Perhaps the only serious danger. The Germans cannot beat us from the air. Invasion is out of the question, at least for the foreseeable future.'

... I was disinclined to be too pessimistic about British prospects in the naval war.

'You see,' I explained, 'it is difficult to defeat a great nation in its own element. Your element is the sea, the German element is land. That's why I don't believe the Germans can beat you at sea. You'll manage somehow. You'll work something out. On the other hand, I doubt your ability to beat Germany on land, for land has been the Germans' element for millennia. And how could it be otherwise? Your army is basically an amateur army. You don't have the skills and traditions of land warfare. You don't have real military science and a good general staff. You only have the experience of colonial wars to fall back on. That does not suit Europe. That is why I regard with scepticism all these cries of "war to the end" or "war till the crushing of Hitlerism". But as for the sea... You'll manage somehow at sea. You'll think of something.'

Lloyd George laughed and looked at me slyly.

'There is much truth in what you say,' he said suddenly. 'Yes, the sea is our home. The sea is in our blood. Take Megan: there is no greater delight for her than the sea. She adores water and swims like a fish. Or Gwilym. He is crazy about yachting. The more turbulent the sea, the more he likes it. Yes, we'll manage somehow at sea.'

... Lloyd George waved his hand and added: 'Winston is waging a "Tory war". He wants to win without infringing the privileges of the ruling upper crust. This won't do. Something has to be forfeited: either the victory or the privileges. As a matter of fact, it seems to me that the War Cabinet does not have a "general plan" for the conduct of war. I'm sure they have never discussed such a plan seriously. They think the plan is hidden in Winston's head. I doubt it.'

Pausing for a while, the old man concluded: 'Winston has become a hostage of the Conservative Party and swims with the current. I've told you more than once that I see only one way of gaining a real victory over Germany: by drawing the Soviet Union over to our side. But this is just what the British Government doesn't want. The Government is awfully afraid of the possible effects of such an "alliance" on the internal life of the country. Better to lose the war than to "pave the way for Bolshevism".'

... I told Lloyd George about Churchill's demeanour in his recent talk with Shigemitsu.[11] Judging by the prime minister's behaviour, one can hardly expect a compromise peace.

'Tears in his eyes?' Lloyd George smiled. 'Yes, that happens to Winston. He is a very emotional man. So what?... Now he has tears because he wants to crush Hitler. Within a year he may have tears because of the shock of the horrors of the war... Things change.'

Lloyd George suddenly remembered something and burst into peals of laughter: 'If you remember, I twice lunched with Winston in December. His wife was with us at the table. She is a fairly intelligent woman, and above all she has plenty of typically English *common sense*... Winston was being very noisy about fighting to the end. He will not agree to peace until Germany is defeated. He will not sign a treaty with Hitler, etc. I argued with him, saying that the future is a closed book. There may come a time when tactics will need to be revised. One shouldn't tie one's hands for good. Winston, however, continued to growl. Suddenly Mrs Churchill interrupted our conversation and, addressing her husband, said with a smile: "Are we not allowed to change our mind if the moment requires it?" Winston wheezed, but said nothing in reply... Oh, the lady is clever! And Winston listens to her.'

... I felt somewhat sad taking my leave of Lloyd George. His wife has just died. Neither Megan, nor Gwilym, nor any other of his relations lives with him. His home is empty. Two housemaids tend to the old man. And he keeps raising a handkerchief to his face with a trembling hand...

---

[11] Mamoru Shigemitsu, Japan's vice-minister of foreign affairs, 1933–36; ambassador to Moscow, 1936–38, and to London, 1938–41.

From Lloyd George we drove to the Webbs for tea. ... We discussed current events. What impressed me most was the amazing coincidence of their and Lloyd George's opinions. The Webbs, too, do not believe in the likelihood of an *invasion* and regard the German 'blockade' of England as the main danger. They, too, do not know how England can emerge 'victorious' over Germany ... the sole chance for England to 'win' lies in drawing the USSR over to its side, but the British ruling circles will never do so out of fear of Bolshevism. ...

2 March (2)

And so, Bulgaria has capitulated: yesterday the protocol of Bulgaria's adherence to the Axis was signed, and German troops began marching into Sofia. ...

Subbotić came by. In a very anxious frame of mind.

'The situation in the Balkans is bad, very bad,' he said, and went on to explain. 'Now that Bulgaria has joined the Axis, Yugoslavia is surrounded on three sides. Hopes for effective Soviet support have proved unwarranted. The Yugoslav Government has to manoeuvre to gain time, but this is becoming increasingly difficult with each passing day. Yugoslavia is prepared to trade with Germany and develop economic relations to the maximum (all the more so as the German market is the sole external market for Yugoslavia today), but she does not want to go any further. Does not want to become a member of the 'Axis' or to allow the passage of German troops through her territory against England and Greece. Wants instead to remain absolutely neutral. But Germany demands more. How to behave? What should be done?'

... I tried to console Subbotić and explain our position to him. I said: 'Just wait! Everything will not be over today!'

... It looks as though Cripps is turning into our enemy due to his political failures, failures resulting from the British Government's reluctance to move towards rapprochement with us. I warned Cripps when he was leaving for Moscow that he might find himself in an awkward position through London's fault. An ambassador, after all, is akin to a travelling salesman. When he sells good commodities, he will be successful even if his personal qualities are quite ordinary. When he sells bad commodities, he is doomed to fail even if his personal qualities are excellent. Cripps has basically had nothing to sell for these past ten months. This is the source of his failure. But instead of directing his anger at his boss, who has not provided him with decent goods, Cripps prefers to curse his buyer, who for very good reasons has no wish to buy rotten stuff. Very short-sighted. But even clever people are often like that.[12]

---

[12] Cripps returned to Moscow from Ankara firmly convinced that Russia and Germany would be at war 'before summer ... not later than the end of June'.

12 March

I arranged a lunch for Beaverbrook and Alexander, inviting Prytz and his wife, Monckton, Strang, Cunliffe-Owen[13] and others.

Beaverbrook looked quite well, but he was very angry. He barked and fumed his way through lunch. ... Beaverbrook hardly believes in the threat of an invasion, but he is most anxious about attacks on British commercial shipping. He consoles himself with the hope that the United States will formally enter the war in the near future.

... Monckton told Novikov[14] that Cripps had been in an 'awful' mood before his visit to Ankara. He saw not the slightest grounds for hope. But he cheered up after meeting with Eden. He sent Monckton a telegram the other day in which he says, among other things, that Eden will take up the question of Anglo-Soviet relations in all earnestness upon his return to London. We shall see.

[On 20 February Maisky was elected a candidate member of the Central Committee of the Communist Party of the Soviet Union (CPSU). Trying to boost his rather precarious standing in England, he boasted to Butler about the 'great honour' which was 'a sign of approval of my work in general and here in London in particular'. His independence and manoeuvrability were, however, seriously curtailed in early March with the arrival of a new counsellor, Novikov, most likely working for the NKVD, who was ordered to be present at all of Maisky's top-level meetings. Novikov, observed Eden in their first encounter, was clearly a 'Kremlin watch-dog upon Maisky'.[15]]

13 March

The new US ambassador (John Winant[16]) has paid me his first visit. ... Winant makes a somewhat strange impression. Tall, dark-haired, with slow, demure manners, a listless, barely audible voice, and a pensive, introspective look, he is the polar opposite of his predecessor, the vociferous, jaunty, loquacious and flighty Joe Kennedy. I had to strain my ears to catch Winant's words.

---

[13] Sir Hugo Cunliffe-Owen was chairman of an aircraft construction company bearing his name which produced parts for Spitfires in the Second World War.

[14] Kirill Vasilevich Novikov, recruited to the NKID in 1937 after pursuing a successful career in the metal industry; counsellor at the Soviet embassy in Great Britain 1939–42; head of the Second European department of NKID, 1942–47; ambassador in India, 1947–53.

[15] See entry on p. 360.

[16] John Gilbert Winant, US ambassador to Britain, 1941–46.

15 Match

Apparently we are facing a new flare-up of the war, a new battle between two mighty enemies. It is difficult to foresee the outcome of this second 'trial of strength', but it is possible to make an assessment of what the belligerents have at their disposal entering the 1941 'war season'. It is rather tricky to assess Germany's potential from London. But what about England? What will England take into the cruel battles that lie ahead?

... The 'national front' has survived as a united force. ... Temporary 'calm' has been restored in India with the help of repressions. It is not stable, but it may well last for the duration of the current 'war season'. So it would seem that no major complications threaten the British Government in the immediate future either at home or in the Empire ...

Morale among the broad masses of the population is now very strong. The victories in Africa, the insignificant human losses at the front, the respite in the air war over England in the last three or four months, the absence of epidemics, the tolerable food situation (worse than last year, but by no means catastrophic) and, finally, the Government's position – all this and much else creates an atmosphere of great confidence across the nation and a willingness to fight. The USA's open allegiance with England strengthens these feelings still further. The clear position of Churchill & Co. to 'fight to the end' does have an effect on both the state apparatus and the masses. Nothing remains to remind one of the era of Chamberlain, when the air was thick with corrosive rumours, gossip and reports (not always unfounded) about doubts, hesitation and indecision 'at the top'. ...

24 March

I paid Winant a return visit. The American ambassador has decided to play the democrat: he has abandoned the luxurious house in which the representative of the USA usually resides and has settled in a modest three-room apartment above his office on Grosvenor Square. His wife will arrive soon, but he doesn't intend to change his residence even then. We shall see.

... Winant started lavishing compliments on me. In our conversation in Geneva in 1939, I had demonstrated outstanding foresight concerning the European situation. Now, in the embassy archives, he has found a record of my conversation with Counsellor Herschel Johnson on 1 March 1938. My statements of that time have proved most prophetic (I have a poor memory, incidentally, of the conversation with Johnson). Winant concluded half in jest: 'Should you happen to be in a prophetic mood again, please send for me.'

My general impression of Winant is quite clear: he is an advocate of US entry into the war, but is still trying to veil his opinion. His minister Harriman,[17] however, who is busy setting up a special 'department' at the embassy to supervise US supplies to England, is quite brazen in this respect. A few days ago, at a meeting of American journalists, Harriman declared 'off the record' that he hoped to see the United States at war within the next few months.[18]

... A visit from Simopoulos[19] ... The English, in Simopoulos's opinion, have decided to fight in the Balkans in earnest, but he does not know how many British troops have landed in Greece. He says that the English conceal this even from the Greek Government. He believes that the British Government has earmarked considerable forces for Greece. Why does he think so? Because during the negotiations in Athens between Eden, Dill and the Greek Government, the latter said unequivocally: either serious aid with land forces or no aid at all.

... I tried to discuss the strategic situation in the Balkans with Simopoulos, but to no avail: the old man understands nothing about strategy, mixes up mountains and plains, and doesn't know the difference between a division and a corps. When you ask him anything related to military strategy, he spreads his arms in perplexity and mumbles helplessly: 'You'd better ask my military attaché. I'm clueless in these matters.'

A rum job at a time when diplomacy has become strategy.

4 April

The Czechs report:

(1) Eden can't pull off a tripartite bloc of Yugoslavia, Greece and Turkey because of Turkey's position.

(2) The British have already landed six divisions in Greece, fully armed and equipped, with a large quantity of aircraft. Reinforcements continue to arrive.

(3) A great quantity of troops is passing through Prague in the direction of the Soviet border. There is a Geographical Institute in Prague which passed into German hands long ago. This Institute is now urgently engaged in producing detailed maps of the Ukraine. ...

---

[17] William Averell Harriman, President Roosevelt's special representative in Great Britain with the rank of minister, March 1941; US ambassador to USSR, 1943–46.
[18] This conversation led Maisky to suggest to Butler two days later that 'war ... would probably spread and America would come in'. He believed it was advantageous if 'one great nation, namely Russia, remained neutral and was available at the end of the war to act as a makeweight'.
[19] Charalambos Simopoulos, Greek ambassador to London, 1935–42.

6 April

Early this morning Germany attacked Yugoslavia and Greece.

Two days ago Comrade Molotov summoned Schulenburg and, having informed him of the forthcoming signing of a Soviet–Yugoslavian pact of friendship and non-aggression, told the German ambassador that the pact would be concluded in the interests of peace in the Balkans, that peace in the Balkans was in the interests of Germany itself, and that he hoped Germany would observe peace in this part of the world. Schulenburg replied that he had nothing against such a pact between the USSR and Yugoslavia in principle, but found the moment of its conclusion 'unfortunate'.

Today Hitler responded to Comrade Molotov's démarche.

We shall remember this and draw practical conclusions. What conclusions? Time will tell. One thing is clear: through its policy in the Balkans, Germany is taking the fatal action of forcing the USSR to turn its front towards her. This does not mean that the USSR will rush into war against Germany. We shall do our utmost to avoid it. But the USSR is turning its front towards Germany. It cannot afford not to. The USSR cannot resign itself to the presence of German heavy artillery in Constanţa and Burgas as a permanent phenomenon – a presence about which the Germans themselves recently boasted over the wireless.

Why has Hitler's policy recently taken such a turn? Is he consciously picking a fight with the USSR? Or does he not see any other way out of the current situation? Hard to say. But it is increasingly clear that we have played our 'German card' and will get little more from it (for as long as Germany remains in Hitler's hands, at any rate). The time draws near when we shall have to look for other cards.

... It's not easy being a prophet in our days, and I don't want to resort to tea leaves. I'll merely note that the beginning of the 1941 war season differs significantly from that of the season of 1940.

In Germany's favour: Germany possessed only Poland beyond its borders at that time, while now all Europe is subject to it in varying degrees, except for England, the USSR and half of the Balkans. Moreover, the prestige of German military might has been firmly established. ... On land Germany is considered 'invincible'.

In England's favour: the German offensive has entirely lost the element of surprise. Churchill has replaced Chamberlain as head of the Government. England has become much stronger in the air and on land during the past year and has defeated Italy in Africa. England has preserved its mastery of the sea. The USA has openly moved into England's camp. ...

Yes, there is a difference, but what will be the upshot of the current military season?

The events of the next three or four weeks may give us a clue. All will depend on whether or not the Germans succeed with their Blitzkrieg in the Balkans. Much will become clearer after that.

There is one more factor in the current situation, a factor of great significance – the Soviet Union. The position of the USSR is somewhat different from what it was a year ago, and it may change still further under certain conditions.

[On 25 March the Yugoslavs were forced by Hitler's familiar combination of threats and cajoling to join the Axis. The cards, however, were reshuffled two days later, when a bloodless military coup in Belgrade installed the 17-year-old Prince Peter[20] on the throne. On the night of 4–5 April, the Yugoslavs and the Russians concluded a friendship and non-aggression pact, which in retrospect has been hailed as courageous defiance of Germany. Stalin regarded the pact as a mere demonstration of solidarity with Yugoslavia which, he hoped, would suffice to deter Hitler from attacking her and draw him back to the negotiating table. Hitler, however, reacted swiftly, with a ferocious bombardment of Belgrade and a lightning campaign which brought the whole country under his control within less than a fortnight, followed by a swift occupation of Greece.

The German offensive coincided with an incessant stream of precise intelligence reports to the Kremlin about the increased German deployment on the Soviet border. The vulnerability and deficiencies of the Soviet armed forces' defence had been exposed in the January war games. The games induced Stalin to seek to extend the scope of the Molotov–Ribbentrop Pact. This led to the hasty conclusion of a neutrality pact with Japan in the Kremlin on 13 April. In hindsight, the agreement seems to have been a tremendous coup, as it removed the threat of a second front in the event of Germany launching an attack on the Soviet Union. However, Stalin's pressing objective (overlooked by historians) was the wish, as he told Matsuoka,[21] the Japanese foreign minister, 'to collaborate extensively with the Tripartite Pact partners'.]

7 April

I called on Subbotić.

I congratulated him on the pact of friendship and non-aggression between the USSR and Yugoslavia, signed on the night of 5 April. Subbotić was deeply moved: he embraced and kissed me, and there were tears in his eyes. 'The pact,' he exclaimed, 'has saved Yugoslavia's soul. Hardships and suffering may await our people, and the Germans may temporarily seize our country – it doesn't matter. Every Yugoslavian, and every Serbian in particular, will now know:

---

[20] Born in 1923, Peter II ruled through his regent, Prince Paul, from 1934 until 1941, when he was enthroned following a coup d'état.
[21] Yosuke Matsuoka, foreign minister of Japan, 1940–41; signed the non-aggression treaty with the Russians in Moscow in April 1941.

Russia is thinking about us and, sooner or later, will save us. I'm not a communist, but I bow low to Stalin on the occasion of this pact.'

... Subbotić complained that he was experiencing great difficulties in
maintaining contact with his government. The Belgrade radio station was
wrecked by the Germans on the first day of their attack. The Yugoslavian
Government was evacuated from the capital. Where to? Subbotić himself has
no idea.

9 April

Subbotić called to give me some very alarming news from the front. The
Germans have broken through to Saloniki and Üsküb. The former defence
plans are in tatters. New ones have to be improvised in haste. The main reason
for the German success, according to Subbotić, is the new tank which can
travel over mountains. The Germans employed a large quantity of such tanks
and broke through the Yugoslavian lines. The Yugoslavian army doesn't know
how to respond to the mountain tanks. It is becoming ever clearer that the
Germans plan to deliver a blow in a westward direction, that is, towards
Albania. If they succeed in this, Yugoslavia will be cut off completely from
Greece and from the English.

* * *

In Parliament to hear Churchill's speech. Churchill was evidently in low spirits.
No wonder: the Germans occupied Saloniki early this morning. No hint of
defeatism, however. On the contrary, he displayed anger and redoubled hatred
towards Germany. The House shares this mood, to judge by MPs' remarks and
comments during Churchill's speech and by their conversations in the lobbies.
The political barometer still clearly indicates: 'Fight!'

On the whole, then, there is no panic, only anxiety. ... English dissatisfaction with Turkey is all too evident. ... Also evident are the attempts to take our
pulse in connection with the new turn of events. Brendan Bracken talked with
me on this subject in the lobby today. He said half in jest: 'You'd better remove
road signs in the Ukraine double quick.'

Vansittart (I called on him yesterday) spoke in the same vein, predicting an
early German attack on the USSR. But Vansittart is a little unstable these days:
after his *Black Record*[22] he sees Germans everywhere, even under his bed.

---

[22] Refers to Vansittart's *Black Record: Germans Past and Present*, published in 1941, in which he
suggested that German history had always been marked by militarism and aggression, of which Nazism
was only the latest phase. He advocated harsh treatment of Germany after the war.

I reply to all our unexpected and unbidden well-wishers that I fail to see any causes that render a clash between Germany and the USSR inevitable; but should such a clash nevertheless occur, the Soviet Union will take care of itself.

[Stalin's desire to seek an agreement with Germany at all costs was strongly motivated by fear that British provocation might entangle Russia in war. Contrary to Churchill's account, the massive concentration of German troops in the east was consistently misinterpreted by British intelligence, too, until just a week before the invasion. It was dismissed as 'a war of nerves' mounted by the Germans to secure positive results in negotiations, which (it was supposed in Britain) must be impending with Russia. Rather than revealing the German intention of attacking Russia, Churchill's famous, albeit cryptic, message to Stalin in early April pointed to a German decision to postpone deployment against the Russians and divert the war to the Balkans. Such a decision, Churchill believed, exposed Germany's inability to simultaneously prosecute a war against Yugoslavia and Turkey, on the one hand, and Russia on the other. He hoped Stalin would use the lull to align the Soviet Union with Britain in forging a Balkan bloc. The warning had the opposite effect: it fed Stalin's suspicion that the rumours of war were fabricated in London in an attempt to involve Russia in the war. Well attuned to the Kremlin, Maisky reported a well-orchestrated campaign by the British Government and the press to 'scare the Soviet Union with Germany'. He was particularly disturbed by Churchill's speeches in Parliament on 9 and 27 April, in which he predicted a German attack on Russia.]

10 April

Sylvester called and asked me to visit Lloyd George. The old man had come to London for a day and wanted to talk to me.

When I entered his office, Lloyd George had just come back from lunch with Churchill. He said the prime minister was concerned, perhaps even somewhat *depressed*. The situation in Libya has taken a more serious turn than was initially anticipated. The British relied excessively on the obstacle provided by the Sicilian Channel and exposed Cyrenaica. The Germans, contrary to all expectations, assembled a relatively large force in Tripoli ... and the results are there for all to see: Benghazi has fallen, and there are German tanks on the Egyptian border. The British Government, of course, is responding, but does it have time? And can one count on the Sicilian Channel any longer?

The situation in the Balkans is even graver. The swift success of the Germans in the Balkans came as a great surprise to Churchill. ... The old man fumed and cursed the British ruling circles for being 'blinded by class'. He made no exception even for Churchill. It seems that the prime minister now reasons in the following way: a German attack on the Soviet Union in the very near future is inevitable – because of the Ukraine, because of Baku – and then the USSR will fall like a 'ripe fruit' into Churchill's basket. So is there any point in making efforts to attract the USSR? Is there any point in trying to court it? It will all happen by itself.

L-G does not share this confidence in things taking their own course. He does not believe that Hitler will turn eastward against us. To do so he would have to employ nearly his entire army. What would happen in Western Europe then?...

The old man, nonetheless, thinks that we, too, are in a very difficult position. What if Hitler attacks Turkey? Will the USSR be able to observe German seizure of the Straits with equanimity?

I replied in my usual spirit: namely, we can take care of ourselves. The old man shook his head and answered: 'Don't play with fire! The German army is a terrible machine. Once the Balkan campaign is over, there will be no force left in Europe which could even conceive of opposing Germany on land, except for you. Will Hitler accept such a state of affairs? I doubt it. Hitler, after all, strives for global domination. Moreover, he will be left with an idle army of several million, intoxicated with success and demanding employment. Will Hitler be able to resist the temptation to divert it to the east?'

11 April

Quo Tai-chi came by for his farewell visit. In a few days he will be leaving England and heading for his new post in Chungking via the USA. We shall see what kind of foreign minister he will make.

... Quo Tai-chi's visit made me somewhat sad. He came to London three months before me, and we have been good colleagues throughout these eight years. We've seen each other often, had long talks and got used to one other. Relations of trust have been established between us (as far as trust is possible, of course, between a Soviet and a bourgeois diplomat). Quo Tai-chi never deceived or misled me. Naturally enough, he didn't tell me everything and preferred to maintain silence on some topics; but when he did tell me something, I knew it to be true. I repaid him in the same coin. We also met several times in Geneva, which he frequently visited as a Chinese delegate. There, too, on the shores of Lac Léman, we retained a friendly tone in our relations. So many of my memories of diplomatic life here are associated with Quo Tai-chi: receptions in the palace, ministerial dinners, fashionable 'garden parties', political lunches, semi-official 'weekends'...

Eight years of orderly routine and habit – and now Quo Tai-chi is leaving London *for good*! His departure serves to remind me of the time that has passed since I first set foot on English soil as *Ambassador*. It also reminds me that nothing lasts for ever and that the time will soon come when I, too, will have to leave London *for good*. Well, I'm always ready. To tell the truth, coming to London in October 1932 I never thought I'd be stuck here for so long. I thought I might remain in London for five years or so, but as for staying longer – it didn't even cross my mind!

Bidding farewell to Quo Tai-chi, I made a comment in this spirit. ... The twists and turns of fate! 'Some are no more, others are far away'...

15 April

I've just returned from the grand reception given by Quo Tai-chi to bid 'Adieu!' to his numerous friends and acquaintances. ... There is nothing remarkable about Quo Tai-chi's appearance: a short, miniature, almost skinny Chinese with a round, typically Oriental face, a rather flat nose, and a pair of big horn-rimmed glasses resting on his nose. When he takes off his glasses (which happens from time to time), his eye sockets look terribly small and his face absolutely flat. One cannot guess his age by his appearance: he may be 35 and he may be 60. In fact, he is about 50. Quo Tai-chi's movements are even, unhurried and smooth. They reflect his temperament and his nationality. As with many other Chinese people, I was always most impressed by a kind of subconscious sense of the venerability of his race, a kind of majestic serenity nurtured by the thousand-year history of his nation. How many times during our conversations did I fly into a rage, become irritated or indignant at one or other action by the British Government, one or other machination on the part of Japan? But Quo Tai-chi always preserved an imperturbable calmness and merely observed: 'It will pass...', 'It will change...', 'One must not lose one's patience...'

All the time I had the feeling that, gazing at me from the height of the five-thousand-year history of his people and smiling to himself like a wise old man before an excited youngster, Quo Tai-chi wanted to say: 'Yes, many things have happened in my life... Many things... Good and bad... I used to get excited, too, like this youngster, but not any more. Life has its own equilibrium. One must learn to wait – and it will come... It will come!'

Indeed, aren't all European nations (even the German, French and English, to say nothing of young Russia) greenhorns compared with the Chinese? The English measure their precedents by the century, while the Chinese measure them by the millennium. A Chinaman, speaking about the most recent events, will let slip: 'There was an incident at the time of the T'ang dynasty...' Or: 'Poet so-and-so said two thousand years ago...'

And so on and so forth.

... Needless to say, Quo Tai-chi had his weaknesses, too. He was a sybarite and grew ever more accustomed to the effete bourgeois lifestyle. He had some shady sources of income: I nurture grave suspicions that he exploited his diplomatic status to make some money on the side through contraband. Strange things also went on in his family life. He sought to keep his wife (a fat, uncultured and rather common Chinese woman) at a distance, whether in China or America. Here in London, he always had young and pretty compatriots following him around. But, after all, Quo Tai-chi is a bourgeois diplomat, and a Chinese one at that – it would be absurd to apply the standards of communist morals to him. ...

26 April

It was only 20 days ago, while noting the beginning of the German attack against Yugoslavia, that I posed the question: will the Germans succeed with their Blitzkrieg in the Balkans?

Today there can be no room for doubt: yes, the German Blitzkrieg was a success. Perhaps even more so than previous ones.

How quickly events unfold in our days! Merely 20 days have passed, and Yugoslavia no longer exists, and within another 2–3 days Greece will be no more.

... The capture of Yugoslavia and Greece, i.e. of the whole Balkans (together with the earlier *gleichgeschalteten*[23] of Rumania and Bulgaria) by the Germans poses a whole host of serious problems. The most important of them is: what will be Hitler's next move?

It seems to me that there are two likely alternatives. The first: pressure will begin to be exerted on Turkey, so as to seize her diplomatically or by force, and advance through her to Asia Minor and Egypt. The second: Germany will leave Turkey in peace for the time being, draw Spain (even better, Spain and France) into a triple pact, march to Gibraltar, cross the Strait, seize Morocco, Algeria and Tunisia, capture Egypt via North Africa, and press on to Iraq and Iran. The second alternative looks more probable. ... One thing is clear: the war is entering a new and exceptionally important phase. The next six months may prove to be a turning point not only in the history of the war, but in the history of mankind as well. We shall see.

29 April

When I talked with Quo a few days ago, I remarked: 'I'm certain of one thing at least: the present "Polish Government" will never ride into Warsaw.'

---

[23] Maisky means probably *Gleichschaltung* – 'forcible-coordination', a Nazi term used for establishing their authoritarian rule on occupied territories.

Quo laughed and said: 'As if that's what they want! They live just fine in London.'

Quo furnished me with interesting details about the life and behaviour of members of the 'Polish Government' in London. They spend heaps of money. They really are puttin' on the Ritz. All of them have cars, secretaries, aides-de-camps, servants or batmen. They drink and eat in the most extravagant London restaurants. They try to make the acquaintance of only the most aristocratic families (without always succeeding). The 'official representatives of Poland', that's to say, squander their money and live fast. And of the 17,000-strong Polish corps defending a section of the Scottish shore against invasion, there are 6,500 officers!

How all this resembles the old Polish szlachta![24] I recall that when Poland sent an embassy to England in the 1670s, it numbered no fewer than 1,600 people! This at a time when Sweden, Germany and other countries would send no more than 70 to 100. The Polish 'Pans', don't you know! They won't be outdone by anyone!...

30 April

Brendan Bracken came for lunch. I have not seen him for 3–4 months. We had much to talk about. He was here for nearly three hours. Our conversation mostly circled around two issues: Anglo-Soviet relations and the war.

... I asked Bracken: what may we expect in Anglo-Soviet relations in the near future?

Bracken replied that Eden is undoubtedly striving to improve relations, but Bracken is not sure that he will be successful. Why? For two reasons. (1) Eden is often too cautious: he does not want to take risks and assume responsibility. (2) It is not clear whether the USSR wants an improvement in relations?

I objected to the second point: the USSR was ready to maintain good relations on the basis of reciprocity with all states, be they belligerent or otherwise. Bracken listened to me with great interest and said: 'In Conservative circles one often hears the following argument. If Germany attacks the Soviet Union (as many now believe will happen), the USSR will come to us of its own accord. If Germany does not attack the USSR, it will do nothing for us anyway. So is it worth courting the USSR?'

I burst out laughing and noted that the British Government had not even tried to court us, so how can it know what effect its courting might have on the conduct of the Soviet Government? Then I strongly condemned the tendency,

---

[24] An association of the Polish and Lithuanian land nobility which had enjoyed institutional and economic privileges since the fifteenth century.

prevalent in the press and among British politicians, to frighten us with Germany. I mentioned Churchill's recent speeches (9 and 27 April) in this connection, in which he, too, paid his due to this popular craze. I can only regret such speeches. What is their purpose? Why has Churchill suddenly begun taking Soviet interests to heart? We can take care of our interests ourselves, can't we? The Soviet Union needs no outside mentors. The prime minister's remarks sound very infelicitous and even tactless in the current situation. They produce an effect in Moscow quite opposed to the one he intends.

My words seemed to impress Bracken. He even remarked: 'Yes, sometimes it's better not to mention certain things aloud.'

I inquired whether the British Government had any exact information about Hitler's intention to attack the USSR, or whether this was all just theoretical speculation based on *wishful thinking*.

Bracken had to admit that the British Government has, in essence, no specific information concerning Germany's preparations for an attack. There are only suppositions based on various signs and on conversations between Hitler and trustworthy individuals. As an example of the latter group, Bracken named Cudahy,[25] former US ambassador in Belgium, who, as a high-ranking journalist, recently visited Berlin and had a long talk with the Führer. Cudahy is a great admirer of Hitler, so his testimony, in Bracken's opinion, deserves special attention. Hitler spoke sharply about the USSR in this conversation, saying that his present policy towards Moscow was just a 'war-time manoeuvre' and that his words in *Mein Kampf* would be realized to the letter. ...

Then Hitler allegedly added: 'The Soviet–Finnish war taught us a lot. I have no doubt that my armies will cut through Russia like a knife through butter.'

... It was clear that the campaign waged by the British Government and the press about the forthcoming German attack on the USSR has no solid foundation whatsoever and follows the model, *Der Wunsch ist der Vater des Gedankens*.[26] ...

6 May

Stalin has been appointed chairman of the Council of People's Commissars, Molotov – his deputy and people's commissar for foreign affairs. We return to Lenin's times, when the leader of our party and of the peoples of the USSR held the post of chairman of the Council of People's Commissars.

---

[25] John Clarence Cudahy, American ambassador to Poland, 1933–37; Ireland 1937–40; Belgium, 1940; and Luxembourg, 1940.

[26] The proverb 'The wish is father to the thought' derives from Shakespeare's *King Henry IV Part 2*, but it has become much more common in the German language – to the extent that Maisky, who uses it often throughout the diary, assumes it to be German.

This is a signal. The threat of war is approaching our frontiers. The time is approaching for major and significant decisions. It is necessary for Stalin himself to be at the helm.

[The looming prospect of war led Stalin to keep his cards even closer to his chest. He resorted to 'divide and rule' tactics, keeping the military ignorant of his political moves. Neither were the diplomats trusted – and particularly not Maisky, whom Molotov, ever since his appointment, had been keeping at arm's length. Maisky was deliberately kept in the dark about the political initiatives taken by Stalin to avoid war. Left to guess what Stalin's intentions were, and seeking to conform to them, Maisky's cautious reports unwittingly contributed to the Kremlin's fatal misjudgement of German intentions on the eve of the war.

Schulenburg, who encountered the Führer fuming about the Soviet pact with Yugoslavia during his visit to Berlin, was resolved to repair the damage. Inadvertently, he also misled Stalin into believing that it was still possible to avert war. His scheme was to prod Stalin to 'involve Hitler in negotiations which would rob him, for the time being, of all pretexts for military actions'. This he did at three clandestine meetings with Dekanozov,[27] Stalin's ambassador in Berlin, at his own residency in Moscow, away from potential informers in the embassy – on 5, 9 and 12 May.

Possessing little straw to make his bricks, Schulenburg chose to convey to Dekanozov his impression that 'rumours of an imminent war between the Soviet Union and Germany are of explosive nature, and should be suppressed, broken to the bones'. This accounts for Stalin's obsessive fear henceforth that an overt and effective deployment of troops on the border might be conceived as provocation in Berlin. His initiative, however, did not go far. 'No diplomacy,' Hitler instructed his ambassador, 'would make him change his mind about Russia's attitude.' On 12 May, Dekanozov returned to Schulenburg's apartment for their third breakfast meeting inside a week, confirming Stalin's agreement to send a personal letter to Hitler. He encountered 'an impassive' Schulenburg, who confessed that he had been conversing with him 'privately' and that his overtures were made 'on his own initiative without authority'.

The strange blend of constant hints about the likelihood of war, equally persuasive attempts to maintain the momentum, and disinformation added to the already confused state of mind at the Kremlin. Baffled, Stalin could easily assume that a cautious policy might still yield an agreement. However, it could just as well be a trap set for Russia, whereby a premature approach might be used as a trump card in future German negotiations with Britain. Indeed, during the meeting Schulenburg made the entirely speculative assessment that 'in his own opinion the day was not far off when England and Germany were bound to reach agreement and bring the calamity and

---

[27] Vladimir Georgievich Dekanozov, deputy people's commissar for foreign affairs, 1939–40, and Soviet ambassador in Berlin, 1940–41. Before embarking on his diplomatic career, Dekanozov was a prominent official in the NKVD. A close associate of Beria, he was arrested with him and shot in December 1953.

destruction and bombing of their cities to an end'. This statement was surely scruti-
nized in the Kremlin in the evening, when news came on Radio Berlin of the flight of
Hitler's deputy, Rudolf Hess, to Britain on a self-appointed peace mission. The fact that
both Schulenburg and Cripps had been alluding in their conversations in the Kremlin to
the possibility of a separate peace alerted Stalin to the need to forestall it by further
appeasing Hitler. The 'appeasement' of Germany and the uncertainty were taking their
toll on Maisky. Alexander (the Labourite first lord of the Admiralty, whom Maisky came
to see 'as an old friend') gained the impression that he was 'rather anxious as to his own
position ... although, of course, he did not say this'.]

7 May

I spent yesterday and today in Parliament. Major debates about the course of
the war, mostly prompted by the British failures in Greece. Looking down from
the diplomatic box at the so-familiar chamber, I unconsciously drew a parallel
with similar debates held a year ago (8–9 May) after Norway, which dragged
the Chamberlain Government to its grave. Drawing this parallel, I asked
myself: is it the same as before or not?

No, of course not. There's a big difference.

... The general inference to be drawn from the debate is that the British
ruling classes do not want peace, preferring to fight against Germany.

Why?

Because peace today would mean peace on the basis of Germany's present
gains. In other words, Germany would come out of the war on the European
continent west of the USSR in possession of all the material, technical and other
resources of the countries it had occupied or subjugated. This, in turn, would
enable Germany, over a period of five years or so, to build a fleet not inferior to
that of the English, which would signify the end of the British Empire.

It cannot be ruled out, however, that in spite of the above considerations the
ruling classes of England might prefer peace to war at a certain moment, but
when? In two cases: (1) if England were to suffer crushing defeats and its position became hopeless, or (2) if the soil of society were to catch fire under the
feet of the English bourgeoisie at home or in the Empire. Neither case is to be
observed at present.

That is the general background, against which the personality of Churchill
plays a very major role. The prime minister was undoubtedly born too late. By
nature he is an adventurist on a historical scale, strong-willed and resolute, a
romantic of British imperialism and war. Had he lived in previous centuries, he
would have been a match for Cortes or Admiral Drake, a conqueror of new
lands or a celebrated pirate. ... It is not without reason that Churchill reveres his
ancestor, the duke of Marlborough, who lived at the turn of the seventeenth

century and was a brilliant military leader, a political chameleon, and protago-
nist of the most shameless love affairs. Indeed, the prime minister has dedicated four fat volumes to the career of the duke of Marlborough.

Churchill has told me more than once over the years, and I have no grounds
not to believe him, that the British Empire is his alpha and omega. In 1918–20,
Churchill organized a crusade against 'Bolshevism', which he considered a
major menace to the British Empire at that time. ...

Churchill is just as keen on wars. Megan Lloyd George told me once that
ever since childhood she had heard stories about how Churchill, when visiting
her father, would always talk about battles, military campaigns and conquests
with great enthusiasm and excitement. He always imagined himself in the role
of a great military leader who flung armies from one end of Europe to another,
conquered kingdoms and won brilliant victories. Today – I know this from the
most reliable sources – Churchill is totally engrossed in the war. Fortune has
smiled on him at last. He has 'his own' war, a gigantic war in which he, like a
fanatical chess player, swears to checkmate Hitler. In this war, Churchill is
commander-in-chief, chief of the general staff, and leader of the troops. He
won't surrender 'his' war to anyone. And now, when the British bourgeoisie
wants to continue the war, Churchill has become its godsend. But he may
become an obstacle if and when it desires peace.

All this, however, is just the 'music of the future'. Today Churchill has a
massive role to play in England. He is surely 'master' of the country, for he is a
cut above all other political leaders, except Lloyd George (who is 78!). Moreover,
Churchill is a talented writer and orator – extremely important qualities for a
major 'historical adventurist' of our days.

... This has much relevance to Anglo-Soviet relations as well. My general
impression is that Eden sincerely wants an improvement in this regard, but
cannot do much about it. ... Eden has two difficulties. The first is Churchill.
The prime minister reasons in the following way. If he could count on the
immediate entry of the Soviet Union into the war, efforts might be taken to
improve relations. Since he cannot count on this, Churchill ceases to care about
the Soviet Union and says that the problem of Anglo-Soviet relations does not
interest him for now. Also, Churchill suffers from an obsession that a war
between Germany and the USSR is inevitable. This being the case, he just has
to wait: the USSR will approach England of its own accord as soon as German
guns start firing on its borders. No cause for concern. Such reasoning is very
strange and nonsensical.[28] ... The USA is Eden's second difficulty. Eden tested

---

[28] Maisky was spot on. Churchill instructed Eden that the Russians 'knew perfectly well their dangers
and also that we need their aid. You will get much more out of them by letting these forces work than by
frantic efforts to assure them of your love.'

the ground in Washington after our talk on 16 April, but did not meet with any sympathy for his plan for resolving the Baltic question.

9 May

I lunched with Prytz, who is going to fly to Stockholm in a strange and risky way – by British plane across German lines. ... In connection with his departure, Prytz expressed his wish to see Churchill. The prime minister invited him and his wife to lunch (there were half a dozen guests). ... Prytz asked Churchill how he envisaged the further development of the war. ... In reply, Churchill told Prytz the following 'fable'.

There lived two frogs – an optimist and a pessimist. One evening they were jumping over some grass and detected the wonderful smell of fresh milk emanating from a nearby dairy. The frogs were tempted and jumped into the dairy through an open window. They miscalculated and flopped directly into a large jar of milk. What to do?... The pessimist looked around and, seeing that the walls of the jar were high and sheer and that it was not possible to climb up, fell into despair. He turned on his back, folded his legs and sank to the bottom. The optimist did not want to perish so disgracefully. He also saw the high and sheer walls, but decided to flounder while he could. All night long he swam, beat the milk energetically with his legs, and displayed varied forms of activity. And?... By the time morning came, the optimistic frog had, quite unawares, churned a big knob of butter out of the milk and thereby saved his life. The same will happen to the British Empire.

Churchill's 'fable' was very good from the literary point of view, but could not, of course, fully satisfy Prytz. However, all his attempts to learn something more definite about the 'general strategy' of the British Government in this war were in vain.[29]

... In his talk with Prytz, Churchill mentioned, among other things, the impending clash between the USSR and Germany (this is Churchill's recent 'tick'). Prytz expressed his anxiety in this connection, for Sweden would find itself between the devil and the deep blue sea, as both belligerents would want to use its territory for themselves. He then asked if this meant that, in the event of conflict with Germany, the USSR would automatically become an ally of England.

Churchill reddened, his eyes became bloodshot, and he cried with fury in his voice: 'To crush Germany I am prepared to enter into an alliance with anyone, even the devil!'

---

[29] In Maisky's memoirs, with obvious hindsight, he uses the tale to depict a heroic Churchill who stood firm against all odds. But the impression he and Prytz had at the time was entirely different.

[The flight of Rudolf Hess, Hitler's deputy, on a peace mission to Britain on 10 May is vital to any understanding of the Soviet attitude to the approaching conflict. The British archives reveal a clandestine operation by MI6, endorsed by the Foreign Office, to use covert channels to pass on disinformation to Moscow in an attempt to discourage Stalin from committing himself further to Germany. Maisky's unenviable task, hardly assisted by the growing rumours of an impending war, was to assess Hess's mission objectively, while remaining attentive to the entrenched concepts prevailing in Moscow. His normally assiduous entries in the diary were suspended for ten days, while his sparse dispatches to Narkomindel stood in sharp contrast to the intensive meetings he held in an attempt to make sense of the affair. At the Foreign Office, Maisky gleaned from Butler that as a result of a quarrel between Hess and Hitler, 'Hess decided to make his flight to England in the hope that here he would succeed in finding influential circles prepared to make peace with Germany'. He came to believe (as did Stalin) that Hess had either been lured by British intelligence or had come with the full knowledge of the German Government, which had been misled by German intelligence into assuming that he would find 'a strong party ready to negotiate with Hitler'. Though convinced that Churchill would not succumb, he failed to advise his government unequivocally what the British response might be.]

22 May

We visited the Webbs. I wanted to drink from the 'fount of wisdom' regarding the British political *mentality* and acquire some notion of what one may expect of England in the near future. I well remember how, in response to my question about a year ago as to what England would do if France were to quit the battlefield, the Webbs answered without the slightest hesitation: 'She will fight alone.'

Events have fully corroborated their prognosis.

Today I asked the Webbs another question: what will England do if she loses Egypt and her positions in the Middle East? Their answer this time was just as categorical: 'England will continue the war, for until this island is conquered by the Germans (and the leaders seem to be sure that invasion is impossible), there is always the hope that the loss of Egypt and so on is temporary – till the end of the war. Besides, Hitler's constant victories irritate and enrage our bourgeoisie. They can't reconcile themselves to his successes. They are stubborn and will do their utmost to beat Germany.'

I was interested to find out whether the attitudes of the British ruling elite are affected by the growing *unrest* in the mother country or in the British Empire. For the unrest will inevitably increase with every passing month of the war. Won't this circumstance make the British bourgeoisie more acquiescent in the matter of peace with Germany? The Webbs gave me a quite definite answer to this question as well: 'There is no serious *unrest* among the masses at the moment and it is doubtful whether it will manifest itself soon.' ...

3 June

Beaverbrook came for lunch (there were three of us: Beaverbrook, I and Agniya). ... I asked Beaverbrook what he thinks of Hess. Beaverbrook answered without hesitation: 'Oh, Hess, of course, is Hitler's emissary.'

There are many proofs, but Beaverbrook considers two to be the most convincing: an additional fuel tank was attached to Hess's plane, and he flew from Germany to Scotland assisted by a Pelengator.[30] Hess (i.e. Hitler) was counting on British 'Quislings' – the duke of Hamilton,[31] the duke of Buccleuch[32] and others. It is not without reason that Hess landed near Hamilton's estate. Judging by all the available evidence, Hess expected to spend 2–3 days in England, negotiate with the local 'Quislings' and fly back home. Hess offered England a peace on 'honourable' terms: the British Empire would remain *intact*, the European continent would go to Germany, plus some colonies in Africa, a non-aggression pact for 25 years. All this was served up with a spicy anti-Soviet sauce in defence of 'civilization against Bolshevist barbarism'. However, the precondition for peace and for an agreement was the removal of Churchill from power. Hess is convinced that as long as Churchill heads the Government, there can be no 'friendship' between Germany and England. Beaverbrook remarked sarcastically: 'Hess probably thought that as soon as he presented his plan to the dukes they would run to the king, overthrow Churchill and set up a "reasonable government"... Idiot!'

Hess's gamble on the British 'Quislings' has failed. From being an 'emissary' he has become a 'prisoner of war'. Churchill, according to Beaverbrook, does not fully agree with his theory. However, the PM does not himself have a clear view of the 'Hess incident' and so does not want to speak in Parliament on this matter.

Beaverbrook spoke about Hitler's plans. Hitler undoubtedly wants peace. He proposed peace ('on honourable terms') through Sweden right after the collapse of France, he proposed peace through Hess, and is now launching a major 'peace offensive' in the United States – nothing has come or will come of all this! In particular, Roosevelt will not play the role of peace-maker, whatever the Germans may think. The pope, on the other hand, does seem to be seeking ways of drawing closer to Hitler. But this will not help him on the question of peace.

---

[30] Radio direction finder.
[31] Douglas Douglas-Hamilton (14th duke of Hamilton), Royal Air Force, 1939–45; Conservative MP, 1930–40.
[32] Walter John Montagu Douglas Scott (8th duke of Buccleuch), a Tory peer.

Beaverbrook thinks that Hitler's present strategic plan is the following: first, an attack on Egypt and the Suez Channel, then the capture of Gibraltar, and then the liquidation of the British fleet in the Mediterranean.

... Beaverbrook launched a vicious attack on the English: they are carefree and sluggish, underestimate the severity of the situation, do not look ahead, are always late, have grown accustomed to the quiet life and don't want to give up their comforts. They are capable of doing so many stupid things! Examples? There are plenty.

... Why was Crete lost? Certainly not because the Germans were especially strong or especially capable. It happened for the simple reason that, despite Crete being in British hands for seven months, the Middle East Command did nothing to fortify it. As a result, it fell to the Germans.

The military command in the Middle East? Who are they? Wavell? Just think of the eulogies bestowed on him so recently! And now? *Sic transit gloria mundi.*

On the whole, the English, according to Beaverbrook (he himself is a Canadian!), are asleep. They need to be woken up. They need to be struck hard on the head. ...

3 June

Together with Novikov, I paid a visit to Leathers,[33] the new minister of war transport. ... I heard the following colourful story about the appointment of Leathers as minister of war transport. His appointment came as a total surprise to him. He himself confirmed to me in our conversation that he had to accept his post with *24 hours notice.* He has been in coal and transport all his life. I don't know who recommended Leathers to the prime minister as a suitable candidate for leading the war transport ministry, but what is certain is that a month ago Churchill summoned him and offered him the newly established post. Leathers' first reaction was negative: he said he had never been engaged in politics before, that he was scared of Parliament, which he didn't understand at all, and that he preferred to remain what he had always been, a *business man.*

The prime minister glanced askance at him and said: 'You are afraid of the House of Commons? Hm... I see... But there is a way out: we shall make you a Lord.'

'A Lord?' echoed Leathers, somewhat perplexed. He had not expected such a turn of events.

Nevertheless, he liked the prime minister's offer and agreed to take the post of minister of war transport.

---

[33] Frederick James Leathers, minister of war transport, 1941–45.

Coming back to his office Leathers called his wife: '*Darling*, prepare a bottle of champagne for dinner.'

'What for?' his wife asked in amazement.

'*Darling*, you'll be a baroness tomorrow.'

And that's what happened.

[Maisky glosses over a most important meeting he had with Eden on 2 June. Eden unveiled to Maisky intelligence reports concerning the German deployment on the Soviet borders, though – in order not to compromise the Enigma source – he remained somewhat aloof. Pressed by Maisky, however, he conceded that the concentrations might be 'part of a war of nerves' in an attempt to 'force from the Soviet Government concessions'. Eden noted, though, that while Maisky emphatically denied the rumours, it seemed 'that he might be trying to convince himself as he went along'. Within days, Cripps was unexpectedly rushed back to London for consultations on the German threat that would face the British in the Middle East if the Russians were to conclude a military alliance with Germany. The fact that the announcement of his recall was withheld, together with the hints dropped by Cripps during his last meeting with Vyshinsky that if circumstances changed he might not return to his post in Moscow, fuelled a wave of rumours. Maisky was anxious to establish whether the recall came against the background of Hess's mission and indicated connivance in the German move eastwards.]

10 June

Less than a month has passed since the last general debate on the war in Parliament (6–7 May), and so many changes have already occurred! Time now flies not like an express train, but like a high-speed fighter plane. ... It would be wrong to speak of a growing mood in favour of peace. This is not yet the case. Regardless of Crete, the determination to fight, to fight until 'victory', still dominates both government circles and public opinion.

... There has not been such a heated debate for a long time – not since Churchill came to power at any rate. ... How did the prime minister respond? Very nervously. He was annoyed and irritated, less eloquent than usual, and even made some tactical errors when arguing with his opponents (with Hore-Belisha in particular). But, on the whole, Churchill rebuffed the attack successfully, although today there was nothing to recall the evening of 7 May, when agitated MPs gave the PM a stormy ovation.

... The general conclusion: today's debate shows that the Government's stocks (Churchill's too) have fallen a little, but that the Cabinet is not yet in any serious danger. For deep down everybody understands (without wishing to state openly) the main reason for England's failures and at the same time everyone understands that the country's position is, despite everything, much stronger and more secure than a year ago.

... In the corridors of Parliament, I met Lloyd George (who did not speak today) and we exchanged a few words concerning the current situation over a cup of tea.

The old man is gloomy and anxious. He, at least, is under no illusions. In view of the present position of the USSR (for which he lays great blame on the British Government), Lloyd George excludes the possibility of a British victory. This means that a compromise peace must be sought. On what terms? Lloyd George thinks that peace could be reached if Hitler were to declare himself satisfied with a *Greater Germany.*

... I asked Lloyd George what he thought of the peace terms proposed by Hess.

'Absolutely unacceptable,' the old man answered categorically. 'If Hitler decides to insist on these terms, continuation of the war is inevitable.'

10 June

Conversation with Eden

(1) In reply to Eden's question concerning an 'alliance' between Hitler and the USSR, I declared that there has been neither a new agreement nor a dissolution of the old one between us. Powerful impressions and mistrust. Eden says he has information suggesting that the most serious negotiations, on matters of immense importance, are being conducted between Germany and the USSR. I: 'One should not believe every rumour.' ...

(2) Eden: Have I received a reply to his démarche of 2 June concerning the Middle East? No! My personal opinion: considering the present state of relations between England and the USSR, it would be difficult to respond to this démarche. ...

(3) I ask about the fate of Hess. Eden replies that he will have to spend some time in England – until the end of the war. Eden's theory: Hess fled because of a quarrel not with Hitler, but with another dignitary (Ribbentrop or Himmler[34]). All those men are at each other's throats. ...

12 June

The press is conducting a vast campaign, focusing on the massing of German troops on the Soviet border and the inevitability of war between the USSR and Germany...

---

[34] Heinrich Himmler, head of the Gestapo from 1936.

Here is what I have just learned about the hidden history of this campaign. On 7 June Churchill summoned the editors of the London newspapers and briefed them on the war situation in the spirit of his speech in Parliament on 10 June. The PM's speech gave little cause for cheer. Above all, the listeners couldn't see how and when England might win.

One of the editors asked Churchill a question concerning relations between the British and Soviet governments. Churchill replied that the Soviet Government resembles a crocodile, which bites whether you beat it or pat it. The British Government, he said, had tried various means of improving relations with the Soviet Union and had sought to influence it, but all to no avail. Eventually, the British Government had come to the conclusion that it would be better to let things follow their natural course. A collision between Germany and the USSR is inevitable. The massing of German troops on the Soviet border proceeds apace. One must wait...

13 June

Eden telephoned, invited me and asked me to come alone, because Eden would be alone. I answered him that I did not see any reason not to bring Novikov with me. When we were in the reception area, the secretary emerged and stated that it would be better for N. to wait in the reception area. However, I went in to see E. with N. Seeing us together, E. flushed deeply with irritation, which I had never seen in him so far, and shouted: 'I don't want to be rude, but it should be said that today's invitation is for the ambassador alone, not for the ambassador and the counsellor.' I replied that there were no secrets between me and N., and I did not understand why he could not accompany me in the discussions. E. heatedly said that he had no personal animosity towards N., but that he could not set an undesirable precedent; if the Soviet ambassador could arrive with his counsellor, then other ambassadors can do the same. If one can take counsellors, why not take two or three secretaries as well. Then whole delegations will come, not ambassadors. This is inconvenient. Eden has always received ambassadors alone. And he is not about to change his routine. I shrugged my shoulders. N. stayed, but Eden was red-faced and sulky during the whole conversation. An abnormal situation was created. If such a scene is repeated, I will have to bow and go back to the embassy.[35]

---

[35] Regardless of the tone of his entry, Maisky was most embarrassed by the incident. Upon returning to the embassy, he hastened to send Eden 'warm greetings' for his birthday. 'May the coming years,' he concluded, 'bring you good health and luck; and the faculty to find the right way in the very complicated circumstances of our time.'

(1) Eden informed me on behalf of the prime minister that the concentration of German troops on the Soviet borders has intensified, particularly during the past 48 hours. The aim of the concentration: war or a war of nerves? In case it turned out to be war, the British Government wished to bring it to the notice of the Soviet Government that if Germany attacked, the British Government will be prepared to provide assistance using its air force units in the Middle East, to send to Moscow a military mission to share the experiences gained during the war, and to develop economic cooperation in every possible way (through the Persian Gulf and Vladivostok).

(2) I suggested that the proposed measures hinted at a level of friendship between the two countries which presently does not exist.

(3) Even if there was a concentration of troops on the border, I do not believe the Germans will attack the Soviet Union.

(4) I attracted Eden's attention to the press campaign connected with Cripps's return to England. What a pity they were busy speculating.

[In his memoirs, Maisky overplays his own warnings to Stalin. He has successfully deluded historians into believing that on 10 June he transmitted to Moscow an 'urgent' ciphered telegram with specific intelligence he had obtained from Cadogan. He claims, therefore, that it was with 'extreme amazement' that he reacted to Stalin's response in the form of the communiqué released on the evening of 13 June, denying the rumours of an impending war between Germany and Russia. The communiqué, however, was in fact a logical culmination of his own appraisals. His emphasis conceals the fact that the significant meeting with Cadogan at which he received the detailed evidence of German troop concentrations took place not on 10 June, as he claims, but rather on 16 June. Maisky blatantly misconstrued his narrative to cover up his own contribution to the self-deception and delusion which affected the Kremlin on the eve of war.

On 13 June, Eden summoned Maisky to inform him of the increasing flow of reliable intelligence in the previous 48 hours, which now left the Joint Intelligence Committee convinced that Hitler 'has made up his mind to have done with Soviet obstruction and intends to attack her'. Still under the influence of the press campaign following Cripps's return from Moscow, Maisky paid no heed to Eden's frantic attempts to point out that the information had been obtained from extremely reliable sources. Burdened nonetheless with the heavy responsibility of weighing the significance of the intelligence, Maisky pressed Eden for specific details 'at an early date, either today or during the week-end'.

The decision to part with momentous evidence obtained through Enigma was finally sanctioned by Churchill late on Sunday, 15 June. It included a map that depicted in minute detail the deployment of the German forces on the border. Maisky was astounded when he was subjected to Cadogan's detached and monotonous recital of 'precise and concrete' evidence. What disturbed him was not so much the realization, subsequently so graphically depicted in his memoirs, that 'this avalanche, breathing fire and death, was at any moment to descend' upon Russia, but rather the content of his previous misleading communications, which had led to the publication of the communiqué denying rumours of war. He hastened therefore to cable Moscow, reversing his earlier assessments. Indeed, when Cripps dined with Maisky on 18 June, he formed the distinct impression that Maisky 'seemed much less confident that there would not be a war' than he had been at their meeting a few days earlier. He noticed that their conversation had brought about 'a complete deflation of the Soviet Ambassador who now seemed very depressed'.]

18 June

A week after his arrival in London, Cripps and his wife visited Agniya and me. We lunched together at the embassy.

What mood are the Crippses in?

... Cripps is absolutely convinced of the inevitability of a German attack on us and is certain this will happen very soon.

'If this does not happen before the middle of July,' he noted, 'I'll be greatly surprised.'

Cripps added that, according to the British Government's information, Hitler has amassed 147 divisions on the Soviet borders.

I set about disproving this. The point of my objection was that, to my mind, Hitler is not yet ready for suicide. A campaign against the Soviet Union is, after all, tantamount to suicide. That is why it is difficult for me to believe in a German attack on the Soviet Union, especially in the next few days. It is difficult to deny the concentration of German troops on our borders, but I deem this more likely to be one of Hitler's moves in the 'war of nerves'. I cannot rule out the possibility that Hitler may start making demands to us concerning supplies and trade. Politicians seek to create a suitable psychological atmosphere to lend extra weight to their demands. But war? An invasion? An attack?... I can't believe it! It would be madness.

... Cripps would not agree with me. He adduced the following arguments. Hitler cannot plunge into a final and decisive battle against England until the potential threat to Germany from the east has been eliminated. This must be done this year. For the Red Army is a serious force. It will be too late to attack the USSR in 1942, because all the defects exposed by the Finnish campaign will have been rectified by then. The Red Army will be too strong, while the strength of the Reichswehr is more likely to start diminishing. Today, after eight campaigns (Austria, Czechoslovakia, Poland, Norway, France, Holland, Belgium and the Balkans), the Reichswehr is at its zenith. Army morale is exceptionally high and vast experience has been accumulated. True, the USSR has more men and machines, but the Germans are better at organizing than the Russians. Cripps, comparing the two sides objectively, finds it difficult to foretell the outcome of Germany's clash with the USSR. One thing is clear, however: Hitler's chances of success are much higher now than they will be in a year's time. That is why Cripps is so sure that Hitler will strike. Moreover, Cripps possesses absolutely reliable information that this is just what Hitler is planning. If he manages to defeat the Soviet Union, he will then bring all Germany's might down on England. Cripps has spoken to some members of the British Government who think that before attacking the USSR Hitler will present us with an ultimatum. Cripps does not agree. Hitler will attack us without prior warning because he is interested not so much in getting food, raw materials, etc. from the USSR, as in the destruction of the country and the elimination of the Red Army.

We had a long argument. Cripps stuck to his line.

I asked Cripps when he was going to return to Moscow. He shrugged his shoulders and said this depended on many circumstances. He started elaborating. First, he mentioned the TASS communiqué of 13 June which, in Cripps's view, was issued to please Schulenburg. Its meaning is clear: the Soviet Government lets it be known that Cripps is no longer 'persona grata' and had better leave Moscow. I objected, assuring Cripps that the Soviet Government has a high opinion of him personally and that all his difficulties in the USSR have stemmed from the policy of the British Government. Cripps, however, did not agree with this and by way of proof cited a telegram he received today from Moscow, which says that the Moscow diplomatic corps considers the communiqué to be a 'polite hint' on the part of the Soviet Government aimed at showing Cripps the door. Cripps kept returning over and over again to Schulenburg as the cause of all his troubles in Moscow. It was obvious that Schulenburg vexes Cripps greatly.

... After Cripps left, I fell to pondering: 'Is Cripps right? Will Hitler really attack us?'

I did not reach any certain conclusion. It seemed improbable to me that Hitler could attack, knowing our might and our determination to resist. But does he know of them?...

21 June (Bovingdon)

The morning

A wonderful summer's day. Bright sun. Hot. Today we wore light suits and cycled. I'm making remarkable progress in this art.

Then I lay on the grass, resting my head on my hands, and gazed into the deep blue skies. I lay and wondered: 'Will there really be war?'

In the past 2–3 weeks the atmosphere in London has been thick with anticipation of a German attack on the Soviet Union. The press writes about it, it is
discussed in the corridors of Parliament, Churchill has spoken about it in
public more than once, offering us the British Government's assistance, and
Cripps told me about it with absolute confidence just three days ago...

... To tell the truth, I am disinclined to believe that Hitler will attack us.
Fighting Russia has always been hard. Invasions have always ended in sorrow
for their initiators. It is enough to recall the Poles (during the Time of Troubles),
Charles XII, Napoleon, and the Kaiser in 1918. The diesel motor has, of course,
introduced great changes in the methods and possibilities of the art of war, but
still... Russian geography remains the same. ...

The evening

After lunch, I was hastily summoned to London at Cripps's request. He came to
see me at 4.30 p.m.

He again spoke of the inevitability of a German attack on the USSR.
Very soon.

'To tell the truth,' he said, 'I expected the attack to occur this "weekend" –
tomorrow, the 22nd – but Hitler has evidently delayed it till next Sunday, the
29th.'

I asked: 'Why till "Sunday" exactly?'

'Because Hitler,' replied Cripps, 'generally likes to attack his victims on
Sundays. After all, it gives him a small advantage: the enemy is somewhat less
prepared on Sundays than usual.'

Being convinced of the inevitability of war between the USSR and Germany,
Cripps has already undertaken some preliminary measures. He has arranged
with the British Government for a military and economic mission to be sent to
Moscow immediately following the outbreak of hostilities.

... But Cripps wanted to know what attitude the Soviet Government would
take towards such plans. Would the Soviet Government find it possible to
cooperate with England in the event of a German invasion? Or would it prefer
to act quite independently?

I could not give Cripps a definite answer and promised to liaise with
Moscow at once.

On parting, Cripps said: 'I am now off to the country. I need to have some
rest before things get going.'

Towards eight in the evening I returned to Bovingdon. Negrín and I walked
together around the garden for a long while, discussing the situation. Negrín,
like Cripps, is also almost certain that war between Germany and the USSR is
at hand.

Later I kept turning over in my head all the arguments for and against an imminent attack. It seemed improbable – not in general, but right now. Nonetheless, a puzzling question haunted me: 'Will there really be war?'

By the time I went to bed I had almost convinced myself that Hitler was not bluffing this time, but intended a serious invasion. Still, I did not want to believe it.

22 June

War!

I was woken at 8 a.m. by a telephone call from the embassy. In a breathless, agitated voice, Novikov informed me that Hitler had declared war on the USSR and that German troops had crossed our border at 4 a.m.

I woke up Agniya. There was, of course, no question of going back to sleep. We dressed quickly and went down to hear the nine o'clock news on English radio. Novikov had called for the second time a few minutes earlier: Eden wished to see me at 11.30.

We had a hasty breakfast, listened to the nine o'clock news, which added nothing to what we already knew, and set off for London. In the embassy we encountered a crowd of people, noise, commotion and general excitement. It resembled a disturbed beehive.

When I was getting into the car, to drive to Eden's office, I was told that Comrade Molotov would be going on the air at 11.30. I asked Eden to postpone our meeting by half an hour so that I could listen to the people's commissar. Eden willingly agreed. Sitting next to the radio, pencil in hand, I listened to what Comrade Molotov had to say and took down a few notes.

I arrived at the Foreign Office at midday. I was led into Eden's office. This was without doubt a major, serious and historical moment. One might have been forgiven for thinking, had one closed one's eyes, that everything should be somehow unusual, solemn and majestic at such a moment. The reality was otherwise. Eden rose from his armchair as usual, and with an affable expression took a few steps towards me. He was wearing a plain grey suit, a plain soft tie, and his left hand had been hastily bound with a white rag of some sort. He must have cut his palm with something. The rag kept sliding off, and Eden kept adjusting it while we talked. Eden's countenance, his suit, his tie, and especially that white piece of cloth entirely removed from our meeting any trace of the 'historical'. That modest dose of solemnity which I felt in my heart on crossing the threshold of Eden's office quite evaporated at the sight of that rag. Everything became rather simple, ordinary and prosaic. This impression was further enhanced when Eden began our conversation by asking me in the most humdrum fashion about the events at the front and the content of Comrade

52. Maisky informed of the German invasion of Russia through Molotov's radio speech.

Molotov's speech. This 'humdrum' tone was sustained for our entire meeting. I couldn't help but recall the sitting of Parliament on 3 September 1939, when Chamberlain informed the House about the outbreak of the war. At the time that sitting also struck me as being too simple and ordinary, lacking the appropriate 'historical solemnity'. In real life, it seems, everything is far more straightforward than it is in novels and history books.

... At 9 p.m. I listened to Churchill's broadcast with bated breath. A forceful speech! A fine performance! The prime minister had to play it safe, of course, in all that concerned communism – whether for the sake of America or his own party. But these are mere details. On the whole, Churchill's speech was bellicose and resolute: no compromises or agreements! War to the bitter end! Precisely what is most needed today.

At the same time, the response came through from Moscow to the question posed by Cripps yesterday: the Soviet Government is prepared to cooperate with England and has no objection to the arrival of British missions in the USSR.

I called Eden and asked him to communicate to Churchill my complete satisfaction with his speech. I also agreed to meet Eden the next morning.

So, it's war! Is Hitler really seeking his own death?

We did not want war; we did not want it at all. We did all we could to avoid it. But now that German fascism has imposed war on us, we shall give no quarter. We shall fight hard, resolutely, and stubbornly to the end, as befits Bolsheviks. Against German fascism first of all; later, we will see.

[Well into the morning of 22 June, Stalin did not exclude the possibility that Russia was being intimidated into political submission by the Germans. Stalin's miscalculation hinged on the belief that Hitler would attack only if he succeeded in reaching a peace agreement with Britain. When war broke out, recalled Litvinov, 'all believed that the British fleet was steaming up the North Sea for joint attack with Hitler on Leningrad and Kronstadt'. This explains the ominous silence and confusion which engulfed Maisky in the early days of the war. It is indeed most revealing that when Maisky met Eden on the day of the invasion, he was entirely haunted by the likelihood of an imminent Anglo-German peace: 'could the Soviet Government be assured that our war effort would not slacken?' Maisky urged Churchill to dispel the rumours of peace (which had been so prominent since Hess's arrival in Britain) in his radio speech to the nation which was scheduled for the evening.

Britain was no better prepared for the new reality of an alliance of sorts. The Molotov–Ribbentrop Pact had entrenched a fatalistic political concept, meticulously cultivated at the Foreign Office, that the Soviet Union was 'a potential enemy rather than a potential ally'. Once war became almost a certainty (a mere week before the German attack) the chiefs of staff evaluated that the Wehrmacht would cut through Russia 'like a hot knife through butter' within 3–6 weeks, leading to the capture of Moscow. The British Government's gloomy prognosis of Soviet prospects, which at best afforded Britain a breathing space and allowed her to pursue the peripheral strategy, did not encompass a full-blooded alliance, but rather, as Eden put it, 'a rapprochement of some sort … automatically forced upon us'.

Churchill's famous speech of 22 June addressed varying quarters and brilliantly concealed his determination to avoid major commitments. Churchill had readily acceded to a request by both the chiefs of staff and the Foreign Office not to refer to the Russians as 'allies'. His firm verbal support for Russia reinforced his grip in the domestic domain – weakened as a result of the chain of military fiascos in North Africa, Greece and Crete against the background of the heavy German bombing of Britain. For the moment, the Russians were satisfied with the denial of any connivance in the German attack and with a public undertaking to pursue the war right to the end.

Churchill's genuine objective was to avoid a revision of his grand strategy, which might affect the Middle Eastern arena. While drafting the speech, he hastened to issue directives on assistance to Russia which allowed for supplies and military operations, so long as they did not interfere with British deployment in other theatres or endanger British operations in planning or execution.]

27 June

The fifth day of the war. One may draw the following conclusions about the English situation in general.

(1) The first round of political support for the war, if we are talking about Great Britain and the British Empire, has been won. Hitler's calculation was quite clear: to strike to the east, to revive his glory as 'saviour of European civilization from Bolshevik barbarism', to cause a split in the public opinion of the 'democracies' and to secure either a favourable peace with them or, at the very least, their effective withdrawal from the war until he has finished dealing with the Bolsheviks. So far, this plan has entirely failed. ...

(2) Against this background, Churchill has played an extremely prominent and positive role. His fable about the optimistic frog has proved unexpectedly prescient. Without a moment's hesitation, he brought all his influence and eloquence to bear on the situation. Not only was the prime minister's radio broadcast on 22 June remarkable for its form and inner force: it also presented the case for fighting to the last and offering maximum aid to the USSR with the utmost clarity and implacability. ...

(3) So, the first round has been won. England is with us. Hitler's hopes for a separate peace with the 'democracies' have so far failed. All this is good. But some grey areas remain. First, what will England's aid consist of? And will it really be serious? I'm not sure. ... Second, *bewilderment* is still palpable in the minds of the public. Psychologically, this is quite understandable. Only recently 'Russia' was considered a covert ally of Germany, all but an enemy. And suddenly, within 24 hours, it has become a friend! This transition was too abrupt, and the British *mentality* has yet to adjust to the new state of affairs.

(4) Thirdly and lastly, great scepticism concerning the Red Army's efficacy may be observed in all quarters. People in the War Ministry believe that our resistance will last no more than 4–6 weeks.

[Maisky was quick off the mark, fighting fit after his long diplomatic seclusion and alienation from the Kremlin, which had lasted since the signing of the Molotov–Ribbentrop Pact. Not only did he regain confidence – enough to shake Novikov off his tail even at his first meeting with Eden – but he also managed to convey the sense that his implicit critical attitude towards association with the Germans had been borne out. 'As you know from my preceding communications,' he reminded Molotov, rather embellishing his stance on the eve of the war, 'I regarded the British will to war as fairly strong and did not anticipate an Anglo-German deal in the foreseeable future.' The 'expeditiousness and decisiveness' with which the British Government had acted, he added smugly, 'came to me as a pleasant surprise'. He further hailed Churchill, Eden and

Beaverbrook, the 'troika of friends of Russia', whom he had cultivated over the years, for the 'firm and favourable position they have adopted towards us'.]

6 July (Bovingdon)

The second week of the war has ended. I feel somewhat relieved. Of course, it is a great pity that our best forces, our young generation, perish in their thousands on the battlefields, that a sea of blood waters our Soviet land. But on the other hand, it has been proved not only in our patriotically motivated imagination, but also in deeds, that the Red Army can measure up to the Reichswehr, that it can withstand the crushing onslaught of the mechanized German Attila. I was sure of that before as well, but observing how often *wishful thinking* distorted the English perspective, I sometimes asked myself: wasn't I also exhibiting certain elements of *wishful thinking* in respect of the Red Army?

Now my doubts have been dispelled. True, we have suffered great losses in men, tanks, planes and territories. In the second week of the war, the Germans crossed the Western Dvina, reached Ostrov, crossed the Prut, entered Bessarabia, advanced towards Berezina and the region of Novograd-Volynsk, but this is not what matters. What matters is that nowhere did the Germans succeed in seriously breaking through our lines and crushing the Red Army's resistance. ...

It is already quite clear, however, that this is a case of diamond cut diamond. For the first time, Hitler has encountered an army that measures up to his own in terms of arms, methods of warfare and tactical techniques, and that surpasses his army in strength and morale. Moreover, Hitler has, for the first time, come up against a country that is monolithic within and whose leadership far surpasses his own in firmness, wisdom and confidence. The speech by Comrade Stalin, which I heard on the radio in the small hours of the morning of 3 July, is a document of the greatest historical significance. Its basic idea can be simply formulated: a patriotic war to the end! Until victory! No wavering! No compromises! Not a pound of bread, not a litre of petrol to the enemy! ...

[Despite the critical situation at the front, the Russians were adamant from the outset that the war aims, the post-war settlement and the strategic priorities needed to be defined. The Anglo-Soviet agreement, signed on 12 July, was of a purely allusive nature, pledging assistance 'without defining quantity and quality'; but most telling from the Soviet point of view was a mutual undertaking not to conclude a separate peace.

The Soviet military mission, headed by General Golikov,[36] the deputy chief of staff and head of Soviet Military Intelligence, arrived in London in the second week of July.

---

[36] Filipp Ivanovich Golikov, from July 1940 deputy chief of the general staff, head of the GRU (Soviet Military Intelligence); head of the military mission to the United Kingdom and Washington, 1941.

53. Maisky and the Soviet military mission headed by General Golikov and Admiral Kharlamov, watched over by the ubiquitous Novikov.

General Dill, the chief of staff, regarded the association with the Russians mostly as a liability: 'It is the Russians who are asking for assistance: we are not ... All our forces are now being devoted to the accomplishment of a definite strategy for winning the war *without* having allowed for Russian aid.' Indeed, Eden was duly worried 'at the lack of support of the Chiefs of Staff and even of the P.M. who, for all his brave words, is reluctant to agree to raids'.]

13 July (Bovingdon)

The third week of the war is over. ... Today, at 2 p.m., a momentous statement was broadcast over the radio in London and in Moscow: an agreement about a military alliance was signed yesterday evening in Moscow between the USSR and England. The parties undertake to assist one another in every way during the war and to conclude neither a separate armistice nor a separate peace.

Very good!

I remember that about two years ago, when the Anglo-French military delegation went to Moscow to negotiate a mutual assistance pact, I wrote in my diary that the logic of things, despite the subjective aspirations of the two sides, was driving the USSR and England to form a bloc against Germany. Such was the international situation. I made the reservation, though, that the two countries might cease to share common interests and that their paths might diverge, if and when questions surrounding the final division between capitalism and socialism became the order of the day. After I wrote these lines in my diary, many events occurred which seemed to refute my theory entirely: the non-aggression pact with Germany, rapprochement with Berlin along economic and political lines, confrontation with England during the Soviet–Finnish war, and the cold, hostile relations between London and Moscow in the course of last year... More than once during this period I asked myself the question: did I make a wrong prognosis? Was the theory recorded in my diary in August 1939 correct? Shouldn't I amend it?

But an inner voice kept repeating: no, you were not wrong! Your theory is correct! And I did not make any amendments. Now life has proved me right: the USSR and England are allies. They have joined forces to wage a deadly struggle against Germany.

Both countries can say: 'Our paths have converged.' But nothing is forever. The 'paths' can diverge... Under a variety of circumstances. Especially if and when the problem of capitalism and socialism is placed on the agenda in one form or another.

Cripps must be triumphant! His life's dream (since the war broke out, at least) has been fulfilled. What's more, the success is his. This massively strengthens his position. He will return to England as a hero, to the great displeasure and embarrassment of such men as Citrine, Bevin and Attlee, who sent him to Moscow last year, hoping to get rid of a restless and dangerous rival, and who did so much in the past year to prevent Cripps from achieving even a crumb of success in the matter of improving Anglo-Soviet relations.

The world is in the grip of the most severe contradictions. Today brought a vivid illustration of this fact.

Ever since the USSR entered the war, a tragicomic *controversy* has flared up in England. The BBC introduced the following practice last year: the national anthems of all Allies are played on Sundays before the nine o'clock news broadcast. Naturally, after 22 June, the question arose: should the 'Internationale' be played over the wireless or not? The answer would seem obvious: it should. But do, please, remember: the 'Internationale' is not only the national anthem of the USSR, but is also the militant song of the international proletariat, and in particular of the British Communist Party. The hair of thousands of British Blimps stands on end when they hear it. It came to blows – in the press, in Parliament, in society. ... Duff Cooper rang me up on 11 July and asked whether we might be able to find some other Soviet or Russian song to replace it. He, for instance, had heard an orchestra playing 'Kutuzov's March' after Molotov's speech on 22 June – couldn't that be substituted for the 'Internationale'? Needless to say, I categorically opposed the idea. On the 12th, I visited Duff Cooper. ... I learned from my conversation with Duff Cooper that Churchill himself is behind all this. He declares: I am ready to do anything for Russia, but I will not allow the communists to make political capital from the 'Internationale'. ...

The conclusion of a military alliance between the USSR and Great Britain was announced today at two o'clock. I was waiting with curiosity to hear what the BBC would offer at 8.45 in the evening. And? The first item in the programme of national anthems was... a very beautiful but little-known Soviet song. There was no 'Internationale'. After that song, all the other national anthems were played one after another.

... We were at the dinner table when the BBC demonstrated the British Government's cowardice and foolishness. Agniya got terribly worked up, while being cross with me for being calm and finding it all amusing (I was mocking the British Government). She exclaimed: 'I see we have spent these nine years in England for nothing!'

Unable to contain herself, she leapt to her feet and ran out of the room in tears. It took me some time to calm her down. ...

20 July

Yesterday morning I received Stalin's 'personal message' to Churchill with a request to translate it into English and hand it over at once. It was Saturday. I met Eden in the morning, on matters concerning Iran, and asked him to arrange an appointment for me with the prime minister. Eden asked me in confidence whether he should be present when I handed over the 'message'. I replied that the 'message' dealt with military-strategic issues. Eden exclaimed: 'If so, the business can be handled without me.'

... At around one o'clock, Eden called me from the Foreign Office and said that Churchill would receive me at five in the afternoon, but asked me to come to Chequers where he was spending the 'weekend'. Having completed the translation of the message and typed it up (to maintain secrecy I did it all myself), I took off to the countryside. The weather was capricious, with rain giving way to bright sunshine. Teterev, who had not been to Chequers before, lost his way and took the wrong turn. When we finally reached the PM's country residence, it was already nearly 5.30. It was embarrassing, but nothing could be done.

A young secretary met me at the door and led me to the prime minister.

'They are having tea,' he uttered on the way.

Dark halls, old paintings, strange staircases... How it should be in a respectful, solid English house several centuries old. Not that I know how old Chequers is. Maybe it is relatively young – by English standards, of course.

Eventually, the secretary flung a door wide open and I found myself in a large lit room in the shape of an extended rectangle. It was noisy and full of life. Mrs Churchill sat at the table and poured the tea. There were several young people of both sexes at the table and near it. General Ismay[37] sat to one side, by a window. Everyone was talking, laughing, exchanging remarks. The air was filled with chatter. Churchill, dressed in strange grey-blue overalls and a belt (a cross between a bricklayer's work clothes and an outfit suitable for a bomb shelter), was sitting in the other corner of the room and playing *Halma* with some pretty young girl. He gave my hand a friendly shake and replied good-humouredly to my apologies for being late: 'That's all right. Have a cup of tea while I finish the game.'

Mrs Churchill sat me next to her very hospitably, while Randolph's red-haired wife set about offering me biscuits. I drank two cups. Ate a few biscuits. Randolph was mentioned. His wife complained that she had little hope of seeing him soon. She said proudly that 'baby Winston' had started to walk.

Finally the prime minister ended the game, stood up, nodded to the guests and led me downstairs to a somewhat large and dreary *drawing-room*. We sat on a sofa at the fireplace and I presented Churchill with Stalin's 'personal message'. The prime minister started reading it slowly, attentively, now and then consulting a geographical map which was close at hand. He was evidently pleased – pleased at the very fact of having received a 'personal message' – and did not try to conceal it. When Churchill came to the paragraph where Stalin said that the position of our army would now be immeasurably worse had they had to begin their defence at the old borders of the USSR and not the new ones, he stopped and exclaimed: 'Quite right! I've always understood and sought to justify the policy of "limited expansion" which Stalin has pursued in the last two years.'

When the prime minister finished reading the message, I asked him what he thought of it. Churchill replied that first he had to consult HQ. He could make just a few preliminary comments. He likes the idea of a northern front in Norway.

... As if to prove his point, Churchill picked up the telephone and asked to speak to Admiral Pound,[38] chief of the naval staff. He began asking him about the preparations for Admiral Vian's[39] naval operation and the aircraft carrier operation in the area of Petsamo – they are scheduled for the end of the month.

---

[37] General Hastings Ismay, military adviser to Churchill and deputy secretary (military) to the War Cabinet 1940–45.

[38] Admiral Sir (Alfred) Dudley Pound, admiral of the fleet, 1939; first sea lord and chief of naval staff, 1939–43.

[39] Admiral Sir Philip Louis Vian, led the attack on the battleship *Bismarck*, May 1941; promoted to rear-admiral and sent to Russia for naval cooperation in the evacuation of Russians from Spitzbergen, July 1941.

He pressed Pound to act fast and gave him orders in a sharp, somewhat irritated tone.

But on the matter of a second front in France, Churchill immediately took a negative stand. This cannot be done. It's risky. It will end in disaster for England, bringing no benefits at all. All the prime minister's arguments are expounded in detail in his reply to Stalin's 'personal message'. To vindicate his position, Churchill appealed to Ismay, who had just entered the room where we were talking. Ismay fully backed the PM. ... Perhaps in order to soften the impression made by his refusal, the prime minister began to talk about an air offensive against Germany from the west.

'We shall bomb Germany mercilessly,' he exclaimed emphatically. 'Day after day, week after week, month after month! We will keep expanding our raids and increasing the strength of our strikes. In the end we will overwhelm Germany with bombs. We will break the morale of the population.'

Then Churchill suddenly shifted to Iran, repeating everything I had heard from Eden this morning, but in a sharper and more resolute form.

'The Shah must not be allowed to pursue *monkey tricks*,' the prime minister uttered heatedly. 'Persia must be with us! The Shah must choose one way or the other.'

Churchill added that if the Shah persisted, a military occupation of Persia by Anglo-Soviet forces would be necessary. He hinted, moreover, that the Persian operation, along with Norway, could also be a sort of 'second front'.

Since it was clear that there could be no talk of a landing operation on the other side of the Channel for now, I turned to questions of supplies, emphasizing their importance.

... Then Churchill started asserting that victory was possible only with the active participation of the United States in the war, noting that on questions of supply the USSR should count first and foremost on the USA. He promised to facilitate our access to the American armaments market, if necessary.

... When our conversation was coming to an end, Hopkins,[40] who was spending the 'weekend' at Chequers as the prime minister's guest, entered the room. We greeted each other, but talked little. I asked Hopkins about certain American supplies with which we had encountered difficulties. He promised to make inquiries and inform me of the results. It's strange, but Hopkins reminds me – in his countenance, manners and dress – of a Zemstvo statistician of olden times.

Churchill and I parted warmly and amicably. As I was leaving, I heard his secretary summoning chiefs of staff for a conference that evening. Churchill

---

[40] Harry Lloyd Hopkins, secretary of commerce, 1938–40; special adviser and personal assistant to Roosevelt throughout the war.

promised to dispatch an urgent reply to Stalin through Cripps, and to send me a copy.

Admiral Pound called on me at 11 p.m. today and did indeed present me with a copy of the PM's reply. In it I found everything I had heard from his lips yesterday. In general, it gives little cause for comfort. No second front in France for now. The entire burden of fighting against the German war machine rests on our shoulders. But at least the PM's stance is now clear to me. That is important. Illusions must be avoided! *Wishful thinking* is worst of all.

[Eden and Beaverbrook challenged Churchill's Russian policy. It was Beaverbrook who had first raised the idea of a second front at his meeting with Maisky on 27 June. Eden had often wished to shake off his image as Churchill's pampered heir. His earlier attempts to assert his independence led nowhere. The German invasion of Russia afforded Eden, reputed to be held in high esteem by the Russians, an opportunity to improve his political standing. Apprehensive lest Eden commit Britain too far, Churchill, who had hitherto shown only a marginal interest in Russia, drove him off the scene and resorted to direct correspondence with Stalin. In private, Eden expressed repugnance at Churchill's 'sentimental and florid' telegrams, which were bound to lead Stalin to the correct conclusion that 'guff no substitute for guns'.]

29 July

So, Harry Hopkins is in Moscow! What a remarkable story this has turned out to be.

On 25 July, I met Hopkins at the American embassy. Winant was present. Molotov had asked me to discuss with Hopkins the possibility of providing us with a range of material and fighters which the Americans had sent to the Middle East for the English. My talk on this subject with the president's 'personal emissary' brought little success. ... True, Hopkins assured me that Roosevelt was ready to provide the USSR with every kind of support in the struggle against Hitler, but warned me at the same time against cultivating any illusions regarding the speed and scope of American armaments aid.

... Once this topic was exhausted, Hopkins suddenly asked: what could be done to bring Roosevelt and Stalin closer?

I did not understand Hopkins right away. He then started explaining that Stalin was little more than a name for Roosevelt. The abstract head, perhaps, of the Soviet Government. There is nothing concrete, material or personal in Roosevelt's perception of Stalin. ... It was evident that Hopkins was very pre-occupied by the matter of 'acquaintance' between Roosevelt and Stalin and that he had been doing some serious thinking.

... On the 27th I was in Bovingdon. At around ten in the evening a telephone call came from the embassy and I was informed that Winant wanted to see me urgently on important business. I set off to town straightaway. When I entered the embassy building it was ten past eleven. Winant was sitting in my office and talking with Novikov. It turned out that Winant had brought along the passports of Hopkins and his two assistants. He asked me to put visas on their passports immediately as the three of them were leaving for the USSR in half an hour. I did not understand what he was talking about. But Winant exclaimed impatiently: 'I'll explain everything to you afterwards. For now just give me the visas. The train departs for Scotland at 11.40. Hopkins is already at the station. I must give him the passports with the visas before the train departs.'

That's easy to say: give me the visas! All the stamps and seals were at the consulate. Driving to the consulate would take a quarter of an hour, and there would probably be no one there anyway at such a late hour. What to do?

I adjusted quickly, in the Bolshevik style. After all, Hopkins' visit to Moscow could not be delayed on account of a few paragraphs in the consular instructions! I took Hopkins' passport and wrote on a blank leaf by hand: 'I request that Mr Harry Hopkins be allowed through without inspection of his luggage. Ambassador of the USSR to Great Britain I. Maisky. 27 July 1941.' Then I called Lepekhin and attached our seal. I did the same with the other two passports. I expect the head of the NKID consular department to faint when he sees 'my visa'. Such a visa, I imagine, has never been recorded in the annals of our diplomacy. But why worry? Even Peter the Great used to say: 'The law itself can be changed if the need requires it.' Here the 'need' was unquestionable.

Winant took the passports and left. He came back at midnight.

'I only just made it,' he exclaimed on entering my office. 'The train was already moving.'

[Hopkins, Roosevelt's powerful close adviser, left Churchill in no doubt that the president attached supreme significance to the breathing space achieved through the war in the East, was unhappy about the heavy burden that the campaign in North Africa imposed on the United States, and favoured a redistribution of resources. Hopkins' arrival in Moscow as Churchill's envoy made it possible for Cripps to intervene and persuade Hopkins that the *sine qua non* for an alliance was immediate military cooperation, sustained by long-term political agreements. He proposed a conference, at which the United States, the Soviet Union and Britain would 'fully and jointly explore the relative interests of each front'. The assistance to Russia was to be granted not as 'merely sparing to a partner or ally what we feel we can spare but rather as the point upon which we should concentrate all our efforts'. Cripps even provided Hopkins with a draft telegram to Stalin, which Churchill reluctantly endorsed at his first summit meeting with Roosevelt at Placentia Bay a fortnight later.]

30 July

Today at long last we signed the Soviet–Polish treaty! I can barely believe it.

Novikov, Korzh, Zinchenko,[41] Zonov[42] and I arrived in the F[oreign] O[ffice] at 4.15 this afternoon. The rain was pouring down, dull grey clouds scuttled over the sky. We entered the reception room. I started telling our young men that meetings on 'non-intervention' in Spain had once been held in this room. Before I had finished my story Sikorski appeared in his general's uniform, accompanied by the chairman of the Polish Sejm and also some ministers. ...

Eden glanced at his watch and said rapidly: 'The prime minister has not yet come...'

Then, as if to apologize, he added: 'You know, the prime minister likes to take an hour's nap after lunch. Such is his habit. He will be here any moment.'

Then Eden laid his hand on Sikorski's shoulder, led him aside and whispered a few words to the Polish prime minister. After that he came to me, laid his hand on my shoulder in similar fashion, and said in a subdued voice and with slight embarrassment: 'Please forgive my foolish question. During the signing at the table, I'll sit in the middle... Do you mind the general sitting to the right of me, and you on the left? He is the prime minister, after all...'

I laughed heartily and replied: 'No, I don't mind. It's not the place that makes the man...'

Eden sighed with relief and added cheerfully: 'Thank you so much.'

Still no Churchill. Those present wandered about Eden's room rather aimlessly. Strang and Novikov fussed around the table where the signing was to take place. This table, which was long and covered with a cloth, stood to one side, to the right of the table at which Eden usually received his guests, along the wall displaying Pitt's bust.

Sikorski addressed me in French. He was delighted that we were signing the treaty. He came to the conclusion long ago that Poland could not balance between its neighbours in the west and in the east for ever. It had to choose: either with Germany against Russia, or with Russia against Germany. Sikorski himself has always thought that Poland must be with Russia against Germany.

... Suddenly, it was as if a gust of wind had swept through the room. Everyone fell silent and turned their gaze to the door: the prime minister had appeared in the doorway. Eden's warning proved apposite. Churchill really had just got out of bed. This could be seen from his sagging face, his red, somewhat watery

---

[41] Konstantin Emelianovich Zinchenko, from 1940 to 1942 second, then first, secretary at the Soviet embassy in Great Britain; central organ of NKID in Moscow, 1942–44.
[42] Vasily Matveevich Zonov, head of the consular section at the Soviet embassy in Great Britain, 1939–41; second secretary at the embassy, 1941–44.

54. No love lost – Sikorski and Maisky signing the Soviet–Polish treaty.

eyes, and his generally sleepy appearance.[43] Dressed in a black coat and striped
trousers, broad-shouldered, thickset, his head obstinately lowered – a real
English bulldog – the prime minister inspected the scene with a furtive smile.
Eden hurried to greet him and led him into the middle of the room. Sikorski
introduced his 'retinue' to Churchill, and I introduced mine.

    We then got down to business. It was already half past four. We took our
seats at the table for the signing of the treaty. Eden sat in the middle and
Churchill on his left. I sat further to the left at the corner, while Sikorski took
his seat to the right of Eden. The Polish Pan had schemed in vain, for fate had
tricked him: he may have sat to the right of Eden, but I sat next to Churchill.

    ... At last, the signing procedure is complete. ... We shake hands and say
goodbye to one another. The camera-men want to film Sikorski and me shaking
hands. We do as they ask. On parting, Churchill says to me: 'I'm ready to help
you however I can. If you have any thoughts on this score, come and see me.
We'll have a talk.'

---

[43] The Poles, too, noted that 'Churchill looked tired, and he was deeply and visibly moved. There were
quivers in his voice, and tears in his eyes.'

3 August

Hopkins' visit to Moscow has evidently been a success. We will, of course, only be able to judge its outcome later (how will the American deliveries go?), but the situation at present seems satisfactory.

Hopkins met Comrade Stalin twice, on 30 and 31 July. Their talks were long and detailed. Hopkins stated on behalf of Roosevelt that the United States would provide all manner of aid to us without concluding a special agreement. Comrade Stalin thanked Hopkins for his statement and then set out to him the list of our requirements (mostly heavy machine-guns and small antiaircraft guns). Comrade Stalin also asked that the $500 million loan granted to us by the US Government be expedited. This would also serve to demonstrate openly the existence of the bloc of the United States, the Soviet Union and Great Britain. Hopkins agreed to this and promised to telegraph Roosevelt promptly in the same vein. Comrade Stalin also gave Hopkins firm assurance that our victory is inevitable and that Hitler and his gang must be removed from power, because they lack 'gentlemanliness' and violate all agreements. The observance of such agreements is especially important in view of the existence of different systems of government in different countries.

Comrade Stalin made a very strong impression on Hopkins. Winant, who saw Hopkins upon his return to Scotland (Hopkins departed for America without coming to London), told me that Roosevelt's *special envoy* left Moscow having drawn the following conclusions. Comrade Stalin has an exceptionally clear mind and is most realistic. He knows what he wants and is a true master of the situation. He knows the front like the palm of his hand. He is wholly confident of victory. Stalin does not ask for the impossible, and he did not lose heart when Hopkins told him that there was not much the USA could give the USSR at the present moment. On the contrary, he began calmly discussing with Hopkins a programme for the future and various possibilities for supplying the USSR by the spring of 1942. This gave Hopkins the impression that the Red Army has a sufficiently solid base of its own and that in general the USSR is a trustworthy partner, with whom the USA can do business. ...

10 August (Bovingdon)

Seven weeks of war.

The future is hidden, of course, but some very important things are clear even now. The main thing is that the Red Army has held firm against the Reichswehr. The Hitlerite war machine proved unable to overrun, overthrow and grind down the Red Army as it had done to all other armies, including the

French. It was unable to do so in the first 2–3 weeks of the war, when it had every advantage on its side. ...

The idea of a second front in the west, which Comrade Stalin proposed to Churchill, has been rejected in view of the difficulties involved in its attainment. The idea of a joint front in the north has been accepted in principle, but its implementation is going on so slowly and sparingly that our navy and army men are falling into despair. Air attacks on Germany from the west are carried out, but, first, they cannot have a strong impact on the withdrawal of forces from the eastern front and, second, they too are somewhat anaemic. Even in the sphere of supplies the English try to limit themselves to the absolute minimum. They don't want to grant us sufficient loans, and they don't want to provide us with the weapons we need most badly (small-calibre antiaircraft guns, fighters, etc.). I wrested 200 American *Tomahawks* from them with the greatest difficulty – now they can't forget about it and boast about it as a symbol of their generosity at every opportunity, suitable or otherwise. They all say: we ourselves don't have them! It's a lame excuse as often as not. The point of the matter is that ... members of the Government, including Churchill, still keep to the course of that 'defensive strategy' which they have pursued for the last year and which was quite natural and reasonable before we entered the war, but became an anachronism after 22 June.

As a result, a mood of *complacency* is widespread in the country, infecting the workers as well to a certain extent. On 2 August, a *Bank Holiday*, there were huge crowds of people at the railway stations bound for the *country*, just as in peacetime. More than 300 extra trains left London, carrying 'holiday-makers'. Does one need any further proof of widespread complacency?

That is why I do not expect full-fledged aid from England in the near future either, with the possible exception of the Middle East. In the main we must rely on ourselves.

26 August

Eden asked me about the mood in the USSR.

I replied in my private capacity (not on behalf of the Government).

Britain's conduct arouses growing bewilderment and disappointment among the broad Soviet masses. We've been waging a terrible struggle against the most powerful war machine in history for ten weeks. Alone! The people and the army are fighting bravely, but the losses are huge: 700,000 people, 5,500 tanks, 4,500 planes, 1,500 guns, as well as territories, some of which are valuable and important.

And what has England been doing all this time? Our proposal – a second front in the west – was declined in July.

... Something is happening, sure. Thanks. But... it's not enough to pinch the rabid beast's tail; it must be hit round the head with a club! The British bombers haven't forced the Germans to withdraw a single squadron from the east... Much enthusiasm, *admiration*, etc. It's pleasant, but platonic. I often think: 'I'd swap the admiration for more fighter planes!' No wonder the Soviet citizen feels disappointed and bewildered. As the ambassador, who is... etc., I deem it necessary to warn Eden about such sentiments.

Strong impression on Eden. A *half-hearted* defence (he himself an advocate of a second front): England is not prepared for invasion, USA lingers with supplies. Britain pursues an air offensive, cooperation of Britain and USSR in Iran. Good prospects in the Middle East. Forthcoming operations in Libya.

I replied. Iran and Libya are secondary tasks.[44] The main one: how to beat Germany?

... I said: 'If the British Government really wants to improve relations, here is some good advice: don't make important declarations (*deus ex machina*) in the middle of the Atlantic Ocean. It's not about the content (that's OK), but the way they originate. The impression has been created that Britain and the USA imagine themselves lords and masters, judging the rest of the sinful world, including the USSR. You can't forge friendship on such a basis.'

30 August

My initiative struck home. My conversation with Eden on the 26th made an impression in Moscow. The response from D.I.[45] started with the words: 'Your conversation with Eden on strategy fully reflects the mood of the Soviet people. I am glad you caught that mood so well.' There then follow considerations of a political nature. Hitler's aim is to beat his enemies one by one, the Russians today, the British tomorrow. The passivity of the British Government at present plays straight into Hitler's hands. True, the British applaud us and hurl verbal abuse at the latter. But, in practice, this doesn't change a thing. Do the British understand this? Of course they understand. So what do they want? Evidently,

---

[44] When the German armies invaded Russia and approached the Caucasus, fears arose that the Germans might turn southwards towards Iran, thus threatening the entire British position and assets in the area. To counter such a threat, a joint Anglo-Russian invasion of the country was launched on 25 August. The stated objectives of the operation, to counter German 'Fifth Columnists' in the country and to open a supply line to Russia, thinly veiled the genuine objective of forcing a division of Persia on the 1907 Anglo-Russian partition lines. Churchill told his son Randolph that the 'questionable' operation was 'like taking a leaf out of the German book'. Eden 'ashamed of himself', regarded the invasion as Britain's 'first act of "naked aggression"'.

[45] The abbreviation is for 'instantsia' which in Russian connotes *vlast* – the power or authority. In earlier days, instructions from the Central Committee of the CPSU were handed down under this title, before it was appropriated by Stalin. It was most unusual for Stalin to communicate directly with an ambassador, and it clearly flattered Maisky, whose stock had sunk low in the previous two years.

they want to see us weakened. If so, we must be very wary in our dealings with them.

D.I. gave me some information about the situation at the front. Lately, the situation in the Ukraine and near Leningrad has worsened. The reason: the Germans have transferred 30 more divisions from the west. If we include the 20 Finnish and 22 Rumanian divisions, we now face close to 300 divisions. The Germans consider the threat in the west to be a bluff, so they are quite happy to remove from there every half-decent unit. Where does the Germans' confidence come from?... Unless the English rouse themselves very soon, our situation will become critical. Will the British gain from this? No, I think they will lose.

D.I.'s conclusions are very gloomy: if a second front is not established in Europe within 3–4 weeks, we and our allies may lose everything. It's sad, but it may become a reality.

Having received such a message, I paced my room back and forth for a long time and pondered. D.I., of course, knows the situation better, but I nonetheless find it difficult to believe that we may suffer defeat. I have been firmly convinced of our ultimate victory since the very beginning of the war. For me, it was only the cost of victory that was uncertain. I still stick by my conviction. But D.I.'s words attest to the fact that the situation has become extremely strained. Efforts must be made to relieve the tension, or at least to exploit it in order to 'rouse' the English. Reckoning more on the latter, I immediately replied in that spirit.

I explained that if the situation was so serious, one more attempt should be made to urge the British Government to open a second front in France or in the Balkans. At the same time, I added: I don't want to create any groundless illusions. At such a moment as now, you need more than ever to know the facts as they stand. So let me tell you in advance that, to judge by my own impressions, the atmosphere in governmental quarters (but not among the masses) is hardly in favour of a second front. This was confirmed, in particular, by my conversation with the prime minister at lunch on 29 August. A complicated knot of motives underlies such attitudes: the hypnotic effect of Germany's invincibility on land; the growing *complacency* caused by our powerful resistance (many say: the Russians are fighting well, so we can mark time and steadily fulfil our plans for a decisive offensive in 1942 or 1943); the desire to weaken the USSR (a significant wing of the Conservatives definitely has such a wish); the ill-preparedness of the British for large-scale landing operations; and the fear of a new Dunkirk (which might undermine the Government's position from the inside and damage its prestige in the USA). This is an analysis of the afore-stated mood, not its justification. Proceeding from the given situation, it seems to me that we stand a better chance of 'rousing' the British in the area of supplies.

... Nevertheless, considering the menace to the USSR, the question of a second front could be put before the British Government once more. Churchill and others must understand at long last that if the USSR leaves the stage, the British Empire is finished. ... However, we must also consider the other side of the coin: if the British do not open a second front and we reveal to them the critical nature of our situation, this may have an adverse impact on issues of supply. The British may decide: since it is useless helping the Russians, we'd better keep the available tanks and planes for ourselves. All the pluses and minuses of the démarche which I am proposing must be weighed. If it is undertaken, two forms are possible: (1) a personal message from Stalin to Churchill, and (2) an extensive conversation between me and Churchill about the current situation. To my mind, the first form would be better and more effective.

[Cripps received Stalin's message to Churchill on 4 September. 'It is such a grave document,' he wrote in his diary, 'that it leaves me completely *bouleversé*. ... Unless we can do something most immediately and effectively to help them the game is up at any rate for a long time if not *all together*. They will not be able to hold out for the winter. If now Russia collapses we shall be left without the possibility of victory ... I took the decision to return at once to London and to take General Mason-Macfarlane[46] with me.' Churchill was determined to deter Cripps from carrying out a *fait accompli*. However, no longer able to ignore Cripps's challenge, he addressed him personally with a lengthy recitation of the arguments against direct assistance to the Russians and ridiculing his call for a superhuman effort, which he took to mean 'an effort rising superior to space, time and geography'. The letter heralded a long and acrimonious correspondence between the two, culminating in Cripps's bid for power after his return from Moscow.

Churchill's estrangement from Cripps on the eve of the Moscow conference coincided with a growing crisis on the Russian front. On 8–9 September, the Germans resumed their thrust on the outskirts of Leningrad. Meanwhile, much against the opinion of his generals, Hitler had decided on 21 August to halt the advance on Moscow. After a fierce but swift armoured battle, Guderian[47] succeeded on 7 September in ripping apart the Russian defences of the Bryansk and south-eastern fronts. On 11 September, the legendary General Budenny[48] found himself trapped in the Kiev salient;

---

[46] Lieutenant General Sir Frank Noel Mason-Macfarlane, military attaché in Berlin and Copenhagen, 1937–39, and head of the British military mission to Moscow, 1941–42.
[47] Colonel General Heinz Guderian, the architect of the German armoured corps' doctrine and victory in the west and in the early stages of the campaign in Russia. A critic of the conduct of the war in the east, he was dismissed by Hitler in the winter of 1941 but reinstated in command in 1943.
[48] Marshal Semen Budenny, a former tsarist cavalryman, his association with Stalin during the Civil War saved his life during the purges. Was commander-in-chief of the Russian army in the Ukraine and Bessarabia at the outset of the war, but was removed from his command after the disastrous defeats inflicted on his troops in summer 1941.

his request to withdraw saw him immediately relieved of command and Marshal Timoshenko[49] appointed in his place. A few days later, Guderian and Field Marshal Ewald von Kleist[50] linked in a pincer movement some 100 miles east of Kiev, trapping Timoshenko's troops. Shaposhnikov[51] cabled the general staff on that day: 'This is the beginning as you know of catastrophe – a matter of a couple of days.' Kiev indeed fell on 18 September, and the bulk of the Soviet army on that front was either annihilated or captured. The situation on the southern front seemed just as bleak, with the German forces encircling Odessa and threatening the Crimea.]

4 September

My proposal has been accepted. This morning I received the text of Stalin's personal message to the prime minister. Firm, clear and ruthless words. No illusions, no sweeteners. The facts as they stand. The threats as they loom. A remarkable document.[52]

I came to Cadogan's office at about 4 p.m. to discuss the Iranian affair. I informed him that I must hand Stalin's personal message to Churchill and asked to arrange a meeting with the prime minister in the evening, if possible, or tomorrow morning. ... I also asked Cadogan that Eden be present at my meeting with the prime minister.

'I'm very sorry,' I added, 'that it is necessary to disturb the foreign minister's rest, but the matter is quite serious and I think he will bear no hard feelings towards me on this score.' ...

Eden had left a few days earlier for a week in the country, for his *holidays*.

Cadogan thought he would get a reply from the prime minister's secretary while we were discussing Iranian affairs, but the response was somehow delayed. I decided to go home and asked Cadogan to inform me by phone about the time and place of my meeting with the PM. The telephone rang as soon as I got back to the embassy. Cadogan said the PM would receive me at ten o'clock in the evening at 10, Downing Street and that Eden would be present at the meeting.

---

[49] Semen Konstantinovich Timoshenko, marshal of the Soviet Union, people's commissar for defence, May 1940 to July 1941; deputy people's commissar for defence July–September 1941; commander of the Stalingrad front July 1942, and of the north-western front October 1942 to March 1943.

[50] Field Marshal Paul Ewald von Kleist was commander of the First Panzer Group fighting in the Ukraine in 1941 and charged with the capture of the Baku oil fields in 1942.

[51] Boris Mikhailovich Shaposhnikov, chief of staff of the Red Army, 1928–31, 1937–40 and 1941; deputy commissar of defence, 1941–43.

[52] Stalin presented a grave view of the situation on the front, ending with a plea to open, already in 1941, a second front in the Balkans or in France, which would draw 30–40 German divisions from the eastern front, as well as to provide for the delivery to the USSR of 30,000 tons of aluminium and a minimum of 400 planes and 500 tanks monthly by October. Without these two kinds of aid, he warned, the Soviet Union may either suffer a debacle or be weakened to such an extent that it would not be able to give active support to its allies in their struggle against Hitlerism for a long period of time.

I left home a quarter of an hour before the appointed time. The moon shone brightly. Fantastically shaped clouds raced from west to east. When they blotted the moon and their edges were touched with red and black, the whole picture appeared gloomy and ominous. As if the world was on the eve of its destruction. I drove along the familiar streets and thought: 'A few more minutes, and an important, perhaps decisive historical moment, fraught with the gravest consequences, will be upon us. Will I rise to the occasion? Do I possess sufficient strength, energy, cunning, agility and wit to play my role with maximum success for the USSR and for all mankind?'...

I entered the hall of the famous house in a heightened mood, filled with a kind of resonant, inner tension. Prosaic life immediately brought me down to earth with a crash. The porter, a most ordinary English porter in livery, bowed low and took my hat. Another porter, indistinguishable from the first, led me through a poorly lit corridor along which dashed young men and girls, probably the prime minister's secretaries and typists. They then sat me at a small table and went to report my arrival. This entire, ordinary routine, so familiar to me from the experience of many years, felt like a tub of cold water poured over my soul.

I was then ushered into the PM's office, or, to be more precise, the Government's meeting room. Churchill, wearing a dinner jacket and with the habitual cigar between his teeth, was sitting halfway down a long table covered with a green cloth, amid a long row of empty chairs. Eden, dressed in a dark-grey suit of light material, sat near the PM. Churchill looked at me distrustfully, puffed at his cigar and growled like a bulldog: 'Bearing good news?'

'I fear not,' I replied, handing the prime minister the envelope with Stalin's message.

He took out the letter, put on his glasses and began to read it carefully. Having read a page, he would hand it over to Eden. I sat beside the prime minister, keeping silent and observing his expression. When Churchill finished reading, it was clear that Stalin's message had made a powerful impression on him.

I began to speak: 'So now, Mr Churchill, you and the British Government know the real state of affairs. We have withstood the terrible assault of the German war machine on our own for eleven weeks now. The Germans have massed up to 300 divisions on our front. Nobody helps us in this struggle. The situation has become difficult and menacing. It is still not too late to change it. But to do so it is essential to carry out quickly and resolutely what Stalin writes about. If the right measures are not taken immediately, the moment may be lost. ... Either you take firm and decisive steps to provide the USSR with the help it needs – then the war will be won, Hitlerism will be crushed, and the opportunity for free and progressive development will open before mankind.

Or, if you don't provide us with the aid we need, the USSR will face the risk of defeat with all the ensuing consequences.'

... While I spoke, the prime minister sucked on his cigar and listened, merely responding to my words every now and again with gestures or facial expressions, while Eden pored over Stalin's message and made some notes on the margins.

Then Churchill started responding. ... 'I have no doubt,' Churchill exclaimed, 'that Hitler still wishes to pursue his old policy of beating his enemies one by one... I would be ready to sacrifice 50,000 English lives if, in so doing, I could draw even just 20 German divisions from your front!'

Unfortunately, England currently lacks the strength to establish a second front in France. Here, Churchill repeated everything he had told me on this matter in July and which he had then set out in his reply to Stalin's July message.

'The Channel, which prevents Germany from jumping over into England,' the prime minister added, 'likewise prevents England from jumping over into occupied France.'

Churchill considers a second front in the Balkans to be impossible at present. The British lack the necessary troops, aircraft and tonnage.

'Just think,' Churchill exclaimed, 'it took us a full seven weeks to transfer 3–4 divisions from Egypt to Greece in the spring. And this on the basis of Greece being not a hostile, but a friendly country! No, no! We can't walk into certain defeat either in France or in the Balkans!'

... Seeing that there was no point arguing any further on the question of a second front, I fell back on my 'second line', putting special emphasis on matters of military supplies. Here the PM was far more amenable, as I had expected. He promised to consider Stalin's request concerning tanks and planes with the utmost goodwill and then to give a definite answer.

'Only don't expect too much from us!' Churchill warned. 'We, too, are short of arms. More than a million British soldiers are still unarmed.'

Like a schoolboy boasting of how skilfully he has tricked his classmate, Churchill told me with a twinkle in his eye how, at the Atlantic conference, he had managed to wangle 150,000 rifles out of Roosevelt. 150,000! So these are the kind of figures we have to argue about today. As for tanks, 500 a month is out of the question. The entire output of tanks in England does not reach this number!

'I don't want to mislead you,' Churchill concluded. 'I'll be frank. We'll not be able to provide you with any essential aid before the winter, either by creating a second front, or through abundant supplies. All we are capable of sending you at present – tanks, planes, etc. – are trifles compared with your needs. This is painful for me to say, but the truth must come first. The future is a different matter. In 1942, the situation will change. Both we and the Americans will be able to give you a lot in 1942. But for now...'

And Churchill concluded with half a smile: 'Only God, in whom you don't believe, can help you in the next 6–7 weeks. Besides, even if we sent tanks and planes to you now, they would not arrive before winter.'

Here I turned to another question that has long been weighing heavy on my heart. 'The USSR and England,' I said, 'are allies. They are waging a common war against a common enemy. This, one might have thought, would assume the existence of a joint strategic plan for the war (if only in its basic outline). Do they have such a plan? No, they don't. We don't know how the British intend to defeat Hitler, and the British don't know how we envisage doing the same. There are no military negotiations between the chiefs of staff. Nor even so much as a suggestion of serious military cooperation. This is not normal. Couldn't the parameters of the forthcoming Moscow conference be extended to discuss not only matters relating to supplies, but also those relating to a common strategy?'

Churchill agreed with me in principle, albeit without much enthusiasm. He declared that he was ready to develop a general strategic plan together with us.

I asked how the prime minister perceives the further course and outcome of the war.

... 'My plans for 1942 are very modest,' Churchill replied. 'Here they are: to keep a firm hold of the mother country and not permit an invasion, to hold the Nile valley and the Middle East, to win back Libya (and take Tripoli, if we can), to secure supplies to the USSR via Iran and other routes, to draw Turkey onto our side, to bomb Germany incessantly, and to conduct a relentless submarine war. For the rest: to prepare the army, strengthen the air force, develop arms production, reinforce the Middle East. I plan to have 750,000 troops in that part of the world by the end of this year (there are about 600,000 now), and about a million by the spring of 1942.'

What Churchill was saying, essentially, was that 1942 should be merely a 'preparatory' year. No major landing operations. No attempts to bring the war to a conclusion. Then 1943 may be the decisive year, when England, aided by the USA, will raise the number of its tanks to 20,000. However, this, too, is merely hypothetical. One cannot exclude the possibility that the denouement may have to be postponed until 1944.

... It was a quarter to twelve when I left the prime minister. We had talked for nearly two hours. The moon had set, and the London streets, plunged into 'black-out', were filled with an ominous silence. Summing things up, I wondered: 'What will the result of it all be?'[53]

---

[53] Maisky deliberately concealed in both his report to Moscow and the diary that Churchill, sensing the 'underlying air of menace' in the appeal, was enraged, telling Maisky that 'Whatever happens and whatever you do, you of all people have no right to make reproaches to us', having collaborated with Nazi Germany before the war.

5 September

Today at 11 a.m. the meeting proposed by Churchill with the chiefs of staff took place in Eden's office. It was chaired by Eden. Present were Admiral Pound, General Dill, Air Marshal Portal[54] and 2–3 other military men. On our side there was myself and Kharlamov,[55] with Baranov acting as the admiral's interpreter. It lasted about two hours. We discussed the feasibility or otherwise of a second front in France from a purely strategic point of view. I was greatly disappointed – not by the fact that the chiefs of staff deemed such an operation impossible (everything had prepared me for this), but by the poverty and triteness of their arguments.[56] Absolutely nothing new, nothing more convincing than what I had heard a dozen times before from others, beginning with the prime minister and ending with ordinary journalists. One could sense that the chiefs of staff are simply hypnotized by the might of the German war machine and wholly deprived of initiative and boldness. Dill made the best impression on me and Pound the worse. Eden merely presided and barely expressed his views. We finished just before 'lunch'. The verdict of the chiefs of staff is that a second front is impossible, either in France or in the Balkans.

... I asked Eden: 'As I understand it, the British Government is considering expanding its aid to us in the way of supplies. On what basis will this be done? For cash? On credit?'

My question took Eden unawares and he said he would ask the prime minister. I added: 'Since you are going to talk with Churchill on this matter, couldn't you raise the question of the supplies being granted to us on the basis of *Lease and Lend*?' ... Eden livened up and said he agreed with me. It was evident that he liked my idea. He promised to mention my proposal during his talk with the prime minister.

At six o'clock I was expected to make a short speech at the civil funeral ceremony for Tagore. ... I had barely finished speaking when a message from the embassy was handed to me: Churchill asked me to come immediately to *10, Downing Street*. I had to make my apologies to the chairman and the gathering and leave.

I sat for some ten minutes in the prime minister's reception room. Eden put his head round the door at one point and said: 'Sorry for the delay. The reply is being typed up.'

---

[54] Charles Portal, chief of the air staff, 1940–45.
[55] Admiral Nikolai Mikhailovich Kharlamov, from June 1941 naval attaché and head of the Soviet military mission in Great Britain; deputy chief of the general staff of the navy from 1944.
[56] Eden gained the wrong impression that Maisky 'had at the finish a clearer perception of our weakness and limitations'.

55. Maisky conferring with the clandestine opposition, Lloyd George and Anthony Eden.

Then he added with a half-apologetic smile: 'We couldn't satisfy you fully, but we did what we could... You'll see for yourself.'

Eden left and I began speculating what the British concessions might be.

Eventually, they ushered me in. The same long room with a table covered by a green cloth. Churchill and Eden sat at the table, with a bottle of whisky on the table and some soda water. The prime minister, with his customary cigar between his teeth, made a cordial gesture inviting me to sit down and poured out a whisky and soda. Then he grinned and said: 'The text of the message will be brought in a minute... In the meantime I'd like to touch upon another matter.'

It transpired that Churchill had seen Lloyd George just the other day. The old man criticized Churchill's policy towards the USSR and mentioned in passing that the British Government was not even supplying us properly. ... Churchill is under the impression that I complained about the British Government to Lloyd George. This stung him to the quick.

'If you're unhappy about something,' the PM said, 'come to me, to Eden or to Max (Beaverbrook), and we shall try to do what we can. But why appeal to the opposition?... After all, Lloyd George represents the opposition to the

Government. It is more advantageous for you to work with the Government. The opposition now is nothing...'

Eventually, they brought in a copy of the PM's reply to Comrade Stalin. Churchill handed the document over to me and said with a slightly conceited grin: 'This is what we can do now. I think it will be of some help to you after all.'

I quickly glanced through the reply. I found my proposals reflected in it: the agreement in principle to discuss joint war plans and the agreement to apply the lend-lease principle in the sphere of supplies. This was pleasing. What was not pleasing was the categorical rejection of a second front.

15 September

A new message from Comrade Stalin to Churchill, in reply to Churchill's message to Comrade Stalin of 5 September, arrived today. Its main point: if the British Government considers a second front in the west impossible, let it send 25–30 divisions to the USSR to fight against the Germans side by side with our soldiers.

... Eden was not present at the meeting and my conversation with the prime minister was conducted *tête-à-tête*.

Having read Comrade Stalin's message, Churchill began 'thinking aloud'. His 'thoughts' boiled down to the following.

In principle, Churchill would be willing to carry out Stalin's request and send British troops to the USSR. He would even consider it a matter of honour to do so. But he must discuss this question in advance with his colleagues and advisers.

The prime minister envisages two difficulties in fulfilling Comrade Stalin's request. The first: from where should he draw the troops for such an expedition? The British have about 600,000 troops in the Middle East and hope to bring their number to 750,000 by Christmas. Churchill had already told me about this. The number of trained and armed troops at home does not exceed 1 million (excluding the Home Guard, antiaircraft defence, coastal defence, etc.). An offensive in Libya is currently being prepared. Is it possible under these circumstances to allocate serious forces for an expeditionary corps in the USSR? Of course, 25–30 divisions are out of the question – that is beyond England's capability today – but can anything *substantial* still be found to send to the USSR? Churchill was uncertain.

... Then I asked: may I assume that the British Government agrees in principle to meet Stalin's request? If that is the case, practical military negotiations could be opened in Moscow or in London without delay. The prime minister avoided a direct response to my question and only repeated that he would urgently discuss this question with his advisers and would notify me promptly.

This sounds suspicious to me. The 'advisers' (I immediately imagined the faces of Pound, Dill and Portal) will, of course, be against Comrade Stalin's suggestion or, even if they don't say so openly, will raise a barbed-wire fence of unfeasible conditions around its implementation – will Churchill be able to stand his ground? I fear that little will come of it all. But we shall see.

Churchill summed up the situation in the following way: 'I repeat what I told you at our last meeting: I don't want to mislead you. Even if the British Government decides to send an expeditionary force to you, it will not arrive before winter. I am afraid the next six weeks will be a hard time for you, but I won't be able to help you with anything substantial in this period. This is sad, but, unfortunately, that's how it is.'

The prime minister glanced through Comrade Stalin's message once again and added with a contented smile: 'It is very good that Mr Stalin has at last come to believe in our good intentions vis-à-vis the USSR. Yes, we want your victory, for it will be our victory, too. And I'm prepared to do all I can for your victory. The trouble is that there is a limit to what I can do. Please understand this!'

And then, after a moment's thought, Churchill added: 'I believe in our cooperation. I believe Mr Stalin. I believe for two reasons. First, because our interests coincide: we face mortal peril from one and the same enemy. Second, because I know that so far the Soviet Government has always kept its word.'

I supported the prime minister on both accounts.

22 September

At the factories. Rallies.[57]

From platform in front of the tanks. 'Stalin' is the 1st to roll out.

The crowd's mood like at our meetings in the years of the revolution.

Shop stewards' meeting – all promise *'not to let us down'.*

Crafty Beaverbrook. He organized everything, including *shop stewards'* meeting. He's not afraid.

Is it worth helping increase production in England? On condition that a firm % goes our way.

My *broadcast* on 27 Sept.

'Russian tank week' brought a 20% rise in production.

---

[57] Beaverbrook initiated the 'Tanks for Russia Week', which was launched at a factory in Birmingham, where Agniya 'pulled a string to release the red flag that covered a part of the tank', revealing the name given to this first offering (by Maisky in advance) – 'Stalin'. In his speech, shown on newsreels all over the country, Maisky castigated the British Government, suggesting that 'These good machines will not rust in idleness. They will go into the battle line against the Nazis.'

56. Maisky thanking workers for 'Stalin', the first tank destined for the Russian front to roll off the Birmingham factory production line.

23 September

... Moscow conference

Eden said on 24 September at the Inter-Allied Conference that the Moscow conference should end in approximately 7–10 days. Everything is well prepared. Such is Churchill's line – Beaverbrook also told me before leaving that he hoped to complete the main job in a few days ('it is necessary to act, not investigate'). 'I admire the Russians' bravery and resilience. They are a true people. You told me on the first day of the war: we will fight like devils. I went to the PM and said: "Maisky says the Russians will fight like devils. We must help them!" It turned out like you said.'

[On 29 September, a day before the Germans launched their decisive offensive on Moscow, Beaverbrook and Averell Harriman, Roosevelt's coordinator of American supply to Britain, arrived in Moscow. Maisky was led to believe by Eden that General Ismay would be empowered to discuss the transfer of British troops to the eastern front. Beaverbrook, however, was barred by Churchill from conducting any political or strategic talks. Determined nonetheless to profit from the tremendous popular support for Russia at home and to enhance his political standing in London, he staged the conference as a 'Christmas Party', at which the United States and Britain were 'presenting poor Russia with gifts'. By extending 'lend-lease' to Russia and sweeping under the carpet the contentious issues, he hoped to divert Stalin from the 'second front' and post-war arrangements.

Quite a bit of gossip was exchanged between Stalin and Beaverbrook, and this allows a rare glimpse into Stalin's personal attitude to Maisky. Beaverbrook apparently extolled the virtues of Maisky as an ambassador, complaining only that he 'came on too strong at times'. Stalin seemed more worried about Maisky's habit of lecturing the British 'on matters of Communist doctrine'. 'What about our fellow?' Beaverbrook asked, 'barely concealing his personal distaste for Cripps'. Stalin simply shrugged his shoulders: 'Oh, he's all right.' 'The modified acceptance of Cripps,' Beaverbrook reported to Churchill, had led Beaverbrook to observe that there was nothing wrong with Cripps, but that he was a bore. '"In that respect," asked Stalin, "is he comparable to Maisky?" I answered, "No, to Madame Maisky." Stalin liked the joke immensely.']

12 October (Bovingdon)

A hard week! These last seven days form a gloomy chain in my memory. In his last speech, Hitler was not only apologizing and bragging. He was also advertising the huge offensive against Moscow. The greatest offensive in this war. And indeed, in the course of the first 6–7 days, he really did achieve major successes: Timoshenko's army was forced to make a 70–80 kilometre retreat, Orel was captured by the Germans, the fighting goes on at Vyazma and Bryansk, and in the south Berdyansk and Mariupol have been captured. True, in the last 3–4 days we have managed to slow the speed of the German drive in the centre significantly, but it has not yet been stopped. Our further retreat 'to new positions' has been announced today. Will we manage to hold on to the new positions? Will we manage to halt the enemy's advance? Will we manage to hold Moscow?

Some inner feeling tells me that we shall be able to hold Moscow, albeit by dint of great effort and immense losses. But inner feelings are a poor guarantee. Time will tell. My expectations with regard to the south are far gloomier. Will we hold the Donbass? I don't know. Some feebleness can be sensed in our resistance on the Ukrainian front. ...

The events on our front elicit a complex reaction in England. ... Disappointment at the inability to bring the war to a convenient conclusion, without huge and arduous efforts on the part of England itself, and anxiety about the course of events in the east and the course and outcome of the whole war. These feelings have intensified during the past week. Thursday, 9 October, was the worst day. The newspapers came out with panicky headlines. The whole Soviet front, it seemed, was collapsing like a pack of cards. A wave of pessimism rose high in social circles. Rumours (surely emanating from German sources) were abroad in the city that 'Russia' had actually withdrawn from the war and that negotiations between Berlin and Moscow on an armistice were already in progress. Many could find only one, rather dubious, consolation: 'How lucky that Hitler's diabolic machine, the entire might of which we've only seen now, fell not on us but on Russia!'

... That is one facet of the English reaction. There is another, running in parallel to the first. I mean the colossal growth of goodwill and compassion towards the USSR, especially (but not solely) among the lower classes. ...

... Everything 'Russian' is in vogue today: Russian songs, Russian music, Russian films, and books about the USSR: 75,000 copies of a booklet of Stalin's and Molotov's speeches on the war ... sold out instantly. Goodwill towards us has grown particularly strongly over the last 2–3 weeks. 'The Russian Tank Week' organized by Beaverbrook prior to his departure to Moscow was a brilliant success. The mayor of Kensington arranged a special reception for Agniya and me: some 500 guests attended, including many diplomats, political and public figures, the clergy, and all sorts of aristocrats. ... On 10 October I was invited as a guest of honour to the Livery Club, the City's holy of holies: they gave me a real ovation. The Athenaeum and the St James Club have elected me their honorary member.[58] My greetings to the large international youth demonstration in the Albert Hall on 11 October were met with loud applause, while the welcomes given by the king, Churchill, Beneš, the archbishop of York[59] and others were met with deathly silence.

... Along with this goodwill and sympathy, a disturbing question sounds louder and louder among the broad masses: 'Has England done everything it can to help the USSR?'

And many, not without foundation, find this to be far from the case. ... Will the campaign for a second front bring practical consequences? I doubt it. ... Churchill himself is against a second front in Europe. ... It seems to me that Churchill is simply afraid of the might of the German war machine and, besides, he listens too much to his 'military advisers', particularly Admiral Pound.

---

[58] *The Times* described the event: 'The glass eyes of the slightly moth-eaten stuffed bear on the staircase of London's St James's Club should have bugged out last week. ... Founded in 1757, St James's is famed for its claret, its caricatures by Sir Joshua Reynolds and the exclusiveness of its membership, mostly confined to diplomats from the topmost social drawer. ... Last week's tradition-shattering new member was short, thick, athletic Ivan Mikhailovich Maisky, 57, Soviet Ambassador to the Court of St James's, whose moon face, chuckling dark eyes and ragged imperial whiskers make him look like a small-time conjurer of the old school.'

[59] William Temple, archbishop of York, 1929–42; archbishop of Canterbury, 1942–44.

Can pressure from below change the Government's line? I don't know. For now it does not seem so.

13 October

When we had finished with business (a tripartite treaty of alliance between the USSR, England and Iran), Eden suddenly stretched out in his armchair and asked in a homely kind of way: 'A whisky and soda?'

'I won't say no,' I replied.

It was about eight in the evening. Eden's office was only dimly lit. The atmosphere lent itself to intimacy and heart-to-heart conversation.

Eden took two bottles from a handsome cabinet by the window and put them on his desk. I filled two glasses with the classic English mixture. Eden moved his armchair closer to the fireplace and said: 'Yes, it's a terrible time we are living through! The whole world is in a state of chaos and war.'

He thought for a moment and added: 'We have our share of the blame, too... I mean my country... Our policy has not always been wise or successful.'

I took a sip of whisky and soda and replied: 'Yes, I agree. There are two men who bear especially great responsibility for what is happening today. I am convinced that history will judge them harshly.'

'Who are they?' Eden asked with obvious interest.

'Baldwin and Chamberlain.'

I paused and added: 'To my mind, they bear even more responsibility than Hitler. For they nurtured Hitler with their policy.' ...

'And you think agreement was possible?' Eden asked a little doubtfully.

It seemed to me, though, that Eden did not really have any doubts on the matter: he merely wished to hear me confirm his own thoughts.

'Of course it was possible,' I replied with conviction.

'I also think so,' Eden confessed. 'Do you know what I did during the talks?... When I learned that Halifax was going to send Strang to Moscow, I came to him and said: "Don't do it! No good will come of such a move!" I must confess I was indignant. Why? After Chamberlain and Halifax had been to Rome, after the prime minister and the foreign secretary – both! – had "gone to Canossa", to send Strang to Moscow after all that... It would be tantamount to an insult! I understood all this, I understood what feelings such a decision might raise in Moscow, and I wanted to prevent the negotiations collapsing. So I asked Halifax not to send Strang, but to go himself. Halifax objected, saying he could not go, he was very busy, etc. Then I proposed myself as a *special envoy* to conduct negotiations. I told Halifax this would be better and that, as far as I could judge, Moscow's attitude to me was not unfavourable – so let me test myself in this exceptionally important matter! Halifax promised to think it over. A few days later he told me it would be difficult to implement my plan. I understood what the matter was: Chamberlain, of course, was against my going to Moscow. Strang went in my place.'

'So you think it was all Chamberlain's doing?' I asked Eden, before continuing: 'I think a great deal of the blame should be shared by Halifax, too. I'll tell you why. On 12 June 1939, on the very day of Strang's departure for Moscow, I visited Halifax and, after we had dealt with various routine matters, I asked him here in this room: "Lord Halifax, don't you think the difficulties with the negotiations might be eased considerably should you yourself go to Moscow? I have serious grounds to suggest that the Soviet Government would welcome your visit to us." True, I did not tell Halifax at the time that I had instructions from Moscow to say what I said, but that was not required. If an ambassador of a foreign state makes a statement such as mine, what minister of foreign affairs would not understand that there must be a good reason behind it?'

'Did you really say all this to Halifax?' Eden exclaimed in great agitation.

'Yes, of course I did,' I replied, 'and with great emphasis at that. To misunderstand me would have been impossible.'

'I never heard that story,' Eden went on. 'And how did Halifax react to your statement?'

'Halifax replied that my idea was very interesting and he would *bear it in mind*. That was all. Halifax never returned to the question. So Halifax's visit to Moscow never happened. I consider 12 June, when I suggested to Halifax that he visit Moscow, to be the turning point in the entire history of the negotiations. Or, to be more precise, not 12 June, but the following few days.'

... At this moment the telephone on Eden's table rang. It was his wife. She was calling from the 'foreign secretary's private residence' where Eden presently lives, and asked what he was doing. Having heard that I was with Eden and that the official part of my visit was over, Beatrice invited both of us upstairs (the 'private residence' is two storeys above the foreign secretary's office). There we met the famous author of light comedies Noël Coward,[60] who has just staged his new work. Eden's wife was dressed in a short crimson dress and looked very striking. I had not seen her for a long time, since for the past year she has been driving up and down the country with her military *Canteen* and appears in London quite rarely.

We talked about the stage, literature and art. It was a pleasant break from war and politics. I posed the question: whom did they consider to be the

---

[60] Sir Noël Coward, popular playwright and producer of a series of wartime films.

greatest playwright, the greatest novelist and the greatest poet of all time and all nations?

All agreed on the playwright: Shakespeare. And on the novelist: Leo Tolstoy. But opinions about the poet differed. Coward said he held Shakespeare to be the greatest playwright and also the greatest poet (I disagreed with him). Eden, after a moment's hesitation, named Dante. Eden's wife refused to commit herself at all. My preference went to Goethe. This was met with objections from Eden and Coward. They do not like Goethe. I replied that I do not like Goethe all that much myself, and that my favourite German poet is Heine, but, without fear or favour, I must name Goethe as the greatest (albeit not the most loved) of the poets I know. We argued for a good while, without finding anyone whom we could all consider to be the greatest poet of all time and all nations.

[Operation Typhoon, which the Germans launched on 2 October 1941, led to the capture of Orel in the south and Torzhok in the north, and finally to the annihilation of the forces trapped in the pocket of Vyazma. The reserve forces on the Mozhaisk defence line proved no match for the sweeping German armoured divisions. On 13 October, Kaluga fell on the southern flank, and two days later Kalinin, a key town on the approaches to Moscow. The Moscow defence zone was now, in places, only 60 miles from the capital. Anti-tank ditches were frenziedly dug by battalions of recruited civilians, while barricades and road blocks were built and tank traps set in the main city streets leading to the Kremlin. Discipline and morale sank low in Moscow, and what had been, until that point, a trickle of civilians fleeing from the capital turned into swarms of refugees. The rapidly deteriorating situation led to a hasty evacuation of various ministries and the diplomatic corps from Moscow to Kuibyshev, a small city on the Volga, where Maisky had spent a couple of years of his childhood. Its population was to double in the next couple of days – from half a million to a million.]

19 October

We didn't go to Bovingdon this weekend. Agniya is making a speech today at a meeting about Red Cross aid to the USSR. I stay in town and think.

One more week has passed. It has not proved to be decisive. But the situation has not improved; if anything, it has deteriorated. ... In the south we have evacuated Odessa. This did not come as a surprise to me. Beaverbrook told me that Stalin was weighing up the possibility of abandoning Odessa if the Crimea needed strengthening. ... However, I consider the main deterioration of our position to lie not so much in events at the front as in events in international politics. ...

I saw Eden several times on the 16th and 17th and enquired about the possibility of England and the USA 'warning' Japan that any attempt to attack the USSR would mean war between Japan and the English-speaking democracies. Eden sent a telegraphic message to this effect to Washington and spoke with Winant. I have no idea what the outcome will be, but I am not very optimistic...

... The Soviet Government moved from Moscow to Kuibyshev. This event is both positive and negative at the same time. Positive as an indicator of firm belief in final victory and negative as an indicator of the fact that Moscow is in great danger. No official statement concerning this change has been made yet, and on the whole the situation looks somewhat confused and unclear. ... On the morning of the 17th I received a telegram from Molotov in Moscow in which he informed me that on the night of 15–16 October most of the government departments and the diplomatic corps had left for Kuibyshev, but he himself was remaining in Moscow. Molotov also promised that an official statement about the evacuation of the Soviet Government would 'probably' appear on the 17th. However, no such statement has yet been made. In the last two days I have not received any telegrams, either from Moscow or from Kuibyshev.

What is happening? Most likely, the top leadership is being transferred from Moscow to Kuibyshev, and our communications with the Government are temporarily interrupted. This, of course, will not last long.

20 October

Agniya and I saw *Sorochintsy Fair*[61] at the *Savoy* theatre. The play is performed by a company of Whites under the direction of 'the King of the Black Exchange' – a certain Pomeroy, a clever Jew from Kharkov. All the revenue from the show goes to the Red Cross for the needs of the USSR. We were given seats in a special box. With us in the box were Churchill's wife, and Baron Iliffe[62] and his wife. '*God Save the King*' and the 'Internationale' were played before the beginning of the performance. All stood. Mrs Churchill was standing, too, even though it was her husband who forbade the 'Internationale' from being played over the radio, together with the other anthems of the Allies. The audience clapped the prime minister's spouse, but Agniya and I received even more applause. How this war has jumbled things up! The Soviet ambassador attends a performance by a White company, the White company gathers money for the Red Army [*sic*], and the wife of the British prime minister blesses this undertaking.

---

[61] An incomplete opera by Mussorgsky, based on a short story by Gogol.
[62] Edward Mauger Iliffe (1st Baron Iliffe), newspaper and periodical proprietor; Conservative MP, 1923–29.

... We had tea during the interval, and Mrs Churchill disclosed a few interesting details about her husband's way of life. Before the war, in peacetime, he used to go to bed at midnight and get up at eight. But now there's no chance for him to sleep his usual eight hours. He almost always goes to bed at two or three in the morning and has to get up at eight, as before. Which means no more than 5–6 hours of sleep. It's not enough. The prime minister makes up for it after lunch: he undresses, lies down in bed in complete darkness, and sleeps for an hour or an hour and a half. Experience has shown that this short daytime rest gives him a lot of strength, and he values it highly. If Churchill does not have any meetings or more or less official engagements in the morning, he stays in bed until lunch, summons his secretary and works with him.

... As I was leaving Parliament, some young man in soldier's uniform approached me and said with pain in his voice: 'Mr Maisky, I would just like to tell you I'm ashamed of my country, of its conduct at this time.'

I gave the youth a firm handshake.

23 October

Today I spent half the day in Parliament. The course of the war was discussed. There were comparatively few people present, but passions ran high.

... Aneurin Bevan[63] was particularly harsh, delivering a truly belligerent speech in which, *inter alia*, he attacked Halifax for the public statement he made in America that an 'invasion of the Continent' was now impossible because of the lack of shipping and arms. Bevan called Halifax's conduct 'all but high treason' (particularly so because he said all that just as Hitler was preparing his full-scale offensive against Moscow). Addressing the Government, Bevan shouted several times: 'If you can't change your policy, then step down!'

It all had a powerful effect: such words had not been heard in the Commons since the time of the crisis which brought about Chamberlain's resignation in May 1940.

3 November

The city is awash with rumours about the 'restructuring' of the Government and above all the possible resignation of Beaverbrook. ... Beaverbrook's resignation at present would be most inconvenient for us! I visited Eden that same morning and at the end of our conversation asked him what was behind the above-mentioned information. Eden shrugged his shoulders and said he knew nothing about it. He was inclined, however, to assume that Beaverbrook was in

---

[63] Aneurin Bevan, Labour MP, 1929–60; minister of health, 1945–51.

57. Maisky pampered by his left-wing friends, Bevan (seated on the ground to his right) and Gollancz (wearing a hat).

one of his moods, which usually coincide with bad attacks of asthma. I did not hide from Eden my own view on the matter of the minister of supply's resignation.

The same day, after *lunch*, I paid a visit to Beaverbrook and asked him right away: 'What does this mean?'

Beaverbrook was in a bad mood. On hearing my question, his face turned sallow and he suddenly banged the table viciously with his fist.

'I will not resign if the Cabinet says I ought not to!'

He turned towards me sharply and shouted: 'The *public* will not let me resign!'

Later in the conversation it became clear to me that while Beaverbrook was still on excellent terms with Churchill, he had been at loggerheads with a number of other ministers recently. Beaverbrook would not reveal their names, but remarked: 'Right now I'm on bad terms with Eden.'

'Why?' I asked in surprise.

'Why?' Beaverbrook repeated my question and replied: '*He hasn't got the guts!* He often deserts me in my hour of need.'

... I did my best to convince Beaverbrook that his resignation would have the direst consequences for England and Anglo-Soviet relations, especially now, right after the Moscow conference. It would be interpreted in the USSR as the abandonment or, at the very least, the weakening of the policy of cooperation between our two countries that alone could lead to victory. In saying that, I was of course aware that I was putting a trump card in Beaverbrook's hands, but I had nothing against this. On the contrary, I had privately decided to do all I could to support Beaverbrook, for at the present time we couldn't have a better minister of supply. Beaverbrook was very glad. My words were a balm to his soul.

[Beaverbrook concealed from Maisky that the reason for the crisis was in fact his mishandling of the Moscow talks and his intrigues against Cripps, which had just come to light through a series of private letters addressed to Eden by the ambassador. By mid-October, Churchill encountered a fierce debate in the Cabinet, prompted by unprecedentedly harsh criticism from Cripps, who warned that the failure to deploy force on the Russian front meant that Britain was 'trying to carry on two relatively unrelated wars to the great benefit of Hitler instead of a single war upon the basis of a combined plan'. 'The Soviet Government,' he added, 'was treated without trust and as inferiors rather than as trusted allies.'

Eden, too, was concerned by Churchill's 'very evident signs of anti-Bolshevik sentiments'. The Defence Committee (formed by Churchill to ensure his undisputed control of the war) now gave a positive hearing to Cripps's proposals. Churchill wasted little time in reinstating his authority. His personal instructions to Cripps unequivocally reiterated his intention not to alter British strategy, as 'we shall presently be fighting ourselves as the result of long-prepared plans'. Next he secured the overdue resignation of General Dill and the appointment as chief of staff of his own trusted adviser, General Alan Brooke.[64] By late November, Churchill's efforts bore fruit, when the restructured chiefs of staff recognized that, 'since assistance to Russia raised very delicate political issues, the final decision must rest entirely with the Prime Minister'.]

9 November (Bovingdon)

One more week. The twentieth week of war.

The situation seems to be somewhat better. True, the Germans have captured the greater part of the Crimea and are approaching Sevastopol and Kerch. ... The main thing, however, is that the Germans have been stopped on the Moscow front. ... It looks as if the German offensive on this front is running out of steam – particularly with the advent of winter. Still: once bitten, twice shy. I am afraid to draw any conclusions.

... The past week brought me two joyful events. The first – the main one – was Stalin's speech on the occasion of the 24th anniversary. It was awfully

---

[64] Alan Brooke (1st Viscount Alanbrooke), commander-in-chief home forces, 1940–41; chief of imperial general staff, 1941–46.

pleasant that on the evening of 6 November Stalin spoke at a ceremonial public meeting in the Bolshoi Theatre, and that on the morning of 7 November there was a splendid military parade on Red Square, which was made so much more brilliant by Stalin's short second speech. It is said that Hitler had reckoned on reviewing his troops on Red Square on 7 November.

... The second joyful event, albeit on a much smaller scale, was the appointment of Litvinov as ambassador to the USA. My telegram sent ten days ago, stressing the necessity of immediately sending an ambassador to Washington, obviously played its part in hastening the resolution of this matter. ... M.M. will surely be in the right place in America. Today more than ever before, we need a reliable, strong and influential figure there. ...

11 November

It seems that we've come to the first crisis in relations between the 'allies'!

Today I handed the prime minister Stalin's reply to his message of 4 November. Churchill received me in his office in Parliament. Eden was also present at my request. We had come together from the Foreign Office, where I had had a preliminary talk with Eden on various issues of the day. When we entered the prime minister's office, Churchill stood up to greet us and, shaking my hand, said with a friendly smile: '*Let us have a good talk.*'

We sat down at the long table covered in green cloth at which Cabinet meetings are usually held, and I handed Churchill the package I had brought with me. He took out the letter and began reading. I observed his facial expression: it became increasingly dark. Churchill reached the last line and passed the document to Eden in silence. Then, also in silence, he jumped up from his chair and quickly paced the room a couple of times. It was difficult to recognize the prime minister: his face was as white as chalk and he was breathing heavily. He was obviously enraged. Finally, having gained a measure of control over himself, Churchill uttered: '*Grave message!*'[65]

And added icily: 'I don't want to answer this message now! I have to consult my colleagues.'

It was said in such a tone that I thought it better to rise and take my leave. But Eden held me back and I remained.

Churchill did not maintain his outward restraint for long. He again paced the room a couple of times, getting more and more worked up. Eventually, he could keep silent no longer: 'So, Stalin wants to know our post-war plans? We

---

[65] Churchill had informed Stalin on 4 November of the Government's decision not to declare war on Finland and Hungary, whose troops were fighting the Russians. Stalin was also bitter about Churchill's failure to respond to his request for British troops to be deployed on the Russian front.

do have such plans – the *Atlantic Charter*! What else can be said at the present moment?'

I objected that the *Atlantic Charter* was too general a document and that within its framework (for we also recognize the *Atlantic Charter*) a number of points could be usefully clarified. Just one example: about three weeks ago Eden, referring to the question Stalin had asked Beaverbrook during the Moscow conference, told me that the British Government would like to build post-war relations between England and the USSR on the basis of friendly cooperation. Couldn't this matter be profitably solved within the framework of an agreement about the post-war plans of both powers?

'It's true that I spoke with you about it,' Eden commented, 'but I asked Mr Stalin to express his own thoughts on this matter.'

'I am inclined to interpret point (a) of Stalin's wishes,' I countered, 'as a reply to the message you conveyed to me.'

Eden smiled sceptically.

Churchill suddenly flared up again and exclaimed: 'If you want to turn England into a communist state in your post-war plans, you should know you'll never succeed!'

'What makes you think so!' I protested with a suppressed laugh. 'Stalin's last speech should have quite reassured you in this respect.'

The prime minister again took Stalin's message in his hands and glanced at the second sheet. It was as if he had been scorched.

'Hm!' Churchill cried out in fury. 'I send two of my chief commanders to him but he can't find the time to see them unless they are authorized to conclude those agreements...'

And the PM poked his finger in vexation at the passage where Stalin mentions the absence of agreements between England and the Soviet Union on mutual military assistance and post-war plans.

'No, I am not going to propose any more military negotiations!' continued Churchill in the same tone. 'Enough!'

The prime minister rapidly paced his office once more and added: 'And why was it necessary for Stalin to assume such a tone in our correspondence? I am not going to stand for it. I could well say things, too! Who will profit from it? Neither we, nor you – only Hitler!'

I remarked that I could see no grounds for such *excitement*. What Stalin is now suggesting is essentially what I discussed with Churchill more than two months ago – a joint strategic plan for the conduct of the war. Is that so unreasonable?

'What strategic plan can there be today?' Churchill exclaimed with irritation. 'We are still on the defensive, you are still on the defensive, and the initiative is still in Hitler's hands... What joint strategic plan can there be under such circumstances? Only to hold out until the moment arrives when we can snatch the initiative from our enemy's hands – that is our plan!'

'I agree that for the moment both you and we have to think about defence,' I interjected, 'but even defence requires a plan. What will we do in 1942, for instance – you and us? Wouldn't it be a good idea to agree on that?'

... Churchill flared up again as if he had touched white-hot iron, and shouted bitterly: 'It was me who acted without hesitation on 22 June and offered you my hand, although only a few weeks earlier I had had no idea what you would do! Perhaps you were going to go with Germany?... Who needs all these disputes and disagreements?... After all, we are fighting for our lives and will keep on fighting for our lives whatever happens!'

'We're fighting for our lives too,' I replied. 'And not badly at that.'

'You're fighting superbly!' exclaimed Churchill with passion.

He thought for a minute, glanced at Eden, who had kept silent throughout, and finally added: 'Right now I don't wish to respond to Stalin... I might say a lot of undesirable things in the heat of the moment... I'll consult our people, calm down and then write... You will be duly informed.'

'Whether or not you like Stalin's message,' I remarked in conclusion, 'there's little sense in excessive *excitement*. One must keep a sober and cool head. We have a common cause and a common struggle. If I can help in building bridges, I am entirely at your service.'

12 November

Beaverbrook called me today on the phone and blurted out in his typical style: 'Maisky! What a disgrace! We must find a way of clearing up this *mess*! Come over, we'll have a talk.'

When I entered Beaverbrook's office I found Bennett[66] (former prime minister of Canada) sitting there. He gave me a firm handshake and expressed his great admiration for the Red Army and the resistance of the Soviet people. He then left and Beaverbrook and I remained alone.

'What has made Stalin so angry?' Beaverbrook asked straight off. 'Finland?'

'And why do you think he is angry?' I replied, repeating his question.

'Well, you tell me!' Beaverbrook exclaimed. 'I know what he's like! I can see he's angry, that he's peeved with us... Is it because of Finland?'

I answered that the British Government's behaviour on the question of Finland and other German vassals could hardly put Stalin in a good mood.

---

[66] Richard Bedford Bennett, Canadian prime minister and minister of external affairs, 1930–35; moved to England in 1938.

Neither could he be cheered by the evasive behaviour of the British Government in the matter of sending an expeditionary corps. Stalin is a true realist. He does not care much for words and understands only deeds. And what were the deeds of the British Government in both cases?

'Yes, but when it comes to supplies,' Beaverbrook protested, 'we are doing so much right now. I'm prepared to do anything to fulfil my promises. You'll receive everything. If you have complaints or requests regarding supplies, don't hesitate to come straight to me. Tell Stalin to wire me directly. I chair the committee for supplies to the USSR. I'll not feel offended by anything. I have a thick skin... Stalin is my friend. I'll do anything for him. Have you read my Manchester speech?'

I confirmed that I had read it and that I found it very good.

'But of course!' Beaverbrook brightened up, pleasantly flattered by my words. 'I've provided such a good advertisement for Stalin, haven't I!... Ha-ha-ha!'

And Beaverbrook burst into satisfied laughter. Then he became more serious and added: 'We shouldn't upset our prime minister with complaints about broken aircraft or missing ammunition! He takes it too much to heart! Let Stalin wire me directly. I'll sweep away with an iron broom all those saboteurs who fail to pack our cargos in the proper way.'

Beaverbrook paused for a moment.

'Having said that,' he continued expressively, 'we must do all we can to settle this disagreement between the heads of our governments!... Stalin's letter is, after all, rather *harsh*... This must be admitted. Churchill is awfully touchy and stubborn. How can we smooth things over?'

Beaverbrook cast me an inquiring look.

I answered that, in my view, it was not so difficult to settle the matter. First of all, we must remove the problem of Finland, Rumania and Hungary. ...

... 'The problem is that Stalin wants negotiations of both questions to be conducted by the generals... What sort of post-war problems can generals discuss? This is not their sphere. Here, people say: if Stalin wants it done this way, it means he doesn't want negotiations at all.'

I laughed and said that this was a false conclusion. Of course, the generals are not best placed to discuss matters concerning the post-war reconstruction of Europe, but why couldn't politicians and diplomats discuss them here in London, or in Moscow?

Beaverbrook jumped at the idea and exclaimed: 'I'll definitely support the holding of such negotiations in London.'

'As for military negotiations,' I went on, 'you really ought to *make up your mind*. If you want to send an expeditionary corps to the USSR – very well. Then it makes sense for the generals to go to Moscow.' ...

I stood up to take my leave. Beaverbrook saw me to the lift and, shaking my hand, said: 'All this was *off the record*, of course. I trust you and share my thoughts and feelings with you. But nobody should know about it.'

I swore complete secrecy.

At seven in the evening I was in Eden's office at his request. The foreign minister obviously felt ill at ease and, having invited me to sit down, said he wanted to make the following official statement to me:[67] 'Mr Stalin's message is being considered by the Cabinet. At the present moment I am not in a position to respond to it, as it raises such serious questions. However, I can't conceal from you the fact that the prime minister as well as the members of the Cabinet were surprised and put out by the tone and content of the message.'

Eden delivered the statement aloud, while glancing at a piece of paper in front of him. I asked Eden to repeat it and wrote it down word for word.

'That is all I can tell you officially for now,' he added.

This was said in such a way for me to understand: 'And now, if you are inclined to speak unofficially, I'm at your service.'

... Eden acknowledged that there was nothing unacceptable or unreasonable in Stalin's proposals as such. He merely expressed some doubts as to the possibility of saying anything specific at the present time on the question of the organization of the world after the war. ... Eden also said that Beaverbrook had helped him a great deal in dealing with the situation that had arisen, but kept emphasizing the touchiness and stubbornness of the prime minister. It was obvious – and Eden did not try to conceal it – that he was very upset by the incident and that he felt very troubled by Stalin's mistrust of the Churchill Government.

... 'Please help me patch up this unpleasant incident. I, for my part, will do all I can to achieve this.'

I answered: 'You may be sure of my goodwill.' ...

[On 24 November, German troops occupied Klin, a key point on the north-western approaches to Moscow. Four days later, the Germans advanced further, to a distance of only 20 miles from the Kremlin. Meanwhile Panzer Commander General Guderian was meticulously executing a pincer move on a wide front in the south, pressing on to Kashira, beyond which there was not a single Soviet formation to prevent the capture of Moscow. The final German thrust was attempted on 1 December by Field Marshal von Kluge[68] along the Minsk–Moscow highway in fierce winter conditions. The next

---

[67] Eden was instructed by Churchill 'to be fairly stiff with Maisky'.
[68] Field Marshal Günther von Kluge, succeeded as the commander of the Fourth Army in the battles of Poland and France, but was forced to retreat in December 1941 from the outskirts of Moscow; later excelled as commander of the central front and finally commander-in-chief of the west.

day, however, General Zhukov[69] made his bid and successfully drove the Germans back to positions they had occupied a few days earlier. Taking advantage of the parrying of the German offensive, Zhukov mounted a counter-strike on 5 December in temperatures that dipped to −30°C. By 9 December, the Germans had been driven back to positions they held before the major assault, after which they were subjected to continued harassment in their rear and a second counter-offensive at the end of the month.]

23 November (Bovingdon)

... Last week (18 November) the British finally started their long-awaited offensive in Libya ... Eden is in an optimistic mood. If the British manage a successful Blitzkrieg in Libya, it may have serious consequences for the general course of the war, because this time they will surely not stop at Benghazi but will go on to Tripoli and possibly even Tunisia. This would be of immense importance for North Africa, would ease the shipping situation in the Mediterranean and would open routes for attacking Sicily, Sardinia and Italy. A second front in Europe could be opened before spring. But can the British launch a Blitzkrieg? I am not sure. Well, we'll see.

30 November

We have not gone to Bovingdon. Much to do in London.

Developments on the front are taking a turn for the better. Hitler continues to tread water near Moscow. Suffers massive losses. The general impression is that the Germans are not strong enough to break through to Moscow.

... I am going to Moscow. To accompany Eden and take part in the negotiations! Hurrah! ...

[There are no further entries in the diary for 1941. Maisky, who was actively involved (at Eden's request) in the preparatory stages of the conference in London, joined the foreign secretary on his trip to Moscow during 7–30 December. Never sure as to what was in store, he made sure he took along 'a considerable quantity of Dunhill's best' for Stalin. On the whole, Eden shared Molotov's hopes of concluding the conference with two agreements, one defining the common strategy and relationship during the war, and the other the nature and borders of Europe in the aftermath of the war (though he did not wish the second to be specific and detailed). At Eden's instigation, the Foreign

---

[69] Marshal Georgy Konstantinovich Zhukov, as chief of the general staff of the Red Army, halted the German offensive at the gates of Moscow in December 1941; appointed deputy people's commissar for defence, 1942, and conducted the counter-offensive operations which brought him at the head of the Red Army to Berlin; Soviet minister of defence, 1955–57.

58. Arriving in Moscow with Eden.

Office embarked on the drafting of the so-called 'Volga Charter', to be incorporated into the 'Atlantic Charter', recognizing the Soviet demand for a buffer zone in the Baltic and East Poland. This, they insisted, did not reflect expansionist ambitions, but was a 'legitimate security claim'. Once again, Churchill considered only the tactical and propaganda value of the visit. To prevent undesirable commitments, he timed the visit for after the launch of the offensive in Libya. This offensive, he knew, would stifle any debate on strategic priorities and would enable Eden to claim that Britain had indeed opened a second front.

Eden's visit in early December was overshadowed by two major events. On his way to Russia he was informed of the attack on Pearl Harbor. A day before the attack, Churchill still appeared conciliatory and flexible in his farewell talk with Maisky, embarking in detail on his vision for a post-war Europe in which the Soviet Union was assigned a prominent role. Churchill's hasty departure for Washington a few days after the attack, accompanied by all the chiefs of staff, and the discussion on common strategy at the White House stood in sharp contrast to the perfunctory treatment of Russia.

The second event that overshadowed Eden's visit was the impressive Soviet counter-offensive at the gates of Moscow. While the Russians gained in confidence, Eden lost a great deal of his bargaining power. As anticipated, he was confronted with the issues of frontiers and strategic collaboration. The initial cordial atmosphere, again coloured by Soviet expectations, soon gave way to frustration and conflict. The intensive negotiations reached deadlock, but a final noncommittal joint declaration and an ostentatious farewell reception at the Kremlin served Stalin as a morale booster at home and a display of unity vis-à-vis the Germans.]

1942

[There are barely any entries following Maisky's return from Moscow. This can be attributed only in part to a severe bout of recurring malaria and the immense burden of work he was subjected to. Not unlike in 1939, the main reasons for the protracted periods of silence were his qualms about the Kremlin's policies. The diary only alludes to the dramatic soul-searching going on in Moscow in the first quarter of 1942.

Maisky was enticed by Eden's favourable response to Stalin's post-war schemes and the impression he left in Moscow that the British Government would 'raise no difficulties'. The draft agreement brought along by Eden was first discussed in Cabinet only on 5 and 6 February. Beaverbrook alone spoke strongly in favour of acceding to Stalin's demands, describing the Baltic states as 'the Ireland of Russia'. Churchill, whose gaze was fixed on the United States, insisted that Stalin's demands 'should be settled at the Peace Conference'. Maisky shared with Eden a serious concern that the procedure adopted by the Cabinet of consulting the Americans first was bound to lead to procrastination. He therefore defied instructions from Moscow to keep a low profile and conspired with Eden to launch tripartite conversations in London, leading to 'close cooperation, both for the conduct of the war and in the period after the war'.]

31 January[1]

Three-day parliamentary debate (27–28/1) [*sic*] on government policy. Vote of confidence: 464 to 1, with 27 abstentions. A smart move by Churchill: show your confidence! ... Government will have to contend with stormy weather in the near future; many of the present ministers will be thrown overboard, but Churchill will stay. The bourgeois elite does not like or trust him, but can't do without him while war with Germany is still on. No other figure on the British political horizon of Churchill's quality and popularity.

---

[1] A number of entries, written in haste and abbreviated, are expanded here to facilitate reading.

27 February[2]

Dear Maksim Maksimovich [Litvinov],

I deem it necessary to bring the following to your attention: on 2 February Harriman arrived in London from America, he called me on the 4th and invited me to lunch with him on the 5th. We lunched, just the two of us, in Harriman's hotel room. First we discussed various topics, but then Harriman asked whether it would be possible to arrange a meeting between Roosevelt and Stalin. Harriman believes that there is a great deal of distrust between the USA and the USSR, as well as between the USSR and England. The best way of eliminating it would be a personal meeting between Roosevelt and Stalin. Harriman knows that Roosevelt would be eager to meet, but how about Stalin? Harriman suggested either Iceland or the area around the Bering Strait as the location for the meeting, stressing that it makes no odds to Roosevelt whose territory is chosen for the meeting.

... I gained the impression from what Harriman told me that the possibility of a meeting between Roosevelt and Stalin is being discussed not in the State Department, but among people in the president's circle, such as Hopkins, Harriman and others, and that they probably thought it more convenient and less binding to probe our intentions on this issue through London rather than Washington and via the Harriman–Maisky route, rather than the Hull–Litvinov one.[3]

... I reported our conversation to Moscow and received a reply 8 days later stating that the Soviet Government deemed the meeting desirable; but since Stalin could not leave the USSR because of the tense situation at the front, Arkhangelsk or Astrakhan was proposed as the site of the meeting. I informed Harriman of this.

... I wished to inform you about the afore-said in a purely personal manner because the matter lies within your competence and I was involved in it quite against my will and desires. It goes without saying that I'll hand the matter over to Washington at the first opportunity.

I press your hand warmly,

I. Maisky

[For three key players – Halifax and Litvinov in Washington, and Maisky in London – the situation was alarmingly reminiscent of 1939. All three were virtually 'in exile', little trusted by their own governments. Halifax, atoning for mistakes he might have committed on the eve of war, was most eager to forestall a separate Soviet–German

---

[2] The copy of the letter to Litvinov is included in the diary under this date.
[3] Cordell Hull, US secretary of state, 1933–44.

peace and to foster the alliance. Litvinov strove for the same goal, but shared Stalin's and Molotov's distrust of the British, who had let him down in Munich and during the negotiations for a triple alliance. Maisky and Litvinov, arguably the most effective advocates of their country's interests, continued to be deadly rivals of Molotov. Apart from Kollontay, they were the only active survivors of the old school of Soviet diplomacy.]

15 February

What is England's reaction to the military successes of the USSR in the last ten weeks?

... The prestige of the Red Army is growing. Rapturous admiration. The myth of German 'invincibility' has been destroyed. We'll crush the German army soon. The question is asked half in jest, half in earnest: 'Couldn't we borrow a couple of your generals?'

... For as long as our successes remain reasonably modest, the reserves of the ruling class will keep silent. But what if the Red Army starts approaching Berlin? And on their own to boot? A nightmare! Cold sweat!

And such a situation is possible: 1942, 1943. If our calculations prove justified (there are good grounds for them), the Red Army might reach Berlin alone, before England and the USA. To avoid this, the English might race to open a 'second front' at the end of this year. Can they do it? I doubt it. The sabotaging of our supplies is conceivable in order to put off a 'decision' till 1943, when Britain and the USA will be better prepared. ...

18 February

The political atmosphere has remained tense and uneasy. I was in Parliament on the 17th. Churchill spoke about the fall of Singapore.[4] He did not look well, was irritated, easily offended and obstinate. The MPs were caustic and sniffy. They gave Churchill a bad reception and a bad send-off. I've never seen anything like it. Sharp questions made the PM angry.

... The general situation is clear. The role of Churchill personally: he makes it ever more difficult even for his friends to support his Government. 'I answer for everything!' This means that one can't criticize the ministers, generals, etc., although no shortage of fools, mediocrities and potential representatives of the 'fifth column' have gathered under his protective umbrella. 'The War Cabinet is good, no changes are called for!' ...

---

[4] The battle raged between 8 and 15 February. More than 80,000 British troops were taken prisoner.

Who could succeed Churchill if he resigned? Two names are widely touted: Eden and Cripps. Eden has been touted for some time. Cripps's star has risen meteorically of late (particularly after his speeches over the wireless and in Bristol). The reasons: the common man is convinced that Cripps 'brings luck' ('Russia has entered the war'), that he is 'fresh' and 'outside the parties' (the people are sick and tired of parties), progressive, clever, a good orator and, most importantly, has bet on the right horse – the USSR. ...

Personally, I'm for Churchill as PM. He is reliable: against Germany. Strong-willed: he rules on his own. Neither Cripps nor Eden is strong enough. Churchill has his feet firmly on the ground. Seems to be ready to compromise. ... It is possible that after yesterday's sitting of the House, Churchill will make concessions both on the question of the Government and on the question of the military command. The need for this becomes ever more obvious. When I was leaving Parliament yesterday, an MP I know stopped me in the lobby and asked: 'What could lead to an outburst of enthusiasm in England today?' – 'What indeed?' – 'If Marshal Timoshenko were to be appointed commander-in-chief of the British army!'

20 February

... Government reshuffle ... Churchill has agreed to a compromise on the matter of the Cabinet. ... Skilful tactician.

... On the whole, reshuffle is a plus. Beaverbrook – minus. Will Cripps replace him?

Cripps played a good hand. Became member of the War Cabinet and 'leader of the House of Commons' (a good post for him + *limelight*). Has ironic satisfaction of leading the Labour Party (together with the others) which expelled him three years ago. A man without a party is the leader of the House of Commons (under Lloyd George there was Bonar Law). Cripps's story over the last couple of years is an English political fairy-tale. His strong position is all thanks to the reflected light of the USSR's power and the Red Army's heroism.

[Cripps's reception by the public after his return from Moscow was reminiscent of Churchill's 'finest hour' a year earlier. It was reckoned in political circles that 'each week his stature will grow' while Churchill's might 'correspondingly sink'. Cripps's vow not to serve in a Cabinet alongside Beaverbrook eventually forced the resignation of the latter. It was widely assumed, as Winant informed Washington, that Cripps's entry into the War Cabinet signalled the 'intensification of efforts for closer relations with Russia'. No wonder Maisky was quick to congratulate Cripps on his appointment to the War Cabinet – something he hoped would 'augur well for the conduct of the war in general and for relations between the Soviet Union and Great Britain in particular'. But

Beaverbrook was right in claiming that while Cripps was 'playing the Russians up ... in reality *he* was the only genuine supporter of Russia in Cabinet', and that his own resignation meant 'trouble for the Russians'. Churchill fell back on his abundant political experience to sustain his authority. He neutralized Cripps by including him in the War Cabinet and appointing him leader of the House. This role, as Churchill must have known, did not suit Cripps's spartan, righteous and ascetic personality: it was a time-consuming task and it alienated him from his potential supporters. When discussions on Russia gathered momentum in March, Cripps was entrusted with a protracted and forlorn mission to India – 'a masterly stroke' by Churchill which 'had shown him up'. In such circumstances, Cripps's continued presence in the Cabinet, with little to show for it, gradually gnawed away at his credibility. He was the obvious loser when forced to resign his seat in the War Cabinet at the end of the year, following victory at El Alamein.]

26 February

Eden.

I pose the question of additional supplies in March–April to those stipulated by the Moscow protocol: the spring offensive and the danger for lines of communication (ships breaking through). Eden promises to do all he can.

Eden says he handed Winant, who flew off today, a memorandum for Roosevelt in the spirit of my conversation with Winant (although we hadn't agreed on this). Eden is all for speeding up the signing of the treaties. Gives it a month. I said: if he doesn't sign it very soon, the effect of Eden's visit to Moscow will evaporate.

Eden is satisfied with the restructuring of the Government: it has become more amicable and competent. Great hopes for Cripps. His first speech in Parliament was a success.

I voice my impression: the country and Parliament are ready to give the Government 'a chance', but without much enthusiasm. Eden agrees.

28 February

At Beaverbrook's at Cherkley. Dinner. Harriman and his daughter. Mrs R. Churchill, M. Foot[5] and others.

Before dinner – in the study... Portraits of Stalin and Roosevelt and the king on mantelpiece.

Agitated. He wants Stalin to know the truth.[6]

---

[5] Michael Foot, assistant editor, *Tribune*, 1937–38; acting editor, *Evening Standard*, 1942; Labour MP, 1945–55 and 1960–92.
[6] The reasons for his resignation.

2 March

Beaverbrook.

Came in the evening. Utmost support to the USSR. It's easier outside than inside the Government. Stalin will see this. If there's anything Stalin wants, Beaverbrook is always at his disposal... Concentrating on supplies. ... Second front.

... Understands Stalin's resentment: 'I'm fighting alone.'

4 March

Cripps.

Cripps dined at mine.

Cripps is trying hard to conclude arrangements for the treaty. The Cabinet has accepted the 1941 borders, albeit without much enthusiasm.

... 'Unfortunately, about a year ago, when England was fighting alone and wanted to involve the USA in the war, the British Government promised the Americans not to recognize changes in the European borders without prior consultation. England became wholly dependent on the Americans. It's awkward, but what can be done?' The Americans are in no hurry (the proposal for the treaty was sent 3 weeks ago). Cripps's plan to send Eden to the USA failed. Internal crisis. ...

5 March

Eden and Cripps.

Military situation: (1) Libya. The English have good defensive positions and hope to hold them. ... (2) Far East. Dutch Indies are considered lost. Now it's Burma's turn. The British Government will be defending her, but not sure of holding her. ... Japan may strike at India, but it's a big country and the Japanese may well get stuck. Moreover, next week Churchill will make an important statement on India in Parliament. ...

[On 7 March Eden persuaded a reluctant Churchill that 'the only way of tilting the American scale' was through a personal message to Roosevelt. It was necessary to overcome the 'discomfort' in the United States and Russia over the absence of British support, and the resurgence of old suspicions that Britain wished to see Russia 'bled white'. As powerful was the negative argument that only an immediate intervention on the Continent would secure a sufficiently strong presence of Anglo-American forces to 'hinder any possible expansionist plans of the Soviet Government'.

'The increasing gravity of the war,' Churchill cabled to Roosevelt, 'has led me to feel that the principles of the Atlantic Charter ought not to be construed so as to deny Russia the frontiers she occupied when Germany attacked her ... I hope therefore that you will be able to give us a free hand to sign the treaty which Stalin desires as soon as possible.' Heeding the warning of his military planners that keeping Russia at war was 'of primary importance', Roosevelt left Churchill in no doubt that he was eager to see the establishment of a new front in Europe 'this summer'. 'Nothing,' he insisted, 'would be worse than to have the Russians collapse ... I would rather lose New Zealand, Australia or anything else than have the Russians collapse.'

Litvinov was accordingly summoned to the White House on 12 March and bluntly told by the president that, as 'it was difficult to do business with the English and the Foreign Office', he preferred to discuss the Baltic issue directly with Litvinov. Indeed, within a couple of days, Roosevelt introduced a coup in relations with Russia. While appearing to woo Churchill, he mercilessly hammered home the repercussions of the military disasters on Churchill's political standing, in order to justify his independent approach to the Russians:

> I know you will not mind my being brutally frank when I tell you that I think I can personally handle Stalin better than either your Foreign Office or my State Department. Stalin hates the guts of all your top people. He thinks he likes me better, and I hope he will continue to do so.

Taking the lead, he promised to send the prime minister within days 'a more definite plan for a joint attack in Europe itself'.]

10 March

... A second English front in Europe is needed by the time all offensives are launched – or the only chance to win the war may be lost.

Roosevelt summoned Litvinov and spoke about the Baltics. He agrees in essence, but is against any open or secret agreement because of public opinion. R. said bluntly that if the British Government were to conclude a secret agreement of which he was not informed, he would not object. – Moscow had informed L. earlier that it was no longer interested in an agreement.

12 March

Eden handed me a copy of Churchill's message to Stalin of 9 March.

My questions: (1) When did Ch. send the telegram to Roosevelt and what reaction? Telegram sent 7 March. No reaction so far. Halifax communicated today that R. wants to talk with Litvinov on this matter. ... (2) What is meant by 'other means' to alleviate USSR's situation (item 3 of the message)? Eden replied that in the first place – air offensive and raids. I asked: and in the second? Could it be a second front?... Eden neither rejected nor supported a second front. ...

13 March

Eden.

The British Government has accepted the 1941 borders. Approached Washington on the 10th. The question was formulated in such a way as to get a positive reply if possible, i.e. no objections on the part of the USA. Winant supports the British Government but he doesn't know whether he expresses the opinion of the US Government: he hasn't been to the USA for a long time; going in a few days. Promises cooperation. ...

[The failure to set up a common strategic and political platform presented the Russians with a serious dilemma as to how best to confront the looming German spring offensive. Maisky knew that the disasters inflicted on Britain in the Far East had raised doubts in Stalin's mind about the value of British 'assistance, sincerity and determination to fight the war to a finish'. Although he claimed to know better, Maisky dropped ominous hints that 'some, like Stalin, have never been out of Russia and find us [the British] more difficult to understand'. Stalin would tend to assume that the British had 'passed the buck to Roosevelt and are hedging'. This could prove disastrous, as Stalin expected 1942 to be the decisive year of the war and the one in which the Germans could be crushed, were Britain to embark on 'a big enterprise' in Italy or the Balkans – let alone a cross-Channel attack. Maisky strove hard to eliminate the apparent discrepancy in the timetable, convinced that 'the British did not really want to win victory in 1942' and were at best preparing for victory in 1943.

The growing disillusionment in Moscow was confirmed by Molotov's startling strict instructions to Litvinov to avoid raising the second front issue – instructions which the ambassador openly disputed. He was roundly reprimanded by Molotov and again reminded that 'the Soviet Government was not at present pressing the Allies to open a second front'. He was further instructed to 'follow rigorously' directives in the same vein concerning the contemplated political agreement.

The puzzling shift in the Soviet position has been either overlooked or misconstrued by Western scholars, who have often attributed the rumours of a separate peace to Stalin's attempts to scare and 'blackmail' the Western powers into further commitment. The major driving force in the West to harness the Russians to the Allied camp was, as in 1939, fear of a German–Soviet reconciliation. The Soviet Union harboured similar suspicions of a possible Anglo-German separate peace. It is conceivable (and there are indeed indications of the fact) that in desperation Stalin resorted to the same tactics as he had employed in the spring of 1939 and considered an approach to the Germans through Beria. The essence of this would have been cessation of hostilities with Germany by May 1942, coupled with the bait that Russia might join the war against the West by the end of 1943. The reward for the Russians would have been the reinstatement of the territorial arrangements of the Molotov–Ribbentrop Pact, supplemented by the allocation of spheres of influence in the Balkans, and most likely even in Greece. This may explain the nervousness of both Litvinov and Maisky, and cryptic comments in the diary (as well as the prolonged silences).

Such a probability is corroborated by an intriguing set of instructions from Molotov to Litvinov which disclosed the state of mind in the Kremlin. It established the fact that, in view of the failure to reach an agreement in Moscow, the Soviet Government regarded the negotiations 'merely as precursory talks on various topics', and since negotiations had not resumed they were 'no longer interested in continuing them', 'did not consider it expedient to seize the initiative in this matter' nor 'to rush the British'.[7]]

16 March

On Saturday, the 14th, I received Comrade Stalin's message to Churchill. I called the Foreign Office at once and asked for an appointment with the prime minister on Monday the 16th. Within an hour, the FO called to inform me that Churchill would see me on Monday at 5 p.m. Yesterday, Sunday, I received another call from the FO to inform me of a change of plan: the prime minister would not be able to see me at five o'clock on Monday and instead invited me to come to lunch at Chequers that same day. I agreed.

So today, at around one o'clock, I arrived at Chequers. Eden, whom I had asked to be present during my conversation with Churchill, appeared a few minutes later. Upon entering the room where I sat waiting, Eden took me aside and said anxiously: 'I've just received a telegram from Washington that conveys the essence of Roosevelt's statement to Litvinov... A very unpleasant statement. We must discuss it.'

That very moment the prime minister's adjutant arrived and called us into the dining-room. It was, in fact, not exactly a dining-room, but a small corner room on the first floor with a very private feel to it. A small table was set for the three of us: Churchill, Eden and me. The PM, dressed in his habitual *siren suit*, greeted me in jovial, friendly fashion and apologized for his domestic appearance. Having undergone a minor operation today, he had been unable to return to the city and was obliged to receive me at home.

---

[7] It is indeed most telling that this document is not included in the official publication of the Soviet documents, and that there is an ominous gap in the exchanges with Litvinov between 18 February and 12 March.

When we sat down at the table, I handed Churchill the message from C[omrade] Stalin. He quickly read it through and was evidently satisfied. Then it was Eden's turn to read the message. At first our conversation revolved around the latest war news. Then Eden touched upon the question of the treaties. He spoke once again about the telegram from Washington and expressed his fear that the attitude of the USA could complicate the situation.

'This does not mean, of course, that we will not sign the treaties with you,' Eden added, 'but you must understand how important it would be to have America on our side.'

Churchill intervened and defined his position: 'I have, since the very beginning, been reluctant to recognize the 1941 borders, but, as Stalin was so insistent, I eventually agreed to do so... Maybe it's a prejudice, but I'm a great believer in the principle of the free self-determination of nations which was also included in the *Atlantic Charter*, while here...'

'But a broad democratic plebiscite was held in the Baltics,' I interrupted, understanding full well what Churchill was driving at.

Churchill grinned slyly and rejoined: 'Yes, of course there was a plebiscite, but all the same...'

He concluded his phrase with a vague gesture.

'Frankly speaking,' I retorted, 'I don't quite understand the position of the B[ritish] G[overnment] on this issue. As far as I know, the B[ritish] G[overnment] undertook to "consult" the USA, and I stress "consult", on issues relating to European borders, not to seek the USA's permission. As I understand it, "consultation" has already taken place. You made a démarche in Washington which showed there to be a marked difference of opinion between the Am[erican] and the British governments. Very well. What next? I think you should have told the Americans: "We have informed you of our intention to recognize the Soviet borders of 1941. You don't like it, but we maintain that the move is in the interests of our victory over the common enemy. We are taking this step in the hope that you will come to understand and appreciate the correctness of our policy." Our treaties should have been signed right after such a statement was made. In general, the British Government should appeal to its "American uncle" a little less often, and think a bit more about the independence of its policy.'

Churchill and Eden heard me out, but would not commit themselves to anything right away. Churchill merely said: 'Talk with Eden and find an acceptable solution.'

So it was decided: tomorrow, the 17th, I am to meet with Eden and discuss the current situation.

Then I mentioned Comrade Stalin's message and drew Churchill's attention to the paragraph where Comrade Stalin expresses his confidence that 1942 will be the decisive year. I asked Churchill: what were his thoughts on the subject?

Churchill's countenance darkened immediately. He shrugged his shoulders and uttered with slight irritation: 'I don't see how 1942 can become the decisive year.'

I was about to protest, but Churchill cut me short with a sharp question: 'Tell me, how do you feel yourselves to be today – stronger or weaker than in 1941?'

'Stronger, of course,' I answered without hesitation.

'Well, I feel weaker,' Churchill retorted.

And then he added by way of clarification: 'Last year we had to fight against two major powers, this year – against three.'

'But now,' I responded, 'you have two mighty allies.'

Churchill, however, would not agree with me and started raising additional domestic problems, such as India, the press, Parliament, production...

So then I decided to take the bull by the horns and said to Churchill: 'I don't know how you see it, but I think we face a very menacing situation. A crucial moment in the course of the war really is approaching. It's "either or". How do things stand? Germany is preparing an enormous offensive this spring. She is staking everything on this year. If we succeed in defeating the German offensive this spring, then in essence we will have won the war. The backbone of Hitler's war machine would be broken this year. It would only remain for us to finish off the crazed beast. With Germany defeated, everything else would be relatively easy. Now, suppose we fail to defeat Germany's spring offensive. Suppose the Red Army is forced to retreat again, that we begin to lose territories once more, that the Germans break through to the Caucasus – what then? For Hitler will not stop in the Caucasus if that happens. He will go farther – to Iran, Turkey, Egypt, India. He will link hands with Japan somewhere in the Indian Ocean and stretch out his arms towards Africa. Germany's problems with oil, raw materials and food will be resolved. The British Empire will collapse, while the USSR will lose exceptionally important territories. ... What would be our chances of victory? And when?... That is the choice before us! It's now or never!'

Churchill, who had been listening to me with a frowning countenance and his head bent to one side, suddenly straightened up with a jerk and exclaimed in great agitation: 'We would rather die than reconcile ourselves to such a situation!'

Eden added: 'I quite agree with the ambassador. The question is exactly that: now or never!'

I continued: 'The Red Army has certainly become stronger compared to last year, and the German army has weakened. Of course we shall fight savagely this year. But who can vouch for the future? ... Britain and the USA are still deliberating, sizing things up, thinking things over, and are simply unable to decide which is the crucial year: 1942 or 1943. The situation is quite intoler-able. The differing "war schedules" of the USSR, on the one side, and Britain and the USA, on the other, represent the gravest flaw of the Allied strategy. It must be eliminated. Britain and the USA must also place their stake on 1942. This is the year when they must throw into battle all their forces and resources, irrespective of the degree of their preparedness.' ...

Once again Eden was in total agreement.

Churchill sat sunk in thought. Finally, he raised his head and said: 'Perhaps you are right. All the information I have at my disposal testifies that the Germans are preparing an attack in the east. Countless trains are heading east, carrying men and weapons. ... Yes, you will have to withstand a terrible blow this spring. We must help you in every way possible. Do all we can.'

It was clear, however, that arriving at this conclusion had not been easy for Churchill.

Having thus gained victory over Churchill on this matter of principle, I shifted our conversation onto more practical ground. ...

There followed a long, animated, at times even heated, exchange of opin-ions. ... Churchill said he was now studying the question of a second front in Europe. It was clear from this that Eden had already spoken with the PM on this matter, following my conversation with him on 12 March. I tried to develop the matter further and pushed the argument in favour of a second front which had worked so well on Eden (the need to train the British army in an attack-minded spirit). Churchill responded to my argument no less positively than Eden. He even remarked that technically it would be easier to open a second front now, as compared to last year, because the English are currently in posses-sion of a large number of vessels fit for landing operations. Nonetheless, the prime minister resolutely avoided making any specific promises.

... India. I mentioned this problem in passing. Churchill responded with considerable anger and irritation.

'Cripps won't be able to do anything there,' he uttered curtly. 'The Indians won't agree between themselves... From the military point of view it is not so important. From the military point of view, the Caspian–Levantine front is far more impor-tant than India. Politics and emotions are another matter. We shall see.'

Churchill made an abrupt gesture with his hand and continued: 'In general, the Indians are not a historic nation. Who has not conquered them? Whoever came to India from the north became her master. Throughout their history the Indians have barely ever enjoyed true independence. Look at the Indian villages: each stands on a hill. Where did the hill come from? Each village has been building its mud huts for centuries, for millennia. Every year the rainy season washes the huts away. The old ones are replaced by new ones from the same earth. In turn they, too, are washed away. And thus from one generation to another. As a result, the hills have grown higher and higher. What kind of people is it that has not been able to invent something better over the course of millennia?' ...

Churchill took a sip of wine and continued with still more irritation: 'I'm prepared to leave India this very moment. We won't be living there in any case. But what would happen then? You might think: liberty, prosperity, the development of culture and science... How wrong you would be! If we leave, fighting will break out everywhere, there'll be a civil war. Eventually, the Moslems will become masters, because they are warriors, while the Hindus are windbags. Yes, windbags! Oh, of course, when it comes to fine speeches, skilfully balanced resolutions, and legalistic castles in the air, the Hindus are real experts! They're in their element! But when it comes to business, when something must be decided on quickly, implemented, executed – here the Hindus say "pass". Here they immediately reveal their internal flabbiness.'

... I listened to him and couldn't help thinking: 'Of course, Churchill is a considerable man and a major statesman. And yes, he is 67 years old. But nonetheless, something of the small boy lives on in him: Iran is a toy he likes, while India is a toy he dislikes.'

... Churchill spoke about the Red Army with admiration, saying that goodwill towards the USSR had grown immensely in England, along with its prestige. He added with a laugh: 'Just imagine! My own wife is completely Sovietized... All she ever talks about is the Soviet Red Cross, the Soviet army, and the wife of the Soviet ambassador, with whom she corresponds, speaks over the telephone and appears at demonstrations!'

He added with a sly sparkle in his eye: 'Couldn't you elect her to one of your Soviets? She surely deserves it.'

... During today's conversation with the prime minister, I was struck by one feature which I had not observed before: Churchill is in a 'twilight mood'. He even let slip the remark: 'I'm not long for this world... I'll be ashes soon...'

The same note sounded in a number of other statements. But every time Germany was mentioned Churchill flared up and his eyes flashed with sparks of fury. My general impression is that Churchill has an acute sense of being on the wane and is harnessing his remaining strength and energy in pursuit of one fundamental and all-exclusive goal – to win the war. He looks and thinks no further than that.

Seeing me out onto the porch, Eden quickly whispered into my ear: 'You managed to get a lot out of the prime minister today. He was in a good mood. He is being needlessly irritated – Parliament's criticisms and the suspicions of the press exasperate him... Meanwhile, you can see that much is being prepared, though it's too early to speak about it openly... You have many friends here... If you could do something to ease the PM's situation, we'd all gain from it.'

17 March

Eden.

We conferred on the treaties. Halifax has sent the record of Roosevelt's statement to Litvinov; it had been passed on to him by Sumner Welles for his information. The statement is long (two single-spaced pages). Main points: in view of prevalent American public opinion, Roosevelt was 'alarmed' to learn about Anglo-Soviet negotiations concerning the 1941 borders, he would like to study the matter more intensively, could in no way approve a secret treaty, and could not now sign any treaty concerning future borders. ...

Eden asked: what should be done now? In spite of the USA pouring cold water on them, the treaties must be signed quickly. It was obvious, however, that Halifax's telegram had upset him. I set about reassuring him. The British Government must be courageous. Roosevelt's statement is more of an insurance policy than a protest.

... After our discussion, Eden reached the following conclusion: let Stalin reply (the statement is addressed to him), then Eden will reply in the same spirit. Then we shall get down to drafting the treaties. Stalin's reply, according to Eden, should be based on the following ideas: there is no question of a secret treaty, no one has invited the USA to sign; the security requirements of the USSR call for a recognition of the 1941 borders now in order to establish trust between England and the USSR.

I'm asking Moscow to send me a copy of the reply to Roosevelt and details of the talk between Roosevelt and Litvinov.

[Maisky was anxious to prevent the political talks from stalling. Eden concealed in his own report of the conversations the fact that, despite the 'cold shower' from Washington, the two had conspired over how to pursue the political negotiations. The scheme was for Stalin to assure Roosevelt that the treaty would have no secret clauses and that, while his tacit support was welcome, he was not required to be a signatory. Eden hoped Stalin would start the ball rolling by insisting that for the sake of 'establishing mutual trust and steadfast cooperation among the Allies it was essential to recognize the borders now and not after the war'.]

23 March

I informed Eden that in fact the Soviet Government has decided not to respond to Roosevelt's statement to Litvinov, regarding it merely as information, but only to instruct M.M. Litvinov to tell the president that the Soviet Government has taken his statement into consideration. Eden was dumbfounded. I reassured him: we have no obligations in relations to the USA, and have requested nothing from Roosevelt. ...

59. The 'conspirators'.

60. Medals presented by Maisky to Hurricane pilots deployed in northern Russia.

[Again Molotov appeared to be far from keen to pursue the negotiations. He was puzzled, as he informed his ambassador in London, by Eden's approach. In Washington, Litvinov was as baffled as Maisky by the 'incomprehensible' policy pursued by the Kremlin. Expecting Russia to face a 'mighty' United States and a 'weakened and shattered' British Empire at the peace conference, he failed to see the wisdom of pressing the British to sign an agreement against the will of Roosevelt, who was bound to be insulted.[8] It is worth noting, therefore, that rather than specifically demanding a cross-Channel attack at this stage, Moscow was eager for the Allies to put the eastern front at the top of their strategy. 'There is no time,' said Maisky, as he pinned the Order of Lenin on British pilots who had flown in Russia, 'to wait until the last button is sewn on the uniform of the last soldier.']

24 March

Kerr's[9] first visit to Molotov. Molotov remarked that ... we consider 1942 to be the decisive year in the struggle against Germany. Germany is preparing a

---

[8] Typically, Litvinov's assessment is missing from the official published Soviet documents.
[9] Archibald Clark Kerr (1st Baron Inverchapel), British ambassador in China, 1938–42; in the USSR, 1942–46; and in the USA, 1946–48.

spring offensive. We are doing all we can to obstruct the organization of the offensive. Soviet troops are incessantly attacking along the entire front, so as not to give a respite to the Germans anywhere, to frustrate the German offensive plans. If Britain and the USA do the same where they can land blows on the Hitlerites, the aim of reaching a turning point in 1942 will be achieved. ...

5 April (Bovingdon, Easter)

... The situation is unclear. The facts may signify the beginning of the disintegration of the Empire, but they may also simply signify a transitional phase in the transformation of the Empire. All will depend on the English 'spirit', and primarily that of the ruling class. If the leaders fail to show the necessary flexibility and fail to make sufficient concessions in various parts of the Empire in good time, its disintegration as a result of the war will become inevitable. If, on the other hand, the leaders succeed in showing these qualities, the transformation of the Empire is possible. One example: India may become a dominion or even formally an independent state after the war, but if the British Government succeeds in signing proper trade, political and military agreements with her in advance, as well as with Egypt, England will still be able to maintain a significant number of its advantages there. The same goes for other parts of the Empire.

In which of the two directions are events unfolding? My general impression is that events are advancing more in the second direction, i.e. that the leaders are making considerable efforts to save whatever can be saved of their position in the Empire and inside the country.

... It is perfectly clear that the English ruling class is heading towards impoverishment with all the ensuing consequences. It is sliding downhill fast. ... That is why, when drawing up plans for post-war reconstruction, they will only do as much as pressure from the lower classes and the USSR compels them to do. ... And the mood of this class is now very troubled and gloomy. Not long ago I attended a lunch arranged by Rothschild, the banker. I gently pushed the conversation in the direction of post-war prospects. It soon became apparent that I had touched a nerve. A sharp debate developed. ... The host closed the debate with a characteristic remark: 'To avoid sleepless nights, my wife forbids me to think about the future.'

6 April

Continuing the thoughts which I noted down yesterday, I arrive at the following conclusion.

What will the world look like at the end of the war? An end, of course, which we desire and are counting on.

Germany, Italy and Japan will be crushed and weakened for a long time. France will be in the process of a slow and painful recovery, having lost its status as a great power. The British Empire will be significantly weaker (I choose the optimum scenario for her: not disintegration, but transformation). China will be triumphant, but licking her wounds and regaining her strength with great difficulty.

Against this background, two powers will present a somewhat different picture – the USSR and the USA.

The USSR will also have to tend its wounds, but, emerging from the war with a powerful army, a vast industry, mechanized agriculture and a wealth of raw materials, it will be the mightiest international power. The socialist system will help the USSR to overcome the grave consequences of the war faster than other countries.

The USA, in its turn, will become the second-largest power because it will, by all appearances, suffer least from the war and will maintain its strength to a greater degree than anyone else. The American army will probably be ready for serious battle only once the war is over. Together with the mighty navy, air force and military industry, this army will make the USA very powerful.

The USSR and the USA will represent the two social and international poles of socialism and capitalism in the post-war period. For in the USA capitalism will have preserved infinitely more of its vital juices by the end of the war than in England. The USA will become the citadel of capitalism. That is why the post-war period will most probably be marked by a contest between the USSR and the USA rather than between England and the USA. ...

I certainly do not rule out the possibility that Hitler may mark the month of April with novelties of one kind or another. ... I, in any case, think it most probable that Hitler's aim this year will be to conquer the Caucasus, with all the ensuing consequences.

... As we approach the spring–summer campaign, what kind of shape are we in?

The winter offensive had major significance. It gave a big boost to the morale of the Red Army and the entire Soviet population. It gave the Red Army very valuable experience of war. It returned to us a number of our territories. It deprived Hitler of the possibility of calmly waiting out the winter while preparing a tremendous reserve force for the spring. It compelled the Germans to fight through the whole winter, sustaining heavy losses. ... These, of courses, are all pluses. But I am somewhat disappointed that our territorial gains have fallen short of my expectations. I had thought that by the end of winter we would at least have taken Smolensk, driven the Germans from Leningrad and liberated the Crimea. But it hasn't happened and there's nothing you can do about it now.

What are the prospects? It's hard to predict, especially in the absence of any kind of accurate information from the USSR. Hitler has evidently recovered somewhat from the initial confusion sown in the German ranks by our December offensive. By February it was clear that it was too early to speak of the disintegration of the German army. The German troops did not retreat in disarray and panic. ... Meanwhile, we got on with preparing the Red Army for the spring. Reserves were called up, extensive efforts were made to expand military production, and we imported as much as we could from abroad. ...

[There are no further entries in the diary until mid-June, with the exception of an abbreviated record of a meeting with Beaverbrook on 7 May (not reproduced here) and the telegrams exchanged between Stalin and Churchill concerning Molotov's visits to London and Washington in May and early June. The tension that pervaded relations between Maisky and Molotov – tension which came bubbling to the surface a couple of times during and immediately after the latter's visit to London[10] – and the uncertainty over the Kremlin's intentions in the period preceding the resumption of the German offensive probably account for Maisky's ominous silence.

61. Ambassador at work with 'Flo', his devoted communist secretary, and Zinchenko, first secretary.

---

[10] See p. 431.

Eden had explained to Maisky that Churchill was seeking at least tacit American support for the treaty, given that there was 'relatively little' the British could do 'by way of military aid to Russia'. An unintended consequence of the excuse was that it enabled Roosevelt to forestall the political treaty by backing the Russian demands for the second front, thereby diverting the pressure onto Britain. Inundated by intelligence reports on the state of 'anxiety, despondence, and pessimism' in Britain, Roosevelt wondered whether Churchill was losing his grip on the domestic scene. What was desired above all was 'an offensive attitude on the part of the fighting forces instead of continual retreat and defense, efficient and strong leadership at home towards a real total war effort'. Since his visit to Moscow, Hopkins had been urging Roosevelt to adopt General Marshall's[11] carefully worked-out plans for a cross-Channel offensive and impose them on Churchill. Such a decision, he insisted, had to be taken '*now*' to ensure that all necessary logistical and deployment preparations were completed in time for an operation at the beginning of April 1943. In the meantime, he presented a contingency plan for an offensive in September 1942, 'a sacrifice for the common good'.[12]

When Marshall and Stimson,[13] the First World War veteran and experienced secretary of war, met Roosevelt over lunch in the White House on 25 March, they prodded the president to submit their plans to Churchill and then 'lean with all your strength on the ruthless rearrangement of shipping allotments and the preparation of landing gear for the ultimate invasion' not later than September. On 1 April, the plans, comprising three distinct operations and culminating in an invasion of Europe on 1 April 1943 were approved by the president. The first was Operation Bolero, under which the Americans would deploy in Britain some 30 divisions, six armoured divisions and 3,250 aircraft. Operation Round Up would see those forces backed by 18 British divisions landed in the stretch between Boulogne and Le Havre. Operation Sledgehammer was an emergency measure aimed at establishing bridgeheads in a French seaport during the early autumn of 1942, particularly if the Soviet Union was on the brink of collapse.

Churchill had justified the decision to conclude the political treaty by his failure to assist Russia on the battlefield. To steal a march on the British prime minister and forestall any agreement, Roosevelt resorted to the military card. He hastily informed Stalin of the 'very important military proposal' he had for 'military action of our forces in a manner to relieve your critical western front'. He urged Stalin to send 'Molotov and a General' to Washington without delay to provide crucial advice before the Americans 'determine with finality' the common strategy and action. He then informed Churchill *en passant* that he was summoning two 'special representatives' from Moscow to

---

[11] George Catlett Marshall, chief of staff of the United States army, 1939–45; secretary of state, 1947–49.
[12] Maisky remained sceptical about the Allies doing 'their *utmost* to win the war by sacrifice of men and wealth to the common cause'.
[13] Henry Stimson was President Hoover's secretary of state from 1929 to 1933 and Roosevelt's secretary of war throughout the Second World War, despite being a Republican and 72 years old.

discuss the plan, which he hoped would be 'greet[ed] with enthusiasm'. Most discon-certed by Roosevelt's lead, Churchill proposed 'to flip over' to Hyde Park (Roosevelt's estate in upstate New York) for a weekend as there was 'so much to settle that would go easily in talk'.

On 8 April, Maisky was informed by Eden that, despite Roosevelt's reservations, the Cabinet was now prepared to negotiate 'a treaty on the lines desired by M. Stalin', with only some minor modification to accommodate American sensibilities. Amidst growing concern that there would be either a separate Soviet–German peace agreement or a successful Soviet offensive which would pave the Russians' way to Berlin, Eden was anxious for Molotov to come to London, too. A major bone of contention, however, remained Stalin's insistence on recognition of the Curzon Line as Russia's future border with Poland. Eden suggested, probably after consulting Maisky, that if Molotov was indisposed, the ambassador would be authorized to sign the agreement. Molotov indeed did prefer that Maisky should stand in for him at the negotiations (ominously reminiscent of when, in May 1939, the ambassador replaced Molotov as chairman of the League of Nations). Eden was told that, much as Molotov appreciated the invita-tion, he had been charged by Stalin 'with more important' issues.

Marshall and Stimson were increasingly alarmed by British dithering. Though they attributed the reservations to the absence of sufficient resources, the genuine objections seemed to stem to a large extent from Churchill's determination not to slacken off on the North African campaign and to make sure that supplies earmarked for the Mediterranean theatre were not diverted to the eastern front. It was obvious that the prime minister remained sceptical about the feasibility of a cross-Channel attack even in 1943.

At his meeting with the British chiefs of staff in London on 12 and 13 April, General Marshall dug in his heels, insisting that the Americans 'did not wish to see possible reverses and additional commitments in other theatres affecting the full execution of the plan, once accepted'. Hopkins left Churchill in no doubt that the 'United States was prepared to take great risks to save the Russian front'. The desultory debate which followed the visit cast doubt on the implementation of the plan, so long as Churchill continued to insist that 'it was essential to carry on the defence of India and the Middle East'. Britain could not 'entirely lay aside everything in furtherance of the main object proposed by General Marshall'.

Marshall, however, returned to Washington believing that a 'complete agreement' had been achieved, at least on the need to launch a cross-Channel offensive in 1943. However, while both sides seemed to be unanimous about the primacy of the European theatre, the British peripheral strategy would hardly allow an offensive across the Channel to become 'ripe' before May 1943. For the time being, Roosevelt sided with his advisers in accepting the Soviet view that, regardless of the obvious obstacles, the sacrifice was worthwhile. While the Americans gave an impetus to the preparations for a second front, Churchill assured the Cabinet that Britain was 'not committed to carry out such an operation this year'.

No wonder Maisky was distressed to learn from Eden that although an agreement in principle had been reached in the Defence Committee during Marshall's visit, 'no precise' decision had yet been taken on the actual opening of the second front, which required close coordination with the Americans. His vast experience allowed him to see through Churchill's manoeuvres. He was quick to discern that the declaration specified neither 'when nor where'.

On 20 April, Stalin, pinning his hopes on the Americans, welcomed Roosevelt's invitation for Molotov to go to Washington and exchange ideas about the creation of a second front. He further announced that Molotov would stop over in London. Roosevelt enthusiastically assured Litvinov that the Americans were set on creating a second front 'now'. He hoped Molotov would visit London on the way back as well, where he could 'exert double pressure' on the British, speaking also on behalf of the American president. Molotov did not appear to be particularly enthusiastic about an agreement with the British which he did not expect to address Soviet demands. In a harsh and almost brutal reaction to Maisky's positive reports, he preferred to 'interrupt the negotiations ... and postpone them indefinitely' rather than make 'more obsequious concessions'. Consequently Maisky found himself in a conundrum, reminiscent of the turbulent 1938–39 period. He desperately needed an agreement which would ensure his continued precarious presence in London, and indeed his survival.

62. A pugnacious Molotov in pilot's gear, arriving in Scotland for the London conference.

There was no one of stature to greet Molotov when he finally arrived on 20 May, on board the highly sophisticated TB-7 Soviet bomber, of which there were only six in existence. The plane had undertaken a test flight to England four days earlier on the same route, carrying on board Stalin's personal interpreter and a number of Molotov's aides. Pavlov[14] was charged with delivering to Maisky the latest revised Soviet draft agreement. Soviet suspicion had reached such a state that the draft was sewn into his waistcoat and he was instructed to encrypt it personally in Moscow and decipher it at the embassy in London. Maisky joined Molotov only halfway to London, most likely after Pavlov had had ample time to pander to the foreign minister's disdain for the ambassador, giving him a disparaging account of his sojourn at the embassy. His testimony concerning Maisky, together with Litvinov's row with Molotov in Washington a few weeks later, presaged the two ambassadors' removal from office a year later and therefore deserves to be quoted in full:

> I.M. Maisky suggested that I stay in his apartment in the embassy to await the arrival in England of V.M. Molotov. I endured one night, but was uncomfortable, as I felt that my presence had disrupted the English daily routine of my hosts. I therefore 'ran away' to A.E. Bogomolov,[15] the ambassador for the governments in exile. He warmly welcomed me.
>
> I was left with a particularly bad impression from a lunch at Maisky's home, to which the prominent members of the embassy were invited. The conversation at table focused on the difficult situation at the Soviet–German front in the summer of 1941. Spurred on by the conversation, and concerned about her husband's and her own fate, the wife of I.M. Maisky, Agniya Aleksandrovna, said to I.M. Maisky: 'Vanechka, I think that the English will take care of us in much the same way as they looked after the Austrian ambassador to London following the German occupation of Austria in March 1938.' Maisky did not respond. These were the thoughts which were turning over in A.A. Maisky's head.

The negotiations came unstuck over the question of the Soviet demand for an immediate recognition of the Soviet–Polish frontier as it had existed prior to the German invasion of Russia. On a personal level, Molotov hardly seemed to possess the diplomatic virtues which Litvinov and Maisky could boast. He had, observed Cadogan,

---

[14] Vladimir Nikolaevich Pavlov, recruited by Molotov in 1939, he served as first secretary in the Berlin embassy, 1939–41, and alternated as interpreter for Molotov and Stalin during the Second World War. Associated with the Molotov–Ribbentrop Pact, he was side-tracked by Khrushchev to work at the Progress publishing house.

[15] Aleksandr Efremovich Bogomolov, general secretary and head of the First Western Department of the People's Commissariat for Foreign Affairs, 1939–40; counsellor and then ambassador in France, 1940–41; Soviet ambassador for the governments in exile, 1941–43; Soviet ambassador representative to the French National Liberation Committee, 1943–44; Soviet ambassador in France, 1944–50.

'all the grace and conciliation of a totem pole'. This was in stark contrast to Maisky, whom Churchill found to be 'the best of interpreters, translating quickly and easily, and possessing a wide knowledge of affairs'. While committing himself in principle to a second front, from the outset Churchill expressed reservations, promising to launch the operation 'as soon as the adequate conditions existed', but dwelling at length on the constraints under which the Government was acting.

Maisky's optimistic expectations, again dovetailing with his outlook in 1939, certainly did not conform to Molotov's. Once again they reflected his wishful thinking, perhaps an existentialist instinct, enhanced by a growing confidence in his own ability to manipulate the British. He believed, as he wrote to Kollontay, that the Western Allies were now firmly committed to the second front, and he was confident that the answer to the crucial question of the timing of the attack was 'sometime this year'. His pressing task was 'to hasten its birth'. Molotov, however, was despondent, informing Stalin that he found Churchill to be 'manifestly unsympathetic'. His impression was that Churchill preferred to watch events unfold on the Russian front and 'was not in a hurry' to reach any agreement.

While the negotiations ground to a halt, the situation at the front, Stalin briefed Molotov, was deteriorating fast. Marshal Timoshenko's counter-offensive at Kharkov 'resulted unfavourably' and the German easy success in the Crimea 'had rather surprised' the Kremlin. Since the gap between the Soviet and the British expectations appeared unbridgeable, Eden had proposed an alternative agreement of a very general nature. On the evening of 24 May, Molotov was unexpectedly instructed by Stalin to adopt Eden's declarative treaty. It provided for a 20-year alliance, reaffirmed mutual military assistance, and set vague general principles for post-war collaboration, while avoiding the contentious frontiers issue. Far from sharing Molotov's view of the treaty ('an empty declaration'), Stalin thought it was 'an important document' – a morale booster at home and a display of Allied unity vis-à-vis Germany. More significantly (and here he revealed again the lingering suspicions among the Allies) he believed it would forestall a potential separate Anglo-German peace. Stalin further put Molotov's mind at rest by assuring him that, as Eden had indeed dreaded, the failure to define the post-war borders would leave Russia with 'free hands' in the future.

'It is desirable,' Stalin wound up his new instructions to Molotov, 'to hastily conclude the treaty, after which fly to America.' The trade-off he expected from concluding the watered-down treaty was the backing of Roosevelt, an ardent supporter of a second front, who had vehemently opposed the original draft agreement. The gamble in adopting the new treaty, which had received American blessing, indeed seemed to pay off. Churchill, however, was bent on deterring Roosevelt from committing himself to a second front. Hardly had the Russians taken off for Washington than he hastened to send the president a telegram, attached to which was a record of his meeting with Molotov at which he had expounded the obstacles to mounting a second front. But as was Churchill's custom, the most important message appeared at the end: he was

63. Molotov on a tour of the garden of 10, Downing Street (left to right: Cadogan, Attlee, Maisky, Molotov, Eden and Churchill).

looking forward to 'the trial of strength' posed by Rommel's[16] renewed offensive in Libya, for which fresh resources would have to be allocated. 'We must never let gymnast[17] pass from our mind,' he concluded. 'All other preparations would help if need be towards that.'

When the negotiations opened in Washington on the evening of 29 May, Molotov went out of his way to court Roosevelt. The president reasserted that personally he was prepared to experience another Dunkirk, even if it meant sacrificing '100,000–120,000'

---

[16] Field Marshal Erwin Rommel, nicknamed 'Desert Fox' by the British for his leadership of German and Italian forces in the North African campaign, 1940–43.
[17] The planned invasion of French North Africa.

people. But his proposal to deploy at best 8–10 divisions on the Continent hardly satis-fied Molotov, whose instructions were to seek the diversion of at least 40 German divisions from the eastern front. Molotov's subsequent gloomy and frank description of the situation at the front, however, convinced the president that unless there was a massive invasion of France in 1942, the Russians might need to retreat from Moscow and the Baku oil fields, thereby aggravating the situation for the Western Allies. 'We are willing to open the second front in 1942,' he told the commissar. 'This is our hope. This is our wish.' And yet, Roosevelt was obviously still wavering, sharing Marshall's doubts as to the feasibility of transferring American troops first to Great Britain, and then across the Channel. Roosevelt finally asked Marshall point blank whether he could tell Stalin that the Americans were 'preparing a second front'. The general replied in the affirmative. But it all depended on the British, who were expected to provide most of the troops for the offensive. The president then 'authorized Mr Molotov to inform Mr Stalin that we expect the formation of a second front this year'.

Roosevelt now passed the buck to Churchill, hoping that he would be able 'to bring to an end that part of the work which was left uncompleted'. Molotov left the United States 'much happier than he had come, and was entirely satisfied'. He confided to Ambassador Davies[18] that the second front had been 'settled and agreed upon'. His optimism was not shared by Litvinov, who wrote to Maisky: 'I am, of course, depressed by the poor results of the London negotiations on the second front ... I fear the military will delay this issue until it no longer will produce the desired effect.' Litvinov alerted the Kremlin that 'great attention should be given to the role of the United States both during the war and in its aftermath'. Litvinov was so disillusioned by the West and so out of tune with Moscow that he had decided, as he wrote to Maisky, 'to maintain silence until the day of victory, if it ever happens in the course of my own lifetime'. His scepticism – similar to the feeling he had had about British politics in 1938–39 – led him to the correct conclusion that 'for political and Empire reasons' Churchill was now set against a second front in 1942.

Counting on Roosevelt's commitment to a cross-Channel attack, which now hinged on British approval, Stalin pursued his divide-and-rule politics, instructing Molotov to 'exert pressure on Churchill to organize a second front and carry it out already in this year'. Back at Downing Street, Molotov followed Stalin's instructions to the letter. Familiar with what had transpired in Washington, Churchill hastened to fend off the chiefs of staff's inclination to launch raids on the Continent in 1942. He dismissed such endeavours as a response to a 'cri de coeur' from Russia, rather than 'the calm determi-nation and common sense of professional advisers'. He, unlike Roosevelt (as he later told Molotov as well), did not approve of an operation which was bound to waste

---

[18] A political ally of Roosevelt, Joseph E. Davies was ambassador in Moscow, 1936–38. His popular diary and memoirs of his stay in Moscow gloss over the purges. In May 1943, Roosevelt sent Davies on a special mission to Stalin, stealing a march on Churchill, who was seeking advantageous agreements in Moscow.

valuable lives and material, and would make 'ourselves and our capacity for making war ridiculous throughout the world'. Though bound by the American communiqué, Churchill left Molotov in no doubt that he did not consider the date of the operation to be binding. Pledging to continue the preparations for the second front, his final aide-mémoire would make 'no promise in the matter'.

The success of Molotov's visit was vital for Maisky against the backdrop of growing alienation between him and Narkomindel. The ambassador toiled behind the scenes to reduce the conflicts to a minimum and secure the signing of the Alliance Treaty, while ensuring that Molotov was given the royal treatment. Indeed he was praised by leading British politicians for having made the Soviet embassy 'the centre of world affairs'. His success, however, smacked of the power he had accumulated in London, his direct access to the top politicians, autonomy and growing public popularity. Generally an asset, in Stalin's authoritarian Russia this paradoxically heralded his downfall.]

13 June

Visited Lloyd George in Churt. We talked about many things, in particular the Anglo-Soviet treaty. Lloyd George thanked me for my *suggestion* (which I had conveyed through Sylvester) that he should speak in Parliament with regard to Eden's communication concerning the treaty and Molotov's visit. Lloyd George had not intended to speak on the matter, but after receiving my message he thought: 'Well, perhaps it would be worth saying a few words.'

And so he did. I complimented him on his performance. The old man was pleased. ...

21 June (Bovingdon)

A hot and oppressive sunny day, just like a year ago...

I can't help recalling the thoughts, feelings and sensations that engulfed me on the eve of the German attack on the USSR. Much has changed since then. The main change, it seems, is this.

A year ago the Germans were convinced they would win – the only question was <u>when</u>? Now they have lost that belief. They don't yet perceive their defeat as inevitable, but its terrible spectre already troubles their minds. It is no accident that, to judge by the latest information, the main topic of conversation in Germany this summer is How to avoid defeat? and not What will we do once we win? ...

24 June

Last 'weekend' brought the anniversary of the German–Soviet war. England greeted it noisily, with fervour and enthusiasm...

... I myself attended a 10,000-strong mass-meeting in the Empress Hall, where Cripps was the main speaker. His speech was fairly decent on the whole. He drew most applause when he let it be understood that the British Government was preparing a second front this year. Very energetic clapping also accompanied the moment when, to my embarrassment, Cripps showered me with praise. The English just can't do without compliments! Agniya and I were sitting on the dais in the front row and the audience gave us a real ovation. When Cripps finished his speech I reprimanded him for his indiscretion, but it was hard to get through to him.

'Just what was needed!' he replied innocently.

Then he asked me somewhat anxiously: 'Do you have the full text of my speech... for Moscow?'

I said I did not. He then pulled the original copy of his speech out of his pocket and gave it to me.

... The past 'weekend' has clearly shown the idea of a second front to be ripe among the masses. I'll bear it in mind. It's useful to know this in my negotiations on the matter with the British Government. What about the British Government, incidentally? I wonder what Churchill will bring back from America...

Yes, there are shifts in England, and big ones at that. National patriotism is mixed up with socio-political radicalism, and all this is clothed in fervent Sovietophilia. We shall see what comes next.

29 June

The situation in Libya is now critical. I saw Eden today and asked him to brief me about the situation. By way of a reply, Eden asked his secretary to bring in Auchinleck's[19] cipher messages of the last few days and gave them to me to read. Gloomy reading!

Mersa Matruh, which had been considered the main British stronghold in Egypt, fell over some three days. Rommel outflanked it from the south. The British beat a hasty retreat to Fuka, where they are now engaged in desperate *delaying action* against the Germans. Further east, 60–70 miles from Alexandria, there is one more fortified position, El Alamein. Its advantage lies in the fact that here, between the coast and the Qattara Depression, there is a narrow 'neck' some 40 metres wide. It offers a relatively narrow front, which is easier to defend. That's where the British intend to make a firm *stand*. Will they succeed?

---

[19] Field Marshal Sir Claude John Auchinleck, commander-in-chief India, 1941 and 1943–47; commander-in-chief Middle East Command, 1941–42.

I don't know. The British defeats on land (and they have already had plenty) render me sceptical. Particularly after learning the details. Among the cipher messages from Cairo there was one which truly appalled me. The commanders in Cairo gave their assessment of the situation and drew up provisional plans for the immediate future – what a terrible document! Not a word about an attack or an offensive, nor even of their determination to hold one or other position at all costs! Quite the reverse: constant talk of evacuation, retreat and the abandoning of positions... 'We shall defend El Alamein... If it proves impossible to hold on to El Alamein, we shall retreat in two columns: one towards Cairo and another towards Alexandria... We are forming special units for the defence of the Nile delta... If they fail to check Rommel we shall make a fighting retreat to the Suez Canal', etc. etc. That's more or less the spirit of the thing... The devil knows what! Sheer defeatism! And it's all set out so evenly, so calmly and methodically, as if these were the calculations of a land surveyor...

As I read the message I couldn't help recalling the Austrian general Weyrother in Tolstoy's *War and Peace*, who, on the eve of the Battle of Austerlitz, monotonously reads out his 'disposition' for the next day to the war council: 'Die erste Kolonne marschiert' ... 'Die zweite Kolonne marschiert' ... At least Weyrother was planning to march forwards; Auchinleck is planning to march back... Contemptible!

With the high command in this sort of mood, you're not likely to win!

That much is clear. Tobruk fell within 24 hours.

... Eden added a revealing detail. This morning he received a telegram from Cairo with the request: 'What to do with the Egyptian Government?' To where should it be evacuated, should the need arise?

I expressed my feelings in the frankest terms. Eden did not even try to defend Cairo (where, it should be said, there are some 160 British generals!). On the contrary, he set about assuring me that Churchill would deal a crushing blow to the defeatist attitudes of Auchinleck and Co. Eden also said that he had already sent a very sharp telegram in reply to the inquiry concerning the Egyptian Government, making it clear that he refuses even to discuss the matter... So much the better!

But where does the root of the Libyan disaster lie?

... Among the cipher messages from Cairo, I found a quite interesting one which shed some light on the matter. It turns out that a few days ago the War Cabinet sent Auchinleck a detailed questionnaire about the events in Libya, and he submitted his replies. The documents are long and detailed. But in essence they boil down to the following: at the root of the disaster, according to Auchinleck, lie two critical elements – the 'greenness' of the British army and the inferiority of its arms.

On the first point, Auchinleck states quite plainly: 'Our army of amateurs is up against an army of professionals.' A valuable admission! And a justified one if it refers also to the lack of an 'offensive' spirit.

As for the second point, Auchinleck emphasizes in particular the weakness of British tanks (2-pound guns against German 88-mm guns) and affirms unequivocally that the *Crusader, Stewart* [*sic*], *Valentina* [*sic*] and *Matilda* operating in North Africa are entirely useless.

... I asked Eden: 'So what are the British Government's plans?'

Eden shrugged his shoulders and replied: 'To hold El Alamein and defend Egypt. We are bringing up reinforcements. A fresh armoured division (350 tanks with 2-pound guns) has just arrived.'

I argued that the British Government must revise its strategy: it must switch to active defence in the Middle East and concentrate all its offensive energy in Europe. We had a long talk on this subject. Eden agreed with me on the whole, but what about Churchill? At bottom, everything depends on him.

It seems unlikely that Churchill will agree. Today I asked Eden about the results of the Roosevelt–Churchill meeting, particularly on the issue of a second front. Eden said that everything was as it was, that is, as it was during Churchill's talks with Molotov on 9–10 June. Events in the Middle East do not affect the British Government's plans for a second front in any way. The prime minister asked Eden specially to convey this to me.

I inquired: 'No date for opening a second front was set during Molotov's talks with Churchill. Are you able to tell me anything more definite in the wake of Churchill's visit to Washington?'

Eden could not and suggested that I should go and see the prime minister myself. I agreed. But this all sounds bad. I fear that a second front will not be opened in 1942 and that Churchill, together with Roosevelt, will try to make 1943 the 'decisive year'.

2 July

Spent two days sitting in Parliament. The conduct of the war was being debated in connection with a resolution of no confidence submitted by a group of 21 deputies headed by Sir John Wardlaw-Milne.[20]

Conclusions?

The main and essential conclusion is that the country is very alarmed and vexed about the disaster in Libya. The mood is close to that which followed Dunkirk. ... In Libya, there were no 'extenuating' circumstances. This was the best

---

[20] Sir John Wardlaw-Milne, chairman of the Conservative Foreign Affairs Committee, 1939–45; Conservative MP, 1922–45.

British front, the PM's very own '*darling*', which was never refused anything and was built up stubbornly and systematically over the last two years. Churchill spoke openly about this today: in the period in question, the B[ritish] G[overnment] dispatched to the Middle East 950,000 troops, 6,000 aircraft, 4,500 tanks, 5,000 guns, 50,000 machine-guns, and so on. What more could have been done?

Yet it was on this very '*darling front*' that in the last few days the British suffered their most decisive defeat! They were defeated in spite of the fact that not only were they not at a numerical disadvantage at the beginning of the battle, but even had a certain superiority (100,000 British and 90,000 Germans, British superiority in the air, a 7:5 advantage in tanks and 8:5 in artillery). How to explain this?

It's hard to find any sort of adequate explanation. ...

The situation in Parliament in itself, however, did not pose any danger to Churchill. Party discipline played its role here. So, too, did the MPs' fear of revealing any internal discord to the outside world (to the enemy, in particular) at such a trying time. Lastly, one should note the disparate and feeble character of the official opposition. Among these 21 could be found the most diverse elements – such as the diehard Wardlaw-Milne, the Left Labourite A. Bevan, and the offended careerist Hore-Belisha.[21] ... It was all too easy for a masterly parliamentary strategist and speaker such as Churchill to see off his opponents. And that's precisely what happened. The prime minister's closing speech was very forceful and imposing, and the voting went as follows: 476 for the Government, 25 against, about 30 abstentions.

So, Churchill has won a brilliant victory in Parliament. But he shouldn't get carried away. In fact, the overwhelming majority in the House is in a very anxious and critical mood, blaming the Government for the long chain of military defeats that has ended, for now, in Libya. This feeling is yet stronger among the masses. ... Personally, I consider Churchill, for all his failings, to be the best of all possible prime ministers today. That is why I take a 'pro-Churchill' line. However, it should be borne in mind that today's voting in no way relieves the prime minister of his enormous responsibility for how events unfold in the immediate future. ...

3 July

Today, at long last, I had the detailed conversation with Churchill that I have been hoping for ever since he returned from America. I've been wanting to learn what effect his meeting with Roosevelt had on the prospects for a second

---

[21] Bevan's harsh words were: 'the country is now more concerned with the Prime Minister winning the war than with his winning a Debate in the House of Commons. The Prime Minister wins Debate after Debate and loses battle after battle. The country is beginning to say that he fights Debates like a war and the war like a Debate'.

front. But Churchill isn't having much luck with his trips to the USA: as soon as he gets back, he is greeted by a domestic political storm. So it was in January and so it was in June. While he was engrossed in overcoming this most recent storm, it was difficult to reach him. But yesterday the storm was silenced – for the time being, at least. And today I went to see the prime minister.

He asked me to come at 12.45. When I arrived, the Cabinet was still in session. I was kept waiting in the reception room for some 20 minutes. Soon after one o'clock Churchill summoned me at last. He apologized for the delay, glanced at his watch, and said: 'You know what?... Let's have lunch together! I've kept you waiting so long. Are you free?'

It was a bit awkward for me, as I was meant to be seeing Vansittart, Lobkovich and others for lunch today, but when a prime minister invites you, you can hardly say no. Besides, I very much needed to talk to him. I called Agniya at home, told her I couldn't come to lunch with Vansittart, asked her to represent me there, and remained at *10, Downing Street*.

Before sitting down to lunch, I congratulated the prime minister on his victory in Parliament yesterday. A smile of satisfaction crossed his face before he replied with emphatic modesty: 'Such victories are not the hardest things in our life.'

... Churchill sees the world in terms of the effect of a parliamentary perform-ance. And is it any surprise? Parliament is in the blood of every Englishman, and Churchill has been warming the benches of Westminster for more than 40 years.

The prime minister asked what impression the debates had made on me. I replied that the current opposition presented no danger to the Government for the simple reason that it was such a motley crew. ... Churchill liked my remark very much, and he exclaimed with a laugh of approval: 'Precisely!'

But then I added: 'Still, the situation is grave. In spite of your victory yesterday.'

The prime minister immediately turned red and frowned. Rising abruptly from his seat, he said: 'Let's go and find Mrs Churchill! She must be fed up with waiting for us.'

We found Mrs Churchill seated in the garden beneath the broad branches of a tree. She was writing something in pencil in a notebook. Her cousin was with her. The PM left us for a minute, and Mrs Churchill started talking to me about the recent events in Parliament. She was most perturbed. Yesterday's vote was a victory for the Government, of course, but...

'If the situation at the front does not improve,' Mrs Churchill continued, 'who knows what may happen?'

There were four of us at the table: Churchill, his wife, his wife's cousin and myself. Entering the dining-room, the prime minister asked somewhat anxiously: 'And where is Mary?'

'Mary *is lunching out*,' answered Mrs Churchill.

The PM said nothing, but his disappointment was obvious: Churchill certainly loves his youngest daughter!

The conversation over lunch was of a more general nature.

... After lunch Churchill and I retired to his office. And there our conversation started in earnest.

I asked Churchill what news he had brought back from America about the second front.

Churchill replied that he had none. Everything is as it was at the moment of Molotov's departure, i.e. as set out in the memorandum of 10 June.

This did not satisfy me, of course, and I tried to make the prime minister shift from his position. ... We must face the facts. It is absolutely clear that for the moment one must abandon all notion of the British Government fulfilling its original, wide-ranging plans for North Africa. They are beyond its power for now. So those plans must be jettisoned and Britain must go on to the *defensive* – not static defence, of course, but active defence, which does not exclude but, on the contrary, presupposes offensive operations on a more limited scale. For instance, to guarantee the security of Egypt, it is essential to win back Mersa Matruh, or better still Sollum, from the Germans. It is also necessary to establish more effective control over the central part of the Mediterranean. On the whole, though, it would be advisable for the British in the Middle East *to dig in* and to reduce the quantity of troops and materiel sent out there accordingly.

... Instead of large-scale plans in North Africa, it would be better to focus attention and efforts on major objectives closer to home – aims which would have a more direct and more decisive effect on the general course of the war than operations in Egypt and Libya. I consider a second front in Europe, and specifically in France, Belgium and Holland, to be just such an objective. It would hit the target directly and it would also yield many considerable advantages: *shipping difficulties* here would be minimal (the distance from England to the second front would be measured in dozens of nautical miles instead of the many thousands separating her from the Middle East), commanding the front would be easier, frequent visits to the front from London would be possible, and the psychological effect in Britain would be massive. The country would immediately feel that it was really fighting.

'In a word,' I concluded, 'I believe Egypt must be defended now not in Egypt but in France.'

Churchill listened to me attentively, then set about making his case: it is, of course, quite possible that Britain will have to curtail its operations in North Africa and *dig in*, but this has no direct bearing on a second front. Preparations for the latter are in full swing. Trial landing operations are being undertaken and will continue to be undertaken. But there is neither sense nor profit in plunging into an adventure that is doomed to fail.

Churchill spoke to Roosevelt a lot about a second front. Roosevelt is entirely in favour of it, but US troops in Britain still number less than 80,000. ... Owing to the shipping situation, the more or less regular transfer of US troops to Britain can begin only in September, and even then in quantities of no more than 90,000 a month. ... And the British deem it impossible to launch a second front without the Americans.

'I repeat once again,' Churchill added, 'that I'll do all I can to expedite the opening of a second front. Should the possibility present itself in any form, we shall open a second front in 1942, but I can't make you any firm promises. I told Molotov and I tell you once again: one has to deceive one's enemy, one can sometimes deceive the general public for its own good, but one must never deceive one's ally. I don't want to deceive you, and I don't want to mislead you. That is why I refuse to make pledges which I am unsure of being able to honour.'[22]

I indicated, in a somewhat veiled form, the psychological impact which the failure to open a second front in 1942 might have in the USSR, but the prime minister remained unmoved.

... Then Churchill spoke of the *Middle East*. He immediately came to life. It was obvious that the Middle East is his '*darling*', that it dominates his mind. ... 'Yes, we shall fight,' Churchill continued. 'We shall fight for El Alamein, we shall fight in the Delta if need be, and beyond the Delta, in Sinai, Palestine, Arabia... We shall fight!'

Then the prime minister added emphatically: 'We shall protect your left flank at all costs! We are defending it now in Egypt. If necessary, we will defend it in Asia Minor and in the Middle East.'

I asked Churchill how he explains the British failures in Africa.

'The Germans wage war better than we do,' Churchill answered frankly. 'Especially tank wars... Also, we lack the "Russian spirit": die but don't surrender!'

I enquired about the circumstances leading to the fall of Tobruk. Churchill turned a deep shade of red, as always happens with him when he is very angry, and said that Tobruk was a shameful page in the history of the British military. In Tobruk there were sufficient troops, ammunition and supplies (enough for three months!). Tobruk could have resisted no worse than Sevastopol, but the Tobruk commander, the South African General Klopper,[23] got cold feet and waved the white flag 24 hours after the German attack began.

'I'd have shot a general like that on the spot!' I blurted out.

---

[22] Eden was more truthful, though, telling Bruce Lockhart: 'We are in a jam over this second front business. We have to try to "bluff" the Germans; to do so we must deceive our friends at the same time.'
[23] General Hendrik Balthazar Klopper, a South African, commanded the 3rd Infantry Brigade in North Africa. He was officially exonerated for the Tobruk disaster.

'I'd have done the same,' Churchill responded. 'But just you try!'

I looked at the PM in bewilderment. He understood me and explained that Klopper was South African and that the South Africans (including Smuts) raise hell whenever anyone tries to call Klopper's action by its real name: 'Hands off the heroes of Tobruk!'

Churchill angrily snatched his customary cigar out of his mouth, as if he wanted to say: 'See how difficult it is to conduct a war!'

So what are my conclusions from my conversation with Churchill today?

Less than rosy. Churchill's visit to America has not yielded a favourable outcome with respect to a second front. If anything, the opposite is the case: Churchill has convinced Roosevelt not to be in too much of a hurry about this. At the same time *the spell of the Middle East* still holds the PM in its grip. He still hopes for a sudden turn of events which will provide England with the opportunity to realize its initial ambitions in North Africa.

I met Churchill on this same day two years ago, on 3 July 1940, and we talked about the military situation. It was a tragic moment. France had just collapsed. Britain was left alone – without allies, without friends, without an army, and without weapons. ... Then I asked the prime minister: 'What is your general strategy in this war?'

His face broke into an even broader grin and he uttered: 'My general strategy is to survive the next three months.'

How the situation has changed since then! There can be no comparison with England's present position – it has improved immensely. But even if we take a general overview of the war and compare the balance of forces between the fascist and anti-fascist camps, then, notwithstanding all our present problems, the future looks infinitely better and brighter than in 1940!

This is our source of hope for victory and confidence in the future.

[Although he claimed that nothing had changed since Molotov's departure, Eden encouraged Maisky to glean directly from the prime minister what had transpired in Washington. Churchill, who came across as being frank, nonetheless deceived Maisky. Following Mountbatten's[24] face-to-face talks in the White House (within days of Molotov's departure) Churchill had become aware that Roosevelt's advocacy of a second front was due not only to his anxieties about the Russian front, but also to the fact that he was itching 'to get into the war and get his troops fighting'. Churchill's blitz visit was motivated by a desire to counter the impact of the Soviet foreign minister's visit by shifting the emphasis from Operation Sledgehammer to Operation Round-Up, the preparations for a cross-Channel invasion in 1943. As if oblivious to Marshall's fierce

---

[24] Lord Louis Francis Albert Mountbatten, chief of combined operations, 1942–43; supreme allied commander, South-East Asia, 1943–46; viceroy of India, 1947.

and well-argued opposition, Roosevelt 'in his foxy way to forestall trouble that is now on the ocean coming towards us in the shape of a new British visitor' urged his War Cabinet 'to take up the case of *Gymnast* again'.

As was feared by the military, Churchill arrived in Washington 'full of discouragement and new proposals for diversions'. He was 'pessimistic regarding *Bolero* and interested in August *Gymnast*'. He flew straight away to Hyde Park to meet Roosevelt, to the manifest dismay of the president's war secretary, who could not 'help feeling a little bit uneasy about the influence of the Prime Minister on the President'. And rightly so. Churchill later recalled how he was welcomed personally by Roosevelt, who insisted on driving him alone around his splendid estate and 'all the time we talked business ... we made more progress than we might have done in formal conference'. That evening, the president hastened to send Marshall a list of queries posed by Churchill. This practically wrote off operations on the Continent in 1942, while introducing 'some other operation by which we may gain positions of advantage'. To make the proposal attractive to the Americans, it was presented as a move which would 'directly or indirectly take some of the weight off Russia'.

Marshall held fast to his appraisal that dispersing the forces might jeopardize an invasion of the Continent even in 1943. But his opposition was superseded by the dramatic defeat of the British at Tobruk, of which Churchill and Roosevelt became aware on their return to Washington. It was, as Churchill later recalled, 'one of the heaviest blows' inflicted on him during the war. Inadvertently, however, the timing was most propitious. It allowed him to brilliantly overcome the stiff opposition of the American military to his efforts to forsake a second front in 1942 in favour of operations in the Middle East. Churchill wasted little time in launching 'a terrific attack on *Bolero*' in the presence of Marshall and Hopkins, and taking up Operation Gymnast, 'knowing perfectly well that it was the President's great secret baby'. The president, it turned out, had proposed to Churchill to send a major force to sustain the denuded Middle Eastern front. The repercussions which a diversion might have on the Russian front – hardly a week after Molotov had left Washington, convinced that the Americans were committed to a second front – were entirely overlooked.

Two days after meeting Maisky, Churchill addressed the chiefs of staff with incisive arguments against Operation Sledgehammer. 'A premature action,' he argued, was likely to end in disaster and 'decisively injure the prospects of well-organised, large-scale action in 1943'. But such arguments were just a prelude to the reintroduction of Operation Gymnast as the main thrust for 1942. In private, Churchill admitted bluntly that his policy was 'to bluff the Germans into believing we shall have second front this year and to conceal from Russians that we can't!']

9 July

I have drawn the following conclusion from my life experience: 'Never say never in politics.'

And one thing more: *Hitler has victories but he has no victory*, and that's all there is to it.

11 July

Sometimes I want to tear myself away from the blood-stained sea of the present and travel in thought to the distant future, when the brilliance of human genius will be expended not on the invention of the most sophisticated means of self-destruction, but on truly creative, constructive deeds...

Today I am in just such a mood. And this is what I have been thinking.

In the 21st or 22nd century, when fully developed communism will be established everywhere, the problem of creating a unified humanity will come to the fore. It's not that national distinctions should be entirely eliminated – no, that would be difficult, and even perhaps undesirable. Let there be diversity in the world. Let there be different characters, different faces, different songs, different tastes. Life would be very dull without this, and human progress would be hampered.

At the same time, it will be necessary to find a way of merging those motley national streams in a single, bursting river of humanity. It will be necessary to create forms of life whereby national distinctions enrich the common life of mankind, instead of dividing it into mutually hostile elements. Communism, of course, will forge a solid economic foundation for the edifice of a unified humanity, yet 'vestiges of the past' may still persist in people's minds. Perhaps we will have to think of some special measures to accelerate the process of creating a unified humanity. ...

How distant is all this from the present day![25]

12 July (Bovingdon)

The Germans have finally launched their major summer offensive. Fierce fighting has been under way for two weeks already in the Kursk–Kharkov region. It flared up right after the heroic fall of Sevastopol (what an unprecedented lesson in heroism this city has given us!). The German side has had indisputable success. They assembled huge quantities of tanks and aircraft (the figure of 8,000 tanks is mentioned, though this seems exaggerated to me), broke through our lines at Kursk and fought their way to Voronezh. ... Were the Allies to establish an effective second front in the west this summer, we could

---

[25] Maisky's confidante, Beatrice Webb, had observed a few days earlier: '... he maintains a strangely aloof attitude towards dogmatic communism; he is no marxist, not bigoted, he does not idolise Lenin or Stalin'.

risk a major strategic offensive in 1942 (or, to be more precise, in the summer of 1942) with the aim of breaking Hitler's backbone now and ending the war in Europe in 1943. Unfortunately, no effective second front is to be expected in the west either in summer or in early autumn. My conversation with Churchill on 3 July made this quite clear. From everything that I see, hear and read here, there seems little doubt that the British and the Americans have no serious intention of opening a second front before 1943.

... If the war is going to drag on, we cannot take too great a risk in the summer of 1942, fighting alone against the entire might of the German war machine. We must save our strength so as not to bleed ourselves dry, so as not to cross the finishing line in total exhaustion (as the Americans and the British would be so keen for us to do).

Hence the conclusion: we cannot risk a major offensive against Germany now. We have to remain in an essentially defensive position. ...

14 July

Went to see Eden this morning. He told me that very unpleasant news had arrived from the north: convoy No. 17 has been badly wrecked by the Germans. Out of 35 ships, 19 have been sunk (this is known for certain), 4 have made it to Arkhangelsk, 5 are in Novaya Zemlya, 2 in Iceland, while the fate of 5 is still unknown. This terrible experience puts in serious doubt the possibility of sending further convoys, at least until the nights draw in in the Arctic zone. The Admiralty, according to Eden, is against sending more convoys. But no decision has yet been taken.

I was greatly disturbed by this and asked Eden whether a meeting could be arranged before a decision was taken, to be attended by himself, Alexander, Pound, me, Kharlamov and Morozovsky.[26] Eden agreed, and promised to speak with the people concerned about the date and time of the meeting. Eden, as if thinking aloud, observed that it wouldn't be a bad thing for Churchill to attend the meeting as well. I, of course, had no objections. ...[27]

[On 20 April, the Admiralty demanded that 'convoys to North Russia should be suspended during months of continuous light unless the very high percentage of losses can be accepted or sufficient air protection can be provided'. Left with only a few cards to play – once the proposed political agreement had been pared to the bone and

---

[26] Admiral N.G. Morozovsky, Soviet naval attaché in London, 1942–45.
[27] Maisky's objective was to impress on Eden the 'very grave' situation on the Russian front. Russian manpower, he warned 'was not inexhaustible'. He was bitter about the withdrawal of the British promise to launch the second front and warned that the effect of a suspension of convoys 'on Russian resistance at this time must be very serious'.

64. Maisky presents a medal to Mrs Woodward, the widow of a naval officer killed in action in the Arctic convoys, who is holding her five-month-old daughter.

a second front in 1942 ruled out — Churchill conceded that postponement of the convoys was bound to 'weaken our influence with both our major Allies'. Convoy PQ 16 was accordingly ordered to sail. Despite heavy attacks, it sustained relatively minor losses. As for the tragic fate of PQ 17, Churchill never felt comfortable with the Admiralty's decision to withdraw the six destroyers from PQ 17 and then order it to scatter when wrong information suggested that the *Tirpitz* had left its berthing place in Norway, heading towards the convoy.]

15 July

... Yesterday, at about four in the afternoon, I had a call from the prime minister's office inviting me and my wife for dinner that same evening. I accepted. We dined on the lower floor of *10, Downing Street*. Seated around the table were Churchill and his wife, I and my wife, and... Admiral Pound. I realized at once that matters had taken a serious turn. I was not mistaken. Eden arrived after dinner. But by then nothing remained to be discussed.

Churchill spoke first. He mentioned Convoy No. 17 and related those details about its fate which I had already heard from Eden in the morning.

'What shall we do now?' Churchill went on. 'The seamen advised us not to send Convoy 17. They took the view that the danger was too great. The War Cabinet disregarded their advice and ordered that the convoy depart. We thought that even if a mere half of the ships reached Arkhangelsk the game would be worth the candle. It came out worse than we had expected: three-quarters of the convoy perished – 400 tanks and 300 planes lie on the sea-bed!... My heart bleeds.'

The prime minister emitted an angry wheeze and banged his fist on the table. Then he continued: 'But all the same, what should we do? There's no sense in sending tanks and planes to certain ruin. We might just as well sink them in the Thames.' ...

... I strongly objected. What's that? Stop supplying the USSR? When? At the very moment when it is fighting for its life? When it needs arms more than even before? What effect would such a step have on the fate of the war? What impact would it have on the psychology of my country?... Stopping the convoys is out of the question.

... I said that the story of Convoy 17 had left me with many puzzling questions. Why, for instance, did the escort comprise, at the critical moment, only destroyers, corvettes and submarines, with no big ships anywhere in the vicinity? We know that two battleships, one aircraft carrier, and seventeen destroyers were cruising 400 miles from the site of the catastrophe. Why, once it became known that the *Tirpitz* had left the Norwegian fjords and was moving north, was the weak escort accompanying the convoy hastily withdrawn, to say nothing of the failure to send a powerful fleet to intercept the *Tirpitz*? Why was the slow-moving convoy ordered to scatter after this, when it was quite obvious that effective dispersal was no longer possible? Why doesn't the Admiralty block the exits from the fjords where the *Tirpitz* and other German ships are moored with mines and submarines? Why doesn't the Admiralty carry out special reconnaissance expeditions while the convoy is on the move? Why aren't aircraft carriers deployed to accompany the convoys?... These and many other questions arise when one analyses the fate of Convoy 17. I, of course, am not a seaman and am prepared to admit that answers of one kind of another may exist to all these questions; but I'm convinced of one thing: that the protection of the convoys can be organized better than has been the case hitherto. One merely needs the will and requisite courage to do so.

Pound set about answering my objections once again. The problem, don't you see, is that the British have only one aircraft carrier in northern waters, and they cannot risk it. Besides, the carrier's planes are greatly inferior to those of the German coastal air force. The escort was withdrawn because it was no match for the *Tirpitz* and would have been sunk to no purpose. The major fleet was 400 miles away from the site of the catastrophe so as not to fall victim to

German bombers. The order was given for the convoy to 'scatter', as otherwise the *Tirpitz* would have sunk every single vessel within an hour or so.

... The PM supported Pound, though without much enthusiasm. ... Churchill thought for a moment and then, as if making a concession, replied that he would ask the Americans about it. As more than 22 ships in Convoy 18 are to be American, let them decide: if they want to take the risk, the British Government will provide the escort.

... The situation was quite clear to me: Pound, of course, would give the Americans a good fright and that would be the end of Convoy 18.

'So,' I concluded, 'you are ceasing the delivery of military supplies at the most critical moment for us. In that case, the question of a second front becomes all the more urgent. What are the prospects here?'

Churchill replied that we were familiar with his position on this matter. It was stated in the memorandum of 10 June handed to Molotov. He reaffirmed it during our conversation on 3 July.

'I know this,' I rejoined, 'but the situation has dramatically changed not only since 10 June, but also since 3 July. The last ten days have been of momentous significance. They have shown that Hitler has succeeded in assembling more forces for his offensive than had been anticipated. Also, our failures at the front were far greater than we had expected. The situation on the Soviet–German front is now perilous. The Red Army will, of course, fight heroically, as it has done throughout, but there is a limit to everything. Who knows what may happen? If the USSR does not receive prompt support from the west in the form of a second front, a retreat far to the east cannot be excluded.'

... Churchill listened to me attentively. Then he said: 'Yes, I agree with you. I have already heard those arguments during Molotov's visit. It's quite possible that you'll have to retreat further to the east. It's quite possible that in the spring of 1943 we'll face on the Continent not the 25 second-rate divisions that are presently protecting France and Belgium, but 50 or 60 first-line German divisions... I understand all of this... But what is to be done?... In 1942 we are simply in no condition to undertake serious operations in order to open a second front. There is no sense getting involved in an absurd adventure which is bound to end in disaster. This will help neither you nor us. Only the Germans will profit from it.'

Pound, grinning in self-satisfaction, hastened to take the prime minister's side. I took the greatest exception to him. This gouty 65-year-old, who has won not a single battle in his entire life but has proved very adept at winning high positions and decorations in ministerial quarters, had stretched my patience to the limit. Churchill intervened in our dispute and said: 'We are ready to assist you any way we can. For instance, we are ready to take part in the northern operation with every kind of weaponry at our disposal.' ...

Churchill then said: '*My worries* may be arranged in the following order. In the first place, the battle in Russia. That is the main thing. In the second place, the situation at sea. Then finally, after a significant, indeed a most significant interval, the battle in Egypt.'

After dinner we moved to a small, neighbouring room. We smoked. Pound puffed away haughtily at his cigar, releasing rings of smoke into the air. Eden arrived. He looked embarrassed. He asked Churchill: 'So, shall we discuss the convoys and the northern operation?'

'We already have,' Churchill muttered gloomily.

Conversation stalled. Mrs Churchill, who was not herself during the dinner, was striving heroically to keep the conversation alive. Poor Mrs Churchill! She was very upset and made several cautious attempts over dinner to support me. But the PM would roar and she would fall silent. Churchill himself was in a gloomy mood. He had to force the words out and spoke roughly, indistinctly, with obvious irritation – either at himself or at the circumstances that were forcing bad acts upon him.

Agniya asked Churchill: 'So how can you help us now?'

Churchill's reply was sullen and carefully measured: 'Unfortunately we can do very little, Mrs Maisky, very little.'

... Then he added with sudden animation: 'But we shall still celebrate victory together!'

It was evident that the PM felt ill at ease.

Only Pound felt on top of the world – smoking, laughing, telling jokes. No wonder: he'd done his job!

It's people like Pound, these top bureaucrats tied by thousands of threads to the top bourgeoisie, who rule England, not the ministers who come and go! Yesterday's dinner was a fine illustration of this fact...

I returned home full of oppressive thoughts. I felt troubled and uneasy.

16 July

... After lunch, I went to see Beaverbrook and talked to him, too, about the convoys. ... He displayed great anxiety about the situation on our front ('I never expected the Germans to reach the Don valley by July') and, assuming a mysterious air, added that developments in the USSR could have major repercussions in England.

... Beaverbrook's ploy is clear enough: he aspires to be prime minister and is waiting for Soviet failures, along with Churchill's reluctance to open a second front immediately, to create a situation in the country such that Churchill will have to go. Churchill's ploy is also obvious: he wants Beaverbrook in the

Government so as to tie his hands. Personal designs against the background of a global tragedy.

19 July (Bovingdon)

A hard week!

The situation at the front is extremely grave. ... The German offensive in the Don valley has made rapid and successful progress over the past week, and Rostov is clearly under threat. It is quite obvious that the Germans are headed for Stalingrad, with the aim of breaking through the Volga line and tearing the Caucasus from the rest of the USSR. If they were to succeed, the situation would become critical. Will they succeed? Some inner feeling tells me they will not. ... But in the meantime we must acknowledge the fact that we stand before a deadly danger to our country, to the revolution, and to the entire future of humanity.

But it was not only at the front that this past week proved difficult. It was also hard here in London. My talks with Churchill, Eden, Cripps, Beaverbrook and others, and everything I heard, saw and read here, led me to the following conclusions:

(1) There will be no second front in 1942.

(2) Supplies to the USSR from Britain and the USA will be reduced (because of the difficulty of continuing with the northern convoys).[28]

(3) Possibilities include: a northern operation (Petsamo, etc.), a landing across the Channel, as discussed during Molotov's visit (though I would make no guarantee of its implementation), the intensification of air bombing over Germany and of raids on the French coast (provided we exert serious pressure). ...

Translated into plain language, this means that we can only count on ourselves during this year's campaign. In other words, our allies have abandoned us to the mercy of fate at the most critical moment. This is a most unpleasant truth, but there is no point in closing our eyes to it. It must be taken into account in all our plans and calculations. And it must be remembered for the future.

[Maisky was again spot on. Stimson and Marshall were infuriated by Churchill's determination to 'reverse the decision which was so laboriously accomplished' during his visit, thereby diverting the American strength 'into a channel in which we cannot effectively use it, namely the Middle East'. Likewise the joint chiefs of staff, never certain of the president's inner thoughts, were strongly opposed to the shift, convinced that it would

---

[28] In the wake of the dismal fate of PQ 17, Churchill informed Stalin on 15 July that the convoys would be suspended.

mean 'definitely no Bolero in 1942' and 'probably make the execution of Bolero in 1943 out of the question'. 'Marshall believes,' General Dill alerted the prime minister, 'that your first love is "Gymnast" just as his is "Bolero", and that with the smallest provocation you always revert to your old love.'

To prevent Britain and the United States from drifting apart, Roosevelt sent Marshall and Hopkins to London to sort out the conflicting strategies within a week. He cunningly preferred to have Churchill discourage his emissaries. In the notes Churchill prepared for the meeting with the American guests, he indeed discarded the second front altogether, shifting the entire weight to the operation in North Africa. 'Just because the Americans can't have a massacre in France this year,' he complained in private, 'they want to sulk and bathe in the Pacific!']

21 July

I spent last weekend in Bovingdon contemplating a plan of action for the immediate future. One question plagued me: what else can I, the Soviet ambassador in England, do to help my country at this critical time? What can I do to rouse the ruling circles in England from their dangerous lethargy, to mobilize the forces stuck in this country, and to hasten the launching of a second front?

Turning these questions over in my mind, I strolled around the garden and lay down on the grass, gazing into the blue and distant sky and exposing my face, neck, arms and chest to the hot sun, whose appearances in England are such a rarity. And I came up with the following plan:

(1) Stalin should confront Churchill with the matter of the convoys and the second front. ...

(2) Once Stalin sends such a message to Churchill I shall speak in the same vein at an informal meeting of MPs and before the editors of the London newspapers. ...

I have suggested the plan to Moscow and am waiting for a reply.

My calculation: this plan could have a certain impact on the situation and help hasten a second front. At the very least, it could facilitate the implementation of secondary measures, such as the resumption of convoys, the intensification of air raids on Germany, etc.

Finally, *if the worst comes to the worst*, my plan will serve as a vindication of the Soviet Government before our people and history, in so far as it will show that the Soviet Government did all that was humanly possible to rouse the British ruling circles from their lethargy, and that it was not our fault if this did not happen.

[Increasingly isolated, Maisky reverted to his old practice of initiating policy. On 16 July, he suggested to Molotov that as Churchill had avoided mentioning the second front in his message to Stalin, it was 'necessary to establish that we were in fact being left to the mercy of fate by our Allies in the most critical moment for us'. The scheme he concocted was for Stalin to harshly reproach Churchill and then seek reconciliation through a meeting of the two leaders. His plan paved the way for Operation Bracelet, Churchill's first meeting with Stalin in Moscow, in early August.]

23 July

Moscow has accepted my plan.

Late in the evening today I handed Stalin's message to Churchill. It is somewhat gentler than I had expected, but strong and resolute enough.[29] ... Churchill was in his *siren suit* and in a bad mood. As I was soon to learn, he had just received disheartening news from Egypt. The British attack, on which the PM had pinned so many hopes, has come to nothing. ... In his distress, Churchill must have had a drop too much whisky. I could tell from his face, eyes and gestures. At times his head shook in a strange way, betraying the fact that in essence he is already an old man and that it won't be long before he starts sliding downhill fast. It is only by a terrific exertion of will and mind that Churchill remains fit for the fight.

Stalin's message produced the impression I had expected on the PM. He was depressed and offended at the same time. The PM's self-esteem was seriously wounded (especially by Stalin's charge that he had failed to fulfil his obligations) and the thought even seemed to flash through his mind that the USSR might withdraw from the war, because he said out of the blue: 'Well, we have been alone before... We still fought... It's a miracle that our little island survived... But...'

'Drop this nonsense!' I interrupted Churchill brusquely. 'The thought of laying down arms has not crossed the mind of any of us. Our path has been defined once and for all – *to the bitter end*. But the present situation must be taken into account: in 1942 we are, in all probability, stronger than we shall be in 1943. Neither we nor you should ignore this fact!'

Churchill calmed down, but he continued to argue for a good long while that he was doing all he could and that, as far as the matter of the second front was concerned, the memorandum of 10 June remained in force. ...

In conclusion, the prime minister said that he would report Stalin's message to the War Cabinet and only then might he be in a position to say something.

---

[29] Stalin contested the reasons of the British naval experts for suspending the convoys and expressed his opinion 'frankly and honestly ... in the most emphatic manner' that in view of the critical situation at the front his Government could not 'acquiesce in the postponement of a second front in Europe until 1943'.

In the course of the conversation, I took advantage of the impression which Stalin's message had produced on Churchill to raise the issue of the resumption of convoys and the intensification of the air bombardment of Germany. It proved a good ploy: Churchill was now ready to agree that Convoy No. 17 should not serve as a precedent for the future, for the Admiralty's actions may not have been the best in this instance, and he was inclining to the idea of sending the next convoy in September. I argued in favour of August, but to no avail. ...

24 July

On his return from Nottingham, Eden summoned me and said that he had acquainted himself with Stalin's message. Churchill is very *hurt* and in some distress about it. At the same time, the prime minister is tormented by the thought that at this difficult hour there is so little he can do for his ally. The War Cabinet also feels wounded by Stalin's message. To avoid further exacerbation and further polemical exchanges, Eden thinks it better to leave Stalin's last message unanswered. Better to allow the passions to subside and the atmosphere to become calmer.

'After all,' Eden added, 'you expect a response from us not in words but in deeds. Let's wait for the deeds.'

Then he remarked with a faint smile: 'Two great men have clashed... They've had a tiff... You and I need to reconcile them... Too bad they've never met face to face!'

This all sounded fine. So far everything is going as I'd expected.

Churchill is hot-tempered, but he is easily appeased. After his initial emotional reaction he begins to think and calculate like a statesman, and, even more so, a parliamentarian. And in the end he arrives at the necessary conclusions. The stronger the shock, the greater the chances that Churchill will do the right thing. I remember the case of Stalin's missive of 8 November last year. First Churchill flew into a rage – right in front of me. Then Eden and Beaverbrook tried to calm him down. Then he himself began to think and work things out. As a result, Churchill made the suggestion to Stalin of sending Eden to Moscow, and peace was restored. This led to Eden's visit in December 1941, talks in the Kremlin, Molotov's visit to London, and the signing of the Anglo-Soviet treaty.

What will be the outcome this time? I don't know. My calculations, at any rate, have proved correct so far. We shall see.

I promised Eden my assistance in restoring 'peace' between the two great men. ...

26 July (Bovingdon)

Yet another hard week!

Our troops continue to retreat. The Germans continue to capture one region after another. Rostov has fallen. The enemy crossed the lower reaches of the Don near Tsimlyansk. The fascist hordes are drawing ever closer to Stalingrad. Ever closer to the Caucasus. Will we really prove unable to contain the Germans? Will they really cut us off from the Caucasus and gain a firm footing on the Volga? It seems like a nightmare from a horrifying fairy-tale. ...

30 July

A hot day, and one fraught, perhaps, with far-reaching consequences!

At three in the afternoon I delivered my speech in Parliament. ... There were about 300 people present, and the 'old-timers' assure me that this is unprecedented in the history of such meetings. ... While I spoke you could have heard a pin drop, and the audience hung on every word – which was also an unusual thing at such meetings, if the elders are to be believed. I felt that my words were 'hitting home'. At times my speech was interrupted by loud applause – when, for instance, I said that what the Allies need above all is a joint strategy. ... When I mentioned that we first raised the question of a second front in July 1941, it was as if an electric current coursed through the audience.

After the meeting, Lloyd George led me into his room in Parliament. Megan dropped by. It was already 4.15 (the meeting had lasted just over an hour). Tea was served. We drank and talked. The old man said that among the many meetings he had attended throughout his long life in Parliament, he remembered few like today's in terms of the numbers present, the attentiveness of the audience, and the impression made by the speaker.

... Lloyd George expressed his opinion that such a meeting cannot fail to exert some influence on the Government.

'But what practical outcome can follow?' I asked, before adding: 'Of course I am pleased with the success of my speech, but oratorical skill is not the point here. ... Will the meeting hasten the opening of a second front?'

Lloyd George shrugged his shoulders. ... It seems to Lloyd George that Churchill currently finds himself in a mental state that precludes him from taking a major decision. This happens to Churchill now and then. It's a great shame.

'He has,' Lloyd George continued, 'some sort of *inferiority complex* when it comes to offensive operations. He was "bruised" already in the last war by the Dardanelles. He's not had much luck in this war either: Norway, Greece, Libya... Churchill fears offensive operations.'

... At 12.30 a.m. a call came from the prime minister's office. His secretary asked me to come to *10, Downing Street* right away. What's the matter? What's happened? All sorts of thoughts ran through my mind. An inner voice was telling me that this midnight invitation to see the prime minister was connected one way or another with today's meeting. ... Churchill's secretary met me in the corridor and we were joined by Bracken a few seconds later. The three of us sat in the reception room, chatting about various issues of the day. Eventually, Bracken said: 'I would like to hear your predictions for the future. You have often proved right. What do you expect to happen in the next two months?'

I had no time to answer him, for at this very moment I was ushered in to see the prime minister. Churchill was sitting at the Government's conference table. He was wearing his customary *siren suit*, on top of which he had thrown a gay, black-and-grey dressing gown. Eden was sitting next to him in slippers and the green velvet jacket which he wears 'at home' in the evening. Both looked tired but excited. The prime minister was in one of those moods when his wit begins to sparkle with benevolent irony and when he becomes awfully charming.

'Take a look. Is it any use?' Churchill asked with a smile, passing me a sheet of paper.

It was the text of his message to Stalin. I quickly ran my eyes over the document.

'But of course! It's worth a great deal, a very great deal!' I responded after reading the message.

And how! A meeting between Churchill and Stalin could have very important consequences. I supported the prime minister's intention in every possible way. He smiled, drank whisky and puffed away at his irreplaceable cigar. I was looking at him and thinking: 'My calculations have been fully vindicated. Not a trace has remained of the irritation Churchill displayed upon receiving Stalin's message of 23 July. The PM has cooled down. Now he is preoccupied with thoughts about his trip to the USSR and his meeting with Stalin. So much the better.'

... I promised to wire the news to Moscow right away. As Churchill was planning to fly overseas on 1 August, he asked for Stalin's reply to be handed to Eden in his absence.

Eden saw me to the door. On parting, he said casually: 'It would be so good if you could go with the PM!'

I answered that I would very much like to go, but that was for the Soviet Government to decide.

31 July

Eden summoned me at 12.30. He expressed great satisfaction about the prime minister's decision to visit the USSR, although the PM would be flying off to

Egypt before the reply was received – for a few days, possibly a week. The Air Ministry will have a plane at the ready for me.

I thanked Eden and said I had nothing to tell him as yet about the matter that interested him. Everything depends on Moscow.

Speaking about the prime minister's forthcoming visit, Eden expressed his hope that Churchill and Stalin would get on well and understand each other.

'It would be so good if you could be their interpreter! One must be able to translate not the words, but the spirit of a conversation! You have that gift! The prime minister was telling me that when you interpreted during our talks with Molotov, he had the impression that the language barrier between him and Molotov had fallen, that it no longer existed.'

I repeated once again that the decision on this matter rested with Moscow...

[The diary for 1942 ends abruptly at this dramatic and fateful moment, most likely because Maisky's hopes of participating in the summit meeting and influencing the course of the events failed to materialize. As we have seen, the meeting was part of the subversive scheme plotted by Eden and Maisky. Only a successful summit could arrest Maisky's fast-declining influence in Moscow. He now staked the considerable power he had gained in mobilizing public opinion to exert pressure on Churchill. However, the resort to an unprecedented emotional appeal to the Members of Parliament, over the head of the Government, seemed to some to be 'a speech of a man in a desperate position'. Never since Gondomar,[30] it was observed, 'have we allowed a foreign ambassador to interfere so much in our domestic affairs'. So far Maisky had successfully convinced Moscow that, despite his personal reservations and scepticism about his military capability, Churchill was still 'the most likely premier to keep [Britain] in the war', while any successor might turn out to be 'a stopgap leading very shortly to appeasement and a separate peace'.

Maisky was gambling on Churchill's need to bolster his political standing at home through a display of unity with Stalin. He failed to realize that Churchill's overriding objective was to achieve a breathing space, during which he could pursue unhindered his preparations for the invasion of North Africa, while deflecting pressure for a second front and securing continued Russian resistance on the battlefield.

So far Churchill had resisted with tenacity any attempt by his new Russian and American allies to alter his peripheral strategy. He had successfully imposed it on reluctant chiefs of staff (though only after purging the top brass) as well as on Roosevelt, against the better judgement of the president's professional military advisers. As much

---

[30] Diego Sarmiento de Acuña, Count of Gondomar, Spanish ambassador to London from 1613–22, saw his embassy as an isle in a hostile land. He did, however, cultivate numerous powerful intimate friends at the Court of King James I through whom he exercised great influence on British politics. He was judged to be 'a cleverer man than any in England'.

as he abhorred the idea of going to Moscow, Churchill assumed that a *tête-à-tête* meeting would convince Stalin of the insurmountable difficulties involved in launching a cross-Channel attack and would convert him to the Mediterranean campaign as the genuine second front.

Maisky's hopes of enhancing his own position in the Kremlin as the go-between – a role he had successfully assumed during Eden's two earlier visits to Moscow and Molotov's London visit – were cruelly dashed. In seeking Eden's intervention to secure his own presence in Moscow, Maisky merely aggravated his position. On 4 August, the humiliated Soviet ambassador not only conceded to Eden that he would not be going to Moscow, but pleaded with him 'not to make further representations to his government in the matter'. In his memoirs, Maisky prefers to deflect the reader's attention from the genuine reasons for his exclusion, attributing it to 'the Soviet Government's dissatisfaction with Britain's conduct' on the issue of the second front. It was, however, a severe personal blow, which Maisky evidently associated with the reproaches over his supposedly defeatist outlook that was exposed during Molotov's visit. Maisky tried to absolve himself in the eyes of the Kremlin, using every possible channel to display his loyalty and commitment to the war effort.

He was little helped by Churchill's promotion of his case. Churchill, who in Moscow was frustrated by the language barrier, lamented to Attlee that Pavlov, 'the little interpreter, was a very poor substitute for Maisky'. In his final candid conversations with Stalin at his Kremlin apartment, Churchill was surprised to discover that Stalin was 'very critical of Maisky'. When Churchill commended Maisky as 'a good Ambassador', he seemed only to increase the host's suspicions as to where Maisky's loyalties lay. Stalin, reported Churchill, 'agreed, but said that he might be better; he spoke too much and could not keep his tongue between his teeth'. Churchill returned to London convinced, as he told Cripps, that the Soviet Government would recall Maisky, who 'talked too much' and would be replaced by a minor figure.

Maisky nonetheless sought to have an impact on the negotiations by 'taking the liberty' of addressing Stalin personally, in a long and detailed brief on Churchill's objectives. He gambled on his unparalleled familiarity with the prime minister to dare to submit to Stalin precise recommendations on how he should handle Churchill. Fearing the worst, it was now vital for him to dispel any illusions (which he himself had cultivated in the Kremlin) about the likelihood that Churchill would agree to a second front. Indeed, in a personal letter to Litvinov on the same day, Maisky stressed twice that he was 'not feeling particularly optimistic', and believed Churchill would postpone the second front to 1943. However, it was as important for him to try and overturn the ideologically oriented appraisal, prevalent in Moscow since Molotov's return from London and Washington, that Churchill and Roosevelt were deliberately avoiding a second front and thereby seeking to weaken Russia. He knew that such thoughts, which he did not share, might lead to Soviet disengagement and further strategic retreat, or still worse to a separate peace.

Maisky would find it increasingly difficult to dent the new narrative which was taking firm hold in the Kremlin. While proposing to maintain the pressure in favour of a cross-Channel attack, he advocated the 'more feasible... subsidiary demands', such as increased supplies and military assistance in the north and the Caucasus; but above all, he advocated the forging of a long-term political and military association with Churchill. Despite his personal dislike of Maisky, Stalin lent a guileful ear to his ambassador's advice. It was not the first time that Stalin had adopted the ideas of an opponent as his own, and then disposed of the draughtsman.

The long-anticipated encounter between the two leaders took place on 12 August, in the evening, shortly after Churchill arrived in the Soviet capital. Stalin's face, according to the British ambassador in Moscow, 'crumpled up into a frown' a couple of times as Churchill conceded that there would be no second front in 1942. He was particularly upset about the breach of the promises made to Molotov, though Churchill insisted that he had endorsed those only with serious reservations. Stalin took heed of Maisky's advice, seeking to end the first round of the discussions by noting that, while he was not entitled to demand the second front, 'he was bound to say that he did not agree with Mr Churchill's arguments'.

Churchill now enthusiastically plunged into a protracted presentation of Operation Torch as an alternative second front, which 'did not necessarily have to be embarked upon in Europe'. Waving a drawing of a crocodile that he had made while Stalin was talking, Churchill explained that it was his intention 'to attack the soft belly of the crocodile as [the Russians] attacked his hard snout'. Taking his leave, Churchill stopped by a globe in the middle of the room to expound on the immense advantages of clearing the Germans out of the Mediterranean. He returned to the guest house in the woods convinced that he had succeeded in swaying Stalin. The British ambassador enthusiastically (but alas prematurely) informed Eden that Churchill's method of approach was 'masterly'. The bluntness with which he had demolished the prospects of the second front 'on which Stalin had set his heart made that which the Prime Minister now set before him appear all the more attractive'. The visit, he concluded, 'promises very well'.

Churchill, still in euphoric mood, could hardly wait for the opportunity to discuss 'Torch' further with Molotov the following morning. Oblivious both to the microphones installed in the dacha and to the presence of the Russian staff, he was beside himself over lunch, describing Stalin 'as just a peasant' whom he 'knew exactly how to tackle'. To his chagrin, Churchill found the Soviet foreign minister elusive and preferring to defer the thorny issues for Churchill's meeting with Stalin that evening. Arriving at the Kremlin in the evening, Churchill was confronted by Stalin with an acrimonious aide-mémoire remonstrating against the decision to scrap the second front operation in 1942, and paying no heed to Operation Torch. Lulled by a feeling that he had succeeded in masterly manner in diverting Stalin from the second front on the Continent to the North African campaign, Churchill, who had emerged from the first meeting convinced that the rest of the talks would be 'plain sailing', was knocked off balance and was shattered by Stalin's callous dismissal of his case. But the Soviet leader did not leave it there.

To deflect Stalin from an ideologically oriented interpretation of Churchill's dithering, Maisky had produced for him a psychological profile of the prime minister. He attributed Churchill's indecisiveness to the haunting memories of the crushing and costly defeats he had suffered in the Dardanelles in the First World War and in Norway, Crete, Singapore and France in the present one. Making full use of this, Stalin resorted to blunt and ironic language in castigating the prime minister, suggesting that the British should not be 'afraid of the Germans, if they fought against them they would find out they were not invincible, soldiers had to be blooded'. A string of accusations followed. Finally, Stalin, who did not find disagreement between the Allies to be 'tragic', vehemently objected to any suggestion that the operation in North Africa – even if it was 'right from the military point of view' – had any relevance for the Soviet Union.

In his reports to Roosevelt and the Cabinet, Churchill described the 'most unpleasant discussion', during which Stalin said 'a great many insulting things'. These, boasted Churchill, he had repulsed 'without taunts of any kind'. This was hardly the case. He emerged from the talks, observed his doctor, 'like a bull in the ring maddened by the pricks of picadors'. While making much of his mistreatment at the Kremlin, he brilliantly concealed from his entourage – as well as from the Cabinet and future historians – that what really troubled him was that his plan to convert Stalin to 'Torch' had been quashed. The fear of the reaction at home was uppermost in his mind, particularly when he was confronted with the Russian draft communiqué summing up the talks, which avoided any mention of the desert offensive but announced the failure to reach an agreement on the cross-Channel operation. To forestall the reopening of the strategic debate, he reassured the Cabinet and Roosevelt that 'in his heart, so far as he has one, Stalin knows we are right' and his 'sure-footed and quick military judgment' made him 'a strong supporter of TORCH'.

Sulking, Churchill made up his mind to return to London first thing the following morning. It was left to the British ambassador to awaken Churchill 'from the intense, and alas, no longer very actual, family and natitude [sic] pride'. Kerr left a bitter description of Churchill's demeanour, full of recriminations. 'I don't like to see a man in whose hands lies the fate of whole peoples,' he wrote in his diary, 'behave like a spoilt child. I don't like to have to shake a great leader of men out of whimsicalities or rather out of sheer folly.' In a most extraordinarily frank conversation, Kerr convinced Churchill that he 'couldn't leave Russia in the lurch whatever Stalin had said to hurt his pride. He would have to swallow his pride if only to save young lives.'[31]

---

[31] In a letter to Kerr, Churchill later acknowledged the 'wise advice' he had received.

The third scene of the drama was about to unfold. Maisky had advised Stalin that the key to Churchill's heart was 'a purely private chat on varied themes', in the course of which it was possible to gain his confidence and establish a closer understanding. After about an hour of futile meetings at Stalin's office in the Kremlin, on the last evening of the visit the Soviet leader made an unprecedented gesture, inviting Churchill to his private quarters for 'a drink'. Stalin had deliberately withheld his response to Churchill's request for a final meeting, but at the same time hastily set the scene at home, ordering an elaborate dinner and laying the table for three (Molotov was to join them later), while requesting his daughter to be available to meet the prominent guest.

There, 'sitting with a heavily laden board between them: food of all kinds crowned by a suckling pig, and innumerable bottles', it all 'seemed to be as merry as a marriage bell'. Stalin went out of his way throughout the intimate dinner (which went on until 3 a.m.) to charm his guest, avoiding the pitfall of the second front. He secured what Maisky had called the 'soft second line' assistance, but, considering his ever-growing fear of a separate peace, perhaps more significant was an undertaking he extracted from Churchill that Prussian militarism would be smashed and Germany disarmed after the war.

The prime minister returned to the dacha jubilant, convinced that he had been 'taken into the family', having 'seen the daughter and drink, food and jokes'. Henceforth he was 'all for Uncle Joe', certain that he had 'established with Stalin a personal relationship of the same kind as he had already built up with President Roosevelt'. Churchill left Moscow boasting that the disappointing news concerning the second front could not have been imparted except by him 'personally without leading to really serious drifting apart'. More significant was the effort he invested in deluding both the Cabinet and Roosevelt into believing that, once reconciled to the bad news, Stalin was 'entirely convinced of the great advantages of TORCH', which, Churchill added, he hoped was 'being driven forward with super-human energy on both sides of the ocean'. It did not take long, however, for this version to be discredited. The demands for the second front resurfaced when Maisky explained to Eden that it was 'difficult to persuade the Russian people that any operations which we might undertake in Africa were of equivalent value to the creation of a second front in Europe'. Maisky kept spreading to the press 'pessimistic accounts' of Churchill's visit. He regarded the absence of a second front as a 'calamity' and, notwithstanding his 'great personal admiration for the Prime Minister', he warned, it 'would be remembered as the greatest mistake of his career'.

Nonetheless Maisky made a last-ditch attempt to convince Molotov that Churchill's visit, which he had contrived, was perceived in London as a great success. The excerpts from Churchill's telegrams which Eden had read to him extolled 'the real Stalin' he had come to know and the latter's 'profound understanding of military matters'. He had been assured by Eden that the amicable comradeship established in Moscow was bound to 'produce even better results in the future'. But Maisky's influence was fast waning. Molotov, who sensed that the ambassador was again bent on launching personal initiatives, as he had done in 1939, warned him in unequivocal terms that the idea he had raised on 'devising a unified strategy' had been deliberately left out of the talks in Moscow because, as long as Russia was fighting alone, it was absolutely 'unacceptable'. 'You should not,' he was warned, 'put forward this idea to the British. You have never been given, you could not have been given, directions to that effect from us.'

The disagreeable role he was now assigned was to diminish the impression projected by Churchill that the Moscow negotiations had been successful, while reviving the agitation for a second front. He resorted to 'seriatim' meetings with the editors of all leading London papers. Inevitably this put him on a collision course with his allies in the British Government. The fact that he was 'intriguing everywhere with the ignorant and disgruntled' drove Eden to file a complaint with Churchill that 'Maisky was overstepping bounds of an Ambassador's privilege' and demand that he be reprimanded. Meanwhile Maisky was swiftly losing his grip on the media and public opinion. The disastrous raid on Dieppe in late August turned out to be a deathblow to his campaign in favour of a second front. 'The workers,' noted Brendan Bracken, Churchill's confidant, were being 'very good ... not very responsive to Stalin's appeals for a second front'.

The successful Anglo-American landing in North Africa and the victory at El Alamein in early November literally brought to an end the 'Second Front Now' movement, so laboriously set up by Maisky, and on which he had staked his diplomatic career, if not indeed his survival. The Soviet victory in Stalingrad gave Stalin a boost and ironically further reduced the likelihood that a unified Allied strategy might ever be attained in the war. Maisky's assets were fast dwindling. He disclosed to the ageing Webbs the intense suspicion in the Kremlin that the British generals and governing class were 'anxious that the German and Russian armies should exterminate each other' and thus enable Britain and the United States to dominate the peace-making process. Perhaps in a mirror image of the Soviet consideration of an arrangement with Germany earlier, he feared that the Government 'might come to terms, not with Hitler and his Nazi Party, but with the German capitalists glad to resume control of Germany'. Absurd accusations were raised by the Russians that Hess was being detained in Britain without trial to serve as a go-between in negotiations with Hitler's Germany or a post-war government in Germany which would be friendly to Great Britain 'after Russia had been bled white in defeating Hitler's Army'.

Maisky's confrontation with the Kremlin placed him in an increasingly awkward situation in Britain, too, where he seemed to be 'behaving in a very odd and indeed alarming way'. The derogatory attitude of Stalin to his own ambassador now led the British to assume that his criticisms and outbursts came 'off his own bat'. Eden was 'bored' with Maisky, whom he found to be increasingly 'troublesome' and 'very difficult'. When Maisky expressed gratitude for assistance given to Russia, the foreign secretary was heard muttering: 'I have never known the little blighter say thank you for anything before.' For Maisky, however, the intimacy he had established with Churchill remained vital for his political survival and continued stay in London – particularly in view of a new wave of rumours suggesting he was 'being moved to Stockholm'. He now desperately clung to Churchill, corresponding with him privately and reminding him of their 'long and friendly association' which 'existed in the past, exists now and, I sincerely hope, will exist in the future'. Alas, it only evoked a noncommittal polite response from the prime minister 'cordially reciprocating the sentiments'.

On 18 October, Maisky reported to Moscow that he had succeeded in foiling attempts by the British Government to convince the public that Stalin had accepted Churchill's reasoning for abandoning the second front in 1942 and replacing it with operations in North Africa. The following day, Stalin rushed a telegram to his ambassador, expressing his view that Churchill's opposition to the second front clearly reflected a wish to see the Soviet Union defeated 'in order to then come to terms with the Germany of Hitler or Brüning[32] at the expense of Britain'. He also referred to Hess as a potential intermediary in the negotiations with Germany.

After a couple of probably sleepless nights, Maisky cautiously addressed to Stalin a long and well-argued rebuttal. Maisky might have been encouraged by Montgomery's[33] offensive at El Alamein which opened on that day and led to victory over Rommel by 11 November. He challenged Stalin, insisting that Churchill could not possibly be craving the defeat of the USSR, which would 'inevitably mean the end of the British Empire' once Germany became the hegemonic power in Europe, if not in large parts of Asia and Africa. The reason he did not put Hess on trial was to prevent Hitler from taking retaliatory measures against British prisoners of war. Displaying an uncharacteristic temerity, Maisky told Stalin that he had drawn some 'practical conclusions' concerning Soviet 'policy and strategy', which he promised to impart in due course. Stalin, however, put an end to the discussion, waving away the arguments. 'Being the champion of an easy war,' he instructed Maisky, 'Churchill is clearly under the influence of those who are interested in the defeat of the Soviet Union ... and a compromise with Germany.' Clairvoyantly, he dismissed the promises made to him by Churchill to launch the cross-Channel attack in 1943, as he 'belonged to those political figures who easily make promises, only to forget or break them as easily'.

Indeed, in early December Churchill told Maisky that although he favoured the idea of a second front in 1943, he did not think the Americans would be able to complete their deployment in England by then. This was far from the truth. Rather than respond directly to Stalin's repeated queries about the likelihood of a second front in 1943, Churchill and Roosevelt now proposed to discuss future strategy with him at a summit meeting. Aware, however, that all they wished was to impart the sombre news that the operations on the Continent would have to be further postponed, Stalin preferred not to join their summit in Casablanca, scheduled for the new year.]

---

[32] Heinrich Brüning, German chancellor in the waning days of the Weimar Republic.
[33] Field Marshal Bernard Law Montgomery, commander of the Eighth Army, July 1942–43, in North Africa, during which he defeated the Germans and Italians at El Alamein (November 1942) and captured Tripoli and Tunisia (1943); commanded the invasion of Italy, September 1943.

1943

1 January

1 January 1943. The old year has died, a new one is born.

We welcomed the New Year with good cheer. The mood was quite different from a year ago. The main difference is this: over the course of these twelve months we have tested ourselves against the enemy in every department, we have sensed his strength and we have sensed our own, we have compared our strength with his and are firmly convinced that ours is the greater. True, much time and effort will still be needed to crush the enemy, but the outcome is certain. The crucial thing now is to ensure that in the course of beating the enemy we do not overstrain ourselves and reach the finishing line in a state of complete exhaustion. For this, skilful tactical manoeuvring is required – on the battlefield and in the <u>sphere</u> of diplomacy. Will we succeed in this? I think we shall. Stalin has shown that he has a superb understanding of the art of the calculated manoeuvre.

My thoughts involuntarily run ahead.

First of all, when should we expect the war in Europe to <u>end</u>?

I stand by the opinion which I first expressed back in October that the end of the war in Europe can be expected no earlier than 1944. And even then only if things go well for the Allies; if, that is, there is no split between them, no frictions which might paralyse the effectiveness of their joint operations, and if a proper front is established in Europe in 1943.

And the prospects for 1943? I hope that in the course of the winter we shall liberate the Volga, the Don, the northern Caucasus and perhaps the Donets Basin, and lift the Leningrad blockade. I also hope we shall recapture Rzhev, Vyazma and perhaps Smolensk. ... No more can be expected during the winter. ... What we intend to do this summer and autumn is not yet clear. To me, at least. Much will depend on the conduct of Britain and the USA. ... Here, all is still fuzzy. It seems as if Churchill and the British Government are currently in favour of establishing a serious second front in France in the spring. Roosevelt and the American Government are evidently not so keen on the idea at present.

London and Washington apparently have swapped positions in comparison with 1942. As the British won't open a second front in France without the Americans, it would be risky to count on an effective second front being established this spring. It may be opened, and it may not. Of course, were the Red Army to start approaching Poland's borders this winter, the British and the Americans would positively race to open a second front in France. ... But I doubt that the Red Army can get that far by spring.

... Now to politics. One must expect political issues to come ever more prominently to the fore in 1943. For two reasons. First, because the world increasingly recognizes that the tide is turning in the war, with the Allies' eventual victory becoming more and more obvious; so post-war problems are becoming a good deal more tangible. Second, because the outcome of the war for the Germans is less and less a question of warfare (they can't win by military means) and ever more one of politics (to avoid defeat by concluding a separate or compromise peace).

From the political point of view the most important thing is to consolidate the alliance between the USSR, Britain and the USA. I hope this objective will be achieved. However, there are dangers here, too. The weakest link is the USA.

I don't expect any serious complications in relations between the USSR and Britain at this stage. We have an alliance treaty and, which is yet more important, England is more dependent on us in matters of war and peace, while its bourgeoisie possesses enough experience and flexibility to recognize the need for cordial relations with the USSR. Churchill, as head of the British Government, and Eden, as head of the Foreign Office, represent the embodiments of this tendency.

The USA is a different matter. This country is, to all appearances, entering a period of frenzied imperialist expansion ... the USA wants to play a major role in Europe. With this in mind, it is already preparing a political base for itself in Europe through various Conservative–Catholic elements. ... I'm increasingly convinced that, contrary to the grandiloquent Atlantic Charters, the 'war aims' of the USA are to establish a Great American Empire in Africa and Asia. The more so since, as is well known, the Americans are very passionate when it comes to the struggle against Japan and very cool when it comes to the struggle against Germany.

... As for the future peace conference (if there is going to be one at all), the USSR will come to it possessing the most powerful army in the world, provided we manage to pursue tactics to avoid total exhaustion. The reason for this is that the British army, despite being stronger, will still be a far less effective military machine than the Red Army, while the US army, despite its size and equipment, will be too 'green' and 'raw' to undertake serious, large-scale operations.

The prospect is not bad. But the key to it is skilful manoeuvring.

3 January (Bovingdon)

Victories on the fronts. We have achieved much during this six-week offensive. Stalingrad has been liberated, and 22 enemy divisions have been encircled and are slowly perishing near Stalingrad. Nearly the entire Don Bend has been regained. ... In the Caucasus we have recaptured Mozdok and launched a successful offensive at Nalchik. On the central front we took Velikie Luki and have almost completely encircled Rzhev. Colossal losses in men and materiel have been inflicted on the Germans. Our human losses are relatively small, while the quantity of materiel increases. In the Don region, for instance, we seized more than 500 undamaged planes and 2,000 undamaged tanks from the Germans. We'll make the most of them.

Certainly, things are very, very different from how they were in summer and autumn, when the Germans were advancing and I had to record our failures every week with bitterness and a heavy heart. Stalin was right when he said that our turn for celebrating will come. ... The first sunrays have broken through the dark heavy clouds on the horizon.

6 January

Eden.

... (5) Eden is concerned about the weakening of Roosevelt's position and growing isolationism in the USA. He says: 'It would be tragic if the history of the last war were to be repeated and isolationists were to gain power just at the moment when the position of the USA in world politics was becoming especially important. This makes cooperation between our two countries all the more valuable. This is our only hope, the only anchor for our countries, for Europe, for Asia.'

[Now that his campaign for a second front lay in ruins, Maisky's stay in London hinged on his ability to persuade the British to cooperate with the Russians in the organization of the post-war reconstruction. 'I think the most important thing for us,' he advised Vernon Bartlett, a leading journalist and Member of Parliament, 'is not to bother too much about the past but to be concerned with the future.' As was his habit, he attributed his own initiative to Eden when reporting to Moscow. Maisky, according to Eden, anxiously remarked that 'if America continued to be interested in Europe, so much the better; but we must face the possibility that her interest might fade'. That, he argued, made it 'more than ever necessary' that the two countries 'should work closely together'. 'I agreed,' noted Eden. Maisky's continued remonstrations, however, eroded his relations with Churchill, who from Casablanca instructed Eden to inform Maisky that he was 'getting to the end of [his] tether with these repeated Russian naggings' and that it was 'not the slightest use trying to knock [him] about any more'.]

7 January

Churchill and Roosevelt are to meet very soon to discuss war plans for 1943. There are two alternatives:

(1) to invade France in spring or in summer, and

(2) to capture Sicily with subsequent landings in southern Italy.

The question of operations in the Balkans is not yet on the table: it would be relevant only if Turkey were to join, but Turkey, to all appearances, is not about to change her position.

According to Eden, Churchill has a definite preference for the French option, while Roosevelt and his advisers seem inclined to gamble on Sicily and Italy.

I fear the question will be resolved in favour of the second option, as it is easier from the military point of view; what's more, the British and Americans have various political reasons for postponing an effective second front in Europe.

17 January (Bovingdon)

Things are going well on the front! We have lived to see the day.

The 22 German divisions encircled at Stalingrad on 23 November are nearing their complete destruction. As a result of the fighting, hunger and cold their strength has been reduced by two-thirds and now stands at 70–80,000. On 8 January, our command delivered an ultimatum: either surrender on honourable terms (including repatriation after the war) or total destruction. The Germans refused to capitulate. Their liquidation is now taking place. Another week or two and it will all be over. Glorious Stalingrad will be liberated once and for all.

... We have a marvellous people, a marvellous army, and a marvellous leader!

Yet a colossal task, great difficulties, and heavy losses still lie ahead of us. The Germans have already lost the war, but we have not yet won it. To win the war as quickly and easily as possible we need a second front, we need the English and the Americans.

... Lloyd George is 80 today. The newspapers carry articles about him and photographs. Lord Winterton spoke about him over the radio (Lord Winterton is the eldest MP in terms of uninterrupted membership of the Commons – since 1904), Lloyd George was saluted in Welsh, and a concert of Welsh music was broadcast in the evening.

[Maisky, who had become reticent in his private correspondence, nonetheless sent Lloyd George an exceptionally warm letter expressing his life-long admiration, and stating 'without any flattery, that in my estimation you are probably the most outstanding statesman Great Britain has produced throughout this period'. He was grateful for the guidance, 'good advice and the valuable information' Lloyd George had offered him throughout his ambassadorship. It evoked an effusive response from 'the Welsh wizard' hailing the recent successes of the Soviet Red Army, which, he believed, might 'yet revolutionise the whole prospect of European democracy, and the influence may even extend to America'. This seemed to reinforce Maisky's fears that the British continued to perceive Soviet policy as revolutionary, thereby ignoring the realpolitik aspects of its foreign policy. He was quick, therefore, to correct Lloyd George. While sharing the hope that the Soviet Union would be able 'to exercise strong influence in shaping the coming peace', he denied any desire to 'revolutionise' the European scene. Such views dovetailed with Stalin's outlook, as was shortly manifested by the dissolution of Comintern in May 1943, thus paving the way for collaboration on a post-war European order.[1]]

18 January

Those Americans are a strange lot!

Roosevelt has sent several messages to Stalin. They amount to the following: a promise of 200 transport aircraft (many thanks for that); the expression of his wish to transfer 100 bombers with American personnel to our Far East right now 'just in case' Japan should attack the USSR; and the statement that General Bradley[2] and a few other officers appointed by Roosevelt should start negotiations with Soviet representatives immediately, carry out a 'preliminary inspection' in the Far East and draw up plans together with our men. Roosevelt reports that in the very near future he intends to send General Marshall (the chief of staff) to Moscow to brief us about the state of affairs in Africa and about the military operations planned for 1943.

Stalin produced a good reply. He sent Roosevelt a message the other day in which he thanks him for the 200 transport planes, but expresses bewilderment at Roosevelt's intention to send a fleet of 100 bombers to the Far East. First, we have told the Americans more than once that we need machines, not pilots. Second, we require planes not in the Far East, where we are not at war, but on the Soviet–German front, where the need for aircraft is very acute.

... Roosevelt will probably take offence. It can't be helped! The Americans need to be taught a lesson. They really do fancy themselves to be the salt of the earth and the mentors of the world.

---

[1] See pp. 522–3.
[2] General Omar Nelson Bradley, commanded II United States Corps in northern Tunisia and in Sicily, April–September 1943; commanded US troops in the invasion of France, June 1944.

19 January

I turn 59 today. Another year and I'll be celebrating my 60th.

I have mixed feelings. On the one hand, cold, sober reason tells me that the autumn of my life is upon me. On the other, my subjective sense of my physical and spiritual state does not register any twilight symptoms or moods. My health is *all right*, my capacity for work has not diminished, and my acuity of mind even seems to have grown (though the latter may be the result of accumulated experience).

My mind tells me: 'You're nearing old age.'

But my body replies: 'You are still far from old.'

Four years ago, when I turned 55, I wrote that, taking the average human span as my guide, I still had some 20 years ahead of me. It was then that I sketched a rough 'plan' for those 20 years: the first 10 years (till 65) would be devoted to active political work, and the next 10 (till 75) to bringing my life's journey to completion.

... I'm not looking beyond 75. What for?

I know several outstanding people here older than 75: Bernard Shaw and his wife – he's 87 and she must be about 89.

The Webbs – she's 85, he's 83 and a half.

Lloyd George is 80.

Looking at them, I have no desire to reach their age.

... Yesterday evening it was announced over the wireless that the blockade of Leningrad has been lifted. What joy! And what a wonderful gift on my birthday!

21 January

I had two interesting conversations with Eden this week: one on the 18th and one today.

Churchill and Roosevelt have met: the two of them have been in Morocco, near Marrakesh, since the end of last week. It was Churchill's idea to meet there. The chiefs of staff and other senior army and navy men are with them. So far the results of the meeting are as follows:

(1) <u>Military affairs in North Africa</u>. The Eighth Army's campaign is coming to an end. Montgomery plans to reach Tripoli on 22 or 23 January. ... In essence, the Churchill–Roosevelt decisions on this matter represent recognition that the US army is still too 'green' to wage serious military operations and that the English influence in the Anglo-American combination has grown. Judging by the tone of Churchill's telegrams (Eden acquainted me with them), the prime minister is extremely pleased. He is particularly glad that General Alexander,

whom he summoned to the conference from the front, made a good impression on the Americans and established good relations with Eisenhower.[3]

(2) <u>General strategy for 1943</u>. It has been decided that immediately after the completion of the Tunisia campaign, the Allies will launch a military operation in Sicily. At the same time it has been decided to start massing large forces on the British Isles immediately, with the aim of 'a return to the European continent' in the course of this year. But the following remains unclear from Churchill's telegrams: will the Allies proceed to Italy if they seize Sicily? When do they intend to make their 'return to the European continent' – concurrently with the operation in Sicily or after it? Where is this 'return to the European continent' expected to occur? With which forces? I sought a reply to these questions from Eden, but failed to receive one. Eden evidently does not yet know himself. I'll have to wait for the prime minister's return to learn more about the Anglo-American plans for Europe. ...

65. A caricacture by David Low.

---

[3] General Dwight David Eisenhower, sent to England as commander of European Theatre of Operations in March 1942; commander-in-chief allied forces in North Africa, November, 1942–44; supreme commander of the Allied Expeditionary Force in Western Europe, 1944–45.

[In his telegrams to the American president and to Churchill, Stalin kept demanding to know when and where the second front was to be established in Europe. He believed a promise had been made for an invasion in 1942, which had now been postponed to 1943. He saw no point in convening a summit conference, as it was his right 'to sit back and demand the fulfilment of the British and American pledges'. Churchill believed, as he informed Roosevelt, that it would be 'fatal' to arrive at the negotiating table with Stalin before a common Anglo-American strategy for 1943 had been devised. Once in Casablanca, General Marshall remained 'most anxious not to become committed to interminable operations in the Mediterranean', while King[4] criticized the British for having no 'definite ideas as to what the next operation should be' and for failing to produce 'an overall plan for the conduct of the war'. Churchill made sure that the military negotiations dragged on, like 'the dripping of water on a stone'. While they dragged on, he was able to sway the president his way, as he had done in Washington the previous May. The 'moderate scale' operation in northern France appeared at the bottom of the list of operations he proposed, while priority continued to be given to operations in North Africa and to the invasion of Sicily, followed by that of Italy, which Churchill now termed 'the soft underbelly of Europe'. Though Stalin's shadow hovered over the conference, there was hardly any reference to the Russian front. From Casablanca the American planners conceded in despair: 'We came, we saw, we were conquered.'

Impatient as ever, Churchill wasted little time in exploiting his success. He embarked on an impromptu lightning visit to Turkey, straight from Casablanca (which is referred to later in the diary). Although to Maisky Churchill presented the visit as part of his efforts to assist the Russians, it fitted all too well into his grand-strategy scheme. Turkey's entry into the war would pave the way for a Balkan campaign after the completion of Operation Husky (the landing in Sicily) and the likely invasion of Italy. The extension of the war into the Eastern Mediterranean would have significantly delayed the cross-Channel attack. This explains why Churchill went a long way to placate Stalin in his message of 1 February, in which he stressed their common interest in British involvement in Turkey and the Balkans once the North African campaign was over.]

26 January

It had just struck half past seven. Eden's room was dimly lit. A bright flame blazed in the large fireplace.

... I asked whether there had been any 'peace feelers' coming from the German side of late. Eden said there hadn't.

'We do receive reports that German morale is cracking fast,' Eden continued, 'but I don't know how far to trust them. What do you think?'

---

[4] Admiral Ernest King, commander-in-chief of the naval forces in the wake of the Japanese attack on Pearl Harbor, and chief of naval operations from March 1942.

'I'm inclined to take such information with a pinch of salt,' I replied. 'I think that the time for a genuine collapse in morale has not yet arrived.'

'Why not?' Eden enquired.

'You see, Mr Eden,' I began, 'the question of "morale" is a complex one. It cannot be dealt with in generalities. One should differentiate between the various elements that make up Nazi Germany. First, the broad masses. What can be said about their morale? There is no doubt that it is being steadily undermined and corroded. ... But we should be under no illusions: this process is still in its initial stage. The broad German masses know little about what is really going on at the front; they are subject to the unremitting impact from all sides of fascist propaganda, and so it seems premature to me to speak of the imminent collapse of the German population's morale. Nor do I believe that Hitler's own "morale" is truly shattered.'

... 'The men whose "morale" has really suffered as a result of recent events,' I continued, 'are the generals and all those connected to them. The generals know what is going on at the front and they do not share Hitler's mysticism. It must already be clear to them by now that Germany cannot win the war on the battlefield. ... So, if military victory is impossible, what is left for the generals? One thing only: to try to achieve a favourable peace deal for Germany. A separate peace would be best of all; next best is a general, compromise peace settlement. The sooner it happens, the better, as Germany still has many strong cards in her hand, but the tide has turned against her. From here on she will have fewer and fewer cards to play. Hitler himself, of course, is hardly a plus point in the light of such prospects. That is why I wouldn't be at all surprised if, waking up one fine morning, we were to read in the papers that Hitler had committed suicide or died in a "car accident". Hitler's days are numbered: 1943 may well be his last year, politically if not physically. Once Hitler disappears, the possibility of forming a new government will open before the generals. In essence, of course, this will be that same bloodthirsty German fascism in disguise, but who knows – maybe some elements in England and the USA will swallow the bait? Especially if the generals present it, as they are sure to do, as a dish entitled "Bolshevik scarecrow". I have no doubt that this scarecrow will be fetched from the pantry very soon. It may be all moth-eaten and bitten by mice, but who cares? The German bosses can't be choosers. Maybe some small fry in Britain and the USA will take the bait, even such a suspicious one as this?'

'I don't think so,' Eden protested. 'I know which elements you are referring to. I assure you that they are absolutely powerless now.'

'So much the better!' I replied. 'Whatever happens, this is what we should expect in the next few months: first, persistent attempts on the part of the Germans to split the united front – the Allied front, and, second, equally stubborn attempts to test the ground for a compromise peace. Does the British Government understand this? Is it prepared to nip all such attempts in the bud?'

Eden rose in agitation from his armchair and replied with uncharacteristic energy: 'As long as Churchill is prime minister and I am foreign secretary, there will be no compromise with Germany!'

1 February

For all his seriousness, Churchill is a rather amusing man!

Eden called me over today late in the evening. He showed me a heap of ciphered messages from and to the prime minister, concerning the latter's visit to Turkey. They made for interesting reading. Churchill's mood is joyful, cheerful, almost boyish. In fact, boyish is just what it is. Flipping through the telegrams it is sometime hard to believe that they were written by the leader of Great Britain in the heat of the greatest war in history.

First, the background to this visit. Churchill has long nurtured the idea of drawing Turkey over to our side. When he was in Casablanca, it got into his head that a meeting with Inönü[5] would serve this purpose. Roosevelt gave his approval, but London started objecting because:

(1) Churchill's prestige might be damaged should the Turks refuse to fight and

(2) London did not want to subject Churchill to unnecessary risk and fatigue.

'After all, the prime minister is 68!' exclaimed Eden, telling me of the Cabinet's reservations.

Mrs Churchill was also against the trip on the grounds of her husband's health. She even asked a few members of the Government not to agree to his proposal.

But Churchill dug his heels in. And when he digs his heels in, nobody can budge him. It's obvious from his telegrams that he was desperate to go. Not only for reasons of state, but also, and perhaps even more so, because he was fed up with sitting in London and had a rush of blood. He wanted to stretch his limbs and travel the world a bit. In one of the telegrams the Cabinet objected to the trip under the pretext that Parliament was eager to hear his report on the meeting in Casablanca. Getting into the plane, Churchill sent a humorous telegram in reply: I wish you fun shining the dusty benches in Westminster, while I gallivant around Africa and the Middle East to my heart's content. Churchill yielded to the Cabinet on one point only: his meeting with İnönü took place

---

[5] Mustafa İsmet İnönü, prime minister, 1923–24 and 1925–37; president of the Republic of Turkey, 1938–50.

not in Ankara, where an attempt upon the PM's life could easily have been made, but in Adana.

There, to judge by his messages, he was evidently *in high spirits*. İnönü, Saracoğlu,[6] Çakmak,[7] Menemencioğlu[8] and others came to meet him. They had long and detailed talks. ... For some odd reason he refers to them in the ciphered messages as 'the morning thoughts' of a pious man! They are very detailed, these 'thoughts': three single-spaced typewritten pages. Their substance is simple. Clearly and even somewhat cynically, Churchill confronts the Turks with the question: we (Britain, the USSR and the USA) will win – do you wish to be on the side of the winners? If you do, give us assistance during the war. If you do not assist us, you'll find yourself after the war in the position of a neutral, and not a very powerful neutral at that. It's your choice. You say you have no arms? All right, we'll give you some. Once this is done, think it over and decide.

Such are Churchill's 'morning thoughts'. How will the Turks act?

... On his way back, Churchill stopped over in Cyprus. It's not quite clear why. Incidentally, a 'cipher catastrophe' very nearly occurred during the PM's stay in Cyprus. Churchill, who is rather careless about ciphering in general, was on the verge of sending a message for publication from Cyprus, which only had a rather primitive military code. Had the message been published, the code would have been cracked and the Axis would have been able to read all the secrets of the British military command in the Middle East. The FO's cipher department was in panic. But 'catastrophe' was averted at the last moment.

5 February

What is Britain's reaction to our victories?

It is impossible to answer this question in a word or two. For England's reaction to the Red Army's successes is complex and contradictory. I'll try to sum up my impressions.

What strikes me first when I ask myself this question is the general amazement at the might of the USSR and the strength of the Red Army. Nobody expected us to be able to retain such fighting capability after the ordeals of last summer. ... That is why the first and foremost feeling which our victories elicit in England is universal amazement. The feeling is equally strong everywhere, from the top to the bottom of the social pyramid.

The second feeling, aroused by events unfolding in the USSR, is great admiration for the Soviet people, the Red Army and Comrade Stalin personally. But

---

[6] Mehmet Sükrü Saracoğlu, Turkish foreign minister, 1938–42; prime minister, 1942–46.
[7] Marshal Mustafa Fevzi Çakmak, Turkish chief of general staff.
[8] Hüseyin Numan Menemencioğlu, Turkish foreign minister, 1942–44.

this feeling is less sweeping than the amazement described above. Among the masses it is unreserved and unrestrained. Here the prestige of the USSR has soared over the last three months. ... I shall just mention Stalin's popularity. His appearance on the screen always elicits loud cheers, much louder cheers than those given to Churchill or the king. Frank Owen[9] told me the other day (he is in the army now) that Stalin is the soldiers' idol and hope. If a soldier is dissatisfied with something, if he has been offended by the top brass, or if he resents some order or other from above, his reaction tends to be colourful and telling. Raising a menacing hand, he exclaims: 'Just you wait till Uncle Joe gets here! We'll even up with you then!'

The higher the strata of the social pyramid, the more the sense of admiration is mixed up with other feelings, largely ones of a corrosive nature. ... The ruling classes are displeased, or rather disquieted: won't the Bolsheviks get too strong? Won't the prestige of the USSR and the Red Army grow too much? Won't the likelihood of the 'Bolshevization of Europe' rise too high? The more success the Soviet military achieves, the deeper the concern in the hearts of the ruling elite.

These two contradictory feelings live side by side in the bosom of the British ruling class and find expression in the sentiments of its two main groupings, which may be called the Churchillian and Chamberlainian groups, for short.

... Although the Churchillian group is now undoubtedly the dominant one, English policy nevertheless tends to steer a middle course between the two trends just mentioned. The result? The British Government seeks methods and means of continuing to have its war fought by others (i.e. us), while also securing for itself a leading role at the post-war peace conference.

... The question of the second front is rather different. Once again there is internal disagreement here among the ruling class. On the one hand, it would like to postpone the opening of a second front for as long as possible and wait for us to break Germany's backbone, so that the Anglo-American forces can make a 'comfortable' landing in France and march on Berlin with minimum losses. On the other hand, if the delay in opening a western front is too protracted, England (and the USA) may miss the boat and allow the Red Army to be the first to enter Berlin. The ruling class fears this greatly: the spectre of the 'Bolshevization of Europe' looms large in their imagination. So the timing for the opening of the second front is the major tactical question facing the British (and American) Government. They reckon this should be done not too early and not too late – *just in time*. ... For now, my impression is the following: Britain and the USA will not open a second front by spring, while in summer

---

[9] Frank Owen, editor of the *Evening Standard*, 1938–41; lieutenant-colonel in the Royal Armoured Corps, 1942–43.

66. Maisky cutting the railings outside the Soviet embassy as a contribution to the war effort.

and winter they will divert themselves with various secondary operations in the Mediterranean (Sicily, Crete, Dodecanese and other places). Perhaps they will cook up some Dieppe monstrosity or other in the north, but they are hardly likely to undertake a serious invasion of France.

It's unpleasant, but that's how it is. One has to face the facts. This inauspicious prospect may alter, I believe, only under one circumstance: if our successes assume such colossal dimensions that Germany's collapse and the Red Army's entry into Berlin in 1943 become real possibilities. Am I mistaken? Time will tell.

7 February (Bovingdon)

... The most remarkable and certainly dramatic event of the last two weeks was the definitive annihilation of Field Marshal Paulus's[10] Sixth German Army at

---

[10] Field Marshal Friedrich Wilhelm Ernst Paulus, commander of the forlorn Sixth Army's assault on Stalingrad in 1942.

Stalingrad. The 2nd of February is a date to remember. Paulus and two dozen German and Rumanian generals were taken prisoner. Ninety thousand prisoners of war, mostly Germans, were captured between 10 January and 2 February, the period during which our forces launched the decisive offensive after Paulus had refused to surrender. ... The moral and psychological significance of Stalingrad is colossal. Never before in military history has a powerful army, besieging a city, itself become a besieged stronghold that was then annihilated – down to the very last general, the very last soldier.

... And now the second front... If in spite of all our efforts a second front were not to be opened, would this really be an unalloyed misfortune? I doubt it.

True, it would be bad in the short run: the war would drag on and our losses would be greater. But what about in the long run? Here, the balance might well be different. First, should the Allies refuse to play a major role on the field of battle, all the glory for defeating Germany would be ours. This would make for a massive rise in the prestige of the Soviet Union, the revolution and communism – not only now, but also in the future. Second, England and the USA would emerge from the war with weak and inexperienced armies, while the Red Army would become the most powerful army in the world. This could not but tip the international balance of power in our favour. Third, in the absence of a second front in the west, the Red Army would stand a good chance of entering Berlin first and thereby having a decisive influence on the terms of peace and on the situation in the post-war period.

So which course of events would be more advantageous for us in the final analysis?

Hard to say. At first glance, a second front would seem preferable. But is that really the case?

Time will tell.

[Soviet successes on the battlefield, though, were for the moment limited. The Soviet winter offensive of 1943 was a logical outcome of the victory at Stalingrad. After regrouping its forces, the Red Army launched a series of offensives between December 1942 and February 1943 which cleared the German and Axis forces from the south bank of the Don River. Its forces further advanced westward into the Donbas and Kharkov regions, the objective of which was the liberation of Kursk. However, Field Marshal von Manstein[11] manoeuvred his troops brilliantly, exploiting the overextended south-western front to effectively contain the Soviet 'winter offensive' by 6 March. By the end of the month, the *Stavka* had been forced to assume a defensive position in the

---

[11] Field Marshal Erich von Manstein, commander of the 56th Panzer Corps, February 1941, and of the Eleventh Army in Operation Barbarossa; dismissed by Hitler in 1944 following his defeat in the battle of Kursk in 1943 and the Wehrmacht retreat from Russia.

Kursk bulge. The initial ambitious Soviet plans account for the confidence displayed by the Kremlin in the political dialogue with their Allies, as is indeed well reflected in Maisky's diary entries. It accounts for the somewhat premature raising of the post-war agendas and a temporary abandonment of the demands for a second front. Those were resumed as soon as the ferocious German offensive was launched in May, though for the first time since the beginning of the war in the East, the Germans failed to break through the Soviet defences, forcing Hitler to call the offensive off on 17 July 1943. The lessons gained from Stalingrad and the winter offensive dictated prudence, which was displayed by the moderate objective set by the Red Army of reaching the Dnepr River line. This did not prevent Kerr from warning his Government how 'horrible' it would be for British prestige if the Russians entered Berlin in tanks 'and we calmly travel to meet them on the train'.]

9 February

On 7 February Churchill finally returned to London. I was in Bovingdon and didn't go to see him. But then, I hadn't been informed of the date of his return.

When I saw Eden in the afternoon of the 8th, I told him I wanted to hand Churchill the message I had just received from Stalin concerning Turkey. Early in the evening, the PM's secretary notified me that Churchill would receive me at 10.30 p.m.

The meeting took place in the prime minister's private apartment. I was shown through to the study and asked to wait. There was a fire going. A bottle of whisky stood on the table with some soda water. For a few minutes there was nobody but me and I whiled away the time inspecting a large map of the USSR that was hanging on the wall. Finally, Eden walked in (I had asked for him to be present at the conversation).

'Our troops have taken Kursk,' I said, informing Eden of the latest news.

'Wonderful!' Eden responded heartily. 'Wait a sec, I'll just tell Beaverbrook. He's in the next room.'

Eden disappeared for a short while and exclaimed on his return: 'Max is utterly delighted!'

Churchill came in a moment later. He was wearing a dressing gown thrown over his customary *siren suit*. His eyes were not yet fully open. His hair was tousled. It was obvious that he had just got out of bed.

'Welcome home,' I greeted him.

He gave me a friendly smile and then immediately asked with a note of impatience: 'I believe you are bringing me a reply from Stalin?'

I confirmed this and proffered the envelope to the prime minister. As on previous occasions, Churchill asked me before opening it: 'It won't upset me, will it?'

I laughed and answered: 'No, I don't think so.'

Churchill opened the envelope and started reading the message aloud. Stalin's rebuke for the incomplete information about Adana irritated the prime minister, but not for long. Having reached the end, Churchill gave his brief summary: 'A good message!... Is it not?'

The question was addressed to Eden. Eden hastened to agree.

Churchill was in a good mood now and started to speak about his meeting with the Turks. ... But I was much more interested in the military plans adopted in Casablanca. I already knew a few things from my previous talks with Eden and from the Roosevelt–Churchill message to Stalin on this matter. However, there were some salient gaps in this information and I decided to try to get to the bottom of it all.

I asked Churchill what he could tell me about the Anglo-American military plans for 1943. The prime minister was evidently expecting this question. He asked for the relevant documents from the secretariat, and read to me his telegram to Roosevelt and Roosevelt's reply on the matter that interested me. Churchill's telegram included the outline of a draft reply to Stalin's message of 30 January. Roosevelt, in his telegram, offered some (insignificant) amendments to Churchill's proposals.

What does the plan amount to?

The main points are as follows:

(1) The operation in Tunisia is expected to be concluded by April at the latest.

(2) Next, approximately in June or July, comes the operation for the capture of Sicily, which is linked to the capture of Italy's 'boot'. After that, one of two things may happen. If the Italians' resistance proves weak or a pro-Allied coup happens in Italy by that time, the British and the Americans will make for the north of the Apennine Peninsula, and from there head west to southern France and east to the Balkans. If the Italians, backed up by the Germans, put up serious resistance, or if a pro-Allied coup fails to materialize, the British and the Americans will move from Italy, Apulia and Calabria to Yugoslavia and Greece, that is, to the western part of the Balkans.

(3) Somewhat later, an operation (of secondary importance) to seize the Dodecanese, possibly Crete.

(4) At some time in August or September, and independently of the operations in the Mediterranean, a landing operation will be carried out across the Channel in France.

(5) Anglo-American forces will intensify the air offensive against Germany and Italy.

(6) Extremely vigorous anti-submarine warfare.

I asked Churchill which forces would be available to carry out the said operations in the south and in the north.

Churchill replied that, after capturing Tunisia, the British and the Americans would be able to assign 300–400,000 men to other operations in the Mediterranean.

'As far as the cross-Channel operation is concerned,' the PM continued, 'I honestly can't say anything definite for the moment. We, the English, would be able to assign 12–15 divisions for this purpose. But the Americans?...'

Here Churchill gave a bewildered shrug of his shoulders and exclaimed: 'Right now the Americans have only one division here!'

'How come only one?' I echoed in surprise. 'You told me in November that one American division was stationed in England... Has nothing been added since then?'

'That is so,' Churchill replied. 'The Americans have sent nothing since November.'

'How many American divisions do you expect by August?' I inquired.

'I wish I knew,' Churchill responded with comical despair. 'When I was in Moscow, I proceeded from the assumption that by spring 1943, the Americans would have dispatched 27 divisions to England, just as they had promised. This was my assumption during my conversations with Stalin. But where are they, those 27 divisions? Now the Americans promise to send only 4–5 divisions by August!... If they keep their word, then the cross-Channel operation will be carried out with 17–20 divisions.'[12]

'What if the Americans deceive you once again?' I asked.

Churchill thought for a moment before answering firmly: 'I'll carry out this operation whatever happens!'

The prime minister, however, did not specify what he would do if the American forces failed to arrive in due time.

Churchill suddenly burst out laughing as if he had recalled something funny and asked me: 'Do you know how many men there are in an American division?'

A little puzzled, I replied: 'I don't know for certain, but I expect about 18–19,000.'

'Right!' Churchill roared still louder. 'If you count the combatants alone... But 50,000 if you count the entire attending personnel!'

I gasped: 'How do you mean, 50,000?'

---

[12] In his memoirs, Maisky suggests that the conversation with Churchill convinced him that 'it was no use reckoning on a second front in Northern France in the spring of 1943'. As we have seen, he had given up on a second front. Stalin, however, returned to the topic later in the month, when he realized that the Soviet offensive would be slower than he had anticipated.

'I mean 50,000!' Churchill exclaimed once more, and then, with blatant sarcasm in his voice, started enumerating. 'What don't you have in an American division!... Of course, there's transport, medical staff, quartermaster service and so on. That's normal. But they also have two laundry battalions, one battalion of milk sterilizers, one battalion of hairdressers, one battalion of tailors, one battalion *for the uplift of the troops and what not!*... Ha-ha-ha!... We've sent nearly half a million combatants to North Africa... But it actually amounts to a mere 10–11 divisions.'

Churchill once again burst out laughing and added: 'We, the English, are poor in this respect, but the Americans are even worse.'

Our conversation jumped from one topic to another. Churchill's thoughts kept leaping this way and that. Some interesting examples: 'Stalin was very sharp with Roosevelt,' Churchill remarked half in derision, half in reproach. 'The president showed me Stalin's last message.'

Then, turning to Eden, he added with a laugh: 'Stalin hasn't always been gentle with me either... Do you remember?... But Roosevelt got it worse...'

'Roosevelt deserved it,' I rejoined. 'Are you familiar with the content of Roosevelt's message, to which Stalin replied with the message you cited?'

'What message was that?' asked Eden, who had clearly never heard about it.

'Oh, it's a remarkable message!' Churchill exclaimed with hilarity. 'I read it, too.'

Churchill then briefly related the content of Roosevelt's message to Stalin, in which Roosevelt suggesting sending 100 bombers to Vladivostok with American personnel 'just in case' and giving the American generals permission to 'inspect' our Far Eastern air and naval bases. Roosevelt also proposed to send General Marshall to Moscow to discuss the 1943 campaign.

Eden's face was a picture of horror when he heard of the proposal to send 100 bombers. His reaction could be interpreted in the following way: 'How clumsy and naive the Americans are!'

'Well,' Churchill went on, 'Roosevelt was, frankly speaking, enraged by Stalin's message and wanted to send an abusive reply. But I managed to talk him out of it. I told him: listen, who is really fighting today?... Stalin alone! And look how he's fighting! We must make allowances... The president eventually agreed and thought better of starting a row with Stalin.'

Churchill took a long drag on his cigar and said, staring at the tongues of flame playing in the fireplace: 'Roosevelt asked me what was the genuine reason for Stalin not attending the conference...'

'But you know the reason,' I interrupted, 'and so does the president.'

'Yes, of course,' Churchill responded. 'He is busy directing military operations and so on... That's right. But that is not all. I responded to Roosevelt's question as follows: Stalin is a realist. You can't catch him with words. Had

Stalin come to Casablanca, the first thing he would have asked you and me would have been: "How many Germans did you kill in 1942? And how many do you intend to kill in 1943?" And what would the two of us have been able to say? We ourselves are not sure what we are going to do in 1943. This was clear to Stalin from the very beginning. So what would have been the point of him coming to the conference?... All the more so as he is accomplishing great things at home.'

But it seems that the 'tiff' between Stalin and Roosevelt is of real concern to Churchill. He explained to me at length how important it is for good relations and mutual understanding to exist between the leaders of the two governments – the USSR and the USA.

'It is important now, and it will be even more important after the war.'

Here Churchill's eyes suddenly became moist and he began speaking in a heartfelt, emotional tone: 'For me, personally, it's all the same... I'm an old man. I'm nearly 70. But the country, the people will remain... When peace arrives, the situation will become exceptionally difficult... I see no other salvation for mankind except close cooperation between the three of us – the USSR, the USA and England. It will be far from easy. The USA is a capitalist country and is moving fast to the Right. The USSR is a socialist country. Britain will have to be the bridge between them. This is why any personal friction between Roosevelt and Stalin is extremely undesirable.'

Churchill grinned and continued: 'England and the USSR need each other too much – in Europe, in Asia and in various common matters. They will always reach an agreement in the end. With America it's different. The Americans think that since they are separated from you and from us by two oceans, they don't need you and us so very much... A gross error! But you know how naive and inexperienced the Americans are in politics. That is why I'm so worried about this conflict between Stalin and Roosevelt. It would be best if they could meet. I've been thinking about it for quite a while...'

Churchill puffed at his cigar again and, pulling a terribly cunning face, asked me slyly: 'Why do you think I made a stopover in Cyprus on my way back from Adana?'

I shrugged.

'The newspapers wrote,' Churchill went on, 'that a regiment I once served in is stationed in Cyprus, and so on. That's right: there is such a regiment. But that's all balderdash! The real reason I stopped in Cyprus was different: I wanted to see whether it would be an appropriate place for a meeting between Stalin and Roosevelt in the future. And it's a jolly good thing I flew there. The island is perfect. Easily cut off from everywhere. Nobody will know a thing. It takes no more than five hours to fly from Tiflis to Cyprus. The president is ready to travel to Cyprus. After his first taste of flying, he's developed a liking for it. He'll get to Cyprus if needs must. I confess, I've already given instructions for a few modest but comfortable buildings to be built on the island to accommodate three delegations.'

Churchill told me all this with manifest excitement, animated gestures and sparkles in his eyes. I could see how much he enjoys all that secrecy, all that romanticism. Truly, there is still something boyish about the prime minister of Great Britain, despite his 68 years.

Then he suddenly gave a start and exclaimed: 'Only please, don't tell a soul about it!'

I promised not to say a word.

Apropos Churchill's boyishness. He described to me in great detail the measures he took to prevent an attempt upon his life during the journey. He had everything you could think of: armoured cars, bullet-proof windows, automatic pistols and revolvers, secret buildings surrounded by armed guards, a sudden change of route, and much more besides. Sounded a bit like vaudeville. Of course, Churchill does have to take security measures. Yet, judging by the way he recounted his adventures, he got quite carried away by all this and approached it with quite boyish exaggeration.

... Churchill mentioned de Gaulle[13] and Giraud[14] in the course of our conversation. The prime minister is highly irritated with de Gaulle, and perhaps that is why he leans towards Giraud. I'm not surprised: Churchill has never liked de Gaulle, and that episode concerning his trip to Casablanca inflamed the prime minister even more.

'I'm fed up with that Jeanne d'Arc in trousers!' Churchill snarled.[15]

Eden made an attempt to mollify Churchill and calm him down, but without much success.

I fear that the entire de Gaulle movement may suffer as a result. We shall see.

Churchill came back several times to our victories and the Red Army. He cannot speak about the Red Army without admiration and emotion. Even his eyes glisten... You can't help but recall 1920! How the wheel of history can turn![16]

---

[13] Charles de Gaulle, commander of the French army in exile after the collapse of France; chief of Free French, then president of the French National Committee, 1940–42.

[14] General Henri Honoré Giraud, commander of the Seventh and Ninth Armies; escaped from France in a British submarine; commanded French forces in North Africa and served as high commissioner; temporarily shared with de Gaulle the chairmanship of the French Committee for National Liberation after the Casablanca summit, but remained commander-in-chief until spring 1944, when the post was abolished.

[15] Making the same allusion in Casablanca, Churchill went on to say: 'and we are looking for some bishops to burn him'.

[16] Churchill was referring to Tukhachevsky's victory over the Polish army which brought the Russians to the gates of Warsaw. General Józef Piłsudski, however, exploited the extended Soviet line and the logistic disarray to repel the Red Army behind the Neman River.

67. Maisky: the go-between.

'Taking all factors into account,' Churchill stated, 'the obvious conclusion presents itself that the Russia of today is five times stronger than the Russia of the last war.'

I teased him a little: 'And how do you explain this phenomenon?'

Churchill understood and replied in the same vein: 'If your system gives the people more happiness than ours, I'm all for it!... Not that I'm greatly interested in what happens after the war: communism, socialism, cataclysm... Isn't it all the same?... So long as the Huns are crushed!'

We shall see.

Churchill is definitely growing old. Yesterday he lost the thread of our conversation several times and, turning to Eden, asked with impatience: 'Remind me – what were we saying?'

I hope Churchill will last till the end of the war. It's very important. England needs him. We need him too.

17 February

Today I handed Churchill Stalin's message, in which the latter insists on the swift opening of a second front in Europe. This message is Stalin's reply to

Churchill's message of 9 February, which summarized all I had heard from the prime minister the previous evening.

I received the message in the afternoon and called Eden immediately to tell him I wanted to see Churchill in the evening, in order to deliver Stalin's message. The appointment was set for ten in the evening. But when I arrived at the PM's apartment, Eden met me and said that Churchill was in bed with a high temperature. He'd been struggling with illness for a few days and now it had confined him to his bed. The nature of Churchill's illness is not yet entirely clear, but evidently it's some ailment of the bronchial tubes and of the respiratory passages in general.[17]

Eden accepted the message from me and took it to the bedroom, where the prime minister was lying. He returned some 20 minutes later and said that Churchill found Stalin's message quite in line with his expectations and that the prime minister would write a reply as soon as he was in a physical condition to do so.

I was about to leave when Eden poured me a whisky and soda, did the same for himself, and proposed that we sit down and have a little chat. This 'little chat' proved quite long.

At first we discussed Stalin's message and the Allies' military plans for the summer. I insisted on the necessity of exploiting the Germans' current confusion to the utmost and of the prompt opening of a second front in Europe. Moreover, I outlined the following concrete plan: to end the operation in Tunisia, postpone further operations in the Mediterranean (Sicily, Italy, etc.), and focus all attention on the cross-Channel operations, transferring the Eighth Army to England for this purpose and appointing Alexander commander-in-chief of the entire offensive operation in France.

Eden liked my plan. He confessed that he had been in favour all along of a cross-Channel operation, found operations in the Mediterranean (with the exception of Tunisia) inexpedient, and considered a direct attack on Germany through France to be undeniably preferable to indirect blows via Italy or the Balkans. Eden promised to bring up this topic with the prime minister the next morning and present my plan to him.

Then we touched upon Eden's forthcoming visit to the USA. He is going because he has not been to the USA since the beginning of the war. Besides, he said, it is very important to maintain contact with the American Government, particularly now that the end of the war is already visible on the horizon (though it won't happen tomorrow).

---

[17] Earlier in the day, Churchill had been diagnosed with acute pneumonia. He reluctantly submitted to the doctors' orders to stay in bed and reduce his workload to a minimum, after being told that the illness was called 'the old man's friend'. 'Why?' he had asked. 'Because it takes them off so quietly.'

... Eden has no luck with America! In 1938, soon after quitting the Chamberlain Government, he made a trip to the United States with his wife. He met all the notables there, starting with Roosevelt, but... he failed to make a good impression on the Americans. He failed to win their hearts.

On returning from Moscow at the end of 1941, Eden tried to arrange a visit to Washington, evidently in the interests of 'balance': he'd been to the Soviet Union, now... spend time in the United States as well. Even though Eden had long ago decided to place his stake on Anglo-Soviet relations, it was important for him as foreign secretary of Great Britain to maintain decent relations with the United States as well. However, though many of the preparations had been made, Eden failed to visit America last year, thanks mostly to sabotage on the part of Halifax (Halifax and Eden are, after all, 'great friends'!).

... We shall see what Eden's visit to America will bring. Will he be able to impress the Americans? Or, on the contrary, will the Americans succeed in influencing Eden? I don't know. The latter, I fear, is more likely: for all his merits, Eden is not a very strong person.

In our conversation today Eden said, among other things: 'I've just had lunch with a group of MPs. They asked me about the prospects for Anglo-Soviet relations in the post-war period. Could the Anglo-Soviet alliance become a reality? Do you know what I replied?'

'What?' I asked.

'I told the MPs,' Eden continued, 'that this depends almost entirely on the role England plays in Hitler's defeat. If her role is substantial – on land as well – then the alliance will become a reality. Otherwise, no guarantees can be given.'

'Quite right,' I responded.

'That's why I am so strongly in favour of the opening of a second front in France,' Eden concluded.

[Eden's positive demeanour is not to be found in his long report, though it seems more than likely that he and Maisky were again plotting behind their leaders' backs. Considering the altering strategic circumstances following the successes of the Red Army on the battlefield, Maisky hoped it might still be possible to reverse the strategic decisions taken in Casablanca, and thus pave the way to conducive political dialogue on post-war Europe. Such dialogue would obviously have vindicated his continued stay in London. He pleaded with Eden, far more forcefully than the diary suggests, to reconsider the postponement of the second front and the launching of Operation Husky.]

21 February

The past week on the front was simply brilliant: we took Rostov, Kharkov, Lozovaya, Krasnograd and Pavlograd. Our troops are reaching the Dnepr line. Zaporozhye and Dnepropetrovsk are the next objectives.

Churchill congratulated Stalin warmly on the capture of Rostov, and Stalin sent him a warm reply.

What are the prospects? It's difficult to say. I'm inclined to think that our advance will slow down a little. First, the season of bad roads is almost upon us. Second, the Germans must make every effort to avoid a second Stalingrad in the Donbas or, worse still, on the Dnepr (which may happen if we take the Dnepr line before the Germans evacuate their troops positioned east of the Dnepr). Third, our troops need to rest and regroup. A three-month winter offensive is not child's play. We shall see.

Today the British Government ceremoniously celebrated the 25th anniversary of the Red Army. A British Government, that is, headed by Churchill, that same Churchill who led the crusade against the Bolsheviks during the Civil War! How times change! History has turned full circle within a quarter of a century.

I attended the event at the Albert Hall. It was all very ceremonious, even majestic. An intricate and beautiful performance was staged. Some details might be criticized from the purely artistic point of view, but that hardly matters very much. On the whole, the spectacle was very, very *impressive*. Especially the episode where a gigantic hammer-and-sickle flag was raised above the stage while, against this background, there rose the figure of a Red Army soldier in uniform and with a rifle.

... Admiration for the Red Army in England is now unstinting. Everywhere – among the masses and in the army. To fight this wave would have been dangerous. So the Government has decided to stand at its head – that is, to ride the wave. It makes it easier to smooth any rough edges. Or even to draw political profit. Hence today's festivities.

One can't help recalling once again the English saying: if you can't beat them, join them. ...

24 February

Complacency and the wish to resume the norms and habits of peacetime, wherever possible, are growing in step with our victories, and are even overtaking them. The Court, of course, is no exception to the general tendency. There had been no receptions at the palace since July 1941, and that party was a very modest affair, with a small quantity of guests. We drank tea and talked about the Soviet–German war that had just begun. Now the palace has decided to arrange three parties (*tea parties*, as it would still be awkward to have a genuine *court* reception), each attended by approximately 300 guests. The first of the three parties was held today. Agniya and I were invited to the palace, together with the Bogomolovs and Kharlamovs.

I was summoned for a talk with the king. I began by thanking the king for his intention to present 'the sword of honour' to Stalingrad. Eden had told me that it was the king's own idea and I thought it would be a good thing to express my appreciation for the king's initiative. All the more so as the idea really appeals to me.

... Then the king asked me about the military situation, the condition of the German army, the internal situation in Germany, the probable line the Germans would try to hold, etc. Moving on to political matters, the king expressed satisfaction with the improvement in Anglo-Soviet relations and asked what, in my opinion, should be done to maintain close cooperation between our countries after the war.

I replied: 'The post-war future of Anglo-Soviet relations is currently being forged on the battlefield. We are conducting a common war against a common enemy. If both nations, the Soviet and the British, come out of this war confident that each has fulfilled its duty to the best of its ability, close alliance and mutual good feeling are guaranteed after the war. If either of the nations does not share this conviction, the outcome will be different. That is why it is so important to establish a second front. It is important from the military point of view, but it is also important from the political point of view.'

The king neither objected to nor approved my remarks. As always, he remained absolutely *noncommittal*. But I had expected nothing else.

26 February

Went to see Eden today. He did not go to the USA after all because of the prime minister's illness. Our talk was not particularly pleasant.

First, Eden told me that Churchill had decided to adhere after all to the military plans adopted in Casablanca. The morning after his evening conversation with me on the 17th, Eden conveyed my scheme to the prime minister. Churchill seemed interested and asked Eden to prepare a memorandum. Eden drafted the memorandum and Churchill passed it on to the general staff for consideration. The general staff presented its comments to the prime minister. Churchill thought over all the relevant details and reached the conclusion that my scheme was impractical. The main argument to this effect was that the troops wouldn't be able to arrive from North Africa to England in time for the cross-Channel operation. Churchill thinks therefore that operations in the Mediterranean (Sicily, Dodecanese, etc.) should be continued after the occupation of Tunisia and that heroic measures should be taken simultaneously – irrespective of the Mediterranean – to prepare the cross-Channel operation. Churchill is prepared to launch this operation even without the Americans, but will, of course, pull out all the stops in order to engage the Americans as early as possible. Eden imparted all this to me by way of preliminary information. Churchill wishes to see me as soon as he recovers and speak to me about it personally.

I don't like the sound of all this. Operations in Tunisia are dragging on because of the Americans' latest defeats and are hardly likely to be completed before April. So operations in the Mediterranean will begin no earlier than June or July. They won't be easy. They will probably drag on as well and I doubt they'll go smoothly. The British will have to concentrate their attention on the transfer of reinforcements to Sicily, the Dodecanese or wherever. Transport ships will be loaded with supplies to be carried thousands of miles from England. As for the cross-Channel operation, the British Government will delay it, size it up, postpone it. I know them only too well!... The English can't do anything quickly. And here they face so many additional obstacles!... What will come of the second front? When will the Red Army get real help at last? No, I don't like this situation one bit.

The second issue I discussed with Eden was Simon's speech in the House of Lords on 23 February. ... Simon was the last to speak on behalf of the British Government and delivered a nasty, truly 'Simonean' speech, the essence of which was: no second front is needed as the British fleet, the air attacks on Germany, the supplies to the USSR and the operations in North Africa already constitute that second front. ... Eden would not commit himself to anything, but promised to raise this matter with Churchill. It seemed to me he was not displeased by my démarche. Hardly surprising: there's no love lost between Eden and Simon!

Simon couldn't attend our reception on the 23rd as he was speaking in the Lords. He did, however, inform us an hour beforehand by telephone. Yesterday I also received a personal, handwritten letter from him in which he expresses his 'deep regret' at not being able to come, for he has a burning desire, don't you know, to express his admiration personally for 'the magnificent feats of the Red Army'. ... Simon! The real Simon! ...[18]

[Eden sympathized with the ideas raised by Maisky. Harvey, his private secretary, noted in his diary that 'a landing in France may be possible against diminished resistance this summer. Under the existing plan all our landing craft would be either wending their way beyond recall round the Cape or engaged in a big but not necessarily determining operation in Sicily.' Considering Churchill's resolve to pursue 'Husky', it is most unlikely that Eden exerted any serious pressure on him to revisit British strategy, beyond recycling a censored version of his talk with Maisky to the Defence Committee. The committee, however, decided to defer the matter until Churchill recovered from his

---

[18] Maisky intimated that Simon's speech was a terrible blow to Moscow and 'had undone all the good of last Sunday's Red Army demonstrations'.

illness. Restive, Churchill quashed the idea at its incipience, instructing the committee from his sick bed: 'There can be no change of plan. I am going to telegraph to M. Stalin in a few days.' In his talks with Hopkins in Washington a month later, Eden alluded approvingly to Maisky's most detailed survey of post-war Europe, which apparently was unfolded during the meeting on 26 February. Eden's only reservation concerned Maisky's opposition to his own vision of federated Europe, an arrangement which Maisky referred to as 'vegetarian – meaning, presumably, innocuous'. Surely the wish to muzzle Soviet criticism and tie British hands accounts for the pressure exerted by Churchill on Eisenhower on 17 February to bring forward Operation Husky through swift conclusion of the campaign in Tunisia.]

26 February

Kerr, having returned to Moscow, has started to display almost feverish levels of activity.[19] On 20 February he paid a visit to Molotov and declared that he was going to engage him in a series of discussions on post-war matters, since the British Government considers it absolutely essential to reach agreement on these matters with the USA and the USSR before the end of the war. ... Kerr then asked Molotov to explain to him the meaning of Stalin's statement, in his address of 6 November 1942, that the USSR is not planning to destroy the German state and the German military. These comments caused bewilderment in London. They seemed to contradict what Stalin told Eden in December 1941.

Molotov evaded Kerr's questions and told him that Stalin would be better placed to reply. Kerr clothed his questions in the form of a letter. On 24 February Stalin received him and gave him a written reply, the essence of which was that there was no point engaging in general non-binding talks on post-war matters, and that it would be far more expedient for official representatives of the two states to meet, discuss these matters and sign a binding agreement on behalf of the two states. This is precisely the method Stalin proposed to Eden in December 1941, but Eden would not commit himself. If the British Government now deems it necessary to arrange such a meeting and to conclude an agreement with the USSR concerning the fate of Germany or other states, we are prepared to play our part.

27 February

Agniya and I attended a football match between England and Wales at Wembley. There were 75,000 people at the stadium. It was a splendid day:

---

[19] This was a bad omen for Maisky. Stalin, who got on well with Kerr, preferred henceforth to conduct negotiations directly through him in Moscow, leaving Maisky in the lurch until his recall.

68. A soft spot for the prime minister's wife Clementine.

sunny and cloudless. We sat in the Royal Box together with the king, the queen, Mrs Churchill, Alexander, Attlee, Morrison, Leathers and other ministers. Tremendous *excitement*. Not for me, of course (I'm always calm on such occasions), but among this gigantic mass of people. The result: England beat Wales 5-3. Had it not been for the regular flow of *Spitfires* guarding the stadium, it would have seemed just like peacetime. Yes, *complacency* is rapidly growing in England in parallel with our victories, and even outpaces them.

Mrs Churchill sat next to me. She is a very pleasant woman and we get along well. Mrs Churchill sometimes talks with me openly on various personal and family themes. Today she shared with me her fears and hopes concerning her husband's health. Churchill fell ill about a fortnight ago. It was only a mild form of pneumonia, but he had a fever. He is a terrible patient. He ignores what the doctors tell him. He refuses to rest. He thinks constantly about various governmental matters. He works. He worked even with a high fever. Now he feels better. His temperature is back to normal. The pneumonia has passed. But the prime minister's bedroom is dark and sunless. Mrs Churchill wants to take her husband to Chequers at the beginning of next week – for the fresh air and sunlight. He'll recover more speedily there and have a rest.

Mrs Churchill said all this quickly, hastily, swallowing her words and laughing infectiously. She always talks like that. Then she thought for a moment and uttered with deep confidence: 'He must get better! Nothing will happen to him: he is destined to lead his country in such times!'

I thought to myself: 'Not bad!'

Mrs Churchill added with a note of bitterness: 'It's a pity the war should have happened now, when he is already 68. It would have been better had he been a bit younger. Well, it can't be helped.'

Yes, this woman believes in fate. There you have it, the bourgeois society of today!

I turned to Mrs Churchill and said: 'Some five or six years ago, long before the war, a friend of mine from Moscow asked me whether your husband had any chance of gaining power. Do you know what I told him?'

'What?' Mrs Churchill asked with the greatest interest.

'I told him: in ordinary circumstances – no, for the mediocrities in the Conservative Party would never let him come to power. They'd be afraid lest he hindered and squashed them. But in a moment of great danger for the country, Churchill would undoubtedly take the reins.'

Mrs Churchill exclaimed with fervour: 'How remarkable! I had exactly the same thoughts. I was always telling my husband: you will be in power when war breaks out.'

She paused and added: 'He was born for it, after all!.. But what a pity he is already 68 years old!' ...

3 March

That was an original way to spend an evening.

The Crippses invited us a while ago to dine with them and then listen to the music of Myra Hess.[20] We arranged to meet this evening. We met them at a French restaurant on *Charlotte Street*. Cripps's daughter, who accompanied her father to Moscow, then worked at the British mission in Tehran, and now has a job at the Ministry of Information, came along too.

We had hardly sat down to dinner than the sirens began to wail. A rare event nowadays! It will soon be two years since the air raids on London ceased. Today was a special occasion: on the night from the 1st to the 2nd March, 700 four-engine English bombers raided Berlin and obviously did a great deal of damage. Göring, of course, could not remain indifferent and this evening 40 German bombers made a 'retaliatory' raid. Forty! Only forty!... Such is the extent to which the Germans have weakened (although if it came to it they could still

69. Attending one of Myra Hess's famous wartime concerts at the National Gallery.

---

[20] Dame (Julia) Myra Hess, British pianist who organized and performed in a series of daily chamber music concerts at the National Gallery in London during the Blitz and throughout the war. Her concerts were attended by over three-quarters of a million people.

muster 100–150 machines for a sortie on London in a single night). Only a few of these 40 'Germans' reached London. The effect of the attack, of course, was negligible. But the antiaircraft barrage from the ground was astonishing. Not at all what it was like in those memorable days of the 'big Blitz' of 1940. It was the barrage fire that kept us in the restaurant until nearly ten o'clock.

But we made our way to Myra Hess's place nonetheless. I liked her apartment very much: two grand pianos, bookcases with a huge musical library, simple but somehow intelligent furniture, portraits of great performers and composers, a fine statuette of Beethoven on the table... All exuding high culture, the peaks of the human spirit...

Myra played us Beethoven's 'Appassionata'. A wonderful interpretation!

I told Myra Hess that this was Ilyich's[21] favourite piece. Myra was greatly impressed by this fact, and the Crippses even more so.

4 March

The Poles are behaving quite idiotically. Not long ago the Polish Government and the Polish 'National Council' adopted an official resolution, later made public, stating that they stand firmly by the basis of the 1939 borders. We responded with a sharp TASS communiqué. ... I think the exchange of pleasantries may end with that, unless the Poles concoct further provocations. I think it would be inexpedient to take it further: why add grist to Goebbels' mill? He is already doing all he can to foment discord in our coalition.

The Poles are a peculiar nation! Throughout their history they have vividly demonstrated a total lack of talent for serious state building (in foreign and domestic policy). ... It is difficult to escape the conclusion that Poland is generally incapable of prolonged and sustained existence as a fully independent and sovereign national organism. The fate of Poland in the period between the two wars and the conduct of Sikorski & Co. in the last 20 months are perfect illustrations of this. Well, we shall see what the future has in store. One thing is already clear: the Polish question will be one of the hardest 'nuts' to crack at the end of the war. ...

9 March

On 6 March the rank of Marshal of the Soviet Union was conferred on Stalin. Excellent. He fully deserves this, the highest military honour – more than anybody else not just in our time, but throughout the long history of our country.

---

[21] Lenin.

What rare happiness has come the way of the Soviet people: to have had two such leaders as Lenin and Stalin over the course of the last 25 years, the most decisive period in our development and that of humanity in general! This is yet further proof of the untapped reserves of talent and energy that lie concealed in the midst of our people. Our people will, without doubt, play a very great role in the destiny of humanity.

11 March

Eden flew off to America today. He plans to be away for 3–4 weeks. We'll have to manage without him. This is somewhat unfortunate: we have established good relations and he tells me a lot. We have also learned to catch one another's drift. This makes our work easier. Still, it can't be helped. I'll have to adjust to the situation.

Yesterday I had a talk with Eden before his departure. An interesting talk.

'Well, what farewell wishes do you have for me?' Eden asked when I had made myself comfortable in the chair opposite him.

'What wishes do I have?' I echoed. 'One wish above all others: don't commit yourself in the USA to any issue which concerns us as well. If you bind yourself with obligations in Washington, you might find yourself in a difficult position with respect to us afterwards... This happened, for instance, during your visit to Moscow in December 1941.'

'You may rest assured in this regard,' Eden said with confidence. 'I won't undertake any obligations in America. We have an alliance with you. We must reach an agreement with you first before arranging tripartite negotiations.'

... Conversation then turned to the main European problems. Before leaving for America, Eden wanted to run over our views on these matters in their general outline. ... The first question concerned Germany. What should its future be after our collective victory?

This was straightforward enough. We recalled the Moscow talks on this matter (December 1941) and further statements made by Stalin and other Soviet representatives. The final conclusion was: Germany must be weakened for a long time after the war to prevent her from even dreaming of any fresh act of aggression. The means for that are disarmament, partition (perhaps in the form of a federation of several German states), and various economic measures, including reparations in kind. Eden fully agreed with this conclusion.

The second question related to Poland. What would its future be? What should be done with it?

'I won't hazard any guesses on this,' I said, 'but one thing at least is already clear to me now: Western Ukraine and Western Belorussia will become part of the Soviet Union. It is out of the question that they might fall under Polish rule again. The British Government, as it happens, is essentially of the same opinion: the Curzon Line generally corresponds to our 1941 borders.'

'But you, it seems, demand more than the Curzon Line – Lvov for instance,' Eden warily retorted.

'Yes, we demand Lvov because it is a Ukrainian, not a Polish city,' I answered. 'However, Lvov is just a minor deviation from the Curzon Line, while we accept the Curzon Line only "in general". ... There is scope for agreement here.' ... Eden hastened to change the topic and expressed his concern for the future of Poland. I shared his anxiety. I said that the future of post-war Poland was genuinely unclear to me. Eden knows our opinion on this matter. I stated it plainly at the very beginning of our talks about a mutual assistance pact with the Poles in 1941. We stand for an independent and free Poland, but within its ethnographic boundaries. We shall willingly help such a Poland; we shall be able to maintain friendly relations with it. We do not intend to interfere in Poland's internal affairs. Let them arrange things as they wish. And as Eden also knows, we are not against bringing East Prussia into the future Poland – with an exchange of population. Once again, that is, we are talking about Poland within its ethnographic boundaries.

'The trouble,' I continued, 'is that the Polish Government in London has quite different ideas... It is full of imperialist ambitions!.. This is very much in the spirit of Polish history down the ages. The Poles have never been able to create a stable and systematically developing state. Why? The reason is clear. The essence of statesmanlike wisdom consists in setting yourself political goals commensurate with the resources and means you have available. The Poles have never acted in accordance with this principle. On the contrary: they have nearly always been chasing the unattainable. To quote a Russian proverb, they've had one kopeck of ammunition for every rouble of ambition. It's enough to recall their attempt at conquering Russia in the seventeenth century. How absurd!... As a result, the Poles have never managed to build a strong and viable state.'

Eden interrupted me: 'There is much truth in what you say. You remember Bismarck's words: "Politics is the art of the possible"?'

'Quite right,' I agreed, 'but does the London Polish Government understand this? No, it does not. Otherwise it would not pursue such an absurd line. It is patently clear that the USSR will be the decisive force in Eastern Europe after the war, so what sense is there in the Polish Government quarrelling with the USSR?'

... From Poland we moved on to the Baltic states.

'When talking with the Americans,' I said, 'let them understand that it's high time to drop all those *monkey tricks* concerning the Baltic question. The fate of the Baltic states has been decided for us once and for all. This question, as far as we are concerned, is simply not up for discussion. If the Americans pose it all the same, nothing will come of it except *bad blood* between the USA and the USSR. Who needs that? The Baltic states will remain part of the USSR whatever happens.'

Eden replied that for him personally the Baltic question had been resolved. He will sound out the Americans' attitudes to this issue during his visit. Then Eden asked: 'And what about Finland?'

I replied that Eden was well acquainted with our point of view from our correspondence and negotiations. We want to reinstate the terms of the Soviet–Finnish peace agreement of 1940, plus Petsamo, plus a mutual assistance pact. We can't accept any less than that. The threat to our state from Finland must be eliminated once and for all. It's our duty towards future generations.

Eden neither objected nor agreed. His attitude, it seemed to me, could be summed up as follows: 'As you like, just so long as it doesn't lead to any complications with the Americans.'

... 'In conclusion,' I said, 'may I ask you to let the Americans understand that the worst way of improving relations between the USA and the USSR is fatherly back-slapping. ... There is a school of thought in America ... which asserts that the twentieth century will be the "American century". I find such slogans to be mistaken in general. Yet, if we have to speak in these terms, I think one would be more justified in saying that the twentieth century will be the "Russian century".'

'Why do you think so?' Eden asked with interest.

'For the following reasons,' I answered. 'If you try to imagine the general, major vectors of historical processes, then what is happening in the world today? It is quite obvious that the era of capitalist civilization is giving way to that of socialist civilization. This began in 1917. I don't know how much time the process of change will take, but there can be no doubt about its basic line. What will the world look like, say, in the twenty-first century? It will, of course, be a socialist world. So the twentieth century will, by all appearances, prove to be a century of transition from capitalism to socialism. It becomes quite clear, from a broad historical perspective, that the USSR represents the rising sun, and the USA the setting sun, a fact which does not exclude the possibility of the relatively lengthy continued existence of the USA as a mighty capitalist power.'

... I don't know whether Eden understood me or not, or whether I succeeded in convincing him with my arguments, but one thing was certain: my thoughts interested him deeply and gave him food for his own reflections.

... Eden smiled and said: 'There is much that is interesting and perhaps correct in what you say... Now, if the USA is a setting sun, then what do we, Britain, represent?'

'You?' I said. 'You, as always, are trying to find a middle course of compromise between two extremes. Will you find it? I don't know. That is your concern.

To judge by the response to Beveridge's[22] report, you still don't quite comprehend the meaning of the radical historical changes which our age is fraught with.'

Eden told me on parting: 'I'm truly grateful to you for this conversation. It will help me a great deal with my talks in America and in general...'

'I wish you every success!' I replied.

We shall see what will come of it. To be sure, Eden has many good intentions and I have no reason to question his sincerity with regard to the Anglo-Soviet alliance. But he is not a very strong or firm man, and I'm rather afraid that the American surroundings may have a negative influence on him. That is why it seemed like a good idea to strengthen Eden's 'backbone' a little before his departure. In essence, I did not tell him anything new. I had articulated the same thoughts to him, piece by piece, many times before on this or that issue. However, repetition (especially in a more comprehensive and finished form) can sometimes prove helpful, if the moment is right. This seemed to be the right moment.

[Maisky's report to Molotov was rather laconic, insisting that he was only a listener – 'at no time did I engage in conversation'. Eden's official report of the meeting dovetails with Maisky's diary entry, though Eden appears to have been entirely passive, while Maisky does all the talking. In his memoirs, Eden reduced the report to a skeleton, removing any trace of his compliance with the gist of Maisky's ideas. However, while in Washington Eden told Sumner Welles that 'Mr Maisky had called upon him and had given him in complete detail the position of the Soviet Union.' Eden recapitulated the position in minute detail, adding that, although he was not coming to Washington as 'Russian Ambassador', he believed that 'the views expressed to him by Mr Maisky could be of value to us'. In his memoirs, over which the Cold War cast a cloud, Eden preferred to dissociate himself from those ideas, concluding with a brief judgemental sentence: 'Most of this was stubbornly negative.' On this occasion, Maisky's *modus operandi* worked to perfection. Eden, on his return to London, described to Maisky in detail the negotiations in Washington and the president's adherence to most of the ideas which, unbeknownst to Moscow, had in fact originated with Maisky himself. Stalin and Molotov displayed great interest in them, allowing Maisky to formulate them at the great length of a 23-page telegram on the possibility of creating a common political platform on post-war Europe. However, the crisis over the Katyn massacre which erupted a couple of days later shuffled the cards and, following the Soviet triumph in the battle of Kursk, the negotiations resumed in Moscow in a completely different atmosphere when the foreign ministers met in the autumn. By then Maisky had already been recalled.

---

[22] William Henry Beveridge, economist and social reformer. His report on Britain's social services focused on unemployment, health care and poverty and eventually became the blueprint for the 'welfare state' legislation of 1944 to 1948.

While progress was achieved on the political front, the differences on strategy remained unresolved. On the day Eden met Maisky, Churchill, who was convalescing, responded to Stalin's queries concerning the strategic plans for 1943 formulated in Casablanca. Although it was 'the earnest wish' of the president and himself to see the troops in battle in Europe, he regretted that the need to sustain the campaign in North Africa had cut supplies to Britain 'to the bone', and the second front could be mounted only if Germany weakened sufficiently. He reserved for himself the 'freedom of decision' nearer the summer.

The attitude towards Russia in London was clearly fluctuating. The enthusiasm for a second front receded considerably after the British victories in the desert war – certainly among diehard Conservatives in Parliament. Prominent among these, Sir Cuthbert Headlam complained in his diary that the Russians were refusing to admit that the North African campaign was 'clearly becoming "a second front" for Hitler'; 'I see that that little swine Maisky is still suggesting that we are not doing all we can to help his people – I distrust this man greatly: from all I hear of him he is a real danger in this country politically.' Roosevelt, too, was getting impatient with Litvinov's 'second front zeal'. He asked Harriman to call him to order 'even to the point of saying we might ask for his recall'.]

14 March (Bovingdon)

The situation on the front has worsened in the past week.

On the one hand, we have further successes in the centre: we took Vyazma and continue to advance westward. In recent weeks the Germans have lost three important 'hedgehogs': Rzhev, Gzhatsk and Vyazma. The road to Smolensk grows ever wider.

But on the other hand, the Germans had a number of major successes in the south: they have not only checked our progress towards the Dnepr but have even pressed us back considerably in the Donbas and at Kharkov. We evacuated Pavlograd, Krasnograd, Krasnoarmeisk, Kramatorsk, Barvenkovo and other centres. The Germans have reached the Donets again, but have failed to cross it as yet. The Germans have also broken through to Kharkov and are fighting on the approaches to the city and, if the Germans are to be believed, inside the city, too.

... Such is life: war is a good teacher. And the present failure will certainly prove a good lesson for us. But it is unpleasant all the same. And another thing: anger towards the English and the Americans grows all the while. Had they opened a second front, the whole situation would be different.

16 March

Today I handed Churchill the message from Stalin concerning the American offer of mediation between the USSR and Finland.

Churchill's reaction was quick and spontaneous. 'This is entirely your own business,' he exclaimed. 'Finland did not attack either us or the Americans. Finland attacked you. So, it is for you to decide when and how to conclude peace with her.' ... 'At any rate,' Churchill concluded, 'I don't see why you should have to pay a high price for peace with Finland. The war situation is such that it is not you who should be courting Finland, but Finland who should be courting you. If the Finns want peace, they must address you themselves.'

In connection with Finland, Churchill recalled the Baltic states. With a sly twinkle in his eye, he muttered: 'Once your troops occupy the Baltics, the whole matter will be resolved.'

Churchill has just one piece of advice to give us to 'soften the hearts' of the Americans: allow those Baltic people who do not want to live in the USSR to emigrate with all their belongings.

I shook my head in reply and said that as far as we were concerned the Baltic question had been decided once and for all. To myself I thought: 'But it is worth remembering his advice. Maybe it will come in handy one day.'

We moved on to the topic of Tunisia. I was dumbfounded to learn from Churchill that the Anglo-American troops will evidently need a further 60–70 days to complete their operations. That means dragging things out until mid-May! Disgusting! Churchill hastened to console me with the news that the Sicilian operation would be carried out a month earlier, in June. As for the cross-Channel operation, the plans have not changed: it will take place in August at the earliest. Churchill blames the Americans: they're not sending their divisions to Europe. When you ask why, the reply is always the same: *shipping*. ... I could not agree with Churchill. We argued at length. Churchill, however, stuck to his guns. Bad. ...

29 March

Went to see Churchill. On instructions from Moscow, I informed him of our reply to the Americans on the question of Finland. Molotov gave Standley[23] to understand that he has little faith in the possibility of concluding a separate peace with Finland now on terms acceptable to us. However, in view of the interest displayed by the American Government in this matter, he was ready to formulate for their information our minimum conditions for a separate peace.

... When we had exhausted the Finnish question, I asked Churchill why the March convoy has been delayed. The ships were loaded five days ago, but still no progress.

---

[23] Admiral William Harrison Standley, chief of naval operations, 1933–37; US ambassador to the Soviet Union, 1941–43.

Churchill suddenly frowned and became gloomy.

'There are some complications with the convoy,' said the prime minister.

'Nothing serious, I hope?' I asked, anticipating bad news.

'I can't tell you anything today,' Churchill answered sullenly. 'I'll inform you of the final decision tomorrow. I'm waiting for a reply from Roosevelt.'

I made another attempt to find out what the matter was, but Churchill was unbending.

Well, I'll have to wait till tomorrow. But I don't like this one bit. I fear things will go badly with the convoys.

30 March

Alas, my fears have materialized, and in an even worse form than I had expected.

This evening Cadogan invited me to the Foreign Office and handed me a copy of Churchill's message to Stalin, which was sent to Moscow in the morning. It notifies Stalin that in view of the concentration of large surface ships in Narvik (the *Tirpitz, Scharnhorst, Lutzow* and others) the British Government deems it impossible to send the next convoy to the north; that in view of the forthcoming operations in the Mediterranean it will not be able to send any convoys to Arkhangelsk and Murmansk from May onwards; and that the convoys may be resumed no earlier than in September, provided the disposition of German naval forces and the state of the sea war in the Atlantic permit this.

Very bad. This will be a heavy blow to our people in Moscow. Especially at such a critical moment – on the eve of Germany's spring offensive.

[At Maisky's instigation, the Soviet Government chose this moment to decorate members of the Royal Navy and Merchant Navy for valour and courage shown in sailing the Arctic convoys in appalling conditions. Maisky used the occasion, on which Admiral Pound and other dignitaries were present, to state that it was not only 'an expression of gratitude for past services' but also 'an encouragement to the services of the future'. The Soviet people were expecting that 'in the military campaigns of this year the Western Allies will pull their full weight in the common struggle against our common enemy'.]

31 March

I went to see Churchill again today.

First, I had to deliver Stalin's message, which arrived yesterday. Secondly, I thought it necessary to have a serious talk with him about the convoys.

Churchill met me looking gloomy and beetle-browed. He probably thought I was bringing with me Stalin's reply to yesterday's message concerning the convoys and was expecting something unpleasant. I handed him the envelope. He slowly pulled out the sheet of paper, slowly put on his glasses and slowly began to read. Suddenly the PM's face brightened up. No wonder! Stalin was congratulating Churchill on the successes in Tunisia, expressing his hope that the British mechanized troops would give the retreating enemy vigorous chase, allowing him no respite.

Churchill jumped up from his chair, walked around the long table at which the Cabinet held its meetings, and walked up to the map hanging on the wall. There he began describing to me with fervour and great expressiveness his strategic plan: in about two weeks' time the Germans and Italians would be pressed into the north-eastern corner of Tunisia within a radius of 50 miles from Bizerte, showered with bombs from the air and cut off from the sea by the British fleet.

'It's not enough to drive the enemy out of Tunisia,' Churchill exclaimed. 'The enemy must be annihilated! This must be our Stalingrad!'

I listened to him and thought: 'We shall see. How many times have Churchill's sweeping declarations been frustrated by reality!'

Churchill then returned to his place and continued to read the message, where Stalin informed him that the previous evening he had watched the film *Desert Victory*, which Churchill had sent him. Stalin liked the film very much. And that wasn't all. Stalin wrote that the film superbly portrays how Britain fights while at the same time exposing those 'rascals (there are some in our country too) who claim that Britain does not fight at all but remains on the side-lines'. In conclusion, Stalin informed Churchill that *Desert Victory* would be widely shown to the Red Army at the front and to the masses at home.

I carefully observed Churchill's expression. When he got to the phrase about 'rascals', something strange happened to him. The prime minister's face was convulsed by a spasm, he shut his eyes for a moment, and when he opened them I could see tears. Churchill was so excited that he couldn't remain in his seat. He jumped up from his chair again, walked to the fireplace and exclaimed with feeling: 'The deepest thanks to Stalin!... You have never brought me such a wonderful message before.'

Was all this genuine? Or was it an act? There was a bit of both, it seems to me, in Churchill's behaviour. The phrase about 'rascals' must have touched the prime minister deeply. He must have perceived in it longed-for recognition of his war efforts of these past three years. And from whose lips?... From Stalin's! This could and must have moved Churchill deeply and brought tears to his eyes. The prime minister has an emotional-artistic temperament. Sudden bursts of feeling overwhelm him like inspiration overwhelms a poet. At such moments Churchill somewhat loses control of himself and is capable of giving promises which later, when he is in a more normal and sober mood, he fails to fulfil. But Churchill is also an actor. During his years in opposition he memorized his speeches to Parliament in front of a mirror. That is why at certain moments Churchill, like a good actor, gives vent to his emotional temperament and does not prevent genuine tears from watering his eyes.

Having regained control of himself, Churchill lavished praise on *Stalingrad*, which I had sent to him a few days ago on Stalin's instructions.

... I spoke about Churchill's message of 30 March and said that it had left me simply astounded. After all, what does it mean? That there will definitely be no convoys until September. And I doubt that the convoys will be resumed even then, for there are too many tricky and elastic 'ifs' concerning their resumption. It would seem that the convoys are effectively being suspended until darkness sets in once more, i.e. November–December. This means that for the next eight or nine months we shouldn't count on receiving remotely sufficient supplies. We can't accept this situation at all.

'And what effect,' I continued, 'will it have on the mood of the Red Army and among the population at large?... Put yourself in their shoes. This is the third summer that they are waiting for a second front from their Western Allies. Will there be a second front now or won't there?... You know better than I do. My personal impression is that nothing definite can be said – maybe there will, maybe there won't. And that is the best that can be said today about the opening of a second front...'

... 'Yes, I know,' he exclaimed, 'that this is a heavy blow for you... It's terrible! I fear that the cessation of convoys will have a serious impact on our relations...'

Tears once again appeared in his eyes. He stood up and began pacing the room in agitation.

'But what could I do?'... Churchill continued with great emotion. 'I had no alternative!... Please understand, I have no right to jeopardize the entire course of the war, not even for the sake of your supplies!... I can't do it! I can't!... It seems strange, but our entire naval supremacy is based on the availability of a handful of first-class combat units. Your people may not understand this, but your Government must!'

Churchill made another round of the room and added: 'I considered it my duty to tell Stalin the whole truth. You mustn't deceive an ally. Stalin should know the real situation. One should face even the most unpleasant news with courage. And Stalin is a man of courage.'

... Before I had uttered a word, Churchill came up very close to me and looking straight into my eyes asked hurriedly: 'Tell me honestly, what do you personally think about this situation?... Will it mean a split with Stalin or won't it?'

'I don't deem it possible to speak for Stalin,' I replied. 'He will speak for himself. I know one thing for sure, though: your decision will arouse very strong feelings in Stalin.'

Churchill moved away from me a little. His disappointment was obvious. He sighed, walked round the table once again, and said quickly: 'Anything but a split! I don't want a split. I don't! I want to work with Stalin, and I feel that I can work with him!... If I'm destined to live longer, I can be very useful to you... In settling your relations with America. That is very important. It is exceptionally important. Whatever happens, we, the three great powers – the USSR, the USA and Great Britain – should maintain our friendship and work together after the war. Otherwise the world will perish.

2 April

... Today I handed Churchill Stalin's reply to his message concerning the cessation of convoys (of 30 March). Considering the general situation, I had imagined that Stalin's reply might not be especially sharp, but it turned out to be far milder than I had expected. Stalin acted most wisely: he expressed neither indignation nor irritation. He merely noted the decision by Roosevelt and Churchill to suspend the convoys and pointed out that such a decision could not but affect the position of Soviet troops in the forthcoming summer campaign.

Churchill was staggered by this. He had been very gloomy and tense when I arrived. I could feel that he was expecting a sharp, abusive response. He put on his glasses and slowly, reluctantly unfolded the message, as if trying to postpone the moment when he would have to swallow the bitter pill. And then this!

He could not remain seated. He leapt out of his armchair in a state of extreme excitement and started rapidly pacing the room.

'Tell Stalin,' Churchill finally said, continuing to pace out the distance around the Cabinet table, 'that this is a magnanimous and courageous reply. He has simply crushed me with his response. Such a reply makes me feel doubly obliged to do absolutely all that is humanly possible to compensate him. I'll be working like a horse! And I'll find some solutions.'

Churchill made two more tours of the table, then spoke again: 'With this response Stalin has shown once again how great and wise a man he is. ... I want to work with him without fail! When the war ends I'll spare no effort to help Russia heal its wounds as quickly as possible... We shall also help the world get to its feet as quickly as possible... Stalin *is a man of great size*, Roosevelt *is also a man of great size*... Yes, the three of us can achieve much!'

11 April (Bovingdon)

... Matters seem to be reaching a conclusion in Tunisia. Yesterday the British captured Sfax. The Anglo-American-French troops are approaching Kairouan and Bizerte. Tunis is not far off. It's time! High time! Tunisia has been a great disappointment. Its capture was supposed to be a matter of some 2–3 weeks, but the fighting has dragged on for five months! So much valuable time has been lost! And as a result so many strategic opportunities have been missed! Even though the end there is near, I look ahead without any great enthusiasm. I don't see any prospect of a real second front in 1943, not at any rate this spring or summer, when it will be most needed.

[Maisky's well-informed 'guess' was right. As he was making his way back to London from Bovingdon, the chiefs of staff were impressing on an ostensibly surprised Churchill that the transfer to North Africa of landing craft (indispensable for executing Operation Husky and exploiting its success for an operation in Italy) excluded the possibility of launching a cross-Channel attack in 1943. 'We must recognize,' Churchill insisted, 'that no important Cross-Channel enterprise is possible this year.' Although he continued to sanction the build-up of troops in Britain for a 1944 operation, he remained aloof and made its execution conditional on the existence of circumstances which might allow 'taking advantage of any collapse on the part of the enemy'. He specifically noted that he wished Stalin not to be informed of the decision.]

20 April

Moscow displayed great interest in Eden's reports about his conversations in America. They asked me to convey to Eden the gratitude of the Soviet Government for his information, and I was asked to prepare a detailed record of the talks. ...

23 April

Stalin's message arrived before lunch. It concerns Poland. Stalin informed Churchill that in view of the entirely abnormal relations between the USSR and Poland, an abnormality caused by the conduct of the Polish Government, and in particular by its stance in connection with the recent German provocation (the 'discovery' of the bodies of 10,000 Polish officers near Smolensk), the Soviet Government has been compelled to 'break off' relations with Sikorski's Government. The message further expressed the conviction that an agreement on this matter exists between Sikorski's and Hitler's governments: the campaign about the 'discovery' of the bodies began concurrently in the German and

Polish press. Stalin expressed his hope that the British Government would understand the inevitability of such a move, which was imposed on the Soviet Government by the political line pursued by Sikorski's Government. Stalin sent a similar message to Roosevelt.[24]

Today is 'Good Friday', and it immediately occurred to me that the prime minister was probably out of town. I called his secretary myself. I was quite right: yesterday evening Churchill went to spend Easter at his small country estate Chartwell (30 miles south of London). I had to choose: either to go to Chartwell myself or to forward the message via the prime minister's secretariat. Considering the importance of the matter, I chose the first. The secretary called Churchill and told me the prime minister would expect me for dinner in Chartwell and would send a car for me.

I left the embassy at around 7 p.m., and by 8 p.m. I was already there. Although the car was from the PM's garage and an army driver was at the wheel, we were stopped at the entrance to the estate by military guards. Several fully armed young soldiers shouted 'Halt!', manifesting great zeal and even pointing their bayonets at us. I couldn't help smiling to myself. Later Churchill said with a chuckle: 'I don't need them (the soldiers), but the War Office insists...'

He waved his hand, as if to say: 'Let them amuse themselves. I couldn't care less.'

The main building at Churchill's country estate, where he lived in the years before the war and where I visited him more than once, was closed. Only a small wing near to the main building remained inhabited. Churchill had built it himself (he is a mason, after all!) on the site of the old stables. I remember Churchill proudly showing me his creation (in 1938, if I am not mistaken). Then it served him as his study and studio for painting (for Churchill is also an artist!). Now it houses Churchill's main apartment, where he stays when he occasionally visits his estate.

I was met by one of Churchill's secretaries, who immediately offered me a glass of sherry.

'The prime minister is changing,' the secretary said. 'He will be back soon.'

I couldn't help wondering: 'Has the process of "normalization" really reached the point of Churchill wearing black tie for dinner?'

I asked the secretary whether there was anyone else at home besides the prime minister. The secretary said that Mrs Churchill was at the seaside and the daughters in London. However, Bracken had come to spend the weekend with the prime minister.

---

[24] Stalin's behaviour throughout the crisis was chillingly cynical. The Soviet cover-up of the 1940 massacres persisted unabated until 1990. Beria's proposal that the interned Polish officers should be executed without trial was approved by the Politburo on 5 March 1940.

'The minister of information is taking a bath,' smiled the secretary. 'He too will be down soon.'

As if in confirmation of this, I heard the sound of water draining from a bathtub somewhere close behind the wall.

'And here is the prime minister!' the secretary suddenly exclaimed, rising from his seat and walking towards the door.

In walked Churchill. My fears proved mistaken! The prime minister was wearing his habitual *siren suit*. He greeted me heartily with a firm handshake.

The secretary left and I presented Churchill with Stalin's message. He began reading it, and the further he read the darker his face became. Bracken entered the room just when Churchill had finished reading. ... The minister of information was in a dinner jacket! What the devil!

Churchill passed the message to Bracken without a murmur and then, turning to me, asked: 'What does it mean: breaking off relations?'

I replied that it meant the breaking off of relations *de facto*, without any public statements and without any official documents being handed to the Polish Government. Those, at least, were the instructions we had received here in London. For now. As for the future, I had no idea. Much would depend on the conduct of the Polish Government.

'It is necessary at any rate to take steps to prevent the decision taken by the Soviet Government being publicized,' Churchill continued. 'Publicity would be most unfortunate. Only the Germans would stand to gain by it.'

... At that moment the butler entered the room and announced that dinner was served. We dined in a small room at a small table. There were five of us (Churchill, Bracken, myself, the secretary and the housekeeper) and I can't say there was much space around the table. The menu was almost Spartan: milk soup (edible!), a piece of fried salmon and a bit of asparagus from Churchill's 'own plots'. Afterwards we drank coffee and smoked. Churchill, of course, sucked at his habitual cigar.

During dinner the secretary reported to Churchill that his order had been carried out, and the content of the message had been conveyed to Eden by telephone.

'Eden is very *upset!*' the secretary added.

When dinner was over, the housekeeper and secretary left. The three of us remained, Churchill, Bracken and I. We resumed our conversation about the message.

Churchill said he had just finished writing his message to Stalin today – on the same Polish question! Had I not come, he would have sent it tonight. Now, in the light of Stalin's message, Churchill deemed it necessary to amend his own, or perhaps to write a new one. The prime minister rang his secretary and asked him to bring the text of the unsent document. He gave it to me, saying half-jokingly: 'There you are, if you wish read it. But then forget all about it, for this message no longer exists.'

I laughed, took the message from Churchill and quickly ran my eyes over it. Churchill informed Stalin that the worsening of Polish–Soviet relations which had recently been observed was a great worry to the British Government; that a series of measures undertaken by the Soviet Government (the closure of the Polish aid organization in the USSR, the declaration that all Poles who find themselves in the USSR are Soviet citizens, the refusal to let out the families of Polish soldiers evacuated from the USSR, etc.) causes great distress among Polish units in the Middle East; that while Polish émigrés in Britain and the USA did undoubtedly conduct themselves in a provocative manner, it would be desirable in the interests of the unity of the Allied front to improve Polish–Soviet relations, to which end it would be good to allow the families of the Polish soldiers stationed in the Middle East, as well as the 40,000 Poles fit for military service who are still in the USSR, to leave the Soviet Union.

'A good thing you haven't sent this document,' I remarked, summing up my impression of Churchill's message. 'It would have met with ill-feeling in Moscow.'

'Why?' Churchill asked.

'Simply because the thread running throughout the message is that it is the Soviet side which is most to blame for the deterioration of Polish–Soviet relations. Meanwhile, reality suggests the exact opposite.'

... I then touched upon the Polish Government's conduct in connection with Goebbels' latest provocation and noted that it has exceeded all bounds. The Soviet Government is aware of the significance of maintaining unity among the Allies no less than the British Government. In view of this, the Soviet Government has been demonstrating exceptional patience for more than a year with respect to the Polish Government and Polish émigrés. But there is a limit to everything. This limit has been reached, and the Soviet Government has been forced to react sharply.

Churchill asked Bracken to tell him the particulars of the recent affair. When Bracken mentioned the Polish–German plan of 'investigating' the circumstances of the crime through the Red Cross, the prime minister exclaimed in irritation: 'What nonsense! What kind of investigation can there be under German occupation?'

Then, with a cunning smile, Churchill added: 'Let the Germans first withdraw their troops from that region and then we shall carry out an investigation!... Only I doubt that Hitler would show the necessary altruism!'

I said that the entire plan of 'investigating' should be 'killed' at the outset. Yet the British Government and the British press keep silent, creating the impression that while they may not necessarily favour the project, they at least have nothing against it.

'Bracken!' uttered Churchill. 'This whole idiotic venture must be "killed" at once. Take the necessary measures.'

Bracken promised to fulfil the prime minister's instruction as a matter of urgency.

Churchill continued: 'Nonetheless, the conflict between you and the Poles is an utterly unpleasant affair. It should be resolved as soon as possible. If you were to agree to let the families of Polish soldiers and the 40,000 Poles fit for military service leave the USSR, peace could be restored.'

... Then Churchill, with occasional interruptions and interventions from Bracken, began telling me that Sikorski now finds himself in a critical position. The 'extremists' are waging a vehement campaign against him, accusing him of weakness and servility to the Bolsheviks. It's not clear whether Sikorski will manage to hold on. If not, who will come to power? Those very 'extremists' will take charge of the government. This has led Churchill to the conclusion that the present Polish Government should be treated with care.

Bracken, in his turn, gave a vivid description of the 'American danger': Roosevelt's position is very delicate: there are many Poles in the United States, they represent a substantial electorate, and Catholics, of whom there are 33 million in the United States, may easily choose to support them. The election is at hand. Roosevelt cannot ignore the mood of the Catholics in general and of the Poles in particular. All this may tie the president's hands and lead to a deterioration of relations between the USA and the USSR.

... Churchill kept silent and sucked slowly at his cigar. From time to time he took a sip of whisky and soda from the glass placed in front of him. Finally he said: 'This Polish issue needs our full attention... In the next few days. I'll talk with Eden. And I'll send another message to Stalin. I'll need to think it over.'

I stayed with Churchill until almost midnight. We spoke a lot, discussing many issues. Quite a number of matters were raised besides Poland. Too many to remember. I shall note a few moments of particular interest.

Churchill stressed that of course he does not believe the German lies about the murder of 10,000 Polish officers... But is this so? At one point during our conversation Churchill dropped the following remark: 'Even if the German statements were to prove true, my attitude towards you would not change. You are a brave people, Stalin is a great warrior, and at the moment I approach everything primarily as a soldier who is interested in defeating the common enemy as quickly as possible.'

At a different point in the conversation, Churchill told me that a couple of days earlier he had been informed by Sikorski about several thousand Polish officers 'missing' in the USSR. Sikorski asked Stalin about their fate in December 1941, but 'did not receive a clear answer'.

On a third occasion Churchill suddenly started expounding the thought that 'everything can happen in war' and that lower-rank commanders acting on their own initiative are sometimes capable of 'doing terrible things'.[25]

I criticized Churchill firmly for his half-suspicions. He hastened to assure me that he harboured no suspicions whatsoever. But the impression remained that Churchill had some '*mental reservations*' concerning our innocence in the murder of the Polish officers.

Churchill recalled his meeting with Stalin with great pleasure. ... Churchill is highly impressed not only by Stalin's military prowess, but also by his military rank. There is even a degree of envy. Churchill told me today: 'I no longer call Stalin premier, I call him marshal! Of course, he is marshal and commander-in-chief!'

Then, turning to Bracken, he added with a laugh: 'Maybe I should be marshal too?'

Bracken encouraged Churchill, but the latter retorted: 'No, I can't be marshal... We have no such title. Captain General, perhaps?'

Churchill burst into laughter again, but I could see that the idea of having a high military rank holds him in thrall. Then, addressing me in a more serious tone, he remarked: 'Basically, I am commander-in-chief here. Naturally enough, I can't always carry out what I want, but I can always prevent that which I don't want.' ... I asked Churchill: 'You were a member of the Government during the last war and had dealings with the tsarist government. Now you are head of the Government during this war and have dealings with the Soviet Government. Tell me, do you perceive any difference between the two governments, and if so, what is it?'

Churchill replied: 'Of course I do. The main thing is that the Soviet Government is immeasurably stronger than the tsarist government was.'

He added: 'But what exists for me above all is Russia... Russia... Its people, its fields, its forests, its culture, music, dances... They never change... I deal with Russia, I wage war with Russia, and I want to build the future with Russia...'

And yet in his attitude to communism, Churchill is implacable. At one point he uttered: 'I don't want communism! It goes against our nature, our history, our view of life... If anyone came here wishing to establish communism

---

[25] Churchill may have had a soft spot for Sikorski, but less so for the Polish Government in exile. Earlier in the month, he had expressed in private his impatience with the Poles: 'We see all those elements of instability which have led to the ruin of Poland through so many centuries in spite of the individual qualities and virtues of the Poles.' Churchill conceded to Sikorski that 'the German revelations are probably true. The Bolsheviks can be very cruel.' But his uppermost interest was to suppress the horrific story rather than forgo his alliance with Stalin. 'Grim things happen in war,' he simply told Maisky. 'This affair of the missing Polish officers was indeed grim. But if they were dead they could not be resurrected to life. It was the case of the living Poles in Russia that required attention.'

in our country, I would fight him just as ferociously as I'm fighting the Nazis now!'

Churchill's voice resounded like a trumpet and his eyes burned with a hostile, angry flame.

It was past one in the morning when I returned home.

[The partition of Poland in 1939 had ended with a large number of Polish prisoners of war being interned by the Russians. Most of the prisoners were released in the wake of the Soviet–Polish agreement brokered by Maisky and Sikorski in July 1941. Close to 20,000 officers, however, remained unaccounted for. Stalin went a long way, as the diary shows, to conceal the cold-blooded massacre of those officers, condoned by the Politburo in March 1940. No historian has come up with a conclusive and convincing explanation for the motives behind the massacre. The Germans, who had stumbled across the graves during their campaign, made full use of the affair to sow discord among the Allies. On 12 April, they announced their findings, inviting the Poles to investigate them jointly with the Red Cross. The Katyn affair became a serious source of embarrassment for Stalin. Had the truth about the fate of the prisoners been unearthed, it could have jeopardized the delicate fabric of the precarious alliance, just as the purges had crippled Soviet diplomacy and undermined negotiations with the West in 1939. Stalin therefore reacted violently to any accusations and conducted an aggressive cover-up operation, which even included a misleading post-mortem of the bodies dug from the grave, once the Katyn area was liberated by the Red Army.]

27 April

Yesterday I was summoned urgently from Bovingdon, where Agniya and I were spending Easter.

A new message from Stalin had arrived, which I was to deliver promptly to Churchill. It turned out that, after I had left, Churchill sent Stalin a new message on 24 April concerning the Polish question, in which he asked him not to aggravate the situation, adducing the 'American menace' as his cardinal argument. But his message contained nothing more specific than that.

Stalin replied that the matter of the 'severance' of ties with the Polish Government had already been settled and that Molotov had presented Romer[26] (the Polish ambassador in Moscow) with a note in this vein on 25 April. Moreover: our note to Romer would be published in the Moscow evening press on 26 April.

---

[26] Tadeusz Romer, Polish ambassador to the Soviet Union, 1942–43; minister of foreign affairs, 1943–44.

So, the situation becomes more serious. Our objective, as it seems to me, is to explode Sikorski's Government and clear the way for the creation of a more democratic and friendly Polish Government by the time or at the time when the Red Army enters Polish territory. This course is correct: over the last year and a half I have reached the conclusion that the London émigrés, including Sikorski's Government, are quite hopeless. However, pursuing this line will bring us up against certain difficulties – from the British side and even more so from the side of the USA. Well, we shall have to overcome them. Perhaps some sort of acceptable compromise will emerge along the way. Time will tell.

I draw the following conclusion from our note: on the eve of the military events of the forthcoming summer campaign, the Soviet Government feels very confident and deems this an appropriate moment to inform Britain and the USA through its actions: 'When it comes to Eastern Europe, we are the masters!'

This is pleasing.

28 April

Masaryk told me the following *story*.

Berlin. 1950. A stranger enters a large pub and takes a seat at a table where a German is drinking beer. The stranger also buys a jug of beer. After a while they strike up a conversation. The stranger asks: 'You don't happen to know what became of that strange, loud man, do you? The one with the little moustache?'

'With the little moustache?' the German repeats. 'Ah, perhaps you mean Hitler?'

'Yes, Hitler, Hitler,' nods the stranger.

'But of course I know!' the German replies. 'He's taken up his true occupation again: he's a decorator in Australia.'

The stranger takes two gulps of beer and asks another question: 'And do you know what happened to that big, fat chap?... The one who liked to cover himself with badges and medals whenever he went anywhere?'

'Who? Perhaps you mean Göring?' guesses the German.

'That's right, Göring! Now I remember!' replies the stranger.

'Göring?' repeats the German. 'Oh, Göring's doing all right for himself: he's a pilot for a private airline in South America.'

After another two gulps of beer, the stranger asks again: 'And what about that small, darkish, ugly one with the squeaky voice and the lame leg, where did he end up?'

'Squeaky voice and a lame leg?' asks the German, scratching his head. 'Oh, you mean Goebbels?'

'But of course, Goebbels! How could I forget?'

'Goebbels is just fine,' the German says. 'He edits a newspaper in West Africa.'

For a minute or two neither of them says anything. Eventually, the German addresses the stranger with a question: 'And why are you so interested in all this? Who would you be?'

'Me? I'm Lord Hess,' replies the stranger in perfect German, but with a slight English accent.

29 April

The Polish events are developing apace.

After delivering Stalin's message of 26 April to Churchill, I decided to take a 'wait-and-see' stance. In Polish–British circles, however, there was a flurry of activity. A series of meetings was held between Churchill and Eden on the one side and Sikorski and Raczyński on the other. The main issue concerned how the Polish Government should respond to Molotov's note of 25 April. The Poles were on their high horses and the English were holding them back. The draft of the Polish communiqué was returned to the Polish Government twice for revision. It was said that Churchill had given the Poles an earful for their behaviour. I don't know how true that is. One way or another, the long-awaited and repeatedly re-drafted Polish communiqué finally appeared on the evening of the 28th. Rothstein[27] read the text to me over the phone. It was worse than might have been expected.

At around eleven o'clock in the evening, I received an unexpected call from Eden.

'Your *Soviet War News* is a good newspaper,' he said, 'but why does it attack Sikorski and his government so fiercely? "Hitler's agents"... "The fascists' helpers".'

When this part of the discussion was over, Eden asked: 'Have you read the Polish communiqué that has just been released?... The PM and I really sweated over it!'

'No, I haven't read it, but I heard it over the phone,' I replied.

'And what was your impression?'

'Negative,' I snapped back.

'Negative?' Eden cried in disappointment. 'But why?'

'I would prefer not to comment until I have read the communiqué myself,' I replied.

And that was the end of our telephone conversation.

---

[27] Andrew Rothstein, an active member of the CPGB, he became the representative of TASS in London.

This morning I got an urgent call from Eden to come over and see him. It was our first meeting since I had visited Churchill in... Eden did not keep me posted during the Polish–British talks of 27 and 28 April; I learned bits and pieces from other sources. Now Eden had evidently decided to carry out his duty 'as an ally' and inform me officially.

... Eden looked genuinely distressed.

'In recent weeks,' he continued, 'everything had been going so well. Our relations with you were better than ever before. The prime minister was very satisfied. And all of a sudden such a blow!... I fear that this ill-starred Polish question may complicate relations between our countries. For my part, I'll do all I can for this not to happen, of course, but who knows?... I'd like to ask you, for your part, to help me keep Anglo-Soviet relations on the same friendly course as before.'

I replied that Eden should have no doubts about my help, but that I did not think my assistance was at all necessary. Entirely reasonable people are sitting there in Moscow and they, for their part, will do all they can to localize the complication that had arisen.

... Then I referred to the communiqué. I said I had managed to read it and form a clear impression of this document. My opinion had not changed. I wouldn't start discussing the main points of the communiqué. I just wanted to ask Eden one question: 'The "integrity of the Polish Republic" is underlined several times in the communiqué. Translated into plain language, this means the borders of 1939. Yesterday evening you told me that you and the prime minister had sweated over the communiqué. That seems to imply that you and Churchill are its co-authors. Should I deduce from this that the British Government has recognized the 1939 Polish borders? It is important for me to know this before I advise my Government on how it should interpret the meaning and significance of the communiqué.'

Eden was almost dumbfounded. Evidently it hadn't occurred to him that the events of the last two days might give rise to such an interpretation.

'Nothing of the kind!' Eden exclaimed with uncharacteristic fervour. 'The British Government's stance on the matter of the Polish borders has not changed one bit. Everything remains as it was. It's wrong to name the prime minister and me as co-authors of the communiqué. Wrong! We told Sikorski bluntly: "This is your, Polish, communiqué! We are not responsible for it!" The prime minister and I made a few improvements to the initial Polish draft. That's all. Do you know what was in it? Just Smolensk graves and nothing else. The prime minister told Sikorski: "Stop thinking about the dead. You can't help them anyway! Think about the living, about what you can do for them!" The Poles yielded to our pressure. What has been published is the best that could have been achieved. But neither the prime minister nor I are co-authors.'

I let Eden finish and then said: 'Your distinction between what represents co-authorship and what doesn't is so subtle as to lie beyond my comprehension. But that is not the main point now. The main point is this: what can I tell my Government about the British position regarding the Polish borders?'

'Tell your Government,' Eden answered heatedly, 'that the British Government, as before, does not in any way guarantee the Polish borders of 1939!'

30 April

Today, at five in the morning, Beatrice Webb died!

She had been unwell for the past ten days, lay unconscious for several days, and finally left this world.

What a bitter loss! Beatrice Webb was over 85, of course, but what of that?... She was her usual self just a few weeks ago when we visited *Liphook* – lively, talkative, deeply interested in all that surrounded her. She paid particular attention to the USSR, and to all the developments on the 'Russian front'.

What a sad blow! I had just been planning to visit the Webbs, to see them and talk to them...

So, Beatrice was the first to go of the glorious 'four'. Such a surprise. I did not think she would be the first.[28]

30 April

I received an unexpected summons from Churchill today at about 5 p.m. He asked me to come immediately. ... Churchill declared that he wanted to inform me of a passage to be added to his message to Stalin of 28 April and to be sent to Moscow post factum, following a special decision of the Cabinet. In this passage, Churchill expressed his regret at Comrade Stalin's hasty actions in terminating ties with the Polish Government, so hasty that Churchill was unable even to complete his 'conciliatory' efforts. Having read the passage, Churchill added: 'The Cabinet finds that I leaned too far in your direction and wishes to restore the balance with this addition.'

I couldn't restrain a snigger.

... At that moment Cadogan bent forward to Churchill and whispered something in his ear.

'Yes, and by the way,' the prime minister began again, 'it seems that you are intending to set up a parallel Polish Government in Moscow?... Bear in mind

---

[28] 'We both had a feeling for her,' Maisky wrote to H.G. Wells, 'which it is very difficult to describe, but which contained the elements of admiration, sympathy and warm friendship in the highest degree.'

that we, the British Government, will support Sikorski as before. And the Americans, as far as I know, will do the same.'

Churchill was getting worked up once again and raising his voice. Once again, I answered calmly: 'You shouldn't believe everything you hear! Germans spread false rumours, Poles pick them up, and good-natured Englishmen believe them. It's all complete nonsense. We don't intend to set up any kind of parallel government in Moscow.'

'Really?' Churchill and Cadogan exclaimed, as if they could not believe their ears. They both cheered up immediately.

'Yes, really!' I reassured them. 'I can say this with absolute certainty.'

Just a few hours before my meeting with Churchill I had received a message to that effect from Moscow, asking me to refute the rumours spread by the Germans.

'However,' I continued, 'we shall not be restoring ties with the present Polish Government.'

Churchill's and Cadogan's spirits sank at once.

'But why not?' asked Churchill.

'How do you mean, why not?' I answered in surprise. 'Has not Sikorski's Government revealed its true face through its behaviour? It is hostile, or at best semi-hostile, to the USSR. We could restore ties only with a Polish Government that found ways of establishing cordial relations with us.'

Cadogan intervened and immediately sought to address the question from a practical point of view.

'Tell me, is the present Polish Government unacceptable to you in its entirety? Or do you make exceptions? Sikorski, for instance?'

I replied that the composition of the Polish Government was a matter for the Poles. I would not care to interfere. As for Sikorski personally, he appears to me to be a man who understands the importance of good relations with the USSR, but unfortunately he is too weak.

'Wait a month or two and you'll see changes!' exclaimed Churchill.

On parting, he remarked with admiration: 'Stalin is a wise man!'

Shaking my hand, he added: 'Now I'll leave for the weekend in a calmer state of mind.'

The weekend! Oh, that sacred British institution!

[Although convinced that a massacre had taken place, the British had been consciously engaged in a careful 'cover-up' so as not to damage Anglo-Russian relations. The Poles were urged to withdraw their demand for an inquiry, and the Ministry of Information was instructed to ensure that the British press 'did not canvass the Russo-Polish quarrel'. Although Maisky, too, was asked to exercise restraint, he appeared to be far more fearful of Stalin than of Churchill. The Soviet embassy's *Soviet War News* printed foul attacks on the Polish Government, depicting the Poles as 'accomplices of the cannibal Hitler'. This provoked a strong reaction from both Eden and Churchill. The severity of the reproach is missing both from Maisky's diary and from his reports to Moscow. Cadogan, however, who was present, testifies that Maisky was accused of 'disseminating poison'. 'We kicked Maisky all round the room,' he entered in his diary with manifest delight, 'and it went v. well.']

1 May

A surprise visit. Inspector Wilkinson of Scotland Yard (the very same inspector who guarded Molotov in London last year) came on behalf of the head of the Metropolitan Police, *Sir Philip Game*,[29] to offer me special protection in view of the threats to have me killed that, according to reports at Scotland Yard's disposal, are spreading among circles of 'irresponsible Poles'.

I took a sceptical view of these reports. But Wilkinson insisted. Eventually I consented to there being more policemen on our street, around the embassy (Sikorski's HQ, opposite our embassy, does rather concern me), but I rejected the suggestion that I should be constantly escorted by a police car during my travels about town.

2 May

The clock ticks, and the old near their end...

This thought struck me with particular insistence when Agniya and I went to see the Shaws a few days ago. We hadn't seen them for several months. We had heard from the Webbs that the Shaws were having a hard time of it: sick, down in the dumps, lonely. That they had some *troubles* or other with [ration] cards, petrol, servants. We'd been meaning to visit the old couple for some time – and now here we were.

Not much fun! Mrs Shaw is bed-bound. Agniya went into her room and spoke with her. Mrs Shaw is in a bad way: she has severe curvature of the spine and was all twisted. She's become very small and crooked. Complains of losing her memory: reads all the time and can't remember a word of it. Even forgets the names and faces of friends. She told Agniya that when she was 16 she fell off a horse and injured her spine. Then it passed. Mrs Shaw hurt her back on a few more occasions. While she was still in good health, she barely noticed a thing, but now nature has recalled her old sins and is taking its revenge.

'I can feel that I'm dying,' Mrs Shaw was saying. 'Inch by inch...'

Mrs Shaw is nearly 90, of course, but still... what a shame!

---

[29] Air Vice Marshal Sir Philip Game, commissioner of Police of the Metropolis, 1935–45.

Shaw himself is better. After all, he's <u>only</u> 87! He looks much as he always has done: tall, slim, with a big grey beard and bushy, unruly white brows. His eyes are alive, restless, expressive. Only his complexion has become somehow paler, and a suspicious bluishness has begun to appear around the eyes, beneath the lids. As if his body were short of blood.

His passion for paradox and wit is intact.

'I made a discovery recently,' Shaw exclaimed, with a great sweeping gesture. 'Stalin is the most important Fabian in history!'

'How's that?' I replied with a laugh.

'Because Stalin took the socialism that the Fabians merely dreamed and nattered about and turned it into reality.'

I roared with laughter. Shaw hasn't changed.

Then Shaw launched into a furious diatribe against Pavlov.[30] He's not fond of our great scholar. It's probably because Pavlov cut up dogs and rabbits, and Shaw, as we all know, is an anti-vivisectionist! Shaw won't say this openly, of course, so he tries to smear Pavlov in various roundabout ways. That's why Shaw started trying to convince me that 'Pavlov's so-called discoveries about the conditioned reflex and other such nonsense' are, first of all, not discoveries, and secondly, had been made long before Pavlov... by Shaw himself!

I roared once more.

Shaw hasn't stopped writing. At the moment he is busy compiling a 'Guide' for today's politicians and public figures. He's been working on it for two years now. He complains that the work is moving more slowly than he would like, but at least it is moving. I can just imagine the final result! If I am to believe what Shaw told me about the contents of the 'Guide' (although Shaw's accounts of his own writing are not always to be trusted), it will be a very witty text, dominated by irrepressible paradox. Poor Pavlov gets it in the neck here as well.

Then Shaw fell to reminiscing. Talked at length about his May Day – in 1889! I read about it all a few days later in the pages of *Reynolds News*.

How much longer will this couple hold out? I have a bad feeling about it all.

We thought we should visit the Webbs[31] in the next few days. We gave them our word that we would see the Shaws and distract them a little. That promise has been fulfilled. Now we can get together with the Webbs and have a good chat. Yesterday I heard that Mrs Webb is poorly. So we will have to wait a little.

---

[30] Ivan Petrovich Pavlov was the famous Russian physiologist who introduced the innovative work on conditioning for which he won the Nobel Prize in 1904. For a while Maisky's father worked under him at his laboratory in St Petersburg.

[31] Beatrice Webb died on 30 April. Maisky is writing two days later about the visit to the Shaws which had taken place a couple of days before her death. It must be assumed that here he describes the hopes he had at the time of seeing the Webbs – a visit which never materialized.

Two couples. Our contemporaries. Comrades in their vision of the world, comrades in the struggle. Friends. Both world-famous. Both of similar age. In both, life's candle is burning right to the end...

Sad.

Agniya and I have been in England for so long now! When we arrived in 1932, the Shaws and the Webbs were still so vigorous, active, energetic. Every winter the Shaws would undertake some big *cruise* or other around the globe, during the course of which he would write a new work, while the Webbs were still working hard at their *Soviet Communism* and travelling to the USSR to gather new impressions and material. The Webbs' last trip abroad was in the spring of 1936, for a holiday after the publication of their monumental opus about the USSR. On that occasion they visited the Balearic Islands. I saw them off at the station. They returned on the very eve of the war in Spain. How symbolic! It was then that Europe set foot on the 'path to war'. Never again has the old couple left England.

3 May

Just back from Beatrice Webb's funeral. A private affair. Only members of her extensive family were present, including Stafford Cripps and his wife. An exception was made only for Agniya and me: our friendship with the deceased was extremely close. The body was cremated in Woking. The crematorium is a quiet, solemn place: a modestly sized, handsome building in an enormous park with old, mighty trees. A service preceded the cremation, but it was very short – about five minutes long. The priest read some parting prayers, said some parting words. Then the coffin vanished in the wall, behind which lies the furnace...

The funeral was attended by more than 60 mostly ageing or even elderly people. Lots of grey hair, lots of wrinkles. After the funeral Beatrice's sister – the youngest of the nine Potter sisters and the only one still alive – came up to us. A truly ancient woman! And in appearance nothing like majestic, inspired Beatrice.

Sidney Webb was also there. With his well-made black suit and fine black hat he exuded exceptional solemnity. His grey hair and grey beard stood out sharply against his dark attire. I was struck by Sidney's complexion: bright pink, unusually healthy. ... Healthy? Perhaps this was some trick of nature? Such things happen. But his eyes! They scared me: wide open, lids swollen, filled with pain. When Sidney saw us, they glistened with tears and became even scarier. Even so, he held himself together and didn't give in to his emotions. And in fact, according to Barbara Drake (Beatrice's niece), who was at *Passfield Corner* throughout Beatrice's final days, Sidney showed unexpected reserves of resilience, courage and restraint at this difficult time.

Returning home from Woking, Agniya and I experienced profound sadness. Gone forever was a great person, a strong spirit, a heartfelt friend of the USSR, our own close personal friend, the only one, perhaps, of all our English acquaintances that we truly loved.

[Maisky had learned of Litvinov's recall (which heralded his own) a couple of days before he attended Beatrice Webb's funeral, on a visit to the terminally ill Mrs Shaw, H.G. Wells and Lloyd George). Meeting his long-standing close friends betrayed a strong sense – perhaps a mirror image – of his own ageing and fragility, if not of finality. Having emerged from the funeral, Maisky composed and deposited with Agniya his own political will.]

12 May

... H.G. Wells came for lunch. There were three of us – me, Agniya and our guest.

Wells has aged terribly. His hands shake, he can barely walk. Just one flight of steps to the first floor and he is completely out of breath. Occasionally you can see in his eyes the sparkle of the author of *War of the Worlds* and *The Time Machine*, but for the most part they are clouded by a deathly film. Wells is 76 now and looking at him, I thought: 'Is it worth living to such an age?'

Nevertheless, Wells is still writing. And still writing well. It's enough to read his obituary of Beatrice Webb. It touched me deeply, and I wrote to Wells to say so. He was extremely flattered.

A young man's organism is filled to bursting with vital energy. He has enough of it for everything: writing talented novels, studying foreign languages, playing sports and preserving a radiant complexion. The closer one gets to old age, the more limited are those reserves of vital energy and the more prudently they need to be spent: no more sports, no more foreign languages, no more radiant complexion. Whatever energy remains has to be focused on that one, most important, most essential thing – writing. This is the stage at which Wells currently finds himself. Whatever energy he still has is expended entirely on writing. He is helped, of course, by his immense experience as a writer, by his refined literary technique, by the habits and inertia of a long literary life...

... Wells also said this today: 'What a giant that Lenin was!'

And then, alluding to his meeting with him in 1920, he added: 'He was right then, and I was wrong!'

Thank you for acknowledging the fact! Just a shame that Wells has needed almost a quarter of a century and a second world war to see the error of his ways. A high price!

Then the subject turned to Stalin, and Wells remarked: 'I like "Uncle Joe" very much... He's a great man. I'm not even sure who's greater: Lenin or Stalin. It would be truer to say that each is No. 1 in his own way.'

Well, that's progress: Wells is acknowledging Stalin's greatness now, without waiting for 23 years to elapse.

27 May

Yesterday Agniya and I went to see Lloyd George at Churt.

The old man is becoming more and more decrepit. Age has really caught up with him in the last 5–6 months. This is not the Lloyd George I used to know. How long will he last?...

We drank tea. Chatted. Lloyd George is in an irritable, carping mood. Especially when it comes to Churchill. Lloyd George finds something dark and sinister in whatever Churchill does. Might it be because the old man has been twiddling his thumbs during this war, and now he is taking it out on Churchill? ... Lloyd George drew the conclusion that the war will drag on and require gigantic losses; there can be no question of the war in Europe ending in 1944.

We also spoke about Poland. Lloyd George supports our position and criticizes the Poles. He recalled how many *troubles* the Poles caused in the last war.

'There wasn't one sensible man among them!' Lloyd George exclaimed. 'All dreamers, megalomaniacs, impudent aggressors!... The best of the bunch was Paderewski,[32] but he was clueless when it came to politics and weak in character. Egged on by Clemenceau,[33] the Poles lost all restraint and refused to listen to me or Wilson.[34] The consequences are now plain to see.'

Lloyd George believes that the USSR would be best off ignoring the Polish Government and putting off its 'reorganization', since it would be impossible to make up a satisfactory government in any case: there are no such people outside Poland. When the Red Army restores the 1941 borders, everything will fall into place by itself.

I think Lloyd George is right about this. My thoughts have often leaned in the same direction. ...

---

[32] Ignacy Jan Paderewski, Polish prime minister and foreign minister in 1919, representing Poland at the Paris Peace Conference of 1919.
[33] Georges Benjamin Clemenceau, French prime minister, 1917–20.
[34] Geoffrey Masterman Wilson, Stafford Cripps's secretary; served in the British embassy in Moscow and the Russian department of the Foreign Office, 1940–45.

29 May

A week has passed since the Comintern was dissolved. The upshot?

First and foremost: this is a very important milestone in the development not only of the USSR but of the entire world. It means that we are not counting on revolution after the war. Needless to say, the war can and will result in all manner of disturbances, strikes, uprisings and so on in various countries, but that is something different. A real, full-blooded proletarian revolution is clearly not anticipated. Which is no surprise to me after the conversations I had in Moscow in December 1941.

But if not a proletarian revolution, then what? This still remains vague, and it cannot be otherwise. Time will tell. But I certainly do not rule out the appearance after the war of a new International – not a second and not a third, but some other kind.

Next: why was the Comintern dissolved? The reasons are clear: fundamentally, the Comintern has been dead for a long time, but its ghost created major difficulties in relations between the USSR and other powers, and also in relations between local communist parties and other workers' parties and organizations in various countries. Now, when the most essential task is to consolidate a united front of all forces to destroy Hitler's Germany, this ghost has had to be liquidated.

Thirdly: what was the reaction of the outside world to the dissolution of the Comintern? Most favourable. On the one side, Goebbels is livid (he has been deprived of his most effective propaganda scarecrow); on the other, the average American has sighed with relief (no more scary 'Reds' under his bed). In England, the Conservatives couldn't be happier. Churchill, when asked by a journalist in Washington what he thought of the dissolution of the Comintern, gave a brief but telling reply: '*I like it.*' ...

In Labour circles, by contrast, the dissolution of the Comintern has elicited mixed feelings. ... Bevin came for lunch the other day. In the course of conversation, he asked: 'Tell me, has the Comintern really, properly been dissolved?'

I looked at Bevin in astonishment and replied: 'Why, do you think we are just fooling around?'

Bevin was embarrassed and beat a quick retreat. We moved on to another topic. After a short while, Bevin asked again, as if in passing: 'But do you not think that the dissolution of the Comintern may be followed by the dissolution of the CPSU?'

Once again I looked at Bevin in astonishment and asked in my turn: 'And what will take the place of the CPSU?'

Bevin thought about it and replied without much confidence: 'I don't know, military dictatorship... or something of the kind.'

I laughed at Bevin, but the train of his thoughts was entirely clear to me. After all, wouldn't it be wonderful if the CPSU dissolved itself and in its place there arose a Russian version of the Labour Party! How easy it would be then to do away with all the communist parties in the world, especially the English one!

... A revolution in England would be possible, even inevitable, only in the event of its empire being lost. It is already clear now, however, that England will come out of the war having not just retained, but even augmented its empire, if only in an indirect form. Its ruling class, therefore, will be able to get by without fascism and to continue governing nation and empire with velvet gloves. ...

[The Comintern had been a millstone around the neck of Soviet diplomacy since the late 1920s. In the midst of his desperate attempts to appease Germany in mid-1941, Stalin was resolved to free himself from the ideological shackles which limited his political manoeuvrability by taking initial steps to dissolve the Comintern. The formal dissolution in May 1943 served the same purpose, but now paved the way for a post-war arrangement with the Allies. Maisky went on to explain to officials in the Foreign Office that in reality the Comintern had been 'moribund for years' and its dispersal was a natural result of 'Stalin's policy of nationalism ... Lenin thought the Russian Revolution could only survive if there were world revolution; Stalin thought Russia big enough to make the experiment alone and if she succeeded that would be the best propaganda for communism.' Russia's wish, he told Lloyd George, was 'not to make Communistic revolutions for other countries, but to secure frontiers and generally to secure the restoration of [Russia]'.]

2 June

Butler came for lunch. We spoke a great deal about England's post-war prospects. ... Butler anticipates that Britain's future development will take the following paths:

(1) A mixed type of economy, i.e. some sectors (electricity, the railways, possibly coal) will be nationalized, some (road and sea transport, civil aviation, etc.) will come under *public control*. ...

(2) The 'constitutional factory' will gradually emerge, i.e. factories in which workers' representatives will participate in the management of the business. ...

(3) The education system should be democratized, i.e. almost all *public schools* should be abolished (though Butler would like to keep two or three of them). ...

I asked Butler: 'So you want England to develop along Fabian lines?'

Butler replied: 'Call it what you will. We English, you know, can do revolutionary things, so long as they are done under the old names.'

Fabianism, of course, is not revolution. But for the Conservatives it might as well be. Butler (who undoubtedly reflects the mood of the ruling Tory elite) is clearly thinking of Fabianism, though he doesn't want to name it. ...

3 June

Morrison came for lunch. It so happened that our conversation also revolved for the most part around the subject of post-war problems. ...

The more Morrison spoke, the more I was struck by the convergence of his views with those of Butler. Of course, there are certain differences of nuance and emphasis between the two men, but essentially they share the same fundamental platform. Astonishing! Listening to Morrison, I thought how easy it will be after the war for the Conservatives to reach agreement with Labour on matters of internal reconstruction in England. ...

Morrison said that he is still undecided in his own mind about the question of whether or not to continue the coalition with the Conservatives after the war. He even asked my advice. But I sidestepped the role of counsellor. ...

4 June

Agniya and I went to see Webb.

The house we know so well is still there. But approaching it on this occasion, we were not met, as in the past, by a tall, beautiful old woman with lively eyes and a profoundly spiritual face...

... We went through to the *drawing-room*, where we were such frequent guests in the past. We sat in the armchairs, as in the past. Once again, the lady of the house was not to be seen in her usual place – the low step by the fireplace. But on the bookcase nearby was a large white urn – with the ashes of she-who-was-never-to-return.

'I've found a spot in the woods,' said Webb, slowly, 'which is just right for this urn, but it takes so long for orders to be processed at the moment and I am still waiting for the bronze slab with the inscription...'

Then, after a period of silence, the old man added: 'That's where I will end up, too.'

Webb is clearly unable to shake off thoughts of his own approaching death. I picked up several other signs of this. No wonder: he is 83, five years ago he experienced a stroke from which he has still not fully recovered, and his companion of half a century, with whom he formed a single physical and spiritual whole, has just gone for good.

'I feel very lonely,' he said in passing.

... The old man told me that almost all the books put out by the Webbs were written by him. The idea for the book, the outline, the gathering of material and so on would all be done jointly. But the actual process of writing was Webb's responsibility. Usually, Beatrice would just cast a critical eye over the text, make corrections and additions – after joint discussion, of course. Webb always wrote evenly, assiduously and quickly – by hand. He just couldn't get used to typewriters. An example: the book *Soviet Communism* (more than 1,000 pages long) was written over two years. 'Written' in the narrowest sense of the word. The gathering of material, the thinking, etcetera, took another two and a half years or so.

Webb's account surprised me a little. I already knew that, in this marvellous 'union of two', spiritual primacy belonged to Beatrice. I had observed this in practice on numerous occasions. I also knew that most of the drafting was carried out by Sidney, that Beatrice usually provided the thoughts, the idea, the general outline and plan for the book, which Sidney filled in with figures and facts. I had imagined that Sidney usually wrote most of their books, with Beatrice contributing only the crucial, summarizing chapters. But I had never thought that practically all of the writing fell to Sidney. ...

14 June

A few days ago (9 June) Air Chief Marshal *Sir Arthur Harris*,[35] the head of RAF Bomber Command, came with his wife for lunch. Harris is a striking representative of the camp that believes that the war can be won from the air. I asked Harris whether he continues to hold that view.

'Of course I do!' Harris cried. 'Now more than ever. Everything depends on the number of bombers you are able to deploy. I assure you quite categorically that if I had the capacity to send a thousand heavy bombers to Germany every night that we fly, Germany would surrender within three months at most. And then the entire army of occupation could consist of just three policemen – American, English and Soviet, who would take Berlin not only without meeting resistance, but with the enthusiasm of the local population. ...

16 June

... Eden informed me that [H.] Alexander,[36] who was in England just a few days ago, has been instructed to expedite 'Husky' by every means. It is possible,

---

[35] Arthur Travers Harris, 'Bomber Harris', was air chief marshal of the Royal Air Force; deputy chief of air staff, 1940–41; commander-in-chief of Bomber Command, 1942–45.
[36] Field Marshal Sir Harold Alexander, commander-in-chief of the operations in North Africa since August 1942, and deputy to Eisenhower after the latter's appointment as supreme commander of the Allied Expeditionary Force in the wake of El Alamein.

therefore, that the operation will begin earlier than planned. I wouldn't object, but I doubt it will happen. We'll see. Then Eden said that an agreement has been reached with the Americans about the bombing of Rome's railways (half a year ago Washington was opposed to any bombing of Rome).

I asked about Turkey. Eden was unable to say anything reassuring. The Turks are still 'sitting on the fence'. In recent days they have been emphasizing their neutrality more strongly than ever. ...

[The diary entry on the meeting with Eden (and the subsequent silence) avoids mentioning the bitter clash between Churchill and Stalin which culminated in the recall of Maisky from London. Following the final defeat of the Axis forces in North Africa, Churchill felt confident enough to openly adhere to his peripheral strategy. He now envisaged a post-war world based on a special and equal relationship with the Americans. His impatience with Stalin impacted on Maisky's standing. Even before setting off for Washington for his fifth summit meeting with Roosevelt, Churchill warned Eden that 'it would be a great pity to establish the principle that Ambassador Maisky should receive copies of all telegrams other than operational which I send to Marshal Stalin. I should object very strongly to this.'

Churchill left for the US on 5 May, on board the *Queen Mary*, with an entourage of 150 advisers; 'an amusing form of megalomania on Winston's part,' jotted down Halifax in his diary, 'but he would no doubt feel the war would gravely suffer if he did not move so attended'. Churchill believed he could convert Roosevelt once again to his strategic and political vision, the implication of which was a definite postponement of the second front to spring 1944, at the earliest, and the introduction of various diversions in the Mediterranean, as well as in the Far East. He hoped also to dissuade the president from ending the war with an international structure which included the Soviet Union and perhaps China as equal partners. Eager to gain the president's support for an invasion of Italy, Churchill continued to harp on the unresolved difficulties involved in landing on the Continent – an operation which could only be undertaken once 'a plan offering reasonable prospects of success could be made'. The turbulent summit ended with 'Avalanche', the plan for the Italian campaign, finally confirmed, while the invasion of France was now set for spring 1944. Both Admiral Pound and General Dill complained to Halifax about Churchill's indecisiveness, while Alan Brooke, the chief of staff, grumbled that Churchill was thinking 'one thing at one moment and another at another moment'.

'Isn't he a sly rogue?' was Maisky's reaction to information coming out of Washington. 'Not only does he want to preserve control over the Mediterranean for Britain and not to allow the Americans to look in there, he intends to do it at the expense of US forces and resources.' Indeed, when Maisky met Churchill as soon as he returned to London, his fears that the prime minister now considered the Italian campaign, combined with the air offensive, to be substitutes for the cross-Channel campaign were confirmed. Churchill remained deliberately noncommittal when the possibility of bringing the war to a conclusion in Europe in 1944 was raised by the ambassador.

Having gleaned from Maisky what had transpired in Washington and Algiers, Stalin bitterly remonstrated with Roosevelt about the exclusion of the Soviet Union from the strategic discussions, regardless of the fact that she was facing 'single-handed a still very strong and dangerous enemy'. His indictment of the Allies (a copy of which was transmitted to Churchill on 11 June) warned of the grave consequences that the decision would have on 'the people and the army of the Soviet Union'. With 'Avalanche' now firmly secured, Churchill reminded Stalin of his determination to 'never authorize any cross-Channel attack which ... would lead only to useless massacre'. He could hardly see 'how a great British defeat and slaughter would aid the Soviet Armies'. Stalin retorted with accusations of perfidy on the part of his Western allies, again referring to the 'colossal sacrifices' made by the Red Army. On 26 June, Churchill, warning that his 'own long-suffering patience [was] not inexhaustible', removed the gloves: he recalled that, as a result of the Molotov–Ribbentrop Pact, Britain had been 'left alone to face the worst that Nazi Germany could do to us', and that presently 'a more hopeful and fruitful strategic policy' had opened up 'in another theatre'.

70. Just informed of his recall, a sad Maisky entertains members of the 'Old Vic' after a performance of *The Russians*.

In a frenzy, Maisky now found it difficult to reach Eden, who had been advised by Churchill 'not to have anything to do with him'. When he finally did get through, it was to break the news of his recall to Moscow. However, even at such a dramatic moment, Maisky had not given up on his persistent efforts to defuse the tension between the two leaders. He appealed to Beaverbrook at the eleventh hour to intervene with the prime minister. Finally he secured a meeting with the prime minister on the eve of his departure. According to Churchill, the ambassador was 'extremely civil', repeatedly assuring him that he 'ought not to attach importance to the tone of Stalin's messages'. On the thorny issue of the second front, it quickly transpired that Churchill clung to his belief that the Mediterranean strategy was 'gaining Russia valuable breathing-space to regather her strength'. Depicting the 'great sufferings and losses of Russia', Maisky explained that although Stalin was harsh in scolding the prime minister, there was nothing sinister in his messages. Eager not to return to Moscow empty-handed, he succeeded in extracting from Churchill an undertaking to continue working with Stalin. He wished to ensure that the failure to embark on joint strategy would not impair the negotiations now taking place on the post-war order. Here he was partially successful, encouraging Churchill to send Eden to Moscow, thereby paving the way for the Moscow summit meeting of the Allied foreign ministers in the autumn.]

2 July

Tomorrow I am flying to Moscow.

About a week ago, I received a telegram summoning me to Moscow for consultations on post-war matters. Very good. I'm glad of the chance to see my people and 'touch native soil' once more.

I think, however, that there is more to this than consultations. My recall, it seems to me, may also be a way of expressing our dissatisfaction with the British Government for failing to keep its word on the second front. This is precisely how Eden interpreted the announcement of my departure. He was greatly alarmed and exclaimed: 'What? You are leaving London at such a moment?'

'What particular moment?' I retorted. 'After all, there won't be a second front now. So there is no reason why I should not fly to Moscow for a period of time.'

It took a week to arrange the flight. The British are putting a plane at my disposal in which they will also be sending out some employees bound for their embassy in Moscow. One of our military men, who is returning to the USSR, is flying with me. The route is interesting: Gibraltar – Cairo – Habbaniya – Kuibyshev – Moscow. I've never been to Egypt – I'll see the pyramids!

Bon voyage!

71. A sad farewell to Britain, 15 September 1943.

End of an Era: Maisky's Recall

Both Litvinov and Maisky chose to present their recall to Moscow as a remonstration against the decision to postpone the second front, rather than as a personal rebuff in the protracted struggle between the old school of Soviet diplomacy and Stalin's now fully erected authoritarian edifice. They were most anxious to impress on their interlocutors in the West that their promotion within the ministry (both were appointed deputy foreign minister) reflected the personal appreciation by the Kremlin and their continued relevance. Maisky's confidants, notably Beaverbrook, echoed him in attributing the recall to Stalin's deepening suspicion of British intentions, the fault for which 'lay entirely with the Prime Minister who was fundamentally anti-Russian and who was too old now to change'. Bruce Lockhart, an old Russia hand, describes how Maisky was most anxious to figure out how public opinion in Britain reacted to his recall. When he learned that there were two conflicting schools of thought – one attributing it to Stalin's displeasure and the other suggesting that Stalin 'would benefit from the presence in Moscow of so great a connoisseur of England as himself' – his 'eyes twinkled' as he admitted that 'in Moscow there were also two interpretations'. The third option, of having fallen out of favour, was thus avoided. Litvinov left Under Secretary of State Welles with the impression that it was he who had insisted on returning to Moscow to directly influence Stalin's foreign policy. In the same breath, he complained of being completely 'bereft of any information as to the policy or plans of his own Government'.

Once in Moscow, the unrelenting Maisky was quick to brief the British press about his new 'elevated' position there and the fact that he, as they put it, was 'held in high regard by Joe'. *The Times* reported that Stalin wished him 'to remain at his right hand, with M. Molotov', while Russia was preparing her post-war policy, considering his 'direct knowledge and understanding of Great Britain', as well as his rare and shrewd views on 'Germany, France, and other countries'. The bleaker reality, more accurately surmised by *Time* magazine, was that 'Little Maisky' would 'get lost in the bureaucratic maze of the Narkomindel (signifying that his tireless bouncing around London had displeased his superiors)'. Ironically, it was Maisky who had had a similar observation about Vansittart's 'promotion' in 1938: 'the new appointment will have to be regarded as a demotion or, more precisely, as a retirement ticket, only with uniform, decorations and a pension'.

Molotov had been long seeking the removal of Maisky and Litvinov from London and Washington, which the two ambassadors considered to be their 'personal territory'. Stalin did not, however, shy away from drawing on their unrivalled connections and familiarity with the West, though under close surveillance and within limited scope. Both Maisky and Litvinov entertained no illusions, being well aware that the recall was first and foremost motivated by a desire to deprive them of the relatively free rein they had enjoyed in London and Washington. Neither returned to Moscow willingly. The memory of the horrifying fate of their colleagues who had been summoned to Moscow was still painfully fresh. Averell Harriman remembered Litvinov being 'ebullient' up to the moment of his recall: 'I have never seen a man collapse so completely. His attitude showed that he was in a rather tenuous position with Stalin and he must have feared for his life in the event that his Washington mission ended in disgrace.' Litvinov's wife Ivy, who for a while stayed behind in Washington, confided to friends that she feared she might never see her husband again. In her unpublished memoirs, she describes emphatically how her husband 'went nearly mad ... he wanted to stay ... he started what he longed for more than anything else [writing his memoirs] because he did not want to go back to Russia'. She went on to describe how he 'did nothing but quarrel with Stalin at that time – unappeasably quarrel with Stalin ... he could do nothing but quarrel with everybody ... with Molotov ... with everybody, and nothing they could do was right'. Once in Moscow (and this would apply to Maisky, too), Ivy 'cast a heedful eye on every side. She begged her friends not to send books to Litvinov nor to come and see them, that was "safer for both".'

The presentation of the recall as a protest against the West has led historians down a false track. The decision to withdraw Litvinov, it should be remembered, had already been taken in late April, prior to the eruption of the major conflict between the Allies. It signalled to Maisky that his days in Britain were numbered, too. As soon as he heard the news from Washington, he wasted little time in depositing a political will with his wife:

Dear Agniya,

My instructions for whatever happens:

(1) My notes (the diary, or my Old Lady, as I like to call her), should be sent to Comrade Stalin. They are in my two little suitcases.

(2) You yourself should go through all my papers and sort them out into those which are of public and those which are of personal nature. Those which are of public interest should be given to Comrade Molotov. All these materials are in my personal safe, in the iron cupboard next to the safe, in the small suitcases, as well as in other places in our apartment.

(3) I should like my childhood memoir to be published.

In his memoirs, Gromyko,[1] who at the outset of his career was very much Molotov's protégé, describes how Maisky's appointment to the post in London had 'shocked many: how could someone who had served in the Menshevik government in Saratov during the Civil War assume such a prominent diplomatic position and for such a long period?' His activities in London, Gromyko claimed, 'were always assessed with some reserve ... the political past of this man prevailed over all appraisals of his work'. As the war dragged on, his 'unjustified' long telegrams, describing in detail his meetings with British politicians 'drowned in his own description of the situation', had become 'irritating to the leadership'. Gromyko finally recalls a conversation with Molotov, when the latter and Stalin decided that 'Maisky had to be replaced.'

Back in Moscow, Maisky was nominally put in charge of the commission on reparation, but was kept at arm's length. His request that the commission should 'enjoy sufficient authority and independence' and that he personally should be 'directly subordinated' to Molotov was not heeded. Litvinov fared slightly better. He at least met Stalin five times during 1943, and his expert advice was welcome in the impending meeting of the Allied foreign ministers and at the following summit meeting in Tehran. Maisky was denied access to the Kremlin. 'I asked Stalin to receive me, in order to report to him direct on the British situation and all the problems connected with it,' he remembers, 'but he did not find it necessary to talk with me.' Keeping Litvinov and Maisky in the wings was a typical method used by Stalin for his divide-and-rule tactics – asserting his power and curtailing Molotov's increasing influence in the formulation of foreign policy. A good indicator of Maisky's precarious position was his complicated manoeuvring to avoid Kerr, the British ambassador in Moscow, who was desperately trying to get him, Litvinov and the American ambassador 'to come and dine for a no fig-leaf kind of talk'. Maisky had so many conferences, reported the ambassador, 'that he didn't know what to do' and then he was 'in the country and would let me know when he got back'. Finally, Kerr would meet him only on the official turf of Narkomindel, where Maisky confessed that he did not yet know what his tasks would be. His plans to go back to England made it clear to Kerr 'that there [was] no hurry about his taking up his new job in Moscow'.

Neither Stalin nor Molotov could watch with equanimity the popular cult of Maisky in London, which reached dimensions second only to the cult of Stalin himself. Maisky had always been heedful of being seduced by the bourgeois environment, an inescapable consequence of the nature of the diplomatic profession. The high esteem in which he was held, especially after Molotov's visit in May 1942, could quickly turn against him – a paradox of which he had been fully aware from the outset of his ambassadorship.

---

[1] Andrei Gromyko was one of Molotov's first recruits to the Foreign Ministry after Litvinov's dismissal. He headed the American Department for six months and in 1940 was appointed first secretary to the embassy in Washington, and in 1943 ambassador. He was minister of foreign affairs 1957–85.

While flattered by the cult evolving around him, Maisky was anxious to keep it on the back burner. He was quick to turn down an invitation by the sculptor Epstein to attend the private viewing of his works at Leicester Galleries, using the flimsy excuse that he did 'not think it would be appropriate for me to be present as the bust of my own head will be shown there'. A similar source of discomfort was the publication of his biography, shortly after the recall, by the Russian-born journalist Bilainkin, who had always been welcome at his home. Not only did Maisky dissociate himself from the author, but he appeared extremely anxious to find out from his trusted colleagues at the embassy whether it contained any incriminating information. He likewise declined an offer by Birmingham University to bestow on him an honorary doctorate a few days before he was called back to Moscow.

After the signing of the Treaty of Alliance, following Molotov's visit to London in May 1942, Lord Cecil and other speakers in the House of Lords had gone out of their way to praise Maisky for his 'valuable contribution to Anglo-Russian understanding ... over a long period of years'. They paid tribute to his 'patient and exceedingly difficult work ... under-taken for many years past in London'. In the Commons debate, Eden paid similar tribute to the 'valuable contribution to Anglo-Russian understanding' made by Maisky 'over a long period of years'. Only passing references were made to either Stalin or Molotov. Likewise, a week later, during a formidable rally at the Albert Hall in support of a second front, Cripps mentioned Molotov *en passant*, before going on to say: 'I could not omit in mentioning ... a very special reference to one other Soviet statesman. We regard him more generally as a diplomat but I can assure you that he is a statesman too, Soviet Ambassador, M. Maisky.' Maisky tried in vain to play down such an homage. 'One has to understand,' he explained to his friends, 'that in all these events the first and foremost honour belongs to our great people and to our brilliant leadership.' Even after his depar-ture from London, farewell letters from ministers kept streaming in and surely would have raised an eyebrow or two in the Kremlin. 'I need not say,' wrote Noel-Baker in one such typical letter, 'and I am sure hundreds of other people have already written to you simi-larly – how ever sorry we all are that you and your wife are leaving London; how very much you will be missed; and how long and how gratefully your memory will be kept alive here. As I am sure the Government have said to you officially, we all feel an immense debt of gratitude for your services in bringing our countries closer together.' Under any normal circumstances, such recognition would have endeared an ambassador at home, but in the Kremlin it would have confirmed the independent position Maisky had assumed, certainly not the servile diplomat now characterizing Molotov's Narkomindel.

One of the worse consequences of the uncalled-for cult of personality was a most powerful portrait of Maisky done by the famous Austrian painter Oskar Kokoschka shortly before his withdrawal. The whole experience was far from pleasant for both. Unusually for him, Maisky was uneasy. He 'read *The Times* throughout the sittings,' grumbled Kokoschka in his memoirs. 'I could not get him to talk: perhaps he regarded a portrait as some new form of brainwashing.' However, the worst was yet to come. A benefactor was found who agreed to contribute the sum of the purchase to a Stalingrad Hospital Fund, stipulating, though, that it would care for both German and Russian wounded soldiers. As embarrassing for Maisky was the artist's wish for the painting to be given to the Museum of Contemporary Art in Moscow. The idea of 'a small token of Anglo-Russian goodwill' was raised with Eden, who passed it on to Maisky as soon as he returned to England to wind up his affairs before his final departure.

Sir Edward Beddington-Behrens,[2] the go-between, was urgently invited to the Soviet embassy. He left a most disturbing description of Maisky's state of mind at the time of his recall:

> As I waited outside, a little peephole in the door was opened, from which I saw two eyes peering at me. When at last I was admitted to the Embassy I was followed into the waiting-room by two men, who remained there but did not speak a word to me. Finally, I was shown into the ambassador's room, where I also found Madame Maisky. To my astonishment, the first thing Mr Maisky did was to take the precaution of locking the three doors leading into the room. Then he asked me not to press for the picture by Kokoschka to be sent to the Moscow Art Gallery ... He also asked me to omit any mention of the proposed gift of the portrait in any official communications to the Embassy concerning the generous donation of the money. His wife begged me to do as he wished, and I suddenly realised that Maisky was probably a victim of one of Stalin's ruthless purges. Both of them appeared to be very nervous, and I was quite moved by Madame Maisky's obvious devoted love for her husband, and her anxiety to shield him in any way that lay in her power.

Maisky's fears proved justified when Kokoschka went ahead with his offer, only to be flatly rebuffed by the Soviet Government. The painting was then donated to the Tate Gallery.

Always torn between fear and conceit, Maisky faced a similar conundrum when Epstein offered him a bronze copy of the bust he had made of him three years earlier. The correspondence concerning the gift was conducted with the embassy after Maisky's departure and seems to have embarrassed him, considering the negative impact his popularity in London was having on his relations with the Kremlin. While, in his customary way, he was making meticulous arrangements for the safe shipping of the bust, he tried to persuade his successor that the sculpture was done 'not of my own will, but at [Epstein's] own initiative'. Distressed by the Kokoschka affair, Maisky went on to excuse himself for not taking appropriate precautions concerning Epstein's possible use of the bust, as he had considered him to be 'generally of a progressive leaning and unlikely to misuse it'. He claimed that there was no way of refusing to accept the bust

---

[2] Major Sir Edward Beddington-Behrens, a businessman and patron of the arts.

done by 'the most famous contemporary sculptor in England and on top of that a person with much sympathy towards us'.

Although the political ideas Maisky held were not contested by the Kremlin, the attitude to the messenger, considered to be a remnant of the 'old guard', evinced contempt and personal resentment. Pavlov (the personal interpreter of Stalin and Molotov) left an account of Maisky's recall and the following short trip he undertook to London to make his final arrangements. Significantly, his narrative is bound together with a devastating critique of the ambassador and his wife from the time of Molotov's visit to London in May 1942.[3] In a last-ditch attempt to mollify his masters in Moscow, and to exhibit his new formal status to London, Maisky exploited his short sojourn in London to embark upon a series of lightning unauthorized negotiations with Churchill and Eden. He still hoped that if he could lure Churchill and Eden to Moscow, he would be able to serve as an intermediary and play a prominent role in forging a political alliance for the post-war period. He obviously found it difficult to reconcile himself to the fact that he was no longer the serving ambassador in London and reckoned that a success might make it possible for him to extend his stay in the capital. In no time at all, he was confronted with chillingly cynical advice from Molotov not to 'waste his strength and endanger his health in vain', and was encouraged to return promptly to Moscow. At the same time, the young Soviet chargé d'affaires, Arkady Aleksandrovich Sobolev (one of Molotov's new recruits) was praised for his harsh uncooperative dealings with Eden. Sobolev, though, was to write to Maisky a year later that Gusev was 'no good' and was 'undoing' all the good work done by Maisky.

Notwithstanding his extreme cautiousness, Maisky found it increasingly difficult to conform to the new role assigned to him as a passive ambassador in London. It is hardly a surprise that he was incensed. He had been involved in a losing war against the attempts by Molotov to reduce diplomats to pure messengers. The institutionalism of diplomacy, through the imposition of military order and hierarchy, symbolically deprived diplomats of their individuality and segregated them from their foreign colleagues. It was perhaps an allusion to Peter the Great's 'table of ranks', which had militarized the civil service and secured loyalty to the tsar, service to whom became the only criterion for promotion. The seemingly innocuous measure signalled the emasculation of Soviet diplomats abroad and their growing dependence on Moscow.

Shortly before learning of his recall, Maisky addressed Molotov with a personal rebuff, of the sort the commissar was hardly accustomed to:

Dear Vyacheslav Mikhailovich,

Rumours travel faster than light, and it has reached my ears that a decision concerning uniforms to be worn by diplomats has been reached in Narkomindel – moreover, that the uniform has already been designed and, if

---

[3] See p. 432.

one is to believe the rumours, it even includes ... a dagger! Is it truly, a dagger?[4] I understand that if a sailor carries a dagger it symbolizes to a degree his military profession. But what is the relevance of a dagger to diplomacy? And what is it supposed to symbolize in this case? As far as I can recall, neither English diplomats nor the French, nor the vast majority of diplomats of other nations, carry daggers.

Such an unprecedented and blunt criticism of Molotov hardly endeared him to Moscow and must have further contributed to the decision to recall him – which saved him from wearing the uniform in London, but not in Moscow. In November, now nominally in a high position at Narkomindel, he was given his new uniform. A strange blend of estrangement and suppressed vanity emerges in his diary:

The uniform is better, more comfortable and more handsome than I had expected. But I feel awkward in it just the same. I haven't worn any kind of uniform for 40 years, ever since my expulsion from St Petersburg University in 1902. I've been in civilian clothes all my life. Now, nearly 60, I find myself wearing uniform once more. It's only natural that it should feel a bit strange. I'll have to get used to it. And another thing: I have a high rank and Marshal shoulder-straps, which attract the attention of passers-by. The military salute me. This also feels novel and awkward.

Assuming the withdrawal of the ambassadors to be mainly an expression of protest, the Foreign Office failed to see the significance of the metamorphosis of Narkomindel. Embracing Maisky (as they did at this point) did little but intensify the Kremlin's mistrust of him, and the suspicion that his loyalties no longer lay with Moscow. Indeed such accusations figured prominently in his trial in 1955.[5] Kerr disputed openly with Molotov the wisdom of withdrawing Maisky from London, even if his services were urgently needed in Moscow. Maisky was, Kerr tried to impress on him, enjoying in London 'a position which no ambassador has had ever before'. It was a 'unique position in every sense'. He was 'loved in England by all from the left to the right, for all he [was] trustworthy'. Listening politely, Molotov did not even blink, but proceeded to request an *agrément* for the new ambassador. Kerr did not give up. Although the Soviet Union had 180 million inhabitants, he argued, it would 'be difficult to find among them a successor for Maisky'. 'Eden,' he now resorted to the heavy guns, would 'certainly be sorry to see Maisky go.' When Kerr referred to the love engulfing Maisky in London, Molotov cynically replied that 'we in Moscow also like Maisky'. He mentioned how, during his visit to London, he was able to appreciate the extensive contacts Maisky had forged – a compliment for any ambassador, but not in

---

[4] May well be a reference to Macbeth's famous line: 'Is this a dagger which I see before me?'
[5] See pp. 549 and 554.

72. In uniform, with a marshal's shoulder straps.

Stalin's Russia. Kerr was misled to inform Eden in his brief report of Molotov's 'warm praise of Maisky', which he took at face value. In a follow-up telegram, he criticized Eden for 'reading too much into the appointment' of a new ambassador. He wrongly assumed that as a result of the purges there were 'only a handful of men of the calibre required' in Moscow and Maisky's presence was imperative.

The decision of the Foreign Office 'to make a bid ... to retain him in London' would also have an adverse effect on Maisky. Eden instructed Kerr to tell Molotov 'how much we appreciated M. Maisky's services in the cause of Anglo-Soviet cooperation and how greatly we regret the departure of such an old and trusted friend'. In conversations with the Soviet chargé d'affaires, Eden 'noted with regret' the withdrawal of Maisky. He went even so far as to question whether 'it was really more important to be one of six Assistant Commissars [for Foreign Affairs] than to be an Ambassador in one of the principal capitals'. Unlike Eden, many were misguided enough to assume that Maisky was indeed being promoted. The remonstrations were becoming a source of personal and political embarrassment to Maisky, who brought them to an end in a formal, and hardly sincere, message (most likely dictated to him) which he transmitted to Eden via Kerr:

> We appreciate your feeling but I am sure you will understand how happy I am after so many years abroad to live again in my country and to work at Narkomindel. I will tell you more about it when I will come to London to say good-bye. I hope that you will establish best relations with my successor.

The choice of Fedor Tarasovich Gusev as the new ambassador, despite his apparent lack of experience, was a well-thought-out move. He was the antidote to Maisky, just as Gromyko was to Litvinov in Washington. His appointment signalled what the new profile of Soviet diplomacy would be – a signal lost on the Foreign Office. They opted to ignore Stalin's and Molotov's statements to Kerr that plenipotentiaries were there 'to sign agreements rather than exchanges of views'. Gusev, a loyal party member, had studied law and had worked in various institutes in Leningrad. He was recruited to the ministry during the purges. Following Molotov's takeover, he was put in charge of its West European department. His British interlocutors in Moscow had a poor opinion of his 'abilities & character' and thought he was 'rather uncouth'. His English was 'sparse and peculiar ... he took no initiative and had the appearance of having come from a collective farm after a short course of GPU[6] training'. In a nutshell, Kerr summed up, he was a man 'without grace, and his appearance is distressing'. Insufficient attention was given to the other observation that, when approached, he would refuse to say anything except 'I will refer the matter to my superiors.' When Alan Brooke met Gusev for the first time, at a meal given in Brooke's honour at the end of October, he, too, was little impressed by '"frogface" Gousev, a former butcher', who was 'certainly not as

---

[6] Predecessor of the NKVD and the KGB.

impressive as that ruffian Maisky was!' Few in London entertained any illusions concerning Gusev's appointment. They anticipated that it would 'certainly make any kind of free exchange of views in London virtually impossible'. Slowly it sank in that rather than being promoted, Maisky was 'being demoted, being placed under Molotov in the Moscow Foreign Office', while being succeeded in London by a diplomat who was 'quite unable to replace him for the purpose of any serious political discussions'. Maisky's warnings that a failure on post-war Europe might encourage the Russians 'to plough a lonely furrow' seemed to be materializing.

Until his recall, Maisky had succeeded in masterly fashion at navigating the stormy turns of his career – a career in which diplomatic achievements and personal survival were tightly intertwined. Now the moment of truth had come. The recall threatened to wipe out, at a stroke, his political assets, while compromising his standing at home and in Britain. Ostensibly the recall was a result of the Russians' grievances over their exclusion from Casablanca, Churchill's unannounced visit to Washington and the decision to postpone the offensive across the Channel until spring 1944 without consulting the Soviet Union. Maisky genuinely feared the 'grave' consequences of the lack of a strategic and political dialogue, which would 'endanger our relations not only in the closing stages of the war but in the post-war settlement'. A successful Soviet winter offensive could bring the Russians to the German border and enhance the feeling in Moscow that the Allies had played only a minor part in the victory, thus leading to unilateral arrangements and Soviet isolation. His professional future in Moscow hinged on sustaining the collaboration which he was determined to achieve during a short stay in London.

In a series of private letters and telephone conversations with Molotov (reminiscent in style of his pleadings with Litvinov in the 1920s), Maisky resorted to mundane reasons for seeking permission to return to London for a brief period: he was concerned about Agniya, who had been left behind and could hardly face a journey back alone in the hazardous wartime conditions, about her 'ear condition' which made it hard for her to fly, about her 'susceptibility to sea-sickness', and about the 'vast amount of luggage (I have many books and other things)' which he wished to ship to Russia. His presence in London – he threw the bait to Molotov – could save the Government money, as the British were bound to put at his disposal the appropriate means of transport. Molotov, who decisively opposed Maisky's return to London, argued that it would nullify the protest which the recall evoked. But Maisky persevered. He was certain that the British Government, which had 'become accustomed to linking [his] name with the idea of Anglo-Soviet cooperation' would continue to analyse the departure 'as a symptom of our displeasure at British policy, as a symptom of the fact that some cracks have grown in the Anglo-Soviet relationship'. His sojourn in London, which he promised would be 'a careful farewell', could help 'prepare the ground a little' for Gusev, his successor. True to himself, however, Maisky perceived his recall as a personal setback. His wish to return to England was genuinely motivated by the need (as he wrote in a draft letter to Molotov and then crossed out) to ensure that the 'Soviet Government's discontent with the policy of the British Government would not appear to foreigners, and still less to our Soviet people, to indicate discontent with the Soviet Government's ambassador in London (if, of course, such dissatisfaction actually does not exist)'. In his memoirs, published during the de-Stalinization period, he describes how he looked 'meaningfully' at Molotov, telling him that 'above all' he wished to go to London to forestall the spreading gossip concerning his recall. He goes on to explain that:

> In the years of the great man cult there were many cases when Soviet Ambassadors were unexpectedly recalled to Moscow and then vanished without a trace – either into the grave or behind the bars of some camp. Therefore in the West there had been created the impression that, once a Soviet Ambassador was recalled to Moscow, some unpleasantness or other was awaiting him at home. I wanted to protect myself against this kind of interpretation and suspicion.

Molotov, who could see through Maisky, was determined to remove the final stumbling block to his complete control of the ministry. After almost a month of beseeching, Maisky was granted merely five days to wind up his eleven-year sojourn in London, rendering it impractical for him to engage in extensive political conversations. Placed in a straitjacket, Maisky found it most embarrassing to concede to his British friends the restrictive terms of his return. Former acquaintances who came to bid farewell found him 'sad and depressed' and 'in a subdued mood'. There was 'a queer distant look in his Mongolian eyes which seemed to indicate that he was sad to leave London'. Short of time, he had to resort to flimsy excuses for turning down numerous invitations – even an invitation from Churchill's wife, Clementine, to attend an Allied rally.

Maisky's intentions were, just as they had been in 1939, to return to Moscow with tangible political achievements concerning post-war collaboration and the definition of European borders. During his brief stay in London, he once again plotted with Eden, who was concerned about the way Churchill was becoming 'dangerously Anti-Russian'. The two met on almost a daily basis, at one point three times a day. Maisky was most candid with Eden, expressing his own private views 'off record'. Eden, though, found it difficult to decide whether Maisky's words 'expressed only his own opinion, and to what degree it had reflected the opinion of his chiefs'. Maisky sought a quick agreement – before the military reality on the battlefield dictated the political outcome of the war – leading to the establishment of an indivisible Europe, where both British and Russian interests were taken into account. Personally, he told Eden, he was 'fundamentally opposed to any Russian domination in Central Europe and has always dreaded Pan-Slavism almost as much as he hates Pan-Germanism'. He remained faithful to his enduring belief that no conflict of interests existed between Britain and the Soviet Union on spheres of influence. He visualized the establishment of consensual independent democracies in Europe, expecting them to be centre-left in their orientation. Like Litvinov, he rejected any idea of setting up revolutionary regimes in the liberated countries. Russia's sphere of interests, according to his scheme, went only slightly beyond Russia's 1941 borders, extending into the Balkans and the Black Sea littoral.

Having witnessed at close quarters the extent of the devastation in Russia and the high price paid on the battlefield, Maisky hoped he could help dispel the growing suspicion in Moscow that both Churchill and Roosevelt were interested in prolonging the war. Although he had not been authorized to pursue the matter with Eden, he knew that Stalin and Molotov attached great importance to an imminent convening of the Allied foreign ministers and the setting up of a permanent commission in Sicily to coordinate the strategic conduct of the war. He still favoured a second front in France (this would be Maisky's last appeal in the relentless campaign he had pursued over the previous two years), but he now advocated such a front 'anywhere, including the Balkans', provided it drew away from the Russian front a sufficient number of divisions and brought the war to a quick conclusion. It is worth noting that Eden gained the correct impression that Maisky 'seemed to wish to attend' the projected conference, and therefore hoped it would be held in London. Stalin, however, fully backed by Roosevelt (to Churchill's manifest dismay and Maisky's disappointment), was determined to convene it in Moscow. Maisky met Churchill once again on 9 September to transmit Stalin's response to Churchill's report on his American trip, but alas no record of their last meeting has survived.

Understandably, Maisky was eager to keep a low public profile. 'The less that [is] said in public by either of us, the better,' he pleaded with Eden. He 'seemed relieved' to glean from Eden that there were to be no public speeches at the farewell luncheon the following day. Yet it was as important for him to display in Moscow his powerful standing in London, which could secure for him a favourable role as an influential go-between. Eden's farewell lunch in his honour at the fashionable Dorchester Hotel, attended by Halifax, Lloyd George, Bevin, Brooke, Cripps and many other prominent British politicians, certainly served that end. But the double-edged strategy could not be received with equanimity in Moscow, particularly not by Molotov, who surely resented newspaper headlines such as 'Eden, Maisky Open Wide Talks Today', exalting Maisky's new role in the ministry.

Maisky arrived in Cairo, *en route* to Moscow, with seven trunks full of personal belongings and some 70 pieces of heavy luggage, which required six three-ton trucks for the long drive from Cairo to southern Russia, via Palestine, Iraq and Iran. All attempts to separate Maisky from his luggage were stubbornly rejected, in spite of the long, slow journey ahead at 15 miles per hour. The security arrangements, testified the British intelligence officer in charge of the convoy, were 'out of all proportion for a retiring ambassador'. He could see no reason why anyone would be interested in assassinating him or 'why a grave situation should arise if he was killed'. The convoy consisted of eleven cars. When any of the vehicles broke down, Maisky insisted on stopping the whole convoy while he 'watched the repairs unblinkingly from start to finish'. The British

73. Maisky takes stock of his treasures in Baghdad.

minister in Damascus, Major General Sir Edward Spears, was flabbergasted by the enormous quantity of books and documents which were taken out from the trucks in bundles to Maisky's room, while there were 'always two men involved in each journey, as it was so arranged that never was a single man left in charge of a consignment. And the men looked terrified. I do not suppose I will ever have to describe a line of men in a queue on the steps to the guillotine. If I had to, I would only have to recall the expressions of these Russian couriers.'

Having achieved remarkable progress in defusing the crisis in London and securing Eden's visit to Moscow, Maisky intended to exploit his presence in the Middle East to make a bold move aimed at drawing the Zionist *Yishuv* into the Soviet orbit. His initiative was prompted by information he had gleaned from Weizmann, the president of the World Zionist Organization, on the eve of his departure, concerning Anglo-American plans for the settlement of the Jewish–Arab conflict which left Russia out in the cold. Maisky's confidence seems to have been bolstered by the positive reaction in the Soviet capital to the establishment of diplomatic relations with Egypt, which he had brought about during his July visit to the Middle East. 'When I received a telegram recalling me to Moscow,' he later wrote, 'the idea immediately flashed through my mind: "Aha! When I pass through Cairo I will try and come to an agreement about diplomatic relations directly with Prime Minister Nahhas Pasha." Having already prepared the ground in London, Maisky arrived in Cairo, according to the British ambassador, 'with all his ideas nicely taped: exactly what he wanted to do and when ... As I had expected one of the first items on his agenda was to see our local Prime Minister ... the result was a foregone conclusion, the elimination of all points of difficulty in the way of the immediate opening of relations between Cairo and Moscow.'

On his way home in October, Maisky spent three crucial days in Palestine, which gave him a unique opportunity to gain a first-hand impression of the viability of the Zionist movement in Palestine and of the country's ability to absorb a considerable Jewish immigration. Defying the British high commissioner, Maisky also visited the old religious Jewish quarters in Jerusalem and toured the modern part of the city. He further met Ben-Gurion, Golda Meirson (Meir) and other leaders of the Jewish *Yishuv* in the exemplary kibbutz of Ma'ale HaHamisha and Kiryat Anavim. Despite his lifelong deliberate effort to distance himself from his Jewish origins, the visit appears to have 'captivated him'. Agniya was 'intensively involved; she wanted to know what everything was called in Hebrew'. The affinity was undoubtedly enhanced by the sense of familiarity Maisky must have felt in Palestine. Most of the Zionist leaders he met spoke fluent Russian, displayed confidence in a future Jewish state, once the British left Palestine, and embraced genuine socialist ideas.

As part of his attempt to play up his own status, Maisky misled Ben-Gurion (and subsequent historians) into believing that he was conveying his Government's views. He was now, so he said, 'number three in foreign affairs', after Stalin and Molotov, and as the expert on Europe it was 'up to him' to deal with the future of the region. Oblivious to Maisky's precarious standing at home, the Zionist leaders later maintained that a direct link existed between Maisky's visit to Palestine and the surprising Soviet decision in November 1947 to support partition, paving the way to the creation of the State of Israel. Though apparently Maisky did prepare a glowing report for Stalin, upon his return he found the doors to the Kremlin bolted, while he was pretty much incarcerated in the Ministry for Foreign Affairs, his activities confined to research work on reparations and post-war plans. It is little known that in spring 1947, Stalin in fact instructed the Soviet delegation to the United Nations to advocate the creation of 'a single, independent and democratic Palestine', where the Jews would have been a minority. His dramatic volte-face in support of partition into two states had little to do with the Arab–Zionist conflict as such, but was a result of the emerging Cold War and of Western attempts to exclude him from the arrangements concerning the Middle East.

After two days in Tehran Maisky set off on his arduous but ostensibly exciting trip, finally reaching Tabriz, where he boarded a train to Moscow. There was little, however, to genuinely boost Maisky's standing in Moscow on his return. Although his persistence might have contributed to the convening of the foreign ministers' meeting in October and the follow-up summit meeting in Tehran, he had failed to ensure any Western commitment. In a move that was very reminiscent of Eden's visit to Moscow in 1941, Churchill chased Eden, on his way to the Soviet capital, with a long telegram prohibiting him from raising strategic and supply issues. The prime minister refused even to

74. Maisky confers with Ben-Gurion and leaders of the Zionist movement in Palestine at the kibbutz of Ma'ale HaHamisha.

commit himself to a cross-Channel attack in 1945. He was rather going to follow a 'sound strategy', as he could not rule out 'a startling [German] comeback'.

Maisky arrived in the Soviet capital too late to take part in the conference, which he had laboured so hard to assemble. Within days, his assignments were defined: he was to work together with Litvinov on post-war issues, while 'gathering ammunition for future peace talks'. He was manifestly disappointed to be entrusted with the issue of reparations, while Litvinov was granted the major commission dealing with post-war issues. Gusev, his successor in London, was instructed by him to publicize the fact that both were engaged in work on the peace agreement, but was specifically told to avoid mentioning the nature of the work assigned to each. Maisky tried in vain to establish warm and personal relations with Molotov. On the occasion of his own 60th birthday, Maisky presented Molotov with his youth memoirs. 'It is said,' he wrote to him, 'that writing memoirs is a sign of old age.' Boasting that he still possessed 'enough gunpowder in the cannon', he vowed to continue active work in the service of the party and the nation. It was as important for him to impress on his successor and colleagues in London, who in a flash had cut him out, that he was engaged 'up to the neck' in work on reparations, enjoying the support of the teamwork within Narkomindel. It was equally important for Maisky to maintain the special relations he believed he had forged in London. He sent his memoirs to Churchill as 'one man of letters to another quite apart from our official positions ... reminiscences of a man with whom you were so closely associated in the darkest days of our great struggle against the common foe'. The book to Eden arrived with a short letter highlighting his 'important and interesting job' on post-war problems, which kept him 'fully engaged in planning the future'. All to no avail. He felt deeply humiliated when, on occasion, he was instructed by Molotov to publish in the newspapers highly critical articles on British politics which were hardly congruent with his own views.

Regardless of the dramatic twist in his political fortunes, Maisky did not budge, as he told Eden, from his old belief in the 'similarity' of the historical development of Britain and Russia 'and the complementary nature of our natural interests. We were both on the fringes of Europe. Neither of us wished to dominate Europe, but neither of us would tolerate any other Power doing so.' But this was the sober swan song of the old school of Soviet diplomacy. It was a generation, he wrote to the aged Lloyd George, when presenting his memoirs, 'which so much contributed to the building of the modern Russia – the USSR', but which had vanished. His and Litvinov's removal from London and Washington left unchecked the triumphant march of Stalin's authoritarian foreign policy, just as the gathering clouds of the Cold War appeared on the horizon.

The Price of Fame: A Late Repression

Sequestered in the back rooms of Narkomindel while the anti-cosmopolitan campaign and the drift towards confrontation with the West raged on, Maisky was destined for oblivion – particularly as he was anxious to steer clear of his British acquaintances. When one of them turned up unannounced at his apartment in Moscow, 'Maisky refused to let him in, whispering in urgent tones, "You will only endanger me if you try to see me".' His correspondence with his friends on the British political scene was reduced to brief, infrequent and predictable messages. Churchill's greetings for the new year of 1945 were acknowledged, for example, in a single sentence: 'Sincere thanks for your kind greetings and good wishes for 1945, which we both reciprocate.' When Maisky and Litvinov were visited by the diplomatic correspondent of *The Times*, Litvinov did not hide his frustration: 'You've come to see me to learn about Soviet foreign policy? Why me? What do I know about it? Does my government ever consult me? Oh dear me no. I am only Litvinov. I am only the man who was charged with the conduct of foreign policy for many years, who knows America, who knows Britain. They don't need *my* advice, thank you very much.' The return to Moscow also entailed previously unknown economic hardship. It necessitated coming to terms with an entirely different lifestyle. When Maisky was away at the Yalta conference, Agniya spent his entire salary on new cutlery (as it was becoming 'embarrassing to use the old stuff'); she hesitated to tell him how much it cost, lest he accuse her of thoughtlessness.

The Yalta summit was going to be Maisky's last glorious moment on the international scene. He could be observed by Churchill, Eden and Roosevelt, seated next to Stalin (though mostly as an interpreter). While his expertise on reparations won him great plaudits (admittedly exclusively from the Western side), his apparent prominence was deceptive. In a letter to Agniya, he suggested that the work 'was proceeding better than expected', but he added cautiously that 'one should not count one's chickens before they are hatched'. Being accommodated in 'dull and primitive' lodgings with no bath, he knew where he stood. Molotov, apparently deliberately kept him away from the conference until he was urgently summoned by Stalin to replace Pavlov, whose interpreting was manifestly unsatisfactory. Stalin's rude treatment of Maisky, despite his excellent performance, perhaps best epitomized their relationship. According to Maisky, Stalin turned to him angrily and asked: '"Why didn't you turn up for the first session?" I replied that I had not been told that I was needed in that session. Stalin continued in a rage: "You weren't informed? What do you mean by – you weren't informed? You're simply undisciplined. Following your own will. Your oversight has cost us several lend-leases."'

Maisky still made a brief appearance at the Potsdam summit, but Churchill's defeat in the elections and the 'surprising appearance' of Attlee and Bevin, with whom he had a rather distant (if not hostile) relationship, further underlined his irrelevance. Rather paradoxically, it had been Maisky's high standing with the Conservatives which gained him Stalin's respect, while his relations with the members of the Labour Government could now prove a pitfall. Those in power in the Kremlin (Kollontay explained to Kerr before he left Moscow to take up the Washington embassy) 'could not forget that [Bevin] was a man of the "old International" which had been against the Bolsheviks in 1917', and it would 'take a long time to live this down'. In the new circumstances, Maisky no longer proved an asset, particularly as Soviet mistrust of Labour would rekindle similar suspicions concerning Maisky's own Menshevik past.

Back from Potsdam, Maisky was kept at arm's length in the ministry. Relieved of his position as head of the reparations committee, he was given no new assignment. He could not even secure an audience with Molotov. He was finally received by the foreign minister, after repeated pleas, in March 1946 – only to be castigated for 'passivity in writing and lack of involvement in the everyday working of the People's Commissariat' and for his work on reparations, which was 'weak'. He was further demoted, assigned to a large team which was collectively preparing a Soviet diplomatic dictionary. He surely found the work – a highly censored monument to Molotov's transformation of the ministry – humiliating.

Maisky's survival instincts now led him to refresh his status in the less hazardous, yet prestigious, sphere of the Russian Academy of Science. Sensing earlier that his career at the ministry was drawing to an end, Maisky was quick to take charge of his own destiny. He resorted to flattery, congratulating Stalin personally on being made a 'Hero of the Soviet Union':

> ... my heart is full of joy. I can remember no other occasion than this when the reward so well matched the effort. It is difficult for me to imagine what would have happened to our people, to our party, to all of us if you had not throughout these years, and in particular these terrible last four years, been the leader of the Soviet Union.
>
>   And one more thing: what a marvellous speech it was you made at the last reception in the Kremlin! It was deep and very timely.
>
>   Yours with deep respect
>   I. Maisky

Maisky now made a bold personal appeal to Stalin, arguing that his literary and research skills could be better employed at the Academy of Sciences – an appeal accompanied by two expensive British pipes from a leading manufacturer. At 62, it was 'right to think of a more serious move to the academic and literary environment'. 'If you have no objection to my plan,' he wrote to Stalin, 'I would be most grateful to you were it to be implemented. It so happens that the Academy is committed to reinvigorate its ranks through the recruiting of fresh forces ... candidates' names need to be put forward no later than 24 June.' It did not require much persuasion on the part of Stalin to ensure that a month later Maisky was unanimously voted into the Academy. Though he was brilliantly qualified for such a position – boasting an extensive record of close to 250 publications, and vast experience as a penetrating analyst of contemporary history – the circumstances of his appointment nonetheless raised an eyebrow or two. Endorsing the appointment, Stalin went on amusing himself by offering membership of the Academy to politicians he no longer trusted. While Vyshinsky accepted, both Litvinov and Molotov declined the honour.

The transition was timely: in January 1947, Maisky was relieved of his work at the ministry, and by a unanimous vote was stripped of his candidate membership of the Central Committee of the Communist Party. The stifling atmosphere of the Terror, which resumed to some extent in the early 1950s, hampered any serious work at the Academy. The projects he was entrusted with hardly lifted his spirits. As the nephew of Evgeny Tarle (the famous Russian historian who stood by the Maiskys during his arrest and trial) observed: 'Maisky had turned from a careful but very self-confident diplomat into a know-nothing academician working on some kind of problems of Spanish history that only he knew about and even he didn't care about.'

To observers, Maisky no longer seemed to be 'the careful but very self-confident diplomat' he had been. His cohort of colleagues from the 'Chicherin–Litvinov school of diplomacy' had thinned, through purges, natural causes – and often through 'diversions to other work'. One could still run into a gloomy Litvinov, somewhere in the House on the Embankment. Sensitive acquaintances, who had once adored the grand couple, quickly vanished 'and the inseparable childless couple were left on their own, fearfully waiting'. The anti-cosmopolitanism campaign deplored the 'worship of foreign things', with which Maisky was associated. How sad it was to see the fragile, ageing and sick Kollontay obliged to remove from her walls the portraits of Swedish King Gustaf Adolf and his son, which were given to her as an appreciative souvenir for her services in Stockholm. Over dinner at a friend's dacha, Maisky, 'an avowed story-teller who had been accustomed to assume centre stage, was now dull and passive, while Agniya bloomed like a rose when she felt like an ambassador's wife, but suddenly stopped when she remembered who she really was now'. It was 'hard to shake a sense of fear coming from them'.

* * *

The year 1952 saw the death of Litvinov, Surits and Kollontay. A critical appraisal of Maisky's work in October at the Academy of Sciences was a precursor of things to come. His relations with Molotov had deteriorated to the point where the latter told Khrushchev[1] that he suspected Maisky of being 'an English spy'. On 19 February 1953, Maisky was indeed arrested and accused by his interrogators of 'high treason'. He was quick to 'confess' that he had been recruited as a spy by Churchill. The arrest followed the new wave of purges triggered by the 'Doctors' Plot' of January 1953, when the Kremlin doctors (mostly Jews) were accused of plotting to murder Soviet leaders. The amnesty which followed the death of Stalin on 5 March was not, however, extended to him.

Maisky, who was interned in a cell in the basement of the Lubyanka, was subjected to 36 interrogations prior to Stalin's death. It must have been devastating for the 70-year-old revered diplomat who had so resourcefully steered clear of the worst phases of the repressions in the 1930s. The trauma of finding himself in jail on his seventieth birthday was movingly expressed in a poem he wrote to his wife. In tone it echoes Beethoven's *Fidelio*, alluding to Florestan's cry of solitude from prison, as he longed for his lover and for freedom:[2]

> ... Today I am seventy years old!
> Movements, revolutions, wars, openings-up
> Of our world have I seen over these years!
> In another time this would be enough for three centuries...
> I absorbed all of this
> With the proud thought of a man
> Who knows that it is the course of history that leads him to the place
> Where the banner of communism will shine brightly,
> I spent my life under the banner of work,
> I spent my life believing in the study of optimism...
> I brightly lived, and brightly fought and suffered,
> I did not spare my strength for the battle,
> I lived life in a major key...
> And now my star has flickered out in a dark sky,
> And the way forward is hidden in a dark shroud,
> And I meet this day behind a stone wall;
> ... My darling! Today, on this cherished day,
> From my half-dark room
> I call my greetings to you
> And in my mind hug you to my bosom.
> Thank you so much, my dearest,
> For all the happiness you gave me,

---

[1] Nikita Sergeevich Khrushchev, first secretary of the Communist Party, 1953–64 and chairman of the Council of Ministers, 1958–64.
[2] Translation by Oliver Ready.

For the love which, shining and playing,

Has given me so much warmth and delight

In times of struggle, in times of toil, in times of thought...

The arrest devastated Agniya. Acquaintances recall how all her pretentiousness and self-importance vanished without trace: 'From an English-style lady in trousers she became a downtrodden old lady begging for meetings and trying to find out how he was doing "there".' His image was further tarnished when he was officially declared 'an enemy of the people' by the Institute of General History, while each of his students was called upon to publicly denounce him.

The need to regain his party membership and be fully rehabilitated led Maisky to blot out the short-lived association he had formed with Beria at the time. 'As I have long noted,' commented his student and confidant, the prominent historian Alexander Nekrich, 'I.M. does not like to be questioned about that topic.' His prolific literary output categorically avoided commenting on the period following his return to Moscow in 1943, and particularly his arrest and trial. His friends realized that it was a 'bleak period' in his life and that there were 'considerations on that account which he did not intend to share with [them]'. On the rare occasion when he referred to the accusations, Maisky maintained that throughout his life he had met Beria only twice – at official luncheons at the Kremlin during the war. All he was prepared to volunteer was that 'facing the threat of harsh physical torture' after his arrest, he had 'entered on the road of self-slander ... in a moment of weakness'. He went a long way to impress on his student Nekrich that he had been personally tortured by Beria – though when he expounded the events in a letter to Khrushchev, he claimed to have met Beria for the first time only after Stalin's death and in far more convivial circumstances. Likewise he apparently told Valentin Berezhkov, Stalin's interpreter and later a senior Soviet diplomat, that he had been personally interrogated by Beria and 'hit with a chain and a lash' to force him to confess his spying activities. The interrogation led him to believe that 'Beria was trying to get at Molotov'. Indeed some of his few subordinates in London who had survived the repressions were also arrested and expected to substantiate Stalin's wild theory that when Molotov had a tête-à-tête with Eden on board the train taking him to London from the airport in 1942, he was recruited to British intelligence.[3] Unwillingly Maisky once again found himself on a collision course with Molotov. What Maisky admitted to only a few close friends was that being perceived as Jewish also contributed to his arrest, which happened shortly after the episode of the 'murderers in white gowns'.[4] After all, it was Maisky who had been trying to reconcile Stalin with Zionism.

Maisky was saved by the bell when Stalin died on 5 March. But alas, events turned out to be treacherous, haunting him for the rest of his life. Later, trying to seek his

---

[3] On Molotov's visit see p. 431.

[4] The Doctors' Plot.

rehabilitation, Maisky concocted a story that on 13 May 1953, when he heard of Stalin's death and on his own initiative, he sought an interview with his interrogator, Lieutenant General Petr Fedotov, head of the foreign intelligence, and demanded to recant his earlier false confessions. The interview with the head of counter-intelligence at the Ministry of the Interior was cut short by a personal call from Beria, demanding to see Maisky 'at once'. Maisky insists that this was the only occasion on which he met Beria after his arrest. What exactly happened at this meeting – by no means an interrogation – has been shrouded in mystery. New archival material now makes it possible to reconstruct more faithfully the course of events. It is hardly surprising that throughout the rest of his life Maisky made a supreme effort to conceal the unfortunate association with Beria. Not only did it cost him two more years of incarceration, but it also reinforced the suspicion and hostility towards him due to his Menshevik past, which he would never succeed in discarding.

What is indisputable is that between 15 May and 5 August, the period roughly coinciding with Beria's alleged bid for power, there was, to quote Maisky himself, an inexplicable 'break in the interrogations'. Sergio Beria claims in his memoirs that while his father had a poor opinion of Litvinov (whom he considered 'weak, yielding to pressure from above'), he 'particularly esteemed' Maisky, whom he regarded as 'more quick witted than Litvinov ... a real diplomat who loved his job'. There is no reason to question the testimony of Beria's son concerning Maisky's relations with his father, particularly as Sergio was not particularly fond of the 'agile little Jew who resembled a mouse'. Beria, according to his son, would have preferred to see Maisky replace Litvinov as foreign minister even back in 1939, but he was not yet in a position to make his voice heard. Sergio further claims that during Maisky's sojourn in England, his father 'kept up close relations with him – more frequently than with other diplomats' and Maisky 'used to visit us'. Beria's high esteem of Maisky would fit only too well with his admiration of Britain, his support of the triple alliance in 1939, and his impressive library at home boasting scores of books on British history and culture. After Stalin's death, Beria encountered strong opposition from Molotov over his plans to relax the Soviet grip on Eastern Europe and to seek accommodation with the West. 'Seeing how stupidly obstinate' Molotov was, Beria even proposed that he should be replaced by Maisky. He clashed with Molotov over the conduct of foreign affairs, telling him bluntly: 'If you don't agree, you can resign.' Beria further saw to it that Molotov's power in the ministry was curtailed, insisting that major issues of foreign policy should be dealt with by the Presidium of the Council of Ministers. In his memoirs, Molotov indeed claims that in 1953 Beria intended 'to appoint Maisky as minister of foreign affairs' to replace him. He even recalls their 'sharp clash' during the week following Stalin's death. No wonder Molotov returned to his office from that meeting 'in a highly excited state'.

Maisky had in fact learned about Stalin's death – and vaguely about the political realignment of forces at the Kremlin – much earlier than he would have us believe. On 31 March, he wrote a letter addressed to Georgy Malenkov, the newly elected chairman of the Council of Ministers, in which he admitted his guilt in betraying the motherland and expressed 'a burning desire to do something that could at least to a small degree atone for the evil' he had inflicted on the USSR. He was prepared 'to accept any form of redemption which will be decided by the relevant "instantsia"'. Aware of Maisky's wide net of contacts in Britain, which could be conducive to implementing his grand design for a thaw in relations with the West, Beria withheld the letter.

On 7 May, Maisky, contrary to his later version of events, was summoned by Fedotov for an interrogation where, fearing a provocation, he continued to admit his guilt. Four days later, he sought a second meeting. Far from recanting, as he later suggested, he wished to supplement his initial statement. The third interrogation, on the evening of 13 May, was interrupted by a phone call from Beria summoning him to his office right away. As he entered the room, Beria told him right away: 'you have spun your testimony', letting him understand from the tone of the conversation 'that he believed my testimony had been untrue'. 'By so doing,' explained Maisky to his interrogators, 'Beria encouraged me, if not explicitly told me, to file an official statement renouncing my previous statement.' Beria apparently promised to rehabilitate him, and proposed placing him in charge of work with British intelligence, under the auspices of the Ministry of the Interior. Within a day Maisky had indeed handed in his written recantation.

To facilitate his work, he was to be elected chairman of the Society for Cultural Relations with Foreign Countries. Insisting that he had not 'the slightest shadow of suspicion' concerning Beria's plans for a coup d'état, Maisky happily obliged, submitting to Beria a detailed outline for action shortly before the latter's arrest at the end of June. It is, of course, inconceivable that such plans were prepared by Maisky in his cell. Berezhkov recalls Maisky telling him that he was escorted from the prison cell to Beria's office, where the table was laid with fruit and a bottle of Georgian wine. He was given back his clothes and personal belongings and allowed to go home. There is a grain of truth in this recollection, but the far more likely scenario is that provided by Lieutenant General Pavel Sudoplatov, in charge of counter-intelligence and special operations at the Ministry of the Interior, and confirmed by Beria in his interrogation. Sudoplatov was entrusted by Beria with Maisky, who was described as 'the ideal man to present to the West' the new Soviet foreign policy. Maisky, however, had been implicated by slanderous testimony forced out of the leaders of the Jewish Anti-Fascist Committee before they were executed in 1952. He could not therefore be released before their case had been fully reviewed. The solution found for the interregnum was to keep him 'in hiding', residing with his wife in comfortable conditions, in the rooms adjacent to General Fedotov's office. Agniya went so far as to tell her friends that his conditions 'there' were now excellent and he had even started writing his memoirs. This, alas, was where the ill-disposed Molotov and Malenkov found him after Beria's arrest.

The insurrection of 16 June in East Germany provided Khrushchev with a pretext to rally opposition against Beria and halt his reforms. Beria was arrested on 26 June and placed in military custody to prevent the domestic security forces from coming to his aid. In presenting the case against Beria before a special plenary session of the Central Committee, both Molotov and Khrushchev blamed him for the events in Germany, which they attributed to his attempts to liberalize relations with the West. Beria was accused of 'getting cues from the chiefs of foreign intelligence'. Paradoxically, the new leadership veered towards the détente line which Maisky and Litvinov had been advocating since 1943, but it would take a while for Khrushchev to impose his will on the party and extricate Maisky from the dire situation he had found himself in. Once Beria was detained, Khrushchev and Molotov, fearing a backlash from the Ministry of the Interior, were quick to arrest his associates, too. Given Molotov's deep-seated distaste for Maisky, who, he claimed, had 'given his consent to Beria' to replace him, it is hardly surprising that (as Molotov put it laconically) 'Maisky was checked out too.' Although most documents relating to Maisky's arrest are under lock and key, the little evidence available suggests that Maisky was rearrested as soon as Beria was taken into custody; and hardly surprisingly, he suffered a nervous breakdown. This course of events is confirmed in Ivy Litvinov's unpublished draft autobiography. Apparently she remained Agniya's 'only friend at that time, nobody went to see her, she was absolutely lonely'. From Agniya she learned that 'the reason Maisky got into trouble after Stalin's death was because of Beria, because he was friendly with him'. She gleaned from Agniya that during the agonizing moments of his arrest, 'Maisky had appealed to Beria. He didn't know what he was doing.' This hardly surprised Ivy, who knew that paradoxically 'Maisky couldn't fail to be arrested – because he was friendly with everybody.' Keeping in step with her husband, Agniya later changed her story, arguing that after Stalin's death absurd charges were pressed against Maisky for 'embezzling Government funds'.

The indictment of Beria revealed his alleged plan 'of creating the type of bourgeois order which would be useful to the Eisenhowers, Churchills, and Titos'. 'Skilfully, like a spy,' it continued, Beria 'wove a web of all manner of intrigues' with the aim of placing his own people in key administrative positions. The sentence of the Supreme Court of the USSR, handed down on 24 December 1953, specifically mentioned Beria's 'criminal-treasonous activity' in establishing 'secret ties with foreign espionage'. Maisky – who had been put by Beria in charge of just such activities in Britain, and was presumably destined to be foreign minister – was thus implicated in the eyes of the insurgents, particularly Molotov, his lifelong adversary. Though he was not specifically mentioned in Beria's sentence, Maisky's assumed complicity became public knowledge following a letter that was sent to all party organizations. It suggested that it had been Beria's intention to release 'the British spy' Maisky from imprisonment and install him as his own minister of foreign affairs. It further included excerpts from Maisky's earlier forced confessions that 'having spent so many years working abroad, he had lost the feeling of belonging to his homeland'. When Agniya saw the letter, she turned 'crazy with worry', assuming that it implied Maisky's guilt. She was further humiliated by her own party cell, required to produce an account of her relations with her husband. Others who had placed their bets on Beria, including Dekanozov and Merkulov, the former head of the NKVD, with whom Maisky was now associated, were executed by firing squad. Foreign policy returned to the hands of Molotov.

The interrogation of Maisky resumed on 5 August, when he was placed in the custody of the state procurator, rather than the Ministry of the Interior. He was now charged – according to Article 58/1, 10 and 11 of the penal code – with 'counter-revolutionary' activities, aimed at the overthrow, subversion or weakening of the Soviet state. In one of the few references ever made by Maisky to his arrest, he summed up the grave accusation in the single word 'treason', thereby relating it to the absurd accusations of espionage which had been levelled against him by Stalin's henchmen. However, the new accusations were, as he himself was quick to recognize at the time, an attempt 'to implicate me in the Beria case'. The most serious accusation levelled at Beria, himself under investigation at the time, before his execution in December, was that 'right up to his arrest' he had 'cultivated secret contacts with foreign intelligence services' in preparing his coup d'état. The specific basis for such accusations was Beria's decision to close Maisky's file and put him in charge of communication with Churchill and intelligence circles in England. Maisky was now removed from the Lubyanka to Butyrka prison, where, apparently fearing provocations through inmates, he demanded to remain in solitary confinement. He successfully resisted the attempts of ten interrogators to extract a confession from him, which would have been used in the ongoing proceedings against Beria. The punitive response was the removal of all books from his cell, while he was denied the use of pen and paper for the next two years of his detention.

The abortive protracted interrogations, throughout the summer of 1954 and early 1955, were accompanied by Maisky's repeated pleas to Khrushchev and Voroshilov to drop the accusations and fully rehabilitate him. He remained in jail for another year before charges were formally brought against him. In mid-May 1955, he was finally given the 39-page indictment – and a pencil. Having refused a defence counsellor, he was allowed to use the reverse of the document to prepare his case personally. After Beria's execution, the interrogators had made futile attempts to frame Maisky through confessions which had been extracted from his colleagues in the embassy following their arrest in 1937. They also forced G.A. Deborin, a professor at the Military Academy, to dig into Maisky's confiscated papers and come up with incriminating material concerning his ambassadorship in London.

When Maisky set off for London in 1932, he had been tipped off by Litvinov that his achievements 'would be measured in Moscow by the close personal relations he would forge in London'. His outstanding success, however, now proved his downfall. Once the accusations of espionage and complicity with Beria were dropped, the main corpus of the indictment was based on information which was retrieved from his confiscated diary, allegedly exposing excessive intimacy in his relations with Churchill and Eden, as well as initiatives which he had concealed from his Government. Moreover, he was accused of withholding from it vital information, sending disinformation, and providing wrong advice concerning the triple negotiations and the campaign for a second front. Though generally

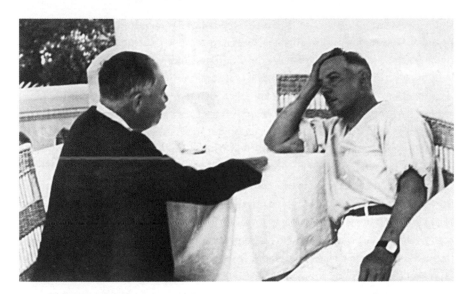

75. Voroshilov and Maisky had seen better days in Sochi in 1934.

absurd, there was a grain of truth in the accusations. Maisky successfully exposed the falsity of what he described as 'Arabian nights fairy-tales', but he found it difficult to convince the court that the intimacy he had established with the British elite was only motivated by 'alter ego' reasons. The inept handling of the case by the procurator, culminating in slanderous and unsubstantiated accusations of treason, could no longer secure indictment in the post-Stalinist period. The more so as no hard evidence was produced, while the historical context of the accusations was never properly explored.

The procurator finally, however, did stumble on a delicate matter which was a source of embarrassment to Maisky. The new indictment, and eventual conviction according to Article 109 of the penal code, cited abuse of his power, 'having allegedly hidden from the Soviet Government a microfilm of the British White Book of 1939 on the triple negotiations between the Soviet Union, Britain and France'. The line of defence pursued by Maisky was to play down the gravity of the offence. Maisky contended that the White Book was an attempt to discredit the Soviet Union, and had been scrapped, as it would also have revealed the conflict between the French and the British concerning the conclusion of a triple alliance. Moreover, he claimed that it was in the second part of July 1941, after the conclusion of the Anglo-Soviet treaty, that he received from 'some English friends of the Soviet Union' a microfilm of the White Book. It being wartime, the courier service was disrupted and it was difficult to pass it on to Moscow. Moreover, he wished to ascertain further that the documents and the commentary had not been falsified. However, because of the burden of work at the time, he set it aside among his papers and forgot about the documents, which he 'did not even read'. His vast archives, he reminded them, contained some 80 large boxes, which were pretty much in a chaotic state. The microfilm, 'the size of a small matchbox, disappeared like a needle in a haystack'. Only during the investigation, he asserted, 'turning over in his head every small detail', did he 'suddenly remember the microfilm' and inform his investigators, of his own volition, of its location. Rather than a deliberate action, it was 'forgetfulness'; rather than 'a crime', it was 'negligence ... a lapse'. He contended that, had he not revealed the existence of the microfilm, it would never have seen the light of day, as 'no one in the London embassy or in Moscow' knew of its existence. But this fevered argument only served to emphasize the significance he had attached to it in the first place, its compromising nature and the secrecy which involved its procurement, most likely back in 1940.[5]

In a draft letter to Khrushchev concerning the incident, shortly after his release from prison, Maisky carefully crossed out certain sentences which might have sounded apologetic, but which nonetheless revealed his true state of mind. The narrative concocted in court was repeated in his personal appeal to Khrushchev for full rehabilitation four years later. It was accepted − with great scepticism − when a final decision on his rehabilitation was approved at the end of 1960. By then, however, the struggle for power within the party had been decided, Molotov had been side-lined, and the issue had lost all political relevance.

Maisky apparently conducted his defence brilliantly. The testimony of former subordinates at the embassy − Kharlamov, the naval attaché, and Zinchenko, the first secretary − was 'somehow toothless' and even supportive of his case. According to Maisky, the virulent Deborin was 'torn to pieces' by him. Exposed as 'a liar and a scoundrel he became confused, lost his composure' and responded to the counter-interrogation with 'complete silence'. Maisky was aware that the political atmosphere was changing when, before being returned to prison, he was offered 'coffee and waffles'.

The summing up of the defence was scheduled for 2 June, but the meeting was postponed. Maisky rightly assumed that the court was 'seeking instructions from the Central Committee which failed to arrive'. Following a second appeal to Voroshilov, he was finally summoned on 12 June to be sentenced. The charge of treason was replaced by Article 109, abuse of power and privileges while at his ambassadorial post, which carried with it six years of internal exile. This appears to have been a compromise reached between Molotov and Khrushchev who, as *primus inter pares*, had established himself firmly in the saddle. These developments unexpectedly played to Maisky's advantage. Although he was convicted and sentenced to six years in exile, Maisky was hastily pardoned by the Presidium of the Supreme Soviet, spared punishment and allowed to return home. A special decree had been issued the day before, specifically excluding Maisky from the amnesty of 27 March 1953, which would have led to his full rehabilitation.

The decision to release Maisky seems to have been motivated by Khrushchev's clash with Molotov over the course of Soviet foreign policy. In July 1955, Khrushchev

---

[5] See Maisky's diary entry of 8 January 1940. Maisky admits to having learned of the contents of the White Book, the exposure of which at the time would have seriously jeopardized his position.

was due to attend a summit meeting in Geneva. Keeping Maisky in prison would have been most embarrassing when he met Anthony Eden (the newly elected prime minister, who was heading the British delegation), who had enjoyed such an intense and close relationship with the former ambassador in London. Full rehabilitation, though, came only in 1960, once Khrushchev had succeeded in consolidating his grip on the party and overcoming the challenges posed to him by Molotov.

Convicted of an administrative rather than a political crime, Maisky was now, at his request, provided with a desk, paper and stationery. He felt now confident enough to complain to the director of the prison that the desk he had been given had 'legs of different lengths and the surface wobbles, and there is no space for me to put my legs as I write. The desk is also too low. Would it not be possible to bring me even the simplest kitchen table, which would at least give me somewhere to put my legs when I write?' His first action was to scribble a plea for clemency to Voroshilov. This was followed two days later by a detailed critique of the verdict, which introduced some 60 corrections to the protocol of the trial. These were accepted by the court and, 'after protracted haggling', he was granted permission to include in the protocol his defence speech and a poem which he had addressed to the judges at the end of the trial:

Beneath a stony vault, on a prison bunk,
I lie abandoned, forgotten, alone...
Confined ... By whom?... Not enemies, no!
Confined by friends under lock and key!
    Oh, such madness! Am I really a foe?
And is this how enemies behave?
Thirty long years we have walked the same road,
Shoulder to shoulder, keeping in step!
    We walked and we struggled, and higher
And higher the victory banner was hoisted.
Many of us died... Yet Communism's flames
Flickered from afar to those who remained.
    Then sudden confusion!... Into the dungeon
I am hurled, cast out, named an enemy.
And why? For what? For which terrible deeds?
By whom am I slandered? And who is rejoicing?
... Oh citizen judges, look with eyes open
At the living truth, as duty commands!
Before you today there stands not a criminal
But an honest Soviet fighter and patriot!

Maisky devoted the rest of his time in jail to penning an allegorical novel he had composed in his head during the two years of prison, *Close and Far Away*

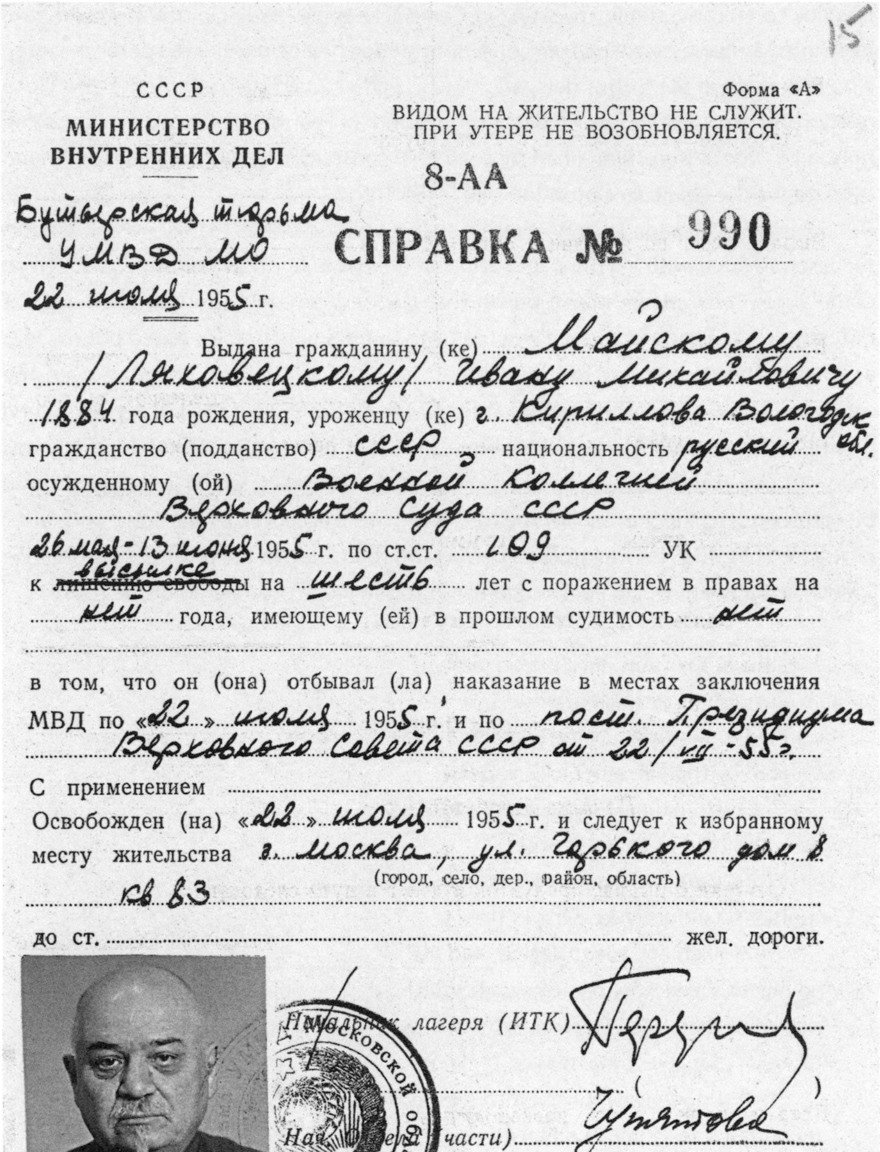

СССР

Форма «А»

МИНИСТЕРСТВО
ВНУТРЕННИХ ДЕЛ

ВИДОМ НА ЖИТЕЛЬСТВО НЕ СЛУЖИТ.
ПРИ УТЕРЕ НЕ ВОЗОБНОВЛЯЕТСЯ.

8-АА

Бутырская тюрьма
УМВД МО

СПРАВКА № 990

22 июля 1955 г.

Выдана гражданину (ке) *Майскому*
(Ляховецкому) Ивану Михайловичу
1884 года рождения, уроженцу (ке) г. *Кириллова Вологодск.*
гражданство (подданство) *СССР* национальность *русский обл.*
осужденному (ой) *Военной Коллегии*
Верховного Суда СССР
26 мая - 13 июня 1955 г. по ст.ст. *199* УК
к лишению свободы на *шесть* лет с поражением в правах на
нет года, имеющему (ей) в прошлом судимость *нет*

в том, что он (она) отбывал (ла) наказание в местах заключения
МВД по «*22*» *июля* 1955 г. и по *пост. Президиума*
Верховного Совета СССР от 22/VII-55г.

С применением

Освобожден (на) «*22*» *июля* 1955 г. и следует к избранному
месту жительства *г. Москва, ул. Горького дом 8*
(город, село, дер., район, область)
кв 83

до ст. _____ жел. дороги.

Н_____к лагеря (ИТК) _____

Нач_____ части) _____

76. Humiliation: the decree on Maisky's release from prison, 22 July 1955.

(*Blizko-Daleko*). On 22 July, the Presidium of the Supreme Soviet of the USSR granted the plea for clemency. Maisky was driven home right away from the Butyrka prison by the officer who had brought the clemency certificate to the prison.

Back at the Academy of Sciences, deprived of many of his rights – including his salary – Maisky was side-lined to work on Spanish history. Only after his full rehabilitation and re-admittance to the party in 1960 (and increasingly after the creation of the Institute of General History) was he able to again steer his career in the direction he had set for himself – writing his memoirs, though always remaining attuned to the winds blowing from the Kremlin. The outpouring of his prolific writings was little affected by a severe stroke he suffered at the age of 81. His convalescence was, however, set back by severe criticism of his work following Khrushchev's fall. A ground-breaking book by his disciple, A.M. Nekrich, *June 22, 1941*, was publicly denounced and the author expelled from the party. The English version of Maisky's own memoirs, which included criticism of Stalin's conduct on the eve of the German invasion of Russia, was condemned as 'subjective'. In an unusual move, the ever-cautious Maisky signed a petition, together with the dissident physicist Andrei Sakharov and others, protesting against attempts to rehabilitate Stalin.

Confined to his dacha outside Moscow, shielded and pampered by Agniya, he remained lucid and continued to write his memoirs until his death on 3 September 1975. Despite his distinguished position at the Academy of Sciences, Maisky remained a solitary figure. He never again rode the crest of the Soviet political and cultural elite, and was forced to dissociate himself from the powerful and close friends he had made in London. Coveting his glory days in London, Maisky appeared envious of his friend, the radical British lawyer and MP Denis Pritt, who was still a 'great globetrotter', while his own life was 'more sedentary', spent in the dacha with his wife 'busy gardening', while he continued to write his memoirs.

How tragic it must have been for Maisky to go on paying a heavy price for his survival until his very last day, forced to atone for his 'ancient' mistakes – forgiven but not forgotten. Only a fragmentary draft was left of his last manuscript, *Memoirs of Churchill, his Circle and his Times*. It was rejected, and then lost, by his publishers, Nauka. 'The blow struck by the publishing house,' Maisky wrote to them, 'is all the more painful as I am now 91 years old and have been working on my book for the last five years, and had hoped that it would be the culmination of my work (I realize that I am now not that far from the end of my life).'

Maisky's long sojourn in London remained undoubtedly his 'finest hour'. The last 20 years of his life at the Russian Academy of Sciences were entirely devoted to recording those formative and dramatic years. 'He sincerely loved Britain and the British,' attested the head of the military mission at the embassy during the war. 'He spoke fluent English, admittedly with a noticeable accent ... [and] he seemed to know every connotation of every word.' His nostalgia is encapsulated in a letter he sent shortly before his death to the then Soviet ambassador in London:

77. The inseparable couple: old age with Agniya at their dacha.

... We spent eleven years in London, and there has been nothing like that! ... and I also spent five years there (1912–1917) as an émigré from tsarist Russia. Naturally, I got attached to this town, and more specifically to particular sites, buildings and monuments ... I find myself even now sometimes wondering: How did he set up his study? And what does their dining room look like? And are there any remnants around from the time of the Blitz in the Second World War?[6] ... We keep remembering the friendships we forged with the Webbs and Bernard Shaw. Of course, the London of your days will be very different from the London of our time...

Visiting Maisky shortly before his death, his loyal student, the renowned historian Nekrich, found him

'moving', literally, pushing a straw chair in front of him and leaning on it, taking heavy steps with one leg and then the other. If it hadn't been for his legs you would never have imagined that I.M. was pushing 90: his dark eyes were mobile, gleaming with thought, and although he spoke slowly and, I would say, slightly

---

[6] The tremendous concrete shelter installed in the gardens of the embassy (see pp. 316–17) proved to be far too expensive to remove, and is still a dominant feature of the grounds.

falteringly, his speech was entirely coherent and logical and it was clear that he had an excellent command of his memory.

Asked by Nekrich how he had managed to survive, being on the brink of catastrophe so often, Maisky looked at him, 'smiled slightly, and said, "I always kept a cool head on my shoulders." And I thought: had Stalin lived just a month or two longer, nothing would have helped Ivan Mikhailovich.'

Illustration Credits

The following images are from the private photo albums of Ivan and Agniya Maisky, deposited in the Archives of the Russian Academy of Sciences and reproduced here by courtesy of the Scheffer-Voskressenski family, the copyright owners: 1, 3–11, 14–17, 20–28, 30, 32, 33, 36, 37, 39, 42–50, 52, 54, 56–58, 60–64 and 66–77. Images 2, 12, 13, 18, 19 and 40 are reproduced courtesy of the Russian Foreign Ministry. I would like to thank Corinna Seeds for 34, the rare photo of her father, Sir William Seeds. Images 31, 51, 53, 55 and 59 are copyright Getty Images. The David Low cartoons – 29, 35, 38, 42 and 65 – are published by permission of the *London Evening Standard*.

Index